POEMS ON AFFAIRS OF STATE

AUGUSTAN SATIRICAL VERSE, 1660–1714

Volume 3: 1682–1685

THE
TRYAL

OF

Tho. Pilkington, Esq; } Sheriffs
Samuel Shute, Esq; } Sheriffs
Henry Cornish, Alderman.
Ford Lord Grey of Werk.
Sir Tho. Player, Knt. Chamberlain of London.
Slingsby Bethel, Esq:
Francis Jenks.

John Deagle.
Richard Freeman.
Richard Goodenough.
Robert Key.
John Wickham.
Samuel Swinock.
John Jekyll, Sen.

FOR THE

RIOT

AT

GUILD-HALL,

On *MIDSOMMER-DAY*, 1682.

BEING THE

Day for Election of SHERIFFS for the Year ensuing.

LONDON,

Printed for *Thomas Dring* at the *Harrow* at the Corner
of *Chancery-Lane* end in *Fleetstreet*, 1683.

The Stuart Counterattack: Title page of the account of the trial of those who opposed the Court in the *bataille rangée* of the shrieval elections.

Poems on Affairs of State

AUGUSTAN SATIRICAL VERSE, 1660–1714

VOLUME 3: 1682–1685

edited by

HOWARD H. SCHLESS

New Haven & London

YALE UNIVERSITY PRESS

1968

EDMÉE

PREFACE

A volume such as this affords its editor many rewards, not the least of which is the opportunity to acknowledge his debts. But where does one begin—or end? My debt to il mio maestro, Fred Johnson, began at Harvard and, happily, continues to grow daily at Columbia. And what of my affection and respect for Marjorie Nicolson, or my fortunate obligations to the wit and learning of A. H. Scouten, to the precision and warmth of Maurice Johnson, to the understanding and instruction of Allen Hazen, or to the encouragement of James Clifford? An apt quotation should be invoked here to permit a decorous coda, but my gratitude must remain as evident as my obligation.

This volume has had many rewards also in the friendships it has brought forth: friendship with James and Helen Sutherland, who have helped since that first richly productive year; friendship with James and Marie Louise Osborn, who have given strength and counsel when the back seemed to be weakening; and friendship with John and Ruth Kaltenbach for Heaven only knows how much concern.

I confess that I have shamefully abused the infinite patience of Miss Marjorie Wynn of the Yale Library, and indeed most of the rest of the staff of that superbly helpful organization. At one time or another I have taken advantage of the thinking of Hugh Amory, Stephen Wise, and Basil Henning on matters critical, legal, and parliamentary. And I gladly join the editors of the two preceding volumes in recording my gratitude to David Vieth not only for the careful reading that he gave the typescript but for the ready help that he so freely offered in the course of research.

So far as the work on this particular volume is concerned, however, my most direct debt is to my fellow editors. They have been ready always to lend a sympathetic ear and a helping hand, to argue sanely and knowledgeably, to evaluate at once with objectivity and concern. In some matters, there has been a divergence of opinion, notably with regard to the form of the text for the present edition.

My own rule of thumb is that texts that are not easily available should be presented in the original; yet, I recognize that the problems of manuscript transmission encountered in the other volumes are so great that modernization may well be the only feasible solution. I hold no brief for those who would print the original merely to sustain the flavor of antiquity; indeed, I should hope that in the vast majority of cases the modernized texts not only clear up accidentals but also give to the modern reader the immediacy that the original text had for its contemporaries. My hesitation comes rather from the fact that there is no way for the reader to check easily on the changes—no matter how small nor how carefully considered—that are inherent in modernization but that have not been considered substantive enough to be noted; it comes too from the inevitable loss of these texts as linguistic and orthographic evidence of Restoration English. I must point out, however, that the majority of the material in the present volume comes from printed texts and therefore my textual problems are relatively simple. I need hardly add that the multiplication of such problems may well constitute a change in degree that becomes a change in kind, and that while modernization might be a matter of choice in the present volume, it would appear to be more a matter of necessity in the others. All things considered, the decision to modernize has much to be said for it, and it is being brought up here only because the strong arguments supporting such a policy for the edition as a whole appear, in the present case, to be less directly relevant.

It is only proper that a preface conclude with some attempt to formulate the aims of the volume. It is my hope that these poems will be of use in three basic ways: first, that they will make more available to the historian, besides a certain amount of factual data, an almost unique source of information concerning the spirit and temper of a relatively neglected period; secondly, that they will supply the student of literature with some sense of the background against which such men as Marvell, Dryden, Pope, and Swift were writing; finally—and most important of all—that they will present a poetry of persuasion whose wit, or zeal, or literary effectiveness will find approval with the reader. If such aims are even partly achieved, the edition will have accomplished a great deal.

CONTENTS

LIST OF ILLUSTRATIONS

The Stuart Counterattack: Title page of the account of the trial [T2331] of those who opposed the Court in the *bataille rangée* of the shrieval elections. *Frontispiece*

Facing page

John Charles, Count Konigsmark, 1682. Engraving by Robert White (1645–1703) in the Pepysian Library. By permission of the Master and Fellows of Magdalene College, Cambridge University. 18

Medal by George Bowers (d. 1690) commemorating the release of Anthony Ashley Cooper, Earl of Shaftesbury, from charges of treason, 1681. By permission of the Trustees of the British Museum. 38

The Oxford Election, 1687, by Egbert Van Heemskerck (1634/5–1704). The Aldermanic Council, compelled by James II's message, accepts a highly unpopular nominee it had previously rejected. By permission of the Oxford City Council. 225

Medals of 1682 by George Bowers (d. 1690) commemorating: (1) James, Duke of York and (2) his escape from the wreck of the *Gloucester;* (3) the arrival of the Moroccan ambassador, Hamet Ben Hadu, for discussions on (4) the port of Tangier; (5) the arrival of the Bantam ambassador, Keay Naia-Wi-Drai. By permission of the Trustees of the British Museum. 387

The Eight Lay Witnesses Slain. Anonymous engraving (probably post-1688) showing "the Whig martyrs": Godfrey (Popish Plot); Essex, Russell, Sidney, Cornish, Armstrong (Rye House Plot); Monmouth, Argyle (1685 uprising). The Pepysian Library. By permission of the Master and Fellows of Magdalene College, Cambridge University. 454

A History of the New Plot: Or, A Prospect of Conspirators, their Designs Damnable, Ends Miserable, Deaths Exemplary. London, Printed for Randolph Taylor, [17 August] 1683 [H2173A]. The broadside contains, beside a brief official account of the Whig Conspiracy, the twenty-seven propositions condemned by the University of Oxford, and a series of Biblical citations (including references to Absa-

xv

WORKS FREQUENTLY CITED

Ailesbury, *Memoirs:* Ailesbury, Earl of (Thomas Bruce), *Memoirs,* ed. W. E. Buckley, 2 vols., Westminster, 1890.

Angliae Notitia: Angliae Notitia, or the Present State of England, together with Divers Reflections upon the Ancient State thereof, compiled and edited by Edward Chamberlayne, London, 14th ed. (1682) [E1830], 15th ed. (1684) [E1831].

Beaven, *Aldermen:* Beaven, Alfred B., *The Aldermen of the City of London,* published by the Corporation of the City of London, 2 vols., London, E. Fisher, 1908–1913.

Bell, *The Great Fire:* Bell, Walter G., *The Great Fire of London,* rev. ed., London, Bodley Head, 1951.

Benham, *Playing Cards:* Benham, Sir William G., *Playing Cards,* London, Ward, Lock, 1931.

Brown, *Fifth Monarchy:* Brown, Louise Fargo, *The Political Activities of the Baptists and Fifth Monarchy Men in England during the Interregnum,* Washington, D.C., American Historical Association, 1912.

Brown, *Shaftesbury:* Brown, Louise Fargo, *The First Earl of Shaftesbury,* New York, Appleton Century, 1933.

Buckingham, *Rehearsal:* Buckingham, 2nd Duke of (George Villiers), (and others), *The Rehearsal, first acted 7. December 1671, published 1672,* mit einleitung hrsg. von Felix Lindner, Heidelberg, C. Winter, 1904; also, ed. Montague Summers, Stratford-upon-Avon, Shakespeare Head Press, 1914.

Buckingham, *Works:* Buckingham, 2nd Duke of (George Villiers), *The Works of George Villiers . . . Duke of Buckingham . . . ,* 3rd ed., 2 vols. London, 1715.

Burnet, *History:* Burnet, Gilbert, *History of My Own Time,* ed. Osmund Airy, 2 vols., Oxford, Clarendon Press, 1897–1900.

CJ: Journals of the House of Commons, vol. 9, 10 October 1667 to 28 April 1687. Printed by order of the House of Commons (n.p., n.d.).

Care, *Weekly Pacquet:* Care, Henry, *Weekly Pacquet of Advice from Rome,* London, Crane and Kaye, *Census,* No. 670.

Carr, John Dickson, *The Murder of Sir Edmund Godfrey*, New York, Harper, 1936.

Case: Case, Arthur E., ed., *A Bibliography of English Poetical Miscellanies, 1521–1750*, Oxford, The Bibliographical Society, 1935.

Chappell, *Popular Music:* Chappell, William, *The Ballad Literature and Popular Music of the Olden Times*, 2 vols., London, 1855–1859.

Christie, *Shaftesbury:* Christie, William D., *A Life of Anthony Ashley Cooper, First Earl of Shaftesbury*, 2 vols., London, 1871.

Clark, G. N., *The Later Stuarts, 1660–1714*, repr. Oxford, Clarendon Press, 1949.

Cotton, *Compleat Gamester:* See entry under *Games and Gamesters.*

Crane and Kaye, *Census:* Crane, R. S., and Kaye, F. B., *A Census of British Newspapers and Periodicals, 1620–1800*, Chapel Hill, University of North Carolina Press, 1927.

Crawfurd, Raymond, *The Last Days of Charles II*, Oxford, Clarendon Press, 1909.

CSPD: Calendar of State Papers Domestic series of the reign of Charles II [1682–Feb. 1685], 6 vols., ed. F. H. B. Daniell, and F. H. B. Daniell and F. Bickley, London, published by His Majesty's Stationers Office, 1921–1938.

Dalrymple, *Memoirs:* Dalrymple, Sir John, *Memoirs of Great Britain and Ireland*, 3 vols., London, 1790.

A Dictionary of the Bible, ed. William Smith, 3 vols., Boston, Little, Brown, 1863.

Dictionary of the Canting Crew: B. E., gent., *A New Dictionary of . . . the Canting Crew . . .* , London, 1690; facsimile reprod. (n.p., n.d.) [E4].

DNB: Dictionary of National Biography, ed. Leslie Stephen and Sidney Lee, 66 vols., New York, Macmillan; London, Smith Elder, 1885–1901.

D'Oyley, *Monmouth:* D'Oyley, Elizabeth, *James, Duke of Monmouth*, London, G. Bles, 1938.

Dryden, John, *The Poems of John Dryden*, ed. James Kinsley, 4 vols., Oxford, Clarendon Press, 1958.

Dryden, John, *The Poetical Works of John Dryden*, ed. G. R. Noyes, Boston, Houghton Mifflin, 1909.

Dryden, John, *Works*, ed. Walter Scott and revised by George Saintsbury, 18 vols., Edinburgh, W. Paterson, 1882–1893.

EB: Encyclopedia Britannica, 13th ed., 32 vols., London and New York, The Encyclopedia Britannica Co., 1926.

Echard, *History:* Echard, Laurence, *The History of England . . . ,* 3 vols., London, 1718.

English Historical Documents (in progress), vol. VIII, 1660–1714, ed. Andrew Browning, London, Eyre and Spottiswoode, 1953.

Evelyn, *Diary:* Evelyn, John, *Diary,* ed. E. S. de Beer, 6 vols., Oxford, Clarendon Press, 1955.

Ferguson, *Ferguson:* Ferguson, James, *Robert Ferguson, the Plotter,* Edinburgh, 1887.

Filmer, Sir Robert, *Patriarchia: or, The Natural Power of Kings,* London, 1680 [F922].

Foxcroft, Helen C., *A Character of the Trimmer,* Cambridge, Cambridge University Press, 1946.

Games and Gamesters of the Restoration: The compleat gamester, by Charles Cotton, 1674; and *Lives of the Gamesters,* by Theophilus Lucas, 1714, with an introduction by Cyril Hughes Hartmann . . . London, G. Routledge, 1930.

Gardner, *Prologues:* Gardner, W. B., *The Prologues and Epilogues of John Dryden,* New York, Columbia University Press, 1951.

Gillett, *Burned Books:* Gillett, Charles R., *Burned Books: Neglected Chapters in British History and Literature,* 2 vols., New York, Columbia University Press, 1932.

Godley, Hon. Eveline C., *The Trial of Count Königsmarck,* London, P. Davies, 1929.

Gough, William, *Londinum Triumphans,* London, 1682 [G1411].

Grew, Nehemiah, *The Anatomy of Plants,* London, 1682 [G1945].

Grose, C. L., "Louis XIV's Financial Arrangements with Charles II and the English Parliament," *Journal of Modern History,* 1 (1929), pp. 177–204.

Hagstrum, Jean H. *The Sister Arts,* Chicago, University of Chicago Press, 1958.

Halifax, *Works:* Halifax, Marquess of (George Savile), *Works,* ed. Walter Raleigh, Oxford, Clarendon Press, 1912.

Heraclitus Ridens: Or, A Discourse between Jest and Earnest, London, Crane and Kaye, *Census,* No. 297.

HMCR: *Historical Manuscripts Commission Reports,* Seventh Report, Manuscript of the House of Lords, Verney Papers, vol. 6, London, 1879.

Howell, *State Trials: A Complete Collection of State Trials,* compiled by T. B. Howell, 21 vols., London, 1816.

Hyde, Harford Montgomery, *Judge Jeffreys,* 2nd ed., London, Butterworth, 1948.

Impartial (True) Protestant Mercury, London, Crane and Kaye, *Census,* No. 896.

Johnson, Samuel, *Julian the Apostate,* London, 1682 [S829].

Journals and Narratives of the Third Dutch War, ed. R. C. Anderson, London, Publications of the Navy Records Society, no. 86, 1946.

Kinsley, *Dryden:* See entry under Dryden.

Kitchin, *L'Estrange:* Kitchin, George, *Sir Roger L'Estrange,* London, Kegan Paul, 1913.

Lane, *Oates:* Lane, Jane (pseud. Lady Elaine Dakers), *Titus Oates,* London, Andrew Dakers, 1949.

Loyal Protestant: Thompson, Nathaniel, *The Loyal Protestant* (formerly *The True Domestick Intelligence*), London, Crane and Kaye, *Census,* No. 179.

The London Gazette, London, Crane and Kaye, *Census,* No. 665.

Luttrell, *Brief Relations:* Luttrell, Narcissus, *A Brief Historical Relation of State Affairs from September 1678 to April 1714,* 6 vols., Oxford, 1857.

Macdonald, *Dryden Bibliography:* Macdonald, Hugh, *John Dryden. A Bibliography of Early Editions and Drydeniana,* Oxford, Clarendon Press, 1939.

Muddiman, *The King's Journalist:* Muddiman, J. G., *The King's Journalist, 1659–1689,* London, John Lane, 1923.

Nicoll, *Restoration Drama:* Nicoll, Allardyce, *A History of Restoration Drama, 1660–1700,* Cambridge, Cambridge University Press, 1928.

North, *Examen:* North, Roger, *Examen: or, An Enquiry into . . . a Pretended Complete History . . . ,* London, 1740.

North, *Lives:* North, Roger, *The Lives of the Norths,* ed. Augustus Jessop, 3 vols., London, 1890.

Noyes, *Dryden:* See entry under Dryden.

Ogg, *Charles II:* Ogg, David, *England in the Reign of Charles II,* 2 vols., 2nd ed., Oxford, Clarendon Press, 1956.

Oldmixon, John, *The History of Addresses. By one very near a kin to the author of The Tale of a Tub . . . ,* 2 vols., London, 1709–1711.

Osborn, *Dryden: Facts and Problems:* Osborn, James M., *John Dryden: Some Biographical Facts and Problems,* New York, Columbia University Press, 1940.

Osborne, Mary Tom, *Advice-to-a-Painter Poems, 1633–1856. An Annotated Finding List,* Austin, University of Texas Press, 1949.

Otway, *Works:* Otway, Thomas, *Works,* ed. J. C. Ghosh, 2 vols., Oxford, Clarendon Press, 1932.

Oxford Companion to English Literature, compiled and edited by Sir Paul Harvey, Oxford, Clarendon Press, 1934.

Oxford Dictionary of English Proverbs, ed. W. G. Smith; 2nd ed. revised by Sir Paul Harvey, Oxford, Clarendon Press, 1948.

OED: Oxford English Dictionary, ed. Sir J. A. H. Murray et al., corrected re-issue, 13 vols., Oxford, Clarendon Press, 1933.

Observator: L'Estrange, Sir Roger, *The Observator in Dialogue,* Crane and Kaye, *Census,* No. 636. Collected, 3 vols. in 2: vol. 1 (Nos. 1–470), London, 1684; vol. 2 (Nos. 471–473, 4–215) and vol. 3 (Nos. 1–246), London, 1687.

Papillon, *Papillon:* Papillon, A. F. W., *Memoirs of Thomas Papillon, of London, Merchant (1623–1702),* Reading, 1887.

Partridge, *Dictionary of Slang:* Partridge, Eric, *A Dictionary of Slang and Unconventional English,* 4th ed., London, Routledge and Kegan Paul, 1956.

Pollock, Sir John, *The Popish Plot,* London, Duckworth, 1903; also, Cambridge, Cambridge University Press, 1944.

Ralph, *History:* Ralph, James, *The History of England . . . ,* 2 vols., London, 1744–1746.

Reresby, *Memoirs:* Reresby, Sir John, *Memoirs and Selected Letters,* ed. Andrew Browning, Glasgow, Jackson, Son, and Co., 1936.

Roberts, *Life:* Roberts, George, *The Life, Progress, and Rebellion of James, Duke of Monmouth,* 2 vols., London, 1844.

Routh, *Tangiers:* Routh, E. M. G., *Tangiers, 1661–1684,* London, John Murray, 1912.

Roxburghe Ballads: The Roxburghe Ballads: Illustrating the Last Years of the Stuarts, ed. J. Woodfall Ebsworth, 8 vols., The Ballad Society, Hertford, 1878–1896. (Vol. 4, 1883; vol. 5, 1885.)

Rump: Rump: or an Exact Collection of the Choicest Poems and Songs Relating to the Late Times. By the Most Eminent Wits, from Anno 1639 to Anno 1661, London, 1662. (Case, No. 128 [c]; facsimile reproduction [1874].)

Seyffert, Oskar, *A Dictionary of Classical Antiquities* . . . , New York, Meridian Books, 1957.

Shadwell, *Works*: Shadwell, Thomas, *Works,* ed. Montague Summers, 5 vols., London, Fortune Press, 1927.

Sharpe, Reginald R., *London and the Kingdom*, 3 vols., London, 1894.

Somers Tracts: A Collection of Scarce and Valuable Tracts, Selected from . . . Private Libraries: Particularly that of . . . Lord Sommers, ed. Sir Walter Scott, 13 vols., London, 1809–1815.

Sprat, *Copies*: Sprat, Thomas, *Copies of the Informations and Original Papers* . . . , London, 1685 [S5029].

Sprat, *True Account*: Sprat, Thomas, *A True Account and Declaration of the Horrid Conspiracy* . . . , London, 1685 [S5066].

S.,–S., *Dryden*: See entry under Dryden.

Thompson: See entry under *Loyal Protestant.*

Tilley, *Proverbs*: Tilley, M. P., *A Dictionary of the Proverbs of England in the Sixteenth and Seventeenth Centuries,* Ann Arbor, University of Michigan Press, 1950.

Warrack, *Scots Dialect Dictionary:* Warrack, Alexander, *A Scots Dialect Dictionary,* London and Edinburgh, W. and R. Chambers, 1911.

Whiting, *Studies in English Puritanism:* Whiting, Charles Edwin, *Studies in English Puritanism from the Restoration to the Revolution, 1660–1688,* London, S. P. C. K., 1931.

Wiley, Autrey N., *Rare Prologues and Epilogues, 1642–1700,* London, Allen and Unwin, 1940.

Wing: *Short Title Catalogue . . . of English Books printed . . . 1641–1700,* compiled by Donald Wing, 3 vols., The Index Society, New York, Columbia University Press, 1945–1951.

Wood, Anthony A, *Athenae Oxoniensis,* ed. Philip Bliss, 4 vols., London, 1813–1820.

Wood, Anthony A, *The Life and Times of Anthony Wood, Antiquary of Oxford, 1632–1695, described by himself,* ed. Andrew Clark, 5 vols., Oxford Historical Society (Nos. 19, 21, 26, 30, 40), Oxford, 1891–1895.

Wright, *A Compendious View:* Wright, James, *A Compendious View of the Late Tumults in this Kingdom, by way of Annals for Seven Years,* London, 1685 [W3692].

Wynne, William, *The Life of Sir Leoline Jenkins* . . . , 2 vols., London, 1724.

Introduction

INTRODUCTION

IN MARCH 1681, Charles II dissolved what proved to be the last parliament of his reign. The effect on the political verse was astonishing, not so much because of the opinions that the event evoked, but because the censorship laws fell into abeyance. To see the change in the poetry, we need only compare the subsequent verse with the satire of the 1640s and of the 1660s. During the Commonwealth period, when the presses were very strictly controlled, the writer of political verse often had first to inform his audience of the event about which he was writing before he could bring in his own polemic views concerning it. The result is a verse that tends to be restricted in its opening stanzas by the expository nature of narrative poetry, and in its closing stanzas by the relatively simple attack of social complaint. With the restoration of Charles II in 1660, political verse flowered, but it did so mainly in the closed circles of the Court and Westminster Hall, and it was further restricted by censorship laws that frequently held its circulation to manuscript copies or to surreptitious printings. As well, the average writer of political verse at this time seems more interested in personal vilification than public issues, more interested in giving his attention to people of quality than to people in quantity. Such broad statements as these naturally invite exceptions: on the one hand, they are only partially applicable to men such as Butler, Marvell, or Dryden; on the other, they fail to point out alternative, less direct, methods by which the government could attempt to control the press. Yet, even granting these and other objections, the fact remains that the verse of the closing years of Charles' reign differs markedly from that which preceded it.

One reason for this change lay in the development of a better informed public, a situation that would certainly seem to come from the wider and more rapid dissemination of news. By the 1680s, not only had the postal system expanded, with the result that correspondence was becoming more rapid and more widely used, but with that expansion, there developed a remarkable increase in the number of manuscript newsletters and printed news-sheets—the former sent out to subscribers, the latter appearing as well in the many taverns and public houses that lined the post roads of England. While both of these media tended to increase from one to three issues per week in accordance with increased postal service, the news-sheets were especially important, carrying a variety of information and opinion throughout London within a matter of hours, and into the farthest corners of the nation within two or three days.

For the writer of political verse, this steady flow of opinionated news meant a wider public aware of both the events and the basic political positions about which he was writing. As a consequence, he was able to attempt more sophisticated satiric effects, using irony, the mask of the persona, wit, rapid allusion to other contemporary events, biblical and classical analogues, and popular slogans or catchwords now charged with meaning for the general reader. As well, the poet seems more and more to be thinking of his audience as limited not merely to a certain group in London, but to all of London, or, better, to London *and* the kingdom. And the same can be said of the events about which he writes: though these events might take place in London, they are considered relevant to the nation as a whole.

Perhaps one reason for this is the gradual acceptance of the idea of parties—as opposed to causes—of national scope. Again, a brief glance backward may serve to point up the shift. During the 1640s, certain members of Parliament reacted as a political unit (i.e. as a party) as a result of their primary commitment to a cause—to what, in fact, was to be aptly named the "Good Old Cause." During this period, religion was the dialectic of politics; that is to say, politics was conceptualized in terms of religion: a religious position was, *ipso facto,* a political position, and the entire spectrum of Protestantism was represented. The 1680s do not present the complete reversal of this situation—that did not come about until the Walpole administration—but the decade does constitute a crucially formative period, the tentative nature of which can be seen not only in the names given parties—Whig and Tory, Country (or Anti-Court) and Court—but even more in the character of the two principal leaders, Shaftesbury and Charles.

Anthony Ashley Cooper rose through the tergiversations of the

Commonwealth and Restoration period to become first Earl of Shaftesbury in 1672. A moving speaker in an age that valued oratory (even his opponents referred to him by the nicely ambiguous title of "Little Sincerity"), he was the spokesman and the rallying point of a strange agglomeration that stood in opposition to the Court. While this group ranged from radical republicans who wished to re-establish a commonwealth to political conservatives who sought to check royal power, its main strength lay in the rapidly disappearing class of moderate Puritans and Parliamentarians that had been the firm foundation of Cromwell's ever more moderate administration. But Shaftesbury seemed fated to be the leader of forces that were just insufficient for victory: to the moderates of both country and city, his party's almost nostalgic appeal to "Liberty and Property" sounded ever more dated in a period when property was suffering nothing but increase and when liberty was being restricted (with at least theoretical impartiality) only for religious extremists of both left and right. Not only was Shaftesbury general of an aging army, but his strongest weapon—exclusion of the Catholic Duke of York from succession—was negative, his only substitute—the bastard Duke of Monmouth—was distinctly illegitimate, and his best field of bat-tle—the Parliament—was increasingly under the control of Charles' prorogations and dissolutions. And, finally, the foremost popular issue—the Popish Plot—had inherently the short life of a sensa-tional event, and so questionable were the motives and revelations of its discoverer, Titus Oates, that it soon changed from a widely held belief to an article of party faith. Try as he might to sustain the life of the Plot, Shaftesbury could not bring even this seed of discord to any positive political fruition, for here, as in the case of Exclusion, the logical end—a restoration of commonwealth govern-ment—was simply out of the question for the overwhelming major-ity of his followers. Although neither the religious zeal of the past nor the political experience of the future existed at this moment with sufficient force to exploit either Exclusion or the Plot, in both instances it is nevertheless clear that Whig frustration intensified the sense of party rather than cause, and that any expression of that pent-up feeling had to take the form of political action, not the armed revolt that a fast-disappearing generation had once pursued with religious zeal.

Time was Shaftesbury's principal adversary. If the familiar forces of the past were constantly receding, those of the future were coming on in a strange guise. These new men appeared following the last great display of Whig power—Shaftesbury's release by a packed grand jury from the Crown's charge of high treason. On the one hand, there was the City leadership, practical and courageous, of the Whig sheriff, Thomas Pilkington, who led the party through the crucial shrieval election of 1682; on the other, there was the national leadership, which was becoming increasingly political (as opposed to religious) both in theory and temper under men such as Sidney, Russell, and Essex, all of whom suffered in 1683 for their connection with the Whig Conspiracy—if we may so designate by a single title both their own plans for an armed uprising and the extremists' plot to assassinate Charles and James at the Rye House. These new leaders that replaced Shaftesbury are representative of the slight but rather critical shift of emphasis that moves us from the end of one era to the beginning of the next as religion is being displaced by politics.

The fact that Shaftesbury and the Whigs were forced into a progressively negative position (that is, they were always becoming more anti-Court) testifies to the astonishing success of Court policy. When Charles returned to England in 1660, he was a king with almost no real power. Indeed, his restoration seemed to have been brought about by equal parts of positive support, fear of anarchy, powerless opposition, and studied indifference. Charles could not have displaced the mellowed and moderate government of Oliver Cromwell's last years by force: he was invited back by Monck, the commander of the last organized force in a rapidly disintegrating government; and, even then, he agreed to issue the Declaration of Breda, leaving in question the vast transfer of property that had taken place during the Commonwealth and putting off those Cavaliers who had sacrificed most in their ardent royalism.

Slowly, Charles built up the royal power, at first by avoiding extremes (vengeance was visited only on the regicides) and then by condemning extremes. In the latter case, this meant, at least in theory, extremes of the left (radical sects and republicans) and extremes of the right (Roman Catholicism and believers in royal absolutism), but with time it became apparent that Charles' inclinations favored the second. The same gradual shift can be seen in the political temper of the reign: in 1660, Charles perforce depended on the moderate left; by 1685, he had developed a strong force in the moderate right sufficiently broad so that England accepted the accession of the Catholic James and firmly rejected the call for a Protestant revolution raised by the invading Duke of Monmouth.

Charles had carefully nurtured this gradual shift throughout his reign; with patient determination he rode out the storms of criticism that centered on Danby and the thunder and lightning of the Popish Plot. The second Charles Stuart had learned thoroughly from history: he was a master of the art of the possible and a brilliant practitioner of the subtle tactic of waiting. Time favored Charles, finally giving him the opportunity to move against London, the center of his opposition, in 1682. As ever, the attack was legalistic in nature. It began quietly enough with Charles' prohibition of the Whig feast of 22 April 1682, reached full scale proportions in the dramatic contention over the shrieval posts during the summer, and ended in 1683 with the crushing defeat of the London municipal government in the Quo Warranto proceedings against the City's charter. Thus began what has been called the "Stuart revenge," a series of legal actions against the principal Whigs that unexpectedly received its most sensational impulse from the two almost separate plans—the republican Rye House Plot for the assassination of Charles and James, and the Whig leaders' plan for an armed uprising—best referred to as the Whig Conspiracy.

Even without this added impetus, the drama of the "Stuart revenge" was almost bound to be set in the law courts, for both Charles I and Charles II as basically conceived of politics in terms of law as their opponents conceived of it in terms of religion. The failure of the two groups to understand each other can be seen in the pathetic lack of communication at the trial of Charles I or (to take an example from the other side) in the Whigs' failure to comprehend until too late the full implications of Charles II's assertion that he would "rule by law." The shrieval elections of 1682 became (in the incisive phrase of the contemporary Roger North), a *bataille rangée* precisely because the Whig sheriffs were threatening Stuart control of the legal structure by impaneling grand juries hostile to Court policy. Charles brought to bear every ounce of pressure in order to capture these insignificant posts which at best were honorific and at all times costly. The full weight of the Court's legal and administrative machinery was set in motion; Ormonde, Halifax, and especially the outstanding Secretary of State for the South, Leoline Jenkins, were employed in advancing the Court's attack. Above all, however, it was Charles who personally directed the entire operation, receiving reports from the election halls, refusing to leave London at times of crisis, and ordering moves that were to immobilize the City Whigs. Basically, the contention was between executive power, represented by John Moore, the Lord Mayor (backed by the Court Party), and elective power, represented by Thomas Pilkington, one of the two incumbent sheriffs (backed by the majority of electors at the polls). Not until the Fall did the Whigs begin to realize that their ultimate weapon, an avenging parliament, had been spiked. Charles, in a "Popish Plot" more far-reaching than any Oates had ever suggested, was receiving just enough subsidy from Louis XIV to avoid summoning a parliament. The shrieval elections in many ways epitomize the course of Restoration politics. As always, Charles' sense of timing was superb, his delegation of authority artfully carried out, and his exploitation of a well-chosen situation pushed to the limits of the possible.

The basic elements of Charles' policy seem eminently simple, though their implementation shows the infinite complexity of a master politician. Charles summed up the most essential element with the characteristically witty remark that he was determined not to go on his "travels" again. His steady assertion of real power during the sixties and seventies insured this. The second element was dynastic. Through all the convolutions of the Exclusion Parliaments, through all the exiles-and-returns meted out with apparent impartiality to York and Monmouth, it is perfectly clear that Charles was determined that the succession would fall to the legitimate but Catholic—as opposed to the illegitimate but Protestant—Stuart heir. The final element was religious. In return for French subsidies, Charles had agreed to do what he could to bring Roman Catholicism to England; but this did not entail any change in policy, indeed it only served to confirm Charles' succession policy and his own covert Catholicism. The success of Charles' policy can be measured by the political temper at the end of his reign; he left to James a nation that could accept a strong monarchy with relatively little difficulty and a Catholic monarch with only slightly more.

Not all of this should be attributed to Charles' political acumen. A new generation had grown up that was as distinct from the Commonwealth in absolute time as the first World War was from the second; and the thirty-six year period since Charles I had been executed by a Commons that considered itself the supreme power is temporally equivalent to that which separates the era of William McKinley from that of Franklin Roosevelt. Not only had Charles II ridden out the winds and storms that had blown across these years, he had successfully brought into port an ever more obsolescent ship —but one that was in far better repair and with a more willing crew than he had had at the start.

In connection with this, two points perhaps need additional explanation. Looking back over three centuries, we may tend to sympathize with the more representative branch of government, the parliament, and may even consider a monarch who sought to check its power as simply wrongheaded. During the seventeenth century, the scales of power were most delicately balanced between parliament and Court, and often the slightest shift or the least addition was sufficient to make them swing to one side or the other. On the Court side, Charles had developed a party which, if not so numerous as the Whigs, received strong support from the civil and legal administrations which the King had so carefully built up. This combination, along with the sacrifices that he was willing to make in order to be financially independent of parliament, gave the King an immense advantage in his last years. Without a parliament, the Whigs could not gain concessions in exchange for subsidies, they could not hope to diminish royal power by attacking "the King's evil counsellors," they could not circumvent the judiciary by calling their opponents to the bar. The "Whig revenge" was to come later, in 1688, and chiefly as a reaction to James II's heavyhanded policy; between 1682 and 1685, however, the scales first wavered slightly and then came down on the King's side.

One reason for the seesawing of power that occurred during the Restoration may be that a critical number of Englishmen stood very near the fulcrum of the seesaw, where even a slight movement could produce major changes in the positions of the opposing parties. This is the other point that may need some explanation. Looked at cursorily, the political verse would seem to bear out the impression that England was clearly divided into Whig and Tory factions; but if we look not so much to the author as to the audience he was addressing, a more realistic picture emerges. Certainly there are verses of mere fulmination which could only convince the convinced, but the more accomplished political verse seeks by logic, wit, analogy, or poetic skill, or (as in Dryden's case) by all of these and more, to persuade. This poetry of persuasion, avoiding the direct aggressiveness of sermon or complaint, most frequently makes use of satire, a mode which depends upon indirection and which therefore forces the reader to supply the implied ethos. And the reader to whom this poetry of persuasion is making its appeal is a member not of any extremist group but of the very large moderate force that supplied the relative stability that is the mark of the English political scene. It would be a mistake, however, to think that the position of the moderates remained fixed and unmoving, a kind of dead center.

Two brief examples illustrate the significant shift in political sentiment of this middle group. The first part of Dryden's *Absalom and Achitophel* appeared in November 1681. At once witty and temperate, the poem aims (to use Dryden's phrase) at "the moderate sort"; it is neither a polemic against the hard-core Whigs nor a manifesto for the conservative Tories. In striking contrast to this poem's attempt to appeal to those of a moderate and slightly left of moderate position, the *Second Part,* which appeared just a year later, is far more aggressive and takes as its audience those whom we might consider as being to the right of center. Too frequently, this change has been attributed to Nahum Tate's presence as a collaborator, but it owes more to that difference in England's political temper that one finds generally in the poetry that appears after the critical *bataille rangée* of the summer of 1682. Indeed, as I have suggested in the headnote to the *Second Part,* there is the distinct possibility that the later poem contains the *disjecta membra* of the earlier one. These are just the passages that would have been inappropriate to the persuasive purpose of the first part, though quite usable once the defeat of the Whigs had created a situation in which Court policy could be more aggressively promulgated. The second example of the shift in political sentiment occurs on 13 November 1682, just three days after the appearance of the Dryden-Tate poem. On that date, Roger L'Estrange's stridently Tory periodical, *The Observator,* significantly changed the speakers of its dialogue-essay from Whig and Tory to Trimmer and Tory. With the obliteration of the more extreme position (that of "Whig"), L'Estrange, like the Court Party he so fervently supported, now concentrated his fire on the next target, those of the moderate left (the Trimmers) who believed that some sort of accommodation with royal power was necessary in order to balance the political forces of the moment. Like the greater boldness of Dryden and Tate, L'Estrange's choice of a new target reflects not only the nullification of the militant left but also the subsequent shift to the right of the whole political structure.

Charles bought this measure of domestic strength at the cost of foreign greatness. Tangier, the dowry of his queen, Catherine of Braganza, constituted the basis of Charles' dream of a Mediterranean empire. Into that port he had poured whatever sums of men, money, and materiel he could get, but the first and last of these were dependent upon the second, and the second depended on subsidies from parliaments that would grant them only at the price of Exclusion. When Charles finally decided to neutralize the Whigs' most powerful weapon by not calling a new parliament, he simultaneously was shattering his hope for English mercantile greatness. Once his funds ran out—and Louis had been careful to give only enough to sustain domestic independence—nothing remained for Charles but the bitter order, given in July 1683, to destroy the town and its outlying fortifications, the harbor and its magnificent new mole; nothing but rubble remained for the warring Sultan of Morocco —and for Charles as well. The King had paid dearly for domestic control in 1682, and he pressed his advantage relentlessly by means of a legal system which he now completely controlled. Not surprisingly, the splintered opposition, frustrated and leaderless, attempted in the Whig Conspiracy just the kind of desperate and sophomoric gamble that swung the vast majority of the kingdom behind not only Charles but also James. The Whig Conspiracy, as well, gave the Court the opportunity of extending its legal attacks both in depth and in degree; it was now the secondary ranks and the potential leaders that could be brought to law and punished not merely with the ruinous fines imposed for *scandalum magnatum* but with the ignominy of a traitor's death.

Once more, however, it must be recalled that England was not simply divided into two camps, Whig and Tory, but rather presented a spectrum in which the numerical majority varied to one side or the other of center. The anti-Court forces that had been so effectively checked by Charles in 1683 were only the opposite end of that spectrum. How large this faction was numerically is almost impossible to determine with any degree of accuracy, but one can say that its political or executive power during these years of 1682 to 1685 was remarkably thin in comparison with the disturbance that it caused. Naturally, in the rural areas, a single Whig (or, for that matter, Tory) magnate wielded far more influence than his counterpart in populous London. At the national level, his influence was manifested most forcefully through a parliament, and once Charles ceased summoning parliaments, the power of the individual magnate became again localized, with no outlet save directly through the favor of Court-controlled executive power or, indirectly, through party pressure at London, the seat of power. It is for this reason, among others, that such mighty forces converge on London and its municipal government, be it on the occasion of a Pope-burning procession or in the matter of the shrieval elections.

In point of fact, the influence of the Whigs in London's corporation represents more a fortuitous concatenation of events than any overwhelming expression of administrative power. The government of the City rested with the aldermanic council; from this body, a lord mayor was chosen and in him the City vested its executive power, a power that was confirmed by the king whose officer he was. The aldermanic council was composed of City magnates, men who had risen to wealth and power, often through the guilds. Contrary to the opinion of some modern historians that class and politics were firmly welded together and that a rising bourgeois was *ipso facto* Whig, the Court of Aldermen was predominantly Tory, and in 1682, according to the contemporary Tory historian Roger North, there were only "five aldermen of the faction" in a body that had twenty-six members. Indeed, in October 1683, after the famous Quo Warranto proceedings which forced London to surrender its charter, Charles replaced only eight aldermen—Alleyn, Frederick, Shorter, Lawrence, Clayton, Ward, Gold, and Cornish (the first two being not so much Whigs as Dissenters)—although he was quite free to choose whom he wished. But, as Beaven has pointed out in his invaluable study on *The Aldermen of the City of London* (2, 109), "the 18 aldermen who retained their seats were all uncompromising Tories." How, then, had the City become such a Whig stronghold in the period just preceding the opening date of this volume? Undoubtedly, the party had a large numerical following, but that had been true formerly. Rather, one feels, the reason lies in the fact that a particular set of circumstances produced consecutively two lord mayors—Robert Clayton (1679–80) and Patience Ward (1680–81)—who, as ardent Whigs, sympathized strongly with those who supported Oates and Exclusion in the City.

The critical moment came with the selection of Ward's successor, for there were few if any Whig aldermen who could be nominated. Lawrence and Clayton had already served; Gold, Shorter, and Cornish had all undertaken the highly expensive shrievalty within the past five years; Ward was retiring as lord mayor, and Pilkington was the incumbent sheriff. In John Moore, the small group of Whig aldermen must have felt they had a malleable figure who could be molded by public pressure and directed by the two incumbent Whig sheriffs, Pilkington and Shute. Moore was, indeed, malleable yet, once formed, quite set in his attitude; but it was the Court, through Secretary Jenkins and ultimately Charles himself, that seized the opportunity and successfully won over the new mayor through flattery, attention, and massive support. Sooner or later, of course, a Tory alderman would have gained the mayoralty, but Jenkins' astuteness saved the Court at least a year's difficulty, in many ways making possible the shrieval victory, the forfeiture of the charter, and the final Stuart triumph. Faced with a combination of the Court's political skill, its control of the judiciary, its check of parliament, and its weight in municipal government, the anti-Court group did remarkably well with surprisingly little. By the end of 1683, Charles had left his opponents very few cards to play—and, in fact, he had left very few opponents.

Charles lived out the last months of his reign in almost a golden glow. In the twenty-five years since the Restoration, he had done much to suppress the faction and anarchy generated during the last years of the Commonwealth; he had returned to the monarchy a great deal of the absolute power it had had under the first Charles, though with that return came the inescapable problems of royal absolutism. Charles II, who surpassed his father in political astuteness, did not live to face those problems; James, who surpassed his father in impolitic righteousness, not only faced them but in many ways aggravated them.

II

The comparative liberty of the press following the expiration of the censorship laws has strongly affected the nature of the contents and the texts of the present volume. With such a degree of freedom, almost every significant event received the immediate attention of political poets intent on persuading the public of the justness of their cause. As a result, we frequently have several interpretations of a specific subject that, through newspapers, pamphlets, and other poems, was thoroughly familiar to the poet's audience. More and more, the poetry broadened to meet the new conditions; it tended to speak to a wider public, to avoid personal scurrility in favor of satire on types or issues, and to replace narrow invective with wit and allusion. Billingsgate attacks on the Court ladies did not entirely cease, and scatological verses still listed the lusts of fops and time-servers, but such screeds became insignificant once an open press could voice the general interest in public affairs.

The texts as well as the contents of this volume also reflect the less stringent censorship. No longer did verses have to be passed around in manuscript copies, each one of which—as we have seen in the first volume of this series—invited a chaos of variant texts; rather, most poetry appeared almost at once in print, frequently only once, with the consequence that many of the difficulties of manuscript transmission disappear in the present volume. Generally speaking, subsequent appearances of such poems derive quite clearly from the original printing; and this tends to be true not only for re-editions of the original, but for reprintings in *POAS* and other collections of the period as well.

This situation has of course strongly influenced my choice of copy text, but an additional factor has been my desire to present the text that the pamphletbuying Englishman would have had in his hand at that time. Naturally, one cannot follow such a rule blindly, but, considering the public and instantaneous effect of these poems, it seems relevant to try, within the limits of this edition, to recreate the conditions of the moment.

A highly important by-product of this process of widespread publication comes to us through the collecting habits of the contemporary Narcissus Luttrell. That formidable chronicler apparently bought a copy of every political poem that appeared in print, add-

ing regularly the price of the item and (even more helpfully) a date
of acquisition which, in most instances, coincides with the date
of publication. As a result, about 70 per cent (forty-two) of the poems
in this volume can be dated precisely; and of the remaining nine-
teen, about one-third (six) can be located within a week or two by
virtue of internal evidence, while the others can only be approxi-
mated within a matter of months.

The fullness of the poetic coverage of events, combined with the
relative exactness of dating, has led to the organization of this vol-
ume mainly on chronological lines, as opposed to the topical group-
ing of the two preceding volumes. With one or two exceptions, I
have varied from chronological presentation only where a specific
event (the shrieval elections, the Quo Warranto proceedings, or the
Whig Conspiracy) evoked a long contention that can be more fully
and easily grasped when the poems are brought together than when
they are spread over the weeks or perhaps months during which they
appeared. In general, however, a chronological arrangement has
been followed, not simply to give a history of the period as the po-
litical versifiers saw it, but, even more, to recreate somewhat the
succession of historical moments in which the poems appeared—to
supply (albeit artificially) some of the setting in which the poem
was first read. Such an attempt is never wholly successful (as Tris-
tram Shandy was to discover), but it must be made, however inade-
quately, if only to give back to the poems some of the allusive force
and literary effectiveness that they had at the time of their appear-
ance.

On the whole, political verse depends for its vitality if not on the
specific occasion that evoked it, at least on the times; and as the
occasion loses its motive and passion or as the times contract into
a paragraph of some history book, the poetry even more rapidly
becomes devitalized. True, the writing of certain poets—of Dryden
and Marvell, for example—seems to succeed by relating the specific
event to a larger theme, by making that event representative of a
more timeless situation. Yet even here we are often in danger of los-
ing the complex conditions of the event and, perhaps, of reading the
poem in just the opposite way (i.e. from the general to the specific)
from that in which the poet expected his audience would read it.
Most of the poems, however, concentrate on immediate situations
that, at first glance, may seem to us insignificant or irrelevant. Only

by attempting to recreate the life of this period can we hope to understand the effectiveness of a particular poetic form, the implications of the tune to which a ballad is set, the wit behind some particular allusion, or the connotations of an apparently innocuous phrase.

III

In keeping with the previous volumes, the texts have been modernized. Punctuation is surely one of the most difficult parts of such a process for several reasons: first, the tendency of the times was to overpunctuate; secondly, pointing practices both of the writer and the compositor were highly idiosyncratic; and, finally, many of the political versifiers composed (and therefore punctuated) basically in an oral rather than written rhetoric. General overpunctuation can be cleared up with comparative ease, and even the idiosyncrasies of a particular poem can be met insofar as that poem is concerned, but we encounter more organic problems when "translating" the looser punctuation (and syntax) of oral rhetoric into the more precise practices of today's written rhetoric. Many of these problems, like the idiosyncrasies of punctuation, can be resolved; but such resolutions should not obliterate the characteristic tone of the poetry by turning it into either closed couplets or dramatic verse. The reader will find, therefore, that the punctuation, rather than being strictly uniform, varies somewhat in order to meet the conditions of the individual poem.

More important changes, those of a substantive nature, have been recorded in the textual notes, but there is no doubt that the definition of "substantive" will vary with the individual reader. Both in punctuation and spelling, what constitutes a substantive change is frequently a matter of personal evaluation. Certain words—for instance *Absalon/Absalom* or *Sanhedrim/Sanhedrin*—are spelled indiscriminately in the original texts; and, indeed, either form may be found as a rhyme word. Or, again, *satyr(e)/satire* may be used interchangeably, though on occasion a poet may allude to the tradition that connects the genre (satire) with the rough-haired, goatfooted beast (satyr). Or, finally, when Dryden refers in the opening of *The Medal* to "all our Antick Sights, and Pageantry," the adjective may be modern *antic* or *antique*—or both. In these and similar instances, the editor of a modernized text must use his discretion in deciding what to give as the form in his texts and what to note as a substantive change.

In accordance with the preceding volumes, the following practices have been observed: (1) Old spellings are retained only when rhyme or meaning would be lost by the change; (2) Proper names, when abbreviated, have been expanded and their spelling has been standardized throughout to that found in the *Dictionary of National Biography;* (3) Definitions come from the *Oxford English Dictionary* unless otherwise indicated; (4) Where no textual notes are given, no substantive textual variants have been found; (5) Wherever possible, specific printed texts are referred to by their Wing number, i.e. the number assigned them in Donald Wing, *Short Title Catalogue . . . 1641–1700.*

1682

The Compleat Swearing-Master

[C 5659]

While *The Compleat Swearing-Master* is not totally accurate in its account of Oates' confused and confusing testimony, it nevertheless represents a witty and incisive analysis of the more blatant discrepancies at a time when Oates' moral and financial credit were beginning to be challenged in the very law courts where he had performed so spectacularly. Nor are these discrepancies first found in this ballad; the chief Tory propagandist, Roger L'Estrange, had been pointing them out in print since 1680 and, with his astonishing ability to combine jest and earnest, had remarked in 1683 that "whoever made him [Oates] a divine spoiled the best romancer in Christendom" (*Observator,* No. 365 [28 June 1683]) . The spirit of ridicule, however, did not predominate until the Popish Plot had passed its real crisis, which, while its date may vary with individual interpretations, probably coincides with the dissolution of the Oxford Parliament on 21 March 1681.

This poem, printed for Allen Banks, may also have been written by him. Banks, a bookseller in Fetter Lane from 1673 to 1682 (H. R. Plomer, *Dictionary of Printers and Booksellers . . . 1668–1725,* ed. A. Esdaile [London, 1922], p. 18), published a ballad of a similar nature, *Titus Tell-Troth* [T 1316]; the Whig reply, *Thompson Tell-Lies* [T 1019A], implies strongly that Banks was the author.

The great contemporary collector, Narcissus Luttrell, obtained his copy of the poem on 18 July 1682. This would be very close to, if not precisely, the date of publication. I have violated chronological order because the poem deals mainly with matters of the preceding year. It was reprinted in *e.*

THE COMPLEAT SWEARING-MASTER

A Rare New Salamanca Ballad
To the Tune of, "Now, Now the Fight's Done"

1.

Once on a time, the Doctor did swear,   1
By the help of his friend the Prince of the Air,
He was busy in consult, one day in Spain,
And on the same day in England again,

Title: "The Compleat————" is the title of innumerable books of the period and
carries the implication of a serious work that is encyclopaedic and definitive.

Salamanca: Oates claimed to have received the degree of Doctor of Divinity from the
University of Salamanca sometime in 1677. L'Estrange printed the total denial by the
University authorities of Oates' self-conferred honor (see *Observator,* No. 225 [17 Oct.
1682] for the Latin text, No. 227 [21 Oct. 1682] for the Latin text with English transla-
tion, and No. 237, [8 Nov. 1682] for the names of the fourteen doctors and three notaries
who swore to the statement), and at about the same time Allen Banks printed a verse
attack entitled *An Address from Salamanca to her Unknown Off-spring Dr. T. O.* ("Son
Titus, for so you strive to be") [A 540]. As Jane Lane remarks, "to the end of his days,
seriously among his admirers, derisively among the rest of his contemporaries, he
remained the Salamanca Doctor" (*Oates,* p. 58) .

2. *Prince of the Air:* The devil.

3–4. Oates dated his movements with extraordinary carelessness. Though the famous
"Grand Consult" of the Jesuits was said to have taken place on 24 April 1678, for
example, the testimony of the accused and also witnesses brought over from Flanders
supported the fact that Oates had been at the Catholic college at St. Omer at this
time. Oates marshalled counter-testimony that he had been seen in London during this
entire period; but there was some question even then of the validity of Oates' witnesses,
several of them being uncertain whether the year was 1677 or 1678. If the entire
affair had occurred in the previous year, Oates would indeed have had to be in both
Spain (at Valladolid) and England simultaneously. It was the question of dates that
caused Oates' conviction for perjury in 1685. Cf. *The Melancholy Complaint of
D[octor] Oates* [M 1634] (London, 1684) where Oates, listing the expenses he has
undergone, includes

> . . . flying horses which could scour
> To France or Spain and back in half an hour,
> With Old Nick's fees for granting me this power
>   (p. 2) .

And the Doctor did swear that Noble Don John,   5
Though little and black, was a tall fair man.

2.

The Doctor swore he brought commissions to town
From Father Oliva to men of renown,
To raise mighty force, the King to destroy,
For which many ruffians the Pope did employ;   10
And the Doctor did swear that little Don John,
And fair and also a very tall man.

3.

That forty thousand pilgrims there were,
Arm'd with black bills, that march'd in the air,

5–6. While there is some variation on the exact wording of Oates' reply to Charles' famous question concerning Don John (see Lane, *Oates*, p. 105), there is general agreement that Oates did not do well at all. The author in this instance follows the version given by Sir John Pollock, *The Popish Plot* (new ed. London, 1944): "He had named in his narrative Don John of Austria as not only cognizant of the plot, but active in it. What was he like? asked Charles. Tall and graceful, with fair hair, Oates replied promptly. Charles had seen Don John and knew him to be short, fat, and dark" (p. 77). See also *An Ironical Encomium*, 52 n.

8. *Father Oliva:* Johannes Paulus de Oliva (1600–81), general of the Society of Jesus. Oates claimed that he had carried sealed commissions from Oliva and the Pope to Thomas Whitebread, the English Provincial, for a popish army of 40,000 men. This occasioned the calling of the famous "General Consult" at the White Horse Tavern on 4 May. For Evelyn's reflections, see *Diary, 4,* 174–75.

10. Oates stated that on 22 August he had seen "£80 counted out and despatched by Harcourt, in the name of the Provincial, for the hire of the Four Irish Ruffians" to "'mind the King's pastures at Windsor'" (Lane, *Oates,* p. 100).

13. Cf. *The Melancholy Complaint:*

> I raised forty thousand of the dead
> Soldiers that from their camp last age were fled. . . .
> Armies of pilgrims I call'd out of Spain
> Embark'd in a nut-shell safely on the main
> And in a trice convey'd them back again.
>
> (p. 7)

14. *black bills:* Oates repeated, at Coleman's trial on 26 Nov. 1678, that 40,000 black bills (i.e. halberds) had been ordered for the rebellion in Ireland (Lane, *Oates,* pp. 93, 147; North, *Examen,* p. 160).

> *march'd in the air:* Cf. *The Melancholy Complaint:*
>
> . . . frighted with the hideous cries
> Of fairy armies fighting in the skies.
>
> (p. 6)

And ready to strike when Pope should command,   15
And carry to Rome poor little England.
And the Doctor did swear, as few others can,
That little Don John is a tall fair man.

4.

And the Doctor did swear he had letters full many,
But for all he swore, he ne'er produc'd any.   20
It's much he kept none to make out the matter,
But it may be he lost them in crossing the water;
But that's all one, the Doctor swore on,
That little Don John was a tall fair man.

5.

He swore two hundred thousand pounds sent   25
To Ireland, which was all to be spent,
In squibs to burn houses, ammunition and bills,
And pay Popish doctors for King-killing pills:
Which he swore had been done if the plot had gone on—
And then swore Don John was a very fair man.   30

6.

And the Doctor did swear he knew not some men,
Yet afterwards swore he knew them again;

19–20. Oates claimed two sources of information: first, the great range of treasonous conversation that he had heard among the Jesuits and, secondly, the many letters that he said he carried between London and St. Omer and London and Madrid. All those that he got hold of (and a few others as well), he claimed to have opened and read, but none, of course, could be produced.

27. *The Melancholy Complaint* echoes the idea:

> That [the Papists] had made the great Vesuvian hills
> Into fire-balls as small as doctors' pills. . . .
> The traitorous Jesuits and their cursed backers
> Had made Mount Aetna in squibs and crackers. . .

(p. 7.)

Not only did Oates give support to the notion that the fire of London (1666) was a Catholic plot, but he swore also that Wapping (a sectarian center) and Westminster were to be burnt with squibs (an explosive firework) and "Tewkesbury mustard balls."

28. Sir George Wakeman, the Queen's physician, was, according to Oates, to be offered up to £15,000 for poisoning Charles II (Lane, *Oates,* p. 97). His acquittal on 18 July 1679 was based principally on his proving that Oates could not have known him and that the documents produced as evidence were indeed forgeries.

31–32. Though Edward Coleman, the secretary to the Duchess of York, had been present when Oates first made his full statement in the Council Chamber, no charge

And the Doctor did swear by fair candlelight,
He could not discern a man from a mite:
But believe him who will, for I hardly can, 35
That little Don John is a tall fair man.

7.

And he swore he always a Protestant was,
And ne'er car'd a fart for Pope or for mass,
And he swore he went to St. Omers to find
What the Jesuits had against England design'd. 40
And the Doctor did swear, deny it who can,
That little Don John is a tall fair man.

8.

And the Doctor did swear a thousand things more,
That discovering the plot had made him so poor,
And he swore himself seven hundred pounds worse— 45
But a pox of all lies, take that with a curse!
But I'll not believ't, although others can,
That little Don John is a tall fair man.

9.

Now if it should please the Doctor to swear,
To keep his hand in, a man is a bear; 50
Or the Doctor will swear his soul to the Devil,
He shall do it for me, I love to be civil;
Every man in his way, let the Doctor swear on—
But I beg his excuse in the size of Don John.

10.

The Doctor may swear the crow to be white, 55
Or a pigmy to be of gigantic height,
Or double his numbers of pilgrims and bills,

---

or identification was made against him at that time. It was only later that Oates accused Coleman with the tragically inadequate excuses that he had not previously identified Coleman because "my sight was had by candlelight," that he had been up for two nights and was weak, and that he had not then mentioned Coleman's horrendous deeds "because I had not been asked." Coleman's letters proved that he had been intriguing with France, but this had no connection with Oates' Popish Plot.

45. Oates' "bill of expenses" totaled £678 12s. 6d. and was the object of much ridicule (e.g. L'Estrange, *Observator*, 2, No. 61 [14 May 1684]).

And swear them drawn up in Lincoln's Inn Fields,
I hear't and believ't as much as I can
That little Don John is a tall fair man.   60

11.

There's no stopping the tide, let the Doctor swear on,
The black is the fair, or the fair the black man,
Or swear what he will, I care not a turd,
I'd as soon as his take another man's word.
So Doctor be damn'd and swear all you can,   65
Don John is not tall, nor yet a fair man.

58. Lincoln's Inn Fields was one of the few remaining open spaces in Westminster
where the trained bands could be drawn up. It was also the scene of public executions.

THOMAS DURFEY

The Whigs' Exaltation

[W 1657]

The use of music to sharpen the ironic tone of a writer's political view is exemplified in Durfey's use of Francis Quarles' famed lyrics of the early 1640s (published posthumously in *The Shepherd's Oracles*, 1646) with its sardonic chorus "And hey then up go we." Quarles' verses (beginning "Know this, my brethren, Heaven is clear") were written to the well-known tune "Cuckolds All A-Row," the original lyrics of which (Chappell, *Popular Music*, p. 340) told a tale of middle-class domestic strife that was quite consonant with the Cavaliers' traditionally disdainful view of their bourgeois foes. Quarles assumes the mask of an extreme Puritan and gains his point by carrying his persona's arguments out to their logical and vicious absurdity. (See Chappell, pp. 428–29, and *The Rump*, pp. 14–16.) Durfey not only uses the highly charged tune but keeps as close to Quarles' original lyrics as possible in order to show that the "new song of 82" should, indeed, be sung "to an old tune of 41." Thus (using the popular version composed of Quarles' verses plus the two concluding stanzas, as given in *The Rump*), lines 1–8 are based on Quarles' 1–8, 9–20 follow closely his 41–52, 21–24 follow somewhat Quarles 53–56, 25–32 follow very closely 57–64, 33–36 follow very closely 25–28, 37–40 follow very closely 21–24, 57–64 follow closely 9–12, and 62–64 follow 70–72.

The implications of the suggested parallel between 82 and 41 did not stop here. The tune had been equally famous during the 1640s under another name, "The Clean Contrary Way." This version had been written by Alexander Brome in 1643 (printed in *Songs and other Poems*, 1644) and entitled "The Saint's Encouragement" (in *The Rump*, pp. 149–51, it is called "Colonel Venne's Encouragement to his Soldiers"). With equally mordant irony it etched out an image of the sanctimonious, pillaging Parliamentarian soldier. Brome's burden "may be traced, in Latin, to the fifteenth century, if not earlier, as, for instance, in a highly popular song 'Of all creatures women be

best,/Cujus contrarium verum est' " (Chappell, p. 426, n. 2). To
emphasize Brome's treatment, as well as to pay tribute to "his chief
forerunner as a writer of political songs" (C. L. Day, *The Songs of
Thomas D'Urfey* [Cambridge, Mass., 1933], p. 35), Durfey put into
his play *The Royalist* (1682) the character of Alexander Brome,
acted by Bowman, who sang five of the stanzas that later appeared in
The Whig's Exaltation.

The idea that new Whig was but old Oliverian writ large was one
of the most effective Tory arguments and certainly did not originate
with Durfey; but his implication that 82 is 41 twice over receives
added force from the witty and incisive way that he handles the main
theme. Thus, in stanzas 1 and 6, the burden refers to mounting in
office; in stanza 2, to mounting in social rank; in stanza 3, to sexual
activity; in stanza 5, to mounting the pulpit; and in stanzas 4, 7, and
8, to mounting the gallows, or hanging, as the cant meaning of the
title's "exaltation" indicates.

The effect of Durfey's verses can be seen in the number of lyrics
that are henceforth set "to the Tune of 41," though the essential
popularity of Quarles' and Brome's original songs never really
flagged. Chappell gives thirteen songs which use this air and follow
the rhetoric of one or the other Civil War poems, concluding that "it
would be no difficult task to add fifty more to the . . . list" (p. 428).

Luttrell acquired his copy of *The Whigs' Exaltation* on 10 Febru-
ary 1682.

THE WHIGS' EXALTATION

A Pleasant New Song of 82 to an Old Tune of 41

1.

Now, now the Tories all shall stoop,
Religion and the laws;
And Whigs on commonwealth get up
To tap the Good Old Cause.

4. *tap:* To open, begin to use; to retail. An allusion, also, to the drain used to
relieve the cyst that afflicted Shaftesbury.
Good Old Cause: The Commonwealth.

Tantivy boys shall all go down,   5
    And haughty monarchy;
The leathern cap shall brave the throne;
    Then hey boys up go we.

2.

When once that anti-Christian crew
    Are crush'd and overthrown,   10
We'll teach the nobles how to bow,
    And keep their gentry down.
Good manners has a bad repute,
    And tends to pride, we see;
We'll therefore cry all breeding down,   15
    And hey boys up go we.

3.

The name of lord shall be abhorr'd,
    For ev'ry man's a brother;
What reason then in church or state
    One man should rule another?   20
Thus having pill'd and plunder'd all,
    And levell'd each degree,
We'll make their plump young daughters fall,
    And hey boys up go we.

4.

What though the King and Parliament   25
    Cannot accord together?
We have good cause to be content;
    This is our sunshine weather.
For if good reason should take place,

5. *Tantivy boys:* The Whigs' derogatory nickname for High Churchmen and Tories. "This arose 1680–81, when a caricature was published in which a number of High-Church clergymen were represented as mounted upon the Church of England and 'riding tantivy' [i.e. at full gallop] to Rome behind the Duke of York" (*OED*).

7. *leathern cap:* Tradesman, mechanic.

9–24. These two stanzas are based on Quarles' ironic treatment of Leveller doctrine. In the context of the 1680s, however, the attack on sectarian egalitarianism would seem to extend itself to include those Whig leaders who, according to the writer, are hypocritically sectarian in order to mask their acquisitive mercantilism.

21. *pill'd:* Pillaged, despoiled.

And they should both agree,   30
'Dzowns, who'd be in a Roundhead's case,
    For hey then up go we?

5.

We'll down with all the versities,
    Where learning is profess'd;
For they still practice and maintain   35
    The language of the beast:
We'll exercise in every grove,
    And preach beneath a tree;
We'll make a pulpit of a tub;
    Then hey boys up go we.   40

6.

The Whigs shall rule committee chair,
    Who will such laws invent
As shall exclude the lawful heir
    By act of parliament.

31. *case:* Condition, state, plight.

33. *versities:* Late seventeenth-century colloquial abbreviation of *universities.*

36. *the beast:* Anti-Christ; specifically, in this context, the Roman Catholic Church.

41. With reference to the Exclusion controversy, this may recall either the Commons committee which, on 2 Nov. 1680, brought in a bill disabling York from inheriting the Crown, or the long debate that began two weeks later in Lords in a committee of the whole House.

42. Undoubtedly an allusion to "the remarkable scene that occurred [on 26 March 1681, during the Oxford Parliament] in the Geometry School where the King was present while the Lords were taking their places" (Ogg, *Charles II,* p. 618). Shaftesbury had the Marquis of Wharton hand to Charles an anonymous letter that he (Shaftesbury) claimed to have received proposing that, in order to guarantee a Protestant succession, the Duke of Monmouth should immediately be declared his successor. According to Barillon, the French Ambassador, who reported the subsequent quasi-public conversation (see Christie, *Shaftesbury,* pp. cxvi–vii), Charles readily owned that he would like "to see a child of his own capable of succeeding him rather than his brother or his brother's children" but also stated that he would in no way act contrary to law and justice. "Lord Shaftesbury replied: 'If you are restrained only by law and justice, place your reliance on us and leave us to act. The laws will be on our side, and we will make laws which will give legality to a thing so necessary for the quiet of the whole nation, and by which great calamities shall be avoided.'" Charles, however, declined the gambit with the assertion that he had on his side, "law and reason, and all right-thinking men . . . [and] the Church."

We'll cut His Royal Highness down,   45
    E'en shorter by the knee,
That he shall never reach the throne;
    Then hey boys up go we.

7.

We'll smite the idol in Guild Hall,
    And then (as we were wont)   50
We'll cry it was a Popish Plot,
    And swear those rogues have done't.
His Royal Highness to unthrone
    Our interest will be,
For if he e'er enjoy his own,   55
    Then hey boys up go we.

8.

We'll break the windows which the whore
    Of Babylon has painted;

45–49. The incident is best summarized in the extreme Tory journal of Nathaniel Thompson, *The Loyal Protestant*, No. 109 (28 Jan. 1682):

> On Wednesday last [i.e. 25 Jan.] some persons (who, 'tis believed, were of the Collegian stamp [i.e. sympathizers of the late Stephen College]) entered into Guild Hall and, having approached the picture of His Royal Highness, cut off its legs a little below the knees, and so departed; but (it's thought) much troubled that they had not his person within their power to act the same malice upon as they did upon his royal father of ever blessed memory.

The allusions to those who had shortened Charles I by a head enforce the basic parallel on which the verses are based. The incident is referred to also in *The True Protestant Mercury*, No. 111 (25–28 Jan.) and by Friday, the 27th, the London officials had offered a £500 reward for the discovery of the offender (*Observator*, No. 95, [1 Feb. 1682]). Otway refers to the "picture mangler" indignantly in the Epilogue to *Venice Preserved* (20–40), with the same allusion to the regicides (Otway, *Works*, 2, 288–89, and n.). See also *A Message from Tory-Land*, 64.

51–52. In the *Observator*, No. 95, when Whig hears of the City's Proclamation, he responds: "Some Papist did it to bring scandal upon the True-Protestants." Durfey and L'Estrange knew well the tactics of their opponents. See also *Impartial Protestant Mercury*, No. 105 (5–9 May 1682).

55. An intentional echo of Martin Parker's famous Civil War ballad "When the King Enjoys His Own Again."

57–58. The Puritans had strongly objected to the ornateness of art, architecture, music, and ritual in the Roman Catholic Church.

And when their bishops are pull'd down,
 Our elders shall be sainted.   60
Thus having quite enslav'd the town,
 Pretending 'tis too free,
At last the gallows claims its own;
 Then hey boys up go we.

59–60. One of the basic aims of the Parliament in 1641 was to pass the Bishops' Exclusion Bill, thus simultaneously breaking the Church's political power and cutting down Charles I's majority in the House of Lords. In 1682 sectarian disdain for High Church policy was no less intense, though few would have gone to the lengths that the "saints" had some four decades before.

At about eight o'clock on the evening of 12 February 1682, Thomas Thynne, Esquire, of Longleat, was returning from a visit to the home of the Duchess of Northumberland, grandmother of the rich, young widow he had married in the summer of 1681. To his contemporaries Tom Thynne was "Tom of Ten Thousand," a title he had acquired popularly by virtue of the wealth of his estates at Longleat. But Thynne was known also as a close friend of James, Duke of Monmouth; indeed, he was one of his great supporters in the western regions of England, where Monmouth's hold was strongest.

A few months before the fateful evening, Thynne had made a brilliant but strange marriage with one of the wealthiest and youngest widows in England. Elizabeth Percy, daughter of the last Earl of Northumberland, had first married, at the age of twelve, the Earl of Ogle, eldest son of the Duke of Newcastle. Two years later, in a mysteriously surreptitious marriage, the young widowed Lady Ogle married Tom Thynne. The marriage had never been consummated, however, and Tom Thynne was now contesting the marriage jointure. The Earl of Essex, according to Luttrell, claimed that the Lady Elizabeth had been betrayed into this marriage by her grandmother; such might well have been the case, for the young married widow had at this time fled to Holland. In all probability, it was this situation that had taken Thynne to the Countess of Northumberland's that evening.

Earlier Monmouth had been with Thynne, but now as the coach came up St. James' street, lit by the flambeaux of Thynne's footmen, he was alone. The description of what happened thereafter was given succinctly but effectively by one of these footmen at the trial which followed shortly afterwards.

> I had a flambeau in my hand and was going before the coach and coming along at the lower end of St. Alban's Street, I heard the blunderbuss go off; so upon that I turned my face back and saw a great smoke and heard my master cry out he was murdered; and I saw three horsemen riding away on the right side of the

coach and I pursued after them and cried out "Murder!"; I ran on to the upper end of the Haymarket till I was quite spent and was able to go no further; and turning back again my master was got into the house and I understood he was wounded. That is all I know.

The three men who had committed this crime were a strange conglomeration. First, there was the leader, the defiantly silent German captain, a soldier of fortune, Christopher Vratz. As accomplices, he had a Swedish lieutenant named Sterne and a "Polander" whose name has been given most often as Borosky. None of these three ever denied his part in the crime, and the trial centered mainly on the astonishing figure who stood behind them, the young adventurous Count Carl Johann of Konigsmarck. Konigsmarck was acquitted as an accessory before the fact, but it was an acquittal that surprised everyone and angered in particular Monmouth's followers.

That Konigsmarck was involved in the crime is undoubted, but what is questionable—indeed, even mysterious—is his motivation. Was he a suitor for the hand of the Lady Elizabeth, and had he become infuriated by Tom Thynne's successfully arranged marriage? There is a good deal of evidence for this. Or had Thynne sent ruffians to the Continent to attack Konigsmarck, and was Konigsmarck merely retaliating in kind? For this, too, there is a certain amount of evidence. Or had the haughty Swedish count received from the English country squire insults so strong that, upon Thynne's refusal to settle the matter honorably, Konigsmarck sent Vratz to deal with him? Here, too, an agglomeration of fact and rumor makes the story possible. Vratz claimed that he was merely seeking an argument, or, better still, a cause for fighting Thynne, and that Borosky, the man who pushed the blunderbuss into the coach window and pulled the trigger, had misunderstood Vratz's orders to him. Next to the case of Sir Edmund Berry Godfrey, the "matchless murder" of Tom Thynne is the period's greatest mystery, at least so far as Konigsmarck's part in it is concerned.

The resemblance to Godfrey's murder was recognized at once, and the Whig pamphleteers gave dark hints that the aim of the plot was actually the murder of the Protestant Duke, James of Monmouth. Echard, writing years later gives his reflection upon it: "As this accident made a great noise, so it was at first looked upon as a party cause,

Mr. Thynne being so deeply engaged with those now called the Whigs and the more upon the account of the acquittal of Count Konigsmarck (*History, 3,* 653)." The hints of the Whig writers suggested a renewal of the Popish Plot. In *A New Discourse about the Fire of London and the Probability of Self-Murder* (London, 1682 [N 621]), the pseudonymous author, Philopolis, wittily assumes the mask of a Catholic Royalist: "When did we Royalists conspire or associate to do mischief? No, if Godfrey is dead, he may thank himself. If a gun lets fly at a man in a coach, dares any say he's murdered? A man may kill or be killed but why should we pry into the mysterious and meritorious contrivers? When men stand in the way, may they not be removed without such a din and clamor and calling the instruments murderers?" (pp. 3–4). And Henry Care (in the Courant section of the *Weekly Pacquet* for 17 Feb. 1681/2) has the following dialogue:

> *Trueman.* . . . There's a new saint lately come over, called Cess process that does daily wonders, Dam Ignoramous is an ass to her.
> *Tory.* What kind of feat does she profess? Can she sham Godfrey's murder and Esquire Thynne's; and make the world believe that they killed themselves or that it was done justly?

That the Popish Plot was dying by 1682, despite all of Oates' attempts to keep it alive, seems beyond doubt. It would probably be unfair to say that the Whig writers saw Tom Thynne's murder only as an occasion to resuscitate the party fervor of the Plot, but they did do their best to underline parallels which were, at the most, fortuitous.

A Hue and Cry after Blood and Murder

[H 3271]

The reactions of the writer of this poem to Thynne's "most barba-rous murder" are not difficult to find: for him, Thynne was a second Godfrey, and he attempted to evoke, in every way possible, the fervor of the first days of the Popish Plot; moreover, "the miraculous es-cape" of Monmouth constituted, for him, further evidence of Heav-en's protection. (See also J. M.'s *Murder Unparallel'd*, "Come and assist my trembling pen" [M 41], a journalistic account from a Whig point of view, with Luttrell's date 17 Feb. 1682.) Divine truth will, on the one hand, have its swift vengeance by revealing the murderers and, on the other, demonstrate its approbation of the Duke's claims. Such an interpretation of events falls well within the uses of history of the religious elements of the period, though the individual inter-pretations could vary. Thus, in *Midsummer Moon*, the author hints darkly at another parallel that "[Argyle's] fall and Thynne's, if rightly understood/ Were only doom'd to flesh the hounds in blood" (25–26; see also the note thereto).

The murder was committed on Sunday evening; by Monday noon, all three assailants had been captured and their depositions taken by Justice Reresby. By Wednesday the 15th—the day when Luttrell ob-tained his copy—the poem had been "printed for Langley Curtis." The present text is taken from *l″* and checked against *h″* and *k″*.

Title. Hue and Cry: Generally, a clamor or shout of pursuit; legally, the outcry calling for the pursuit of a felon, raised by the party aggrieved, by a constable etc. By this time the process (like the analogous but stronger action of outlawry) had become formalized. (For the history of the procedures, see Howard Schless, "Chaucer and Dante," *Critical Approaches to Medieval Literature* [New York, 1959], pp. 141–44 and notes thereto.) Sir John Reresby, at this time J.P. for Westminster and Middlesex, became involved in the Thynne murder on just this point: "At eleven o'clock the same night [of the murder, February 12th], as I was going into bed, Mr. Thynne's gentleman came to me to grant a hue and cry" (*Memoirs*, p. 249). Sir John was soon up, dressed and wholeheartedly "in chase."

Count Coningsmark.

John Charles, Count Konigsmark, 1682. Engraving by Robert White.

A Hue and Cry After Blood and Murder

or

An Elegy on the Most Barbarous Murder
of Thomas Thynne, Esq.

With some thankful Ejaculations to Heaven, for the Miraculous
Escape of his Grace the Duke of Monmouth
from the Hands of the Bloody Ruffians

Whil'st with hot scent, the Popish-Tory crew
A Presbyterian sham-plot do pursue,
Behold a new and true plot of their own
Against a worthy person's life made known.
Blood after blood for God's fresh vengeance calls;   5
Now Monmouth's friend a second victim falls.
The bloody villains skill'd i'th' murderous sin,
Sir Godfrey's murder new act o'er ag'in:
And now the shammers must together plot
To make the world think Thynne himself had shot.   10
What was his crime that thus they sought his life?
Was it because deceived by a wife?
Or was't because that he was Monmouth's friend,

1. A gibe at Roger L'Estrange, the arch-enemy of the Whig pamphleteers, dubbed Towzer, a common name for a large dog, such as was used to bait bears or bulls. L'Estrange was, as always, quick to take this up. He discusses this poem in *Observator*, No. 101 (20 Feb. 1681/2) and on this point remarks that Langley Curtis "will have it to be the act also of the popish-Tory crew, that is to say (according to his key) the Court Party."

2. Very likely the writer has in mind the recent action against Shaftesbury and the Association, but for a complete listing of what the Tories considered Protestant plots, see *Observator*, No. 97 (8 Feb. 1681/2).

8. *Sir Godfrey's.* Sir Edmund Berry Godfrey.

10. The story that the Coroner's Inquest had first found that Godfrey's death was a suicide (*felo de se*) was encouraged at this time by Tory pamphleteers. Indeed, a few days after these lines were written, Nathaniel Thompson, the printer and bookseller, pushed this idea to such lengths in *A Letter to Mr. Miles Prance* (and later in *A Second Letter*, as well as in his *Loyal Protestant Intelligence* for 7 March and 1 April) that he was brought to trial, pilloried, and fined. (Howell, *State Trials, 8*, 1359–89.)

12. With the suggestion (here and in 41–44 below) that Konigsmark had had Thynne murdered at the request of Lady Elizabeth, his paramour, L'Estrange's indignation was uncontrolled: "Nay, the malice of this prostitute libeller carries the plot on (with so many defamatory lies betwixt his teeth) even to a second assassinate, i.e. upon the honor of a lady both as a ———— and a murderess, who is as conspicuous in the world for her generous and unspotted virtue as for her state and quality. And this from the print of

He found so fatal and so sad an end?

 In former times such murders scarce were known.   15
Are we barbarians or fierce Scythians grown?
What impious acts are minted in our age?
What tragic scenes are brought upon the stage?
What e'er the heathen did we now can do
And, though we're Christians call'd, surpass them too. 20
In the last end o'th' Iron Age we live;
A brother won't a brother now forgive;
But for some slight affront or weak offence,
With sword or pistol he is hurried hence.

 These murderous arts by Jesuits hither brought,   25
With their religion they in secret taught:
For murders they have their commission given,
And killing is one gate that leads to heaven.
We may believe it, as we do our creed,
None but some hired Papists did this deed.   30
A deed so horrid, barbarous, and vile
That it will leave a blot upon our Isle,
Which will a spot for our whole age remain
Unless strict vengeance wipe away the stain.
Th' Ambassador whom we barbarian call,   35
When to his barbarous Prince return he shall,
Amongst our crimes with horror will relate
This murder acted near the Palace gate,

---

a despicable scoundrel, viler than the dirt in the kennel" (*Observator*, No. 101 [20 Feb. 1681/2]).

 15. Though Eveline Godley (*The Trial of Count Königsmarck*) suggests that this "matchless murder" could be matched at least by Felton's assassination of Buckingham in 1628, the use of hired killers appears to have been the really shocking element of this particular crime.

 21. *Iron Age:* The last and worst age, succeeding the Golden, Silver and Bronze Ages; a period of wickedness, cruelty, oppression, and debasement. There may be, considering its source, some slight suggestion of Fifth Monarchist thinking behind the use of the image here.

 35. *Ambassador:* Ahmed Hadu headed a small embassy from Morocco that came to make revisions of a treaty relating to Tangiers (see Routh, *Tangiers*, pp. 223–30). Evelyn, who was present at this audience, gives a colorful description of the event (*Diary, 4,* 265–66), which took place on 11 Jan. 1682. Hadu's horsemanship and worldliness, as well as his renegado interpreter, Hamet Lucas (see *Midsummer Moon*, 74 n.), caused a good deal of stir in London throughout his stay (see Luttrell, *Brief Relation*, 1682, *passim*).

 38. *the Palace:* St. James'. Actually, the crime occurred on Pall Mall, at the lower end of St. Albans' Street.

And to his Prince maliciously will say,
Christians can murders act as well as they.   40
    Hard was the fate of this most worthy man,
Whom first a wicked woman did trepan;
And now more hard, if that he lost his life
By murderous means of his disloyal wife.
But God that sees and knows the hearts of all   45
Will soon on guilty heads let vengeance fall;
And those black instruments now laid in hold
Shall all the truth of this black deed unfold.
Where Justice runs down like an unstopp'd flood,
It soon will wash away the stains of blood.   50
The murder'd's friends therefore on Justice cry
And to its sacred throne together fly
That vengeance may both great and small pursue,
O'ertake the hirers and the hired too—
Both those who the damn'd hire for blood receive,   55
And those who to be damn'd their money give.
For if strict vengeance on such be not ta'en,
Our laws for murder will be made in vain;
So impious and so vile now men are grown,
As never in our age before was known.   60
    Who can't but go or ride the streets in fear,
When we have *Bravoes* and *Banditti* here?
Tories who here have shown their murderous skill,
And know the way as well as they to kill.
Under our English cloth men must wear buff,   65
A coat of mail, or armor pistol-proof;

47. Sir John Reresby (*Memoirs*) recounts, with pardonable pride, that "at six o'clock in the morning [of Feb. 13th], having been in chase almost the whole night, I personally took the Captain at the house of a Swedish doctor in Leicester Fields, going first into the room, followed by my Lord Mordaunt, where I found him in bed with his sword at some distance from him upon the table, which I first seized and afterward his person, committing him to two constables" (p. 250). Stern and Borosky were taken by noon.

51. *friends:* Monmouth and his party. It was one of Monmouth's servants who took the disguised Konigsmarck as the latter arrived by sculler at Gravesend. The Count had been planning to leave England the following day aboard a Swedish ship.

54. It was almost immediately admitted that Konigsmarck had hired the men to do the assassination (Reresby, *Memoirs*, p. 252; Luttrell, *Brief Relation, 1*, 164).

65. *buff:* A stout leather made of ox-hide, used especially in military coats of the period.

66. There might be a recollection here of the fear and frenzy at the height of the Popish Plot discoveries.

For fear of some revenge from jilting drabs,
Or else for friendship or religion stabs.
Poison, or bullet, fraud, or force they take,
Both for revenge and for religion's sake.   70
Justice will visit when the murder's past
And overtake the criminals at last,
And such black deeds lie open to God's sight,
Who will the murderous plots bring forth to light.
Then, worthy Thynne, we shall more surely know   75
Who was thy barbarous bloody secret foe
When to the bottom of this plot we see,
And if the villains only aim'd at thee.
    Rest now thy soul in peace, whilst our good King
Your bloody murderers to justice bring;   80
Whilst the scar'd people on thy death debate,
And all thy friends bewail thy sudden fate;
Whilst the good Duke bewails with tears his friend,
Afflicted to behold his sudden end.
But let all loyal hearts to Heaven pay   85

67. *drabs:* Sluts, prostitutes, or strumpets. There is, again, the totally unwarranted attack on Lady Elizabeth.

68. *friendship:* Reresby reports (*Memoirs*) that when Konigsmarck was previously in England wooing Lady Elizabeth, he "resented something as done towards him as an affront from the said Mr. Thynne; and that the said Captain [Vratz], out of friendship to the Count (but as he then pretended not with his privity) was resolved to be revenged of him, to which intent he . . . had committed this so barbarous act" (p. 252).

   religion: The Catholics were said to have murdered Godfrey.

69. A gallimaufry of Oates' original charges, general fears, and the specific event. *Poison* refers to Oates' charge that Sir George Wakeman, the Queen's physician, was to be offered £10,000 (later raised to £15,000) to poison Charles II. *Bullet*, while referring to the assassination of Thynne, is probably meant to recall the endless attempts of Grove and Pickering to shoot the King. *Fraud*, though almost synonomous in this context with Jesuit, may allude to anything from Edward Coleman's dealings with the French to the general apprehension of York. *Force* alludes at once to the specific crime, but, in the wider sense of the Popish Plot, suggests Oates's charge of open invasion by the Spanish and French, rebellion in Ireland, and general massacre.

74, 77. *plots:* The writer leaves little doubt of his interpretation of the events. Fortunately for the Court, the investigation did not fall into the hands of a rabid Whig. Reresby (*Memoirs*) indicates this strongly: "I was glad to find in this whole affair no English person nor interest was concerned, the fanatics having buzzed it already abroad that the design was chiefly against the Duke of Monmouth. And I had the King's thanks oftener than once, my Lord Halifax's, and several others', for my diligent discovery of the true cause and occasion, as well as the authors of this matter" (pp. 252–53).

Their thanks that Monmouth did no longer stay,
That Providence who over him takes care
Had him diverted then from being there.
Who knows what bloody ruffians did intend?
They might perhaps have yet a further end;   90
Revenge might reach both to the Duke and's friend.
But Heaven will hear for him the people's prayer,
And of that noble Prince his life take care
That he may still secure and safely go
And all the plots of Papists overthrow.   95
    May Heav'n preserve the King that he may run
A long, long race, and for his sake his son;
May the Almighty keep the good Duke's life
From Hellish plots, from Popish gun or knife.
And let himself, warn'd, now more watchful be   100
Lest that he fall into like jeopardy.
O Heaven preserve him from a bloody end,
And let him take a warning by his friend.

86. "The truth is," says Reresby (*Memoirs*), "the Duke of Monmouth was gone out of the coach from Mr. Thynne an hour before; but I found by the confession both of Stern and Borosky that they were ordered not to shoot in case the Duke were with him in the coach" (p. 253).

92–93. As in 87, there is the strong implication of divine approval of Monmouth. The same theme—God's discovery of the truth—was at the heart of the much-touted broadsides that told of Monmouth's touching for the "king's evil" at Hinton Park on his Western Progress in Aug. 1680. Two days later, the girl Elizabeth Parcet was cured of what had been considered a hopeless case of scrofula; this was said to be "attested by seven witnesses, including two local clergymen" (Allan Fea, *King Monmouth* [London, 1902], p. 109). For a witty counterblast, see *A True and Wonderful Account of a Cure for the King's Evil, by Mrs. Fanshow* (1681) [T 2584].

99. *gun:* See 69.

knife: In his deposition of 1678, Oates claimed that he had met Father Coniers by chance about 6:00 P.M. on 22 Aug. and that he had shown a knife "a foot long in the blade and half a foot in the haft, with which he intends to slay Charles II through his (Coniers') cloak" (Lane, *Oates*, p. 100). In attempting to build up the proper descent of the crown to Monmouth, the writer makes the enemies of the undoubted ruler (Charles II) those of the Protestant Duke. By implication, of course, these subverters of the English throne are the friends and supporters of the Catholic Duke, James of York.

103. *friend:* i.e. Tom Thynne.

ELKANAH SETTLE

Prologue to "The Heir of Morocco"

[S 2689]

During 1682 Elkanah Settle was going through one of his numerous periods of political transition. His violent attacks on York in the original and (even more) the revised version of *The Character of a Popish Successor* (1681) were to give way to his *Panegyric on . . . Sir George Jeffreys,* when Jeffreys, the Shimei of Settle's *Absalom Senior* (6 April 1682), became Lord Chief Justice (1683). However, in the juvescence of this year, Settle was still with the City, though his position, as given here, is as mildly pro-Whig as it is anti-Dryden.

Prologues, which function as a transition between the actual world and the world of the theater, were a natural medium for the witty, often caustic, comments on the events of the day, and they reflect, as do so many of the plays of the period, the partisan political and literary views of their authors. Thus, Settle's Prologue focuses on two topics: his sporadic ten-year feud with Dryden over this play's predecessor, *The Empress of Morocco,* and the latest event of the town, the hanging, scarcely 24 hours earlier, of Thynne's three assassins. These two topics are unified by Settle's wry view of the decay of the times, whose extremes include at once Dryden's fine-spun dramas of love and honor and the brutal revenge of the disappointed suitor, Konigsmarck; less extreme, perhaps, is the equally ironic comparison of the notorious Rose Alley ambuscade, when Dryden (who, Settle says, will suffer anything for money) was beaten by three hired bullies, with the Pall Mall assassination of Thynne by the three men infamously hired by Konigsmarck to avenge what he (with equal injustice?) considered an affront to his honor. Dryden, then, is twitted, but not too unkindly.

The present text is based on the 1682 quarto of the play [S 2689]. The prologue was printed as a separate half-sheet (Luttrell dates his copy 16 March 1682) by A. [Allen?] Banks with the title *"A Prologue by Mr. Settle to his New Play, called the Emperor* [sic] *of Morocco, with the Life of Gayland.* Acted at the Theatre Royal, the 11th of

March, 1682" [S 2712]. This is reprinted, with its errors, in A. N. Wiley, *Rare Prologues* (London, 1940), pp. 80–83.

PROLOGUE TO *"The Heir of Morocco"*

Acted at the Theatre Royal 11 March 1682

How finely would the sparks be catch'd today
Should a Whig poet write a Tory play!
And you, possess'd with rage before, should send
Your random shot abroad, and maul a friend.
For you, we find, too often, hiss or clap   5
Just as you live, speak, think, and fight—by hap.
And poets, we all know, can change, like you,
And are alone to their own int'rest true;
Can write against all sense, nay even their own—
The vehicle, call'd Pension, makes it down.   10
No fear of cudgels where there's hope of bread;
A well-fill'd paunch forgets a broken head.
But our dull fop on every side is damn'd;
He has his play with love and honor cramm'd.
Rot your old-fashion'd hero in romance,   15
Who in a lady's quarrel breaks a lance;
Give us the modish feat of honor done
With eighteen well-chew'd bullets in one gun.

1. i.e. the young fops (or the small particles of fire) would be surprised and tricked (or ignited).

10. In a marginal note, Luttrell remarks that this is "a touch of Mr. Dryden for writing *Absalom and Achitophel.*" Dryden was created Poet Laureate on 13 April 1668 and confirmed in this as well as in the office of Historiographer Royal on 18 Aug. 1670 at a salary of £200 and a butt of canary per year.

11–12. A reference to the famed Rose Alley assault of 18 Dec. 1679. Luttrell's contemporary account is as follows: "About the same time, Mr. John Dryden was set on in Covent Garden in the evening by three fellows who beat him severely, and on people's coming, they ran away. Tis thought to be done by order of the Duchess of Portsmouth, she being abused in a late libel called *An Essay on Satire*, of which Mr. Dryden is suspected to be the author" (*Brief Relation, 1,* 30). Rochester was also said to have had instigated the attack, for he, too, suffered from what was, of course, the Earl of Mulgrave's poem. See discussion in *POAS,* Yale, *1,* 396–401.

18. In his examination of 19 Feb. Stern stated that "the Captain (Vratz) bid him charge the musquetoon with fifteen bullets," but he, not wishing to kill everyone in the vicinity of the coach, used only five or six (Godley, *The Trial of Count Königsmarck,* p. 195). Actually four bullets entered Thynne's body.

Charg'd but with eighteen bullets, did I say?
Damn it! if that won't do, we'll bring one day   20
Queen Bess's pocket pistol into play.
Give us heroic worthies of renown
With a revenging rival's mortal frown,
Not by dividing oceans kept asunder.
Whilst angry spark comes on, like Jove, with thunder,   25
Gives out in *Harlem Gazette,* blood and wounds
In foreign fray, to skulk on English ground,
And scorning duels, a poor prize at sharps,
He only fights for fame in counterscarps.
Do not you follow his revenge and fury,   30
Be you those tender-hearted things, his jury.
Give us Old Bailey mercy for our play.

21. *Queen Bess's pocket pistol:* "A brass cannon of prodigious length at Dover Castle" (*Dictionary of the Canting Crew,* k 1ʳ).

25. See 1 n.; here the sense is also that of the electrical discharge that precedes thunder.

26. Whether this refers to actual accounts of Konigsmarck's military exploits or, figuratively, to the letters of challenge which were said to have been sent to Thynne from Holland is uncertain. There was a *Haarlem Courant* (frequently referred to as a Gazette) which was used by English news-sheets for continental news. As well, the *Haarlem Courant* was being translated, at least during the early part of the year, as *The Compleat Mercury.* In a similar fashion, *blood and wounds* may literally refer to injuries received by Konigsmarck at Malta and Tangiers, or it may be simply the oath. The factual interpretation is the more likely one. See 29 and n.

28. *at sharps:* To play at sharp(s) is to fight with unbated swords, i.e. in earnest.

29. The counterscarp is the forward wall of the ditch that surrounds a fortification. Gibbons, one of Monmouth's men who captured Konigsmarck at Gravesend, testified that the Count had said, "It is a stain upon my blood; but one good action in the wars or one lodging upon a counterscarp will wash away all that" (Godley, *The Trial of Count Königsmarck,* p. 139). The Count's pragmatic ethic was equally shocking to "a Western gentleman" who, about 18 March 1682 (Luttrell's date), had published *Captain Vratz's Ghost to Count Konigsmarck* [C 487]. The ghost warns that a haunted conscience will keep the Count "alone in company" and that

> Not one or two bold actions in the wars,
> Nor soldier's wounds, nor yet ten thousand scars
> Shall e'er wipe off this blot, this infamy,
> Which thus thy scarlet with a deeper dye
> Hath stained: the war-like trophies of thy fame,
> Thy stock, thy much before reputed name.

(21–26)

32. *Old Bailey:* The trial was held on 28 Feb. at the Sessions House of the Old Bailey.

Ah no! no pray'rs nor bribes your hearts can sway,
Your cruel talents lie the other way.
  Critics   35
Are Polish bullies, fire and lightning all,
The blunderbuss goes off, and where you hit you maul.

33. *bribes:* The charge that the jury had been corrupted was made at once. Vratz's ghost (10–11) demands of the Count: "Though men brib'd may be, dost fondly hope/ Vengeance to 'scape?" "Evelyn [as Godley remarks in *The Trial of Count Königsmarck,* p. 181] in a few words sums up the closing scene of the Konigsmarck incident, and the popular verdict on the trial:"

> 10th March, 1682. There was this day executed Col. [sic] Vratz and some of his com-plices, for their execrable murder of Mr. Thynne, set on by the principal Konigs-marck. [He] went to execution like an undaunted hero, as one that had done a friendly office for that base coward, Count Konigsmarck, who had hopes to marry [Thynne's] widow, the rich Lady Ogle, and [who] was quitted by a cor-rupt jury and so got way. Vratz told a friend of mine [probably Burnet] who was accompanying him to the gallows and gave him some advice, that dying he did not value a rush, and hoped and believed God would deal with him like a gentleman. Never man went so gallant and so unconcerned to his sad fate (*Diary, 4,* 274).

36. *Polish bullies:* While it was in fact Borosky who fired the blunderbuss, all were of the opinion of Vratz's ghost that he was "poor ignorant Borosky." According to "the Polander's" confession, Vratz said that he would take full responsibility if they were caught. "Whereupon I thought with myself that it might be here as it is in Poland, viz., where a servant doth a thing by his master's order, the master is to suffer for it and not the servant" (Godley, *The Trial of Count Königsmarck,* p. 203). Settle's phrase may be artistically justifiable in that it brings together the images of lines 1 and 25, but it finds little support in the contemporary accounts.

A Satire in Answer to a Friend

The convention of the satiric epistle tended to disappear during 1682–85, when party politics and a public audience led naturally to the substitution of the ironic persona for the satirist and of the specific issue for the general survey. Nevertheless, here, with all the savagery of Juvenalian satire, the writer inspects both the Courts and the City from a moral rather than a political point of view and shows his ultimate despair by rejecting the corrupt age in which he lives.

The *Satire* apparently circulated only in manuscript during the Stuart reign, which is not surprising when one considers the directness of its personal attacks on Charles, his ministers, mistresses, and hangers-on; however, from 1689 the poem was printed and reprinted in the major collections of political verse.

The date of the poem is uncertain: *B'* gives 1680, while *m, o, s,* and *c'* give 1682; *I, O" X,* and *l* omit any date. Internal evidence, while not definite, would seem to indicate that 1682 is very probably the correct year of composition.

A Satire in Answer to a Friend

'Tis strange that you, to whom I've long been known,
Should ask me why I always rail at th' town!
As a good hound, when he runs near his prey,
With double eagerness is heard to bay,
So, when a coxcomb does offend my sight,   5
To ease my spleen I straight go home and write.
I love to bring vice ill-conceal'd to light,
And I have found that they who satire write,
Alone can season th' useful with the sweet.
Should I write songs and, to cool shades confin'd,   10
Expire with love, who hate all womankind,
Then in my closet, like some fighting sparks,

9. Cf. Horace's famous "utile dulci" (*Ars Poetica*, 343).
12. *sparks:* Spruce, trim, gay fellows (*Dictionary of the Canting Crew*).

Thinking on Phyllis, frigg upon my works?
  I grant I might, with bolder Muse inspir'd,
Some hero sing, worthy to be admir'd.   15
Our King has qualities might entertain
With noblest subjects Waller's lofty pen;
But then you'll own that no man's thought his friend
That does not love the Pope, and York commend;
He who his evil counsellors dislikes,   20
Say what he will, still like a traitor speaks.
Now I dissimulation cannot bear;
Truth and good sense alike my lines must share.
I love to call each creature by his name,
Halifax a knave, Shaftesbury an honest man.   25
With equal scorn I always did abhor
Th' effeminate fops and blust'ring man of war;
The careful face of minister of State
I always judg'd to be a down-right cheat;
The smiling courtier, and the counsellor grave,   30
I always thought two different marks of knave;
They that talk loud and they that draw i'th' pit,

13. *frigg:* To masturbate (Partridge, *Dictionary of Slang*). So, too, *O"*. All other texts have *love* (a not unusual substitution for an obscene term in Restoration texts), and no printed texts have internal punctuation. Such a line can be made meaningful only by emendation (e.g. *lour, look,* etc.) or by supplying a verb after *then* (12) and repunctuating to "Thinking on Phyllis's love, upon my works." *B'* changes *my* to *me*.

17. Edmund Waller (1606–87) enjoyed wide fame during his lifetime for his lofty style, especially in panegyrics. (See, e.g., Rochester's *An Allusion to Horace,* 54–58). His *Works* and his *Poems* alone had been through eight editions by 1682, and his popularity continued despite efforts to embarrass him (along with Dryden and Sprat) by republishing verses written in praise of Cromwell.

19. Charles' brother, James, was heir to the throne and, as a professed Catholic, the hope of those who followed the strong Roman tendencies of the royal family.

20. *evil counsellors:* The traditional attack on the Court was aimed not at the king but his ministers—in this case, those who fought the Exclusion Bill.

25. George Savile, Marquis of Halifax, was to a great degree responsible for the defeat of the Exclusion Bill. On 15 Nov. 1680 he out-debated Shaftesbury and Essex in the House of Lords. (See *Absalom Senior,* 870 n.). All manuscripts supply these names, save X which, in place of *Shaftesbury,* reads *Seymour* (i.e. Edward Seymour, Speaker of the House of Commons but opposed to exclusion). All printed texts give merely H——— and S———. A Yale copy of *m* glosses "Howard" (i.e. Lord Howard of Escrick) and "Sidney" (i.e. Algernon Sidney, the Whig leader).

32. *they that draw i'th' pit:* If the writer has a specific occasion in mind, it may be Sir Thomas Armstrong's killing of Sir Carr Scroope's brother at the Duke's playhouse on 28 Aug. 1675. (See *The Last Will and Testament of Anthony, King of Poland,* 25 n.)

These want of courage show, those want of wit.
Thus all the world endeavors to appear
What they'd be thought to be, not what they are.   35
If any then by most unhappy choice
Seek for content in London's crowd and noise,
Must form his words and manners to the place:
If he'll see ladies, must like Villers dress;
In a soft tone, without one word of sense,   40
Must talk of dancing and the Court of France;
Must praise alike the ugly and the fair,
Bulkeley's good nature, Felton's shape and hair,
Exalt my Lady Portsmouth's birth and wit
And vow she's only for a monarch fit—   45
Although the fawning coxcombs all do know
She's lain with Beaufort and the Count de Sault.

39. *Villers:* Frank Villers, a contemporary fop whose name appears often in the poems on court gossip.

41. *dancing:* Dancing was the favorite amusement of the Court at this time. See Janet Mackay, *Catherine of Braganza* (London, 1937), p. 112.

43. *Bulkeley:* Lady Sophia Bulkeley, younger sister of Frances Teresa, "La Belle Stewart," was herself a Court beauty whom rumor connected with Sidney Godolphin among others.

Felton: Lady Elizabeth Felton, daughter of Barbara Howard, Countess of Suffolk, had the official position at Court of Groom of the Stole to the Queen.

44. *Portsmouth:* Louise de Keroualle, Duchess of Portsmouth and mistress to the King, came from an old, though not noble, Breton family. She was the daughter of Guillaume de Penancoët, sieur de Keroualle. (See Forneron, *Louise de Keroualle* [Paris, 1886], pp. 1–2; and Evelyn, *Diary, 4,* 66.) While her wit may not have been as persistent as that of her predecessor, Castlemaine, nor as native as that of her temporary successor, Nell Gwynne, it was quite adequate, when supported by "the influence of tears" (*DNB,* citing Sidney's *Diary, 2,* 114 n.), to maintain her supremacy until Charles' death.

47. *Beaufort:* Rumor said that Louise had early run away from her aunt's house in Paris and "accompagna sous une déguisement de page le duc de Beaufort dans l'expédition de Candie. Après la mort du duc, elle aurait servi comme page divers capitaines de navire avant de revenir à Paris [vers 10 Octobre 1669]" (Forneron, *Louise de Keroualle,* p. 3; and *The Secret History of the Duchess of Portsmouth,* 1690 [S 2340]).

Count de Sault: While the story about Beaufort is very doubtful as we have it, this affair with the son of the Duc de Lesdignières in 1669 seems more probable. At any rate, "il est certain que la reputation de la Bretonne fut atteinte" (Forneron, *Louise de Keroualle,* p. 5). Cf. "The Cabal," *Roxburghe Ballads, 4,* 583:

> Who got costly Carwell's maidenhead?
> Who got the better on't, the peer or knight?

(24–25)

This method, with some ends of modern plays,
Basely appli'd and dress'd in a French phrase,
To ladies' favors can ev'n Hewet raise.   50
    He that from bus'ness would preferment get,
Plung'd in the toils and infamies of State,
All sense of honor from his breast must drive
And in a course of villanies resolve to live;
Must cringe and flatter the King's owls and curs;   55
Nay, worse, must be obsequious to his whores;
Must always seem t'approve what they commend,
What they dislike, by him must be condemn'd.
And when, at last, by a thousand different crimes,
The monster to his wish'd-for greatness climbs,   60
He must in his continu'd greatness wait,
With guilt and fear, th' imprison'd Danby's fate.
This road have Halifax and Spencer gone
And thus must answer for the ills they've done.
Who then wou'd live in so deprav'd a town,   65
Where pleasure is by folly, power alone
By infamy obtain'd?

50. *Hewet:* Sir George Hewet, a Court fop, was probably the model for Etherege's Sir Fopling Flutter. (See Lucas, *Memoirs of the Lives . . . of the . . . Gamesters,* reprinted in *Compleat Gamester,* esp. pp. 260–69.)

55. For Charles interest in birds, see the final stanza of the version of Marvell's *The King's Vows* in Wilkins, *Political Ballads* [London, 1860], *1,* 235, and Evelyn, *Diary, 3,* 398–90. Charles' spaniels accompanied him everywhere, were allowed to whelp in his bed chamber, and, says Evelyn, "made the whole Court nasty and stinking" (*4,* 410).

62. *Danby:* Thomas Osborne, Earl of Danby, controlled the Administration as Lord High Treasurer from 1673 to 1678. When Montagu revealed his letters to Louis XIV arranging a pension for Charles II, he was forced to resign. In the following year (10 April 1679), he was sent to the Tower on charges of treason and, though his impeachment was never brought to a trial, he remained imprisoned until Feb. 1684.

63. By 1682 Halifax's position was not unlike Danby's prior to his fall. Both Halifax and Robert Spencer, Earl of Sunderland, were particular objects of Whig scorn, since it was felt that the two men had betrayed their earlier Whig ideals for Court favor. Sunderland had voted with the Exclusionists and was discharged from the Privy Council in Feb. 1681; upon his total recantation to York, and with the help of the Duchess of Portsmouth, he was readmitted to the Council on 28 Aug. 1682.

All manuscripts supply *Halifax* and *Spencer,* save X which has *Peterborough* (i.e. Henry Mordaunt) for *Halifax.* For printed variants, see textual notes, where the blanks that are sufficiently open to interpretation are identified (by Musgrave, Pope, and a Yale copy of *m*) as *Halifax* and *Seymour.* In this case Edward Seymour is a distinct possibility, since he had swung away from Whig parliamentarianism and fought beside

Wise Heraclitus all his lifetime griev'd,
Democritus in endless laughter liv'd;
Yet to the first no fears of plots were known,   70
Nor Parliament remov'd to popish town,
Murder not favor'd, virtue not suppress'd,
Laws not derided, Commons not oppress'd,
Nor King who, Claudius-like, expell'd his son,
To make the impious Nero Prince of Rome;   75
Nor yet, to move the other's merry vein,
Did cuckolds (whom each boy i'th' street can name)
Most learned proofs in public daily give
That they themselves do their own shame contrive,
While their lewd wives, scouring from place to place,   80
T'expose their secret members, hide their face.
    But, Lord! how would this sage have burst his spleen
Had he seen whore and fool with merry King,
And minister of State at supper sit,
Mistaking filthy ribaldry for wit!   85
While Charles, with tott'ring crown and empty purse,
Derided by his foes, to's friends a curse,
Abandon'd now by every man of wit,
Avoids himself with any he can get;
Pimps, fools, and parasites make up the rout;   90

Halifax against exclusion; but he did not hold quite the position of power that these
lines imply, nor was he as constant a target as Sunderland.

68–69. The Greek philosophers Heraclitus (fl. 513 B.C.) and Democritus (born c. 460
B.C.) were popularly referred to as "the weeping philosopher" and "the laughing
philosopher" by virtue of their respective attitudes.

71. *popish town:* In order to avoid the pressure of the London Whigs, Charles
removed the Parliament to the staunchly royalist town of Oxford for its brief session in
March 1681.

72. *Murder not favor'd:* Probably a reference to the favored treatment which allowed
Count Konigsmarck to escape punishment for his part in the murder of Tom Thynne.

73. *Laws not derided:* Many of the religious laws which parliament had passed in
order to cripple Catholics were used by the Court to attack sectarian conventicles.

74. *expell'd his son:* Monmouth had been deprived of his offices and banished in 1679.
After his unauthorized return to England in Nov. of that year, he never really regained
Court favor, and his continued appeal to the populace finally led to his arrest in Sept.
1682, while on a "progress."

75. *Nero:* A common Whig sobriquet for the Duke of York, since it hinted darkly
that, as the Roman Emperor had fired his capital, so James had been responsible for
the London fire of 1666.

89. *Avoids:* Empties, voids; ejects by excretion.

For want of wedding garment none's left out.
　　But I shall weary both myself and you
To tell you all the follies that I know:
How a great lord, in numbers soft, thought fit,
Though void of sense, to set up for a wit;   95
And how, with wondrous spirit, he and's friend
An epitaph to cruel Chloris penn'd.
His name I think I hardly need to tell;
For who should't be but the Lord Arundel?
But should I here waste paper to declare   100
The senseless tricks of every silly peer,
I'd as good tell how many several ways
The trusty Duke his country still betrays,
How full the world is stuff'd with knave and fool,
How to be honest is still counted dull,   105
How to speak plain and greatness to despise
Is thought a madness; but flattery is wise,
Dissimulation excellent, to cheat a friend
A very trifle—provided still our end
Be but the snare we call our interest.   110
Then nothing is so bad, but that is best.
I'll therefore end this vain satiric rage,
And leave the bishops to reform the age.

---

91. *For want of wedding garment:* Richard Vowles suggests that this may perhaps be a reference to the fact that "a Court wedding was the occasion for riff-raff to gain entry in the guise of guests" (*Poems on Affairs of State, 1689* [2 vols. unpublished Ph.D. dissertation, Yale University, 1949], *1,* 91).

99. *Arundel:* Despite the explicit statement in these lines, the precise reference remains uncertain. There seem to be two possibilities: 1. Henry Arundell, Baron Arundell of Wardour (1606?–94), one of the five popish lords imprisoned in the Tower. In 1679 five short poems by him of a devotional nature were printed on two sides of a single quarto sheet. They appeared twice again in that year [A 3896–98] and were reprinted in *b.* It seems unlikely that the 76-year-old prisoner, even with the help of a friend, would have penned an epitaph to cruel Chloris. 2. Henry Howard, seventh Duke of Norfolk (1655–1701), succeeded to the title in 1684. For the previous six years, he had been styled the Earl of Arundel, and *X* (though transcribed at least seven years after this poem) glosses the line "Duke of Norfolk." Howard's age is more reasonable, he definitely qualifies as a "great lord," and perhaps the fact that we have no poetry by him explains the presence of "his friend." Vowles notes that poems by an untitled "Mr. Arundell" appear in *South Sea Pills to Purge Court Melancholy,* but this volume has not been investigated.

103. *Duke:* York.

THOMAS OTWAY

The Prologue to Aphra Behn's The City Heiress

[O 561]

For many of the dramatists writing between 1637 and 1737, stage and state were scarcely a letter apart. Not only were new plays frequently constructed on the political and social events of the day, but older works were at times revived or refurbished to give historic precedent to a point of view. The most conventional place for such social comment was, however, the prologue, with its tone of jest and earnest that formed a rhetorical bridge between the actual and the dramatic.

Otway's prologue is unified by the figure of Titus Oates, at once the symbol of a vicious age and the evil spirit behind the actions of the Whig extremists. Whether or not Oates initiated the idea of the Whig Feast (for which, see below p. 174) is difficult to determine, though he would surely have been in sympathy with those men— John Wilmore, John Wickham, and Edward Partridge—who were its principal stewards. Slightly more certain is the suggestion that Oates was at this time in such penury (Lane, *Oates*, p. 287) that he was forced, according to the Tory journal *Heraclitus Ridens* (No. 65 [25 April 1682]), into the ignominy of accepting as charity some of the left-over provisions of the abortive feast.

The prologue did not go unanswered. About six months later (4 Sept. 1682), *The Tory Poets, A Satire* [T 1948] not only parodied several lines (see 36 n.) but also leveled a more general attack:

> Poetess Aphra, though she's damn'd today,
> Tomorrow will put up another play;
> And Otway must be pimp to set her off
> Lest the enraged bully scowl, and scoff,
> And hiss, and laugh, and give not such applause
> To *Th' City Heresy* as *The Good Old Cause*.

The City Heiress, produced at Dorset Gardens in March 1682, was less of a success than Mrs. Behn's earlier play, *The Roundheads,* or *The Good Old Cause,* which had been presented at the same theater three or four months before. This latter play probably helped a good deal to offset the effect of Shadwell's very popular pro-Whig, anti-Catholic *The Lancashire Witches, and Tegue O'Divelly, The Irish Priest,* a play that was finally allowed to be acted (again at Dorset Gardens) in November 1681. This kind of political theater war is not unusual, and it adds some slight weight to the ascription of *The Tory Poets* to Shadwell.

The Prologue to *The City Heiress*

or *Sir Timothy Treatall*

How vain have prov'd the labors of the stage
In striving to reclaim a vicious age!
Poets may write the mischief to impeach;
You care as little what the poets teach
As you regard at church what parsons preach.   5
But where such follies and such vices reign,
What honest pen has patience to refrain?
At church, in pews, ye most devoutly snore,
And here, got dully drunk, ye come to roar;
Ye go to church to gloat and ogle there,   10
And come to meet more lewd convenient here.
With equal zeal ye honor either place
And run so very evenly your race
Y'improve in wit just as you do in grace.
    It must be so, some demon has possess'd   15

1–7. Though the theme is not uncommon, the same comparisons are found in the concluding lines of Fielding's Epilogue to *The Intriguing Chambermaid:*

    —But though our angry poets rail in spite
    Ladies, I own, I think your judgments right:
    Satire, perhaps, may wound some pretty thing. . .
        No, let 'em starve who dare to lash the age,
        And as you've left the pulpit, leave the stage.

9. *roar:* To revel boisterously; to behave in a noisy, riotous manner.
10. *gloat:* To cast amorous or admiring glances.
11. *convenient:* A mistress or concubine.
15. *demon:* i.e. Titus Oates.

Our land, and we have never since been bless'd.
Y'have seen it all, or heard of its renown;
In a reverend shape it stalk'd about the town,
Six yeomen tall attending on its frown.
Sometimes with humble note and zealous lore   20
'Twould play the apostolic function o'er.
But, Heav'n have mercy on us when it swore!
Whene'er it swore, to prove the oaths were true,
Out of its mouth at random halters flew
Round some unwary neck, by magic thrown,   25
Though still the cunning devil sav'd its own;
For when the enchantment could no longer last,
The subtile pug, most dexterously uncast,
Left awful form for one more seeming pious
And in a moment vari'd to defy us: 30
From silken Doctor, homespun Ananias
Left the lewd Cour and did in City fix,
Where still by its old arts it plays new tricks
And fills the heads of fools with politics.
This demon lately drew in many a guest   35

17ff. North's Tory *Examen* complements this description quite well: "I shall . . .
proceed now with our Spanish pretended doctor and his pesadumbres. He was now in
his trine exaltation, his Plot in full force, efficacy, and virtue; he walked about with his
guards (assigned) for fear of the Papists murdering him. He had lodgings at Whitehall
and £1200 per annum pension. . . . He put on episcopal garb (except the lawn
sleeves), silk gown and cassock, great hat, satin hat band and rose, long scarf, and was
called, or most blasphemously called himself, the Savior of the Nation. Whoever he
pointed at was taken up and committed, so that many people got out of his way, as
from a blast, and glad they could prove their two last years' conversation. The very
breath of him was pestilential, and, if it brought not imprisonment or death over such
on whom it fell, it surely poisoned reputation and left good Protestants arrant Papists,
and something worse than that, in danger of being put in the Plot as Traitors" (p. 205).

27. By order of Council, Oates was commanded to leave Whitehall on 30 August 1681;
and, according to Thompson (*Loyal Protestant*, No. 52 [3 Sept. 1681]), an officer was sent
along to "see that none of His Majesty's goods should be embezzled."

28. *pug:* Probably used here in the sense of a small demon, imp, or sprite; for the
connection with fanatics, see Butler, *Hudibras*, III.1.1415–18.

31. *Ananias:* Biblically, either the Jewish high priest who abused Paul (Acts 23) or
the husband of Sapphira who was struck dead because "he lied unto God" (Acts 5).
Literarily, it recalls the Puritan colleague of Tribulation Wholesome in Jonson's
Alchemist.

32. For one version of Oates' arrival and reception in the City, see *Loyal Protestant*,
Nos. 54 and 57 [10 and 20 Sept. 1681].

To part with zealous guinea for—no feast.
Who but the most incorrigible fops,
Forever doom'd in dismal cells call'd shops
To cheat and damn themselves to get their livings,
Who'd lay sweet money out in sham-thanksgivings? 40
Sham-plots you may have paid for o'er and o'er,
But who e'er paid for a sham-treat before?
Had you not better sent your offerings all
Hither to us than Sequestrators Hall?
I, being your steward, justice had been done ye; 45
I could have entertain'd you worth your money.

36. Ghosh (Otway, *Works, 1,* 34) gives three lines from *The Tory Poets* [T 1948], a poem ascribed to Shadwell, which parody this line and 41–42:

> To part with stolen half-crown for—no jest;
> Sham treats you may have paid for o'er and o'er,
> But who e'er paid for a sham-play before?

44. *Sequestrators Hall:* The same phrase is used in Thompson's parody of the ticket of invitation: "in disorderly order to advance to Sequestrators' [marginal note: English Inquisition] Hall on the north of Cheapside in order to propagate a fresh Association" (*Loyal Protestant,* No. 145 [22 April 1682]).

45. *steward:* The person in charge of the entertainment. Thompson (*Loyal Protestant,* No. 144 [20 April 1682]) lists sixteen, but the principal one was the radical Independent John Wilmore, who had been on Stephen College's "Ignoramus" jury. *Heraclitus Ridens,* No. 65 (25 April 1682) suggests that some of the sixteen had their names used against their wills.

Medal Poems

JOHN DRYDEN

The Medal

[D 2311]

The high point of the London Whigs' defiance of the Court came dramatically in the Old Bailey on 24 November 1681 when a carefully selected grand jury refused to accept the indictment of treason against Shaftesbury and returned it "Ignoramus." The joy of the Country Party burst forth at the trial's end and, as the periodicals report, swept through England with celebrations marked by torch-light parades, bell ringing, and bonfires. In London, only Charles' direct orders to the Lord Mayor kept in check the festivities that followed Shaftesbury's release on 1 December. A week later "there were again bonfires; on the tenth, Prince Rupert dined with him; and on the thirteenth, he was feasted by the Skinners' company of which he was a member. A medal was struck to commemorate his release" (Brown, *Shaftesbury,* p. 292), and Whigs triumphantly wore this "effigy of the Grand Patriot"—as the Yorkist author of *A Pane-gyric on their Royal Highnesses* [P 264] remarked in 1682 with bitter irony:

> Nearest their hearts, where late their Georges hung,
> The pale-fac'd Medal with its silver tongue
> Was plac'd, whilst every wearer still express'd
> His joy to harbor there so fam'd a guest.
> The wretch that stamp'd it got immortal fame;
> 'Twas coin'd by stealth, like groats at Bromigham;
> Whilst each possessor with exalted voice
> Cries "England's sav'd, and now let us rejoice!"
>
> (44–51)

He feels, however, that the return of York should evoke a royalist *laetamur,* for

The Shaftesbury Medal by George Bowers.

> . . . in his face you see the rising sun,
> T'other's a comet blazing o'er the town,
> Portending mischiefs seeming to explain
> The former tragic scene design'd again.
>
> (57–60)

It was not tragedy, but the hurly-burly of the shrieval elections that was to be enacted in this city drama. For the royalists, the final scenes of Charles' reign would end with poetic justice; when the principal actors of the *Ignoramus* denouement were hoisted with their own petards, condemned by the courts whose actions they had sought to control.

A delightful anecdote is connected with Dryden's poem. "The story went that Charles, pleased with *Absalom and Achitophel,* condescended to walk with the author in the Mall and said, 'If I was a poet, and I think I am poor enough to be one, I would write a poem in the following manner.' He proceeded to suggest something on the lines of *The Medal,* which Dryden went off and wrote, in exchange for a handsome fee" (Brown, *Shaftesbury,* p. 293). Whether or not the fee was "a hundred broad pieces," as Spence avers (cited in Hugh Macdonald, *John Dryden, A Bibliography. . . ,* [Oxford, 1939], pp. 26–27), there probably was a royal command (see Richard Garnett, *The Age of Dryden* [London, 1912], p. 10).

Dryden's poem appeared on or about 16 March 1682 (Macdonald, pp. 26–27; and No. 206) at just the moment when reaction to Shaftesbury began to make itself heard in the series of Abhorrences that poured in from the country. *The Medal* reflects the change in temperament; it is not like *Absalom and Achitophel,* "a poem" appealing to the uncommitted moderates, but rather "a satire" lashing Shaftesbury and sedition. (For the generic difference, see Bernard Schilling, *Dryden and the Conservative Myth* [New Haven, 1961], p. 137.)

The text and collation are based on *The Poems of John Dryden,* ed. James Kinsley (4 vols. Oxford, 1958). Some suggestions on punctuation have been taken from Noyes, *Dryden's Poetical Works,* (Boston, 1908).

THE MEDAL

A Satire Against Sedition

Per Graium populos, mediaeque per Elidis urbem
Ibat ovans; Divumque sibi poscebat honores

Epistle to the Whigs

For to whom can I dedicate this poem, with so much justice, as to you? 'Tis the representation of your own hero; 'tis the picture drawn at length, which you admire [a] and prize so much in little.[b] None of your ornaments are wanting: neither the landscape of the Tower, nor the rising sun, nor the *Anno Domini* of your new sovereign's coronation.[c] This [d] must needs be a grateful undertaking to your whole party, especially to those who have not been so happy as to purchase the original. I hear the graver [e] has made a good market of it. All his kings are bought up already; or the value of the remainder so enhanced that many a poor Polander [f] who would be glad to worship the image is not able to go to the cost of him, but must be content to see him here. I must confess I am no great artist; but sign-post painting will serve the turn to remember a friend by; especially when better is not to be had. Yet for your comfort the lineaments are true; and though he sat not five times to me, as he did to B[ower] [g], yet I have consulted history, as the Italian painters do when they

Epigraph. Virgil, *Aeneid*, VI, 588–89.

a. *admire:* Regard with wonder mingled with esteem.

b. *in little:* The phrase would seem to contain a slurring reference to Shaftesbury's diminutive size as well as to his portrait on the medal.

c. Medals were regularly issued to commemorate a "new sovereign's coronation"; Dryden, however, is to extend this charge of impudence to the more treasonable matter of tampering with the coinage of the realm (228–29 and n.).

d. *This:* this poem.

e. George Bower, or Bowers, worked in London from 1650 to 1689. In Jan. 1664 he was appointed Engraver to the Royal Mint and Embosser in Ordinary. For a list of his known works, see *Biographical Dictionary of Medallists*, compiler L. Forrer (8 vols. London, 1904–30), *1*, 258–59.

f. Second only to the gibe about his tap was the Tory joke that Shaftesbury had aspired to the throne of Poland in 1675 when John Sobieski was elected. Kinsley, for example, cites allusions in Otway (Prologue to *Venice Preserved*) and Aphra Behn (*City Heiress*, III.1). In 1681, "Tapski" had an entire ministry assigned him in *A Modest Vindication of the Earl of S[haftesbur]y* [S 2375] (Macdonald 198); Dryden (for the panegyric on Cromwell) was to be poet laureate, with Shadwell as his deputy.

g. See *The Medal,* 18–21.

would draw a Nero or a Caligula: [h] though they had not seen the man, they can help their imagination by a statue of him and find out the coloring from Suetonius and Tacitus. Truth is, you might have spared one side of your medal: the head would be seen to more advantage if it were placed on a spike of the Tower [i] a little nearer to the sun, which would then break out to better purpose.

You tell us in your Preface to the *No-protestant Plot* [j] that you shall be forced hereafter to leave off your modesty; I suppose you mean that little which is left you, for it was worn to rags when you put out this medal. Never was there practised such a piece of notorious impudence in the face of an established government. I believe, when he is dead, you will wear him in thumb-rings, as the Turks did Scanderbeg,[k] as if there were virtue in his bones to preserve you against monarchy. Yet all this while you pretend not only zeal for the public good, but a due veneration for the person of the King. But all men who can see an inch before them may easily detect those gross fallacies. That it is necessary for men in your circumstances to pretend both is granted you, for without them there could be no ground to raise a faction. But I would ask you one civil question: what right has any man among you, or any Association of men [l] (to come nearer

h. *a Nero or a Caligula:* Roman emperors (54–68 and 37–41) who were the very types of tyrants, the former renowned for his cruelty and iniquity, the latter for his fits of passion and madness.

i. After execution, the heads of traitors were impaled on spikes either at the Tower or at London Bridge.

j. *No-protestant Plot:* The three Whig tracts [F 756, F 759, F 762] written by Robert Ferguson in 1681–82. (See Burnet, *History, 1,* 542; and Ferguson, *Ferguson.*) Wood, in the *Athenae Oxoniensis* (2, 726), remarked that "Though no name is put to this, yet the general report was that the Earl of Shaftesbury was the author, or at least found materials for it." See Kinsley's note; also *The Second Part of Absalom and Achitophel,* 320 n.

k. *Scanderbeg:* "George Castriota alias Iskander Beg (c. 1404–67), an Albanian who deserted the Turkish Service and fought for his country's independence" (Kinsley). *The History of George Castriot* (1596) tells how the Turks carried pieces of his exhumed body as reliques that would bring them "fortune, felicity and privilege" (p. 496).

l. The Crown's treason charge against Shaftesbury rested mainly on the draft of an Association reputedly found in the Earl's study. While the House of Lords had been considering an Association in Nov. 1680 (see *LJ, 13,* 672), there can be little doubt of the treasonable nature of the document that was presented before the grand jury (see Howell, *State Trials, 8,* 781–87). The countercharge implied by the jury and made explicit by the Whig author of *The Medal of John Bayes* in his "Epistle to the Tories" (see below), was that the Association paper had been planted by those sent by Secretary Jenkins to seize Shaftesbury's papers. See also Kinsley's note.

to you) who, out of parliament, cannot be considered in a public capacity, to meet as you daily do in factious clubs,[m] to vilify the government in your discourses and to libel it in all your writings? Who made you judges [n] in Israel? Or how is it consistent with your zeal of the public welfare to promote sedition? Does your definition of loyal (which is to serve the King according to the laws) allow you the licence of traducing the executive power with which you own he is invested? You complain that His Majesty has lost the love and confidence of his people; and by your very urging it, you endeavour what in you lies to make him lose them.

All good subjects abhor the thought of arbitrary power, whether it be in one or many. If you were the patriots you would seem, you would not at this rate incense the multitude to assume it; for no sober man can fear it, either from the King's disposition or his practice, or even—where you would odiously lay it—from his ministers.[o] Give us leave to enjoy the government and the benefit of laws under which we were born, and which we desire to transmit to our posterity. You are not the trustees of the public liberty; and if you have not right to petition in a crowd,[p] much less have you to intermeddle in the management of affairs, or to arraign [q] what you do not like—which in effect is everything that is done by the King and Council. Can you imagine that any reasonable man will believe you respect the person of His Majesty when 'tis apparent that your seditious pamphlets are stuffed with particular reflections on him? If you have the confidence to deny this, 'tis easy to be evinced from a thousand passages which I only forbear to quote because I desire they should die and be forgotten. I have perused many of your papers; and to show you that I have, the third part of your *No-protestant Plot* is much of it stolen from your dead author's pamphlet called the *Growth of Popery*,[r] as mani-

---

m. The most famous was the Green Ribbon Club. See also *CSPD* 1682, pp. 236–37.

n. *Who made you judges:* Acts 7:27, 35.

o. Cf. *The Medal,* 227 n.

p. "In 1661, Parliament passed an act against tumultuous petitioning (13 Car. II, c. 5) making it illegal to obtain more than twenty signatures, or for more than ten persons to present a petition to Parliament" (Kinsley). At this particular time, the famed paper war between the petitioners (for a new parliament) and abhorrers (of the Association and the petitioners) was occupying England.

q. *arraign:* i.e. in parliament.

r. Andrew Marvell's popular *An Account of the Growth of Popery* [M 860–2] was first published in 1677.

festly as Milton's Defence of the English People is from Buchanan *De Jure Regni Apud Scotos*,[s] or your first Covenant and new Association from the Holy League of the French Guisards.[t]

Anyone who reads Davila [u] may trace your practices all along. There were the same pretences for reformation and loyalty, the same aspersions of the king, and the same grounds of a rebellion. I know not whether you will take the historian's word who says it was reported that Poltrot, a Huguenot, murdered Francis, Duke of Guise, by the instigations of Theodore Beza; [v] or that it was a Huguenot minister, otherwise called a Presbyterian (for our Church abhors so devilish a tenet), who first wrote a treatise of the lawfulness of deposing and murdering kings of a different persuasion in religion; but I am able to prove from the doctrine of Calvin and principles of Buchanan [w] that they set the people above the magistrate, which, if I mistake not, is your own fundamental—and which carries your loyalty no further than your liking. When a vote of the House of Commons goes on your side, you are as ready to observe it as if it were passed into a law; but when you are pinched with any former, and yet unrepealed, act of parliament, you declare that in some cases you will not be obliged by it. The passage is in the same third part of the

s. The *De Jure* (1579) of George Buchanan (1506–82) "was long a text of the opponents of absolutism" (*DNB*). The connection of Milton with Buchanan and Knox was continuously pointed out during this period, particularly on the anniversary of Charles I's execution; see, for example, George Hickes' *A Sermon Preach'd . . . on the 30th of January 1681/2* [H 1864] and Francis Turner's *Sermon Preach'd before the King on the 30th of January 1684/5* [T 3287].

t. See the Prologue to *The Duke of Guise*, 1–2 and n.

u. Enrico Davila's highly successful *Istorie delle guerre civili di Francia* was completed in 1630 and went through more than 200 editions. It was first translated and printed in England in 1647; a second edition appeared in 1678.

v. "Theodore de Bèze (1519–1605) was Calvin's chief co-adjutor and, after 1564, leader of the Genevan church. 'That Beza has been charged by the Papists for having instigated Poltrotius Meraeus to assassinate the Duke of Guise is readily acknowledged; but withal, we know how usual and how meritorious a thing it is with them to brand Protestants with whatsoever they can suppose will render them odious' (*The Medal of John Bayes*, 'Epistle to the Tories')" (Kinsley).

w. "In the Postscript to his translation of Maimbourg's *History of the League* (1684), Dryden draws a parallel between the political ideas of the Jesuits [see Preface to *Religio Laici*, 173ff. n.] and those of the Calvinists Buchanan, Knox, and Goodman: '. . . that when magistrates cease to do their duties, God gives the sword into the people's hands: evil princes ought to be deposed by inferior magistrates; and a private man, having an inward call, may kill a tyrant' (Malone, 2, 449–50)." (Kinsley). The parallel was not unusual (see George Sensabaugh, *That Grand Whig Milton* [Stanford, 1952], pp. 114–25), nor was the appeal to tyrannicide (see *Absalom Senior*, 21 n.).

No-protestant Plot and is too plain to be denied. The late copy of your intended Association you neither wholly justify nor condemn. But, as the Papists, when they are unopposed, fly out into all the pageantries of worship, but in times of war, when they are hard pressed by arguments, lie close entrenched behind the Council of Trent,[x] so now, when your affairs are in a low condition, you dare not pretend that to be a legal combination; but whensoever you are afloat, I doubt not but it will be maintained and justified to purpose. For indeed there is nothing to defend it but the sword; 'tis the proper time to say anything when men have all things in their power.

In the meantime, you would fain be nibbling at a parallel [y] betwixt this Association [z] and that in the time of Queen Elizabeth. But there is this small distance betwixt them: that the ends of the one are directly opposite to the other; one with the Queen's approbation and conjunction, as head of it, the other without either the consent or knowledge of the King, against whose authority it is manifestly designed. Therefore, you do well to have recourse to your last evasion; that it was contrived by your enemies and shuffled into the papers that were seized, which yet you see the nation is not so easy to believe as your own jury.[a] But the matter is not difficult: to find twelve men in Newgate who would acquit a malefactor.

I have one only favor to desire of you at parting: that when you think of answering this poem you would employ the same pens against it who have combatted with so much success against *Absalom and Achitophel*,[b] for then you may assure yourselves of a clear victory, without at least reply.[c] Rail at me abundantly and, not to break a custom, do it without wit; by this method you will gain a consider-

---

x. The Council of Trent (1545–63) made certain dogmatic decisions to oppose Protestant encroachment and attempted a number of reforms of ecclesiastical life.

y. The alleged precedent for an Association was 27 Elizabeth cap. 1 (see *LJ, 13,* 672). For Burnet's rejection, see *History, 2,* 264–65 and n.

z. See n. 1. above.

a. The members of the grand jury and the panel from which they were chosen is given in *The Impartial Protestant Mercury,* No. 62 (22–5 Nov. 1681); Barnardiston, Papillon, and Dubois were to play leading roles in the struggle for power in the following months. For the packing of juries, see, e.g., *CSPD, 1682,* p. 236; Burnet, *History, 2,* 254; Wright, *A Compendious View* [W 3692], p. 146; and the poems on the shrieval elections.

b. For anti-*Absalom* and anti-*Medal* poems, see Macdonald, *Dryden Bibliography,* 199–209, 211.

c. Cf. *The Second Part of Absalom and Achitophel,* 485–88, 496–505.

able point, which is wholly to waive the answer of my arguments.
Never own the bottom of your principles, for fear they should be
treason. Fall severely on the miscarriages of government, for if scan-
dal be not allowed, you are no freeborn subjects. If God has not
blessed you with the talent of rhyming, make use of my poor stock,
and welcome. Let your verses run upon my feet; and for the utmost
refuge of notorious blockheads, reduced to the last extremity of
sense,[d] turn my own lines upon me and, in utter despair of your own
satire, make me satirize myself.[e] (Some of you have been driven to
this bay already.) But, above all the rest, commend me to the Non-
conformist parson who wrote the *Whip and Key.* I am afraid it is not
read so much as the piece deserves, because the bookseller [f] is every
week crying help at the end of his *Gazette* to get it off. You see I am
charitable enough to do him a kindness, that it may be published as
well as printed, and that so much skill in Hebrew derivations may
not lie for wastepaper in the shop. Yet I half suspect he went no
further for his learning than the index of Hebrew names and ety-
mologies which is printed at the end of some English Bibles. If *Achit-
ophel* signify the "brother of a fool," the author of that poem will pass
with his readers for the next of kin, and perhaps 'tis the relation that
makes the kindness. Whatever the verses are, buy 'em up, I beseech
you, out of pity, for I hear the conventicle is shut up and the brother
of Achitophel out of service.

   Now footmen, you know, have the generosity to make a purse [g] for

   d. Dryden was not wholly innocent of this "extremity of sense," as his parodies of
lines from Waller, Cowley, and Shadwell in *Mac Flecknoe* demonstrate.
   e. "At the time of the publication of *The Medal,* the most conspicuous example of
turning Dryden's own lines upon him had been *Azaria and Hushai,* written probably
by Samuel Pordage (Luttrell's copy is marked 17 January 1682). Settle continued the
parodies in *Absalom Senior* (Luttrell's copy is dated 6 April). 'The non-conformist
parson' is Christopher Nesse, a London Calvinist minister and supposed author of
A Whip for the Fool's Back . . . (1681) and *A Key . . . to . . . Absalom and
Achitophel* (Luttrell's copy dated 13 January 1682)" (Kinsley). See also *Absolon's IX
Worthies* (Luttrell: 10 March 1682) and Macdonald's discussion of these pieces
(*Dryden Bibliography,* 202–03). Dryden may also have had in mind the more damaging
reprintings of his elegy in praise of Cromwell (pp. 5–6) and the verses attacking him for
his inconsistency (pp. 224–25).
   f. Macdonald No. 202 was sold by Langley Curtis, and Macdonald No. 203 by
Richard Janeway; at this time the former published *The Weekly Pacquet of Advice
from Rome* and the latter *The Impartial Protestant Mercury.* The only paper with the
title of *Gazette* was *The London Gazette.*
   g. *to make a purse:* To collect a sum of money as a present.

a member of their society who has had his livery pulled over his ears; and even Protestant socks are bought up among you out of veneration to the name. A Dissenter in poetry from sense and English will make as good a Protestant rhymer as a Dissenter from the Church of England a Protestant parson. Besides, if you encourage a young beginner, who knows but he may elevate his style a little, above the vulgar epithets of *prophane,* and *saucy Jack,*[h] and *atheistic scribbler,* with which he treats me when the fit of enthusiasm is strong upon him; by which well-mannered and charitable expressions I was certain of his sect before I knew his name. What would you have more of a man? He has damned me in your cause from Genesis to the Revelations and has half the texts of both the Testaments against me, if you will be so civil to yourselves as to take *him* for your interpreter and not to take *them* for Irish witnesses.[1] After all, perhaps you will tell me that you retained him only for the opening of your cause, and that your main lawyer is yet behind. Now if it so happen he meet with no more reply than his predecessors, you may either conclude that I trust to the goodness of my cause, or fear my adversary, or disdain him, or what you please—for the short on 't is 'tis indifferent to your humble servant, whatever your party says or thinks of him.

The Medal

A SATIRE AGAINST SEDITION

Of all our antic sights and pageantry
Which English idiots run in crowds to see,
The Polish Medal bears the prize alone:
A monster, more the favorite of the town
Than either fairs or theaters have shown.   5
Never did art so well with nature strive,
Nor ever idol seem'd so much alive:
So like the man; so golden to the sight,
So base within, so counterfeit and light.

h. *A Whip* (Macdonald No. 202) refers to *Absalom* as "profane," and *A Key* (Macdonald No. 203) attacks "dirty Jack," his "saucy satyr verse," and so on.

i. See *The Medal,* 149 n., and, as one instance of the general furor, Kinsley's note to this line, with its excerpt from *The Irish Evidence Convicted by Their Own Oaths* (1682) [I 1038].

One side is fill'd with title and with face; 10
And, lest the King should want a regal place,
On the reverse, a tow'r the town surveys,
O'er which our mounting sun his beams displays.
The word, pronounc'd aloud by shrieval voice,
Laetamur, which, in Polish, is rejoice. 15
The day, month, year, to the great act are join'd,
And a new canting holiday design'd.
Five days he sat for every cast and look;
Four more than God to finish Adam took.
But who can tell what essence angels are, 20
Or how long Heav'n was making Lucifer?
O could the style that copi'd every grace
And plow'd such furrows for an eunuch face,
Could it have form'd his ever-changing will,
The various piece had tir'd the graver's skill! 25
A martial hero first, with early care,
Blown, like a pigmy by the winds, to war.
A beardless chief, a rebel ere a man
(So young his hatred to his prince began).
Next this (how wildly will ambition steer!), 30
A vermin wriggling in th' usurper's ear.

14. *shrieval voice:* Thomas Pilkington and Samuel Shute, the two Whig sheriffs of London, empaneled the "Ignoramus" jury that refused to indict Shaftesbury. On 13 Dec. Pilkington and the Skinners' Company feasted Shaftesbury "and the entertainment was generous and splendid" (*Impartial Protestant Mercury,* No. 68 [13–16 Dec. 1681]).

15. *in Polish:* See "Epistle to the Whigs," note b.

17. Days of national fasting and praying were proclaimed by the Parliament during the 1640s in thanksgiving for victories over the King and in order to sustain the people's spirits. For Charles II's reaction to the Whig Feast of 21 April, see below, pp. 174–75.

22. *style:* An engraving tool.

23. *furrows:* Bower's portrait shows deep lines from the side of the nose down to the chin.

26–29. Shaftesbury in 1643 supported Charles I, but at the end of the following year he resigned his commission and obtained command of the parliamentary forces in Dorset. See also Kinsley, *Absalom and Achitophel,* 150 n., and Brown, *Shaftesbury,* p. 96.

27. *pigmy:* Cf. *Absalom and Achitophel,* 157. For an expanded view of the relationship of pigmies with the Whigs and the Association, and their connection with "rebels," see *Heraclitus Ridens,* No. 60 (21 March 1682).

31. The image is that of an earwig, a flatterer, or parasite. Cf. *Midsummer Moon,* 405.

Bart'ring his venal wit for sums of gold,
He cast himself into the saintlike mold;
Groan'd, sigh'd, and pray'd while godliness was gain,
The loudest bagpipe of the squeaking train.   35
But, as 'tis hard to cheat a juggler's eyes,
His open lewdness he could ne'er disguise.
There split the saint; for hypocritic zeal
Allows no sins but those it can conceal.
Whoring to scandal gives too large a scope;   40
Saints must not trade, but they may interlope.
Th' ungodly principle was all the same,
But a gross cheat betrays his partner's game.
Besides, their pace was formal, grave, and slack;
His nimble wit outran the heavy pack.   45
Yet still he found his fortune at a stay,
Whole droves of blockheads choking up his way;
They took, but not rewarded, his advice—
Villain and wit exact a double price.
Pow'r was his aim; but, thrown from that pretense,   50
The wretch turn'd loyal in his own defense,
And malice reconcil'd him to his prince.
Him in the anguish of his soul he serv'd,
Rewarded faster still than he deserv'd.
Behold him now exalted into trust;   55

35. *squeaking train:* Cf. the description of sectarian pulpit style in *Observator*, No.
110 (11 March 1682); also the "squeaking engine" of Crowders in Butler, *Hudibras*,
I.II.113.

37. *His open lewdness:* The charge of *covert* immorality is found regularly in anti-
Shaftesbury writing; indeed, such accusations form a constant theme during the
previous half-century in the attacks on religious sects and those associated with them.
Separating Shaftesbury from his party by his "open lewdness" (as well as by his hypo-
critical use of zealous hypocrites) sharpens Dryden's satiric thrust, though Kinsley's
assumption (*4*, 1909) that such "libertinism" is a matter of fact is hardly borne out
by a phrase from North (*Examen,* p. 60) or the version of an anecdote given in Brown
(*Shaftesbury,* p. 214).

41. *interlope:* To traffic without a proper license. Cf. Prologue to *Amphitryon,* 16–17.

47. Cf. *Mac Flecknoe,* 103.

51–52. Shaftesbury sat for Wiltshire after 1653 and served on the Council of State.
His desire for parliamentary government placed him in opposition to Cromwellian
authoritarianism and caused him to be suspected of royalist sympathies.

55–58. Shaftesbury, while holding important offices during the preceding decade,
attained his highest governmental positions as a member of the Cabal in 1670 and as

His counsel's oft convenient, seldom just.
Ev'n in the most sincere advice he gave,
He had a grudging still to be a knave.
The frauds he learnt in his fanatic years
Made him uneasy in his lawful gears: 60
At best as little honest as he could,
And, like white witches, mischievously good.
To his first bias longingly he leans,
And rather would be great by wicked means.
Thus, fram'd for ill, he loos'd our triple hold   65
(Advice unsafe, precipitous, and bold).
From hence those tears! that Ilium of our woe!
Who helps a pow'rful friend forearms a foe.
What wonder if the waves prevail so far,
When he cut down the banks that made the bar?   70
Seas follow but their nature to invade,
But he by art our native strength betray'd.
So Sampson to his foe his force confess'd
And, to be shorn, lay slumb'ring on her breast.
But when this fatal counsel, found too late,   75
Expos'd its author to the public hate;
When his just sovereign, by no impious way,

Lord Chancellor in 1672, the year he obtained his earldom. His work in this office has received almost general approbation, and Dryden's famous lines in *Absalom and Achitophel* (188–97) contrast strongly with the view he gives here. In Nov. 1673 Shaftesbury was dismissed and moved into the opposition, of which he soon became head.

60. *gears:* Work, situation.

65. *triple hold:* The Triple Alliance of England, Holland, and Sweden (1668), meant to serve as a check to French expansion, was broken by the Anglo-French alliance of 1670, which led to the Third Dutch War (1672–78). Shaftesbury, as a member of the Cabal, supported this move, though he and Buckingham were in ignorance of Charles' further agreement with Louis to reinstate Catholicism with the help of large subsidies. See also *Absalom and Achitophel*, 175–76; and for Dryden's support of the Dutch War, see Prologue and Epilogue to *Amboyna* and Kinsley's note thereto. For Halifax's use of this and the subsequent arguments against Shaftesbury, see Barillon's report in Foxcroft, *A Character of the Trimmer*, p. 119.

68. Dryden, treating the Earl alternately as knave and fool, makes him responsible for the growth of France's power, thus calling into question Shaftesbury's whole anti-French policy.

77. On 15 March 1672, Charles issued the Declaration of Indulgence, but it met with such strong opposition in Commons that, on Louis' advice, it was withdrawn. Dryden again casts doubts on Shaftesbury's sincerity as an anti-Catholic and pro-

Could be seduc'd to arbitrary sway;
Forsaken of that hope, he shifts the sail,
Drives down the current with a pop'lar gale,   80
And shows the fiend confess'd without a veil.
He preaches to the crowd that pow'r is lent
But not convey'd to kingly government,
That claims successive bear no binding force,
That coronation oaths are things of course;   85
Maintains the multitude can never err,
And sets the people in the papal chair.
The reason's obvious: int'rest never lies.
The most have still their int'rest in their eyes;
The pow'r is always theirs, and pow'r is ever wise.   90
Almighty crowd, thou shorten'st all dispute;
Pow'r is thy essence, wit thy attribute!
Nor faith nor reason make thee at a stay,
Thou leap'st o'er all eternal truths in thy Pindaric way!
Athens no doubt did righteously decide,   95
When Phocion and when Socrates were tried:
As righteously they did those dooms repent;
Still they were wise, whatever way they went.
Crowds err not, though to both extremes they run;
To kill the father and recall the son.   100

---

parliamentarian by stressing his work to push the Declaration through the House by stirring up support among the Lords and by defending the King's prerogative in ecclesiastical matters. (See Brown, *Shaftesbury*, pp. 207–10.)

79. The withdrawal of the Declaration was followed by pressure for the Test Bill, which tended to be more lenient to dissenters than to Roman Catholics. Shaftesbury, credited with obtaining this leniency as well as with opposition to the French alliance, was becoming the champion of the Protestant party in mid-1673.

82 ff. Cf. *Absalom and Achitophel*, 409–16.

85. *of course:* Belonging to the ordinary procedure, custom, or way of the world. Here the sense is pejorative; i.e. merely formal, emptily ritualistic.

86–87. Those who claimed to be presenting a moderate viewpoint frequently pointed out the similarity of the extreme right and extreme left, of papal and popular claims to infallibility. See, for example, *Observator*, No. 22 (11 June 1681).

94. Kinsley notes the parallel in Preface to *Ovid's Epistles*, 240–44 and quotes *Heraclitus Ridens*, No. 16 (17 May 1681): "Pindaric, which is the poets' latitudinarian way of liberty of conscience in verse." Dryden's alexandrine line exemplifies the "latitudinarian way" of Pindarics.

96. Phocion was executed for treason (317 B.C.) and Socrates for impiety (399 B.C.). In both cases, the Athenians later repented and punished the accusers.

100. *the father . . . the son:* Charles I and Charles II.

Some think the fools were most, as times went then;
But now the world's o'erstock'd with prudent men.
The common cry is ev'n religion's test:
The Turk's is at Constantinople best,
Idols in India, Popery at Rome,   105
And our own worship only true at home.
And true but for the time; 'tis hard to know
How long we please it shall continue so.
This side today and that tomorrow burns;
So all are God-a'mighties in their turns.   110
A tempting doctrine, plausible and new.
What fools our fathers were, if this be true!
Who, to destroy the seeds of civil war,
Inherent right in monarchs did declare;
And, that a lawful pow'r might never cease,   115
Secur'd succession, to secure our peace.
Thus property and sovereign sway, at last,
In equal balances were justly cast.
But this new Jehu spurs the hot-mouth'd horse,
Instructs the beast to know his native force,   120
To take the bit between his teeth and fly
To the next headlong steep of anarchy.
Too happy England, if our good we knew,
Would we possess the freedom we pursue!
The lavish government can give no more;   125
Yet we repine, and plenty makes us poor.
God tried us once: our rebel fathers fought;
He glutted 'em with all the pow'r they sought,
Till, master'd by their own usurping brave,
The freeborn subject sank into a slave.   130
We loathe our manna, and we long for quails;
Ah, what is man, when his own wish prevails!
How rash, how swift to plunge himself in ill;

119. *Jehu:* Cf. 2 Kings 9:20. Jehu became the type of headlong revolutionary who loosed bestial forces (usually, the mob) which he could not fully control. (See, e.g., Pordage, *The Medal Revers'd,* 124; Settle, *Absalom Senior,* 442).

123–34. Cf. *Absalom and Achitophel,* 51–56, 383–384; Prologue to *The Unhappy Favorite,* 13–34 [Kinsley].

129. *brave:* A bravo, bully; a hired assassin. Here, Oliver Cromwell.

131. Numbers 11:4–34.

Proud of his pow'r and boundless in his will!
That kings can do no wrong, we must believe: 135
None can they do, and must they all receive?
Help, Heaven! or sadly we shall see an hour
When neither right nor wrong are in their pow'r!
Already they have lost their best defense,
The benefit of laws which they dispense: 140
No justice to their righteous cause allow'd,
But baffled by an arbitrary crowd;
And medals grav'd, their conquest to record,
The stamp and coin of their adopted lord.

    The man who laugh'd but once, to see an ass   145
Mumbling to make the crossgrain'd thistles pass,
Might laugh again to see a jury chaw
The prickles of unpalatable law.
The witnesses that, leech-like, liv'd on blood,
Sucking for them were med'cinally good;   150
But when they fasten'd on their fester'd sore,
Then justice and religion they forswore;
Their maiden oaths debauch'd into a whore.
Thus men are rais'd by factions, and decri'd;
And rogue and saint distinguish'd by their side.   155

142. *arbitrary:* Dryden transfers to the crowd the term that the anti-Court party had been applying for fifty years to royal power.

144. *coin:* Coinage bore the portrait of the legitimate ruler.

145. Crassus was reputed to have laughed only once, and that was when he saw an ass eating thistles. The story is often included among the *Fables* of Aesop (No. 5). (See Kinsley's note for some seventeenth-century allusions.)

146. *mumbling:* Chewing or biting softly, as with toothless gums; also [with reference to 147] mauling, maltreating.

147–48. Sir Samuel Barnardiston and Thomas Papillon, respectively the foreman and the most powerful member of the famed "Ignoramus" grand jury, attempted to have the proceedings against Shaftesbury heard in private. The Lord Chief Justice (North) denied the request and upheld the King's right to determine the kind of trial he wished. See Howell, *State Trials, 8,* 771–74.

149. *the witnesses:* A number of Irish witnesses, who had previously sworn to the validity of the Popish Plot, now appeared against Shaftesbury, much to the chagrin of those who had formerly accepted their evidence.

151. *their fester'd sore:* An allusion to the suppurating wound in Shaftesbury's side. All editions print the pronoun in italics, indicating, perhaps, that the antecedent here, as in the preceding line, should be either the Whigs or the Whig jury.

They rack ev'n scripture to confess their cause;
And plead a call to preach, in spite of laws.
But that's no news to the poor injur'd page:
It has been us'd as ill in every age
And is constrain'd, with patience, all to take— 160
For what defense can Greek and Hebrew make?
Happy who can this talking trumpet seize;
They make it speak whatever sense they please!
'Twas fram'd at first our oracle t'enquire;
But, since our sects in prophecy grow higher, 165
The text inspires not them, but they the text inspire.

London, thou great emporium of our isle,
O thou too bounteous, thou too fruitful Nile!
How shall I praise or curse to thy desert!
Or separate thy sound, from thy corrupted part! 170
I call'd thee Nile; the parallel will stand:
Thy tides of wealth o'erflow the fatten'd land;
Yet monsters from thy large increase we find,
Engender'd on the slime thou leav'st behind.
Sedition has not wholly seiz'd on thee; 175
Thy nobler parts are from infection free.
Of Israel's tribes thou hast a numerous band,
But still the Canaanite is in the land.
Thy military chiefs are brave and true,
Nor are thy disenchanted burghers few. 180

156. *rack ev'n scripture:* A common metaphor, in use for well over a century, meaning "to give a forced interpretation to" the text. The charge was frequently leveled against sectarians who sought authority for their religious and political positions in the Bible. For other references in Dryden, see Kinsley's note.

157. *to preach in spite of laws:* i.e. the laws against conventicles.

158. The tender page with horny fist was gall'd,
And he was gifted most that loudest bawl'd.
(*Religio Laici*, 404–05)

162. *talking trumpet:* Probably a speaking trumpet, a conical tube used for increasing the force and carrying power of the voice. The earliest reference in the *OED* is 1696, but as early as 1670, "Sir Samuel Morland had proposed to the Royal Society the question of the best form for a speaking trumpet" (*EB*, 27, 327–28).

168. *Nile:* Cf. *Annus Mirabilis*, 183–84, and Kinsley's note thereto.

179. *military chiefs:* The officers in charge of the London trained bands. For the Court party's purge of the London lieutenancy, see Luttrell, *Brief Relation, 1*, 83.

180. *disenchanted:* i.e. with the Whigs, who had been in control of London since Sir Robert Clayton's mayoralty in 1679.

The head is loyal which thy heart commands,
But what's a head with two such gouty hands?
The wise and wealthy love the surest way
And are content to thrive and to obey.
But wisdom is to sloth too great a slave;   185
None are so busy as the fool and knave.
Those let me curse! What vengeance will they urge,
Whose ordures neither plague nor fire can purge
Nor sharp experience can to duty bring,
Nor angry Heaven, nor a forgiving King!   190
In gospel-phrase their chapmen they betray;
Their shops are dens, the buyer is their prey.
The knack of trades is living on the spoil;
They boast, ev'n when each other they beguile.
Customs to steal is such a trivial thing   195
That 'tis their charter to defraud their king.
All hands unite of every jarring sect;
They cheat the country first, and then infect.
They for God's cause their monarchs dare dethrone,
And they'll be sure to make His cause their own.   200
Whether the plotting Jesuit laid the plan
Of murd'ring kings, or the French Puritan,
Our sacrilegious sects their guides outgo,
And kings and kingly pow'r would murder too.

What means their trait'rous combination less,   205
Too plain t'evade, too shameful to confess!

181, 182. *head:* Sir John Moore, the Lord Mayor.

182. *gouty hands:* The Whig Sheriffs, Thomas Pilkington and Samuel Shute. Cf. *The Second Part of Absalom and Achitophel,* 1131–38. For further information on all three men, see the headnote and poems on the shrieval elections.

188. *plague . . . fire:* The principal events of the "annus mirabilis," 1666.

191–94. Dryden gives the traditional picture of the hypocritical sectarian who combines religiosity and sharp materialism. For one such portrait among many, see Kinsley's note. Dryden, however, examines the political implications of the character and finds municipal corruption that warrants Charles's recent Quo Warranto against the London charter (196) as well as national treason that culminates (203–04) in the reputed remark of the Independent extremist and former sheriff, Slingsby Bethel, that "rather than the old King should have wanted an executioner, he would have done it himself" (Luttrell, *Brief Relation, I,* 187).

201–02. *the plotting Jesuit:* Probably with reference to the plots against Elizabeth; *the French Puritan* is Theodore de Bèze. See "Epistle to the Whigs," n. w.

205. *trait'rous combination:* The Association. See "Epistle to the Whigs," n. l.; also,

But treason is not own'd when 'tis descri'd;
Successful crimes alone are justifi'd.
The men who no conspiracy would find,
Who doubts, but had it taken, they had join'd—   210
Join'd in a mutual cov'nant of defense
At first without, at last against, their prince?
If sovereign right by sovereign pow'r they scan,
The same bold maxim holds in God and man:
God were not safe, his thunder could they shun;   215
He should be forc'd to crown another son.
Thus, when the heir was from the vineyard thrown,
The rich possession was the murd'rer's own.
In vain to sophistry they have recourse:
By proving theirs no plot, they prove 'tis worse—   220
Unmask'd rebellion and audacious force,
Which though not actual, yet all eyes may see
'Tis working in th' immediate pow'r to be;
For from pretended grievances they rise
First to dislike, and after to despise;   225
Then, Cyclop-like, in human flesh to deal,
Chop up a minister at every meal;
Perhaps not wholly to melt down the King,
But clip his regal rights within the ring;
From thence t'assume the pow'r of peace and war,   230

---

for the text of the Association and its importance in the Court's case against Shaftesbury, see Howell, *State Trials, 8,* 759–821.

209. *The men:* The members of the "Ignoramus" jury.

213. *scan:* To judge, examine minutely, criticize, analyze.

216. *another son:* In the context of his analogy of God and King and the Whigs' desire to corrupt both to their own ends, Dryden's allusion would be to the illegitimate Duke of Monmouth, whom the Whigs wished to succeed to the crown.

217–18. Matthew 21:38–39 and 1 Kings 21:1–16.

223. *immediate:* Direct, proximate.

227. i.e. each session ("meal") of parliament feeds upon the King's minister—Clarendon, Danby, Stafford, Lauderdale, or Halifax. Only Stafford was literally chopped up.

228. *clip:* Mutilate current coin by fraudulently paring the edges.

the ring: The circle round the sovereign's image. Coins clipped "within the ring" were no longer legal tender. For other references in Dryden, and for comments on contemporary minting, see Kinsley's note. The anti-monarchical tactics present through line 236 constituted the traditional attack of parliamentarians, most succinctly satirized in the well-known *Commons' Petition to the King* ("In all humility we crave"); see *POAS,* Yale, *2,* 192.

And ease him by degrees of public care.
Yet, to consult his dignity and fame,
He should have leave to exercise the name
And hold the cards while commons play'd the game.
For what can pow'r give more than food and drink,   235
To live at ease, and not be bound to think?
These are the cooler methods of their crime,
But their hot zealots think 'tis loss of time;
On utmost bounds of loyalty they stand
And grin and whet like a Croatian band   240
That waits impatient for the last command.
Thus outlaws open villainy maintain:
They steal not, but in squadrons scour the plain;
And, if their pow'r the passengers subdue,
The most have right, the wrong is in the few.   245
Such impious axioms foolishly they show,
For in some soils republics will not grow:
Our temp'rate isle will no extremes sustain
Of pop'lar sway or arbitrary reign,
But slides between them both into the best,   250
Secure in freedom, in a monarch blest.
And though the climate, vex'd with various winds,
Works through our yielding bodies on our minds,
The wholesome tempest purges what it breeds,
To recommend the calmness that succeeds.   255

  But thou, the pander of the people's hearts,
(O crooked soul, and serpentine in arts!)
Whose blandishments a loyal land have whor'd,

239. *bounds:* Frontiers.

240. Croatia stood at the limits of Christian Europe and marked the farthest point of the Ottoman advance.

243. Croatia divides naturally into two major sections: the rugged highlands of the west, and, to the east, the lowlands of the great Hungarian Plains which contain the fertile, accessible valleys of the Drone and Danube.

252–55. Kinsley cites Lord Halifax's similar statement of this theory: "Our government is like our climate, there are winds which are sometimes loud and unquiet, and yet with all the trouble they give us, we owe great part of our health unto them, they clear the air which else would be like a standing pool. . . . There may be fresh gales of asserting liberty, without turning into such storms of hurricane, as that the state should run any hazard of being cast away" (Halifax, *Works*, p. 63). Kinsley refers to other discussions of "seventeenth century notions of the effects of climate" in Burton and Dennis.

And broke the bonds she plighted to her lord,
What curses on thy blasted name will fall!   260
Which age to age their legacy shall call;
For all must curse the woes that must descend on all.
Religion thou hast none: thy mercury
Has pass'd through every sect, or theirs through thee.
But what thou giv'st, that venom still remains,   265
And the pox'd nation feels thee in their brains.
What else inspires the tongues and swells the breasts
Of all thy bellowing renegado priests
That preach up thee for God, dispense thy laws,
And with thy stum ferment their fainting cause;   270
Fresh fumes of madness raise, and toil and sweat
To make the formidable cripple great?
Yet should thy crimes succeed, should lawless pow'r
Compass those ends thy greedy hopes devour,
Thy canting friend thy mortal foes would be;   275
Thy God and theirs will never long agree.
For thine (if thou hast any) must be one

262. The Luciferian image of the foregoing five lines culminates in a view of political lapsarianism.

263. *Religion thou hast none: Heraclitus Ridens,* No. 37 (11 Oct. 1681) remarked: "There is nobody swears against my Lord Shaftesbury . . . for being a Protestant or being publicly engaged against popery; I never heard that he was accused for being of any religion." See Brown, *Shaftesbury,* pp. 209–10, for an account of Shaftesbury's famed remark (reported by John Toland, *Tetradymus* [London, 1720], part 2, chap. 13) that "wise men are all of the same religion" but "wise men never tell" what religion that is. Evelyn suggests that he was "without much regard to the religion established under the hierarchy" (*Diary, 4,* 328), and Burnet feels he was "a deist at best" (*History 1,* 372).

mercury: An emblem of volatility, inconstancy, wittiness; used also for a cheat or thief. Dryden develops the pharmaceutical meaning as it relates to the cure of venereal disease (226) and to mercurial poisoning from overuse (265).

268. *renegado:* An apostate from any form of religious faith, especially a Christian who becomes a Mohammedan. The term was much used at this time because of the notoriety of the English interpreter of the Moroccan ambassador. See *Midsummer Moon,* 46 n. and 74 n. Dryden's "renegado priests" probably refers to the nonconformist preachers who found it impossible to submit to such laws as the Act of Uniformity (1662) or the Test Act (1673).

270. *stum:* Must used for renewing vapid wines.

272. To his contemporaries, Shaftesbury was "the little, limping peer." Cf. Brown, *Shaftesbury,* p. 268.

277–80. Dryden would seem to be suggesting that Shaftesbury's "religion" is virtually Epicureanism, which in the late seventeenth century was considered nearly synonymous with atheism.

That lets the world and humankind alone:
A jolly god that passes hours too well
To promise heav'n or threaten us with hell;   280
That unconcern'd can at rebellion sit,
And wink at crimes he did himself commit.
A tyrant theirs: the heav'n their priesthood paints
A conventicle of gloomy sullen saints;
A heav'n, like Bedlam, slovenly and sad,   285
Foredoom'd for souls with false religion mad.

Without a vision poets can foreshow
What all but fools by common sense may know:
If true succession from our isle should fail,
And crowds profane with impious arms prevail,   290
Not thou, nor those thy factious arts engage,
Shall reap that harvest of rebellious rage
With which thou flatter'st thy decrepit age.
The swelling poison of the sev'ral sects,
Which, wanting vent, the nation's health infects,   295
Shall burst its bag; and, fighting out their way,
The various venoms on each other prey.
The Presbyter, puff'd up with spiritual pride,
Shall on the necks of the lewd nobles ride,
His brethren damn, the civil pow'r defy,   300
And parcel out republic prelacy.
But short shall be his reign: his rigid yoke
And tyrant pow'r will puny sects provoke;
And frogs and toads and all the tadpole train
Will croak to Heav'n for help from this devouring crane.   305
The cutthroat sword and clamorous gown shall jar

289. *true succession:* Dryden seems to be differentiating "true" from "legal" succession. Burnet explains the latter: "the word *heir* . . . imported that person who by law ought to succeed, and so it fell to any person who by law was declared next in the succession. In England the heir of the king that reigned had been sometimes set aside, and the right of succession was transferred to another person" (*History,* 2, 215). See also *The Medal Revers'd,* 371 n.

297. Cf. *Absalom and Achitophel,* 1012–15 and Kinsley's note thereto.

299. *lewd:* Ignorant, foolish; ill-conditioned.

303–04. The earlier allusion (298) to the Aesopic fable (No. 26) of "The Ox and the Frog" leads into this closer analogue of the fable (No. 36) of "The Frogs Desiring a King."

306. *clamorous gown:* The legal or clerical profession.

In sharing their ill-gotten spoils of war;
Chiefs shall be grudg'd the part which they pretend;
Lords envy lords, and friends with every friend
About their impious merit shall contend.   310
The surly commons shall respect deny
And justle peerage out with property.
Their gen'ral either shall his trust betray
And force the crowd to arbitrary sway;
Or they, suspecting his ambitious aim,   315
In hate of kings shall cast anew the frame—
And thrust out Collatine that bore their name.

Thus inbred broils the factions would engage,
Or wars of exil'd heirs or foreign rage,
Till halting vengeance overtook our age;   320
And our wild labors, wearied into rest,
Reclin'd us on a rightful monarch's breast.

——————Pudet haec opprobria, vobis
Et dici potuisse, et non potuisse refelli.

311. *surly:* Imperious, haughty.

317. The evocation of the Interregnum begins with a reference to the leveling and compounding policies of the rebellious parliament (312), calls up the period of Cromwell (313) and the Major-Generals (315), and culminates in the image of Lucius Tarquinius Collatinus, who (as Kinsley notes) with Lucius Junius Brutus drove the Tarquins from Rome and established the Republic. "But Collatine was abominated because he was himself a Tarquin, and was forced into exile. A like fate, says Dryden, threatens the Stuart Monmouth. He had made a similar point in *His Majesties Declaration Defended,* 1681 (pp. 12–13): '. . . the Protestant successor himself, if he be not wholly governed by the prevailing party, will first be declared no Protestant; and next, no successor. . . . for all the bustle concerning the Duke of Monmouth proceeds from a Commonwealth principle.' Cf. *Absalom and Achitophel,* 82, 220–27, notes; *Heraclitus Ridens,* No. 71, 6 June 1682 . . ."

323–24. Ovid, *Metamorphoses,* I.758–59. The lines are added in the second issue (Macdonald No. 13 a ii). A standard translation (F. J. Miller, Loeb Library) renders this, "Ashamed am I that such an insult could have been uttered and yet could not be answered."

The assertion on the title page that this poem is "By the author of *Azaria and Hushai*" introduces a typical problem of pamphlet ascription. Luttrell, who obtained his copy on 31 March 1682, wrote on it "Sam Pordage," perhaps in keeping with his earlier views of *Azaria* (an answer to Dryden's *Absalom*) which he had marked as "by S. Pordage. 17 Jan." Some additional support comes from *The Observator*, No. 119 (5 April 1682), where L'Estrange, after devoting the first column to a Tory critique of this poem, goes on to other matters and then, starting an attack on Pordage, remarks that "limping Pordage [is] . . . violently suspected for *The Medal Revers'd*."

The interlocking of the two poems only serves to complicate the problem. Dobell (*Literature of the Restoration* [London, 1918], p. 54) notes a copy of *Azaria* with "For my worthy friend Mr. Pordage" inscribed in a hand that is not Settle's, though the poem was generally thought to be his when it first appeared (Wood, *Athenae Oxoniensis, 4,* 687). And second thoughts by contemporaries are equally elusive. *The Second Part of Absalom and Achitophel* very probably refers to Pordage as "lame Mephibosheth," but an allusion to *Azaria* (let alone the authority for it) is far less definite. So, too, in the play *City Politics* (performed 20 Jan. 1683), Crowne has the comic character Craffy ("an ignorant, amorous, pragmatical fop, that pretends to wit and poetry") discuss his two major works in progress, *Azaria and Hushai* and *The Medal Revers'd*. Here the question of the identification of Craffy is colored by Crowne's habit of constructing a character on the basis of more than one historical person. Undoubtedly, the principal model is Settle, but whether he is the sole model, as Macdonald (p. 244) and Ham ("Dryden versus Settle," *MP*, 25 [1928], 414) suggest, is not entirely certain. Ham's thorough analysis of the external evidence gives very strong support to Settle's exclusive authorship of both poems; and one might add that both Macdonald and Yale University have copies of *The Medal Revers'd* with "E. Settle" in manuscript on the title page. Finally, one should not dismiss too quickly the possibility of multiple authorship, a not uncommon practice among pamphleteers, for whom rapid publication was vital. Spence's report that Settle received assistance in writing *Absalom Senior* from "several of the best hands of the time" is not unfeasible in principle, though it may be inaccurate in the specific authors mentioned (see Macdonald, p. 230, n. 2). Some such collaborative effort may well have produced these two poems. Certainly the style of *The Medal Revers'd* could be that of a number of accomplished writers in the Whig idiom: Settle of course, or perhaps his friend Pordage, or even Edmund Hickeringill, whose rhetoric, vocabulary, and phrasing seem at times remarkably similar to the poem's. The tone moves effectively from moderation and generalized indignation to specific warnings that are at once startlingly frank and prophetic.

The text is based on the 1682 quarto (Macdonald 207) and collated with z.

The Medal Revers'd

A Satire against Persecution

How easy 'tis to sail with wind and tide!
Small force will serve upon the stronger side;
Power serves for law, the wrong too oft's made right,
And they are damn'd who against power dare fight.
Wit rides triumphant, in Power's chariot borne,   5
And depress'd opposites beholds with scorn.
This well the author of *The Medal* knew,
When Oliver he for an hero drew.
He then swam with the tide, appear'd a Saint,
Garnish'd the devil with poetic paint.   10
When the tide turn'd, then straight about he veers,
And for the stronger side he still appears.

8. The elegiac verses on the death of Cromwell, written between Sept. 1658 and Jan. 1659, were constantly mentioned by Dryden's opponents and reprinted three times in 1681–82 to embarrass the now Tory poet (Macdonald, *Dryden Bibliography*, pp. 3–6).

9. *Saint:* The term used by certain puritanical sectarians for their adherents, whom they considered as members of the elect under the New Covenant of the New Testament. By those outside the sects, the term was used with obloquy to signify those extremist groups which had given full support to Cromwell's government.

Then in heroics courts the great and high,
And at th' oppress'd he lets his satyrs fly.
But he who stems the tide, if ground he gains,   15
Each stroke he makes must be with wonderous pains:
If he bears up against the current still,
He shows at least he has some art and skill,
When against tide, wind, billows he does strive
And comes at last unto the shore alive.   20
Huzza, my friends! let us our way pursue,
And try what our poetic arms can do.
This latter age with wonders does abound;
Our Prince of Poets has a Medal found,
From whence his pregnant fancy rears a piece   25
Esteem'd to equal those of Rome and Greece.
With piercing eyes he does the Medal view,
And there he finds, as he has told to you,
The hag Sedition, to the life display'd,
Under a statesman's gown (fanci'd or made,   30
That is all one, he doth it so apply);
At it th' artillery of his wit lets fly,
Lets go his satyr at the Medal straight,
Worries the Whigs, and doth Sedition bait.
Let him go on, the Whigs the hag forsake;   35
Her cause they never yet would undertake,
But laugh to see the poet's fond mistake.
But we will turn the Medal; there we see
Another hag, I think as bad as she;
If I am not mistaken, 'tis the same,   40

---

13. The author probably has in mind such poems as *Astrea Redux* (c. 19 June 1660),
To His Sacred Majesty . . . On His Coronation (April 1661), *To My Lord Chancellor*
(1662), and *Annus Mirabilis* (Jan. 1667).

14. *satyrs:* The original spelling has been retained since the writer is making use of
the contemporary confusion of *satire,* the literary genre, and *satyr,* the partly human
and partly bestial woodland god that appeared in Greek drama.

21. *Huzza:* The writer's exclamation is mildly ironic. As North explains, "at all the
Tory healths . . . the cry was reared of 'Huzza!' which, at great and solemn feasts
made no little noise and gave advantage to the Whigs, that liked not such music, to
charge the Tories with brutality and extravagance" (*Examen,* p. 617).

24. *Prince of Poets:* Cf. *The Medal of John Bayes,* 72.

29. While the subtitle of *The Medal* is "A Satire Against Sedition," Dryden does
not actually use the image of the hag.

Christians of old did *Persecution* name;
That's still her name; though now, grown old and wise,
She has new names as well as new disguise.
Let then his satyr with Sedition fight,
And ours the whilst shall Persecution bite.   45
Two hags they are, who parties seem to make;
'Tis time for satyrs them to undertake.

   See her true badge, a prison or the Tower;
For Persecution ever sides with power.
Our satyr dares not worry those he should;   50
But there are some felt, heard, and understood,
Who, substantives of power, stand alone,
And by all seeing men are too well known—
What steps they tread and whither 'tis they drive,
What measures take and by what arts they thrive.   55
But were these little tyrants underfoot,
How bravely o'er them could our satyr strut!
What characters, and justly, could he give,
Of men who scarcely do deserve to live!
Yet these are they some flatterers can court,   60
Who now are Persecution's great support.
We on the Medal see the fatal Tower;
Truth must be silent, for we know their power:
Whilst they, without control, can show their hate,
And whom they please, with grinning satyrs bait.   65
This puts our satyr into fume and chafe;
He could bite sorely could he do it safe.
Since against such he dares not spend his breath,
Th' hag Persecution he will bait to death.

   Old as the world almost, as old as Cain,   70
For by this hag was righteous Abel slain;
In tyrants' courts she ever doth abide,
Accompani'd with Power, with Lust and Pride.
What she has done is to the world well known;
She always made the best of men to groan.   75
Her bloody arts are register'd of old,
And all her cruel policies are told.
All that is past, our Muse shall let alone,

Pass foreign, and speak only of our own;
Our own a dear ugly hag, who now has power   80
To send to Tyburn, Newgate, or the Tower.

If power be in the multitude, not few,
They show that they have faith and reason too,
Leap not their bounds, nor do their power betray,
Since they to laws and government obey.   85
If other power they exercise, 'tis force,
Or rage, that seen in a wild headstrong horse,
The more he's spurr'd or rein'd, the more doth bound,
And leaves not till the rider's on the ground.
But far it seems from our almighty crowd   90
To boast their strength or be of power proud.
Their power they of old had fruitless tri'd
And therefore now take reason for their guide.
Nay, faith they have in their own juster cause,
In their dread Sovereign, and his righteous laws;   95
This makes them thus submit, all power lay by;
For right, for law, for peace they only cry.
For this, by some, they are accounted fools;
So generous horses are mistook for mules,
And some Court Jockeys mount them in their pride   100
And with a satyr's heel spur-gall their hide;
Dull asses they suppose the people are,
Made for their burdens, and not fit for war.

All with the forewind of religious sail;
It to all parties is the common stale.   105
I know you'll grant the devil is no fool;
He can disguise in surplice, cloak, or cowl;

82. See, for example, *The Medal*, 82–83, 91–92.

87–89. The forthright development of the image probably answers Dryden's allusion
to Jehu (119–22), a common symbol of uncontrollable revolt.

90. *almighty crowd:* Cf. *The Medal*, 91.

91. Cf. *The Medal*, 134.

92. *of old:* The reference is to 1640–60. Cf. *The Medal*, 127–30.

93–94. Cf. *The Medal*, 93.

100. *Jockeys:* Colloquially, cheats or fraudulent bargainers. The author employs the
word to refer to Scots generally and, by extension, to the adherents of the Duke of
York, who had been Lord Commissioner of Scotland.

105. *common stale:* A prostitute of the lowest class, employed as a decoy by thieves.

But still he may be known without dispute
By Persecution; 'tis his cloven foot.
Let him be Christian, Pagan, Turk, or Jew,   110
Pretends religious zeal, it can't be true
If 't Persecution raises, or maintains,
Or makes a market of ungodly gains.
When Rome had power here and sat enchair'd,
How cruel and how bloody she appear'd!   115
Our Church Dissenters then did feel the same;
Their bodies serv'd for fuel to the flame:
And can this Church now got into the chair,
A cruel tyrant like to Rome appear?
For bare opinion do their brothers harm,   120
Plague and imprison, 'cause they can't conform?
—But stay; our Church has law upon its side:
And so had Rome, that cannot be deni'd.
And if these Jehus, who so fiercely drive,
In their sinister arts proceed and thrive,   125
We soon shall see our Church receive its doom
And feel again the tyranny of Rome.
To bar succession is th' ungodly sin,
So often broke, so often piec'd ag'in:
O may it here in England never cease,   130
Could we but hope it would secure our peace!
But men with different thoughts possessed are;
We dread th' effects of a new Civil War.
We dread Rome's yoke, to us 'tis hateful grown,
And Rome will seem a monster in our throne.   135

How rarely will a cope the throne bedeck?
A bishop's head set on a prince's neck?
Th' inherent right lies in the sovereign's sway,

117. The allusion is probably to the Marian persecutions that began in 1555.

120–21. Under such laws as the Act of Uniformity, the Conventicle Act, the Five-Mile Act, and the later Test Act (1681), nonconforming sects and bishops were harassed by the government.

124. *Jehus:* 2 Kings 9:20. See 87–89 n. and *The Medal*, 119 n.

128–31. Cf. *The Medal*, 115–16.

136. *cope:* A clerical, or sacerdotal, vestment; also, the special dress of a monk or friar.

But then the monarch must Rome's laws obey.
Head of the Church he must no longer be,   140
But give that place unto Rome's Holy See.
Both of the Church, and him, Rome will take care;
The throne must truckle under papal chair.

    Kings can't do wrong, so does the maxim say,
But ministers of State, their servants, may.   145
Though kings themselves do sit above the law,
Justice still keeps their ministers in awe;
For if they do not make the law their guide,
Great as they are, by law they may be tri'd;
Else we should subject be to every ill,   150
And be made slaves to arbitrary will.
O happy isle where each man justice craves!
Kings can't be tyrants, nor the subjects slaves.
The laws some great ones fear, who rule the State;
When they can't new unto their wills create,   155
They to their minds, with cunning, try to mold,
And, with new images, to stamp the old:
What 'gainst dissenting Papists first was bent,
For Protestants now proves a punishment.
Law! Law! they cry, and then their brother smite,   160
As well upon the left side as the right;
To every jail the Protestants they draw,
And Persecution still is mask'd with law;
We do not know but Rome may have its turn,
And then it will be also law to burn.   165

    This is not all; for some ill men there be,
Who would the laws use in a worse degree:

143. Cf. *The Medal*, 87.

144. Cf. *The Medal*, 135.

145ff. The classic parliamentarian attack against royal prerogative was through the king's "evil counselors." Cf. *The Medal*, 227–31.

158. Parliament enacted certain bills for religious conformity aimed primarily at Roman Catholics; the government, however, enforced them against those of the opposite extreme, the dissenting sectarians.

165. It was not until 8 March 1677 that a bill for taking away of the writ *De Haeritico Comburendo* was introduced in Commons (*CJ, 9,* 394). The bill passed, of course, quite rapidly (ibid., p. 419), but Whig writers alluded to it constantly at this time (cf. *Weekly Pacquet,* 10 Feb., 16 June 1682).

Treason and traitors, plots against the State,
To reach their foes, they cunningly create.
To prison then the innocent they draw,   170
And if they could, their heads would take by law;
But law is just, and Englishmen are good,
And do not love to dip their hands in blood
Of innocents. But this has rais'd the rage
Of some politic actors on our stage,   175
And, spite of justice, law, and reason too,
Their wicked ends by other means pursue.
Those men whom they can neither hang nor draw,
Freed by their country, justice, and the law,
They try to murder with an hireling's pen,   180
By making them the very worst of men.
They've orators and poets at their will,
Who, with their venom, strive their fames to kill.
These rack the laws and Holy Scriptures too,
And fain would make all the old treasons new.   185
They will not let the graves and tombs alone,
But conjure up the ghost of forty-one.
With this they try the ignorant to scare,
For men are apt the worst of things to fear;
Though that ghost is no liker eighty-two,   190
Than a good Christian like a Turk or Jew.

    London, the happy bulwark of our isle,
No smooth and oily words can thee beguile;
Thou know'st thy int'rest, that will never lie;
Eternal as thyself, the men do die.   195

168. *Treason and traitors:* Though closely connected with the second half of the line, the reference here would seem to be to the government's charge of high treason against the Earl of Shaftesbury.

plots against the State: The Meal Tub Plot, according to the Whigs, was a sham plot fabricated by the Catholics in order to incriminate the leaders of the Whig party.

182. *orators:* George Savile, Marquis of Halifax, was credited with having almost singlehandedly defeated the Exclusion Bill on 15 Nov. 1680 by out-debating Shaftesbury.

184. Cf. *The Medal*, 156–57. On the racking of Holy Scriptures, the author is very likely referring to Dryden's use of the Bible in *Absalom and Achitophel.*

187. *ghost of forty-one:* Dryden, like most Tory writers, constantly connected the anti-Court party with the parliamentarians who, in 1641, had taken up arms against Charles I.

192. For Dryden's description of London, see *The Medal*, 167–204.

'Tis truth and justice do thee uphold,
And richer in religion than in gold;
Thy piety has built thy turrets higher
Than e'er, in spite of plague, of war, and fire.
Without a sigh, we can't think on the flame,   200
Nor by what hands, and from what heads, it came.
With envious eyes, they do thy riches view;
When old ways fail, to spoil thee they find new:
No art's untri'd which may thy coffers drain,
For which the subtle lawyer racks his brain.   205
Thy too-old Charters they will new arraign.
Thou must not think thou canst in safety stand
Whilst the false Canaanite swarms in the land.
Some State-physicians cry that thou art sick,
And on thee they would try some quacking trick;   210
As yet their poisonous drugs thou dost not need,
Nor does thy body want to purge or bleed.
Thy head, we hope, with loyalty is crown'd,
Thy heart and entrails we do know are sound:
Thy hands are open, honest, free, and straight,   215
And all thy members pliable and neat.
All think you well in health, and sound within;
Though some few spots appear upon your skin,
They're but the purgings of the sounder part
And are at a great distance from the heart.   220
The wealthy love to thrive the surest way;
For gain perhaps they will like slaves obey,
Give up their Charters, bend their necks, now free,

200–01. In June 1681, following the feverish months of the Popish Plot, the London Common Council ordered that the monument commemorating the fire of London (1666) should be engraved with the declaration that the disaster "was begun and carried on by the treachery and malice of the Popish faction" (Bell, *The Great Fire*, pp. 208–09).

206. In Nov. 1681, Charles II began the Quo Warranto proceedings to recall the London Charter. The case was finally decided in the Court's favor in 1683 (Howell, *State Trials, 8*, 1039–1358).

208. Cf. *The Medal*, 178.

213. *The head:* Sir John Moore, the Lord Mayor, became increasingly attached to the Court during his stormy term in office. Cf. *The Medal*, 181.

215. *Thy hands:* The Whig Sheriffs, Thomas Pilkington and Samuel Shute. Cf. *The Medal*, 182. For further information on these London officials, see the headnote and poems on the shrieval elections.

To servile yokes, and stoop to that degree
As to submit to Rome's curs'd tyranny.   225
But sure the wise, and the religious too,
Will all the just and lawful ways pursue
To keep that freedom unto which they're born
And which so well doth Englishmen adorn;
Which our forefathers did preserve with care   230
And which we, next our souls, do hold most dear.
Let the hot Tories, and their poet, curse!
They spend in vain, and you are ne'er the worse.
Alas! they seem as only made to damn,
And then curse most when they have lost their sham;   235
They are true Shimeis, or the sons of Cham.
Their mouths are open sepulchers; their tongue,
With venom full, is ever speaking wrong.
With oaths and cursings, and with looking big,
They seek to fright some harmless, peaceful Whig;   240
Then boast the conquest, hector, rant, and tear,
And cry, "God-damn 'em! Protestants they are!
All the fanatics are a cursed crew,
Worse than the Papists, or the Moor, or Jew!
The City is a laystall full of mire,   245
And ought again to be new purg'd with fire!"
All honesty, all godliness they hate,
Love strife and war, contention and debate.
These are the men from whom much mischief springs,
Whilst their bad cause they falsely make the King's.   250
These wrong the King, and then to make amends,
With oaths declare they are his only friends;

236. *Shimeis:* The Benjamite Shimei cursed David as the royal party fled from Absalom (2 Samuel 16:5–13). Dryden, in *Absalom and Achitophel* (585–629), had represented the former Whig Sheriff, Slingsby Bethel, under this name. See also *Absalom Senior*, 696 n.

sons of Cham: i.e. descendants of Ham, the second son of Noah. Because of his irreverence to his father, Ham and his race were cursed (Genesis 9:22). Hamites (a term of obloquy) are connected primarily with Egypt, which in political verse usually referred to France.

241. *hector:* To brag, bluster, domineer.

242. Cf. *The Medal*, 110.

245–46. Cf. *The Medal*, 187–88.

laystall: A place where refuse and dung are laid.

But these are they who Coleman would outdo,
Blow up both kings and kingly power too.

For why is all this contest and this strife,   255
This struggling in the State, as 'twere for life,
When all men own'd their enjoy'd happiness,
And daily did their belov'd Monarch bless?
But these ill men all common roads forsake;
O'er hedges, and through standing corn they break;   260
Though ill success they have, they will not cease
Till they have spoil'd the nation's happy peace.
They see none to rebellion are inclin'd,
Yet plots they make, where plots they cannot find.
But their designs they did so idly frame,   265
The evil on their heads return'd with shame;
And though they find their evil projects curs'd,
They keep the impudence they had at first:
'Gainst honesty, law, reason, then they fight,
And falsely cry, *The King can have no right*.   270
The people of their judgment they bereave,
No proof, no circumstance will they believe,
Rebels and traitors they will still create,
And are men-catchers of the highest rate.
With regal rights, these men keep much ado;   275
But, with that stale, their own game they pursue.
Their Monarch's safety, honor, fame, renown,
The great supports and jewels of the crown;
The people's love, their freedom, liberties,
Those they neglect, and these they do despise.   280
What e'er these men pretend, the juggling feat
Is plainly seen: 'tis to grow rich and great,
To rule, to sway, to govern as they please:
The people's grievance, and the land's disease.

253. *Coleman:* The Roman Catholic secretary to the Duchess of York. The discovery of his treasonous correspondence with Père La Chaise led to his execution on 3 Dec. 1678.
264–66. Another allusion to the Meal Tub Plot; see 168 n.
270. *can have:* i.e. is able to obtain.
274. *men-catchers:* Entrappers of men. Edmund Hickeringill, the nonconformist divine and pamphleteer, was particularly fond of this term which he devised from Jeremiah 5:26 and used as the basis of his highly popular sermon (three editions in 1681 and a fourth in 1682), *The Horrid Sin of Man-catching* [H 1811–14].

All men that would oppose their pow'r and sway   285
And will not them, like galley-slaves, obey,
They brand with odious names—although they spring
From fathers ever loyal to their King;
Though they themselves sons of the Church are known,
Would with their blood defend their Monarch's throne,   290
And ready are their lives to sacrifice
For all their King's just rights, which much they prize.
But O the change that's now in England seen!
They who are loyal, and so e'er have been,
Because they will not serve sinister ends,   295
Are rebels call'd, at least call'd traitors' friends.
Thou wicked hag that now art arm'd with pow'r,
That wouldst men's souls and bodies both devour,
That now dost show thy bloody armed paws,
With malice arm'd, and with too rigid laws;   300
With what poetic curse shall I thee paint,
Who art a devil, yet appear'st a saint?
But vengeance for thee still in Heav'n there's store;
Though many bless and thee the Beast adore,
Thou'rt dy'd with blood and art the Scarlet Whore.   305
O Persecution! thou'rt a goddess blind,
That never sparest any human kind;
In every country thou dost footing gain,
In all religions thou desir'st to reign,
But never wast admitted in the True.   310
Hence grow our tears, that here thou shouldst renew
Thy strength and power in this happy realm,
Our quiet and our peace to overwhelm;
When for some years thou hast been banished,
And Protestants believ'd thou hadst been dead;   315
Or that at least, we never more should fear
That thou shouldst live to show thy power here,
Unless (which Heav'n avert) that thou shouldst come
By force, brought in by the curs'd power of Rome.
But griev'd we are to see it in our age,   320

287. *although they spring:* The pronoun refers to those who are unjustly vilified.
304. *the Beast:* Antichrist.
305. *Scarlet Whore:* The whore of Babylon, the Roman Catholic church.

And fear it may a greater ill presage.
Prisons and fines the punishments are now,
But who knows what at last it may come to?
For this damn'd hag longs still for human food,
Ne'er satisfi'd till she is gorg'd with blood.   325
Well may the Papists, when they have their turn,
Rack and imprison, torture, hang, and burn;
When Protestants to Protestants do show
That, had they pow'r, themselves as much would do.
But let the busy ministers take care,   330
They do but vengeance for themselves prepare;
For in all ages it was ever known,
That God His vengeance on their heads pour'd down.

   All but mere fools may easily foresee
What will the fatal end of these things be: 335
If one bigotted in the Romish way
Should once again the English scepter sway,
Then those who in the pulpit are so loud,
Preaching succession to the vulgar crowd,
Must change their croaking notes, their coats must turn;   340
Or, if prove honest, fly the land, or burn.
Whom benefit or ignorance engage
Now to the Party, then shall feel the rage
Of those fierce tyrants, who now undermine
And, hidden, carry on their curs'd design.   345
The proud usurping priest and Popish knaves
Shall be your lords, and all the English slaves;
The nobles then must wear the Romish yoke,
Or heads submit unto the fatal stroke.

322. *punishments:* i.e. for holding illegal conventicles.

330–31. *ministers:* The author seems to have in mind principally (but not exclusively) ministers of State, who (he implies, 375–78) will be brought to the strict justice öf a parliament.

336. *one:* i.e. the Duke of York.

339. The bishops had unanimously voted against the Exclusion Bill. The author's fairly accurate analysis of future events culminates in a surprisingly frank statement of the threat of civil war should York succeed to the throne (361–64). Cf. the prophecy in *The Medal,* 287–317.

342. *whom:* i.e. whomsoever.

348–49. Cf. *The Medal,* 298–99.

Oppression will grow bold, the tadpole priests   350
Shall lift above the lords their priestly crests.
T' attempt or struggle then will be in vain,
For Persecution will a tyrant reign;
Her fatal pow'r will then be understood,
And she will glut herself with martyr's blood.   355
The Pope's supremacy shall then be shown,
No other head in England will be known.
Then shall a general curse flow through the land,
Lord against lord, friend against friend shall stand;
Till at the last, the crowd, in their defence,   360
Provok'd to rage, arm 'gainst their Popish prince.
With words no longer, but with arms they'll jar,
And England will be spoil'd with civil war;
True peace and happiness so long shall want
Till she shall get a monarch Protestant.   365
Thus factious men to civil broils engage,
And with their ferment, make the crowd to rage.
Their madness they in others would increase,
Yet wipe their mouths and cry they are for peace;
For King, for regal rights, and true succession,   370
They in the people's ears still make profession;
Yet for one man, such friends they are, so civil,
They'd send almost three nations to the devil.
But there's no way these mischiefs to prevent,
Unless we have a healing parliament.   375

359. Cf. *The Medal*, 309.
361–62. Cf. *The Medal*, 306–07.
366. Cf. *The Medal*, 318, 290–92.

370. *true succession:* A highly important, though often unnoticed, distinction of the period is that between true succession (i.e., succession solely on the basis of the most immediate consanguinity) and legal succession (i.e. succession to the nearest in line who is not debarred by existing laws). The question at this time was whether York, the nearest in blood, could, as a professed member of the excluded Roman Catholic religion, become head of the State church, which supported the exclusion of Romanism. Cf. *The Medal*, 289 n. and the explanation of legal succession by Burnet (*History*, 2, 215) given there.

372. *one man:* i.e. York.

375. *a healing parliament:* The basic error in Whig strategy during the critical struggles of 1682 was their ever more desperate dependence on what they thought would be "the after-game in parliament" (North, *Examen*, p. 611). Not until far too late did they begin to discover that the real Popish Plot lay in the subsidies which Louis XIV paid to Charles and which were sufficient to make the calling of a parliament unneces-

Of that these faulty men love not to hear;
They've much transgress'd and much they have to fear.
Until that day, England will find no rest,
Though now she slumbers on her Monarch's breast;
But then the nation will be truly bless'd.   380

---

sary. (See Grose's excellent article, "Louis XIV's Financial Relations with Charles II
and the English Parliament," pp. 177–204.)

379. Cf. *The Medal*, 322.

Thomas Shadwell

The Medal of John Bayes

[*S 2860*]

While there is very strong evidence to suggest that this poem is by Thomas Shadwell, its authorship has never been absolutely settled. Contemporary ascription by Luttrell ("By Thomas Shadwell. Agt Mr. Dryden. very severe. 15 May [1682]") and a Trinity College Cambridge MS ("Shadwell is run mad.") militate strongly for Shadwell, but Macdonald's position (pp. 232–33) is only a more recent example of the hesitation that some scholars have felt. D. M. McKeithan's support of Shadwell ("The Authorship of *The Medal of John Bayes,*" *University of Texas Studies in English, 12* [1932], 92–97) on the basis of parallel passages seems definitely weakened by the number of such passages based on contemporary commonplaces; indeed, one could make at least an equal case for Settle's authorship on such internal evidence. The most conclusive evidence for Shadwell's authorship is that presented by James M. Osborn (*John Dryden: Some Biographical Facts and Problems* [New York, 1940], pp. 154–67); his careful analysis of the poem and its epistle presents as strong proof as one can expect from anonymous poems during this period.

The poem and its epistle reply to *The Medal* with a *saeva* and *sancta indignatio* which not only gives us more information (true or false) on Dryden than any other contemporary work but also expresses the high aims of Whig parliamentarianism and its response, however weak, to divine right and "true" succession.

The text is based on the 4⁰, printed for Richard Janeway. In addition to occasional words, certain lines and passages are italicized (22, 39, 78, 82, 87–92, 101–02, 124, 185–86, 193–95, 210, 215, 219–20, 229, 246–47, 260, 265, 322–23, 328–34, 338–40, 347, 356–59, 368–69). Save for an error in 278, Summers carefully reproduces the 4⁰ text in his edition of Shadwell's *Works*. The text given here is based on the 4⁰, though some cuts have been made in the long introductory epistle.

THE MEDAL OF JOHN BAYES

Epistle to the Tories

We here present you with a medal of an heroic author which most properly belongs to you, he being at this time hired to lie and libel in your service and in his last essay has performed it so dully that if you put him away (as it is said of the *Gentleman Usher* ᵃ and the Doctor in *The Rehearsal*) nobody else will take him—no, nobody else will take him. We cannot say his portraiture is done at the full length or has all its ornaments since there are many touches to be added to it which we will reserve for the occasions he shall give us hereafter. But we dare say these rough strokes have made the lineaments and proportions so true that anyone that knows him will find there is a great resemblance of him and will believe that he has sat above five times for it.ᵇ Though indeed he is so liberal of showing himself that in an hour's space he will expose all his parts, and a good drawer in that time may observe enough to make a nudity ᶜ of him.

You may know he is no concealer of himself by a story which he tells of himself, viz. That (when he first came to town) being a young, raw fellow of seven and twenty, as he called himself when he told the story, he, frequenting but one coffee-house, the woman (it seems finding him out) put coffee upon him for chocolate and made him pay three pence a dish for two years together; till at length, by what providence I know not, he discovered the cheat. This stupidity were incredible if he had not told it of himself publicly; but there is somewhat to be said for it, for (as he said of himself at the same time) the opening in his head (which in children usually closes about the age of three) did not close in him till he was seven and twenty—which may be the reason he has had such a devilish soft place there ever since. . . .

As for ready wit, he carries very little or none about him; but, if you draw a bill upon him, like a banker, he can answer you at home; ᵈ and, as bankers do, with the cash that is other men's.

a. *The Gentleman Usher,* a comedy by George Chapman (1606); *The Rehearsal,* II.4, Buckingham's comedy (1672) that ridiculed Dryden.

b. See *The Medal,* "Epistle to the Whigs," n. g.

c. The 4° note explains: "So the painters call a naked picture."

d. *at home:* In addition to the literal there may also be the idiomatic meaning of "directly, effectively, thoroughly."

Whoever has been conversant with Spanish, Italian, French, and classic authors will find all that's tolerably good in him in some of those. He can, indeed, new-trim and disguise a little the clothes he steals.

He has an easiness in rhyme, and a knack at versifying, and can make a slight thing seem pretty and clinquant; [e] and his *forte* is that he is an indifferent good versificator.

If at any time he has wit of his own, 'tis in railing, when the venom of his malice provokes his fancy. His panegyrics are full of such nauseous flattery that they are libels; and he is now become so infamous that his libels will be thought panegyrics.

His prostituted Muse will become as common for hire as his mistress Revesia [f] was, upon whom he spent so many hundred pounds; and of whom (to show his constancy in love) he got three claps, and she was a bawd. Let all his own romantic plays show so true and so heroic a lover.

You who would know him better, go to the coffee-house [g] (where he may be said almost to inhabit) and you shall find him holding forth to half a score [of] young fellows (who clap him on the back, spit in his mouth, and loo [h] him on upon the Whigs, as they call 'em) puffed up and swelling with their praise. And the great subject of his discourse shall be of himself and his poetry, what diet he uses for epic, what for comic, what course he is in for libel, and what for tragedy.

He has never been conversant in any science but poetry. Philosophy of all sorts he has an aversion to, having no rational or argumentative head; but if he be anything, he is a mere poet, and from such an animal, *libera nos* [i] etc. from a man of one business as the Italian proverb says.

'Tis not two years since he consulted with an eminent and learned physician of this town, telling him he was obliged to write a play and, finding himself very dull, desired he would prescribe him a diet and course of physic fit for his malady. The doctor merrily asked

e. *clinquant:* Glittering with gold or silver, and hence with metallic imitations of these; tinseled.

f. Anne Reeves. See 44 n., below.

g. Very likely, Will's. See Osborn, *Dryden: Facts and Problems*, p. 160.

h. *loo:* Incite by shouting "halloo"; urge on by shouts.

i. The concluding words to the supplications in the litany. Libera nos Domine, are found frequently in political verse.

him whether 'twas comedy or tragedy he designed? He answered, tragedy. The doctor replied, the steel diet was most proper for tragedy. Whereupon the poet desired to have it prescribed, and did undergo it for six weeks.[j]

Before the writing of *The Medal,* he might e'en as properly have been prescribed a diet of brass;[k] for (to use his own expression) never was there practiced such a notorious piece of impudence in the face of an established government as the villainous libeling [of] so great a peer[1] so instrumental in the restoring of the King, who has so deservedly borne and so faithfully discharged such great offices in the State, and who is still (in spite of Popish clamors and false witnesses) ready upon all occasions to serve his Majesty and the kingdom with the highest loyalty and integrity. . . .

There is not so vile an employment as that of a hired libeler, an executioner of men's reputations. The hangman is an office of greater dignity. Were all which your poet says of this great peer true, yet the libeler ought to be whipped out of a country for his insolence. But what does he deserve, when he himself knows every word of it to be false! and scarce a Papist in England believes anything of it to be true.

He is as unlucky in his allusion to the Turks' wearing of Scander-beg's bones[m] as he is afterwards in his bungling simile about the feigned Association. They were the Turks, Scanderbeg's enemies, that wore his bones; and therefore he thinks this Lord's friends must do the same. . . .

'Tis you [Tories] that are apparently the faction, since ye are the few that have divided from the many. 'Tis you who in your factious clubs vilify the government by audaciously railing against parliaments, so great and so essential a part of it. They ought to lose the use of speech who dare say anything irreverently of the King or disrespectfully of parliaments. If anything could make the King lose the love and confidence of his people, it would be your unpunished boldness, who presume to call the freeholders of England the rabble and their representatives a crowd, and strike at the

j. For parallels in *The Rehearsal* and elsewhere, see Osborn, *Dryden: Facts and Problems,* p. 161.

k. *brass:* Effrontery, impudence, unblushingness.

l. Shaftesbury. See *The Medal,* 51–52 n.

m. See *The Medal,* "Epistle to the Whigs," n. k.; also Shadwell, *Works, 5,* 438.

very root of all their liberty. Ye are those who abuse our gracious Prince and endeavor to delude him with false numbers, and promising to serve him when ye have no interest, as in all the frequent parliaments (his Majesty has been pleased to promise us) will plainly appear.

If anything could dishonor him, it would be the bloody violence of your spirits, your unpunished exorbitancies and breach of laws; your huzzaing, roaring, quarreling, and damning by much the greater part of the nation and their whole representative body. Who made ye judges [n] in Israel? But whatever ye might have been in Judea, ye will find very few of ye will be made, in England, trustees for the liberty of the people, as your poet says, who (as if he had been hired for the whole Popish Plot) vilely casts dirt upon the best reformed Protestants in his next page. . . .

[There follows a series of objections to Dryden's allusions to Theodore Beza and George Buchanan.]

For the Association,[o] which he next mentions, dropped out of the clouds, entered into and subscribed by nobody, and seen by no one of our party that ever we could hear of (and, we believe, by none of yours but those contrived the putting it into the Earl's closet), it renders you more ridiculous and extravagant than ever ye were to set up an Abhorrence [p] through all England of a paper which you can lay to the charge of no party not at one single man's door; but we doubt not but if you had found or put the libel your poet was cudgell'd for (though few of your loyal closets, perhaps, are without that and other libels upon the King) into the Earl's closet, ye would have set up an Abhorrence of that rather than not have kept up the fermentation and division amongst the people. When this is run out of breath, we suppose ye will set up the ticket for the forbidden dinner,[q] and ye will abhor factious, schismatical, seditious, fanatical, and rebellious dining, or some new red herring out of his Lordship's kitchen will come forth.

The insolence in the same page of your libeler in comparing the Jury that gave in *Ignoramus* to the bill against our noble peer, to a

n. See *The Medal*, "Epistle to the Whigs," n. n.; and Acts 7:27, 35.

o. See *The Medal*, "Epistle to the Whigs." n. l.

p. The addresses to the King expressing abhorrence of the ideas set forth in the Association. See 344 n., below.

q. The Whig Feast of 21 April 1682, prohibited by the King as an encroachment on royal prerogative.

jury taken out of Newgate, deserves the pillory, since 'tis evident
to the whole City [that] they were all men of singular honesty and
integrity in all their dealings, of signal good lives, of good under-
standing, and of great wealth.[r] And in the memory of man, the City
has not seen a jury better qualified; nor was there one Dissenter
amongst them, to prevent your weak cavils. Cavils, I say; for it had
been no objection if they had been all so, since they value their oaths
and consciences as much as any sort of men, and have no dispensa-
tions to go against them.

And this clamor against the jury is because they would not be-
lieve an incredible matter from incredible witnesses who either were
then, or had been lately, most of them Papists; who were so incon-
sistent in their testimony with one another and themselves that I am
confident not one of the reverend bench believed them. If they did,
they must be very shallow and must take this Lord to be little better
than an idiot. If ye look upon the oath of a grand jury man, ye will
find that the meaning of those two words *Billa Vera* is [that] they do
believe the matter of the bill in their consciences to be true; which if
they did not, they must have been perjured if they found the bill.
The law provides that in capital cases a man shall not be wrongfully
accused, and therefore appoints two juries, both [of] which are
bound to find according to their belief; and the injustice is as great,
though the injury be less, for the former to accuse by indictment, if
they believe the party innocent, as for the latter to hang him with
the same belief. . . .

[After attacking pro-Tory court decisions, the Meal Tub Plot, and
those who disbelieve the officially accepted Popish Plot, the Epistle
concludes:]

Now, Tories, fare ye well. Apply your heads to thinking a little,
and do not, like young whelps, run away with a false scent and cry
out *Forty-One* [s] and *Ignoramus;* and in time ye may be wiser. And
let your poet know that the first occasion he gives, he shall hear from
us further.

r. The "Ignoramus" jury was composed largely of Whig magnates.
s. See 383 n., below.

The Medal of John Bayes

A SATIRE AGAINST FOLLY AND KNAVERY

—Facit indignatio versus.

How long shall I endure, without reply,
To hear this Bayes, this hackney-railer, lie?
The fool, uncudgell'd, for one libel swells,
Where not his wit, but sauciness excels;
Whilst with foul words and names which he lets fly,   5
He quite defiles the satire's dignity.
For libel and true satire different be;
This must have truth, and salt, with modesty.
Sparing the persons, this does tax the crimes,
Galls not great men, but vices of the times,   10
With witty and sharp, not blunt and bitter, rhymes.
Methinks the ghost of Horace there I see,
Lashing this cherry-cheek'd dunce of fifty-three;
Who, at that age, so boldly durst profane,
With base hir'd libel, the free satire's vein.   15
Thou styl'st it satire to call names: Rogue, Whore,
Traitor, and Rebel, and a thousand more.
An oyster-wench is sure thy Muse of late,
And all thy Helicon's at Billingsgate.
A libeler's vile name then may'st thou gain,   20
And moderately the writing part maintain;
None can so well the beating part sustain.
Though with thy sword, thou art the last of men,
Thou art a damn'd Boroski with thy pen.

Title: The dropped title gives "or, A satire upon Folly and Knavery." The epigraph comes from Juvenal, I.79.

1. Juvenal I.1: Semper ego auditor tantum? Numquamne reponam.

2. *Bayes:* 1682 note: "His name in the *Rehearsal.*" See also Summer's note in Shadwell, *Works, 5,* 441.

3. *uncudgell'd:* A reference to the famous Rose Alley ambuscade of 18 Dec. 1679. See 95–96 n.

13. Dryden, who was born about 9 Aug. 1631, would have been close to 51 at this time.

19. *Billingsgate:* One of the London gates near which was the fish market famous for its foul vituperative language.

24. *Boroski:* George Borosky, the "Polander" who murdered Tom Thynne by discharging a blunderbuss into Thynne's coach. See p. 16.

As far from satire does thy talent lie   25
As from being cheerful, or good company.
For thou art saturnine, thou dost confess;
A civil word thy dullness to express.
An old gelt mastiff has more mirth than thou,
When thou a kind of paltry mirth would'st show.   30
Good humor thou so awkwardly put'st on,
It sits like modish clothes upon a clown;
While that of gentlemen is brisk and high,   ·
When wine and wit about the room does fly.
Thou never mak'st, but art, a standing jest;   35
Thy mirth by foolish bawdry is express'd,
And so debauch'd, so fulsome, and so odd,
As ——————————
"Let's bugger one another now, by God!"
(When ask'd how they should spend the afternoon)   40
This was the smart reply of the heroic clown.
He boasts of vice (which he did ne'er commit),
Calls himself Whoremaster and Sodomite;
Commends Reeves' arse and says she buggers well,
And silly lies of vicious pranks does tell.   45
This is a sample of his mirth and wit,
Which he for the best company thinks fit.
In a rich soil, the sprightly horse y'have seen,
Run, leap, and wanton o'er the flow'ry green,
Prance and curvet, with pleasure to the sight;   50
But it could never any eyes delight

27. *saturnine:* Summers (Shadwell, *Works*, 5, 441): "In his *Defense of an Essay of Dra-matic Poesy*, prefixed to the second edition of *The Indian Emperor* 4 to, 1668 [D 2289; Macdonald 69 b] . . . Dryden speaking of himself says: 'My conversation is slow and dull, my humor saturnine and reserv'd'."

41. *the smart reply:* 1682 note: "At Windsor, in the company of several persons of quality, Sir G[eorge] E[therege] being present." Lines 35–41, along with 52, might echo Rochester's *An Allusion to Horace:*

> But when he would be sharp, he still was blunt:
> To frisk his frolic fancy, he'd cry "C———!"
>
> (73–74)

44. *Reeves':* Anne Reeves, a minor actress with the King's Company (1670–72), was said to have been Dryden's mistress. See Summers' long note in Shadwell, *Works*, 5, 436–38; also his edition of *The Rehearsal* [Stratford, 1914], pp. 81–83; and Macdonald, *Dryden Bibliography*, esp. pp. 96 and 314.

To see the frisking frolics of a cow;
And such another merry thing art thou.
In verse, thou hast a knack with words to chime,
And had'st a kind of excellence in rhyme: 55
With rhymes like leading-strings, thou walk'dst; but those
Laid by, at every step thou brok'st thy nose.
How low thy farce! and thy blank verse how mean!
How poor, how naked did appear each scene!
Even thou didst blush at thy insipid stuff,   60
And laid thy dullness on poor harmless snuff.
No comic scene or humor hast thou wrought;
Thou'st quibbling bawdy and ill breeding taught;
But rhyme's sad downfall has thy ruin brought.
No piece did ever from thy self begin;   65
Thou can'st no web from thine own bowels spin.
Were from thy works cull'd out what thou'st purloin'd,
Even Durfey would excel what's left behind.
Should all thy borrow'd plumes we from thee tear,
How truly Poet Squab would'st thou appear!   70
Thou call'st thy self, and fools call thee, in rhyme,
The goodly Prince of Poets of thy time;
And sov'reign power thou dost usurp, John Bayes,
And from all poets thou a tax dost raise.
Thou plunder'st all t'advance thy mighty name,   75
Look'st big, and triumph'st with thy borrow'd fame.
But art (while swelling thus thou think'st th' art chief)
A servile imitator and a thief.
All written wit thou seizest on as prize;
But that will not thy ravenous mind suffice;   80

54–55. Cf. Dryden's lines on Doeg (Settle) in *The Second Part of Absalom and Achitophel*, 412–13.

56. *leading-strings*: Formerly used to guide and support children when they were learning to walk.

57. Cf. *Rehearsal*, II.5.

70. *Poet Squab*: In *An Allusion to Horace*, Rochester wrote:

> Dryden in vain tri'd this nice way of wit,
> For he to be a tearing blade thought fit. . . .
> Would give the ladies a dry, bawdy bob,
> And thus he got the name of Poet Squab.
>
> (71–72, 75–76)

72. *Prince of Poets*: The same gibe appears in *The Medal Revers'd*, 23.

Though men from thee their inward thoughts conceal,
Yet thou the words out of their mouths wilt steal.
How little owe we to your native store,
Who all you write have heard or read before?
—Except your libels; and there's something new,   85
For none were e'er so impudent as you.
Some scoundrel poetasters yet there be,
Fools that burlesque the name of Loyalty,
Who, by reviling patriots, think to be
From lousiness and hunger ever free,   90
But will (for all their hopes of swelling bags)
Return to primitive nastiness and rags.
These are blind fools: thou hadst some kind of sight;
Thou sinn'st against thy conscience and the light.
After the drubs, thou didst of late compound,   95
And sold for th' weight in gold each bruise and wound;
Clear was thy sight, and none declaim'd then more
'Gainst Popish Plots and Arbitrary Pow'r.
The ministers thou bluntly wouldst assail,
And it was dangerous to hear thee rail.   100
(Oh may not England stupid be like thee!
Heaven grant it may not feel before it see.)
Now he recants, and on that beating thrives:
Thus poet laureates, and Russian wives,
Do strangely upon beating mend their lives.   105
But how comes Bayes to flag and grovel so?
Sure, your new lords are in their payments slow.
Thou deserv'st whipping thou'rt so dull this time;
Thou'st turn'd the *Observator* into rhyme.

95–96. On the evening of 18 Dec. 1679, Dryden was assaulted by three men in Rose Alley, near Covent Garden, presumably for his part in Mulgrave's *Essay Upon Satire*. Despite recent suggestions that the Duchess of Portsmouth instigated the assault, it is more likely that its author was Rochester. See Summers' note, and Lord's summary of the arguments in *POAS*, Yale, *I*, 396–401. The suggestion that Dryden made capital of this is found in Settle's *Prologue to The Heir of Morocco:*

No fear of cudgels where there's hope of bread;
A well-fill'd paunch forgets a broken head.
(11–12)

109. Dryden's political poems followed the political line and witty tone of the most effective Tory periodical, Sir Roger L'Estrange's *Observator*.

But thou suppliest the want of wit and sense   110
With most malicious lies, and impudence.
At Cambridge first your scurrilous vein began,
When saucily you traduc'd a nobleman,
Who for that crime rebuk'd you on the head,
And you had been expell'd had you not fled.   115
The next step of advancement you began
Was being clerk to Noll's Lord Chamberlain,
A sequestrator and committee-man.
There all your wholesome morals you suck'd in
And got your genteel gaiety and mien.   120
Your loyalty you learn'd in Cromwell's court,
Where first your Muse did make her great effort.
On him you first show'd your poetic strain,
And prais'd his opening the basilic vein.
And were that possible to come again,   125
Thou on that side wouldst draw thy slavish pen.
But he being dead who should the slave prefer,
He turn'd a journey-man t'a bookseller,

112–15. This incident is otherwise unknown. Dryden was admitted to Trinity College
on 11 May 1650 and received his Bachelor's degree in Jan. 1654. Aside from being
discommuned in July 1652 for contumacy to the vice-master (Scott-Saintsbury, *Dryden,*
1, 24–25), there is no official record of any difficulty.

113. *nobleman:* 1682 note: "A lord's son, and all noblemen's sons, are called noble-
men there."

117. *Noll's Lord Chamberlain:* Sir Gilbert Pickering (1613–68), an ardent parlia-
mentarian, member of Cromwell's five Councils of State, Lord Chamberlain to the
Protector and, in 1659, one of the Committee of Safety. His exemption from the Act of
Indemnity was reversed only through the influence of the Earl of Sandwich. Dryden
was cousin-german through both his mother and father (Scott-Saintsbury, *Dryden, 1,*
29 n.).

118. Scott-Saintsbury is undoubtedly correct in suggesting (*Dryden, 1,* 31) that this
line refers to Pickering, not to Dryden. Pickering, early in the war, was on the
parliamentary committee raising troops and money in his county; he served also on the
Northamptonshire Committee of Sequestration (32 n., and the lines from *The Protes-*
tant Poets; also *Protestant Satire* [G'], 115–16, 127 and Summers' note).

123–24. Dryden's elegiac *Heroic Stanzas* on Cromwell (1659) referred to the regicide
in terms his opponents never tired of quoting:

He fought to end our fighting, and essay'd
To staunch the blood by breathing of the vein.

(47–48)

basilic: Kingly, royal, sovereign; the *basilic vein* is the large vein starting at the elbow.

128. *journey-man to a bookseller:* 1682 note: "Mr. Herringman, who kept him in his
house for that purpose." Henry Herringman entered in the Stationer's Register, but

Writ prefaces to books for meat and drink,
And as he paid, he would both write and think.   130
Then by th' assistance of a noble knight,
Th' hadst plenty, ease, and liberty to write.
First like a gentleman he made thee live,
And on his bounty thou didst amply thrive;
But soon thy native swelling venom rose,   135
And thou didst him, who gave thee bread, expose.
'Gainst him a scandalous Preface didst thou write,
Which thou didst soon expunge rather than fight.
When turn'd away by him in some small time,
You in the people's ears began to chime,   140
And please the town with your successful rhyme.

When the best patroness of wit and stage,
The joy, the pride, the wonder of the age,
Sweet Annabel the good, great, witty, fair
(Of all this Northern Court, the brightest star)   145
Did on thee, Bayes, her sacred beams dispense,
Who could do ill under such influence?
She the whole Court brought over to thy side,
And favor flow'd upon thee like a tide.
To her thou soon prov'dst an ungrateful knave;   150

did not publish, Dryden's *Heroic Stanzas*. He was, however, Dryden's publisher from
1660–78. See Macdonald, *Dryden Bibliography*, pp. 3–4 and notes thereto; Scott-Saints-
bury, *Dryden, 1,* 44 n. (Shadwell's comment only) and 45.

131. *a noble knight:* Sir Robert Howard, younger son of the royalist Earl of Berk-
shire, Dryden's patron at this time, and (as of 1 Dec. 1663) his brother-in-law.

137–38. In his *Defense . . . of Dramatic Poesy* (see 27 n.) in answer to Howard's
Preface to his tragedy *The Great Favorite* (1668) [H 2996], Dryden stood by his literary
views strongly. While "scandalous" may be a bit strong, the literary dispute was
undoubtedly becoming more personal. The *Defense* was prefixed only to the second
edition of *The Indian Emperor.*

142. *patroness:* Anne, Duchess of Monmouth; the name of Annabel (144) was given
her in *Absalom and Achitophel,* 34. *The Indian Emperor,* acted in the spring of 1665,
was dedicated to her (Macdonald, *Dryden Bibliography,* p. 92). She and Monmouth
had taken parts in a Court performance of the play (Pepys, 14 Jan. 1668).

150. *an ungrateful knave:* 1682 note: "When he had thrice broken his word, oath,
and bargain with Sir William Davenant, he wrote a letter to this great lady to pass
her word for him to Sir William, who would not take his own; which she did. In his
letter, he wish'd God might never prosper him, his wife or children, if he did not
keep his oath and bargain, which yet in two months he broke, as several of the Duke's
playhouse can testify."

So good was she, not only she forgave,
But did oblige anew, the faithless slave.
And all the gratitude he can afford
Is basely to traduce her princely lord:
A hero worthy of a God-like race,   155
Great in his mind and charming in his face,
Who conquers hearts and unaffected grace.
His mighty virtues are too large for verse,
Gentle as billing doves, as angry lions fierce:
His strength and beauty so united are,   160
Nature design'd him chief, in love and war.
All lovers' victories he did excel,
Succeeding with the beauteous Annabel.
Early in arms his glorious course began,
Which never hero yet so swiftly ran.   165
Wherever danger show'd its dreadful face,
By never-dying acts h'adorn'd his royal race.
Sure the three Edwards' souls beheld with joy
How much thou outdidst man when little more than boy.
And all the princely heroes of thy line   170
Rejoic'd to see so much of their great blood in thine.
So good and so diffusive is his mind,
So loving too, and lov'd by human kind,
He was for vast and general good design'd.
In's height of greatness, he all eyes did glad,   175
And never man departed from him sad.
Sweet and obliging, easy of access,
Wise in his judging, courteous in address.
O'er all the passions he bears so much sway,
No Stoic taught 'em better to obey.   180
And, in his suffering part, he shines more bright

154. *princely lord:* James, Duke of Monmouth; Dryden's Absalom. Throughout the following lines, the author attempts to show that Monmouth's godlike, heroic actions prove him to be the legitimate and logical successor to Charles II.

169. In 1665, Monmouth, then 16 years old, fought at the battle of Lowestoft; in 1672–73, he gained wide acclaim for his courageous action against the Dutch, particularly at the siege of Maestricht.

181. *suffering part:* In 1679, Monmouth was stripped of his offices; his closer ties with the Country party in the following years put him at complete odds with the Court, and shortly after the publication of this poem he was not permitted to associate with the King's servants.

Than he appear'd in all that gaudy light;
Now, now, methinks he makes the bravest show,
And ne'er was greater hero than he's now.
For public good, who wealth and power forsakes,   185
Over himself a glorious conquest makes.
Religion, prince, and laws to him are dear;
And in defense of all, he dares appear.
'Tis he must stand like Scaeva in the breach,
'Gainst what ill ministers do, and furious parsons preach.   190
Were't not for him, how soon some Popish knife
Might rob us of his royal father's life!
We to their fear of thee that blessing owe:
In such a son, happy, great King, art thou,
Who can defend, or can revenge thee so.   195

    Next, for thy *Medal*, Bayes, which does revile
The wisest patriot of our drooping isle,
Who loyally did serve his exil'd Prince,
And with the ablest counsel bless'd him since.
None more than he did stop tyrannic power,   200
Or, in that crisis, did contribute more
To his just rights our Monarch to restore;
And still by wise advice and loyal arts
Would have secur'd him in his subjects' hearts.
You own the mischiefs, sprung from that intrigue,   205
Which fatally dissolv'd the Triple League.

189. *Scaeva:* Either Quintus Mucius Scaevola (usually called Pontifex Maximus), the distinguished Roman public servant and legist, or else Gaius Mucius Scaevola, the legendary hero who, when threatened with torture for attempting to assassinate the leader of the forces besieging Rome, thrust his right hand into the altar fire until it was consumed.

190. *ill ministers:* At this time, Halifax and his adherents.

191. *popish knife:* According to Oates, Father Conyers (among others) planned to kill Charles and had a knife "a foot long in the blade and half a foot in the haft" which he had shown Oates (Lane, *Oates,* p. 100).

197. *patriot:* The Earl of Shaftesbury.

198. Shaftesbury's parliamentarianism led him into increasing opposition to the Commonwealth government; by 1659, he was strongly suspected of sympathy with royalist Presbyterians, and in the following year, he "steadily pursued the design of restoring Charles" (*DNB*). A good analysis of his position is given in Brown, *Shaftesbury.*

199. See *The Medal,* 54–57 n.

206. See *The Medal,* 65 n.

Each of your idol mock-triumv'rate knows
Our patriot strongly did that breach oppose;
Nor did this lord a Dover-journey go,
"From thence our tears, the Ilium of our woe."   210
Had he that interest follow'd, how could he
By those that serv'd it then discarded be?
The French and Papists well his merits know;
Were he a friend, they'd not pursu'd him so.
From both he would our beset King preserve,   215
For which he does eternal wreaths deserve.
His life they first, and now his fame, would take,
For crimes they forge, and secret plots they make.
They by hir'd witnesses the first pursue,
The latter by vile scribblers hir'd like you.   220
Thy infamy will blush at no disgrace,
(With such a harden'd conscience, and a face)
Thou only want'st an evidence's place.
When th' isle was drown'd in a lethargic sleep,
Our vigilant hero still a watch did keep.   225
When all our strength should have been made a prey
To the lewd Babylonish Dalilah,
Methinks I see our watchful hero stand,
Jogging the nodding genius of our land;
Which sometime struggling with sleep's heavy yoke,   230
Awak'd, star'd, and look'd grim, and dreadfully he spoke.
The voice fill'd all the land, and then did fright
The Scarlet Whore from all her works of night.

---

207. *mock triumv'rate:* Probably three of the Cabal; perhaps Clifford, Arlington, and Lauderdale, since Buckingham at this time was in opposition.

209. *Dover-journey:* The French Alliance, which replaced the Triple Alliance, served as a mask for Charles' secret Treaty of Dover. By the 1680s the Treaty was an open secret but one which could only be referred to obliquely.

210. Cf. *The Medal,* 67.

212. Shaftesbury had been dismissed from office in Nov. 1673.

214. There was talk of danger to Shaftesbury's life during the Meal Tub Plot (Brown, *Shaftesbury,* p. 265).

217. A similar idea is found in Settle's *Absalom Senior,* 414–17.

219. See *The Medal,* 149 n.

227. *Babylonish Dalilah:* The French Catholic Louise de Kéroualle, Duchess of Portsmouth.

233. *Scarlet Whore:* The whore of Babylon; the Roman Catholic church.

But ——————
With unseen strengths at home and foreign aid,   235
Too soon she ralli'd and began t'invade,
And many nets she spread, and many toils she laid.
To lull us yet asleep, what pains she takes!
But all in vain, for still our genius wakes,
And now remembers well the dangerous Test   240
Which might have all our liberty oppress'd,
Had not the cover'd snare our hero found
And for some time bravely maintain'd the ground
Till others saw the bondage was design'd
And late with them their straggling forces join'd.   245
A bill then drawn by Buckingham did we see,
A zealous bill against York for Popery.
Then murder'd Godfrey, a lov'd prince's blood,
Ready with precious drops to make a purple flood.
When Popish tyranny shall give command   250
And spread again its darkness o'er the land,
Then bloody plots we find laid at their door,

240. *the dangerous Test:* In April 1675, Shaftesbury strongly attacked Danby's Test
Bill, pointing out the futility of an oath that demanded nonresistance to the king
and support of established government of church and state. (Brown, *Shaftesbury*,
p. 229.) He recognized, as did many at the time, that such laws were more likely to be
applied against the nonconforming sects than against the Roman Catholics.

244. *others:* The reference may be to Buckingham, Halifax, or any of the others
who opposed Danby's bill.

245. *them:* Shaftesbury's faction.

246. "Buckingham" is Summers' suggestion for the 4° "B——————." Though
not unlikely, this makes the 4°'s dating of *A bill* as "Anno 76" rather difficult. Parlia-
ment was prorogued from 22 Nov. 1675–15 Feb. 1676/77, and Buckingham (with
Shaftesbury, Wharton, and Salisbury) was in the Tower on the following day for
questioning the legality of the prorogation. The author may have been thinking of the
second (Oct.–Nov.) session of 1675 and simply erred on the dating. Buckingham was quite
active in that session and may well have sponsored one of the anti-Popish bills, such
as that which would have disabled Popish recusants from sitting in either House of
Parliament (*LJ, 13,* 24). Granting this, Summers' suggestion that the blank in 247 "may
be filled by York" would be quite judicious.

248. After *then,* sc. *did we see* [?]. This and the following lines are syntactically
confused.

The death of Sir Edmund Berry Godfrey, the Westminster Justice of the Peace who
took Oates' first depositions in 1678, gave notoriety and credibility to the Popish Plot.
The cause of his death and the persons involved are still matters of speculation.

252. *their:* the Whigs'. The reference is to the attempt of the Meal Tub Plot to show
that the Popish Plot was devised by the Whigs in order to seize power.

Than whom none e'er has done or suffer'd more,
Or would, to save the Prince they did restore.
Amidst these hellish snares, 'tis time to wake; 255
May never more a sleep our genius take.
These things did soon our glorious city warm,
And for their own and Prince's safety arm.

Thou joy of ours, terror of other lands,
With moderate head, with unpolluted hands, 260
To which the Prince and people safety owe,
From which the uncorrupted streams of justice flow,
Through thickest clouds of perjury you see,
And, ne'er by hackney oaths deceiv'd, will be
Resolv'd to value credibility. 265
Thou vindicat'st the justice of thy Prince,
Which shines most bright by clearing innocence.
While some would subjects of their lives bereave,
By witnesses themselves could ne'er believe,
Though wrongly accus'd, yet at their blood they aim, 270
And, as they were their quarry, think it shame
Not to run down and seize the trembling game.
Thy justice will hereafter be renown'd,
Thy lasting name for loyalty be crown'd,
When 'twill be told who did our Prince restore, 275
Whom thou with zeal didst ever since adore.
How oft hast thou his princely wants suppli'd?
And never was thy needful aid deni'd.
How long his kindness with thy duty strove!
Great thy obedience, and as great his love; 280
And curs'd be they who would his heart remove.
Thou (still the same) with equal zeal will serve;
Maintain his laws, his person wilt preserve.
But some foul monsters thy rich womb does bear,
That, like base vipers, would thy bowels tear; 285
Who would thy ancient charters give away,

259. The apostrophe conflates London, its grand jury, and "its" parliament.
265. The line is cast in the form of a parliamentary resolution.
269. *themselves:* The antecedent is *some* (268).
284. *foul monsters:* the Court party. Cf. *Paradise Lost,* II.795–800.
286. A reference to the Court's Quo Warranto proceedings against the London charter begun in Nov. 1681. The personal crimes (290) of London officers and the City's

And all thy stronger liberties betray:
Those elder customs our great ancestors
Have from the Saxon times convey'd to ours,
Of which no pers'nal crimes a loss can cause,   290
By Magna Charta back'd, and by succeeding laws.
This is the factious brood we should pursue:
For as in schism, so in sedition too,
The many are deserted by the few.
These factious few, for bitter scourges fit,   295
(To show Addressing and Abhorring wit)
Set up a Jack of Lent and throw at it.
But those, alas, false silly measures take,
Who of the few an Association make.
Thou need'st not doubt to triumph o'er these fools,   300
These blindly led, these Jesuited tools,
Whilst bravely thou continu'st to oppose
All would-be Papists, as all Romish foes.
In spite of lawless men and Popish flames,
(Enrich'd by thy much lov'd and bounteous Thames)   305
May into the wealth of nations flow,
And to thy height all Europe's cities bow.
Thou great support of princely dignity!
And bulwark to the people's liberty!
If a good mayor with such good shrives appear,   310
Nor Prince nor people need a danger fear:

---

appeal to law and custom from ancient times can be found in Howell, *State Trials, 8,* esp. 1039–1147.

296. Against the Country party's petitions for a parliament, the Court sympathizers sent in addresses against the petitions and abhorrences of the paper of association found in Shaftesbury's study.

297. *Jack of Lent:* A figure of a man set up to be pelted; a butt for everyone to throw at.

299. 4° note: "Their addressing is plainly making an Association."

304. *Popish flames:* At this time, the fire of London (1666) was considered to have been started by Roman Catholics. The 4° note reads, "See the Chancellor's excellent speech before the sentence on Lord Stafford." Heneage Finch, who was constituted Lord High Steward for Stafford's treason trial in Dec. 1680, remarked in closing, "Does any man now begin to doubt how London was burnt?" At the request of both Houses, the speech was printed [N 1409]; see also Howell, *State Trials, 7,* 1556.

310. A reference to the Whig municipal officers of the previous year (1681), Lord Mayor Ward and Sheriffs Bethel and Cornish, and to the incumbent Whig sheriffs, Pilkington and Shute.

And such we hope for each succeeding year.
Thus thou a glorious city may'st remain,
And all thy ancient liberties retain,
While Albion is surrounded with the main.   315
Go, abject Bayes! and act thy slavish part;
Fawn on those Popish knaves, whose knave thou art:
'Tis not ill writing or worse policy
That can enslave a nation so long free.
Our King's too good to take that rugged course;   320
He'll win by kindness, not subdue by force.
If king of slaves and beasts, not men, he'd be,
A lion were a greater prince than he.
Approach him then let no malicious chit,
No insolent prater, nor a flashy wit;   325
Impeachments make not men for statesmen fit.
But ——————————
Truth, judgment, firmness, and integrity,
With long experience, quick sagacity,
Swift to prevent, as ready to foresee;   330
Knowing the depths from which all action springs,
And by a chain of causes judging things:
That does all weights into the balance cast,
And wisely can foretell the future by the past.
Where'er such virtuous qualities appear,   335
They're patriots worthy of a prince's ear;
To him and subjects they'll alike be dear.
The King's and people's interest they'll make one.
What personal greatness can our Monarch own,
When hearts of subjects must support the throne!   340
And ministers should strive those hearts t' unite,
Unless they had a mind to make us fight.
Who by Addresses thus the realm divide
(All bonds of kindred and of friends unti'd)

324–25. An awkward inversion. Read: "Let no . . . flashy wit approach him then."
326. *impeachments:* accusations, charges; i.e. the accuser does not become a states-
man by slandering others.

344. *Addresses:* A reference both to the pro-Court Addresses of Abhorrence (that
were meant to counterbalance the Whig Petitions for a parliament in 1679–80) and to
those which voiced an abhorrence of the Paper of Association which Shaftesbury was
accused of having written.

Have, in effect, in battle rang'd each side.   345
But Heaven avert those plagues which we deserve:
Intestine jars but Popish ends can serve.
How false and dangerous methods do they take
Who would a king but of Addressers make!
They from protection would throw all the rest   350
And poorly narrow the King's interest.
To make their little party, too, seem great,
They with false musters, like the Spaniards, cheat.
He's king of all, and would have all their hearts,
Were't not for these dividing Popish arts.   355
Statesmen, who his true interest would improve,
Compute his greatness by his people's love:
That may assist our friends, and foes o'ercome;
So much he will be fear'd abroad as lov'd at home.
He at the people's head may great appear,   360
As th' Edwards, Henrys, and Eliza were.
And curs'd be they who would that power divide,
Who would dissolve that sacred knot by which they're ti'd.
Those miscreants who hate a parliament
Would soon destroy our ancient government.   365
Those slaves would make us fit to be o'ercome,
And gladly sell the land to France or Rome.
But Heaven preserve our legal monarchy
And all those laws that keep the people free.
Of all mankind, for ever curs'd be they   370
Who would or king's or people's rights betray,
Or aught would change but by a legislative way.
Be damn'd the most abhorr'd and traitorous race
Who would the best of governments deface.

   Now farewell wretched mercenary Bayes,   375
Who the King libel'd and did Cromwell praise.
Farewell, abandon'd rascal! only fit

353. *false musters:* A fraudulent inclusion in a muster roll of men who are not available for service. Here the implication is that many of the names on the Addresses are invalid.

368. *legal monarchy:* See *The Medal,* 289 n.

376. *who the king libel'd:* Probably a reference to Dryden's witty treatment of Charles II in *Absalom and Achitophel.* Cf. Macdonald, *Dryden Bibliography,* p. 203.

To be abus'd by thy own scurrilous wit,
Which thou wouldst do and, for a moderate sum,
Answer thy *Medal* and thy *Absolom*.   380
Thy piteous hackney pen shall never fright us;
Thou'rt dwindl'd down to Hodge and *Heraclitus*.
Go, "Ignoramus" cry, and "Forty-One,"
And by Sam's parsons be thou prais'd alone.
Pied thing! half wit! half fool! and for a knave,   385
Few men, than this, a better mixture have:
But thou canst add to that, coward and slave.

378. An intentional misreading of Dryden's remark in the *Epistle to the Whigs,*
n.d.

382. *Hodge:* Sir Roger L'Estrange; see 109 n.

Heraclitus: Heraclitus Ridens, the wittiest of the periodicals of this period, has
been variously attributed to Edward Rawlins, Thomas Flatman, and Roger L'Estrange.
Henry Care (*Weekly Pacquet,* 12 May 1682) suggests that it was the work of a group
that met on Sunday at the Sun Tavern in Aldersgate Street.

383. *Forty-one:* The year in which the Civil War against Charles I began. Tory
propagandists frequently pointed out that 82 was 41 twice over.

384. *Sam's parsons:* 4° note: "A coffee-house where the inferior crepe-gown men
[i.e. clergy] meet with their guide Roger to invent lies for the farther carrying on the
Popish Plot." L'Estrange answered this "asterism" in *Observator,* No. 140 (20 May
1682). For a further description of Sam's (as an "Academy of Nonsense" and ante-
chamber of Hell), see Care, *Weekly Pacquet,* 12 May 1682.

The Tories' Confession

[*T 1910*]

The Tories' Confession appeared about 28 March 1682 (Luttrell's date) in answer to Durfey's poem of the previous month, *The Whigs' Exaltation*. While *The Tories' Confession* cannot develop the earlier poem's artful parallels to 1641, it offers a strong condemnation of Tory arguments and a startlingly frank assertion of the sectarian position. The tactic of the poem is, indeed, to take all those arguments put forth in *The Whigs' Exaltation* and, with the same device of assuming the persona of the enemy, to extend them to their logical absurdity. A subsequent Whig poem, *A Looking Glass for a Tory* ("The Devil and we have done brave things") [L 3015], employs the device once more, though in that instance the persona is an Irish witness.

THE TORIES' CONFESSION

or
A Merry Song
In Answer to
The Whigs' Exaltation

1.

A pox on Whigs! We'll now grow wise;
   Let's cry out "Guard the throne!"
By that we'll damn the Good Old Cause
   And make the game our own.
Religion, that shall stoop to us,   5
   And so shall liberty;
We'll make their laws as thin as lawn,
   Such Tory rogues are we.

7. *lawn:* A fine linen resembling cambric; here a metonomy for bishops, whose lawn sleeves were a distinctive part of episcopal dress.

2.

When once that preaching, whining crew
    Are crush'd and quite undone,   10
The poor we'll banish by our laws,
    And all the rest we'll burn.
Then abbey-lands shall be possess'd
    By those whose right they be;
We'll cry up laws, but none we'll use,   15
    Such Tory rogues are we.

3.

The name of Protestant we hate,
    The Whigs they know it well;
And since we can't it longer hide,
    Let's truth genteely tell.   20
Now Damme is good manners grown,
    And tends to gallantry;
We'll s———— the nation out of doors,
    Such cursed rogues are we.

4.

What care we for a parliament?   25
No money comes from thence;

11. While this was a common charge of both parties, it might refer more specifically to the Parliamentary debates on the poor that took place throughout the 1670s (Cobbett, *Parliamentary History of England* [London, 1808], *4*, Appendix xviii, ccv, 22 & 23 Car. II, 16, 18, 20; also *CJ*, *9*, 483).

12. Whig journalists attempted constantly to associate Tory religious sentiment with the harshest decrees of Papal suppression. Thus, Henry Care has "Tory" remark regretfully that "Tis pity that excellent writ *De Haeretico Comburendo* is out of date" (*Weekly Pacquet* [10 Feb. 1682], p. 63) and later, "Trueman," after having heard that Care had been burnt in effigy at Norwich, comments: "O Heavens! how some people's fingers itch to be at fire and faggot. . . . Had not the writ *De Haeretico Comburendo* been unluckily abolished, they would no doubt have been glad to have roasted the poor fool in bad earnest" (ibid. [16 June 1682], p. 207).

While the *statutes* had been repealed as early as 1558, it was not until 8 March 1677 that a bill to take away the Crown's right to the *writ* was introduced in Commons. It passed in that session. (See *CJ*, *9*, 394 et seq.)

13. In the idea that the monastic property seized under Henry VIII would be returned to the Roman Church there might be an echo of the debates on the reassumption of Crown lands that took place in Parliament in 1677.

21. *Damme:* The stock Tory blasphemy, according to their enemies.

23. *s————:* Luttrell fills in the blank with *shite*, but *NN* gives *swear*, as does *r"*(IV).

Would they but give us coin enough,
    We'd spend the nation's pence.
These twopenny statesmen all shall down,
    A goodly sight to see;   30
To finish all, we'll plunder 'em too,
    Such sons of whores are we.

5.

We'll build more universities,
    For there lies all our hope;
And to th' crape gown we'll cringe and creep,   35
    Supposing 'twere a Pope.
Say what he will, we'll him believe,
    If true or false it be;
And while he prays, we'll drink his health,
    Such Tory rogues are we.   40

6.

What pimping Whig shall dare control
    Or check the lawful heir?
We'll take the rascal by the poll
    And pox off all his hair.
Then here goes honest James's health,   45
    Come drink it on your knee;
Dzowns, we'll have none but honest souls,
    Such Tory rogues are we.

7.

These crafty Whigs are subtle knaves,
    To give them all their due;   50

29. *twopenny:* Trifling, worthless. The term would seem to echo the Tory's "twopenny (or ninepenny) esquire," referring to Slingsby Bethel, the former sheriff famous for his extreme Whiggism and parsimony. See *Iter Boreale*, 43.

35. *crape gown:* The clergy.

42. *lawful heir:* James, Duke of York.

43. *poll:* The part of the head on which the hair grows.

44. *pox off: Pox* was used for any one of several eruptive skin diseases, though here the reference would seem to be to syphillis, which causes depilation.

46. Another stock charge, going back to the anti-Cavalier writings of the 1640s, was that the rake-hell Courtiers committed the blasphemy of kneeling as they drank their toasts.

And yet we balk'd the Popish Plot,
   Though they had sworn it true.
For this you know whom we may thank;
   But mum for that! yet we
Are bound to pray and praise him for't,   55
   Such Tory rogues are we.

8.

When all these zealous Whigs are down,
   We'll drink and fall a-roaring,
And then set up the triple crown;
   'Twill saint us all for whoring.   60
When we have quite enslav'd 'em all,
   Ourselves cannot be free;
Then prithee Devil claim thy own,
   For hey to Hell go we.

9.

We'll choose their sheriffs and juries too,   65
   And then pretend 'tis law.
We'll bring more Irish o'er to swear
   'Gainst those they never saw.
We'll seize their charters, then they must

54. *mum for that!:* Not a word about that. The extreme caution of the writer would seem to suggest that he had in mind either the Duke of York or (more likely) the King himself.

59. *triple crown:* The papal tiara.

65. The Tories faced a constant frustration in the face of the Whig sheriffs (Pilkington and Shute) and their carefully selected Grand Juries which culminated in the return of "Ignoramus" to the charge of high treason brought against Shaftesbury on 24 Nov. 1681. The Court party had already attempted unsuccessfully to disqualify the former sheriffs, Bethel and Cornish, and oppose the present sheriffs in Common Hall. The writer seems to anticipate the events that were to begin when the Lord Mayor drank to Dudley North at the Bridge House Feast on 18 May. (See the poems on the shrieval elections.)

67. The Irish witness who gave evidence against Shaftesbury in his treason trial. While some of them appeared on this occasion for the first time, the Crown very cleverly made use of a number of them who had formerly testified to the credibility of the Popish Plot.

69. In Nov. 1681, the Court began a Quo Warranto proceeding against the City of London. While this at first seemed only an inquiry into the tenure of its liberties, it soon became obvious that it was a demand for the surrender of the charter itself. The case was argued on 7 Feb. 1683 and finally adjudged on 12 June, when the court of

Come beg 'em on their knee.   70
If this won't do, we'll call the French,
Such cursed rogues are we.

King's Bench found unanimously for the Crown. The various corporations had, indeed, to "come beg 'em on their knee." For the national implications of the original action, see Gough, *Londinum Triumphans*, pp. 371–72.

71. *call the French:* While Whig propagandists could have known nothing of Charles II's secret alliance with France, their suspicion of an entente was voiced in political verse as early as 1673.

The Loyal Scot

[*L 3366*]

The effective satiric device of the foreigner commenting on a situation is here reinforced by the care with which the author sketches in his commentator's background. This particular Scot cannot be accused of either royalist absolutism or Yorkist leanings; indeed, in his simple and direct speech, he openly admits that he last saw England in 1643—when the Scotch army invaded England at the request of the Parliament and turned the tide of war against Charles I. In admitting, by implication, that his Scot's actions may have had some justification then, the author establishes a plain-dealing Covenanter whose sense of loyalty is so shocked by the hypocrisy and radicalism of Whig politics that his only thought is to return to Scotland. Thus, by means of the persona, the author stresses not only that 1682 is far worse than 1643 but also that the principles of the earlier period have been corrupted beyond all recognition by Shaftesbury and his party. With the most corrosive kind of irony, the Whig claim that there is no connection between 1641 and 1682 emerges with grim insistence as the reader realizes the difference between principled and unprincipled action.

The text is based on *l''* (checked with copies in *f''* and *k''*) but the more consistent dialect of *c* has been incorporated. Luttrell's copy is dated 5 April 1682. The "new Scotch Tune" is printed in *c*.

THE LOYAL SCOT

An Excellent New Song
To An Excellent New Scotch Tune

1.

Bread of Geud! I think the nation's mad,
    And nene but knaves and perjur'd loons do rule the roast;

1. *Bread of Geud!:* Bread of God, i.e. the sacramental bread; an obsolete form of adjuration or oath.
2. *nene:* None.
loons: Rascals; idle, stupid fellows; peasants; persons of low rank (Alexander Warrack, *Scots Dialect Dictionary* [Edinburgh, 1911]).

And for an honest carl ne living's to be had;
    Why sure the deel is landed on the English coast.

I ha' ne'er been here sin' forty-three,   5
    And now thro' Scotland gang to'l see our gracious King;
But wunds a Geud, instead of mirth and merry glee,
    I find aud sniveling Presbyter is coming in.

2.

For they talk of horrid Popish Plots, and Heav'n knows what,
    When au the wiser world knows well what they'd be at;   10
For with sike like seeming sanctity the geudest King
    They did to death and ruin bring.

When on the civil broils they first did enter in,
    (As well ye ken) with *Popery* they did begin;
And with *Liberty* and *Public Geud* was muckle din,   15
    When the deel a bit they meant the thing.

3.

That machine of monstrous policy,
    I'se mean old Shaftesbury for loyalty so fam'd;
The voice of all the Geudly rabble mobile,
    The fausest loon that ever Envy destin'd damn'd.   20

3. *carl:* A man, an old man (Warrack).

4. *deel:* Devil.

5. *forty-three:* In 1643, upon the English Parliament's acceptance of the Solemn League and Covenant, the Scots entered the Civil War against Charles I.

6. *gang:* go.

to'l: i.e. *till,* to, in order to.

7. *wunds a Geud:* Wounds of God, another oath.

8. *aud:* Old.

11. *sike:* Such.

geudest: Best.

15. Much of Parliament's unprecedented assumption of power and prerogative in the opening years of the Civil War was based on the fundamentally republican concepts of "liberty of the subject" and "the common good."

Muckle: Large, great.

16. *thing:* When used with the definite article and a preceding negative, a term of disapprobation (Warrack).

18. *I'se:* Dialectical or archaic abbreviation for *I shall,* and also for *I is* (i.e. *I am*). Its use here is questionable.

19. *Geudly:* Godly; or perhaps, goodly.

mobile: Trisyllabic.

20. *fausest:* Falsest.

Heav'n sure never meant so fou a thing,
    But to inform the world where villainy did dwell:
And sike a traitor beath to Commonwealth and King
    The muckle deel did surely never hatch in Hell.

4.

For, like Roman Catiline, to gain his pious ends,   25
    He pimps for au the loose rebellious fops in toon;
And with treats and treason daily crams his City friends,
    From the link-man to the scarlet goon.

And with high debauchery they carry on the Cause,
    And Geudly Reformation is the sham pretense;   30
And religiously defy divine and human laws,
    With obedience to their rightful prince.

5.

Then as speaker to this Grand Cabal,
    Old Envy Tony seated at the head o'th' board,
His learn'd oration for rebellion makes to all,   35
    Applauded and approv'd by ev'ry factious lord.

Cully Jemmy then they vote for king,
    Whom curse confound for being sike a senseless loon.

---

destin'd: Very likely this is meant to suggest the narrator's Calvinistic sense of predestination.

21. *fou:* Foul.

23. *beath:* Both.

25. *Catiline:* The Roman conspirator, who sought support in every rank from slaves to young aristocrats, was exposed through the efforts of Cicero. The Catalinarian conspiracy and its leader became symbols of rebellion and demagoguery to the writers of the 1680s.

26. *toon:* Town.

27. *treats and treason:* The primary allusion may be to the famous Pope-burning processions of 17 Nov. 1680 and 1681. (See North's excellent, though biased analysis, *Examen,* pp. 570–72, 574–81; also Luttrell, *Brief Relation, I,* 144.) Once the chief municipal offices were in Charles' hand, he prohibited such demonstrations (Luttrell, *I,* 237).

28. *link-man:* One who carries a link, or torch, to light passengers along the street.

scarlet goon: The robes of civic office used on official or ceremonial occasions. The reference here would seem to be to the Lord Mayor (either Robert Clayton or Patience Ward) and the Aldermanic Council.

32. *With:* Along with.

33–34. The description is not unlike those of the meetings of the Green Ribbon Club at the King's Head Tavern (North, *Examen,* pp. 571–72).

37. *Cully:* The slang word for a dupe, gull, or simpleton.

Can they who did their lawful lord to th' scaffold bring
    Be just to him that has no title to a croon?   40

6.

But they find he is a blockhead fitted for their use,
    A fool by nature and a knave by custom grown;
A gay fop-monarch, whom the rabble may abuse;
    And their business done, will soon unthrone.

But Jemmy swears and vows, gan he can get the croon,   45
    He by the laws of forty-ene would guided be;
And profane lawn sleeves and surplices again must doon,
    Then hey for our aud Presbytery.

7.

Buckingham a statesman would be thought,
    And reason geud that he should bear that rev'rend name;   50
Since he was ene of them that first began the Plot,
    How the King might banter and three kingdoms sham.

All the malcontents His Noble Grace
    To this Rehearsal did invite, to hear and see;
But whilst he wittily contriv'd it but a farce,   55
    The busier noddles turn'd it into tragedy.

Jemmy: The dashing, popular James, Duke of Monmouth, was the Whig party's choice for successor to Charles II.

45. *gan:* Probably an abbreviation of *against* (before, in readiness for), though there may be the sense of *an* (before; if).

46. *forty-ene:* i.e. forty-one, the year of the beginning of the Civil War.

47. *lawn sleeves and surplices:* i.e. the Anglican clergy.

49. *Buckingham:* George Villiers, second Duke of Buckingham (1628–87), was second only to Shaftesbury in the Whig hierarchy.

51. Tory writers strongly suspected that Shaftesbury and Buckingham had directed the Popish Plot.

52. Supply *he* (i.e. Buckingham) as subject.

banter: Impose upon; cheat, trick, bamboozle (though this predates the earliest quotation in the *OED*).

sham: Cheat, trick, deceive, delude with false pretenses.

54. *Rehearsal:* The title of Buckingham's comedy attacking Dryden; here referring to the Popish Plot as the forepiece to rebellion.

8.

And now each actor does begin to play his part,
    And, too, so well he cons his geer and takes his cue,
Till they learn to play the rebel so by rote of heart,
    That the fictitious story seems as true.   60

And now, without control, they apprehend and hang;
    And with the nation au is gospel that they swear;
Then, bonny Jockey, prethee back to'l Scotland gang,
    For a loyal lad's in danger here.

58. *cons:* Examines, inspects.

geer: While signifying generally tools, goods, wealth, or accoutrements, there is also the more specific meaning of a sword or a weapon. (See Warrack, sub *geir, geer,* and *gear.*)

63. *Jockey:* A country fellow, a rustic; also a strolling minstrel. While usually employed derisively, the word was applied to any Scotsman.

ELKANAH SETTLE

Absalom Senior

[S 2653]

On 10 January 1682, *Heraclitus Ridens* remarked that "Elkanah promises to vindicate Lucifer's first rebellion for a few guineas. Poor Absalom and Achitophel must e'en hide themselves in the Old Testament again; and I question whether they'll be safe there from the fury of this mighty cacadoggin." Indeed, they were not safe. Settle, though unable to match Dryden's finest satire on poetic grounds, had a distinct advantage in the biblical source and in the political circumstances. Both men were appealing to the uncommitted moderates, whether of the right or of the left; but Dryden, if he had the often dubious advantage in satire of promulgating conservatism on the basis of sweet reason, was essentially writing an apologia; Settle, with a whole battery of specific complaints and suggestive suspicions, could launch a coordinated attack that turned the Absalom analogue against the Court Party most effectively. Nor is Settle's poem totally lacking in poetic quality; many of the passages and portraits are quite accomplished, and Dryden himself, in the frequently quoted description of Settle which followed the *Absalom Senior,* acknowledged that

> Doeg, though without knowing how or why,
> Made still a blund'ring kind of melody.

Charles II's official acceptance of the Popish Plot, his brother's conversion to Catholicism, and his own pro-French policy based on secret but suspected treaties were all factors which Dryden had to avoid by wit but which Settle could exploit with profit. Settle had only to dissociate himself from the Commonwealth extremists, and

Title: Settle probably took the term *Transpros'd* from the attack on Dryden (Bayes) in *The Rehearsal* (see first [1672] and second [1673] editions); the word had also gained wide currency from Marvell's *The Rehearsal Transprosed* (five editions in 1672–73). The 4° reading, *Transpos'd,* would seem to be an error similar to that found in a later printing of *The Rehearsal* (Buckingham, *Works* (1715), 2, 36).

this, in the very nature of his appeal to the moderate left, was easily accomplished. Beyond this, he could press the biblical analogues of the Egyptian (Roman Catholic, French) worship of Baal (idolatry) and its tyranny over Israel (England) prior to the escape (the Reformation); he could make Absalom's (York's) plot not just a vague misdemeanor but an event of national import whose end was the reestablishment of a Catholic prince, ruled by Rome (Babylon) and allied to the idolatrous French.

Though *Absalom Senior,* like the other anti-*Absalom* poems, could marshal convincing arguments, the overwhelming superiority of the original was surely obvious even to those of Whig sympathies. Dryden's opponents must have recognized that the only writer who could possibly nullify his poem's effectiveness was Dryden himself, and therefore, in the months following the publication of *Absalom and Achitophel,* there appeared three editions of Dryden's *Heroic Stanzas* in praise of Oliver Cromwell (first printed in 1659), "to show," as one of the title pages ironically remarked, "the loyalty and integrity of the poet."

Luttrell acquired his copy of *Absalom Senior* on 6 April 1682, and on the title page penned an apt evaluation: "A poem for the Whigs, and running down all the Duke of York's party, and crying up their own particularly, but under borrowed names."

ABSALOM SENIOR

or

Achitophel Transpros'd

In gloomy times, when priestcraft bore the sway
And made Heav'n's gate a lock to their own key;
When ignorant devotes did blindly bow,
All groping to be sav'd they knew not how:
Whilst this Egyptian darkness did o'erwhelm,   5

2. *their own key:* A reference to the papal claim of exclusive inheritance of St. Peter's keys to the Kingdom of Heaven (Matthew 16:19). Dryden rather unfairly misquotes this line in the *Second Part of Absalom and Achitophel* when he claims that Doeg (Settle) "makes Heaven's gate a lock to its own key."

3. *ignorant:* In the literal sense of not knowing.
devotes: Devotees.

5. *Egyptian darkness:* Biblically, the bondage of Israel. See also Isaiah 9:2 and Moses's ninth plague (Exodus 10:21–23). Historically, England prior to the Reformation.

The priest sat pilot even at empire's helm.
Then royal necks were yok'd, and monarchs still
Held but their crowns at his almighty will.
And to defend this high prerogative,
Falsely from Heaven he did that power derive: 10
By a commission forg'd i'th' hand of God,
Turn'd Aaron's blooming wand to Moses' snaky rod.
Whilst princes little scepters overpower'd,
Made but that prey his wider gorge devour'd.
Now to find wealth might his vast pomp supply   15
(For costly roofs befit a lord so high),
No arts were spar'd his luster to support,
But all mines search'd t'enrich his shining Court.
Then Heav'n was bought, religion but a trade,
And temples murder's sanctuary made.   20
By Phineas' spear no bleeding Cozbi groan'd,

6. *priest:* Biblically, the High Priest of Egypt. Historically, the papacy's claim to temporal supremacy, particularly of the Holy Roman Empire. Cf. Milton, *Lycidas,* 109–11:

> Last came, and last did go.
> The Pilot of the Galilean Lake.
> Two massy keys he bore.

9. *high prerogative:* Generally, an extraordinary distinction, privilege, or precedence. In seventeenth-century England, the phrase would have connoted at once "that special pre-eminence which the sovereign, by right of regal dignity, has over all other persons and out of the course of common law" (*OED*). The contention between parliamentary privilege and royal prerogative constituted the basis of the political struggles of the period; when used in sectarian attacks on ecclesiastical questions, "prerogative" referred to the Court-supported policy of High Church Anglicanism which (it was claimed) varied little from Roman Catholicism.

10. In the terms of contemporary politics (see 9 n.), Settle is here strongly attacking the extreme royalist argument of divine right.

11. Historically, an allusion to the famous eighth- or ninth-century forgery, the Donation of Constantine, upon which the papacy based its pretensions to temporal domination from the eleventh century onward. The genuineness of the grant was first attacked by the Italian humanist Lorenzo Valla in 1440, but, though the document was generally rejected by antipapal elements, the defense was not silenced until the close of the eighteenth century.

12. *Aaron's blooming wand:* Numbers 17:1–10. The miraculous confirmation of the divine choice of Aaron and the tribe of Levi as ministers of the tabernacle.

Moses' snaky rod: Exodus 4:2–4.

21. Numbers 25:6–9. Phinehas, the grandson of Aaron, incensed at seeing the Israelite prince Zimri committing whoredom with the Midianitish princess Cozbi at the very time that God was angered with the Israelites for their worship of Baal-Peor, seized a spear and "went after the man of Israel into the tent and thrust both of them

If Cozbi's gold for Cozbi's crimes aton'd.
With these wise arts (for human policy
As well as heav'nly truth mounts priests so high),
'Twixt gentle penance, lazy penitence,   25
A faith that gratifies both soul and sense,
With easy steps to everlasting bliss,
He paves the rugged way to Paradise.
Thus almost all the proselyte world he drives,
Whilst th' universal drones buzz to his hives.   30
Implicit Faith Religion thus convey'd
Through little pipes to his great channel laid,
Till Piety, through such dark conduits led,
Was poison'd by the spring on which it fed.
Here blind Obedience to a blinder guide   35
Nurs'd that Blind Zeal that rais'd the priestly pride;
Whilst to make kings the sovereign prelate own,
Their reason he enslav'd, and then their throne.
The miter thus above the diadem soar'd;
God's humble servant he, but man's proud lord.   40
It was in such church-light Blind Zeal was bred,
By Faith's infatuating meteor led;
Blind Zeal, that can even contradictions join,
A saint in faith, in life a libertine,
Makes Greatness, though in luxury worn down,   45
Bigotted even to th' hazard of a crown;
Ti'd to the girdle of a priest so fast,
And yet religious only to the waist.
But Constancy, atoning Constancy,
Where that once reigns, Devotion may lay by.   50
T'espouse the Church's cause lies in Heav'n's road
More than obeying of the Church's God.

---

through." As a result, God stayed the plague that beset Israel and conferred on
Phinehas "the covenant of an everlasting priesthood" for his zeal. The figure of
Phinehas had been used in the popular extremist pamphlet of a Scots Presbyterian,
Sir James Stewart, *Jus Populi Vindicatum* (1669) [S 5536], which went so far as to
applaud assassination by men who, like Phinehas, had a "call."
    40. The traditional description of the pope is that of "servus servorum Dei."
    41ff. The description of Blind Zeal bears striking similarity to Whig views of the
Catholic James, Duke of York.

And he dares fight for faith is more renown'd,
A zealot militant, than martyr crown'd.
Here the arch-priest, to that ambition blown,   55
Pull'd down God's altars to erect his own:
For not content to publish Heav'n's command,
The sacred law penn'd by th' Almighty Hand,
And Moses-like 'twixt God and Israel go,
Thought Sinai's Mount a pinnacle too low.   60
So charming sweet were incense's fragrant fumes,
So pleas'd his nostrils, till th' aspirer comes
From offering, to receiving, hecatombs;
And ceasing to adore, to be ador'd.
So fell Faith's guide: so loftily he tow'r'd   65
Till, like th' ambitious Lucifer accurst,
Swell'd to a god, into a fiend he burst.

But as great Lucifer by falling gain'd
Dominion, and even in damnation reign'd,
And though from light's bless'd orb forever driven,   70
Yet Prince o'th' Air, h'had that vast scepter giv'n
T'have subjects far more numerous than Heav'n;
And thus enthron'd, with an infernal spite,
The genuine malice of the realms of night,
The Paradise he lost blasphemes, abhors,   75
And against Heav'n proclaims eternal wars.
No art 's untri'd, no hostile step 's untrod,
Both against Truth's adorers, and Truth's God.

So Faith's fall'n guide, now Baal's champion
    reign'd;
Wide was his sway, and mighty his command,   80

53. *he:* He who.

55–56. Biblically, the allusion might be to Aaron and the episode of the golden calf (Exodus 32:1–6). Historically, the arch-priest signifies the pope, who, it was claimed, demanded obedience to the Church above all else.

58. Biblically, either the Decalogue (Exodus 20) or the two tablets of stone which God writes (Exodus 31:18; 32:15–16) and which are broken in anger at the idolatrous worship of the golden calf and then rewritten (Exodus 34:1).

59. The allusion here concentrates on the golden calf episode (Exodus 32:30); throughout the Mosaic books, however, Moses' role is that of intercessor.

68–78. Miltonic overtones dominate the passage. Cf., *inter alios, Paradise Lost* I.84–124, or the Infernal Council of Book II

79. *Faith's fall'n guide:* Historically, the pope, who, in the opinion of sectarians, encouraged idolatry. Baal's lineage is as complex as it is ancient. The word by itself

Whilst with implacable revenge he burn'd
And all his rage against God's Israel turn'd.
Here his envenom'd soul's black gall he flings,
Spots all his snakes, and points his scorpions' stings,
Omits no force or treacherous design   85
Blest Israel to assault or undermine.

But the first sword did his keen malice draw,
Was aim'd against the God-like Deborah.
Deborah, the matchless pride of Judah's crown,
Whose female hand Baal's impious groves cut down,   90
His banish'd wizards from her Israel thrust,
And pounded all their idols into dust.

---

means simply "lord," "master," or "husband," and it is not until the time of Hosea that the application of the general term to Jehovah is condemned (*Abingdon Bible Commentary*, ed. Eiselen, Lewis, and Downey [New York, 1929], p. 364). In the episode of Phinehas (21), Baal-Peor was undoubtedly a Priapic god, connected with Baal, the supreme male divinity of the Phoenician and Canaanitish nations (cf. *A Dictionary of the Bible, 1*, pp. 145–46). This idolatry returned in the succeeding generation (Judges 2:10–13), and, although it was checked under Gideon (Judges 6:25–32), it recommenced immediately upon his death (Judges 8:33–34) and continued until the time of Samuel (Judges 10:10; I Samuel 7:4). Two centuries later, it reasserted itself more strongly than ever (I Kings, 3, 16, 18; II Kings 8, 10–11, 16–18; Jeremiah 7, 9, 11) as the court religion under Ahab, Ahaziah, and Ahaz.

82. *Israel:* England. Settle has in mind the period immediately following the Reformation.

84. The imagery may derive from Revelations 9:10 or Luke 10:19.

89. *Deborah:* Historically, Elizabeth I. The biblical story (Judges 4–5) has some startling parallels with England's victory over the Spanish Armada in 1588. Deborah was a judge and prophetess of the three northern tribes that particularly felt the tyranny of Jabin, king of Hazor. She summoned Barak to aid her in defeating Jabin's general, Sisera, who "had nine hundred chariots of iron; and twenty years he mightily oppressed the children of Israel" (Judges 4:3). Urged on by Deborah, Barak led his little army from their encampment on Mount Tabor (where Sisera's iron chariots could not maneuver) against the unwieldy host of Canaanites. A providential storm fiercely blew wind into the faces of the enemy, "the earth trembled, and the heavens dropped, the clouds also dropped water . . . the stars in their courses fought against Sisera [and] the river Kishon swept them away" (Judges 5:4, 20–21). The victory was decisive: Sisera was killed, Jabin ruined, and a peace of 40 years ensued. (*A Dictionary of the Bible, 1*, 166, 419).

90. Biblically, the line refers to the act of Gideon in the Judges 6:28. Historically, Settle is referring to the reestablishment of Protestantism with Elizabeth's accession (1558) and, perhaps, the subsequent treaties leading up to the adoption of the Thirty-Nine Articles and the Establishment of the Anglican Church (1563).

91. Possibly a reference to the imprisonment of the Catholic bishops in 1559, though other events in the early years of Elizabeth's reign would be equally appropriate.

Her life, with indefatigable pain,
By daggers long and poisons sought in vain;
At length they angry Jabin's rage inflam'd,   95
Hazor's proud king, for iron chariots fam'd;
A warrior powerful, whose most dreadful host
Proclaim'd *Invincible* (were human boast
Infallible), by haughty Sisera led,
'Gainst Deborah their bloody banners spread.   100
But Deborah her Barak calls to war;
Barak, the sun's fam'd fellow-traveler,
Who, wand'ring o'er the earth's surrounded frame,
Had travel'd far as his great mistress Fame.
Here Barak did with Deborah's vengeance fly,   105
And to that swift prodigious victory,
So much by human praises undefin'd
That Fame wants breath, and Wonder lags behind.
To Heav'n's high arch, her sounding glory is rung,
Whilst thus great Deborah and Barak sung: 110

93–94. There were numerous plots—real and imaginary—against Elizabeth, including
the Spanish plot (Guise conspiracy) of Throckmorton and that of William Parry
during 1583–84, the Bakington conspiracy of 1586, and the alleged attempt at poisoning
by Roderigo Lopez, the Queen's physician. Nearly all were connected with the
Spaniards, or the Jesuits, or both.

95. *Jabin:* Philip II of Spain.

96. *Hazor:* Spain.

Iron chariots fam'd: The Spanish men-of-war which, certainly after Lepanto (1571),
had a great reputation.

97. Popularly known as the "Invincible Armada," the Spanish fleet of approximately
130 ships and 2500 cannon set sail from Lisbon on 20 May 1588, under the command
of Don Alfonso Perez de Guzman, Duke of Medina Sidonia. It was defeated by the
English under Lord Howard of Effingham, with Drake, Frobisher, and Hawkins as
subordinate admirals, between 21 and 29 July. About mid-September, in its flight to
the north, the damaged fleet ran into gales which destroyed a great number of the
remaining ships on the coasts of Scotland and Ireland. For Philip II, this was the
final failure in his crusade to establish the supremacy of the Hapsburg dynasty and
the Church of Rome.

99. *Sisera:* i.e. Medina Sidonia, though there are scarcely any parallels to Sisera
either in character or fate.

101. *Barak:* Strictly speaking, this should be Howard, but a copy of the poem in the
editor's possession has the contemporary gloss "Sir Fra[nces Drake]." The subsequent
description bears this out. Drake, in 1586, had sailed to the West Indies, sacked Santo
Domingo and Carthegena, and attacked the Spanish merchant fleets; in 1587, he
inflicted heavy damages on the Spanish fleet at Cadiz. Most historians would find it
difficult to maintain that the relationship of Elizabeth to Drake paralleled very closely
that of the war-like Deborah and the highly cautious Barak.

"Hear, oh ye princes, oh ye kings give ear,
And Israel's great avenger's honor, hear.
When God of hosts, thou Israel's spear and shield,
Went'st out of Seir and marched'st from Edom's field,
Earth trembled, the Heavens dropp'd, the clouds all pour'd;   115
The mountains melted from before the Lord;
Even thy own Sinai melted into streams
At Israel's dazzling God's refulgent beams.
In Shamgar and in Jael's former days,
The wand'ring traveler walk'd through byways.   120
They chose new gods. No spear nor sword was found
To have Idolatry depos'd, Truth crown'd:
Till I alone, against Jehovah's foes,
I, Deborah, I, Israel's mother, rose.
Wake Deborah, wake, raise thy exalted head!   125
Rise Barak, and captivity captive lead,
For to blest Deborah, belov'd of Heav'n,
Over the mighty is dominion giv'n.
Great Barak leads, and Israel's courage warms;
Ephraim and Benjamin march down in arms,   130
Zebulon and Nepthali my thunder bore,
Dan from her ships, and Asher on the shore.
Behold Megiddo's waves, and from afar
See the fierce Jabin's threat'ning storm of war.
But Heav'n 'gainst Sisera fought, and the kind stars   135

111–46. The passage reworks the famous song of Deborah (Judges 5) as follows:
111 = v.3; 112 = v.2; 114–15 = v.4; 116–17 = v.5; 118 = v.31; 119–20 = v.6; 121 = v.8;
124 = v.7; 125–26 = v.12; 128 = v.13; 130–31 = vv.14, 17; 132 = v.17; 133 = v.19;
135–36 = v.20; 138 = v.21; 139–41 = v.23; 143–44 = v.21; 144–46 = v.31.

Specific identification of the biblical proper nouns is difficult. Seir (114) may be
Plymouth, the assembly point of the English fleet. If the tribal names (130–33) refer
to specific persons, then one would have to consider Howard and Hawkins as two
possibilities (inter alios), with the nobility (Thomas Howard, Sheffield, Southwell) and
the famous captains (Frobisher, Fenton, Luke Ward, Raymond, Lancaster, Richard
Hawkins) making up the remainder. Asher might well be Leicester, who was in
command of the land forces which Elizabeth did, in fact, visit at Tilbury. If the
names are to be taken as representative of nations, England, Scotland, and Wales
would probably have been in Settle's mind; and, depending on his view of whether
the Dutch were helpful by blockading the Duke of Parma or cowardly in not joining
the battle directly, one might consider either Dan (132) or Meroz (139) as alluding to
the Netherlands. Meggido (133) in all probability is the English Channel, while
Kishon (138) would be the North Atlantic in the vicinity of the western islands.

Rank'd their embattle'd fires for Deborah's wars,
Shot down their vengeance that miraculous day
When Kishon's torrents swept their hosts away.
But 'Curse ye, Meroz! curse 'em from on high!'
Did the denouncing voice of angels cry;   140
'Accurs'd be they that went not out t'oppose
The mighty—Deborah's, God's, and Israel's foes.'
Victorious Judah! Oh my soul, th'hast trod,
Trod down their strengths. So fall the foes of God.
But they who in His sacred laws delight   145
Be as the Sun when he sets out in might.''

Thus sung, thus conquer'd Deborah; thus fell
Hers, and Heav'n's, foes. But no defeat tames Hell.
By conquest overthrown, but not dismayed,
'Gainst Israel still their private engines play'd;   150
And their dire machinations to fulfill,
Their stings torn out, they kept their poison still.
And now too weak in open force to join,
In close cabals they hatch'd a damn'd design
To light that mine as should the world amaze   155
And set the ruin'd Israel in a blaze.

139. *Curse ye, Meroz:* The text was well known as the basis for sectarian sermons. As Scott noted when explicating Dryden's use of the phrase in *The Vindication of "The Duke of Guise,"* it "was much in vogue among the fanatic preachers in the civil wars. It was preached upon in Guildhall before the Lord Mayor, 9th May 1680, by Edmund Hickeringill, rector of All Saints, Colchester" (Scott-Saintsbury, *Dryden,* 7, 157 n.). See *The Assembly of Moderate Divines* ("Pray, pardon, John Bayes, for I beg your excuse" [A 4018]), stanza 18 (cited by Scott), *r"* (V), p. 438, n. 9, and *Heraclitus Ridens,* No. 28 (9 Aug. 1681). In *The Reformation, A Satire* ("How Roman-like did our old rebel die") [R 740], published 19 Dec. 1683, there seems to be the suggestion that it might have been the text for the sermon at the prohibited Whig Feast of 21 April 1682:

> [Wharton (?)] Seems so to hate the Salamanca trade
> That now a passive lecture he'll digest
> As well as Meroz at forbidden feast
>
>   (43–45)

154. *a damn'd design:* The Gunpowder Plot (5 Nov. 1605), the conspiracy initiated by Robert Catesby and aided by Guy Fawkes and a number of English Catholics to blow up James I and the Parliament. Settle's vague connection of this plot with the Spanish has now some basis in fact.

155. *mine:* A subterranean gallery in which gunpowder is placed for blowing up the enemy's fortifications. Prior to their hiring the vault under the House of Lords, the conspirators had taken a house next door, from the cellar of which they began a mine.

When Judah's Monarch with his princes round,
Amidst his glorious Sanedrin sat crown'd,
Beneath his throne a cavern low, and dark
As their black souls, for the great work they mark.   160
In this lone cell their midnight-hands bestow'd
A Stygian compound, a combustive load
Of mixture wondrous, execution dire,
Ready the touch of their infernal fire.
Have you not seen in yon ethereal road   165
How, at the rage of th' angry driving god,
Beneath the pressure of his furious wheels,
The heav'ns all rattle, and the globe all reels?
So does this thunder's ape its light'ning play,
Keen as Heav'n's fires and scarce less swift than they.   170
A short-liv'd glaring murderer it flies,
In time's least pulse, a moment's wing'd surprise:
'Tis born, looks big, talks loud, breathes death, and dies.
This mixture was th' invention of a priest;
The sulphurous ingredients all the best   175
Of Hell's own growth; for to dire compounds still
Hell finds the minerals, and the priest the skill.

From this curst mine they had that blow decreed,
A moment's dismal blast, as should exceed
All the storms, battles, murders, massacres,   180
And all the strokes of daggers, swords, or spears,
Since first Cain's hand at Abel's head was lift:
A blow more swift than pestilence, more swift
Than ever a destroying angel rode,
To pour the vial of an angry God.   185

157. *Judah's monarch:* James VI, king of Scotland (Judah), afterwards James I, king of England.

158. *Sanedrin:* The parliament. See 371 n.

164. The 36 barrels of powder had been placed in the vaults and covered with coal and faggots by May.

169. *ape:* A counterfeit, an imitation; "to play the ape" is the verbal idiom. The image given here is quite conventional; Roger Bacon's description (1242) of gunpowder is that it produces "a noise like thunder and flashes like lightning."

174. *th' invention of a priest:* The "discovery" of gunpowder was popularly accredited in England to the learned friar Roger Bacon, though it is more generally connected with the name of the German monk Berthold Schwartz.

The train was laid, the very signal giv'n;
But here th'all-seeing Israel's guardian, Heav'n,
Could hold no longer, and to stop their way,
With a kind beam from th' empyrean day,
Disclos'd their hammering thunder at the forge,   190
And made their Cyclop's cave their bolts disgorge.

Discover' thus, thus lost, betray'd, undone,
Yet still untir'd, the restless cause goes on;
And to retrieve a yet auspicious day,
A glowing spark even in their ashes lay,   195
Which thus burst out in flames in Geshur land,
The utmost bound of Israel's command,
Where Judah's planted faith but slowly grew,
A brutal race that Israel's God ne'er knew;
A nation by the conqueror's mercy grac'd,   200
Their gods preserv'd and temples undefac'd;
Yet not content with all the sweets of peace
(Free their estates and free their consciences),
'Gainst Israel those confederate swords they drew,
Which with that vast assassination slew: 205
Two hundred thousand butcher'd victims shar'd
One common doom; no sex nor age was spar'd:
Not kneeling beauties' tears, nor virgins' cries,
Nor infants' smiles. No prey so small but dies.
Alas, the hard-mouth'd bloodhound, Zeal, bites through;   210
Religion hunts, and hungry jaws pursue.

186. *train:* 1. artifice, stratagem; treachery; 2. a line of gunpowder laid so as to convey fire to a mine; 3. a series of consequences.

187. The plot came to official attention on 26 Oct. The inspection of the vaults and the arrest of Fawkes took place on 4 Nov. Catesby and most of the others fled, hoping to raise the countryside, but they were totally unsuccessful and were either captured or killed within four days.

196. *Geshur:* Biblically, probably "a section of the wild and rugged country, now called el-Lejah, among whose rocky fastnesses the Geshurites might dwell in security while the whole surrounding plains were occupied by the Israelites" (*A Dictionary of the Bible, 1,* 683). Historically, Ireland.

198. *Judah's planted faith:* Protestantism, though my copy specifies Puritanism. Ireland was conquered under Elizabeth, who, as always, made a virtue out of necessity and did not seek to wipe out Roman Catholicism. The reference here is probably to the Ulster plantation under James I.

206. The massacres of the Irish Rebellion of 1641.

To what strange rage is superstition driv'n
That man can outdo Hell to fight for Heav'n!
So rebel Geshur fought: so drown'd in gore,
Even Mother Earth blush'd at the sons she bore;   215
And still asham'd of her old staining brand,
Her head shrinks down, and quagmires half their land.
Yet not this blow Baal's empire could enlarge,
For Israel still was Heav'n's peculiar charge:
Unshaken still in all this scene of blood,   220
Truth's temple firm on golden columns stood.
Whilst Saul's revenging arm proud Geshur scourg'd,
From their rank soil their Hydra's poison purg'd.

Yet does not here their vanquish'd spleen give o'er,
But as untir'd and restless as before,   225
Still through whole waiting ages they outdo
At once the chemist's pains and patience too—
Who, though he sees his bursting limbecks crack
And at one blast, one fatal minute's wrack,
The forward hopes of sweating years expire,   230
With sad yet painful hand new-lights his fire:
Pale, lean, and wan, does health, wealth, all consume,
Yet for the great elixir still to come,
Toils and hopes on. No less their plottings cease;
So hope, so toil, the foes of Israel's peace.   235

When, lo, a long-expected day appears,
Sought for above a hundred rolling years;
A day i'th' register of doom set down
Presents 'em with an heir of Israel's crown.

216. *brand:* Various meanings are applicable: stigma; a particular sort or class; torch.
222. *Saul's revenging arm:* Oliver Cromwell's cruelly efficient campaign of 1649–50 reached greatest attrition at Drogheda.
223. *Hydra:* The fabulous, many-headed snake of the marshes of Lerna; used generally for a dragon or any terrific serpent. The connection of Ireland and snakes is traditional.
238. *register of doom:* The phrase probably derives from the Domesday Book, the twelfth-century register of lands.
239. *'em:* i.e. the Roman Catholics.
an heir of Israel's crown: Like Dryden, Settle had to make a number of changes in the biblical history of David, though, of course, these variations differed according to

Here their vast hopes of the rich Israel's spoils   240
Requites the pains of their long ages' toils.
Baal's banners now i'th' face of day shall march
With Heav'n's bright roof for his triumphal arch.
His lurking missioners shall now no more
From foreign schools in borrow'd shapes come o'er,   245
Convert by moonlight, and their mystic rites
Preach to weak female half-soul'd proselytes.
An all-commanding dragon now shall soar
Where the poor serpents only crawl'd before.
Baal's restoration, that most blest design,   250
Now the great work of majesty, shall shine,
Made by his consecrating hand divine.
He shall new-plant their groves with each bless'd tree,
A graft of an imperial nursery.
In the kind air of this new Eden bless'd,   255

---

the political views of the two authors. Both, however, were faced with the difficulty of separating David's earlier career (which had certain strong analogies to the life of Charles I) from his later life (which applied to Charles II). On the whole, Dryden's parallel is far more successful; Settle, trying to turn against Dryden the guns which that poet had captured, concentrates on the word "heir," which, in the matter of succession, did not have to be a son (see Burnet, *History*, 2, 215; and Dryden, *The Medal*, 289 n.). This does violence to the Absalom parallel, but Settle has already announced that he is writing of Absalom Senior. In addition, the partial confusion allows him to make some highly daring suggestions. For example, since the last historical reference was to Cromwell, the reader would undoubtedly have thought for a shocked instant that the reference was to Charles II. That the Whigs suspected the King of at least strong Catholic leanings goes without saying, and Settle drives home this point by holding back precise identification as long as possible.

245. Catholic secular priests and Jesuits, trained frequently at the English Colleges at Rome or St. Omer, were forced to live in disguises while in England.

246. A reference to the extremes to which "hedge-priests" were driven.

247. *half-soul'd:* Probably alludes to the inferior position of women traditionally connected with the anti-feminism of the Catholic Church. On the other hand, Protestant religious sects had, according to their critics, made a concentrated appeal to women and drawn most of their support from them.

248–49. Cf. 223 n. and 263 n. Settle is attempting to connect York and Henrietta Maria as closely as possible with the Irish, who were anathema to the average contemporary Englishman.

250. *Baal's restoration:* The reestablishment of papal power in England. Again, Settle's use of "restoration" would seem to hint at the King.

252. *his:* i.e. Baal's. The reference again is to the popes' claim to temporal power and the right to confirm princes in their offices.

253. Cf. 90.

Perch'd on each bough, and palaces their nest,
No more by frighting laws forc'd t' obscure flight
And gloomy walks, like obscene birds of night,
Their warbling notes like Philomel shall sing,
And like the bird of Paradise their wing.   260
Thus Israel's heir their ravish'd souls all fir'd;
For all things to their ardent hopes conspir'd.

   His very youth a bigot mother bred,
And tainted even the milk on which he fed.
Him only of her sons design'd for Baal's   265
Great champion 'gainst Jerusalem's proud walls;
Him dipp'd in Stygian Lake, by timely craft,
Invulnerable made against Truth's pointed shaft.
But to confirm his early poison'd faith,
'Twas in the cursed foreign tents of Gath,   270
'Twas there that he was lost. There Absalon,

256. *palaces:* i.e. as advisers and directors of the monarchy. Also an allusion to the luxury of ecclesiastical princes.

257. Though discussing the future consequences of York's succession, Settle is undoubtedly hinting at Charles II's Declaration of Indulgence. The "frighting laws" would probably be based upon anti-Catholic interpretation of the Act of Uniformity (1662), the Test Act (1673), and the Papists' Disabling Act (1678), among others.

258. *obscene:* Filthy, foul, loathsome.

259–60. The references are to sectarian objections to music and ornate dress in the Catholic ritual.

263. *a bigot mother:* Because of the twofold nature of the David story (see 239 n.), Settle does not mention his name but does make inaccurate use of II Samuel 3:3 to attack Charles I's wife, the Catholic daughter of Henry IV, Henrietta Maria, and her pro-Irish policy. King David married "Maacah, the daughter of Talmai, king of Geshur"; and "her son Absalom sought refuge among his maternal relatives after the murder of his brother. The wild acts of Absalom's life may have been to some extent the results of maternal training; they were at least characteristic of the stock from which he sprung" (*A Dictionary of the Bible, 1,* 683).

266. *Jerusalem's:* London's. The principal royalist attack at the time of writing was the Quo Warranto proceedings against the London Charter.

270. *Gath:* One of the five royal cities of the Philistines. It was here, among his hereditary enemies, that David, in his flight from Saul, found refuge, service, honor, and friends. Gath's ruler, Achish, was forced to dismiss David because of the distrust of the other Philistine lords, though he had already granted him the city of Ziklag (I Samuel 27–29). Historically, Gath is most likely St. Germain, the home of the English court in exile.

271. *Absalon:* James, Duke of York (1633–1701), had converted to Catholicism by March 1672, though he had long been sympathetic to that religion and probably

By David's fatal banishment undone,
Saw their false gods till in their fires he burn'd,
Truth's manna, for Egyptian fleshpots, scorn'd.
Not David so; for he, Faith's champion lord,   275
Their altars loath'd and prophane rites abhorr'd,
Whilst his firm soul on wings of cherubs rode,
And tun'd his lyre to nought but Abraham's God.
Thus the gay Israel her long tears quite dri'd,
Her restor'd David met in all her pride;   280
Three brothers saw, by miracle brought back,
Like Noah's sons sav'd from the world's great wrack,
An unbelieving Ham grac'd on each hand
'Twixt God-like Shem and pious Japhet, stand.

'Tis true, when David, all his storms blown o'er,   285
Wafted by prodigies to Jordan's shore,
(So swift a revolution, yet so calm)
Had cur'd an age's wounds with one day's balm,
Here the returning Absalom his vows
With Israel joins, and at their altars bows.   290
Perhaps surpris'd at such strange blessings show'r'd,
Such wonders shown both t' Israel's Faith and Lord,

---

delayed his conversion only for political reasons. The extent of Henrietta Maria's influence on his religious beliefs is highly debatable. James' first wife, Anne Hyde, had died as a professed Catholic on 31 March 1671, but James had already made known to his Catholically inclined brother his strong desire to profess the Roman faith (Ogg, *Charles II*, p. 338).

272. Biblically, Absalom is first mentioned during David's seven and a half years' rule of Judah (II Samuel 3:3), prior to his anointment as king of Israel (II Samuel 5:4). Historically, Charles II was crowned in Scotland (5 Feb. 1649) but was decisively defeated at Worcester (3 Sept. 1651) and fled to France. James had escaped from St. James' Palace in April 1648 and served with distinction under Turenne and later with the Spanish forces in Flanders during Charles' exile. He returned with his brothers (280–81) when Charles—like David, at the age of 30—was crowned king of England (Israel).

274. *Egyptian:* French.

283. *Ham:* i.e. York. Ham was the disrespectful second son who was cursed by Noah (Genesis 9:22–27).

284. *god-like Shem:* Noah's oldest son; here, Charles II.

Japheth: Noah's youngest son; here, Henry, Duke of Gloucester (1639–60), third son of Charles I, who was disowned by his mother for not converting to Roman Catholicism. He died of smallpox in London and was buried at Westminster.

286. *Jordan:* The English Channel.

His restoration-miracle he thought
Could by no less than Israel's God be wrought.
Whilst the enlighten'd Absalom thus kneels,   295
Thus dancing to the sound of Aaron's bells,
What dazzling rays did Israel's heir adorn,
So bright his sun in his unclouded morn!
'Twas then his leading hand in battle drew
That sword that David's fam'd ten thousand slew: 300
David's the cause, but Absalom's the arm.
Then he could win all hearts, all tongues could charm:
Whilst with his praise the echoing plains all rung,
A thousand timbrels play'd, a thousand virgins sung;
And in the zeal of every jocund soul,   305
Absalom's health with David's crown'd one bowl.

   Had he fix'd here, yes, Fate, had he fix'd here,
To man so sacred, and to Heav'n so dear,
What could he want that hands, hearts, lives could pay,
Or tributary worlds beneath his feet could lay?   310
What knees, what necks to mount him to a throne;
What gems, what stars to sparkle in a crown?
So pleas'd, so charm'd, had Israel's genius smil'd.
But oh, ye pow'rs, by treacherous snakes beguil'd,
Into a more than Adam's curse he run;   315
Tasting that fruit has Israel's world undone.
Nay, wretched even below his falling state,
Wants Adam's eyes to see his Adam's fate.
In vain were David's harp and Israel's choir,

---

296. *Aaron's bells:* The golden bells on the hem of Aaron's robe of chief priest
(Exodus 28:33–35). Settle probably had in mind the head of the Anglican clergy, the
Archbishop of Canterbury, William Juxon (1582–1663), who, though ill at the time
(Evelyn, *Diary, 3,* 281–84), officiated at the coronation of Charles on 23 April 1661.
299. James, created Lord High Admiral in 1660, achieved great fame for his victories
at Lowestoft (1665) in the first Dutch War and at Sole Bay over De Ruyter (1672) in the
third. The passage of the Test Act (March 1673) forced him to resign the admiralty.
300. Cf. I Samuel 18:8.
302. Cf. II Samuel 15:6.
303–04. Cf. I Samuel 18:6–7.
314. Luttrell: "Duke of York turning papist."
319–23. The sense is unclear; a possible interpretation is: David's harp and Israel's
choir were in vain; for his [York's] conversion [to goodness] they [or f°'s *all*] did in

For his conversion did in vain conspire;   320
For though their influence a while retires,
His own false planets were th' ascendant fires.
Heav'n had no lasting miracle design'd;
It did a while his fatal torrent bind:
As Joshua's wand did Jordan's streams divide,   325
And rang'd the wat'ry mountains on each side;
But when the marching Israel once got o'er,
Down crack the crystal walls, the billows pour,
And in their old impetuous channel roar.

At last this last stroke thus totally o'erthrown,   330
Apostacy now seal'd him all her own.
Here op'd that gaping breach, that fatal door,
Which now let in a thousand ruins more.
All the bright virtues, and each dazzling grace,
Which his rich veins drew from a God-like race—   335
The mercy, and the clemency divine,
Those sacred beams which in mild David shine—
Those royal sparks, his native seeds of light,
Were all put out, and left a starless night.
A long farewell to all that's great and brave: 340
Not cataracts more headstrong; as the grave,
Inexorable; sullen and untun'd
As pride depos'd; scarce Lucifer dethron'd
More unforgiving. His enchanted soul
Had drunk so deep of the bewitching bowl,   345
Till he whose hand, with Judah's standard, bore
Her martial thunder to the Tyrian shore,
Arm'd in her wars, and in her laurels crown'd,
Now, all forgotten, at one stagg'ring wound,

---

vain conspire; for, though their [the malevolent planets'] influence retire for a while,
they [i.e. his own false planets] were the ascendant fires.
319. *Israel's choir:* The Anglican clergy.
325. Cf. Joshua 3–4.
331. *Apostacy:* My copy's gloss reads: "Popery."
338. *native:* Belonging to one as a possession or right by virtue of one's birth.
seeds of light: The image would seem to be based on the emission hypothesis. A seed-spark is the germ of a fire.
345. *bowl:* i.e. of popular approval. Cf. 306.
347. *Tyrian:* Dutch.

Falling from Israel's Faith, from Israel's cause,   350
Peace, honor, int'rest, all at once withdraws.
Nor is he deaf t' a kingdom's groans alone,
But could behold ev'n David's shaking throne;
David, whose bounty rais'd his glittering pride,
The basis of his glory's pyramid.   355
But duty, gratitude, all ruin'd fall;
Zeal blazes, and oblivion swallows all.
So Sodom did both burnt and drown'd expire;
A poison'd lake succeeds a pile of fire.

On this foundation Baal's last hope was built,   360
The sure retreat for all their sallying guilt:
A royal harbor, where the rolling pride
Of Israel's foes might safe at anchor ride,
Defy all dangers, and ev'n tempests scorn,
Though Judah's God should thunder in the storm.   365

Here Israel's laws, the dull Levitic rolls,
At once a clog to empire and to souls,
Are the first martyrs to the fire they doom
To make great Baal's triumphant legends room.
But ere their hands this glorious work can crown,   370
Their long-known foe, the Sanedrin, must down:
Sanedrins, the free-born Israel's sacred right,
That God-like balance of imperial might,
Where subjects are from tyrant-lords set free

352–53. James' conversion, followed by his marriage to Mary of Modena (1673), evoked violent protestations from Commons. His unpopularity increased immeasureably with the anti-French administration that followed the fall of the Cabal and was culminated by evidence of his connection with Coleman (the Duchess of York's secretary) during the early investigations of the Popish Plot. Though he was forced to retire to The Hague, the great uneasiness still felt by many Englishmen encouraged the pretensions of Monmouth and brought on the stormy sessions of the Exclusion parliaments. Cf. *Absalom and Achitophel*, 796.

366–67. *Israel's laws:* Both the laws of succession, which forbid a Catholic monarch (James was the true but not the legal heir), and the religious laws, which were often applied more against nonconforming Protestants than against Catholics. These latter laws would have included a great deal of the "Clarendon Code" as well as the later Test Act (1681).

371. *Sanedrin:* The judicial assembly of the later Jewish commonwealth, said to be derived from the group of seventy elders "whom Moses was directed (Numbers 11:16–

From that wild thing unbounded man would be,   375
Where pow'r and clemency are pois'd so even,
A constitution that resembles Heav'n.
So in th' united great Three-One we find
A saving with a dooming Godhead join'd.
(But why, oh why! if such restraining pow'r   380
Can bind Omnipotence, should kings wish more?)
A constitution so divinely mix'd,
Not Nature's bounded elements more fix'd.
Thus earth's vast frame, with firm and solid ground,
Stands in a foaming ocean circl'd round;   385
Yet this not overflowing, that not drown'd.
But to rebuild their altars, and install
Their molten gods, the Sanedrin must fall;
That constellation of the Jewish pow'r,
All blotted from its orb, must shine no more;   390
Or, stamp'd in Pharaoh's darling mold, must quit
Their native beams for a new-model'd light;
Like Egypt's sanedrins, their influence gone,
Flash but like empty meteors round the throne:
That that new lord may Judah's scepter wield,   395
To whom th' old brickill taskmasters must yield;
Who, to erect new temples for his gods,
Shall th' enslav'd Israel drive with iron rods.

---

17) to associate with him in the government of the Israelites" (*A Dictionary of the Bible*, 2, 1136). For Settle this is, historically, the English parliament.

375. Based in part on *Absalom and Achitophel*, 761–62 and the Hobbesian view (*Leviathan*, Bk. II, ch. 18) discussed there. Settle is replying throughout this passage to Dryden's argument in 753–68.

384–85. The traditional view of the earth.

387. *their:* i.e. the idolatrous followers of Baal.

391. *Pharaoh:* The French king, Louis XIV.

392. *new-model'd:* Settle uses ironically the phrase which the Tory propagandists had taken from Cromwell's hated new-model Army and applied to the many extreme Protestant sects.

393. *Egypt's sanedrins:* The French parlement, whose powers were vigorously curtailed under the personal government of Louis XIV.

395. James was appointed High Commissioner of Scotland, following Charles' illness in Aug. 1679, and replaced Lauderdale's suppressive royalism with a combination of concession and repression that broke the extreme theocrats of Scottish Presbyterianism.

396. *brickill:* Brick kiln. The well-known incident is recounted in Exodus 5:5–19.

If they want bricks for his new walls t' aspire,
To their sad cost, he'll find 'em straw and fire.   400

All this t' effect, and their new fabric build,
Both close cabals and foreign leagues are held:
To Babylon and Egypt they send o'er,
And both their conduct and their gold implore.
By such abettors the sly game was play'd: 405
One of their chiefs—a Jewish renegade,
Highborn in Israel, once Michal's priest,
But now in Babylon's proud scarlet dress'd—
'Tis to his hands the plotting mandates come,
Subscrib'd by the apostate Absalom.   410
Nay, and to keep themselves all danger-proof,
That none might track the Belial by his hoof,
Their correspondence veil'd from prying eyes.
In hieroglyphic figures they disguise.
Hush'd as the night in which their plots combin'd,   415

400. *straw and fire:* i.e. for burning heretics. The writ *De Haeritico Comburendo* was not repealed until 1677. For Whig use of the theme, see *The Tories' Confession,* 12 n.

402. Two of Coleman's letters, seized by the Council on 29 Sept. 1678, were ordered printed along with that of the Duke. All were addressed to Père La Chaise, Louis XIV's confessor and almoner, and bore out Oates' charges of Jesuit "consults" as well as intrigues to have Louis send sufficient money to allow Charles to dissolve the parliament.

403. *Babylon:* Rome. Coleman was also in correspondence with the papal nuncio at Brussels in hopes of obtaining papal support for funds. He was later sent there by York.

406. Coleman also corresponded with Philip Thomas Howard, "known as Cardinal Norfolk, at the Roman court. In 1672, Howard was appointed bishop-elect of England with a see 'in partibus' but not consecrated. In 1675, he was created cardinal by Clement X, and in 1679 was nominated by Innocent XI Cardinal Protector of England and Scotland" (Pollock, *The Popish Plot,* p. 34 and n.). He had been first chaplain and grand almoner to Queen Catherine until popular feeling forced him to leave England in 1674.

407. Cardinal Howard was the third son of Henry, third earl of Arundel.
Michal: Biblically, Saul's second daughter and David's wife. As a result of her reproof of David's dancing uncovered before the Ark, she was cursed with sterility (II Samuel 6:23). Historically, the reference is to Charles II's childless queen, Catherine of Braganza.

412. *Belial:* The spirit of evil personified; used from early times as a name for the Devil or one of the fiends and by Milton as the name of one of the fallen angels. Belial's hoof would, of course, have been cloven.

414. Coleman's correspondence was written in an arbitrary cipher which was understood only because the key to it was found with his letters.

And silent as the graves they had design'd,
Their ripening mischief 's to perfection sprung.
But oh! the much-loath'd David lives too long.
Their vultures cannot mount but from his tomb,
And with too hungry ravenous gorges come   420
To be by airy expectation fed.
No prey, no spoil, before they see him dead.
Yes, dead; the royal sands too slowly pass,
And therefore they're resolved to break the glass;
And to insure Time's tardy, dubious call,   425
Decree their daggers should his scythe forestall.
For th' execrable deed a hireling crew
Their Hell and they pick out; whom to make true,
An oath of force so exquisite they frame,
Sworn in the blood of Israel's paschal lamb.   430
If false, the vengeance of that sword that slew
Egypt's firstborn, their perjur'd heads pursue.
Strong was the oath, the imprecation dire;
And for a viand, lest their guilt should tire,
With promis'd Paradise they cheer their way;   435
And bold 's the soldier who has Heav'n his pay.

    But the ne'er-sleeping Providence that stands
With jealous eyes o'er Truth's up-lifted hands;
That still in its lov'd Israel takes delight,
Their cloud by day and guardian fire by night;   440
A ray from out its fiery pillar cast
That overlook'd their driving Jehu's haste.

426. Besides plans to poison and shoot the King, Oates pointed to at least two schemes to stab him to death: one was to be carried out by Fathers Conyers and Anderton; the other, by the "four Irish ruffians" who were said to have been paid £80. (Lane, *Oates*, pp. 93, 99–100; also summarized in Henry Care's *History of the Damnable Popish Plot* (1680) [C 522], p. 107).

430. *Israel's paschal Lamb:* Cf. *Absalom and Achitophel*, 576, where the reference is to Lord Howard of Escrick's reputed taking of the sacrament while in the Tower by using lamb's wool (hot ale mixed with the pulp of roasted apples) for wine. See Kinsley, ed., *Dryden, 4*, 1891, and *Absolon's IX Worthies*, 1682 [A 110].

431–32. Cf. Exodus 11–12.

441. Luttrell: "discovery of the Popish Plot."

442. *Jehu:* The founder of Israel's fifth dynasty came to the throne through intrepid daring and secret plotting as well as a policy of total extermination of the house of Ahab, his predecessor. Settle refers only to his ruthless rise to power and his fanatic

All's ruin'd and betray'd: their own false slaves
Detect the plot and dig their masters' graves:
Not oaths nor bribes shall bind when great Jehovah saves.   445
The frighted Israelites take the alarm,
Resolve the traitors' sorceries t' uncharm;
Till cursing, raving, mad, and drunk with rage,
In Amnon's blood their frantic hands engage.

Here let the ghost of strangl'd Amnon come,   450
A specter that will strike amazement dumb;
Amnon, the proto-matyr of the plot,
The murder'd Amnon, their eternal blot;
Whose too bold zeal stood like a Pharos light,

---

zeal and dissimulation, not to his destruction of the Baal worship of Ahab. See II Kings
9–10.

443. *their own false slaves:* Settle's phrase is probably intentionally ambiguous. If
meant as approbation of the underlings whom the Jesuits incorrectly considered true
to their cause, it would include Oates, Bedloe, and Prance. If pejorative, it would
refer to Turberville, Dugdale, and Haynes, informers against the Catholics during the
heat of the Plot, who gave evidence against Stephen College, "the Protestant Joiner,"
at his trial in Aug. 1681.

447. *Resolve:* i.e. in the subsequent sessions of the Council and of the Parliament.

449. *Amnon's:* Historically, Sir Edmund Berry Godfrey, the justice who took Oates'
deposition and whose murder, one month later, gave life and substance to the Popish
Plot. Settle's choice of Amnon has at least two arguments that strongly recommend
it, though it would appear at first to include one overwhelming fault. This apparent
difficulty arises from the biblical narrative in which Amnon is guilty of violating
the virgin Tamar (Absalom's sister) and then, revolted by her, of exposing her to
the world in so harsh a manner that Absalom (unable to incite the indignant David
to punish his eldest son) plots and performs his avenging murder. By a particularly
ingenious twist (459), Settle turns this seemingly intractable material to his own end.
Further, he presses two arguments of undoubted force. The first is his implication
not only that James (Absalom) was responsible for plotting Godfrey's murder, but
also that Charles (David) was deeply disturbed by the exposure of the plot, though
he would never have condoned the killing. Both of these suspicions were being hinted
at by Whig writers at this time. Secondly, Settle is capable of keeping to the story
of Absalom in a way that Dryden had avoided, and indeed of suggesting (again, as
Dryden did not wish to do) that with this murder Absalom had entered into a course
of action that would end with rebellion and death. Monmouth's rebellion ironically
proved Dryden as wrong in omitting this argument as James' ascension proved Settle
wrong (ironically) in using it.

450. Godfrey's body was found at the foot of Primrose Hill on Oct. 17; the decision of
the jury was that he had been strangled to death. Settle stresses this point, since
L'Estrange, Thompson, and the extreme Tories were attempting to establish suicide.

454. *Pharos light:* Pharos is an island off Alexandria on which stood a famous tower
lighthouse; the word was used for any lighthouse or beacon to direct mariners.

Israel to warn, and track their deeds of night;   455
Till the sly foe, his unseen game to play,
Put out the beacon to secure his way.
Baal's cabinet-intrigues he open spread,
The ravish'd Tamar for whose sake he bled.
T' unveil their temple and expose their gods   460
Deserv'd their vengeance's severest rods.
Wrath he deserv'd, and had the vial full.
To lay those devils had possess'd his soul,
His silenc'd fiends from his wrung neck they twist;
Whilst his kind murd'rer's but his exorcist.   465
Here draw, bold painter (if thy pencil dare
Unshaking write what Israel quak'd to hear),
A royal altar pregnant with a load
Of human bones beneath a breaden god.
Altars so rich not Moloch's temples show;   470
'Twas Heaven above, and Golgotha below.
Yet are not all the mystic rites yet done:
Their pious fury does not stop so soon,

456, 457. *his:* i.e. the foe.

457. *beacon:* Settle might well be recalling the famous set of Beacon pamphlets of 1652 which had certain vague parallels to the contemporary situation. The first pamphlets (*A Beacon Set on Fire* [Thomason E 675 (14)] and *A Second Beacon Fired* [Thomason E 675 (29)]) attempted to warn against "the vigilancy of Jesuits" and "the former actings of the Papists in their secret plots and now discovering their wicked designs to set up popery." The reply (*The Beacons Quenched* [Thomason E 678 (3)]) claimed that these were "the Macchiavellian designs of the Presbyterians . . . to bring an odium upon the Parliament and army."

459. Settle's arresting device for aligning the biblical story with the historical situation is to make Tamar the embodiment of the entire Popish Plot. In this way, Tamar becomes a Duessa-like object of disapproval, while the ravishment and the violation of false temples receives the fullest praise.

462–65. An ironic presentation of the Jesuits' reasoning.

466. This conventional form is traced by Osborne, *Advice-to-a-Painter Poems, 1633–1856.*

468. The medieval Church made it a rule that no altar could be consecrated unless it contained a relic, a practice that Protestants rejected. Here, Settle implies that Godfrey was a human sacrifice on York's altar of Baal.

469. *breaden god:* A parallel to the molten god, the golden calf, which was the object of the Israelites' idolatry (Exodus 32:1–6 and Deuteronomy 9:12–21). Historically, Settle is alluding to the basic Protestant departure from Rome on the validity of transubstantiation.

470. *Moloch:* A Canaanite idol, the Baal-like fire god of the destructive element, to whom children were sacrificed as burnt offerings (Leviticus 18:21).

But, to pursue the loud-tongu'd wounds they gave,
Resolves to stab his fame beyond the grave   475
And in eternal infamy to brand
With Amnon's murder, Amnon's righteous hand.
Here with a bloodless wound, by hellish art,
With his own sword they gore his lifeless heart.
Thus in a ditch the butcher'd Amnon lay,   480
A deed of night enough to have kept back the day,
Had not the sun in sacred vengeance rose,
Asham'd to see, but prouder to disclose,
Warm'd with new fires, with all his posting speed,
Brought Heav'n's bright lamp to show th' infernal deed.   485

What art thou, Church! when faith to propagate
And crush all bars that stop thy growing state,
Thou break'st through Nature's, God's, and human laws,
Whilst murder 's merit in a church's cause.
How much thy ladder Jacob's does excel,   490
Whose top's in heaven like his, but foot in Hell;
Thy cause's bloody champions to befriend,
For fiends to mount as angels to descend.

This was the stroke did th' alarm'd world surprise,
And even to infidelity lent eyes: 495
Whilst sweating Absalom in Israel pent,
For fresher air was to bleak Hebron sent.
Cold Hebron, warm'd by his approaching sight,
Flush'd with his gold and glow'd with new delight.

475–79. Godfrey's body had been pierced by a sword after—according to medical evidence—his death. This gave rise to the story that he had committed suicide, that his relatives had found him, and that, in order not to lose his estate (which they would have if he had been officially declared a suicide), they had staged the murder.

496–97. Actually, James had withdrawn to Antwerp and then The Hague in March 1679. He returned to England at the time of Charles' illness in Aug., received his post in Scotland at the end of Sept., left Whitehall for the north on 27 Oct., and arrived with his entourage in Edinburgh on 24 Nov. There, "their Royal Highnesses . . . were received with all the splendor and joy imaginable by the Lord Lieutenant, lords of the council, and magistrates of the city" (Luttrell, *Brief Relation, I,* 27).

497. *Hebron:* Biblically, the city where David established the seat of his government during his reign over Judah (II Samuel 5:5). Historically, Edinburgh.

Till sacred all-converting interest   500
To loyalty (their almost unknown guest)
Op'd a broad gate, from whence forth-issuing come
Decrees, Tests, Oaths, for well-sooth'd Absalom.
Spite of that guilt that made even angels fall,
An unbarr'd heir shall reign; in spite of all   505
Apostacy from Heav'n, or Nature's ties,
Though for his throne a Cain-built palace rise.
No wonder Hebron such devotion bears
T' imperial dignity and royal heirs;
For they, whom chronicle so high renowns   510
For selling kings, should know the price of crowns.

    Here, glorious Hushai, let me mourn thy fate,
Thou once great pillar of the Hebron state:
Yet now to dungeons sent, and doom'd t' a grave.
But chains are no new sufferings to the brave.   515

503. Under James's rule, the Scottish Parliament in 1681 passed an act completely securing the legitimate succession without regard for difference of religion. The same parliament passed the complex and contradictory Test Act which favored a royal prerogative and which Argyll accepted only "as far as it was consistent with itself and the Protestant faith."

507. *Cain-built palace:* Settle again connects James with the plots to murder his brother. Toward the end of 1680, the Duke was evidently "willing to entertain a project of civil war, in which he was promptly encouraged by Louis XIV" (*DNB* and references therein).

511. *for selling kings:* On 5 May 1646, Charles I surrendered to the Scottish army at Newark and was taken to Newcastle. For the rest of the year he unsuccessfully tried to play one faction against the other; finally, on 30 Jan. 1647, the Scottish army, having received the first payment due them for their service, marched homeward, leaving Charles in the hands of the English commission that conducted him to Holmby House, his first stage on the road to the block.

512. *Hushai:* Biblically, the friend to whom David "confided the delicate and dangerous part of a pretended adherence to the cause of Absalom. His advice was preferred to that of Achitophel, and speedily brought to pass the ruin which it meditated" (*A Dictionary of the Bible, 1,* 842). Historically, Archibald Campbell, Earl of Argyll, whose opposition to James, culminating in his refusal to accept wholly the Scottish Test, made him a hero and martyr of the Protestant cause. Dryden's Hushai ("the friend of David in distress") is Halifax, Settle's Achitophel.

514. Argyll's trial, "marked by shameless quibbling and illegality on the part of the crown," ended with the equally illegal sentence of death and forfeiture of estates on 23 Dec. 1681 (*DNB*). While Charles intended to suspend the death sentence, it was generally supposed that execution was imminent. Argyll, therefore, escaped from prison in disguise on 20 Dec., making his way eventually to London and Brentford. That Settle does not mention his escape may possibly indicate the date of the passage's composition.

Witness thy pains in six years' bonds endur'd,
For Israel's Faith and David's cause immur'd.
Death, too, thou oft for Judah's crown hast stood,
So bravely fac'd in several fields of blood.
But from fame's pinnacle now headlong cast;   520
Life, honor, all are ruin'd at a blast.
For Absalom's great law thou durst explain,
Where but to pry, bold Lord, was to profane:
A law that did his mystic God-head couch,
Like th' ark of God, and no less death to touch.   525
Forgot are now thy honorable scars,
Thy loyal toils, and wounds in Judah's wars.
Had thy pil'd trophies, Babel-high, reach'd Heav'n,
Yet by one stroke from Absalom's thunder given,
Thy tow'ring glory 's level'd to the ground.   530
A stroke does all thy tongues of fame confound,
And *Traitor* now is all the voice they sound.
True, thou hadst law; that even thy foes allow;
But to thy advocates, as damn'd as thou,
'Twas death to plead it.

      Artless Absalon,   535
The bloody banner to display so soon!
Such killing beams from thy young daybreak shot;
What will the noon be if the morn 's so hot?
Yes, dreadful heir, the crowd Hebron awe.
So the young lion tries his tender paw: 540
At a poor herd of feeble heifers flies

516. In 1656, Argyll (then Lord Lorne) was strongly suspected of being in correspondence with the exiled Charles II. Early in 1657, he refused to take an oath renouncing the Stuarts and adhering to the Commonwealth; as a consequence, he was imprisoned until the Restoration. Again, in 1661, through the influence of Middleton, he was indicted on the capital charge of lease-making, with the sentence of death and forfeiture given on 26 Aug. but with the date of execution left to the king, who held it in suspension. Argyll remained in prison until 1663 when he was restored to his estates and the earldom.

520. Argyll had been captain of Charles II's Scottish lifeguard in 1650, fought at Dunbar, and remained in arms for a while thereafter. He was excepted from Cromwell's act of pardon in May 1654.

522. i.e. the contradictions and questionable legalities of the Test.

525. II Samuel 6:6–7.

534. *advocates:* Lockhart, Dalrymple, and Stuart.

Ere the rough bear, tusk'd boar, or spotted leopard dies.
Thus flush'd, great sir, thy strength in Israel try:
When their cow'd sanedrins shall prostrate lie
And to thy feet their slavish necks shall yield,   545
Then reign the princely savage of the field.

Yes, Israel's Sanedrin; 'twas they alone
That set too high a value on a throne,
Thought they had a God was worthy to be serv'd,
A Faith maintain'd, and liberty preserv'd;   550
And therefore judg'd, for safety and renown
Of Israel's people, altars, laws, and crown,
Th' anointing drops on royal temples shed
Too precious show'rs for an apostate's head.
Then was that great deliberate counsel giv'n,   555
An act of justice both to man and Heav'n,
Israel's conspiring foes to overthrow,
That Absalom should th' hopes of crowns forego.
Debarr'd succession! oh that dismal sound!
A sound at which Baal stagger'd and Hell groan'd;   560
A sound that with such dreadful thunder falls,
'Twas heard even to Semiramis' trembling walls.

But hold! Is this the Plot's last murd'ring blow,
The dire divorce of soul and body? No!
The mangl'd snake, yet warm, to life they'll bring,   565
And each disjointed limb together cling.
Then thus Baal's wise consulting prophets cheer'd
Their pensive sons, and call'd the scatter'd herd.

"Are we quite ruin'd! No, mistaken doom,
Still the great day, yes, that great day, shall come   570
(Oh, rouse, our fainting sons, and droop no more!),
A day whose luster, our long clouds blown o'er,

555. Bills of Exclusion had been introduced in 1679, 1680, and 1681 but had been
stopped by various means.

562. *Semiramis:* An Assyrian princess connected in myth with the fish and the dove
and in legend with the sexual luxury, incest, and corruption of the East. She was
often associated with Babylon and was reputed to have been mannish in her dress
and love of war. Here, the reference is undoubtedly to Rome.

Not all the rage of Israel shall annoy,
No, nor denouncing sanedrins destroy.
See yon North Pole, and mark Boötes Car: 575
Oh! we've those influencing aspects there,
Those friendly pow'rs that drive in that bright Wain,
Shall redeem all and our lost ground regain.
Whilst to our glory their kind aid stands fast,
But one plot more, our greatest and our last."   580

Now for a product of that subtle kind,
As far above their former births refin'd
As firmamental fires t' a taper's ray,
Or prodigies to Nature's common clay.
Empires in blood, or cities in a flame,   585
Are work of vulgar hands, scarce worth a name.
A cake of shewbread from an altar ta'en,
Mix'd but with some Levitical king-bane,
Has sent a martyr'd monarch to his grave.
Nay, a poor mendicant, Church-rake-hell slave   590
Has stabb'd crown'd heads; slight work to hands well-skill'd,

575. The astronomical references are meant to indicate Scotland.
North pole: The northern axis of the earth; also, Polaris, the star in Ursa Minor.
Boötes Car: "A northern constellation, the Wagoner, situated at the tail of Ursa Major. . . . A slow working star in the north pole, near to Charles's Wain, which it follows."
577. Again, Settle hints at Catholic influence on Charles. "Charles's Wain," the seven bright stars in Ursa Major, had long been the phrase connected with the Stuart cause.
585. *cities in a flame:* As officially recorded on the Monument, the fire of London was caused by the Catholics. In 1682, Sheriff Pilkington committed the error of voicing, before witnesses, the current rumor that York had been responsible for the conflagration. The Duke won his £100,000 suit for *scandalum magnatum.*
587. *shewbread:* One of the twelve symbolic loaves of bread placed each Sabbath upon the golden Table of the Lord within the Ark or the sanctuary.
588. *king-bane:* A nonce-word, formed on herbane, rat's bane, etc.; i.e. a poison.
589. *a martyred monarch:* The Holy Roman emperor, Henry VII. One story had him poisoned by the communion wafer, another by the sacramental wine given him by a Dominican friar.
590. François Ravaillac, who unsuccessfully attempted to enter the Feuillants and then the Jesuits, through rumors that Henri IV was planning to war on the Pope was led to assassinate the popular King (14 May 1610). Despite persistent reports that the assassin had been incited by those opposed to Henri's pro-Protestant policy, no evidence has ever been found in corroboration.

Slight as the pebble that Goliah kill'd.
But to make plots no plots, to clear all taints,
Traitors transform to innocents, fiends to saints,
Reason to nonsense, truth to perjury;   595
Nay, make their own attesting records lie,
And even the gaping wounds of murder whole:
Aye, this last masterpiece requires a soul.
Guilt to unmake, and plots annihilate,
Is much a greater work than to create.   600
Nay, both at once to be, and not to be,
Is such a task would pose a deity.
Let Baal do this, and be a god indeed:
Yes, t' his immortal honor 'tis decreed,
His sanguine robe, though dipp'd in reeking gore,   605
With purity and innocence all o'er
Shall dry, and spotless from the purple hue,
The miracle of Gideon's fleece outdo.
Yes, they're resolv'd, in all their foes' despite,
To wash their more than Ethiop treason white.   610

   But now for heads to manage the design,
Fit engineers to labor in this mine:
For their own hands, 'twere fatal to employ;
Should Baal appear, it would Baal's cause destroy.
Alas, should only their own trumpets sound   615
Their innocence, the jealous ears around
All infidels would the loath'd charmer fly,
And through the angel's voice the fiend descry.
No, this last game wants a new plotting set,

593. The reference is to the almost unintelligibly complex maneuverings known as the Meal Tub Plot, which the Whigs considered a sham plot on the Protestants. Probably as clear an explanation as is possible is that given by Pollock, *The Popish Plot*, pp. 204–13.

608. Gideon requested, as a sign and proof of God's salvation of Israel, that a fleece which he left on the ground be covered with dew while the ground itself was dry. On the following night, he asked that the reverse occur, and "it was dry upon the fleece only, and there was dew on all the ground" (Judges 6:36–40).

610. While the phrase "to paint an Ethiop white" was common enough, it became so attached (with the variation from *Ethiop* to *Moor*) to Sir John Moore, the pro-Court Lord Mayor of London at this time, that it is difficult to believe that Settle did not have him in mind here.

And Israel only now can Israel cheat.   620
In this machine their profess'd foes must move,
Whilst Baal, absconding, sits in clouds above,
From whence unseen he guides their hidden way,
For he may prompt, although he must not play.
This to effect, a sort of tools they find,   625
Devotion-rovers, an amphibious kind,
Of no religion, yet like walls of steel,
Strong for the altars where their princes kneel.
Imperial, not celestial, is their Test,
The uppermost, indisputably best.   630
They always in the golden chariot rode,
Honor their heav'n, and interest their god.

Of these than subtle Caleb none more great,
Caleb who shines where his lost father set;
Got by that sire, who, not content alone   635
To shade the brightest jewel in a crown,
Preaching ingratitude t' a court and throne,
But made his politics the baneful root
From whence the springing woes of Israel shoot,

625. *a sort of:* Used in the now obsolete sense of a number of persons associated together in some way; a band, company, group.

632. *honor:* In the sense of worldly position or court distinction.

633. *Caleb:* Biblically, Caleb, as a reward for his spying out Canaan with Joshua and ten others (Numbers 13–14), was promised land by Moses. Years later, when Joshua honored his claim, Caleb, in order to control the land, offered his daughter to whoever would take the city of Debir; Othoniel, his younger brother, succeeded (Joshua, 14:6–15; 15:13–19). Historically, the reference is to Lawrence Hyde, at this time Viscount Hyde of Kenilworth, who had previously (1679) been in the Tory ministry of the "young statesmen" (with Sunderland and Godolphin) known as "the chits." Settle may have heard of the coming marriage (July 1682) of Hyde's eldest daughter Mary to James Butler, Earl of Ossory (later Duke of Ormonde). Since Hyde supported the Exclusion Bill and opposed Halifax, Settle portrays him with little acrimony. The chief minister's "period of greatest power lasted from . . . November 1680 to the return of the Duke of York in May [1682]" (Evelyn, *Diary, 4,* 294 n. 1). Dryden's Caleb may be Arthur Capel, Earl of Essex. (See James Kinsley, "Historical Allusions in *Absalom and Achitophel*" *RES,* N.S. 6 [1955], pp. 292–94.)

634. *lost father:* Edward Hyde, Earl of Clarendon, Charles II's chief minister during the early years of the reign, whose unpopular measures led to his banishment in 1667.

638. Settle might have in mind Clarendon's outmoded view of constitutional monarchy or, more specifically, that series of measures repugnant to the Whigs known as the Clarendon Code.

When his great master's fatal Gordian ti'd,   640
He laid the barren Michal by his side
That the ador'd Absalom's immortal line
Might on Judea's throne forever shine.
Caleb, who does that hardy pilot make,
Steering in that hereditary track,   645
Blind to the sea-mark of a father's wrack.

    Next Jonah stands bull-fac'd, but chicken-soul'd,
Who once the silver Sanedrin controll'd,
Their gold-tipp'd tongue; gold his great council's bawd,
Till by succeeding sanedrins outlaw'd,   650
He was preferr'd to guard the sacred store.
There, lordly rolling in whole mines of ore,
To dicing lords a cully favorite,
He prostitutes whole cargoes in a night.
Here to the top of his ambition come,   655
Fills all his sails for hopeful Absalom.
For his religion 's as the season calls,
God's in possession, in reversion Baal's.
He bears himself a dove to mortal race,
And though not man, he can look Heav'n i'th' face.   660

640. *Gordian:* An indissoluble bond; here, the marriage knot.

642. The marriage of Clarendon's daughter Anne to the Duke of York was concluded 3 Sept. 1660. Clarendon was unjustly accused of having encouraged Charles II's marriage to Catherine of Braganza, knowing beforehand that the future queen was unable to produce an heir.

647 *Jonah:* Edward Seymour (1633–1708), speaker of the House of Commons from 1673, during the Pension Parliament (1661–79). In 1665, he had been made Treasurer of the Navy, and shortly after being elected speaker, he became a member of the Privy Council. His court connections made him suspect to some Whigs, but he was again elected speaker in 1679. Charles, however, rejected him, and he cooperated with Halifax in opposing the Exclusion Bill (1680). Later that year, articles of impeachment were brought in against him for malversation in his office as Treasurer of the Navy, but this action was stopped through dissolution of the Parliament. Over the next two years, he continued to be connected with Halifax. Biblically, the reference is to the famed Hebrew prophet who fled from the Lord. Not only is he associated with the sea, but contemporary metaphor used his name for someone who raised storms in the state, and who must be cast overboard before the tempest can be allayed (see *OED* citation). Dryden connects Jonas with Sir William Jones through a similarity of sound rather than sense.

653. *cully:* A dupe or gull who is cheated by sharpers and strumpets.

Never was compound of more different stuff,
A heart in lambskin, and a conscience buff.

Let not that hideous bulk of honor scape,
Nadab, that sets the gazing crowd agape:
That old kirk-founder, whose coarse croak could sing   665
The Saints, the Cause, No Bishop and No King:
When greatness clear'd his throat, and scour'd his maw,
Roar'd out Succession, and the Penal Law.
Not so of old: another sound went forth,
When in the region from Judea north,   670
By the triumphant Saul he was employ'd,
A huge fang tusk to gore poor David's side.
Like a proboscis in the tyrant's jaw,
To rend and root through government and law.

662. *buff:* A course, stout leather made of ox-hide.

664. *Nadab:* Biblically, Aaron's son, who, with his brother Abihu, was struck by fire for offering "strange fire before the Lord" (Leviticus 10:1–2). Historically, John Maitland (1616–82), Duke of Lauderdale, early (1641–43) an ultra covenanter and one of the commissioners of the Solemn League and Covenant, though he increased his ties with the Royalist cause in the ensuing years and was with Charles II at Worcester. From 1660–80, he was Secretary for Scottish Affairs, with the aim of making the crown absolute there both in state and church.

666. *the Saints:* The term applied to certain Puritanical sects, especially during the Commonwealth. See *The Medal Revers'd*, 9 n.

the Cause: The Good Old Cause, the phrase used by the Commonwealth's men to describe their faction.

No Bishop and No King: The epigram, attributed to James I at the Hampton Court Conference (1604), summarized the interdependence of episcopacy and monarchy. It was a Stuart maxim, confirmed by events, that Scottish Presbyterianism aimed at the overthrow of the crown.

667. Maitland was created Earl of Lauderdale in 1672, though his extreme monarchism had begun some twenty to twenty-five years earlier.

668. Lauderdale naturally favored the succession of York. While he was not pro-Catholic (voting for condemnation of Stafford in 1680), he rigorously suppressed conventicles during his later administration.

671. From 1643 until 1648, Lauderdale was one of the Scottish Commissioners, though his sympathies were far from those of his colleagues whose actions caused the defeat of Charles I.

672. Again, Charles I and II are referred to as David.

673. *proboscis:* Though Settle may be using the word in its literal sense of any appendage for providing food (674), he seems incorrectly to be applying it to a tusk (672).

674. *root:* There would undoubtedly be overtones of the famous "Root and Branch" Petition of 1640 to Settle's contemporaries.

His hand that Hell-penn'd League of Belial drew,   675
That swore down kings, religion overthrew,
Great David banish'd and God's prophets slew.
Nor does the Court's long sun so powerful shine
T' exhale his vapors or his dross refine;
The metal is not mended by the stamp.   680
With his rank oil he feeds the royal lamp.
To sanedrins an everlasting foe,
Resolv'd his mighty hunter's overthrow.
And true to tyranny as th' only gem
That truly sparkles in a diadem,   685
To Absalom's side does his old Covenant bring,
With *State* raz'd out, and interlin'd with *King.*
But Nadab's zeal has too severe a doom;
Whilst serving an ungrateful Absalom,
His strength all spent his greatness to create,   690
He's now laid by, a cast-out drone of state.
He rous'd that game by which he is undone,
By fleeter coursers now so far outrun,
That fiercer, mightier Nimrod in his chase,
Till quite thrown out and lost, he quits the race.   695

   Of low-born tools, we bawling Shimei saw,
Jerusalem's late, loud-tongu'd Mouth of Law.

675. *League of Belial:* The Solemn League and Covenant.

677. *Great David:* Here, Charles II.

God's prophets: The Independent sects, against which the Covenanters fought vigorously. It is possible, but highly doubtful, that Settle is alluding to the other extreme of the religious spectrum, Archbishop Laud and his followers.

680. Coinage bore the sovereign's image.

682. From Jan. 1674, there were unsuccessful attempts by Commons to remove Lauderdale from office.

683. *mighty hunter's:* i.e. Nimrod. Cf. Genesis 10:9 and "that fiercer, mightier Nimrod" (i.e. York), 694. A strong tradition, coming from Josephus, made Nimrod a type of violence and insolence, a hunter of people, and, perhaps through false etymology, a rebel.

690. In 1680, Lauderdale's health gave way. James replaced him as commissioner in 1681, and his other offices were taken in the following year. About four months after this poem's appearance, he died at Tunbridge Wells, "worn out with . . . the toils of his earlier days" (*DNB*).

693. *coursers:* Those who relentlessly chase or pursue, as well as horses or dogs used for hunting.

696. *Shimei:* Biblically, Shimei cursed David, casting stones, dust, and imprecations on the royal party as it fled from Absalom (II Samuel 16:5–13). Very likely a part of

By blessings from almighty bounty given,
Shimei no common favorite of Heaven;
Whom, lest posterity should lose the breed,   700
In five short moons indulgent Heav'n rais'd seed;
Made happy in an early-teeming bride,
And laid a lovely heiress by her side;
Whilst the glad father's so divinely bless'd
That, like the stag proud of his brow so dress'd,   705
He brandishes his lofty City crest.
'Twas in Jerusalem, was Shimei nurs'd;
Jerusalem, by Baal's prophets ever curs'd,
The greatest block that stops 'em in their way,
For which she once in dust and ashes lay.   710
Here to the bar this whiffling lurcher came,

---

his feeling resulted from David's slaughter of the sons of Saul. The King refused to
allow Abushai to attack the Benjamite, and when David returned after his successful
campaign, Shimei, in abject penitence, was the first to meet him at the edge of the
Jordan. In the general amnesty of the restoration, David again protected Shimei
(II Samuel 19:18–23), who, though he eventually found favor at court, was never free
of the King's suspicions (I Kings 2:8–9). Historically, Sir George Jeffreys, whose
"voluble tongue and stentorian voice" had helped him obtain the position of common
sergeant of London (1671). During the next few years, Jeffreys, who was to refer to
himself as "the mouthpiece of the City," increasingly devoted himself to Court in-
terests, becoming York's solicitor general (1677), City Recorder (1678), and Chief
Justice of Chester (1680). His attempt to rally the "Abhorrers" led to a Commons
reprimand and, though he took part in trying some of Oates' victims, he devoted
himself principally to breaking the Whig hold on the City. Jeffreys, who came from
an undistinguished Welsh family, received his knighthood in 1671 and a baronecy
ten years later. See also *Midsummer Moon*, 174–224 and notes thereto. Dryden's
Shimei is the Whig sheriff, Slingsby Bethel.

701. Jeffreys' second marriage to Lady Ann Jones, the widowed daughter of the
former Lord Mayor, Sir Thomas Bludworth, produced a daughter within eight months.
Rumor had it that the child's father was Sir John Trevor, Jeffreys' cousin. See Hyde,
Judge Jeffreys, pp. 87–90; also, *A Westminster Wedding, or the Town Mouth* (" 'Tis
said when George did dragon slay") (1679), 43ff.

702–03. Probably an allusion to Jeffreys' first marriage to Sarah Neesham (1667),
which produced at least seven children in eleven years. Sarah had been the com-
panion of a rich heiress whom Jeffreys, then a poor law student, courted surrepti-
tiously. When the affair was discovered, Sarah, who had acted as go-between, was
dismissed; Jeffreys is said to have married her out of a sense of his responsibility for
her distress.

705. i.e. with horns, the sign of a cuckold.

710. A reference to the fire of London.

711. *whiffling:* Swaggering, bragging; also vacillating; used for a contemptlible or
shifty person.

And bark'd to rouse the nobler hunter's game.
But Shimei's lungs might well be stretch'd so far;
For, steering by a Court-ascendant star,
For daily oracles, he does address   715
To the Egyptian beauteous sorceress.
For Pharaoh, when he wisely did essay
To bear the long-sought golden prize away,
That fair enchantress sent whose magic skill
Should keep great Israel's sleeping dragon still.   720
Thus by her powerful inspirations fed,
To bite their heels, this City-snake was bred,
Till Absalom got strength to bruise their head.
Of all the heroes since the world began,
To Shimei, Joshua was the bravest man.   725
To him, his tutelar saint, he prays, ". . . and oh,
That great Jerusalem were like Jericho!"
Then bellowing loud, for Joshua's spirit calls,
Because his ram's horn blew down city walls.

    In the same role have we grave Corah seen,   730
Corah, the late chief scarlet abbethdin;

---

lurcher: One who pilfers or filches in a mean manner; a petty thief, swindler, or rogue. Also, a cross-breed dog used by poachers.

712. *nobler hunter's:* i.e. York's.

716. *Egyptian sorceress:* Louise de Kéroualle, Duchess of Portsmouth and Charles II's mistress. Her influence was, to a great extent, responsible for Jeffreys's advance. See *Midsummer Moon,* 221 and n.

729. A reference to Jeffreys' part in developing the attack on the London corporation through the writ of Quo Warranto, delivered in Dec. 1681.

730. *same role:* Of king's sergeant.

Corah: Biblically, the leader of the revolt against Moses and Aaron. He and his 250 followers, angered at having only inferior offices or being totally excluded from the priesthood, challenged Moses and, as a result, were consumed by Jehovah's fire while their households were swallowed up in an earthquake. The destruction of the bold, haughty, and ambitious leader firmly established the priesthood in Aaron's line (Numbers 16). Historically, Sir William Scroggs, whose early support of Oates and the Popish Plot turned, with suspicious speed at Wakeman's trial, to a questioning of the validity of the evidence of both Oates and Bedloe as well as (during the Meal Tub Plot) that of Dangerfield. His servility to the Court led to an unsuccessful attempt at impeachment (7 Jan. 1681), but he was nevertheless removed as lord chief justice in April 1681. Settle's suggestion is, perhaps, that Scroggs and the other Court-appointed justices were attempting to take from the parliament judicial supremacy of England. Dryden's Corah is Titus Oates.

731. *abbethdin:* "A rabbinical term for a certain officer of the high court of justice

Corah, who luckily i'th' Bench was got
To rate the bloodhounds off to save the Plot;
Corah, who once against Baal's impious cause
Stood strong for Israel's Faith and David's laws.   735
He pois'd his scales and shook his ponderous sword,
Loud as his father's Bashan-bulls he roar'd;
Till by a dose of foreign ophir drench'd,
The fever of his burning zeal was quench'd.
Ophir, that rescu'd the Court-drugster's fate,   740
Sent in the nick to gild his pills of state;
Whilst the kind skill of our law-empiric
Sublim'd his mercury to save his neck.

---

of the Jews" (Noyes's note to *Absalom and Achitophel*, 188). See also *The Second Part of Absalom and Achitophel*, 1014 n.

733. *To rate:* In hunting, to reprove or scold a dog vehemently.

the Plot: i.e. the so-called Protestant Plot.

734. Scroggs had presided over the Popish Plot trials of Staley, of Coleman, of Ireland, Pickering, and Grove, of Green, Berry, and Hill, of Whitehead, Harcourt, Fenwick, Gavan, and Turner, and of Langhorne between 18 Nov. 1678 and 14 June 1679. His intimidation of these defendants had made him a hero to the rabidly anti-Catholic.

737. *his father's Bashan bulls:* Scroggs "was the son of a one-eyed butcher near Smithfield Bars," according to Dugdale and others (cf. *DNB*). The "strong bulls of Bashan" were of almost proverbial fame (e.g. Psalm 22:12–13).

738. *Ophir:* A seaport, probably in Arabia, from which the Hebrews in the time of Solomon obtained gold. By itself, the word is used to denote fine gold (See *A Dictionary of the Bible*, 2, 637–42).

740. According to Oates, Sir George Wakeman, the Roman Catholic physician to Queen Catherine, was to receive up to £15,000 for poisoning Charles II. When he was tried on 18 July 1679, Scroggs totally reversed his previous position, now casting his opprobrium on Oates, Bedloe, and the entire plot.

The rumors that flew through London following the Court physician's acquittal are summed up by Luttrell (*Brief Relation, 1*, 17–18): "Sir George Wakeman, since his acquittal, is gone beyond the sea, thinking it not safe to stay here, people murmuring very much at his acquittal. And 'tis said that there was no fair dealing in that affair, for the Lord Chief Justice Scroggs was at Windsor about it . . . and the Portuguese Ambassador was to wait on [him] the day after Wakeman's acquittal. Some scruple not to say his Lordship had store of gold for this good piece of service." (For another, more political, explanation of Scroggs's *volte-face*, see North, *Examen*, p. 568.)

742. *empiric:* In the later seventeenth century, this adjective tended to have the opprobrious sense of being ignorantly presumptuous, being guided by mere experience without scientific knowledge; having to do with charlatanism and quackery.

743. *Sublim'd:* In alchemy, to heat a substance to a vapor, which then resolidifies on cooling; also, raised to an elevated or exalted position.

mercury: Figuratively used, mercury is an emblem of volatility of temperament, inconstancy. Alchemically, sublimed mercury is common or corrosive sublimate.

In law, they say, he had but a slender mite,
And sense he had less: for, as historians write,   745
The Arabian legate laid a snare so gay,
As spirited his little wits away.
Of the records of law, he fanci'd none
Like the Commandment Tables grav'd in stone;
And wish'd the Talmud such that sovereign sway,   750
When once displeas'd, might th' angry Moses play.
Only his law was brittle i'th' wrong place:
For had our Corah been in Moses' case,
The fury of his zeal had been employ'd
To build that calf which th' other's rage destroy'd.   755
Thus Corah, Baal's true fairy changeling made,
He bleated only as the Pharisees pray'd,
All to advance that future tyrant pow'r,
Should widows' houses gorge and orphans' tears devour.

Nor are these all their instruments. To prop   760
Their mighty cause and Israel's murmurs stop,
They find a sort of academic tools
Who, by the politic doctrine of their schools,
Betwixt reward, pride, avarice, hope, and fear,
Prizing their Heav'n too cheap, the world too dear,   765
Stand bold and strong for Absalom's defense:
Int'rest the thing, but conscience the pretense.

746. *Arabian legate:* The Portuguese ambassador.

750–51. *Talmud:* The body of Jewish civil and ceremonial law. The meaning here would seem to be that Scroggs would like to have civil law likewise graved on stone so that, when the sovereign power (Scroggs as head of the judiciary or Charles as head of the realm) is displeased with it, he might play the angry Moses and destroy it as Moses destroyed the tablets upon finding the Israelites worshipping the golden calf.

762ff. The doctrine of submission to the divinely appointed ruler "was supported by the Universities with all the collective authority they possessed. In 1681 the University of Cambridge presented an address to King Charles II, and took the opportunity to set forth in uncompromising terms the doctrine of divine right and passive obedience. 'We will still believe and maintain,' they declared, 'that our kings derive not their title from the people but from God; that to Him only they are accountable; that it belongs not to subjects either to create or to censure, but to honor and obey their sovereign, who comes to be so by a fundamental hereditary right of succession, which no religion, no law, no fault or forfeiture can alter or diminish'" (G. R. Cragg, *From Puritanism to the Age of Reason* [Cambridge, 1950], p. 164. Cragg notes that the Address is "printed in the *History of Passive Obedience,* p. 108").

These, to insure him for their Sion's king,
A right divine quite down from Adam bring,
That old Levitic engine of renown   770
That makes no taint of souls a bar t' a crown.
'Tis true, religion's constant champion vow'd,
Each open-mouth'd, with pulpit-thunder loud,
Against false gods and idol temples bawls;
Yet lays the very stones that raise their walls.   775
They preach up Hell to those that Baal adore,
Yet make 't damnation to oppose his pow'r.
So far this paradox of conscience run,
Till Israel's Faith pulls Israel's altars down.
Grant Heav'n they don't to Baal so far make way,   780
Those fatal wands before their sheepfolds lay;
Such motley principles amongst them thrown
Shall nurse that piebald flock that's half his own.
Nor may they say, when Moloch's hands draw nigher,
We built the pile, whilst Baal gives it fire.   785

   If monarchy in Adam first began,
When the world's monarch dug and his queen span,
His fig leaves his first coronation robe,
His spade his scepter and her wheel his globe,

768. *Sion's:* One of the hills of Jerusalem which became the center of Jewish life and worship; hence referring to the Israelites' religious system, the Christian Church, etc. The Universities were, of course, the training ground for the Anglican clergy.

771. Settle, alluding to the position given in the Cambridge Address (762 n.), is silently but effectively countering the Duke of Monmouth's taint of blood with the Duke of York's "taint of soul."

772. *religion's constant champion:* i.e. the Anglican clergy.

774. *idol:* Counterfeit, sham.

781. *wands:* Emblems of pastoral care.

783. *piebald:* Composed of irregular patches of black and white; mixed, motley, mongrel. The implication is that Anglicanism, particularly as taught by the Universities, tends strongly towards Romanism.

787. Settle counters the argument of direct descent of divine right by showing that such arguments give support to the Royalists' worst enemies, the Levellers. This latter group, being fully in the tradition of medieval egalitarianism, frequently made use of the doctrines of the earlier period, even to echoing the famous slogan associated with the Lollards:

   When Adam delved and Eve span,
   Who was then a gentleman?

789. *wheel:* Spinning wheel.

And royal birthright (as their schools assert),   790
Not kings themselves with conscience can divert;
How came the world possess'd by Adam's sons,
Such various principalities, powers, thrones,
When each went out and chose what lands he pleas'd,
Whilst a new family new kingdoms rais'd?   795
His sons assuming what he could not give,
Their sovereign sire's right heir they did deprive;
And from rebellion all their pow'r derive:
For were there an original majesty
Upheld by right divine, the world should be   800
Only one universal monarchy.
Oh cruel right divine, more full of fate
Than th' angel's flaming sword at Eden's gate,
Such early treason through mankind convey'd,
And at the door of infant Nature laid.   805
For right divine in Esau's just defense,
Why don't they quarrel with Omnipotence?
The firstborn Esau's right to Jacob giv'n,
And God's gift too, injustice charge on Heav'n.
Nay, let Heav'n answer this one fact alone,   810
Mounting a bastard, Jephtha, on a throne.
If kings and sanedrins those laws could make
Which from offending heirs their heads can take,
And a firstborn can forfeit life and throne,
And all by law, why not a crown alone?   815

790. *their:* i.e. the supporters of divine right.

806. Though Jacob received the Covenant blessing by deception from his father Isaac, nonetheless Esau, the older of the twins, bitterly recognized that divine approval rested with his younger brother when God granted him Canaan (Genesis 27–28).

811. Jephtha, the son of Gilead and a harlot, was cast out of his father's house by the legitimate children. He dwelt in Tob, at the head of a band, until the Gileadite elders called him back to save them from the invading Ammonites. Jephtha agreed to return if they would afterwards acknowledge his leadership. This they agreed to, and, with "the Spirit of the Lord upon him," he conquered and ruled. A more frequent use of this obvious analogy to Monmouth may have been avoided by the Whig writers of the times because of the terrible consequences of Jephtha's vow, which Settle very carefully omits. (See Judges 11.)

812–15. Since, argues Settle, English history affords precedents of princes and royal heirs being executed through the act of a (conquering) king or parliament, the passage of a bill that merely excludes York from the throne is perfectly legal and comparatively mild.

Strange-bounded lawmakers! whose pow'r can throw
The deadlier bolt, can't give the weaker blow.
A treasonous act—nay, but a treasonous *breath*—
Against offended majesty is death.
But, oh! the wondrous church-distinction given   820
Between the majesty of kings and Heav'n!
The venial sinner here, he that intrigues
With Egypt, Babylon; cabals, plots, leagues
With Israel's foes her altars to destroy,
A hair untouch'd, shall health, peace, crowns enjoy.   825

Truth's temple thus the exhalations bred
From her own bowels to obscure her head;
And Absalom already had subdu'd
Whole crowds of the unthinking multitude.
But through these wiles too weak to catch the wise,   830
Thin as their ephod-lawn, a cobweb net for flies,
The searching Sanedrin saw; and to dispel
Th' engend'ring mists that threat'ned Israel,
They still resolv'd their plotting foes' defeat
By barring Absalom th' imperial seat.   835

But here's his greatest tug. Could he but make
Th' excluding Sanedrin's resolves once shake,
Nay, make the smallest breach, or clashing jar
In their great council, push but home so far,

825. *crowns:* Settle himself comes dangerously close to treason here. While "crowns" can, of course, refer to coins (and thus to such men as Wakeman allegedly was), there is undoubtedly the suggestion that Charles was kept (and James shall inherit) his three kingdoms through secret leagues with France and Rome.

827. *head:* The higher clergy and, ultimately, the King as head of the Church.

831. *their ephod-lawn:* i.e., the priestly influence (signified by the ephod, the Jewish priests' garment) of the bishops (who wore lawn, or fine linen).

835. The Exclusion Bill was first read on 15 May 1679, and when it overrode the strong opposition, Charles dissolved the Parliament. At the next session, it again passed the Commons but was rejected by the Lords by a vote of 63 to 30, mainly through the efforts and influence of Halifax. In Jan. 1681, the Commons voted that no supplies should be granted until the Exclusion Bill passed, and that the Bill's opponents were traitors bought with French money; Charles dissolved the Parliament on the 18 Jan. Again, at the Oxford Parliament in March, an Exclusion Bill was pushed forward, and dissolution followed rapidly. The Bill proposed that, on Charles' death, the crown would pass to York's heirs, as if the Duke himself were dead.

And the great point's secur'd. —And lo! among   840
The princely heads of that illustrious throng,
He saw rich veins with noble blood new fill'd;
Others who honor from dependence held;
Some with exhausted fortunes to support
Their greatness, propp'd with crutches from a Court.   845
These for their country's right their votes still pass,
Mov'd like the water in a weather-glass,
Higher or lower, as the powerful charm
O'th' sovereign hand is either cool or warm.
Here must th' attack be made: for well we know   850
Reason and titles from one fountain flow:
Whilst favor men, no less than fortunes, builds,
And honor ever molds as well as gilds.
Honor, that still does even new souls inspire,
Honor, more powerful than the Heav'n-stol'n fire;   855
These must be wrought to Absalom's defense;
For though to baffle the whole Sanedrin's sense,
T' attempt impossibles, would be in vain,
Yet 'tis enough but to divide and reign.

Here, though small force such easy converts draws,   860
Yet 'tis thought fit in glory to their cause,
Some learned champion of prodigious sense,
With mighty and long-studi'd eloquence,
Should with a kind of inspiration rise
And the unguarded Sanedrin surprise;   865
And such resistless conquering reasons press
To charm their vanquish'd souls, that the success
Might look like conscience, though 'tis nothing less.

For this design, no head nor tongue so well
As that of the profound Achitophel.   870
—How! Great Achitophel? his hand? his tongue?

847. *weather-glass:* An early form of thermometer, used to measure temperature
of the air.
870ff. *Achitophel:* Biblically, one of David's privy councillors who, upon Absalom's
revolt, joined with the rebel and urged him to public acts that made reconciliation
impossible. To counteract his former confidant's advice, David sent Hushai, whose
counsel of caution prevailed. Achitophel, now despairing of success, returned to his

Babylon's mortal foe? he who so long
With haughty sullenness and scornful low'r,
Had loath'd false gods and arbitrary pow'r?
'Gainst Baal, no combatant more fierce than he   875
For Israel's asserted liberty;
No man more bold, with generous rage inflam'd,
Against the old ensnaring Test declaim'd.
Besides, he bore a most peculiar hate
To sleeping pilots, all earth-clods of State.   880
None more abhorr'd the sycophant, buffoon,
And parasite, th' excrescence of a throne;
Creatures who their creating sun disgrace,
A brood more abject than Nile's slime-born race.
Such was the brave Achitophel; a mind   885
(If but the heart and face were of a kind)
So far from being by one base thought deprav'd,
That sure half ten such souls had Sodom sav'd.
Here Baal's cabal Achitophel survey'd,
And dash'd with wonder, half despairing said,   890
"Is this the hand that Absalom must crown,
The founder of his temples, palace, throne?

---

home and hung himself (II Samuel 15:12–17:23). Historically, the statesman and
privy councillor, George Savile, Marquis of Halifax (1633–95), whose ideas coincided
with those of Shaftesbury's group until mid-1679. He had been active against the Test
Act, had supported Clarendon's motion prohibiting the marriage of future heirs to
Catholics, had angered Danby, and had been even more violently critical of the Cabal
than Shaftesbury, with whom he worked in procuring Lauderdale's dismissal. On the
question of succession, they parted company, for Halifax's objections to York were
only surpassed by his objections to Monmouth. Though favoring William of Orange
in theory, he was forced by the circumstances of the King's illness (Aug. 1679) to
counteract Shaftesbury by secretly summoning York from the Continent. Monmouth's
subsequent fall from favor put Halifax in the undesirable position of being the
champion of James' hereditary claim, even though he was opposed to exclusion and
to the power that its adoption would give the opposition. On 15 Nov. 1680, he bril-
liantly out-debated Shaftesbury and Essex, but his plan for a regency was defeated
and Commons' request that he be removed from the King's counsels was avoided by
dissolution. His anti-French, anti-Catholic views made him definitely disliked by York,
whose return from Edinburgh in mid-1682 marked the end of the Marquis's supremacy
at Court. Dryden's Achitophel is Halifax's political foe, Shaftesbury.

880–82. These may be specific references to Danby, to Lauderdale, and to "the
chits" (Hyde, Godolphin, and Sunderland).

884. *Nile's slime-born race:* The French ministry.

This, this, the mighty convert we must make?
Gods, h' has a soul not all our arts can shake."

At this a wiser, graver head stepp'd out,   895
And with this language chid their groundless doubt:
"For shame! No more! What is't that frights you thus?
Is it his hatred of our god, and us,
Makes him so formidable in your eye?
Or is't his wit, sense, honor, bravery?   900
Give him a thousand virtues more, and plant
Them round him like a wall of adamant,
Strong as the gates of Heaven, we'll reach his heart.
Cheer, cheer, my friends; I've found one mortal part:
For he has pride, a vast insatiate pride.   905
Kind stars, he's vulnerable on that side.
Pride that made angels fall, and pride that hurl'd
Entail'd destruction through a ruin'd world.
Adam from pride to disobedience ran:
To be like gods, made a lost, wretched man.   910
There, there, my sons, let our pour'd strength all fly!
For some bold tempter now to rap him high,
From pinnacles to mountain tops, and show
The gaudy glories of the world below."

At which the consult came to this design,   915
To work him by a kind of touch divine,
To raise some holy sprite to do the feat.
Nothing like dreams and visions to the great.
Did not a little Witch of Endor bring
A visionary seer t' a cheated king?   920

908. *Entail'd destruction:* The transmission, as an inalienable inheritance, of primal sin.

912. *to rap:* To take up and carry off, to transport.

913–14. Matthew 4:5, 8–9, recounts the temptation of Christ by the devil, who sets him on the pinnacle of the temple, and then on "an exceeding high mountain, and sheweth him all the kingdoms of the world, and the glory of them."

915. *consult:* The term constantly used by Oates to describe the surreptitious meetings of the Jesuits to carry out the Popish Plot.

919. *Witch of Endor:* On the eve of Saul's last engagement and at his request, she raised the spirit of Samuel, who foretold his downfall (I Samuel 28:7–23).

And shall their greater magic wants success,
Their more illustrious sorceries do less!

   This final resolution made, at last
Some mystic words and invocations pass'd,
They call'd the spirit of a late Court scribe,   925
Once a true servant of the plotting tribe
When both with foreign and domestic cost
He play'd the feasted Sanedrin's kind host.
H' had scribbled much, and, like a patriot bold,
Bid high for Israel's peace with Egypt's gold.   930
But since a martyr (Why! as writers think,
His master's hand had over-gall'd his ink.)
And by protesting Absalom's wise care,
Popp'd into brimstone ere he was aware.
Him from the grave they rais'd, in ample kind,   935
His sever'd head to his sere quarters join'd;
Then cas'd his chin in a false beard so well
As made him pass for Father Samuel.
Him thus equipp'd in a religious cloak,
They thus his new-made reverence bespoke: 940

925. *a late Court scribe:* Edward Coleman, the Duchess of York's Catholic secretary, whose treasonable correspondence with the French was seized as a result of Oates' accusation. He was tried on 27 Nov. 1678 and executed six days later. See also 402 n. and 406 n.

931. *martyr:* He was so addressed in an elegy found in the pocket of Henry Neville, a priest who was apprehended at Westminster in Dec. 1678. The poem, "To that Glorious Saint and Martyr, Mr. Edward Coleman," is reprinted in Care's *History of the Damnable Popish Plot* (1680), pp. 153–54.

932. The fourth of the five letters produced as evidence at Coleman's trial was "written as it were by the Duke of York, but really by Coleman (as the latter confessed to the House of Lords), adding his Highness' persuasions to Coleman's to obtain a loan from France." (Lane, *Oates,* p. 115; the letter is given in Howell, *State Trials, 7,* 54–55.)

934. Rumor had it that Coleman, even as he mounted the gallows, "had been made to believe that he should be pardoned . . . [but] finding himself deceived, he was heard to say, 'there is no faith in man'" (Howell, *State Trials, 7,* 78). This Macchiavellian tactic, not unlike that used by Lorenzo in *The Spanish Tragedy* (III, iv–vi), would have been attributed to York.

936. The brutal punishment for high treason included hanging, being cut down while still alive, emasculation, disemboweling, decapitation, and quartering. Coleman's family had been allowed to bury his remains.

sere: 1. dry, withered; 2. separate, distinct, various.

938. *Father Samuel:* See 919 n.

"Go, awful sprite, haste to Achitophel,
Rouse his great soul, use every art, charm, spell:
For Absalom thy utmost rhet'ric try.
Preach him Succession, roar'd Succession cry,
Succession dress'd in all her glorious pride,   945
Succession worshipp'd, sainted, deifi'd.
Conjure him by divine and human pow'rs,
Convince, convert, confound, make him but ours,
That Absalom may mount on Judah's throne,
Whilst all the world before us is our own."   950

The forward sprite but few instructions lack'd,
Straight by the moon's pale light away he pack'd,
And in a trice, his curtains open'd wide,
He sat him by Achitophel's bedside.
And in this style his artful accents ran: 955

"Hear, Israel's hope! thou more than happy man!
Belov'd on high, witness this honor done
By Father Samuel, and believe me, son,
'Tis by no common mandate of a god,
A soul beatifi'd, the blest abode   960
Thus low deserting, quits immortal thrones
And from his grave resumes his sleeping bones.
But Heav'n 's the guide, and wondrous is the way,
Divine the embassy: hear, and obey.
How long, Achitophel, and how profound   965
A mist of hell has thy lost reason drown'd?
Can the apostasy from Israel's Faith,
In Israel's heir, deserve a murmuring breath?
Or to preserve religion, liberty,
Peace, nations, souls, is that a cause so high   970
As the right heir from empire to debar?
Forbid it Heav'n, and guard him every star.
Alas, what if an heir of royal race
God's glory and his temples will deface,
And make a prey of your estates, lives, laws;   975

967ff. The arguments of passive obedience propounded by Coleman's ghost are startlingly similar to those voiced in the Cambridge Address. See 762ff. n.

Nay, give your sons to Moloch's burning paws;
Shall you exclude him? Hold that impious hand!
As Abraham gave his son at God's command,
Think still he does by divine right succeed.
God bids him reign, and you should bid them bleed.   980
'Tis true, as Heav'n's elected flock, you may
For his conversion, and your safety, pray.
But pray'rs are all. To disinherit him,
The very thought, nay, word itself 's a crime.
For that's the *means* of safety: but forbear,   985
For means are impious in the sons of pray'r.
To miracles alone your safety owe;
And Abraham's angel wait to stop the blow.
Yes, what if his polluted throne be strow'd
With sacrilege, idolatry, and blood;   990
And 'tis you mount him there, you're innocent still:
For he's a king, and kings can do no ill.
Oh Royal Birthright, 'tis a sacred name!
Rouse then, Achitophel; rouse up, for shame!
Let not this lethargy thy soul benumb;   995
But wake and save the God-like Absalom.
And to reward thee for a deed so great,
Glut thy desires, thy full-crown'd wishes meet;
Be with accumulated honors bless'd,
And grasp a Star t' adorn thy shining crest."   1000

     Achitophel, before his eyes could ope,
Dreamt of an ephod, miter, and a cope.
Those visionary robes t' his eyes appear'd;
For priestly all was the great sense he heard.
But priest or prophet, right divine, or all   1005
Together, 'twas not at their feebler call,
'Twas at the Star he wak'd; the Star but nam'd,
Flash'd in his eyes, and his rous'd soul inflam'd.

---

978. Cf. Genesis 22:1–2.

  982. *his conversion:* Halifax, in mid-1681, had gone far beyond prayer in his attempt
to have York give at least token recognition to Protestantism (Foxcroft, *A Character
of the Trimmer*, pp. 140–41).

  1000. *Star:* Most likely a reference to the insigne of the Order of the Garter.

A Star, whose influence had more powerful light
Than that miraculous wanderer of the night   1010
Decreed to guide the eastern sages' way:
Theirs to adore a God, his to betray.

Here the new convert, more than half inspir'd,
Straight to his closet and his books retir'd.
There, for all needful arts in this extreme,   1015
For knotty sophistry t' a limber theme,
Long brooding ere the mass to shape was brought,
And after many a tugging, heaving thought,
Together a well-order'd speech he draws,
With ponderous sounds for his much-labor'd cause.   1020
Then the astonish'd Sanedrin he storm'd,
And with such doughty strength the tug perform'd;
Fate did the work with so much conquest bless,
Wondrous the champion, glorious the success.
So powerful eloquence, so strong was wit;   1025
And with such force the easy windfalls hit.

But the entirest hearts his cause could steal
Were the Levitic chiefs of Israel.
None with more rage the impious thought runs down
Of barring Absalom pow'r, wishes, crown,   1030
With so much vehemence, such fiery zeal!
Oh, poor unhappy Church of Israel!
Thou feel'st the fate of the archangels' wars,
The Dragon's tail sweeps down thy falling stars.
Nay, the black vote 'gainst Absalom appear'd   1035
So monst'rous that they damn'd it ere 'twas heard.
For prelates ne'er in Sanedrins debate,
They argue in the Church, but not i'th' State;
And when their thoughts aslant towards Heav'n they turn,
They weigh each grain of incense that they burn;   1040
But t' Heaven's vicegerents, soul, sense, reason, all,

1028. The bishops in the House of Lords all voted against the Exclusion Bill.

1034. *Dragon's tail:* In astronomy, the descending node of the moon's orbit with the ecliptic.

1040. Incense, church organs, and absolution in High Church Anglicanism were elements of Roman ritual to which the sectarians had long and vehemently objected.

Or right, or wrong, like hecatombs must fall.
And when State business calls their thoughts below,
Then like their own church-organ-pipes they go.
Not David's lyre could more his touch obey;   1045
For as their princes breathe and strike, they play.
'Gainst royal will, they never can dispute,
But, by a strange tarantula struck mute,
Dance to no other tune but *Absolute*.
All acts of supreme power they still admire: 1050
'Tis sacred, though to set the world on fire;
Through Church infallibility they explode
As making human knowledge equal God,
Infallible in a new name goes down,
Not in the miter lodged, but in the crown.   1055
'Tis true, blest Deborah's laws they could forget
(But want of memory commends their wit!)
Where 'twas enacted treason not to own
Hers and her Sanedrin's right to place the crown.
But her weak heads o'th' Church, mistaken fools,   1060
Wanted the light of their sublimer schools,
For divine right could no such forces bring.
But wisdom now expands her wider wing,
And streams are ever deeper than the spring.
Besides, they've sense of honor; and who knows   1065
How far the gratitude of priest-craft goes?
And what if now like old Elisha fed,
To praise the sooty bird that brought 'em bread,
In pure acknowledgment, though in despite
Of their own sense, they paint the raven white.   1070

1048–49. Tarantism, or often tarantulism, was an hysterical malady characterized by an extreme impulse to dance; it prevailed as an epidemic in southern Italy from the fifteenth to the seventeenth century and was popularly attributed to the sting of a tarantula. The best cure was said to be music. Settle's tarantula is "strange" in that the symptoms ordinarily included a good deal of singing and occasional fits of laughing.

1058. The "laws" (1056) would probably include 13 Elizabeth c. 2 (1571), which was meant to offset the papal excommunication, and the famous Instrument of Association of 1584.

1067. *Elisha:* This should, of course, be Elijah (I Kings 17:6). Since Settle has here been corrosively setting forth the arguments of what is for him a cynical and pseudo-learned Anglican clergy, the common confusion of Elijah and Elisha may well be intentional.

Achitophel, charm'd with kind Fortune's smiles,
Flush'd with success, now glows for bolder toils.
Great wits perverted greatest mischiefs hold,
As poisonous vapors spring from mines of gold.
And proud to see himself with triumph bless'd,   1075
Thus to great Absalom himself address'd:

"Illustrious Terror of the World, all hail!
Forever like your conquering self prevail.
In spite of malice, in full luster shine;
Be your each action, word, and look, divine.   1080
Nay, though our altars you've so long forborne,
To your derided foes' defeat and scorn,
For your renown, we have those trumpets found,
Shall ev'n this deed your highest glory sound,
That, spite of the ill-judging world's mistake,   1085
Your soul still owns those temples you forsake.
Only by all-commanding honor driven,
This self-denial you have made with Heav'n;
Quitting our altars 'cause the insolence
Of profane sanedrins has driven you thence.   1090
A prince his Faith to such low slaves reveal?
'Twas treason though to God to bid you kneel!
And what though senseless, barking murmurers scold
And with a rage too blasphemously bold
Say Israel's crown 's for Esau's pottage sold?   1095
Let 'em rail on! and to strike envy dumb,
May the slaves live till that great day shall come
When their hush'd rage shall your keen vengeance fly
And, silenc'd with your royal thunder, die.
Nay, to outsoar your weak forefathers' wings,   1100
And to be all that Nature first meant kings,
Damn'd be the law that majesty confines,

1077. Settle's version of Halifax's views on the parliament and on succession is, of
course, colored by contemporary rumor, popular antipathy, and political enmity. For
the counter-arguments, see Foxcroft, *A Character of the Trimmer*, esp. chaps. VI–IX.
1095. Cf. Genesis 25:30–34. In concluding *The History of the Damnable Popish
Plot* (1680), Care employs the same idea: "For what shall the lay Roman Catholics
and their posterity get by exchanging their natural English birthright for slavery?"
(p. 363).

But doubly damn'd accursed sanedrins,
Invented only to eclipse a crown.
Oh, throw that dull Mosaic landmark down.   1105
The making sanedrins a part of pow'r
Nurs'd but those vipers which its sire devour.
Lodg'd in the palace, towards the throne they press,
For pow'r's enjoyment does its lust increase.
Allegiance only is in chains held fast;   1110
Make men ne'er thirst, is ne'er to let 'em taste.
Then, Royal Sir, be sanedrins no more;
Lop off that rank, luxurious branch of pow'r,
Those hungry scions, from the cedar's root,
That its imperial head towards Heav'n may shoot.   1115
When lordly sanedrins with kings give law,
And thus in yokes like mules together draw,
From Judah's arms the royal lion race
And Issachar's dull ass supply the place.
If kings o'er common mankind have this odds,   1120
Are God's vicegerents, let 'em act like gods.
As man is Heav'n's own clay, which it may mold
For honor or dishonor, uncontroll'd,
And monarchy is mov'd by heav'nly springs,
Why is not human fate i'th' breath of kings?   1125
Then, Sir, from Heav'n your great example take,
And be th' unbounded lord a king should make;
Resume what bold, invading slaves engross'd,
And only pow'r's effeminacy lost."

To this kind Absalom but little spoke,   1130
Only return'd a nod and gracious look:

1106–07. i.e., to have granted to parliament a part of royal power only nursed its
viprous inclination to devour its sire.
1114. *scions:* Suckers, shoots, or twigs.
1118. *race:* Scrape out, alter by erasure, tear or root out.
1119. *Issachar:* Cf. Genesis 49:14–15. Henry Care, attacking those whose materialistic
interests have made them "lukewarm Laodiceans," warns that Romanism is a "plot
upon the purse" and that "these crouching sons of Issachar . . . must bear as heavy
burdens as any" (*The History of the Damnable Popish Plot*, pp. 358–60). Settle's
Halifax scathingly alludes to the Country party's economic background; Dryden uses
the specific example of Tom Thynne.

For though recorded fame with pride has told
Of his great actings, wonders manifold,
And his great thinkings most diviners guess,
Yet his great speakings no records express.   1135

   All things thus safe; and now for one last blow,
To give his foes a total overthrow;
A blow not in Hell's legends match'd before:
The remov'd Plot 's laid at the enemy's door.
The old Plot forg'd against the saints of Baal   1140
(Cheat, perjury, and subornation all!),
Whilst with a more damn'd treason of their own,
Like working moles, they're digging round the throne;
Baal, Baal, the cry, and Absalom the name,
But David's glory, life, and crown the aim.   1145
Nay, if but a petition peep abroad,
Though for the glory both of Church and God
And to preserve even their yet unborn heirs,
There's blood and treason in their very prayers.
This unexampled impudence upheld,   1150
The government's best friends, the crown's best shield,
The great and brave, with equal treason brands.
Faith, honor, and allegiance, strongest bands
All broken, like the cords of Sampson, fall

1136ff. Though the really serious Whig would hardly have been so restrained (see, for example, *The History of Popish-Sham-Plots*, 1682 [H 2133]), Settle wisely restricts himself to the most important of the so-called Protestant Plots, the confused and confusing Meal Tub Plot. Happily, he approaches this "Ethnic Plot" (1160) on the comparatively simple lines of Dangerfield's two *Narratives* [D 192–93] on the Meal Tub Plot. Briefly, the Catholics are said to have concocted a sham Protestant plot which, with great denunciations of York and the papists, was to reestablish a commonwealth. This "plot" was to be discovered, thus discrediting Shaftesbury and his group. Like the original Popish Plot (*Dryden's* "ethnic plot"), this sham plot had a certain plausibility though even less basis in fact.

1140. *forg'd:* Made in fraudulent imitation of something else; made or devised in order to pass the spurious off as genuine.

1146. The petitions of the Country party for the sitting of a parliament were countered by the Court party with addresses of abhorrence of those petitions. The latter claimed that there was an invasion of royal prerogative and a threat of civil disobedience, while the former urged the danger to King, religion, and government from the Popish Plot.

1148, 1149. *their:* i.e. those who "earnestly pray" for a parliament.

Whilst th' universal leprosy taints all.   1155
These poisonous shafts with greater spleen they draw
Than the outrageous wife of Potiphar;
So the chaste Joseph, unseduc'd to her
Adult'ries, was pronounc'd a ravisher.

    This hellish Ethnic Plot the Court alarms;   1160
The traitors, seventy thousand strong, in arms,
Near Endor town lay ready at a call,
And garrison'd in airy castles all.
These warriors on a sort of coursers rid,
Ne'er lodg'd in stables, or by man bestrid.   1165
What though the steel with which the rebels fought
No forge e'er felt, or anvil ever wrought?
Yet this magnetic Plot, for black designs,
Can raise cold iron from the very mines.
To this were twenty underplots contriv'd   1170
By malice and by ignorance believ'd,
Till shams met shams, and plots with plots so cross'd,
That the true Plot amongst the false was lost.

    Of all the much-wrong'd worthies of the land
Whom this contagious infamy profan'd,   1175

1155. Cf. Pope's conclusion to *The Dunciad,* IV.656.

1157. On 7 Jan. 1680 Elizabeth Cellier, the Popish midwife who was the moving spirit of the Meal Tub Plot, and John Gadbury, the astrologer who was an accessory, stated that Sir Robert Peyton, wishing to associate himself with the Yorkists, had claimed that he could raise 20,000 men in two days time and 60,000 within a week (*The London Gazette,* No. 1476 [8–12 Jan. 1680]). While this charge was soon abandoned, it illustrates the plausibility to the contemporary of an alliance between the extreme left and right.

1162. Settle employs against the Court party one of its most effective bits of anti-Plot criticism. Oates, desirous of showing a clear and present danger, claimed that an army of foreigners had landed in Scotland and an army of Spanish pilgrims in England. Their precise location and maintenance was a matter of mystery, as *The Compleat Swearing-Master* remarked: "Forty thousand pilgrims there were,/Arm'd with black bills, that march'd in the air." Settle chides the Tories in his introductory Epistle to this poem: "Nay, you are so far now from your former niceties . . . about raising of armies . . . that you can swallow the raising of a whole Protestant army without either commission or commission officer. Nay, the very when, and how are no part of your consideration."

In the first rank the youthful Ithream stood,
His princely veins fill'd with great David's blood.
With so much manly beauty in his face,
Scarce his high birth could lend a nobler grace.
And for a mind fit for this shrine of gold,   1180
Heav'n cast his soul in the same beauteous mold;
With all the sweets of prideless greatness bless'd,
As affable as Abraham's angel-guest.
But when in wars his glittering steel he drew,
No chief more bold with fiercer lightning flew;   1185
Witness his trial of an arm divine,
Passing the ordeal of a burning mine:
Such forward courage did his bosom fill,
Starting from nothing, but from doing ill.
Still with such heat in honor's race he run,   1190
Such wonders by his early valor done,
Enough to charm a second Joshua's sun.
But he has foes; his fatal enemies
To a strange monster his fair truth disguise,
And show the Gorgon even to royal eyes.   1195
To their false perspectives, his fate he owes;

1176. *Ithream:* The sixth son born to David in Hebron. Settle probably chose this otherwise obscure name because Eglah, the mother of Ithream, is alone called David's wife (II Samuel 3:5; I Chronicles 3:3). Historically, James, Duke of Monmouth, the popular, handsome "Protestant Duke," born in 1649, the son of Charles II and Lucy Water. Rumors of a secret marriage of his parents had circulated for many years and culminated in the famous story of the Black Box, which was said to contain the marriage papers. Though Charles thrice denied Monmouth's legitimacy, the story was kept alive by the Country party's support of the young duke as successor to Charles.

1183. Cf. Genesis 18:1–22.

1184. Monmouth's most recent military victory had been over the Scottish rebels at Bothwell Bridge (1679).

1187. The heroism of Monmouth at the siege of Maastricht (1673) was noteworthy indeed. Not only did he daringly capture the counterscarp, but when the enemy sprang a mine which killed two officers and fifty men, it was he who rallied the forces and led the recapture of the position (See D'Oyley, *Monmouth,* p. 89).

1189. *starting:* Flinching, recoiling.

1192. Joshua's valor found such favor with God that He made the sun stand still "in the midst of Heaven" so that there would be sufficient light to carry out vengeance on the Amorites (Joshua 10:13).

1194. *disguise:* To transform, alter in appearance, disfigure.

1196. *perspectives:* Telescopes.

The spot 's i'th' glass, not in the star it shows.
Yet when by the imperial sentence doom'd,
The royal hand the princely youth unplum'd,
He his hard fate without a murmur took,   1200
And stood, with that calm, duteous, humble look,
Of all his shining honors unarray'd,
Like Isaac's head on Abraham's altar laid.
Yes, Absalom, thou hast him in the toil,
Rifled, and lost; now triumph in the spoil.   1205
His zeal too high for Israel's temples soar'd,
His God-like youth by prostrate hearts ador'd,
Till thy revenge from spite and fear began,
And, too near Heaven, took care to make him man.
Though Israel's King, God, laws, share all his soul,   1210
Adorn'd with all that heroes can enroll,
Yet vow'd succession's cruel sacrifice,
Great Judah's son, like Jephtha's daughter, dies.
Yes, like a monument of wrath he stands;
Such ruin Absalom's revenge demands.   1215
His curiosity his doom assign'd,
For 'twas a crime of as destructive kind
To pry how Babylon's burning zeal aspires
As to look back on Sodom's blazing fires.
But spoil'd and robb'd, his drossier glories gone,   1220
His virtue and his truth are still his own.
No rifling hands can that bright treasure take,
Nor all his foes that royal charter shake.

1198. In the month following the King's illness (Sept. 1679), the influence of York and Halifax led Charles to strip Monmouth of his various offices and order him beyond the sea. Monmouth complied but was not so submissive as Settle suggests (D'Oyley, *Monmouth*, pp. 139–41).

1203. The type of the submissive son is found in Genesis 22:6–9.

1212. *vow'd succession's:* Settle refers to Charles II's determination to enforce true, if not legal, succession.

1213. Jephtha vowed that he would sacrifice "whatsoever cometh forth of the doors of my house to meet me when I return" if he conquered the Ammonites. It was his only daughter who came joyously out to greet him (Judges 11:29–40). Cf. 811.

1219. "Then the Lord rained upon Sodom and upon Gomorrah brimstone and fire. . . . But [Lot's] wife looked back from behind him, and she became a pillar of salt" (Genesis 19:24, 26).

1220. *spoil'd:* Stripped or despoiled.

The dreadful'st foe their engines must subdue,
The strongest rock through which their arts must hew,   1225
Was great Barzillai. Could they reach his head,
Their fears all hush'd, they had struck danger dead.
That second Moses-guide resolv'd to free
Our Israel from her threat'ning slavery,
Idolatry and chains; both from the rods   1230
Of Pharaoh-masters and Egyptian gods;
And from that wilderness of error freed,
Where Dog-stars scorch, and killing serpents breed;
That Israel's liberty and truth may grow,
The Canaan whence our milk and honey flow.   1235
Such our Barzillai; but Barzillai, too,
With Moses' fate does Moses' zeal pursue;
Leads to that bliss which his silver hairs
Shall never reach, rich only to his heirs.
Kind patriot, who, to plant us banks of flow'rs,   1240
With purling streams, cool shades, and summer bow'rs,
His age's needful rest away does fling,
Exhausts his autumn to adorn our spring,
Whilst his last hours in toils and storms are hurl'd,
And only to enrich th' inheriting world,   1245
Thus prodigally throws his life's short span
To play his country's generous pelican.
But oh, that all-be-devill'd Paper, fram'd,

1226. *Barzillai:* Biblically, "a wealthy Gileadite who showed hospitality to David when he fled from Absalom (II Samuel 17:27). On the score of his age, and probably from a feeling of independence, he declined the King's offer of ending his days at Court (II Samuel 19:32–39)" (*A Dictionary of the Bible, 1,* 169). Historically, Anthony Ashley Cooper, Earl of Shaftesbury (1621–83), the leader of the Country party who was at this time deprived of all offices. His strongly anti-French and anti-Roman views made him the rallying point for the Protestants and sectarians, both in Parliament and in London. Dryden's Barzillai is James Butler, Duke of Ormonde.

1247. *pelican:* According to legend, the pelican would pierce its own breast in order to feed its young on the blood. It became a symbol of self-sacrifice, of the redemption, and of the Eucharist.

1248. *that all-be-devill'd paper:* Luttrell's marginal gloss reads, "The Association paper said to be found in his closet." This was the principal basis of the treason charge entered against Shaftesbury. The signer pledged himself to reject York and to fight, if need be, under the leadership of those members of Parliament who were signatory.

fram'd: Both (1) shaped and   (2) contrived, invented, fabricated.

No doubt, in Hell; that mass of treason damn'd;
By Esau's hands, and Jacob's voice disclos'd;   1250
And timely to th' abhorring world expos'd!
Nay, what's more wondrous, this waste-paper tool,
A nameless, unsubscrib'd, and useless scroll,
Was, by a politician great in fame
(His chains foreseen a month before they came),   1255
Preserv'd on purpose, by his prudent care,
To brand his soul, and ev'n his life ensnare.
But then the Geshuritish troop, well-oath'd,
And for the sprucer face, well-fed and cloth'd,
These to the Bar obedient swearers go,   1260
With all the wind their manag'd lungs can blow.
So have I seen from bellows' brazen snout,
The breath drawn in, and by th' same hand squeez'd out.
But helping oaths may innocently fly,
When in a Faith where dying vows can lie.   1265
Were treason and democracy his ends,
Why was't not prov'd by his revolting friends?
Why did not th' oaths of his once-great colleagues,
Achitophel and the rest, prove his intrigues?
Why at the Bar appear'd such sordid scum,   1270
And all those nobler tongues of honor, dumb?

1250. It is not impossible that Settle has in mind the part played by the royal
brothers, Charles and James.
1251. *timely:* At the right moment.
abhorring: Following the discovery of the Paper of Association, a flood of abhor-
rences of its principles were sent in from those with Court party sympathies.
1254. *a politician:* i.e. Shaftesbury.
1255. A month before his own arrest on 2 July, Shaftesbury had been extremely
active in the defense of Stephen College, the zealous "Protestant joiner" (Brown,
Shaftesbury, p. 286), but he must have realized, as soon as the Oxford Parliament was
dissolved (28 March), that he was in danger. "In anticipation of attack, he secured his
estate to his family by careful settlement, and granted copyhold estates for their lives
to several of his servants" (*DNB*). During June, charges of subornation of witnesses
and treasonable letters were registered with the government (Brown, *Shaftesbury,* pp.
282–83 and n.); and by 21 June, Halifax and Clarendon were urging his arrest (*DNB*).
1257. *his . . . his:* i.e. Shaftesbury's.
1258. *Geshuritish troop:* The Irish witnesses against Shaftesbury.
1265. *dying vows:* Much to the chagrin of those who had been exploiting the Popish
Plot, not one of its victims was willing to buy his life at the cost of admitting such a
plot existed, nor did a single one recant on the gallows.

Could he his plots t'his great allies conceal,
He durst to leaky starving wretches tell?
(Such ignorant princes, and such knowing slaves—
His Babel-building tools from such poor knaves!)   1275
Were he that monster his new foes would make
Th' unreasoning world believe, his soul so black
That they in conscience did his side forego,
Knowing him guilty, they could prove him so.
Then 'twas not conscience made 'em change their side.   1280
Or if they knew, yet did his treasons hide,
In not exposing his detested crime
They're greater monsters than they dare think him.
Are these the proselytes renown'd so high,
Converts to duty, honor, loyalty?   1285
Poorly they change, who in their change stand mute:
Converts to truth ought falsehood to confute.
To conquering Truth, they but small glory give,
Who turn to God, yet let the Dagon live.

But who can Amiel's charming wit withstand,   1290
The great State-pillar of the Muses' land.
For lawless and ungovern'd, had the age
The nine wild sisters seen run mad with rage,
Debauch'd to savages, till his keen pen

1281. *his treasons:* i.e. his alleged treasons.

1289. *Dagon:* The deity, half man and half fish, of the ancient Philistines; an idol or object of idolatrous worship.

1290. *Amiel's:* A proper biblical analogue is difficult to establish, since there are four Amiels. The least likely reference would seem to be I Chronicles 26:5, which, though no more than a name, is cited in Kinsley's edition of Dryden. Almost equally unlikely are I Chronicles 3:5 (Bathsheba's father) and Numbers 13:12 (one of the twelve men who, with Joshua and Caleb, searched out Canaan). Finally, in II Samuel 9:45 and 17:27, we find the name in the context of the David story, but only as the father of Machir. In the latter instance, Machir (along with Barzillai and Shobi) houses David and his followers in their flight from Absalom. Though none of these references seems particularly applicable, the last would at least appear to conform to Settle's intention (expressed in his introductory remarks "To the Tories") to avoid the anachronisms of Dryden's poem. Historically, Amiel is George Villiers, the second duke of Buckingham (1628–87), whom Dryden had brilliantly satirized in the character of Zimri. As a Court Wit, Buckingham wrote a number of satires and lampoons, but his best work is undoubtedly *The Rehearsal*, an anti-heroic play whose chief target was Dryden (Bayes). Here Settle echoes the opening (899) of Dryden's portrait of Amiel (Edward Seymour): "For Amiel, who can Amiel's praise refuse?"

Brought their long banish'd reason back again,   1295
Driven by his satyres into Nature's fence,
And lash'd the idle rovers into sense.
Nay, his sly Muse, in style prophetic, wrote
The whole intrigue of Israel's Ethnic Plot;
Form'd strange battalions, in stupendous-wise,   1300
Whole camps in masquerade, and armies in disguise.
Amiel, whose generous gallantry, whilst Fame
Shall have a tongue, shall never want a name;
Who, whilst his pomp his lavish gold consumes,
Molted his wings to lend a throne his plumes,   1305
Whilst an ungrateful Court he did attend,
Too poor to pay what it had pride to spend.

　　But, Amiel has, alas, the fate to hear
　　An angry poet play his chronicler;

1295. Epilogue to *The Rehearsal*, 17–18:

　Let's have at least, once in our lives, a time
　When we may hear some reason, not all Rhyme.

1296. *satyres:* The original spelling has been kept in order to preserve the word play possible under the tradition that related *satire* and *satyr*.

1298–1301. In *The Rehearsal*, one of Bayes's characters, Prince Volscius, is suddenly taken up with a design "to head the army that lies concealed for him at Knightsbridge." Smith, one of the gentlemen observing the rehearsal, eventually inquires, "Is not this difficult . . . to keep an army thus conceal'd in Knightsbridge?" (III.5). After deciding that the army must all be friends of the innkeepers at Knightsbridge, the matter is dropped until the last act, when the two kings of Brentford (usually taken to be Charles II and York) are warned that it has marched up from Knightsbridge in disguise, whereupon they flee for shelter before the comic battle takes place. *The Rehearsal* was acted on 7 Dec. 1671 (though composition may have been begun as early as 1665), but it "prophesies" (1160–69) Gadbury's story of Sir Robert Peyton.

1302–03. Buckingham, who had been a member of the Cabal, changed to the Country party after his scandalous downfall in 1674. His new life led him to a full attack on the Test, on the bishops, and on the illegality of Charles' fifteen-month prorogation of Parliament. In this last, he was supported by Shaftesbury, Wharton, and Salisbury, and all four were sent to the Tower for their stand. He soon moved to the City and worked assiduously for Whig candidates; he never really led the party, however, and on the question of exclusion, he was carefully absent from the House. Though he had zealously supported the Popish Plot, he was drawing away from Shaftesbury's group at the time that Settle was writing.

1304. Buckingham's prodigality was awesome. By the time of his death, he had managed to spend almost entirely his vast estate.

1305. Probably an allusion to Buckingham's losses in the Royalist cause during the Civil War (See *Fairfax Correspondence, 4,* 249).

1309. *an angry poet:* Dryden, whose devastating portrait of the Duke as Zimri is

A poet rais'd above oblivion's shade,   1310
By his recorded verse immortal made.
But, Sir, his livelier figure to engrave,
With branches added to the Bays you gave
(No Muse could more heroic feats rehearse!):
Had, with an equal all-applauding verse,   1315
Great David's scepter and Saul's javelin prais'd:
A pyramid to his saint, Interest, rais'd—
For which religiously no change he miss'd,
From Commonwealth's-man up to Royalist.
Nay, would have been his own loath'd thing call'd Priest: 1320
Priest, whom with so much gall he does describe,
'Cause once unworthy thought of Levi's tribe.
Near those bright tow'rs where art has wonders done,
Where David's sight glads the blest summer's sun

---

justly considered a masterpiece of verse satire, may well have been motivated in part by Buckingham's corrosive treatment of him in *The Rehearsal*.

1316. In 1659, Dryden had published his *Heroic Stanzas, Consecrated to the Glorious Memory of his Most Serene and Renowned Highness Oliver Late Lord Protector of this Commonwealth etc. Written after the Celebration of his Funeral;* in the following year, he wrote *Astrea Redux. A Poem on the Happy Restoration and Return of His Sacred Majesty Charles the Second.* Dryden's antagonists effectively replied to the "author of Absalom and Achitophel" by bringing out, in 1681 and 1682, three separate editions of his *Heroic Stanzas*.

Saul's javelin: "And Saul sought to smite David even to the wall with the javelin" (I Samuel 19:10).

1320. Though Legouis ("Dryden and Eton," *MLN, 53* [1937], p. 113) suggests that these lines should be read with reference to 1331, it would seem, as his own note suggests (p. 114, n. 8), that there was gossip about town in 1676 that Dryden might be considering the priesthood in order to obtain a post at Oxford (E. S. de Beer, "Dryden's Anti-Clericalism," *N&Q,* 179 [1940], 254–57). *A Session of the Poets* (c. 1676; see *POAS,* Yale, *1,* 353), which has been attributed to Rochester, to Buckingham, and to Settle, states:

> But Apollo has heard a story i'the town
> Of his quitting the Muses to wear a black gown,
> And so gave him leave, now his poetry's done,
> To let him turn priest, when Reeves is turn'd nun.
>
> (11–14)

See also 1333 n.

1321. Perhaps an allusion to *The Spanish Friar* (performed 8 March 1680; printed 1681). See 1330–31 n.

1323. Windsor Castle, rising above the Thames (1325), was enlarged, redecorated, and improved by Charles II (the Star Building was completed under Hugh May, ceilings in some of the state apartments were painted by Antonio Verrio, Grinling

And at his feet proud Jordan's waters run,   1325
A cell there stands by pious founders rais'd,
Both for its wealth and learned rabbins prais'd:
To this did an ambitious bard aspire,
To be no less than lord of that blest choir;
Till Wisdom deem'd so sacred a command   1330
A prize too great for his unhallow'd hand.
Besides, lewd Fame had told his plighted vow
To Laura's cooing love perch'd on a dropping bough.
Laura, in faithful constancy confin'd
To Ethiop's envoy, and to all mankind;   1335
Laura, though rotten, yet of mold divine;

Gibbons was engaged to do his "incomparable carvings," the Long Walk and Cumberland Lodge were added to the parks), though the large-scale plan of Sir Christopher Wren was not carried out. For a full account and appreciation of the artistry and work, see Evelyn, *Diary, 3–4,* passim.

1326. *A cell:* Eton College, which lies just across the Thames from Windsor, was founded by Henry VI in 1440.

1328–29. Investigating this passage, Legouis ("Dryden and Eton," p. 112) demonstrated that Dryden most certainly attempted to become provost of Eton College, probably between 28 Jan. and 24 Feb. 1681. There are, however, still certain confusions on date; see p. 113 of Legouis' article and Evelyn, *Diary, 4,* 176.

1330–31. Dryden may have been unsuccessful because, as with Waller in 1665 (?), it was decided that the post should be held only by a clergyman (Legouis, "Dryden and Eton," p. 113, citing Johnson, *Lives,* ed. Hill, *1,* 273–74). This would offer one explanation of the "unhallow'd hands" and might, according to Legouis, explain 1320–22 above. An additional reason for Dryden's rejection is offered in Macdonald's note on Settle's passage (*Dryden Bibliography,* p. 231 n. 1): "In Oldys's Langbaine (B.M.C. 28. g. 1), p. 171, against ll. 8–9, '. . . ever since a certain worthy bishop refused orders to a certain poet . . . ,' there is a note: "he missed his Eton preferment which seems to be after he wrote *The Spanish Friar* 1681 and also after his *Religio Laici* 1682.' In another annotated Langbaine (Bodl. Bliss B. 121) against the same lines there is the note, 'Bishop Compton to Bayes.'" Since the *Religio Laici* did not appear until Nov. 1682, the first note must be treated with some caution.

1333. While the meaning of many of the allusions in these lines lies hidden by time, Legouis' and Macdonald's inability to identify the central theme is strange. It seems to me undoubted that Laura is Anne Reeves, an actress in the King's Company, who reputedly was Dryden's mistress. About 1675 or 1676, there are references to her becoming a nun (see 1320 n., above; also the contemporary references given in J. H. Wilson, *All the King's Ladies* [Chicago, 1958], p. 184), but since there are also references to her being a bawd, one must keep in mind the slang meaning of a nunnery as a brothel. Whichever reading one gives, the affair was still being referred to in 1682. *The Medal of John Bayes* [S 2860], probably by Shadwell, a highly scurrilous, highly informative attack on Dryden published in May 1682, states in the Preface:

His prostituted Muse will become as common for hire as his Mistress Revesia was upon whom he spent so many hundred pounds, and of whom (to show his

He had all her claps, and she had all his coin.
Her wit so far his purse and sense could drain,
Till every pox was sweet'n'd to a strain.
And if at last his nature can reform,   1340
A-weary grown of love's tumultuous storm,
'Tis age's fault, not his; of pow'r bereft,
He left not whoring, but of that was left.

But wand'ring Muse, bear up thy flagging wing;
To thy more glorious theme return, and sing   1345
Brave Jotham's worth, impartial, great, and just,
Of unbrib'd faith, and of unshaken trust;
Once Geshur's lord, their throne so nobly fill'd,
As if, to th' borrow'd scepter that he held,
Th' inspiring David yet more generous grew   1350
And lent him his imperial genius too.
Nor has he worn the royal image more
In Israel's Viceroy than Ambassador:
Witness his gallantry that resolute hour
When, to uphold the sacred pride of pow'r,   1355

---

constancy in love) he got three claps and she was a bawd. Let all his own
romantic plays show so true and so heroic a lover

The striking parallels need not be put aside because of 1334–45, which are certainly
meant ironically. It does not seem too absurd to suggest that "Ethiop's envoy"—an
allusion which so puzzles Legouis ("Dryden and Eton," pp. 111–12, n. 3)—might very
well be the Moroccan ambassador whose escapades during the first half of 1682 were
duly recorded in the diaries and newspapers of the day.

1339. *a strain:* A passage of song or poetry.

1342–43. Cf. the concluding lines of Dryden's portrait of Zimri (567–68)

Thus, wicked but in will, of means bereft
He left not faction, but of that was left.

1346. *Jotham:* Biblically, the youngest son of Gideon, who escaped when his 70
brothers were slain by their half-brother, Abimelech, who thus was elected king.
Jotham defiantly stood on Mount Gerizim and, telling the parable of the bramble,
protested eloquently against both the usurper and those who had brought him to
power (Judges 9:1–21). Historically, Arthur Capel, Earl of Essex (1631–83), whose
excellent administration of Ireland (1672–77) and of the Treasury (1679) angered the
King's favorites. He strongly supported Shaftesbury on the Exclusion Bill, and upon
its defeat, his plan for an association was considered. In 1681, he spoke out equally
vehemently against holding parliament at Oxford and against the popish lords. It was
also believed that he had written a defense of Shaftesbury's "Ignoramus" jury. Dry-
den's Jotham is Halifax, with whom Essex had previously been aligned.

His stubborn flags, from the Sydonian shore,
The angry storms of thund'ring castles bore.
But these are virtues Fame must less admire,
Because deriv'd from that heroic sire
Who, on a block, a dauntless martyr di'd   1360
With all the sweetness of a smiling bride;
Charm'd with the thought of honor's starry pole,
With joy laid down a head to mount a soul.

Of all the champions rich in honor's scars,
Whose loyalty through David's ancient wars   1365
(In spite of the triumphant tyrant's pride)
Was to his lowest ebb of fortune ti'd,
No link more strong in all that chain of gold
Than Amasai, the constant, and the bold;
That warlike general whose avenging sword,   1370
Through all the battles of his royal lord,
Pour'd all the fires that loyal zeal could light;
No brighter star in the lost David's night.

No less the lordly Zeleck's glory sound,
For courage and for constancy renown'd.   1375

1356. *Sydonian:* Danish. Essex, on his first assignment as ambassador to Christian V, had refused to strike his colors as he sailed under the guns of Kronenborg. On landing, he demonstrated the preparation he had made for the embassy by justifying his defiance on the basis of former treaties which excepted English warships. His action was acclaimed by the English court.

1359. *heroic sire:* Essex's father, Arthur, Lord Capel of Hadham, was beheaded on 9 March 1649 for his leadership of the Royalist cause. His courageous conduct on the scaffold drew the admiration of a number of writers at the time. Compare the following lines with Marvell, *Horatian Ode*, 57–64.

1369. *Amasai:* Biblically, the chief of the captains who early joined David in his struggle against Saul (I Chronicles 12:18). Historically, Charles Gerard, Earl of Macclesfield, one of Charles I's most vigorous commanders, who was wounded at least three times in the course of the many campaigns in which he took part. He followed Charles II into exile, engaging himself just as actively in advancing his monarch's cause. By 1679, he was one of Monmouth's strongest backers, protesting against the rejection of the Exclusion Bill in 1680 and even, according to Lord Grey, suggesting in 1681 that York be murdered. In August, he lost his position as gentleman of the bedchamber, but his support of Monmouth was unflagging.

1374. The portrait of Zeleck first appears in the quarto and replaces 1374–77 of the folio:

No less with laurels Ashur's brows adorn,
That mangl'd brave, who with Tyre's thunder torn,

Though once in nought but borrow'd plumes adorn'd,
So much all servile flattery he scorn'd
That, though he held his being and support
By that weak thread, the favor of a Court,
In sanedrins unbrib'd, he, firmly bold,   1380
Durst truth and Israel's right, unmov'd, uphold.
In spite of Fortune, still to Honor wed;
By Justice steer'd, though by Dependence fed.

With reverence the religious Helon treat,
Refin'd from all the looseness of the great;   1385
Helon who sees his line of virtues run
Beyond the center of his grave, his own
Unfinish'd luster sparkling in his son;
A son so high in sanedrins renown'd,
In Israel's int'rest strong, in sense profound.   1390
Under one roof, here Truth a goddess dwells;
The pious father builds her shrines and cells,
And in the son she speaks her oracles.

In the same list, young Adriel's praise record;
Adriel, the academic neighbor lord;   1395

Brought a dismember'd load of honor home
And lives to make both th' earth and seas his tomb.

I am unable satisfactorily to identify either Ashur or Zeleck.

1384. *Helon:* Biblically, Helon is mentioned several times, but only as the father of Eliab, the chief of the tribe of Zebulon (Numbers 1:9; 2:7; 7:24; 29; 10:16). Historically, William Russell, Earl of Bedford (1613–1700), who, though never a major political figure, voted steadily against Danby's non-resistance oath (1675), was on the subcommittee which was to prepare Essex's Protestant Association (1680), signed the petition against holding a parliament in Oxford (1681), and, within the scope of parliamentary action, followed Shaftesbury's lead on the Exclusion Bill.

1389. *A son:* William, Lord Russell (1639–83), third and only surviving son of the Earl of Bedford, led the Country party's attack on York and was one of the central figures of the Shaftesbury faction. In the year following this poem, he was found guilty of treason in the Rye House Plot and executed.

1394. *Adriel:* Biblically, the husband of Merab, Saul's daughter, who had previously been promised to David (I Samuel 18:19). The relation to the historical person, John, Baron Lovelace of Hurley (1638?–93) is unclear. Hurley is about 53 miles from Oxford, where Lovelace matriculated in 1655 and was created M.A. in 1661, and this may qualify him as "the academic neighbor lord." Lovelace was a zealous Whig, and perhaps he became so through the influence of Robert Owen, the famous Independent

Adriel, ennobled by a grandfather
And uncle, both those glorious sons of war,
Both generals, and both exiles with their lord,
Till with the royal wanderer restor'd,
They liv'd to see his coronation pride,   1400
Then, surfeiting on too much transport, di'd.
O'er Adriel's head these heroes' spirits shine,
His soul with so much loyal blood fenc'd in;
Such native virtues his great mind adorn,
Whilst under their congenial influence born.   1405

   In this record, let Camrie's name appear,
The great Barzillai's fellow sufferer;
From unknown hands, of unknown crimes accus'd,
Till th' hunted shadow lost, his chains unloos'd.

   Now to the sweet-tongu'd Amram's praise be just,   1410
Once the State Advocate, that wealthy trust,
Till flattery, the price of dear-bought gold,
His innocence for palaces unsold;
To naked truth's more shining beauties true,
Th' embroider'd mantle from his neck he threw.   1415

---

whom Lovelace's ardently Royalist father had rather surprisingly engaged as his chaplain during the 1640s. Lovelace was strongly anti-Catholic and, though afterwards discharged, was arrested in connection with the Rye House Plot in 1683. Dryden's Adriel is his patron, the Earl of Mulgrave.

1396–97. His grandfather was one of the Elizabethan "worthies," Sir Richard Lovelace, knighted at Dublin in 1659; his uncle was the famous Thomas Wentworth, Earl of Cleveland.

1406. *Camrie:* William, third Baron Howard of Escrick (1626?–94), during the Commonwealth allied himself to the radical republicans and Anabaptists and during the Popish Plot fully credited Oates' accounts. In 1681, he suffered his third imprisonment, this time on the false charges of Edward Fitzharris. Ironically, it was Algernon Sidney who obtained his release in Feb. 1682; in the Rye House Plot the following year, it was largely Howard's evidence that convicted Russell and ruined Sidney.

1410. *Amram:* The father of Moses, Aaron, and Miriam (Exodus 6:20; Numbers 26:59). Historically, Sir William Jones (1631–82), an eminent lawyer who (Nov. 1679) resigned the attorney generalship to which he had been appointed four years earlier and became strongly anti-Court. He was the Commons' manager for Stafford's trial and did much to get the Exclusion Bill through that house. Though reputedly not friendly with Shaftesbury, he was very close to Russell. For Dryden, he is "Bull-fac'd Jonas."

Next Hothriel write, Baal's watchful foe, and late
Jerusalem's protecting Magistrate,
Who, when false jurors were to frenzy charm'd,
And against innocence even tribunals arm'd,
Saw deprav'd Justice ope her ravenous jaw,   1420
And timely broke her canine teeth of law.

Amongst th' asserters of his country's cause,
Give the bold Micah his deserv'd applause,
The grateful sanedrins' repeated choice,
Of two great Councils the successive voice.   1425
Of that old hardy tribe of Israel born;
Fear their disdain, and flattery their scorn,
Too proud to truckle, and too tough to bend.

Of the same tribe was Hanan, Ithream's friend;
From that fam'd sire, the long robe's glory, sprung;   1430
In sanedrins his country's pillar long.

1416. *Hothriel:* Biblically uncertain, though Settle may have meant Othniel, who
became the first judge of the Israelites after Joshua's death and their deliverer from
their first servitude (Judges 3:9–11; but see also 633 n.). Historically, as well, the refer-
ence is uncertain. Luttrell's marginal gloss supplies the names of Sir Robert Clayton
or Sir Patience Ward, and the marginalia of my copy suggest Slingsby Bethel or Sir
Patience Ward. The lines deal with both (1) the rejection of Dangerfield's evidence
(because of his criminal record) and the consequent acquittal of Cellier (11 June 1680)
and Castlemaine (23 June 1680) by their juries of treason in the Meal Tub Plot and
(2) the Whig counterattack against these reputedly bribed ("false") juries by the use
of "Ignoramus" Grand Juries that refused to allow cases to come to trial; one can
therefore reject Clayton, the first Whig Lord Mayor (29 Oct. 1679–29 Oct. 1680), since
he was unable to block the acquittals that occurred during his office. The man re-
sponsible for packing the Grand Juries was Slingsby Bethel, one of the two Whig
sheriffs from June 1680–June 1681; however, "late Jerusalem's . . . magistrate" seems
to indicate the unshared office of Lord Mayor. Ward, whose mayoralty terminated on
29 Oct. 1681, may well have been responsible for the maneuver, so often used during
his term of office, of controlling the City through its Grand Juries. Certainly, the
Whigs at this time were unhappy with his successor, Sir John Moore, and their worst
fears were to be realized when, six weeks later, the struggle for the shrieval posts began.

1422. *Micah:* Biblically, the prophet Micah attempted to establish a religious house,
but his sacred objects were taken forcibly from him by the raiding Danites (Judges
17–18). Historically, Sir William Williams (1634–1700), speaker of the House of Com-
mons in 1680 and 1681 and a staunch defender of parliamentary privilege against
royal encroachment. His defiance not only of the King's sympathizers but of the King
himself was stopped only by Charles's dissolution of the House.

1429. *Hanan:* The reference is probably to Nehemiah 8:7 where one of the persons
who helps Ezra interpret the law is so named. Historically, according to Luttrell,

Long had he fathom'd all the depths of State;
Could with that strength that ponderous sense debate
As turn'd the scale of nations with the weight;
Till subtly made by spiteful honor great,   1435
Preferr'd to Israel's chief tribunal seat,
Made in a higher orb his beams dispense,
To hush his formidable eloquence.

   But Israel's numerous worthies are too long
And great a theme for one continued song.   1440
Yet these by bold flagitious tongues run down,
Made all conspirers against David's crown.

   Nay, and there was a time, had Hell prevail'd,
Nor perjury and subornation fail'd,
When a long list of names, for treason doom'd,   1445
Had Israel's patriots in one grave entomb'd;
A list, with such fair loyal colors laid,
Even to no less than royal hands convey'd.
And the great mover in this pious fraud,
A dungeon slave, redeem'd by a midnight bawd,   1450
Then made by art a swearer of renown,
Nurs'd and embrac'd by th' heir of Judah's crown,
Encourag'd too by pension for reward,

Heneage Finch, Earl of Nottingham and, after 19 Dec. 1674, Lord Chancellor of England (cf. 1436). While it is true that Finch's father was also a lawyer (of "the long robe"), and while he himself was famed for his eloquence (1438), it is curious indeed to find him in such Whiggish company and singled out as Monmouth's friend. Finch's opinion did coincide with that of the Country party on occasion, and he did propose limitation of the Catholic successor; nevertheless, if Luttrell's identification is correct, one can only attribute Settle's praise either to Finch's probity and discretion or to information which we no longer have.

   1441. *bold, flagitious tongues:* i.e. of those involved in the Meal Tub Plot.

   1445–46. The list of names contained in the Meal Tub Papers included most of Settle's "worthies."

   1448. *royal hands:* Dangerfield was brought to Charles II by York.

   1450. *a dungeon slave:* Dangerfield had been bailed out of Newgate by Elizabeth Cellier, the midwife. In contemporary cant, a mother midnight is a midwife or a bawd, and Cellier by her own statement was the first and by Dangerfield's confession the second.

   1452. According to York and Lord Peterborough, they received from Dangerfield the story of the Protestant Plot; according to Dangerfield, he concocted it at their request.

With his forg'd scrolls for guiltless blood prepar'd.
Poor engine for a greatness so sublime: 1455
But oh, a cause by which their Baal must climb
Ennobles both the actor and the crime.

  Yet this, and all things else, now quite blown o'er,
And Absalom, his Israel's fear no more,
Luster and pride shall hem his radiant brow,   1460
All knees shall fall, and prostrate nations bow.
By Heav'ns, he is, he will, he must, he shall
Be Israel's hero, friend, saint, idol, all.
What though provok'd with all the crying sins
Of murmuring slaves, excluding Sanedrins,   1465
By profane crowds in dirt his prophets spurn'd,
And ev'n his gods in mock processions burn'd,
Himself from Israel into Hebron sent
And doom'd to little less than banishment;
In spite of all his scrolls to Babylon,   1470
And all the promis'd wonders to be done,
When Egypt's frogs should croak on Judah's throne;
Though of a Faith that propagates in blood,
Of passions unforgiving, less withstood
Than seas and tempests, and as deaf as they;   1475
Yet all divine shall be his God-like sway,

1466. *prophets:* The Roman Catholic secular priests and Jesuits.

1467. On 17 Nov. 1681, the anniversary in commemoration of Queen Elizabeth proved particularly eventful. That night, says Luttrell, there were bonfires and a cavalcade with "the effigies of Sir Edmund Berry Godfrey on horseback and held up by a Jesuit; then the effigies of the Observator [i.e. L'Estrange], several friars, popish bishops, and cardinals in their proper habits; then the effigies of suborned persons [i.e., witnesses]; and lastly the pope . . . on a sledge . . . in all his pontificalibus; thus they set out from Whitechapel attended with many thousands of people and some hundreds of links . . . to Smithfield where the Pope was burnt in a great fire prepared on purpose; and store of fireworks concluded the solemnity" (*Brief Relation, I*, 144).

1468-69. After returning from The Hague at the time of the King's illness, York was sent to Scotland as High Commissioner (1679); he returned the following year but was again forced to retire. At about the time that this poem appeared, James had again been allowed to come to England, principally through Portsmouth's influence, which James had bought by granting her a portion of his postal monopoly. Settle's ironic call to complacency may indicate that he had heard that James would be staying in England.

And his calm reign but one long halcyon day,—
And this great truth he's damn'd that dares deny;
'Gainst Absalom even oracles would lie,
Though sense and reason preach 'tis blasphemy.   1480
Then let our dull mistaken terror cease,
When even our comets speak all health and peace.

1479. i.e. even oracles, if they spoke against Absalom, would have to be considered false.

1480. *'tis.* The antecedent is *truth,* 1478.

1482. *comets:* Generally, comets were thought to portend ill fortune and were considered malevolent exhalations.

Charles II's first substantial move against Shaftesbury's forces in London was a remarkably successful and politically astute maneuver. With excellent timing and from a firm position of legality, he caused the maximum embarrassment with the minimum risk.

About Easter (16 April), the Opposition decided to hold a public feast of thanksgiving on Friday the 21st, occasioned (to quote from the tickets of invitation) by God's protection "of His Majesty's person, the Protestant Religion, and English liberties (hitherto) from the hellish and frequent attempts of their enemies (the Papists) ." To this were invited those who wished "to meet many of the loyal Protestant nobility, gentry, clergy, and citizens," meaning, as Luttrell points out (*1*, 179), Monmouth, Shaftesbury, Essex, and the party leaders. The political complexion of the feast can be seen in its principal stewards: John Wilmore, the sectarian who, but lately come from a treason charge, was soon to be prosecuted for kidnapping; and John Wickham, an "Ignoramus" juryman who was to be tried with Pilkington and others for riot during the 1682 shrieval elections. Whether the initial idea sprang, as Otway claims in his Prologue to *The City Heiress* (35–36), from the fertile brain of Oates is less certain.

Charles countered this with two effective moves. First, to the feast of the Artillery Company at Merchant-Tailors' Hall on 20 April, the Duke of York was formally invited, entering the City with his guard, "many coaches of persons of quality and foreign ministers" (*Impartial Protestant Mercury*, No. 104 [18–21 April 1682]). Whether it was, as L'Estrange reported (*Observator*, No. 129 [27 April 1682]), "the most magnificent . . . entertainment that has been known this many a day within the Walls of the City," or whether it was the sad, hireling miscarriage, as Care narrates (*Impartial Protestant Mercury*), where the "noise was not extraordinary and the great showers much incommoded the bravery of the day," depends on one's point of view. What did rankle the Whigs was Charles' order, issued in Council on

the previous day (19 April), prohibiting the Whig feast as a "mani-
fest derogation of his right" to set such public holidays, and as "tend-
ing to Sedition, and raising distinctions and confederacies." As a re-
sult, the Lord Mayor and Aldermen publicly forbade the meeting
and on "the day [the Whigs] should have met, four companies of the
trained bands and several guards of constables and watchmen were
placed at divers parts of the City" (Luttrell).

The resulting confusion in the Whig party was complete. Since it
was too late to cancel the feast for which somewhere between 300 and
800 sympathizers had each paid his guinea, the Whigs were forced
to dispose of a "great part of their provisions to the Compters etc.
prisons." In lieu of the monster rallies that were to have taken place
at Haberdashers' and Goldsmiths' Halls, there was only impotent
frustration—"some of them dining at separate places with the rest of
the provisions" (Luttrell, *1*, 180).

Tory pamphleteers triumphed in the event, not only because their
opponents had been made to look so ridiculous, but, more particu-
larly, because it represented the first counterattack that the Court
had made against the very core of Whig strength, the City of London.
The Whig writers, on the other hand, stressed the pettiness of the act
and the absurdity of the charges; for them, the whole affair demon-
strated yet once more the Court party's irresponsible vindictiveness.

A Congratulatory Poem on the
Whigs' Entertainment

[C 5830]

This delightfully ironic Whig poem portrays the Tory extremist from his outward arrogance to his inner papism. The Whig point of view is never stated, though it stands in sharp contrast to the alleged hypocrisy of the Jesuitical mind and the "demonstrated" absurdity of Tory arguments. Indeed, the basic device of the poem is to extend this absurdity, pari passu, to the point where it redounds on the Tories, who become not only the "threatened" fools of the feast (the woodcocks, geese and calves) but also the ultimate examples of duplicity in their hypocritical statements on Godfrey's death.

Luttrell, who obtained his copy on 22 April 1682, must have read only the opening lines of the poem which so effectively parody the Tory approach that he penned a brief "Against them [i.e. the Whigs]" beside the title.

A CONGRATULATORY POEM ON THE
WHIGS' ENTERTAINMENT

"Hollow boys, hollow, hollow once again!
T'other half crown shall then reward your pain."
Alas, poor Whig, where wilt thou sneaking go?
Thy wine is spilt, thy pies and cakes are dough.
Down go the coppers, tables, shelves, and all,   5

1. In describing the Artillery Company's feast at Merchant-Tailors Hall, the Whig *Impartial Protestant Mercury*, No. 104 (18–21 April 1682) claimed that "several of the Guard were often pleased to put the boys and mobile in mind of their duty to shout and hallow."

2. The anti-Court word play would seem to be based on the Whig report that "a parcel of blades being planted in the balcony threw out money to the rabble, bidding them cry out 'A York!' which they did as long as they got liquor" (*Impartial Protestant Mercury*, No. 105 [21–25 April 1682]).

5. *the coppers:* Large copper boilers made for cooking; also perhaps a mug or vessel for liquor. There may also be a play on the sense of penny or halfpenny.

176

And so farewell to Haberdashers' Hall!
Damn'd Protestants! that, when the court abhor't,
Dare eat and drink without a patent for't—
And what true Catholics, no doubt, will say
Was ten times worse, upon a fasting day!　　　　10
No northern healths would with *huzzas* be crown'd,
No loyal *dammes* there would rend the ground.
These hungry covenanting curs contrive
To gobble up the King's perogative.
In pasties, plots, in custard, treason lies,　　　　15
And hot rebellion lurks in pudding-pies.
Fear always through a perspective looks, and thus
A sausage must be dubb'd a blunderbuss;
Poor woodcocks, loyal subjects counted be,
Condemn'd by sly fanatics' treachery.　　　　20

7. *abhor't:* In 1679–80, the pro-Court party answered the Whigs' petitions for an early meeting of parliament with addresses abhorring any pressure on royal prerogative to summon that body at will. The two groups were known as "Petitioners" and "Abhorrers."

8. *patent:* An official document confirming some privilege, right, or office.

10. The Whig feast was to have taken place on Friday 21 April.

11. *northern:* Probably an allusion to James' role as Commissioner of Scotland as well as Duke of York.

huzzas: "At all the Tory healths, as they were called, the cry was reared of 'Huzza!' which at great and solemn feasts made no little noise and gave advantage to the Whigs, that liked not such music, to charge the Tories with brutality and extravagance" (North, *Examen*, p. 617).

12. *dammes:* The imprecation, according to the Whigs, that was regularly used by the Court adherents.

13. *covenanting:* A reference to the Solemn League and Covenant taken by the Parliamentary party at the insistence of the Scotch prior to the latter's entrance into the Civil War against Charles I in 1643. Tory pamphleteers were constantly suggesting a parallel between the old Commonwealthsmen and the contemporary Whigs, between the old Covenant and the new Association. When the tickets to the Whig thanksgiving said that the feast was for "improving love and charity among such as are sensible thereof," L'Estrange (*Observator*, No. 129 [27 April 1682]) seized on the phrase: "This same 'mutual love and charity' handed to the press by John Wilmore looks like the egg of an Association."

14. The King's prohibition of the feast stated that "Whereas the appointing of public fasts and thanksgiving is matter of state and belongs only to His Majesty by prerogative," he looked upon the gathering as "an insolent attempt" to derogate his right.

17. *perspective:* Magnifying glass, spyglass, telescope, etc.

19. *woodcocks:* The game bird, but also, colloquially, a fool, simpleton, or dupe.

20. *fanatics':* From the writer's ridiculing point of view, the Tories thus condemn anyone who is not of their opinion.

Spits rapiers are to stab obedient geese;
A stately pasty is a mortar-piece;
Glasses are hand grenadoes, which may fall
At Charing Cross or fire the milky Hall.
Cooks' shops hatch close designs upon the state   25
'Gainst calves and capons to associate;
Which if the traitors freely won't confess,
Our juries them shall all-to-be-address.
Those that were never marked by the beast
Shall neither buy, nor sell, nor fast, nor feast;   30
Whilst this indulgence we to friends afford,
Change rusty cassocks for a glittering sword.
But if they have nor coat nor gown to sell,
Godfrey's cravat will do the job as well.

21. *geese:* Stupid, foolish people; simpletons.

22. *pasty:* A meat pie, often made with venison, seasoned and enclosed in a crust of pastry.

24. *Charing Cross:* The location of the brass statue of Charles I.

milky: Timorous, effeminate, weakly amiable.

Hall: i.e. Goldsmiths' Hall, the scene of the Tory feast.

25. *close:* Secret, concealed, occult.

26. *calves:* Stupid fellows, dolts; sometimes meek, inoffensive persons.

capon: When applied to persons, the word refers not only to eunuchs but also to someone who is particularly stupid or dull.

28. *all-to:* Wholly, completely, utterly, soundly, especially with verbs in *be-*. In the storm of Petitions (from the Country party, desiring a Parliament or a Protestant succession) and Addresses (of loyalty to the King, in abhorrence of the Association, or in support of York) that raged through the 1680s, the Addresses very frequently came from the Grand Juries of the counties. See Luttrell, *Brief Relation,* passim.

29. *the beast:* Antichrist or the Antichristian power, from the Apocalypse of St. John.

31. An allusion to the Tory feast on the previous day. The use of "indulgence," with its Roman overtones, is probably intentional.

32. Probably a suggestion that the Artillery Company was strongly Catholic in fact as well as in sympathy, and that those who must ordinarily skulk as hedge-priests can, on this occasion, bravely deck themselves in their officer's garb.

34. *Godfrey's:* Sir Edmund Berry Godfrey, the J.P. whose death was laid to the Catholics involved in the Popish Plot. Extreme Tories, such as Nathaniel Thompson, asserted that Godfrey had hanged himself.

[TOM DURFEY]

The Whig Feast

[*W 1648*]

Yale's copy of this song bears a tentative ascription to Tom Durfey, and, while quite conjectural, a certain amount of circumstantial evidence might be exhibited in support. We know, for example, that Durfey was interested in the event. Janeway's *Impartial Protestant Mercury* (No. 105 [21–25 April 1682]), in giving its Whig account of the Tories' Artillery Company Feast of 20 April, stressed the political nature of the gathering: "Amongst the rest of their entertainment, one Durfey, a poet, sang several Tory songs and was very much applauded." Though this was probably not one of those songs (lines 37–40 refer to events that were happening that evening), nonetheless the use of scotch dialect in the lyrics is to be found in other verses by Durfey.

"Songs in imitation of the Scottish dialect," says Chappell, "seem to have been confined to the stage till about the years 1679 and 1680, when the Duke of York, afterwards James II, was sent to govern Scotland, pending the discussion of the Exclusion Bill. . . . The Whigs were endeavoring to debar him from succession . . . while the most influential Scotch and English loyalists were as warmly espousing his cause" (*Popular Music*, p. 612; see note b thereto).

Dialect songs (even as late as Burns) frequently change to London English as they reach the "moralitas," since dialect, like the tune of a ballad, is often used to establish extraverbally the writer's point of view.

The text is from *l″*, and checked against *k″* and Luttrell's copy (*f″*) of 24 April 1682. It was "Printed for Joseph Hindermarsh at the Black Bull in Cornhill."

THE WHIG FEAST

A Scotch Ballad, made to the Tune of a new and pleasant Scotch Dance

1.

Woons! what noo is the matter?
Gud feth 'tis wonderous strange,
The Whigs do keep sike a clatter,
    That nean can pass th'Exchange.
They cry, 'Bread! 'tis pity   5
    Their numbers are no more;
The Duke does dine in the City,
    And muckle they fear his power.
They begin the awd trick agen,
And cabal like Old Nick agen,   10
Feast three hundred pound thick agen,
    Sike a height they soar:

Ah, bonny London! thou'rt undone,
    If e'er thou art in their power.

2.

Th' wise old Earl with the spigot,   15
    That ne'er knew rest or ease,
Udsbread! is grown sike a bigot,

1. *Woons!:* An abbreviated form of the attenuated oath, "By God's wounds," i.e. the wounds received in the crucifixion.

3. *sike:* Such.

4. *th'Exchange:* The Royal Exchange was the center of England's mercantile life, and the London merchants were traditionally Whig in their sympathies.

5. *'Bread!:* Like *Udsbread!* (17), an abbreviated form of another attenuated oath, "By God's bread," i.e. the sacramental bread.

7. *the Duke:* James, Duke of York.

8. *muckle:* Greatly.

9. *awd:* Old. A reference to the alignments that preceded the Civil War.

10. *cabal:* To intrigue privately.

11. Perhaps a reference to the parliamentary thanksgivings proclaimed after military victories, but there may also be an echo of the phrase, "thick and threefold," i.e. vehemently, fervently, impetuously.

15. The stock allusion to the tap inserted for draining the liver cyst from which Shaftesbury suffered. See Brown, *Shaftesbury,* p. 185.

The nation has his disease.
More o'th' tribe I can name ye,
  That make this Raree-Show,   20
Bold George, and Politic Jemmy,
  Converted by Doctor T.O.
Both the Sheriffs there should ha bin,
Then how merry they would ha bin,
Met for National Good agen,   25
  As they were before:

Ah, bonny London! thou'rt undone,
If long thou art in their power.

3.

More to show us what ninnies
  Are all rebellious beasts,   30
The cuckolds sent in their guineas,
  To make this jolly Feast;
Never caring, or thinking,
  What insolence was done,
Or that their plotting and drinking   35
  Should e'er be oppos'd so soon.
But when they knew they were barr'd agen,

19. *tribe:* Roughly equivalent to the modern "gang."

20. *Raree-Show:* Generally, any peep show, but at this time, specifically used in reference to Stephen College's libelous ballad of that name.

21. *George:* George Villiers, second Duke of Buckingham (1628–87) and the Zimri of Dryden's *Absalom and Achitophel.*

Jemmy: James, Duke of Monmouth.

22. *Doctor T.O.:* Titus Oates. The reference to his doctorate is, of course, satirical, since the University of Salamanca denied ever having conferred a degree on him.

23. *Sheriffs:* Thomas Pilkington and Samuel Shute, the Whig Sheriffs who had empaneled Shaftesbury's "Ignoramus" jury.

29. *ninnies:* Simpletons, fools.

30. *beasts:* Generally, any evil spirits; more specifically, Antichrist or the Antichristian powers. There is, as well, the inevitable allusion to the horned cuckold, traditionally (though not inevitably) connected with the London merchants.

31. *guineas:* The minimum charge for the Whig Feast was one guinea (Luttrell, *Brief Relation, 1,* 179).

36. *so soon:* Either in the general sense that Charles felt that he could move against the Whig stronghold or in the more particular sense that he reacted within a matter of days. The tickets must have been issued sometime after 14 April, and Charles' prohibition was issued on 19 April.

They sent out the Black Guard agen,
All our bonfires were marr'd agen,
    Slaves did shout and roar: 40

Ah, bonny London! thou'rt undone,
    If e'er thou art in their power.

4.

Right and Royalty governs,
    Which rebels would overthrow.
They once were fatal to sovereigns;   45
    Ah, let 'em no more be so!
But to baffle oppression,
    Inspir'd by Fate Divine,
Defend the crown and succession,
    And keep it in the right line.   50
Every soldier will fight for it,
Each bold Genius will write for it,
And the Whigs hang in spite for it,
    Losing regal power:

And, bonny London, they're undone,
    That thought to usurp once more.

---

38. *Black Guard:* The lowest menials of a (noble) household, who had charge of the kitchen utensils and, during journeys, rode in the end of the train; the scullions and kitchen knaves; the rabble of camp servants and followers; the vagabond or criminal class of a community. All these meanings seem to apply, since the writer is contrasting the Whigs' Black Guard with the trained bands (whose regiments were denoted by colors) called out on 21 April to enforce Charles' prohibition.

39–40. The *Impartial Protestant Mercury* (No. 105 [21–25 April 1682]), writing of the Tories' Artillery Company Feast, says that "In the evening, some bonfires were kindled, especially one before the Wonder Tavern in Ludgate Street. . . . At last, a company of young men came and threw abroad the fire, flinging part of the brands in at the tavern windows, and cried out 'No Papist! No Papist!'"

To this Whig version, L'Estrange (*Observator*, No. 133 [6 May 1682]) replied scathingly: "The 'young men,' he calls them. Do but see how gently he handles these mutinous and schismatical sprouts of a bastard reformation. These fellows would have made rare sport if the triumphant Anti-Feast had gone at the two plundering, sequestering Halls." (The Whigs had unfortunately chosen Goldsmiths' and Haberdashers' Hall, the seats of the Committees of Compounding and Sequestration during the Commonwealth period.)

49. *Fate Divine:* An allusion to the sectarians' appeal to the Calvinist doctrine of predestination.

[Nahum Tate]

Old England

So far as is known, *Old England* first appeared in 1685 in *Miscellany, Being a Collection of Poems By several Hands,* compiled by, and featuring the work of, that notable female worthy, Aphra Behn. Although the poem appeared anonymously, it seems fairly certain that its author was Nahum Tate (1652–1715), the future laureate, who, at the time of this poem (May 1682), was beginning to identify himself closely with the Court party.

The ascription is based on three points: First, the survey of history in *Old England* bears a striking resemblance to a similar survey in Tate's *On the Assembling of a New Parliament the 6th of March, 1682* (certainly an error for 6 March 1679), which was printed in *Poems Written on Several occasions, By N. Tate . . . London . . . 1684* (an expanded edition of his first publication, *Poems,* 1677). Here the resemblance is not only in the phraseology and in the selection of certain historical events, but, even more, in the appeal to England to reassert her ancient military grandeur and her historical destiny by once more halting French aggression. Secondly, the use of the names Asaph and Doeg for Dryden and Settle is found in Tate and Dryden's *A & A II* (published in Nov. 1682), and it would seem reasonable to assume that the coauthors each exploited the happy choice of biblical pseudonyms (Tate expanding his tribute to Dryden, Dryden writing his corrosive portrait of Settle) that had first been used in *Old England.* Again, it must be recalled that, so far as we know, *Old England* had not yet been published, and therefore the chance of the biblical pseudonyms' being common knowledge is slight. Thirdly, Tate's tribute to Asaph in *A & A II* bears a striking resemblance in rhetoric, theme, and (on one occasion) image to that found six months earlier in *Old England.* While other details could be pointed out (e.g. the similarity of Moore's portrait as the "loyal praetor" in *Old England* and as Ziloah in *A & A II*), full evidence for ascription would involve a comparison too minute to be given here.

The question of why Tate never acknowledged authorship of the poem brings us to the political position he takes in *Old England*, which, however unrealistic or illogical it may appear now, must not have been uncommon in May 1682. Basically, Tate strongly supports the Court, prerogative, and succession, though he is not an extreme Yorkist. He condemns popular interference of any sort and ardently rejects the zeal of both the sectarians and the Jesuits. While Tate's respect for the established order leads him to accept York as the legitimate successor, he cannot bring himself to admit that such an event would give tremendous encouragement to those very Roman Catholic extremists he has just condemned. His view depends, of course, as much on the irrational as the rational, but it would appear to have been a perilous balance that many had to live with just at this time. Two years later, when *Poems Written on Several Occasions* was published, Tate must have seen not only how close to Catholicism much of the Court was, but also how unwise it would be for an aspiring poet to acknowledge the strong anti-Jesuitism and rashly anti-Stuart remarks of *Old England*. To be anti-French in 1684 was still acceptable (particularly in view of Louis XIV's opportunistic attack on the Spanish Netherlands at the time of the Siege of Vienna), and therefore Tate would have had no qualms about including as his own the poem *On the Assembling of a New Parliament;* but *Old England* contained a good many other sentiments that the intervening months had made too perilous to own. Tate and the times had altered: in 1682, the conservative could still conjure up visions of a moderate Catholic prince ruling an obedient Protestant England; in 1684, the reality of Court policy and Opposition error had eliminated such fine shadowing and left hardly any choice save that of black and white.

One final word might here be added on the form of *Old England*. The convention of the political Advice-to-a-Painter poems allowed the writer to do more than merely hold "a mirror up to actuality" (as Jean Hagstrum suggests on p. 121 of *The Sister Arts*) or to express his "opinions, prejudices, and emotions" (as Mary Tom Osborne has stated in her bibliography of *Advice-to-a-Painter Poems 1633–1856,* where *Old England* is item 28); more than this, it permitted him, by selection and juxtaposition, to present a surrealistic picture of a contemporary situation. By choosing those details which he thought significant, by ordering his scenes to give the total effect that he wanted, by coloring his subjects often to the point of caricature, the writer created a tableau which, for him, was *more* real than actuality. Cer-

tainly the convention goes back to Horace's "ut pictura poesis" and
Simonides' "poetry [is] a speaking picture", but the *pictura* was not
meant to be photographic: indeed, much of the painting of the pe-
riod was highly allegorical, and the artist (whether graphic or literary)
was expected to create a higher truth through his interpretation and
vision.

OLD ENGLAND

Or New Advice to a Painter
A Poem

Quis iniqua
Tam patiens Urbis tam ferrens ut teneat se?

Come Painter, you and I, you know, dare do
What our licentious fancy leads us to.
Talk is but talk; let Court and Country see
None has such arbitrary pow'r as we.
Let's club, then, for a piece to hit the times,   5
While your poetic paint sets off my rhymes.
Old England for the love of virtue draw—
Hold, not our brazen-fac'd Britannica!
Let Agincourt present a warlike scene,
Abbeville Ford, or the fam'd Crécy's plain;   10

2. *licentious:* Free; unrestrained by law or decorum.

3. *Court and Country:* Tate would seem to have in mind the two major political
groups, referred to contemporaneously as Court and Country or (increasingly) as Tory
and Whig. "Country" is a particularly misleading appellation, since the center of that
group's strength lay in London. Court and Anti-Court would perhaps describe the
forces somewhat more accurately.

5. *club:* To join together in common action.

8. *brazen-fac'd Britannica:* i.e. the fanatic aspect of Britain. "Brazen-faced" was a
phrase frequently applied to Oates specifically and to anti-Court politicians and evi-
dences in general. "Britannica" is an unusual variant (not in *OED*) for "Britannia."

9. *Agincourt:* The scene of Henry V's signal victory over the numerically superior
French forces on 25 Oct. 1415. The success of the engagement paved the way for the
reconquest of Normandy and an advance to the gates of Paris (12).

10. On the evening of Thursday, 24 Aug. 1346, Edward III led his small, and ap-
parently trapped, army across the Somme at Blanquetaque—the ford near Abbeville—
after a sharp struggle against Godemar du Fay. This maneuver allowed Edward to
enter Ponthieu and choose his own ground for fighting King Philip. On 26 Aug. he
established a brilliant defensive position on high ground, with his right wing covered
by the river Maye and the village of Crécy. It was this deployment which led to the
crushing defeat of the French forces.

Let the Black Prince his English flag advance,
Or let Fifth Harry march o'er conquer'd France;
Show me those sons of Mars, for I'm afraid
Their race is lost, their valor quite decay'd.
Give the just lines and the proportion fit,   15
None but a hero for this piece can sit.

Hold, Painter, hold! thy forward hand does run
Beyond advice. What is it thou hast done?
What crowds of pimps and parasites are here!
Ha! what a politic fop drinks coffee there!   20
See how th' apostate plies his trait'rous text,
The Gospel wrack'd, and Church-historians vex'd.
Look, look, the sovereign people here dispense
The laws of empire to an absolute prince;
Their will is law divine, themselves being own'd   25
To the Almighty in the spiritual fund.
Religious rogues! new light, new worship teach,

11. While this line could refer to any one of Prince Edward's numerous exploits, it most probably alludes to his conduct at Crécy, when he left his position to charge the enemy's second line, a bold but dangerous maneuver that led him into Alençon's charging division. When King Edward learned that his son was unwounded, he refused to send assistance, "for he would that the lad should win his spurs . . . , that the day should be his, and that he and those who had charge of him should have the honor of it" (*DNB*). It was after the battle of Crécy that the sixteen-year-old prince received the name of the Black Prince, chosen because of the black armor he wore at the time.

20. Numerous attempts were made to suppress, or at least control, coffee-houses, which, as can be seen throughout L'Estrange's *Observator*, tended to become meeting places for political groups. North reviews the attempted suppression in 1675–76 (*Examen*, pp. 138–41) and Ogg gives an excellent summary (*Charles II*, pp. 100–02).

21. *th'apostate:* The reference is probably to the famous Whig attack on a popish successor, *Julian the Apostate* [J 829], written by the "political divine" Samuel Johnson (1649–1703) and published about May 1682 (Wood, *Life and Times, 3*, 18–19). The chief arguments of the book and the legal action taken against the author may be found in Gillett, *Burned Books*, pp. 496–502.

25. *Their will is law divine:* Tate ironically presses the argument which underlay so much of the political agitation especially during the reign of Charles I, i.e. *vox populi vox Dei.*

25–26. *themselves . . . fund:* i.e. they are willing to acknowledge their relationship (and virtual equality) to God. As well, Tate plays with the contemporary conflation of *owe* and *own*, thus creating a picture of sectarian saints who surpass even the most ardent Catholic's view of the "Treasure of the Church" and indulgences.

Some St. Teresia, some St. Beckman preach;
Your very prophets here hang between both,
'Twixt God and Baal, I and Astaroth;   30
Your feather'd buff is valiant but to fight,
Clodius within, or his soft Catamite;
But your promiscuous rout, at change o' th' moon,
Are Tory, Trimmer, Whig, fool, knave, buffoon.
Unhappy isle! who thus can view thy face   35
And not lament thy base degenerate race?
Those lines of majesty that Europe aw'd
Now show a cast-off miss, late turn'd to bawd.
'Twas not from hence those worthies fill'd their veins,
That led at once two potent kings in chains;   40

28. *St. Teresia:* Trances, and striking visions, and angelic messages led St. Theresa (1515–82) to establish a reformed order, the Descalzas, among the Carmelites. Theresa was canonized by Gregory XV in 1622, principally for "her asceticism and mystic visions" (*EB*). The parallel between the Catholic saint and the dissenting preachers is pointed out again below in *Cethegus' Apology*, 37.

St. Beckman: Unidentified.

30. *Baal:* The chief male deity of the Phoenician and Canaanitish nations; hence, a false god.

I: The parallel structure would suggest that this be expanded to *Iesus*, or perhaps emended to *aye*.

Astaroth: Or Ashtoreth, or Astarte, was the principal female divinity of the Phoenicians, as Baal was the principal male divinity.

31. *feather'd buff:* a dandified fellow, a foppish boaster.

32. *Clodius:* Publius Clodius (c. 93–52 B.C.), surnamed Pulcher, was a Roman politician who, being bribed by Catiline to procure an acquittal for a charge of extortion, later joined Cicero in prosecuting the Catilinarian conspiracy. Cicero broke with Clodius in Dec. 62 B.C., when the latter invaded the rites of the Bona Dea "dressed as a woman (men were not admitted to the mysteries) . . . in order to carry on an intrigue with Caesar's wife" (*EB*). He escaped condemnation by bribing the jury and, renouncing his patrician's rank, became leader of the popular party and virtual master of Rome after Caesar's departure for Gaul. The degeneration of the Bona Dea ritual and Clodius' intrusion are commemorated by Juvenal, *Satire VI* (314–45). Clodius is also mentioned in *Satire II* (27), though not in connection with the unnatural lust mentioned in the second half of this line. This latter reference might indicate an oblique allusion to Oates, who, according to Lane (*Oates*, pp. 30–31, 66, 224–26), had homosexual tendencies; or Tate may have had in mind the Emperor Claudius (10 B.C.–A.D. 54), under whom the favorites Narcissus and Pallas gained control of the Roman bureaucracy.

39. *from hence:* i.e. from the sovereign mob.

40. *two potent kings:* King David II of Scotland was in prison until ransomed on 3 Oct. 1357; and King John of France, taken by the Black Prince on 19 Sept. 1356, was in England from 3 March 1357 as a captive. Edward III feasted them both on Christmas 1358 (*DNB*, sub Edward III).

That cropp'd the Flow'r-de-Luce with greater pride
Than ever Tarquin switch'd a poppy's head;
Made lion rampant couch, that long did reign,
The pride o' th' wood and terror of the plain;
Brought Cyprus' king a willing captive here,   45
While Britain did another world appear;
Gave laws to all the land, and then with ease
Led their triumphant flag o'er all the seas.
Curse on that man of mode who, with his wine,
Debauch'd and so debas'd the British line.   50
Turn thy style, Painter; let one gracious blot
Hide all that's stain'd with zealot, villain, Scot.
Try thy skill once again. England, alas!
Draw as it is, if't can't be as it was.

First let Confusion her dear self display,   55
To whom th' unthinking crowd obedience pay;

42. When Sextus, the son of Tarquinius Superbus, became commander of the armies of the Gabii, he "sent to consult his father as to his conduct; [Tarquin] returned no answer to the messenger, but cut off with a stick the tallest poppies in his garden. His son, taking the hint, put to death the most powerful citizens of Gabii" (*Oxford Companion to English Literature*, p. 766).

43. *lion rampant:* While a common heraldic figure, the reference here would seem to be to the Scottish lion.

couch: To cause to lie down; of animals, specifically, to lie in their lair. Tate continues, also, the heraldic language seen in the figure of the lion couchant.

45. *Cyprus' king:* Possibly Peter of Lusignan, who acceded to the throne of Cyprus in Nov. 1358 and came to England in the winter of 1363 to persuade Edward III to join a crusade on Jerusalem. During these months, Edward entertained, as well, the kings of Scotland, France, and Denmark, commemorating his jubilee with great huntings and rich jousts.

49–52. Identifications here are somewhat difficult. Assuming that Tate is still referring primarily to specific persons and not to types (i.e. not to fops and Scots in general), this might be taken to allude to John of Gaunt (1340–99), who strongly opposed his brother (and Tate's hero) the Black Prince and whose third marriage (to his mistress, Catherine Swynford) eventually led (through their illegitimate offspring John Beaufort, Earl of Somerset, and by his daughter Mary Beaufort, Countess of Richmond) to Henry VII, who defeated Richard III at Bosworth, ending the Plantagenet line and establishing the Tudors. For Gaunt as a "man of mode," see Chaucer's portrait of him in the *Book of the Duchess*; consequently, 51–52 may be a rather bold attack on the next, and then reigning, house, the Stuarts.

51. *style:* Stylus; engraving tool. The phrase "to turn one's style" means "to change *to* another subject; also, to speak on the other side" (*OED*).

Next Horror, who the flying standard bears,
Deck'd with this motto, *Jealousies and Fears;*
Here let the rabble in allegiance meet,
With lives and fortunes at their idol's feet;   60
Arm every brigadier with sacred sword,
Inscrib'd, *Come fight the battle of the Lord!*
Let trumpets now proclaim immortal hate
Against all order in the Church and State.
Show not the victim that did lately fall   65
By fool or rogues, the sons of Belial;
But let a curtain of black murder hide,
Till time, or kinder fate, shall draw't aside.
Haste ye infernal pow'rs from your dark cell;
Pour out the vials that were fill'd in Hell;   70
The plagues of the Black Box the world invade,
Fathers by their unnatural sons betray'd.
When thus the kingdom's by confusion rent,
Let youths of Gotham steer the government
By kind address or wise petition sent.   75
Here, Painter, let the royal eagle fly
In state through her dominions of the sky;
Let all the feather'd legions of her train,

57–64. Tate rapidly reviews the situation that led to Civil War in phrases of the period: the "jealousies and fears" expressed by the parliamentarians of Charles I's government; the subsequent popular support, with "lives and fortunes" of the Parliamentary Cause; and the final call to "fight the battle of the Lord" which marked open insurrection.

65. *victim:* Charles I was beheaded on 30 Jan. 1649, after having been condemned for treason by a high court of justice established by the purged Parliament.

71. *Black Box:* In early 1680, the supporters of "the Protestant Duke," Monmouth, received great encouragement from the rumor that the marriage contract of Monmouth's parents, Charles II and Lucy Walter, was "contained in a black box entrusted by Cosin, afterwards bishop of Durham, to his son-in-law, Sir Gilbert Gerard" (*DNB;* also Luttrell, *Brief Relation, 1,* 42–43). Despite the King's repeated official denials of such a marriage, this Pandora's box helped to spread the discontent of exclusion and succession.

72. *unnatural:* Monmouth was a natural (i.e. illegitimate) son by birth, but unnatural in joining the anti-Court forces opposed to his father.

74. *Gotham:* The name of a village proverbial for the folly of its inhabitants.

75. Tate, who objects to all popular party incursion on royal prerogative, condemns both the Tories, who sent in loyal addresses supporting the Court, and the Whigs, who sent in petitions for a new parliament.

March at a distance o'er th'ethereal plain.
Some few through zeal too near their sovereign press,   80
Offending by a plausible address;
Others their grievances aloud declare,
Filling with cries each region of the air,
"The tyrant does her innocent subjects tear."
Let still the mighty monarch steer her way,   85
Regardless what or those or these can say;
Her divine prudence and abounded skill
Will make all happy, though against their will.

Now let the moral to this fable say:
Let none presume to rule who should obey;   90
Yet if all err, let's err the safer way.
Indentures give no right to shake a throne,
Nor must profane hands stay a tott'ring one;
In vain does Caesar vindicate the seas,
That men may traffic to what coast they please.   95
If universal mart thus proudly brag
That the court-sails must lower to city-flag,
If large concessions from successive kings
Be such desirable, such pow'rful things,
Pity that e'er to cities they were made,   100
Whose charter dares prerogative invade.
Sure gratitude is but an empty name,
Or pow'r would guard that hand from whence it came;

92. *Indentures:* The contracts by which apprentices are bound to masters who undertake to teach them a trade. Apprentices had constituted a major force during the disturbances just prior to the Civil War; they were being wooed by both parties during 1682 (see poems on the Whig Feast).

93. Cf. the fate of Uzzah (II Samuel 6:6–7).

96–101. At the end of 1681, Charles moved against the London Charter, on the grounds that the City had gone beyond its rights and invaded the area of royal prerogative. This major legal contest was prepared by both sides throughout 1682, the Court changing the specific charges from violation of its rights in the shrieval election to violation of its right to collect market money and incitement to disloyalty in the matter of a petition for a parliament which the aldermen had supported during the mayoralty of the Whig Sir Robert Clayton. The City, on the other hand, based its defense on "large concessions from successive kings," which it argued were its rights. The case was twice argued in 1683, and the court decided for the King. See the poems on Quo Warranto, and Howell, *State Trials, 8,* 1039–1358.

The coffee-drums beat *Privilege* aloud,
While duty is not heard among the crowd.   105
The law, whose influence is kind to all,
Admits distinctions when a saint should fall—
Then Magna Charta is apocryphal.
Poor loyal hearts, they plot no other thing
Than first to save, then make a glorious king.   110
Yet against evil counsellors, I hope,
Force may be us'd, and so against the Pope;
That was the word, when once, for public good,
Three kingdoms innocently flow'd in blood;
So felons when pursu'd, "Stop thief!" they cry,   115
And by that stratagem they safely fly.
Read well these men, you'll find for many years,
Who Caesar's favor wants, is sure of theirs.
Who flies disgrac'd from Court here popular grows,
And still where Caesar frowns the city bows;   120
The blackest traitors here a refuge find,
For City painters ne'er draw justice blind.

Now cross thyself, my dear, for now is come
Sir Pacolet with his Advice from Rome.

104. *Privilege:* Parliamentary privilege was set against royal prerogative.

106–08. Tate's ironic comment is aimed at the Whig "Ignoramus" juries which refused, on hairsplitting grounds, to indict members of their own party, such as Rouse, Wilmore, College, or Shaftesbury; while at the same time, they attacked all royal prerogative on the grounds of Magna Charta. See Christopher Hill, "The Norman Yoke," reprinted in *Puritanism and Revolution* (London, 1958), pp. 50–122.

110–11. The usual tactic employed by aggressive parliaments was to attack the king through his "evil counsellors" and so seek to "save" him by replacing them with persons of their own faction. The most notable case had been the trial of Thomas Wentworth, Earl of Strafford, in 1641.

112. Tate satirizes the 1641 parliament's argument that led from the specific indictment to a generalized attack.

113. Again, Tate subjects to heavy irony the claim of the rebellious parliament of Charles I that they were acting "for public good."

118. Tate would seem to have in mind such leaders of the anti-Court party as Shaftesbury, Buckingham, and Monmouth.

124. *Sir Pacolet:* Henry Care's popular Whig periodical ran from 3 Dec. 1678 until 13 July 1683 under several titles (all containing the word "pacquet") but chiefly as the *Weekly Pacquet of Advice from Rome* (see Crane and Kaye, *Census*, p. 84). In the early French romance of *Valentine and Orson*, Pacolet is the dwarf servant of Lady Clerimond who possesses a little magic winged horse of wood which carries him instantly wherever he wishes.

Saddle a broomstaff, tie it to his side,   125
For now 'tis nothing but get up and ride;
Yet if that nag don't Pacolet befit,
Paint Pegasus, for Pacolet aims at wit;
Through all the liquid plains o' th' air he flies
And dances a Coranto 'bove the skies;   130
His racer does outstrip the eastern wind
And leaves the horses of the sun behind;
Swifter than thought, from Tiber he's at Thames;
Good Lord! what castles of the air he names,
What vast discoveries does he there descry,   135
Unseen by all but Salamanca's eye!
What lady's there distress'd, what knight's in wall
Lock'd up, yet Pacolet still frees 'em all.
Talk not of Rome's Zamzummins; he no more
Will make of them, than Bellarmine before.   140
Windmills and castles in the air must down,
Quickset and Hudibras here meet in one.
Is one romantic hero not enough?
Join Protestanti, Cardinalo Puffe.

130. *Coranto: 1.* A very quick dance done to a tune in triple time; *2.* A letter or paper containing public news, a gazette, newsletter, or newspaper; *3.* Care added to the *Weekly Pacquet*'s news a dialogue section entitled *The Courant,* which rather successfully countered L'Estrange's Tory *Observator* and the delightful *Heraclitus Ridens.*

131. *eastern wind:* Probably that which comes from Rome, the theoretical place of origin of the *Weekly Pacquet.* The suggestion here and in the following line is that Care gets his news before it happens.

136. *Salamanca's:* Titus Oates, the principal discoverer of the Popish Plot, claimed a doctorate in theology from the University of Salamanca despite the fact that he had been there only briefly and that the University firmly denied his right to any degree. See *Observator,* Nos. 225, 227, 237 (17, 21 Oct., 8 Nov. 1682), for the text, translation, and discussion of the University's statement.

139. *Zamzummins:* A name of "a people great, and many, and tall, as the Anakims" (Deuteronomy 2:21). This use postdates the last entry in *OED* by approximately 22 years.

140. *Bellarmine:* Robert Bellarmine (1542–1621), the Italian cardinal and theologian, was considered by advocates of Protestantism to be "the champion of the papacy, and a vindication of Protestantism generally took the form of an answer to his works" (*EB*).

142. *Quickset:* i.e. Quixote.

Hudibras: The Presbyterian knight who, accompanied by his Independent squire Ralpho, ventures forth "a-colonelling" in Butler's fine tetrameter satire which appeared in three parts (1663, 1664, 1678) and was modeled somewhat on Cervantes' work.

These lead in chains that pagan priest that first   145
Invented surplice, ever since accurs'd:
For pagan priest of old wore vests of white;
Ergo, the surplice is a pagan rite.
By the same logic, they might thus infer:
Pagans built temples, offer'd praise and pray'r;   150
Ergo, prayer, praise, and temples, pagan are.
Good God! that such unthinking things as these
Should once pretend to write, and writing please!
Some little use might of their books be made
If Smithfield fires they duly had display'd;   155
If they expos'd by telling miracles
Of legendary saints in nasty cells;
Had their impartial writings rendered plain
Mariana's politics, and Mary's reign;
Had they in point of doctrine errors show'd,   160
Idolatry in point of worship, good!
But against Rome while they proclaim their war,
The Church of England does their fury bear;
She wears the mark o' th' beast upon her seal,
For Titus does as well as John reveal.   165
Sir Pacolet, now boast that the holy fire
In all our candlesticks does e'en expire.
Hence, thou profane, those are above thy reach!

155. *Smithfield fires:* Tate is referring to the burning of Protestants that took place at the London market during the persecutions of Mary Tudor.

158. *impartial:* This, like "modest," was a word much used in the titles of anti-Court writings. In *Observator,* No. 162 (29 June 1682), Whig protests, "There's no harm, I hope, in the publishing of an *Impartial Account";* to which Tory replies, "No, none at all, Whig; but you have no luck in the world with your *Modests* and *Impartials,* for they are commonly the most shameless and partial of all the pamphlets we have to do withall."

159. Tate might be distinguishing here between Mary Stuart, Queen of Scots, and Mary Tudor, Queen of England and Ireland.

164. Protestant writers had interpreted Revelation 17:1, 3 of St. John the Divine as the Roman Catholic Church ("the great whore") seated upon Antichrist ("the scarlet coloured beast"). The "mark of the beast" is "upon them which worshipped his image," and upon them is poured the first vial of God's wrath (16:2). Titus Oates (and radical sectarians in general) often used St. John's mystical language when they attacked the higher Anglican clergy for Roman inclinations.

167. *candlesticks:* See Revelation, esp. 2:5 and 11:4.

Why should one danmn'd to th' cart presume to preach?
Solicit on for some ignoble fee,   170
For I know Simon, Simon too knows me.
Come, Painter, to th' crowd this thingum show,
And to Saint Pacolet let London bow.
Yet let a loyal praetor sway the sword
That's never rais'd but to exalt its Lord;   175
Happy to future ages be his name,
And may it sound from all the trumps of fame.
No popular breath can steer his prosp'rous sails,
No bribes of zealous gold does turn his scales;
He sits like Justice in his chair of state,   180
Weighing the City's, and the Kingdom's fate,
So is the realm of London swol'n of late.
To th' height of glory justly he aspires;
Thrice happy is the knight, not so his squires;
They with a diff'rent zeal from his do burn,   185
And to the faction would the balance turn.
No care to duty or allegiance had,
Yet one is more unfortunate than bad:

169. On 2 July 1680, Henry Care was found guilty of libel for his remarks on Chief
Justice Scroggs in the *Courant* section of the *Weekly Pacquet* for 1 Aug. 1679 (see
Howell, *State Trials*, 7, 1111-30, and Luttrell, *Brief Relation, 1,* 50).

171. The allusion would seem to be to Simon Magus and the practice (derived from
his name) of simony, or trafficking in sacred things.

172. *thingum:* A contemptuous reference to something or someone that the speaker
does not think fit to name. In *Heraclitus Ridens,* No. 45 (6 Dec. 1681), the same word
is applied to Care:

> *Jest.* . . . But is there no news from the thingum in the Old Bailey?
> *Earnest.* Yes, yes. Harry finds the pence coming in, and he blunders on, sometimes
> in, sometimes out.

173. *Saint:* The term was applied by certain sects to their members, who were con-
sidered among the elect under the New Covenant. Nonsectarians very quickly turned it
into a term of derision.

174. *a loyal praetor:* After 366 B.C., the praetor was the annually elected curule
magistrate of Rome; in the seventeenth century, the word was used for a mayor or
chief magistrate. This reference is to Sir John Moore, the lord mayor of London,
whose increasing sympathy for the Court was an important factor in Charles' recap-
turing of the municipal offices. See the headnote and poems on the shrieval elections.

184. *his squires:* Thomas Pilkington and Samuel Shute were the Whig Sheriffs who,
as officers in charge of the election, led the struggle against the Court candidates.

188. *one:* Thomas Pilkington was, in point of fact, the active leader of the Whig
party during these critical months. Little is known about him (see the poems on the
shrieval elections), but it is reasonably clear that he acted with courage and conviction

So meek his mien, so circumspectly low,
That he has taught his very horse to bow;   190
Yields to the Church, conforms to all her laws,
Yet still embarks in the dissenters' cause;
To Roman idols he'll ne'er say his beads,
Yet if mistaken zeal this vot'ry leads,
He'll split upon the very rock he dreads.   195
His tongue speaks naked swords, his passion flames,
Not to be quench'd by all the floods of Thames;
But yet that tongue that once had felt the smart,
Holds no great correspondence with his heart.
He from himself does strangely disagree,   200
Lives not that thing he talks himself to be;
His goodly fabric has been long possess'd,
And wants the help of some kind exorcist;
Clear is his soul from all this clamorous din,
'Tis some fanatic demon raves within.   205
T'other, by Bacchus well inspir'd, can see
The mystic charms of lawless prophecy;
When he is warm with wine and drunk with zeal,
He'll with an *euoi* to his synagogue reel,
And the indwellings of the spirit reveal.   210

---

despite the legal threats which were eventually carried out. Tate, indeed, has difficulty in sustaining indignation and seems more to pity than censure.

191. In order to hold a public office, a candidate had to show that he had taken the oaths and communion according to the Anglican Church within the previous six months. This had become an issue in the case of Pilkington's predecessor, the radically sectarian Slingsby Bethel (Luttrell, *Brief Relation, 1,* 49).

194. Though Tate may mean that Pilkington's zeal to hold the shrieval post has led him to take the oath and Anglican communion (191) or that Pilkington's zeal for the rights of his office will ultimately destroy that office (202), he is more probably using the conventional Tory argument that the sectarians are merely the equal and opposite of the Catholics (217ff.).

206. *T'other:* Samuel Shute, who was far less active, is regularly charged by Tory writers with excessive drinking. Cf. *The Cavalier's Litany* [C 1577] of 3 Nov. 1682 (found in *f", k", l"*) beginning, "From shuttlecock Shute that to Nantz [i.e. brandy] is inclined."

209. *euoi:* From the Greek εὐοῖ, the Bacchanalian expression, usually written *evoe*. *synagogue:* A place of worship, often used disparagingly in connection with sectarians who tended to base themselves on the Old Testament and Hebraic studies.

210. Sectarians, and particularly Quakers, emphasized the inner search for "the indwellings of the spirit."

From kings' commands, by drink and charter, free,
He can distinguish our mix'd monarchy:
Ill politics that empire can decide
Between the sov'reign and the subject's side.
Nor Pope, nor people do this scepter sway,   215
Whate'er the Leman Lake or Tiber say.

  Now, Painter, draw two factions both alli'd
In blood and ruin, though they now divide.
Those make for Rome and brisk winds fill their sails,
These for Anticyra with equal gales;   220
Both with fanatic zeal, yet here's the odds,
Those make, then worship, and then eat their gods;
These brutish bigots most unwilling come
To th' God of Heaven, 'cause he's God of Rome;
With that devotion to their chaos bow,   225
That those to painted deities do owe.
Both parties boast a star to lead their train,
One but of late dropp'd out of Charles his wain.
Unhappy prince! (by Tapomursky led)
To feed on husks, before thy father's bread!   230

216. *Leman Lake:* i.e. Geneva, the center of Calvinism.
Tiber: i.e. Rome.

220. *Anticyra:* A city in Greece of considerable importance in ancient times. It was "famous for its black hellebore, a herb which was regarded as a cure for insanity. This circumstance gave rise to a number of proverbial expressions, like ''Αντικυρας σε δει' or 'naviget Anticyram' and to frequent allusions in the Greek and Roman writers" (*EB*).

222. The comment on transubstantiation was not unusual. Lord Chief Justice Scroggs, summing up the evidence for the jury in the trial of Ireland, Pickering, and Grove, remarked of Catholics, "They eat their God, they kill their King, and saint the murderer" (Howell, *State Trials, 7,* 134). See also Dryden, *Absalom and Achitophel,* 119–21.

227. *a star:* There may be a dual sense of a person of brilliant reputation or talents and the insigne marking the Order of the Garter. Cf. *Absalom Senior,* 1000.

228. *One:* James, Duke of Monmouth.
Charles his wain: Charles' Wain is the group of seven bright stars in Ursa Major; known also as the Plough. During the closing months of 1679, Monmouth had been deprived of his chief military and civil posts; Charles' disfavor grew with Monmouth's popularity and was virtually complete at the time of this poem.

229. *Tapomursky:* i.e. Shaftesbury. The Tory nickname was based, first, on the tap which Shaftesbury had in his side for the draining of a liver cyst and, secondly, on the rumor that he had aspired to the elective kingship of Poland. For contemporary explanation of the variant "Potapski," see the headnote to *The Last Will and Testament of Anthony, King of Poland.*

230–31. For the story of the prodigal son, see Luke 15:11–32, esp. 16–17, 20.

Fly to his arms, he like th' Almighty stands,
Inviting penitents with both his hands.
Let the True Protestant frogs croak for a king,
Be not that block, that despicable thing;
Disdain the sham of an Utopian crown,   235
Put on those laurels you so early won;
Let Caesar's lawful line the scepter sway,
Thine is as great a glory to obey.
If, by that other star Rome's pilot steer
O'er sands and rocks, that soon will disappear,   240
And leave 'em to be swallow'd in despair.
The Jesuit politics ne'er found a seat
In that brave soul, that is divinely great.
May he still next to Caesar sit at helm,
Assisting to confirm this floating realm.   245
Delos at last on a firm basis stood,
Checking the rage of an impetuous flood;

233. *True Protestant:* A phrase which, when used derisively by Tory writers, applies generally to Whig dissenters.

233–34. The allusion is to the frequently cited Aesopic fable of the frogs who desired a king. When, with time, they rejected the log ("block," 234), Jupiter sent them for their discontent a stork that devoured them all.

235. Tate would seem to be warning Monmouth that the Whigs are only supporting his accession to the crown as a sham, since a Harringtonian Utopia expressly rejects monarchy for republicanism.

236. Cf. *Absalom and Achitophel,* 23. Monmouth had served at sea during 1664–66, with the French in Holland in 1672–73, and as commander in the Scottish campaign of 1679. In all, he showed great personal bravery and received particular commendation.

239. *that other star:* James, Duke of York.

Rome's pilot. The Pope; cf. Milton, *Lycidas,* 109.

240. There may be an allusion to York's escape from shipwreck on 6 May 1682 or to his exploits during the Third Dutch War. See *Midsummer Moon,* 33 n.

243. *that brave soul:* i.e. York's.

245. *confirm:* To make firm or more firm, to add strength to, to settle, establish firmly.

floating: In addition to the more literal meaning developed in the following line, Tate seems to make a political and social application of the word in its sense of "fluctuating, variable, unstable" (*OED*).

245–47. Delos, the smallest but most famous of the Cyclades in the Aegean, was said to have been raised from the sea as a floating island by Poseidon. Leto (or Latona), pregnant by Zeus and pursued by Python, the serpent sent by the jealous and enraged Hera, found refuge on the desolate island, which Zeus thereupon fixed firmly on four pillars of adamant. It was on Delos that Leto gave birth to Apollo and Artemis.

Tate may well be attempting a royalist explication of lines from the Harringtonian

So the fair sons of Leda still dispense
A happy fate, by their joint influence.
Who knows the weight of an imperial crown   250
Would not for ever bear it all alone.
When the celestial globe, from age to age,
Atlas his shoulders singly did engage,
None ever envi'd him a little ease,
To sit and rest, and admire Hercules;   255
Both poles, and all the gods he stoutly bore,
Ev'n those that squeez'd to make his burden more.
The Church on both hands threat'ning danger sees,
Like Jason's ship 'twixt the Symplegades;
Nor doth this panic fear less seize the State,   260
Content to perish in one common fate.
Meanwhile lock Caesar's temples fast asleep;
So slept the almighty pilot on the deep
When wind and waves the sacred vessel toss'd,
When faith was sinking, the ship almost lost.   265

---

poem *Oceana and Britannia* (*POAS*, Yale, 2, 396), where Oceana begs Britannia to allow her refuge:

> To me a Delos, on my childbed smile;
> My happy seed shall fix thy floating isle
>   (15–16)

248. *the fair sons of Leda:* Leda, impregnated by Zeus, who came to her in the form of a swan, gave birth to Castor and Pollux. Here, the brothers would signify Charles and James.

249. *influence:* In astrology, the supposed flowing or streaming from the stars or heavens of an ethereal fluid acting upon the character and destiny of men and affecting sublunary things generally. Castor and Pollux form one of the twelve constellations of the zodiac.

252–57. Atlas, whose burden it was to support the tall pillars which keep heaven and earth asunder, was thought by Hesiod to stand at the western end of the earth, near the dwelling place of the Hesperides. Hercules, carrying out his eleventh labor, the search for the golden apples of the Hesperides, asked Atlas to get them from the garden for him. The Titan agreed, provided that Hercules would bear his burden in the meantime; but, having obtained the apples, Atlas refused to reassume his task and had to be tricked into doing so by Hercules. (Seyffert, *Dictionary of Classical Antiquities,* pp. 83, 282.)

259. *Symplegades.* "In Greek mythology, two cliffs or floating islands near the entrance of the Black Sea, which crushed all vessels that tried to pass between them. The Argonauts, with the help of Hera (or Athene) were the first to succeed in passing through; after this, the rocks became immovably fixed" (Seyffert, *Dictionary of Classical Antiquities,* p. 608).

263–65. Luke 8:22–25.

Sleep gently glide and calm those raging storms
That daily wrack his soul with fresh alarms;
Serene be all his dreams, happy his rest,
No politic fright disturb his thoughtful breast.
This to secure, let the Cyllenian god   270
Stroke both his temples with his charming rod;
Let Morpheus at an awful distance stand,
Observant of his mighty lord's command.

Now Painter, if thou'rt learn'd, with keen effort
Give a bold dash of Pluto's dismal court;   275
Arm that black guard t'attempt great Caesar's life
With consecrated gun, devoted knife.
Let all the factious spirits i'th' Furies' train
Shake all their snakes, and all their rods in vain;
While a wing'd boy, with a triumphant smile,   280
The mighty genius of this British Isle,
Defend all danger, this loose sleeping while.
Let all the Titans, those bold sons of earth,
That challenge Heaven by their right of birth,
With fire and thunder their own force annoy,   285
Aegeon's hundred hands himself destroy;

270. *Cyllenian.* Of Mercury, or Hermes. The god was born upon the Arcadian mountain of Cyllene. This reference antedates the single quotation in the *OED* by approximately 56 years.

271. *rod:* The caduceus "was originally an enchanter's wand, a symbol of the power that produces wealth and prosperity, and also an emblem of influence over the living and the dead. But even in early times it was regarded as a herald's staff and an emblem of peaceful intercourse" (Seyffert, *Dictionary of Classical Antiquities*, p. 288).

272. *Morpheus:* The god of dreams, who was under the authority of Hermes.

276. *that black guard:* i.e. those involved in the assassination attempts on Charles II, as described by Oates in his discovery of the Popish Plot.

277. According to Oates, Pickering and Grove (among others) were hired to shoot Charles, while Father Conyers was ordered to stab him to death (see, *inter alia*, Lane, *Oates*, pp. 77, 79, 99, 100). A pistol had been found by Sir William Waller when he searched Pickering's lodgings in the Savoy (Luttrell, *Brief Relation*, *1*, 7).

282. *loose:* Relaxed, free, untroubled, unhampered.

285. *annoy:* Injure, hurt, harm.

286. *Aegeon:* The three Hecatoncheires ("hundred-handed ones") were Briareus, Cottus, and Gyes. "Homer mentions Briareus, called by men Aegeon, as the son of Poseidon, and mightier than his father" (Seyffert, *Dictionary of Classical Antiquities*, p. 272).

Let 'em all die by one another's sword—
So fall the enemies of my dreadful Lord!
Then let the angel o'er the throne appear,
And with soft accents strike his sacred ear.   290
Here if to paint a sound be a hard thing
Give me this label Painter——

To the King.

"Awake, great sir, thy guardian prays thee wake,
Who to secure thy rest, no rest can take;
See the globe reels, the scepter's tumbling down;   295
One such another nod may lose a crown.
Awake, great care of Heav'n, rise, pay thy vows
To him that neither sleep nor slumber knows;
Yet if thy weari'd head more rest must have,
Secure the Crosier, so the Crown you save.   300
The crowds of thy Court parasites are gone
With early zeal to meet the rising sun.
That prince that shar'd thy banishment must now,

287. This destruction of opposites is found also in *Absalom and Achitophel*:

> Their Belial with their Belzebub will fight;
> Thus on my foes, my foes shall do me right.
>
> (1016–17)

302. *the rising sun:* Either a pun on "son," with an allusion to Monmouth's growing popularity as evidenced in the crowds that met him on his "progresses," or a reference to the famous medal which appeared at the time of the Whig celebrations over Shaftesbury's release. Cf. *The Medal,* 12–13:

> On the reverse, a Tower the town surveys,
> O'er which our mounting sun his beams displays

303. *That prince:* York had shared his brother's exile in France during the Common-wealth period.

303–04. *must now . . . an exile go:* We must conjecture that Tate believed that York's departure for Scotland on 3 May 1682 was to be another "exile" similar to those of 4 March 1679 (when York retired to Brussels in the face of the uproar over the Popish Plot and the first Exclusion Bill), 27 Oct. 1679 (when he first went to Scotland as High Commissioner), and 21 Oct. 1680 (when he was once more forced to return to Scotland in the face of an imminent parliament and a second Exclusion Bill). Tate may have considered that the growing Whig aggressiveness over the coming shrieval elections had led Charles once more to send his brother out of England, in which case he would have treated with some skepticism the short notice in *The London Gazette,* No. 1717 (1–4 May 1682): "Windsor, May 3. This morning early the Duke parted from hence in order to his embarking for Scotland. His Royal Highness will make a very little stay there, and in a short time will be back here with the

To yield to popular rage, an exile go,
Till kinder Providence commission me   305
To bring him safe to 's country and to thee;
Then will appear the greatness of his mind,
Like gold that in the fire is thrice refin'd.
Some friends are left, whose importunity
Will give no rest either to Heav'n or thee;   310
See a poor few, alas, at silent prayers,
No rhetoric sure, like that of sighs and tears;
Those soft addresses they will ne'er forsake—
Nor I my just alarms. Caesar awake!
Awake great care of Heav'n, rise, pay thy vows   315
To him who neither sleep nor slumber knows."

   Now, Painter, force thy art, thy utmost try;
Let day arise from Caesar's waking eye;
And while he grasps the scepter, put in's hand
The long-lost reins of sovereign command;   320
Thus let the beams of majesty outrun
The morn, and be more glorious than the sun.
Once, Painter, when the blust'ring winds grew rough
And o'er the seas did domineer and huff,
Great Neptune then, thinking himself betray'd,   325
Since his prerogative they durst invade,

Duchess." Luttrell, too, may have been skeptical, for, though he mentions the Duke's
voyage, he gives no indication that he accepts the official statement on it (*Brief
Relation, 1,* 182).

306. The loss of the *Gloucester* made people more aware of York's movements
during these weeks, and it is perhaps to this event that Tate refers, but the Duke's
return was probably not fully accepted until his actual arrival on 27 May. If this
conjecture is correct, we could date *Old England* between 3–27 May, which would
seem to be in agreement with the other references in the poem.

308. *thrice:* Possibly a reference to York's three major "exiles," in France, Brussels,
and Scotland.

309. *Some friends:* At this time, this would probably have included Rochester,
Halifax, and the Duchess of Portsmouth.

315–16. In the printed text, the preceding 22 lines begin with quotation marks,
which these two lines lack, though space was left for them. Nor is the quotation closed,
though the paragraphing and change of subject following these lines, which repeat
297–98, properly belong here or constitute an error on the part of the typesetter.

323–30. Tate's description is based on Virgil, *Aeneid,* I.124–56, where Neptune finds
his realm invaded by the winds sent by Aeolus, at Juno's request, to destroy the
Trojans.

Sprung from the deep and, with an awful nod,
Confin'd the slaves of the Aeolian god;
Straight the proud billows from their tumults cease,
And all his wat'ry subjects flow in peace.   330
Let Caesar thus arise, and thus the world,
That was to ruin and confusion hurl'd,
Retire to order, and allegiance pay
In the most loyal and submissive way.

Now let the piece with thy best colors shine,   335
While every man sits under his own vine.
Ye sisters, run this thread t' an endless date;
Now ev'ry one carves to himself his fate;
None are unhappy but who force their woe,
Make themselves wretched lest chance make 'em so,   340
As Fannius kill'd himself t' escape the foe.
Now justice flows to all in equal streams,
Whilst Liberty and Property, those themes
Canted by politic bigots, quit the schools,
Blushing their patrons are such bawling fools.   345
Let the two factions in one interest join,
And that fall'n star in his first glory shine.
Restore those lights to their own sphere again,
That falling Lucifer drew in his train.
Let Court and Country now be understood   350
One heart, one hand, one purse, one common good.
Let ev'ry faithful shepherd tune his lays
To fold his sheep, and to recall his strays;
Let him search ev'ry down, climb ev'ry rock,

336. Cf. Jonah 4:6: "And the Lord God prepared a gourd, and made it to come up over Jonah, that it might be a shadow over his head, to deliver him from his grief. So Jonah was exceeding glad of the gourd."

337. *sisters:* The three Parcae, or Fates, Clotho (who spins the thread of life), Lachesis (who determines its length), and Atropos (who cuts it off).

341. *Fannius:* Possibly the Roman annalist, consul in 122 B.C. I have been unable to locate the incident.

343. *Liberty and Property:* These republican themes, discussed by Harrington and Locke among others, were watchwords of the Whig party.

347. *fall'n star:* i.e. Monmouth. See 228.

349. *Lucifer:* Tate is probably alluding to the Earl of Shaftesbury.

350. *understood:* Regarded as, considered.

And lead his stragglers to the Cath'lic flock.   355
Let Towzer range the plains (so some of late
Have term'd Il Pastor Fido's constant mate);
Staunch to his scent, no tonsure can disguise
The fox; the wolf, though clad in sheepskin, dies;
None of more service, or of better use,   360
When Tityrus thinks fit to let him loose.
Let the plains laugh and sing, the hills rejoice,
While ev'ry sheep hears her own shepherd's voice.
Religion wears her proper dress again.
Oh happy fate, that thus has chang'd the scene!   365
Such is the force of kings, when there's no cloud
To hide their pow'r from the tumultuous crowd.
So Julius, when his legions once rebell'd,
With but a word, a look, the mutiny quell'd.

355. *Cath'lic:* Though the epithet was claimed by Rome for that part of the Western Church which remained under its obedience, Anglicans held that it was not so limited but included the Church of England as the continuation, in its proper historical sense, of the Ancient and Western Church.

356. *Towser:* A common name for a large dog, such as was used to bait bears or bulls. The name was applied to Roger L'Estrange, the most prolific and aggressive of the Tory propagandists, about 1680 by his Whig opponents, who burnt him in effigy during the Pope-burning procession of 17 Nov. 1680.

357. *Il Pastor Fido:* Tate would not seem to be alluding to Sir Richard Fanshawe, whose translation of Guarini's work appeared in 1647, and certainly not to Settle, whose version came out in 1679 but who was, at this time, still writing for the Whigs; rather, he would seem to be employing the phrase merely as a pastoral sobriquet for Charles, the shepherd of the country (cf. 361). L'Estrange, an ardent Royalist, had been imprisoned for his activities during the Civil War and had fled to Holland but had returned prior to the Restoration. After Charles' return, the volume of his controversial writing increased, though the main themes continued to be a support of High Church Anglicanism and an attack on the "fanatics." His largest and most successful undertaking was *The Observator,* a periodical in dialogue that ran from 13 April 1681–9 March 1687.

358. *Staunch:* Of a sporting dog: that may be trusted to find or follow the scent or mark the game; dependable.

358–59. L'Estrange insisted, as does Tate in this poem, that the sectarian zealot (the wolf) who preached republicanism was just as dangerous, though a Protestant, as the Roman Catholic priest (the fox).

361. *Tityrus:* The name of a shepherd in Virgil's *Eclogues;* a shepherd; Virgil himself or his *Eclogues.* Here, it would seem to refer to the King.

368–69. The incident is recounted by Suetonius in *The Lives of the Twelve Caesars* (trans. A. Thomson, rev. T. Forester [London, 1903]):

LXX. When the soldiers of the tenth legion at Rome demanded their discharge and rewards for their service, with violent threats and no small danger to the

Awake my lute, of Caesar is my song.   370
Ah! Painter, why did'st let him sleep so long?
Caesar gives life to nature, fills each soul
With peace and joy, while plenty crowns each bowl.
Let great Apollo strike his Delphic lyre,
With all the well-tun'd virgins of the choir;   375
Infuse ye goddesses a loyal vein
On all th' attendants of the Hippocrene;
Let not th' infection of uneasy times
Pollute the fountain with seditious rhymes;
Restrain licentious prophets, and let none   380
Come with unhallow'd lays to Helicon;
May still fresh laurels round his temples spring,
That to the royal harp does sit and sing.
On wretched Oates, Doeg his lips shall wear,

---

city, although the war was then raging in Africa, he did not hesitate, contrary
to the advice of his friends, to meet the legion, and disband it. But addressing
them by the title of 'Quirites,' instead of 'Soldiers,' he by this single word so
thoroughly brought them round and changed their determination, that they
immediately cried out, they were his 'soldiers,' and followed him to Africa, al-
though he had refused their service. He nevertheless punished the most mutinous
among them, with the loss of a third of their share in the plunder, and the land
destined for them.

377. *Hippocrene:* The fountain on Mount Helicon, struck forth by the hoof of
Pegasus and sacred to the Muses; hence, used allusively in reference to poetic or
literary inspiration.

380. *licentious:* See 2 n.

384. *Doeg:* Saul's chief herdsman, who informed on David and Ahimelech and,
when others refused, carried out Saul's orders to destroy the priests and their families
(I Samuel 21:7; 22:9–10, 17–22). Here, Doeg stands for Elkanah Settle, at this time the
principal Whig poet and organizer of the famous Pope-burning procession of 1680;
he had regularly attacked York (as in *The Character of a Popish Successor*, 1681
[S 2670–2]) and attempted to answer Tory literary attacks (see *Absalom Senior*). Tate,
like Dryden in his later portrait of Settle (*Absalom and Architophel II*, 412–56), prob-
ably found the excoriation of Doeg in Psalm 52 particularly appropriate.

Thy tongue deviseth mischiefs; like a sharp razor, working deceitfully./ Thou
lovest evil more than good; and lying rather than to speak righteousness./ Thou
lovest all devouring words, O thou deceitful tongue./ . . . Lo, this is the man
that made not God his strength; but trusted in the abundance of his riches,
and strengthened himself in his wickedness. (vv. 2–4, 7)

The witty lash of *Heraclitus Ridens* had also struck Settle (No. 50 [10 Jan. 1682]),
who is *Dux Phanaticorum, Whiggorum, Ignoramorum, Dapplorum* and will "vindicate
Lucifer's first rebellion for a few guineas." In 1683, Settle went over to the Tory side,
exposing the perjuries of Oates and attacking the Whigs in *A Narrative of the Popish
Plot* [S 2700].

wear: Wear out, waste away, exhaust.

And murder his ill tunes that fright the ear,   385
Beneath Apollo or the Muses' care.
When thus the poet shall his notes divide
And never play but to the juster side,
The painter shall his trembling pencil bring
To serve the most august and God-like King;   390
Yet all his colors can't set off this scene;
Art, in a piece of nature, is a stain.

Now the great month proceeds; this is that spring
The Sibyll and the Mantuan bard did sing.
Let Saturn envy Caesar's greater bliss;   395
His Golden Age was but a type of this.
Now all the spheres in peaceful measures move;
The very sectaries do order love.
Old England I no more shall long to see;
We're just as happy as we please to be.   400
No prostituted oaths our fears create,
No pilgrims' march alarms the Church or State.

Asaph record these times; no more refuse
The pow'rful impulse of thy charming muse;

393. An allusion to Virgil's *Fourth Eclogue:*

Ultima Cumaei venit iam carminis aetas;
Magnus ab integro saeclorum nascitur ordo.
Iam redit et Virgo, redeunt Saturnia regna.
(4–6)

402. Part of the frenzy caused by the Popish Plot discoveries arose from rumors
that an "army of foreigners landed in Ireland and an army of Spanish pilgrims in
England" (*The Dissenter Unmask'd*, London, 1683 [D 1683]). The pilgrims were said
to come from St. Iago (see *r*" V, p. 345) and to have landed on Barnstead Downs
(*Somers Tracts, 8,* 394). These highly ephemeral pilgrims were ridiculed regularly
by Court poets (e.g. Otway, in the prologue to *Venice Preserv'd*, 15–16; or *The Com-
pleat Swearing-Master*, 13–18).

404. *Asaph.* One of the leaders of David's choir (I Chronicles 6:39) to whom a
number of the psalms are attributed. He was later celebrated as a seer as well as a
musical composer, and was put on a par with David (II Chronicles 29:30; Nehemiah
12:16). Here Asaph represents Dryden, and Tate's tribute bears striking resemblance
to that which he penned for *Absalom and Achitophel II* (1037–64). There, the theme
is that "the song of Asaph shall forever last" (1042, 1048, 1058, 1064), and he con-
cludes the encomiastic portrait with lines that parallel the rhetoric, and even the
imagery, of that given here:

What praise for such rich strains shall we allow?
What just rewards the grateful Crown bestow?
While bees in flow'rs rejoice, and flow'rs in dew,

Those royal heroes that attend the King,   405
None but an Asaph may presume to sing.
When Hybla to the bee shall dew deny,
When suppliants in vain to Caesar fly,
Then shall this age be lost i'th' rolls of time;
Then Asaph's song shall be like Doeg's rhyme.   410

While stars and fountains to their course are true,
While Judah's throne and Sion's rock stand fast,
The song of Asaph and the fame shall last.
                                        (1059–64)

Despite the excellent survey of Reginald Sharpe and the wealth of information given by the Rev. Alfred Beaven, a detailed history of the municipal politics of seventeenth-century London, and their effect on the kingdom, has yet to be written. Certainly one of the most arresting moments would be that fateful 18th of May 1682 when the (until then) mildly royalist mayor, Sir John Moore, exercised his traditional right [1] at the Bridge House banquet and drank to Dudley North, thereby nominating him one of the two sheriffs for the coming year. The Court party, fully aware that control of London was a great step towards control of Commons, knew well that the effective power of the Corporation was vested traditionally in the lord mayor and practically in the two sheriffs of the City of London and the County of Middlesex. The importance of the shrieval offices had been made painfully manifest to the Tories, for the sheriffs, with their power to impanel juries, virtually controlled the legal machinery, despite the fact that the appointed judges tended to side with the government. The Court had received a tremendous setback from the "Ignoramus" that had freed Shaftesbury; they had been forced to move the trial of Stephen College to Oxford in order to get a sympathetic jury; indeed, so overtly prejudiced were juries that Shaftesbury, in 1682, dropped his case of scandalum magnatum against Craddock, and of conspiracy against Graham, when the court ruled that the trials should be held elsewhere because of the partiality of London juries.[2]

To understand the nature of the contest, one must first understand the municipal election procedure. The term of office for both the lord mayor and the sheriffs was one year: the former was selected, ordinarily by seniority, from the Aldermanic Council; the latter came usually, though not invariably,[3] from the same group. The

1. Sharpe, *London and the Kingdom*, 2, pp. 468–72.

2. Echard, *History*, 3, 658–59.

3. Slingsby Bethel, for example, tried unsuccessfully to become an alderman on five different occasions. Cf. Beaven, *Aldermen*, 2, xlv, where it is suggested that "his

overlapping tenure of the offices has caused a great deal of confusion. The Lord Mayor was elected on Michaelmas Day (29 Sept.) and installed on Lord Mayor's Day, one month later (29 Oct.). His sheriffs were those that had been elected and/or confirmed on the previous Midsummer Day (24 June), during the term of his predecessor. About three or four months before the end of his mayoralty, he in turn would nominate a sheriff at the Bridge House banquet by drinking to him (or, if the person were absent, sending the cup to him formally). A Common Hall (i.e. a meeting of the liverymen of the various guilds) was then convoked for Midsummer Day, at which time there was ordinarily confirmation of the mayor's candidate and election of a second sheriff. By custom, the Mayor and Aldermen withdrew during the election (a fact of great importance during the 1682 contest), which was run by the incumbent sheriffs with the help of the common serjeant, the common cryer, and the city recorder.[4] Those chosen were installed on Michaelmas Eve (28 Sept.) and were in charge of the mayoral election the following day. Since the shrieval posts were full-time jobs, many of those elected would "fine off" by paying £400 rather than allow their personal affairs to go neglected for a full year.[5]

In the years immediately preceding the mayoralty of Moore, Charles had unsuccessfully attempted to move against the Whig-controlled municipality. The difficulties had become critical during the term (1680) of Sir Robert Clayton, an ardent Whig. Sir Robert's nominee for sheriff, George Hockenhall, fined off; "the Commons thereupon stepped in and elected Slingsby Bethel, leatherseller, and Henry Cornish, haberdasher. At this juncture, political influence was brought to bear upon the elections. Bethel was particularly an

---

parsimony and his Puritanism [combined] to make him a persona ingrata to the Court of Alderman."

4. For a contemporary discussion of the election procedure, see "The Trial of Thomas Pilkington, Esq., Samuel Shute, Esq., Sheriffs; Henry Cornish, Alderman; Ford Lord Grey of Werk; Sir Thomas Player, Knt., Chamberlain of London; Slingsby Bethel, Esq.; Francis Jenks; John Deagle; Richard Freeman; Richard Goodenough; Robert Key; John Wickham; Samuel Swinock; John Jekyll, Senior; at Nisi Prius at the Guildhall of London, for a Riot, and an Assault and Battery on Sir John Moore, then Lord Mayor, A.D. 1683" in Howell, *State Trials, 9,* 219–94.

5. The prevalence of this practice is strikingly illustrated by Sir George Jeffreys' remark that when he "was common serjeant, there were £5,000 fines one year." (Howell, *State Trials, 9,* 244.)

object of aversion to the Court Party." [6] Certain delays followed, but at a second election on 14 July Bethel and Cornish won over Ralph Box, grocer, and Humphrey Nicholson, merchant taylor, "who, although . . . nominated by the commonalty, were in reality candidates put forward by the Court Party." [7] Jeffreys later remarked, during a famous trial that grew out of the 1682 election, "Ay, in Bethel and Cornish's time, then began the bustle." [8] The "bustle" had, indeed, begun. In the following year (1681), under the mayoralty of the equally extreme Whig Sir Patience Ward, the defeat of the Court party was even more pronounced. Ward had selected Thomas Pilkington, but, in what was to prove an historical irony,[9] a poll was demanded for all candidates. Pilkington received 3,144 votes and his Whig colleague, Shute, 2,245, while the Court candidates, Box and Nicholson, had only 1,266 and 82 votes, respectively. Charles must have felt the defeat keenly. Indeed, four months later, when the two sheriffs and the City Recorder (Treby) invited him to the Lord Mayor's banquet in honor of the recently elected Moore, the King replied, "Mr. Recorder, an invitation from my Lord Mayor and the City is very acceptable to me, and to show that it is so, notwithstanding that it is brought by messengers that are so unwelcome to me as these sheriffs are, yet I accept it." [10]

But Charles had gained, at this very moment, the opening he needed in order to capture control of the City's legal and political machinery. True, Sir John Moore, as Senior Alderman, should not have had to stand to a poll; but he had nonetheless won the office, and the King was quick to exploit the situation. Anyone who still labors under the misapprehension that Charles or the Court were unable

6. Sharpe, *London and the Kingdom*, 2, 472.

7. Ibid., p. 473.

8. Howell, *State Trials*, 9, 240.

9. Sharpe (*London and the Kingdom*, 2, 474, n. 1) notes that "The Court of Aldermen considered the demand for a poll as to Pilkington's election to be an invasion of the Lord Mayor's prerogative, he being already in the opinion of the Court duly elected and confirmed according to ancient usage. It passed a resolution, therefore, that before the poll was opened Alderman Pilkington should be immediately called out on the husting and returned into the exchequer as one of the sheriffs for the ensuing year (Repertory 86, fo. 153)." Pilkington was to run directly into this very confirmation of prerogative in his attempt to deny the shrieval office to Moore's nominee, Dudley North.

10. Sharpe, *London and the Kingdom*, 2, 474 n. 1: "Journal 49, fos. 254, 255b, 261b; Kennet, iii, 401."

to act with a determination bordering on the ruthless need only look at the events of the ensuing months. By January the government called into question the whole corporate and political structure of the City by a Quo Warranto, a device which Charles had used to recall the charters of other cities but which he had not seen fit to level against London until he felt comparatively certain of having a sympathetic municipal officialdom. Such an action made all the more necessary the control of the shrieval posts, as both parties realized. The Whigs, fighting desperately at bay, were behind Pilkington, the man who would be in charge of the election; the Tories, having achieved an opening, supported Moore, the man through whom the election could be legalistically controlled.

The government increased its pressure on the opposition. To the delight of the Tory pamphleteers, the Privy Council ordered Moore to prohibit as seditious the Whig Feast at Haberdashers' Hall on 21 April, to which Monmouth, Shaftesbury, and the supporters of the opposition were contributing their money and their efforts. The Tory banquet at the Merchant Taylors' Hall on the previous day had, of course, gone undisturbed though hardly unregarded by the Court which considered it an expression of loyalty worthy of acceptance by the Duke of York himself. The use of James during the election was a dangerous but clever move calculated both to offset the popularity of Monmouth and to associate York more closely with Court policy towards the City. James made one more well-timed maneuver. In early June, just prior to the elections, he brought a charge of scandalum magnatum against Pilkington, claiming damages of £50,000. If this action was not meant as a direct subornation of Pilkington, it was at least intended to drive him into hiding and so reduce his effectiveness as an opposition organizer. Perhaps it was also hoped that fear of the writ would keep him away from the Common Hall and so give Moore and Charles greater warrant for outright selection of Dudley North and Ralph Box; but if this was the assumption, the Court party had radically underestimated the integrity and character of the Whig sheriff. Pilkington would soon be in the Tower, but before he went he would force Moore, and, through Moore, the King himself, to take such absolute and arbitrary steps that the election would stand blatantly exposed as a piece of legalistic chicanery.

The enigma of the Lord Mayor hovers over the whole history of this period. North, in the *Examen* (p. 596), quite rightly saw that "very much depended on the character of the single citizen, Sir John Moore." After commenting on his honesty in business and orthodoxy in religion, North drew a precise though partisan picture:

> He was by nature not only careful but also very fearful of consequences; but being once satisfied of the justice in what concerned him to do, he wanted no resolution or courage to perform it. In the meantime, his being suspicious, dubious, cautelous, and not soon determined, but hesitatory of unusual occurrences in his office, made him pass for a person timidous, and of a fickle, irresolute temper . . . He was forward in nothing and, being sensible of his soft, unsteady elocution, inclined to silence. But his behavior was always modest and respectful to all and, by his words or carriage, offending none, but to his betters extreme submiss.

And, noting Moore's general air of irresolution and despondency, North concludes:

> All which made it wonderful that . . . he should carry himself with such firmness and perseverance in all the substantial points of his difficulties, as he did. . . . Which character was cut out for his time and public occasion; for nothing but such firmness of mind and manifest goodness, with a seeming passive disposition, could have protected him from the rages of violence as very often threatened him, which probably had broke loose upon anyone in his post that had carried matters with a stern and minatory behavior.

Beneath this obvious bias, there lies a fairly subtle analysis of Moore's personality. Burnet's Whig view seizes on many of the same characteristics, but he speaks of the Lord Mayor as "one whom the Court could easily manage . . . a flexible and faint-hearted man" (2, 335). Papillon's biographer sees him as, at best, a bumbling incompetent and more usually as a mere court jockey (pp. 203–28). That Moore looked to the Court for guidance is a matter of record, but for a Tory to seek such direction is no more surprising than is its condemnation by Whig historians. Nor does this alter the essential problem of Moore's character, a problem made all the more important by the critical role he played.

Nor is it yet absolutely clear who at Court was directing the campaign in the City. That Sir Leoline Jenkins, Secretary of State for the South, was Moore's principal contact with the Court is proven amply by the *CSPD;* but whether or not Jenkins was the strategist is a little more difficult to tell. There is a good chance that he was, for Burnet (2, 339) states that Moore, because of the Whig opposition to his own election, "became in all things compliant to the Court, in particular to Secretary Jenkins, who took him into his own management." And, with reference to the election of Moore's successor, he says flatly:

> Jenkins managed the whole business of the City with so many indirect practices that the reputation he had for probity was much blemished by it. He seemed to think it was necessary to bring the City to dependence on the Court in the fairest method he could fall on; and if these did not succeed, that then he was to take the most effectual ones, hoping that a good intention would excuse bad practices.

Jenkins' biographer Wynne vehemently denies this charge (*1*, xlvii–xlviii) and cites the Secretary's letter to York (2, 684) dissuading the Duke from attempting to seize the City charter. But Wynne's chief argument was Burnet's lack of evidence, and this has been amply supplied by *CSPD*, 1682. It is here that we trace the course of Jenkins' role. On 1 May—just ten days after Moore had pledged to North—Jenkins heard that the Whigs were "combining against ratifying the election" and wrote to Hyde asking permission to "apply [himself] wholly to that one point" (p. 190). Jenkins' notes [11] indicate that it was he who planned the basic strategy, albeit upon consultation with Charles (p. 304) and the Council.[12]

There has been a persistent statement that the real mentor was the Duke of Ormonde; and, indeed, the suggestion is not implausible, since, as the Earl of Langford had written the Duke on the previous 3 Sept., "Mr. Secretary Jenkins is entirely your Grace's creature and I am sure to the utmost of his power and skill will on all occasions serve your Grace." [13] This suggestion, which has been re-

11. Cf. *CSPD,* 1682, pp. 265, 268, 270, 280–81, 293, 302, et al.

12. Cf. Francis North's legal advice, *CSPD,* 1682, p. 278; also North, *Examen,* pp. 610–11.

13. *HMC, Ormonde MSS.,* New Series, 6, 143–44.

peated through the years, [14] apparently has its source in the assertion of Ormonde's biographer, Thomas Carte. His gloss—"Services done by his Grace to the King of England" and "particularly in the City elections"—and his statements in the text are quite unequivocal:

> Sir John Moore, the Lord Mayor at this time, was a very honest man; but timorous in some cases and doubtful of exerting his authority. The Duke of Ormonde was the person that inspired him with courage; he generally dined with him twice or thrice a week during the contests which now happened; and was the only person about Court employed on these occasions.[15]

This last statement, as the *CSPD* shows, is manifestly untrue, and we must bring against Carte the same charge that Wynne brought against Burnet, namely that no evidence is offered in support. Indeed, F. Elrington Ball, the editor of the relevant volume of the Ormonde MSS, remarks in his introduction: "But on the great exertions made by Ormonde in the following year to obtain the election of members of the Court Party to civic offices, to which Carte alludes, the correspondence in this volume does not throw much fresh light." [16] While the contest is frequently mentioned, there is, in fact, no indication of anything more than current knowledge and opinion.

When the first hint of Box's fining off came to Jenkins, he wrote at once to Windsor. The Earl of Conway's reply, sent within two hours of the receipt of the Secretary's letter, reveals a good deal of the inner workings of the Court Party:

> The Earl of Conway to Secretary Jenkins. I received yours about 6 and went with it immediately to his Majesty, who was walking in the Park, Lord Halifax with him. He commanded me to write to you that he does not think Mr. Box offers any reasonable excuse, being he is elected by the major part sheriff

14. See, for example, *DNB*, *3*, 512 (sub Butler); *DNB*, *13*, 806 (sub Moore); Keith Feiling, *A History of the Tory Party, 1640–1714* (Oxford, 1924), p. 194; Leopold von Ranke, *A History of England Principally in the Seventeenth Century* (6 vols. Oxford, 1875), *4*, 161; H. C. Foxcroft, *The Life and Letters of Sir George Savile, Bart., First Marquis of Halifax* (2 vols. London, 1898), *1*, 376, n. 1. It should be noted that both von Ranke and Foxcroft mention Jenkins along with Ormonde.

15. Thomas Carte, *An History of the Life of James, Duke of Ormonde* . . . (2 vols. London, 1736), *2*, 522.

16. *HMC, Ormonde MSS., New Series, 6*, xiii.

according to the laws and customs of the City. What the other party would have been we know not nor can take notice of. But, because Mr. Box has scruples which his Majesty is desirous to satisfy, he conceives Lord Hyde, Lord Chief Justice North and yourself, when you have advised together, are the fittest persons to give him satisfaction, and this he desires you to do with all possible expedition and he will make good whatever you undertake.

He desires you to have all possible care of the Lord Mayor. He looks on the actions against him as inconsiderable and approves of your conduct in appointing one to take all the trouble and charge of them from him and desires you to assure him and such as shall be concerned that he will always do so.

Lord Hyde went hence to London before your letter arrived, but I hope what I have written will be sufficient to engage him and all of you to persuade Mr. Box to hold his shrivealty [sic].

His Majesty has ordered the Council to be put off next Thursday at Hampton Court and to meet there Thursday sennight. I have returned you the three letters signed by his Majesty.[17]

No mention is made here of Ormonde, who was at Windsor; on the contrary, the specific charge to Jenkins to "have all possible care of the Lord Mayor" would seem to confirm Burnet's suggestion that it was the Secretary who had taken Moore "into his own management." Jenkins' planning included a number of preliminary notes on the possibility of keeping Moore as Lord Mayor for an unprecedented second term.[18]

Foxcroft is probably correct in saying that "in these manipulations Lord Halifax does not seem to have taken a conspicuous part—though of course the contemporary lampooners credited him with a share in these, as in all other, unpopular courses." [19] She cites the relevant lines from *Midsummer Madness* but rejects their implications with the conventional remark that "the Duke of Ormonde and Jenkins were the most active agents." [20] Her evaluation of Halifax's role is quite judicious, though, as principal adviser to the King at this

17. *CSPD*, 1682, p. 304.
18. See Ibid., p. 302.
19. *Life, 1,* 375–76; see also Foxcroft, *A Character of the Trimmer,* p. 173.
20. *Life, 1,* 376, n. 1.

time, the Marquis probably had given more than just "tacit sanction" to the Court's policy. There is a highly suggestive entry in the *CSPD* for 21 June, just three days prior to the election date:

> Secretary Jenkins to Mr. Box. Requesting him to call on him about 7 that afternoon at his office in Whitehall, where he will find the Earl of Halifax about that time. His lordship and he have some business of public consequence to speak to him about. (p. 259)

The conversation that took place at Whitehall on that June evening, like the one that was to occur at about the same hour just four weeks later in the park at Windsor, lie just beyond our range of hearing, tantalizing us with imagined sounds. Yet, though these are lacking, contemporary accounts and state papers seem to give overwhelming evidence that it was Secretary Jenkins who, with the advice of Charles and certain privy-councillors, "managed the whole business of the city."

The Whigs, despite the tremendous pressure of the Court, felt that total victory would eventually be theirs by virtue of their ultimate weapon—a Parliament. For this reason, they refused to compromise by confirming North and voting for just one sheriff. Six times in three weeks the Common Halls showed their support of the Whig candidates, Papillon and Dubois, and six times Moore managed to nullify their choice, finally declaring North and Box the legally elected sheriffs.

> But Box was frighted at the double election, for so it was termed, and the disputes with the anti-sheriffs, as might happen, and so fined off; and then Sir Peter Rich was chosen, and the election declared for North and Rich. It was wondered at by many why the [Whig] faction did not interpose to trouble this latter election and, as they might have one, joined one of their own party; for it might (and really it did so) happen that a friend in a corner had been of great service to them. But they considered, wisely enough, that it was better to stand the after-game in Parliament, which would make clear work, and, in the meantime, not hurt their title to two sheriffs by coming in for one; and if they did, their officer would have a sour time of it, having the Court, the

law, and the officers against them, for the latter would certainly obey my Lord Mayor's sheriff.[21]

Roger North's *Examen* can hardly be called unbiased, and yet, allowing for the author's partiality, the analyses therein are remarkably acute. Both sides recognized the national implications of the contest; North's Tory view was as follows:

> Some may think that an account of these city squabbles are but low history; but if such as these are low, I am at a loss to know what is high. For was it not a *battail rangée* between the King and Council, with the ministry and loyal party on one side, and the whole antimonarchial and rebellious party on the other? And at a time when the latter were puffed up in conceit they had the advantage, and that the other was blown and must soon render or be cut off? (p. 616)

North's opening phrase underscores the interesting though probably not surprising fact that, from the very inception of the party system, national policy has ultimately depended on ward politics.

21. North, *Examen,* p. 611.

An Ironical Encomium

The *Ironical Encomium* has been found only in *POAS,* and the texts, with minor exceptions, are consistent. In addition to its sustained irony, the poem is unified by its frequent reference to the Catilinarian conspiracy, drawing specifically from the opening lines of Jonson's *Catiline* (1611). The classical analogy must have been quite attractive to the Court party. In 1682, Sulla's ghost rises in odd places (see 77–78 n.) and evokes the ghost of the "Hotspur" of the conspiracy, Cethegus. In the following year, 1683, the Rye House plot not only produced a *Sulla's Ghost, A Satyr Against Ambition and the Last Horrid Plot,* by C. C. (Caleb Calle?) [C 18] but in all probability inspired at least two translations of the Catilinarian conspiracy. One, *The History of Catiline's Conspiracy* [H 2116], is based on the usual classical authors, though it opens "with some General Observations For assisting the Interests of Peace and Virtue"; the other, *Patriae Parricida: or, the History of the Horrid Conspiracy of Catiline against the Commonwealth of Rome* [S 409], again by C. C. (Caleb Calle), is very freely translated from Sallust and quite unashamedly seeks to parallel the times, beginning with an epigraph on the title page taken from Dryden's *Absalom and Achitophel* (83–84) and continuing not only in the Epistle Dedicatory but in the use of such terms as "Reformation," "Association," and "Conventicle."

AN IRONICAL ENCOMIUM

On the Unparallel'd Proceedings of the Incomparable Couple
of Whiggish Walloons.

> Go on, brave heroes, you whose merits claim
> Eternal plaudit from the trump of Fame,

Title: Whiggish Walloons. The reference is to the French background of Papillon and Dubois. Thus, in an autographed MS. Papillon tells of a meeting on 25 April 1683 at the house of the then Lord Mayor, Sir Henry Tulse, one of whose adherents, Sir James Smith, "said some opprobrious words to Mr. Papillon and Mr. Dubois, that they were French or Walloon Protestants that came into this nation for refuge, and had got estates, and would overthrow the Government, and cut our throats &c"

Beyond the daring hector that aspir'd
To leave a name, when he the temple fir'd,
For after ages; and let nothing pall   5
Your well-fix'd resolutions; not though all
The seas were heap'd on seas, and hills on hills:
Small are secur'd by doing greater ills.

(*Papillon,* pp. 231). When Papillon refused to be provoked, Sir James repeated his
charge, adding to the Lord Mayor that "now there is come over a great many more
of late, and in a little time they will be the same as these are. To which my Lord
Mayor replied, 'I hope the King will take a course to send them back again to their
country'" (pp. 231–32). Undoubtedly both the Lord Mayor and Sir James were aware
that Papillon was the respected treasurer of a company of "adventurers in the Stock
raised for setting the poor French Protestants on work at Ipswich on the linen
manufacture," which included men who were the most bitter political opponents.
Thus, scarcely a month before this (pp. 117–19), we find such names as Dubois and
Box, Sir Patience Ward and Sir John Moore, Henry Cornish and Sir William Prichard,
Sir Robert Clayton and the Bishop of London, voicing their "thanks to Mr. Papillon
for his great charity, care and pains . . . in this affair," and continuing him in office
at a commission assessed on the profits.

2. *trump:* Fame's trumpet was bifurcated, one bell sounding *bona fama* and the
other *mala fama.*

3. *hector:* A swaggerer, braggart, bully.

4. A favorite image of the period. Herostratus is said to have burned the temple
to Artemis in Oct. 365 B.C. in order to acquire eternal fame, even if that fame was
based upon a great crime.

5. Case 211 (3) (a) reads *paul* and may indicate a play on words. Cf. *Massinello, or a
Satyr Against the Association and the Guild hall Riot* (London, 1683) [M 1043]:

> Yet he's [i.e., Shaftesbury] rê vera but an anti-Paul
> Who to gain some becomes all things to all.
>
> (p. 4)

5–10. This passage borrows heavily from the opening lines of Catiline's first speech
in Jonson's *Catiline,* following the prologue of Sulla's ghost (cf. 77):

> It is decreed. Nor shall thy fate, O Rome,
> Resist my vow. Though hills were set on hills
> And seas met seas to guard thee; I would through:
> Aye, plough up rocks, steep as the Alps, in dust,
> And lave the Tyrrhene waters into clouds,
> But I would reach thy head, thy head, proud city.
> The ills that I have done cannot be safe
> But by attempting greater . . .
>
> (73–80)

8. Though derived from Jonson, the line is paralleled in *A True Protestant Con-
jurer to Cethegus' Ghost to appear Septemb. 19. 1682:*

> The ills that we've committed safe can't be
> Without attempting worse for liberty.
>
> (5–6)

Cf. Seneca, *Agamemnon;* "Per scelera semper sceleribus tutum est iter" (116).

Go on, and may your tow'ring deeds outshine
The high achievements of blest Catiline.   10
And let the echoes of your acts by all
Be heard as loud as those were at Guildhall.
What! Shall a puny patriot balk your flight,
And formal fops your dawning days benight?
Shall laws confine, or lawyers you withstand,   15
That have both law and lawyers in your hand?
Shall gilded chains beshackle you with fears?
Tear, tear their gowns and chains from off their ears,
And hang their Worships in them; let the curs
Be swing'd in scarlet and go rot in furs.   20
Damn 'em for dogs to put such worthies by,
Just i'th' nick of our tranquillity;
Just as the Saints with forty thousand men

13. *patriot:* Sir John Moore, the Lord Mayor.

14. The form referred to was probably the time-honored right of the Lord Mayor to select a sheriff by drinking to him.

15. *laws:* i.e. the Lord Mayor's power to adjourn a common hall as well as Moore's insistence that only his books could be used to take a legal poll.

lawyers. Moore was backed up by Serjeant Jeffreys, the Attorney General, Sir Robert Sawyer, and Lord Chief Justice North, among others (Cf. North, *Examen,* pp. 607 and 610).

16. The reference is to the subversion of the law through "Ignoramus" juries. So Jeffreys, sitting as Lord Chief Justice in the action of Sir William Prichard against Papillon in 1683, indignantly referred to "the last past years" as worse than any villainy of the Commonwealth: "The very methods of justice have been corrupted, and all to serve the main design of subverting the government." It was a time "when traitors at the Bar were in less danger of being convicted of their treasons, than the judges were of their lives. . . . Nay, so far were the proceedings in courts of justice tainted, that in no common action whatsoever that came here to be tried, but cropped hair, and a demure look were the best signs of a good evidence; and the business of an oath signified nothing, provided the Party were to be propped up, and the Faction to receive an advantage by it" (*An Exact Account of the Trial between Sir William Prichard . . . and Thomas Papillon . . . on Thursday the 6th of November, 1684 . . . Before Sir George Jeffreys . . .* [London, 1689], pp. 28–29).

17. *chains:* i.e. the chains of office.

20. *swing'd:* Beaten.

scarlet . . . furs: The color and trim of the robe of office. Jeffreys remarked, "I know Mr. Papillon's humor so well that I am confident he would much rather have been contented to sit in his counting-house than in Guild-hall in a scarlet gown" (*An Exact Account . . . ,* p. 30).

23. A reference to one of the many sham plots used to keep the public stirred up. Cf. L'Estrange, *Observator,* No. 9 (4 May 1681), where Answer tells of his dreams of London's downfall, of "fires, rapes, massacres, idols, invasions, the clanging of trumpets,

Were furnish'd for a Holy War again.
Rally once more, and cry them in the crowd,   25
The mobile's your own; give out aloud
For Reformation, and the town's your own,
Else *Liberty and Property* are gone.
Caesar's abroad; go seize the Senate, do;
And if he comes, faith, seize brave Caesar too!   30
Let nothing be too sacred for your arms
(Love and revenge are never fill'd by charms);
By greatest acts your greatest glory gather,
And he's no more immortal than his father.
Serve him as Brutus did, and in his room   35
Put up young Perkin, now the time is come
That ten may chase a thousand; now or never:
Lose but this time and you are lost for ever.
A deed more bold than Blood's, more brave than them

---

clattering of arms, the screams of children." After a few comic revelations of his sub-
conscious, he continues, "Just upon the neck of this comes in an express, methought,
with news for certain that forty thousand French had made a descent at Devil's Ditch
and entrenched themselves. What did I do but presently, with the Covenant in one
hand, an Association in the other, and a leading-staff betwixt my teeth, fall in upon
them and, in one word, methought, I had the chase of them to the very walls of New-
Market." (Devil's Ditch intersects the race course at New Market, one of Charles II's
favorite spots.)

28. "Liberty and Property" was, like "No Popery, No Slavery," one of the political
catchwords of the period. So Jeffreys, attacking the "specious pretence . . . of Law'
and the subversive "whine and snivel and cant," cites one of the previous Whig
sheriffs: " 'Alack-a-day,' as Mr. Pilkington said, 'I am for the preservation of the
liberty and properties of the subject, and I am for law . . .' " (*An Exact Account . . .*
p. 31).

29–31. There is, here, a strong analogy to the evidence for the charge of treason
brought against Shaftesbury. See *The Proceedings at the Sessions House . . . on
Thursday the 24th of November, 1681 . . . upon the Bill of Indictment for High-
Treason against Anthony Earl of Shaftesbury* [P 3563] (London, 1681).

34. Charles I, beheaded 30 Jan. 1649 by order of the High Court of Parliament.

35. Probably a reference to Marcus Brutus, but cf. *A Summons . . . to Cethegus'
Ghost*, 11, where the author would appear to have L. Junius Brutus in mind.

36. *young Perkin:* James, Duke of Monmouth. Perkin Warbeck claimed to be
Richard, Duke of York, the second son of Edward IV. His intrigues, invasions, and
plots for the crown of England were finally ended by his hanging in 1499. Monmouth
is said to have received the prophetic title of Prince Perkin from Nell Gwynne in 1680
(D'Oyley, *Monmouth*, p. 155).

39. *Blood's:* Colonel Blood, the notorious adventurer, attempted, among other nota-
ble exploits, to steal the crown, orb, and scepter from the Tower in 1671.

That slyly sneak'd to steal a diadem: 40
For sure that soul deserves much more renown
That kills a king than he that takes his crown.
The Ides of March are past, and Gadbury
Proclaims a downfall of our monarchy;
Who saw the last conjunction did portend   45
That crowns and kingdoms tumble to their end.
A Commonwealth shall rise and splendid grow,
As now predicted by the wise T.O.
Who can foretell, forestall, forswear, foresee,
Through an inch-board, or through an oaken tree;   50
Whose optics o'er the mighty main have gone,

40. Cf. *Hamlet*, III.iv.100–01: "That from the shelf the precious diadem stole/ And put it in his pocket."

43. *Ides of March:* The prophesied date of Julius Caesar's assassination. John Gadbury (1627–1704) was, along with William Lilly and John Partridge, one of the foremost astrologers of his day. With the Restoration, Gadbury became increasingly Royalist and Roman, until by 1679 he had written at least the first half of the four-part narrative *Ballad upon the Popish Plot* [C 75] and, despite his *Magna Veritas: or John Gadbury . . . not a Papist* (1680) [C 87], probably converted to Catholicism. He was implicated with Mrs. Cellier in the Meal Tub Plot on the evidence of Thomas Dangerfield.

45. The reference here is probably to Gadbury's annual *Ephemerides*. Throughout the seventeenth century, the political effect of the almanacs on the populace had been recognized. Gadbury not only used the conjunctions to suggest coming events but elaborated on his predictions in the opening of his 1682 Almanac. (See the reply of Thomas Dangerfield, *Animadversions upon Mr. John Gadbury's Almanack . . . for . . . 1682* (1682) [D 181].) The "last conjunction" may simply refer to Gadbury's two-part Commonwealth tract *Coelestis Legatus, or the Celestial Ambassador, astronomically predicting the grand Catastrophe that is to befall the most of the Kingdoms and Countries of Europe* (1656).

48. *T.O.:* Titus Oates.

49–50. These lines have multiple meanings. The "foretell" and "forestall" probably refer to Oates' confused testimony against the Queen and Sir George Wakeman. Oates had claimed to be hidden behind the door of an adjoining room when he overheard the treasonous conversation. When asked how he could, then, make identification, Oates had first said he had looked into the room, but later claimed that the Queen had given him an audience at which time he recognized her voice and saw Sir George. See also Tilley, *Proverbs*, *1*, 61: "He will swear (look) through an inch board." Although Tilley's earliest example is 1623, his three later quotations are remarkably relevant: "1658 Franck *North Mem.* p. 191: It's thought they would have sworn through a double deal-board, they seem'd so enraged. 1666 Tor. Proverbial Phrases, s.v. Sole, p. 195: As the English say of a pillory, To make one to look through an inch board. 1678 Ray p. 271 [a 1680] 1759 S. Butler *Gen. Rem.*, II, 363, He will swear his ears through an inch-board."

The "oaken tree" usually refers to the gallows.

And brought destruction on the great Don John.
Titus, whose skill in swearing doth excel
The monstrous monarch Rhadamanth of Hell,
And sent more souls to their untimely grave   55
Than the destroying angels lately have:
A walking plague, a breathing pestilence,
A cockatrice that kills a mile from thence.
Go on, brave Sirs, the gaping crowds attend;
They watch the word, the Saints their thimbles send.   60
The cushion's cuff'd, the trumpet sounds to war,
Our dying hopes in you revived are;
The people's choice, with you they'll live and die,
The guardian angels of their sanctuary.
The groans are grievous, and the hawks and hums,   65

52. Don John of Austria. When Charles II first interviewed Oates before the Privy
Council on 29 Sept. 1678, he asked but two questions, to both of which Oates gave
incorrect answers. One was on the location of the Jesuits' house in Paris; the other and
more famous concerned Don John, whom Oates claimed he had seen give £10,000 to
some Jesuits as a bribe to Wakeman to kill Charles. "The King asked him quick 'What
manner of man Don Juan was?' Oates, knowing the Spaniards are commonly reputed
tall and black answered 'He was a tall, black man' at which the King fell into a laugh,
for he had known Don Juan personally in Flanders, and he happened to be a low,
reddish-haired man" (North, *Examen*, pp. 175–76). See also, *The Compleat Swearing-
Master*, 5–6 n.

54. *Rhadamanth:* One of the judges of the dead in the lower world.

57. So North, describing Oates "in his trine exaltation," remarks that "the very
breath of him was pestilential and if it brought not imprisonment or death over such
on whom it fell, it surely poisoned reputation . . ." (*Examen*, p. 205).

58. *cockatrice:* A serpent, identified with the basilisk, fabulously said to kill by its
mere glance. Cf. Tilley, *Proverbs*, C 495.

59. *Sirs:* i.e. Papillon and Dubois.

60. *watch the word:* Probably in the dual sense of sectarian exegetical practice as
well as awaiting the preconcerted signal to begin an attack (cf. *OED, watchword* 2.).
Saints: Cant term for a sectarian.
thimbles: It was a stock charge that the appeal of the sectarian preacher was to the
middle-class female, who was constantly pictured with her thimble and bodkin (67).
The thimble, frequently of gold or silver, would be donated to the cause in much the
same way that plate had been given to the royalist cause during the Civil War.

61. *The cushion's cuff'd:* A cushion cuffer or cushion thumper is a preacher who
indulges in violent action.

64. i.e. the sheriffs of London.

65. Groaning, hawking (clearing the throat noisily), and humming (an inarticulate
murmur in a pause of speaking) were constantly associated with sectarian preachers.
Cf. Butler's "Character of an Hypocritical Nonconformist" (*Genuine Remains*, 2, 44–
45): "The painful heavings and strainings that he uses to express himself pass for the

And pulpits rattle too like kettle drums.
The sisters snivel, and their bodkins melt;
They're grop'd in darkness, and in pleasure felt.
More than in Pharaoh's time, the souls are sick,
And cry for light. Alas, the candlestick   70
Is quite remov'd. Oh! they're lost, they're gone,
They see that Whore, the Bawd of Babylon,
Is just approaching. Oh! the Popish Jade
Will tear away their teachers, and their trade!
    Call a Cabal for resolution hearty,   75
The blessed brethren of the sober party.
Let Sulla's ghost inform you in the fact;
Rouse him to earth; and in this glorious act
Consult with Pluto, let Old Noll ascend,

---

agonies of those that deliver oracles." The more usual phrase is to hawk and hem,
i.e. give a short, sharp cough (cf. *OED Hawk* v.3, ex.3, and *Hem* v.2, ex.2).
  66. Cf. Butler, *Hudibras:*

> When Gospel-Trumpeter, surrounded
> With long-ear'd rout, to battle sounded;
> And pulpit, drum ecclesiastic,
> Was beat with fist instead of a stick.
>   (I.i. 9–12)

  67. *Sisters:* Like *brethren* (76), a sectarian form of address.
  77–78. *Sulla's ghost:* Jonson's *Catiline* uses Sulla's ghost for its prologue. Rising from
Hell to earth, Sulla attempts to inspire Catiline to greater treachery:

> Let the long-hid seeds
> Of treason in thee now shoot forth in deeds
> Ranker than horror; and thy former facts
> Not fall in mention but to urge new acts.

Cf. Lucan, *Pharsalia:*

> Et medio visi consurgere Campo
> Tristia Sulloni cecinere oracula manes.
>   (I.580–81)

The renewed popularity of the image is seen in the court libel, *Mrs. Nelly's Complaint*
(1682), which begins: "If Sulla's ghost made bloody Catiline start/ And shook the fabric
of his marble heart;" as well as *Sulla's Ghost* by C. C. [C 18] in 1683, following the Rye
House Plot. The texts read *Segla*, perhaps a misreading from manuscript of *Sylla*, a
seventeenth-century form of *Sulla*.
  79. *Consult with Pluto:* Cf. Jonson, *Catiline:*

> Pluto be at thy councils, and into
> Thy darker bosom enter Sulla's spirit;
> All that was mine, and bad, thy breast inherit.
>   (I.16–18)

And if 't be possible the new-made friend.   80
Our much miss'd oracle, let Owen know
The Devil's here as well as those below.
And speed for Bethel; bid him not defer;
Tell him we want an executioner:
For royal blood's in chase, and none but he   85
To act the villian in a tragedy.
The rogue will leap for joy, such news admire;
The son's as sweet as was his sacred sire;
For he's a raving Nimrod will not start
To bathe his hands in such a royal heart.   90

Old Noll: Oliver Cromwell.

80. *new-made friend:* The reference is uncertain; however, John Dean in *Iter Boreale, or Tyburn in Mourning for the Loss of a Saint* (1682) [D 493], has the line "Take with you your new friend Pa[pillon]."

81. *Owen:* John Owen (1616–83), theologian, Independent controversialist, who came to the fore under Cromwell and continued as one of the most eminent of Puritan divines after the Restoration.

82. Cf. Jonson, *Catiline:*

All the names
Of thy confederates, too, be no less great
In hell, than here.

(I.66–68)

83. *Bethel:* Slingsby Bethel, Dryden's Shimei who "loved his wicked neighbor as himself," the Whig Sheriff (with Cornish), 1680–81. Luttrell remarks that on his election several pamphlets "fly out against him, as . . . that he should say, rather than the old king should have wanted an executioner, he would have done it himself" (*Brief Relation 1,* 49). He is said to have been "an assistant at scaffold when King Charles was executed." Bethel brought an "action of scandal against one Mr. Harvey" two years later in May 1682 (Ibid., *1,* 187), but by 22 July he had fled to Hamburg.

89. "Nimrod would suggest to a Jew or Syrian the idea of 'rebel', mrd = rebel; but this is not likely to be the etymology. . . . Many later legends gathered around Nimrod; Philo, *De gigantibus,* sect. 15, allegorizes *more suo.* Nimrod stands for treachery or desertion. . . . According to Josephus, . . . Nimrod built the Tower of Babel. According to the Rabbis, . . . Nimrod cast Abraham into the fire because he refused to worship idols. God, however, delivered him" (*EB*).

The Oxford Election, 1687,
by Egbert Van Heemskerck.

A Game at Cards

A Game at Cards is at once a witty and informative expression of Whig feeling on events that occurred between Shaftesbury's indictment for treason and the Whig defeat in the shrieval elections of 1682. The use of cards for social and political comment during the century was, of course, not unusual. Samuel Rowlands (1570?–1630) had employed the four knaves during the first two decades of the century in order to describe London's "madmen, knaves, and fools" in three pamphlets; [1] and in the early years of the Civil War (c. 1642–43), there appeared an eight-page Royalist tract: "The bloody Game at Cards as it was played betwixt the King of Hearts and the rest of his suit against the residue of the pack of cards wherein is discussed where fair play was played and where foul. Shuffled at London, cut at Westminster, dealt at York, and played in the open field by the City Clubs, the country Spade men, rich Diamond men, and loyal Hearted men." [2]

Playing cards themselves were used to illustrate political events. In 1679, two such packs were printed, each card containing a scene from "The Horrid Popish Plot" as Oates had described it.[3] Other pictorial packs gave "a complete political satire of the Common-

1. *A Merry Meeting or Tis Merry when Knaves Meet* (1600), burnt by the Stationers Company but reissued for W. Fereband in 1609 and again by E. Allde in 1611 as *The Knave of Clubs; The Knave of Hearts. Hail Fellow, well met,* printed for T. S. in 1612, and reprinted for John Back in 1613; and *More Knaves Yet? The Knaves of Spades and Diamonds,* printed for John Toye, 1613. Rowlands' *Works* were edited by Gosse for the Hunterian Club, 1880; and the *Four Knaves* was printed for the Percy Society in 1842 with an introduction by E. F. Rimbault. For a discussion of Rowlands' use of cards, see Benham, *Playing Cards,* pp. 44–54.

2. See Benham, pp. 77–78. The King of Hearts, almost from the first, had been Charlemagne; the transfer to Charles I of England was inevitable and immediate.

3. *True Domestick Intelligence,* No. 35 [4 Nov. 1679] and No. 50 [26 Dec. 1679]. For examples of the cards, see H. T. Morley, *Old and Curious Playing Cards* (London, 1931), pp. 169–71. Many of the scenes appear in *A True Narrative of the Horrid Hellish Popish Plot, The Second Part,* 1680, reproduced in Lane, p. 144. The pack is reproduced in full in John Dickson Carr's *The Murder of Sir Edmund Godfrey* (New York, 1936), and alluded to in Anthony à Wood's *Life and Times,* 2, 468 ("Plot cards came out also for children"), while Richard Duke's *An Epithalamium on the Marriage of Capt. William Bedloe (POAS,* Yale, 2, 134) states:

wealth"; [4] another, in favor of the Duke of Monmouth, illustrates the Rye House Plot; [5] another (c. 1685), Monmouth's rebellion; [6] and 1688 produced a great number illustrating events from William Parry's plot to murder Elizabeth (1585) up to the arrival of William of Orange (1688).[7] This device, which continued through the century and on into the reigns of Anne and George I,[8] reached its highest artistic point in the famous Ombre scene of Pope's *Rape of the Lock.*

A Game at Cards is based principally on an early version of three-card Lanterlu (or Lu), a highly popular and apparently quite fashionable game of the period. There are, as well, numerous secondary references to the somewhat analogous but lower-class game of Put.[9] Indeed, a reconstruction of the hands and the play suggests that a few of the features of Put influenced the more courtly Lu, or at least the version which we would seem to have here, a three-card Pam-Lu. Ordinarily the use of Pam (the knave of clubs as the highest trump) is associated with five-card Lu, but that the game was in a state of rapid development can be seen from the fact that Cotton, in 1674, describes the five-card game without mentioning Pam,[10] while eleven years later, in the third act of *Sir Courtly Nice,* Crowne has the line, "Thou art the very court card women love to play with; the very pam at Lanterlu, the knave that picks up all."

In Pam-Lu, the "Pam is the knave of clubs and ranks above every card in the pack. It is subject to no laws; but may be played on any suit at any time, even though you have in your hand the suit which

----

And when, as now in Christmas, all
For a new pack of cards do call,
Another Popish pack comes out
To please the cits and charm the rout,
Thou, mighty queen [i.e. Bedloe's bride], shalt
        a whole suit command,
A crown upon thy head, and scepter in thy hand.
                                                        (80–85)

4. *A Pack of Cavalier Playing Cards temp. Charles II forming a Complete Political Satire of the Commonwealth,* ed. Edmund Goldsmid (Edinburgh, 1886). Two of the cards are reproduced in Morley, p. 174.

5. Benham, p. 159.

6. Morley, pp. 176–77.

7. Ibid., pp. 172–73, 177–81; Benham, pp. 159–60.

8. Morley, pp. 182–85; Benham, p. 159.

9. There are possible allusions to a third game called Don or Don Pedro (6), and a fourth game, Brag (38).

10. Charles Cotton, *The Complete Gamester* (London, 1674), reprinted with Theophilus Lucas, *Lives of the Gamesters* (London, 1714), in *Games and Gamesters of the Restoration,* introd. C. H. Hartmann, The English Library, (London, 1930), pp. 68–70.

is led. . . . If you hold pam, you cannot be lued [i.e. penalized a set amount]. If pam is turned for the trump card, clubs are trumps." [11] First of all, there is a pool which may consist of the money "paid for the deals and of the sums forfeited by those who were lued the preceding hand" for making mistakes in play or for not making a single trick. The pool is won by the player with the highest flush (i.e. all one suit) or blaze (i.e. all court cards), the hands ranking (1) pam-flush or pam-blaze, i.e. with the "wild" pam as one of the cards (2) a trump flush, (3) any other flush, and (4) blaze. In some cases (as in 93), a separate box is established on the basis of an extra charge for the deal and a proportion of the lues, and these "gradually accumulate till someone has a pam-flush, which entitles him to the whole." [12] In addition, there is a pool for the hand which consists of a lu of a certain amount plus, quite often, the amount charged for the deal. The stakes are almost always three (see 70) or multiples of three—in more modern games, three for the deal and six for a lu [13]—since this is divided in proportion to the number of tricks won.

In the particular version that we have here, the dealer gives three cards to each hand and then turns up one as trumps. As in ordinary pam-lu,[14] the trump card belongs to the dealer and may replace one of his cards, becoming a regular part of his hand (see 85). Usually, the players have the option of standing or not , as they choose, save in the case where there is Club Law [15] or where (as in the present case, cf. 28 and the chorus line) there is a Bold Stand,[16] in which case all are forced to stay. The players then play out their hand, trick by trick, following suit when they can or trumping, if they wish, when void (see 29). Here, as in Put, you "must keep up your cards very close, for the least discovery of any one of them is a great advantage to him that sees it," and, as Cotton goes on to remark, "rooks" will frequently employ accomplices who stand behind "the innocent Col" to force the game on to higher stakes.[17]

11. The fullest description of Pam-Lu is in *Hoyle's Games Improved* (New York, 1821), pp. 146–60. This gives an explanation of five-card Lu, and I have modified its rules in accordance with rules given elsewhere for three-card Lu.

12. Ibid., p. 147.

13. I am here following the discussions of Round Games by "Baxter-Wray" in *The Handbook of Games* (London, 1891), pp. 17–18.

14. Hoyle, p. 146.

15. "Baxter-Wray," p. 26.

16. "Trumps" [W. B. Dick], *The Modern Pocket Hoyle* (New York, n.d.), pp. 182–84.

17. Cotton, pp. 64–65.

We can reconstruct the present game as follows: There are here
two sides, and either we can consider the whole of the poem as repre-
senting a single hand or we can see it as two separate hands, one be-
tween Shaftesbury and the Tories concerning his indictment and the
second between the four shrieval candidates (two Whigs and two
Tories) in 1682. Probably the single game is intended, since the
chorus line remains the same throughout, since a single hand can be
reconstructed for the whole of the poem, and since Shaftesbury was
practically synonymous with the Whig party. Though it is perfectly
simple to divide the hand in two (and there would be rules to cover
this), the reconstruction here given assumes that the author was try-
ing to epitomize the Whig position as a whole. At the beginning, the
Tories are dealing and Shaftesbury leads. He exposes their previous
cheating at Put (20–22) and stakes everything since this is the first
deal and both players must be bold. With the deal, the Tories are
in confusion and must risk everything on the turn of the trump (28–
30). The vicious "discoveries" of their confederate, Teague, make the
situation even more desperate. At this point, the suggestions in 85
and 88 would supply plausible playing hands. Shaftesbury would
have a flush, probably all clubs, made up of the 2, 3, and 4; the Tories
would have a king and queen of one suit (not clubs) and a third
(noncourt) card of another suit. Since they have neither blaze nor
flush, all hangs for them on the turn of the trump card. To their
great delight and surprise, the "knave of clubs is the trump," giving
them a pam-flush (with the king and queen), the only thing that
could beat Shaftesbury's trump-flush. They realize that they have the
winning hand so far as the pool is concerned, and they begin to brag
(29). The betting is quite in keeping with the rules, since it can be
evenly divided by three (70), and there is then the actual playing of
the hand, though the situation is shifted to include the shrieval elec-
tions. Since the hand must be played out, it would begin with the
Whigs' lead. They would take the first and second trick with trumps
and lose the third to the knave. Though the score had been two to
one (79), the Tories, with their pam-flush, would then take both the
pool and the box, and so win the game.

While the above reconstruction is highly conjectural and, indeed,
depends on seeing the game as informing the whole poem, it does
nevertheless present a consistent and logical image which is sup-
ported by the political events to which it has reference.

A GAME AT CARDS

To the tune of "Youth, youth, thou hadst better been
starved at nurse, etc."

1.

An old game at cards left off by Old Harry
And never play'd out since Philip and Mary,
In little Old England was late bringing in
By Pope, Priest, and Deel and the rest of the kin;
    All engines just ready   5
    With don, lord, and lady
And all the fair gamesters that Hell ever made ye;
Then brave dammee boys, come caper and jump
That the bold Tory knave of clubs shall be trump.

1. *Old Harry:* Henry VIII separated from Rome and made himself head of the Church of England in 1533.

2. *Philip and Mary:* Queen Mary (1516–58), whose marriage to Philip II of Spain marked the bloodiest period of persecution of Protestant Reformers in England.

3. *late bringing in:* Introduced in recent times.

4. *Deel:* Obsolete and northern form of "devil." Scots and northern dialect is present throughout the poem.

5. *engines:* Used in the pejorative sense of evil machinations or instruments of war or torture. The reference is probably to the famous "forty thousand black bills," "Tewkesbury mustard balls," and the like in Oates' disclosures.

6. *don:* The possibilities here are twofold. 1. A Spanish lord or gentleman; a Spaniard. Such a meaning would derive from line 2 as well as the traditional English fear of Spain's aggressive Catholic policy. 2. An obsolete and rare form of Dan or Dom, a monk.

8. *dammee boys:* Profane swearers. The phrase had been applied during the past half century to cavaliers, then to Royalists, and finally to those of the Court party.

9. The selection in numerous games of the knave of clubs as an exceptional card is not, I feel, difficult to understand. Not only was he "both in French and English packs . . . the chief swaggerer" (Benham, *Playing Cards*, p. 121), but, even more important, he was a card that was easily picked out. Despite the fact that there had been a "Worshipful Company of Makers of Playing Cards" since 1628, the English continued to buy the far superior French packs. "For many generations this Valet (*Trèfle* or Clubs) was the one Valet in the French packs without a name. This was due to the early custom, which became a legal obligation in 1613, of printing the name of the card-maker on this particular card—the 'duty card'" (ibid., p. 122).

2.

Through gibbets and pillories and other such gears,   10
Some ventur'd their necks and some but their ears;
Whole fortunes were stak'd, and all gamesters were met,
From little Nat Thompson to Coleman the great,
      With Gadb'ry and Celliers,
      All sorts of well willers   15
From rogue, whore, and bawd, to blind fortunetellers.
Then brave dammee boys, come caper and jump,
That the bold Tory knave of clubs shall be trump.

3.

Old politic Tony who long time had smelt
How these cunning sly rooks had shuffl'd and dealt,   20
Seen Godfrey's lost hand and hard game at Put,

11. The writer might have in mind some of the Whig martyrs: Stephen College (1635–81) in the case of hanging, William Prynne (1600–69) and Henry Burton (1578–1648) in the case of mutilation for seditious preaching and publication.

13. Nathaniel Thompson, the printer, along with William Pain and John Farwell, was brought to trial for his part in producing *A Letter to Miles Prance* [F 537], *A Second Letter . . . in reply to the Ghost of Sir Edmundbury Godfrey* [P 192], and *The Loyal Protestant Intelligence* (Nos. 125 and 127), all of which claimed that Godfrey had killed himself, that the witnesses in the famous Berry, Hill, and Green trial were perjured, and that the three men had been executed unjustly. Thompson, Farwell, and Pain were found guilty on 20 June 1682, the first two being sentenced to the pillory and a fine of £100 while the last was merely fined. A full account of the trial is given in Howell, *State Trials*, 8, 1359–98. Thompson, as far as the Whigs were concerned, was a mercenary Papist; see, for example, *More Work for the Popish Implements, Nat. Thompson and the Observator* (1682) [M 2718], *Sir Edmondbury Godfrey's Apparition to Nat. Thompson* (1682) [S 3875], and *A Letter from Lucifer to his Roman Agents N.T., W.P., J.F., R.L.,* (1682) [L 1488].

Edward Coleman (d. 1678) was the Catholic secretary to the Duchess of York, whose correspondence with France led to his execution in the early days of the Popish Plot.

14. John Gadbury, the astrologer, was implicated by Thomas Dangerfield in the Meal Tub Plot with Elizabeth Celliers, "the Popish midwife." Both were acquitted, but see Dangerfield's restatement of the charges in *Animadversions upon Mr. John Gadbury's Almanac . . . for . . . 1682* (1682) [D 181].

19. *Tony:* The usual Whig nickname for Shaftesbury (Anthony Ashley Cooper).

20. Though the writer uses only the term "bullies" (23, 28, 92), Cotton is far more expressive: "This [darkness] is the time (when ravenous beasts usually seek their prey) wherein comes shoals of Huffs, Hectors, Setters, Gilts, Pads, Biters, Divers, Lifters, Filers, Budgies, Droppers, Crossbiters, etc., and these may all pass under the general and common appellation of Rooks" (*Compleat Gamester*, p. 3).

21. *Godfrey:* For an interesting account of this endlessly fascinating crime, see Carr, *The Murder of Sir Edmund Godfrey.*

"Put," says Cotton, "is the ordinary rooking game of every place" (*Compleat Game-*

With Coleman's false card and the Devil's new cut,
    Cri'd, "Hold, bullies, stay!
      I bar all foul play,
For little Old England my life I dare lay.   25
I'll set and I'll stake my old bones to the stump
Though the bold Tory knave of clubs turns up trump."

4.

At such a bold gamester, in doleful sad dumps,
The frighted Rome-bullies were put to their trumps,
All puzzl'd and dash'd, till, to help out the matter,   30
The kind Irish Teague, that honest bog-trotter,
    Came pat in good season
    To cut his old weazon,

---

ster, p. 62). In two-handed Put, three cards are dealt and the eldest, "if he hath a good game and thinks it better than his adversary's, puts to him; if the other will not, or dare not, see him, he then wins one, but if he will see him, they play it out and he that wins two tricks or all three wins the whole set. . . . The game consists very much in daring; for a right gamester will put boldly upon very bad cards sometimes" (ibid., p. 63). The order of cards is 3, 2, ace, king, etc., to the 4, which is lowest.

22. *false card:* A card played contrary to rule in order to take an adversary.

cut: There would appear to be a number of plays on the word. Besides referring to the actual cutting of the pack, it may be used in the sense of "fashion" or "style" or of "lot" or "fortune"; with reference to a particular game at cards of the turn of the century called Swig or New Cut; or finally, as an allusion to New Cut, an area of bad repute. The phrase appears also in the epilogue to Rowlands' *Knave of Clubs* (1609) and again (though probably as *fashion*) in the opening lines of his *Knave of Hearts* (1613). For the great advantages to be gained at Put from a dishonest cut, see Cotton's explanation of the bent, the slick, and the brief (*Compleat Gamester,* pp. 63–64).

28. *put to their trumps:* Probably in the figurative sense of "put to the last expedient," though the technical meaning of obliging a cardplayer to play his trumps is also quite applicable in Lu (see "Baxter-Wray," p. 21). Lacking a flush or blaze, the Tories are obliged to depend on their luck with the trump suit. The same phrase is used for the same situation in Roger Coke's *A Detection of the Court and State of England* (1694) [C 4973]: "This difficulty [of Whig juries], after my Lord Shaftesbury's case, put the court to their trumps, and at present a stop to their proceedings. The assistance of the Duke of York was necessary, but at this time he was busy in Scotland" (p. 308).

31. Which of the Irish witnesses is being referred to—Brian Haines, Bernard Dennis, or John Macnamarra—is difficult to determine.

32. *pat:* Opportunely, in the very nick of time, in a manner that exactly fits the purpose or occasion.

33. *his:* i.e. Shaftesbury's.

weazon: Scot. dial. for *wizen,* the gullet, throat, or windpipe (Joseph Wright, *The English Dialect Dictionary* [7 vols. London, 1898]).

Swear his tap's in the plot and his spigot runs treason,
And sham him with Commonwealth, Cromwell, and Rump,   35
For the bold Tory knave of clubs is the trump.

5.

And now have at all. Their forces they muster;
Their winning hand's in, and they swagger and bluster;
The City of London with Old Noll is run down
And, stinking of Bradshaw and Ireton, is undone.   40
  The brisk Roman-hater,
  Betwixt wind and water,
By an Irish chain shot is sunk for a traitor.
Then brave dammee boys, come caper and jump,
For the bold Tory knave of clubs turns up trump.   45

6.

Young Jemmy the Valiant, the loyal and brave,
Whose life and allegiance can have but one grave,

34. *tap's:* An allusion to the tap which had been applied when an ulcer broke out. The references to it are endless.

35. *sham:* To cheat, delude with false pretences, impose upon.

Rump: The selected remnant of the Long Parliament that sat between Pride's Purge (Dec. 1648) and the dissolution by Cromwell (April 1653); also, that remnant restored in May 1659 and dissolved by Monck in Feb. 1660.

39. *Old Noll:* Cromwell's principal center and source of power had been the City of London.

40. John Bradshaw (1602–59), regicide, was president of the Court of High Commission which tried and condemned Charles I. Henry Ireton (1611–51), regicide, was Cromwell's son-in-law and a zealous force in the establishment of the Commonwealth; he took an active part in Pride's Purge and in bringing Charles I to trial. "On 4 Dec. 1660 Parliament directed that the bodies of Bradshaw, Cromwell, and Ireton should be taken up from Westminster and hanged in their coffins at Tyburn. The indignity was duly perpetrated 30 [28?] Jan. 1660/61. The regicides' heads were subsequently exposed in Westminster Hall and their bodies reburied beneath the gallows" (*DNB* sub Bradshaw). There is probably an echo of the chorus line of *The Whig Feast* (1682), [W 1648], ascribed to Tom Durfey: "Ah, bonny London, thou'rt undone."

41. *Roman-hater:* i.e. Shaftesbury. On 2 July 1681, he was arrested on charges of treason, the principal witnesses being the Irish "evidences" who had formerly sworn to the truth of the Popish Plot. Shaftesbury was released by the famous "Ignoramus" Jury on 24 Nov. 1681.

42. *betwixt wind and water:* Referring to that part of a ship's side which is sometimes above water and sometimes submerged, in which part a shot is peculiarly dangerous; hence, in a figurative phrase, expressing serious injury or attack.

43. *chain shot:* A shot formed of two balls or half-balls, connected by a chain, chiefly used in naval warfare to destroy masts, rigging and sails.

46. *Young Jemmy:* James, Duke of Monmouth, was the "Protestant Duke" and the

Oh now all his glories are quite out of door,
And Bothwell and Maestricht's remember'd no more.
      The Tories run high,   50
      And his honor must die;
The Hero's forgot, and *A Traitor*'s the cry.
Then brave dammee boys, come caper and jump,
For the bold Tory knave of clubs is the trump.

7.

To dine in the City, that mark of the beast,   55
Is all o'er Geneva and treason at least;
Such downright rebellion that some men are able
To prove a whole magazine at one table,
      Where marrow-bone dishes
      Were all mortar pieces,   60
With turnips grenadoes just pat to their wishes.
Oh brave dammee boys, come caper and jump,
For the bold Tory knave of clubs turns up trump.

8.

But Death and the cobbler in desperate case,
He ran for the plate at a country horse race   65

Whigs' choice for succession. The highly popular Whig ballad *Young Jemmy* appeared in 1681; the title was copied in a second ballad *Young Jemmy, or the Princely Shepherd* [Y 102]; the tune was used in *Jemmy and Anthony* (1682) [J 553]; and Aphra Behn's song "Young Jemmy was a fine lad" was included in her *Poems upon Several Occasions* (1684) [B 1757]. For the music, history and location of texts, see Chappell, *Popular Music*, pp. 523–25, 785.

49. Monmouth took an active part in the siege of Maestricht (1673) and commanded the army that defeated the Scots at Bothwell Bridge (22 June 1679).

55. Charles' first move against the City faction was to prohibit as an impingement on prerogative the Whig feast scheduled for 21 April 1682 at Haberdashers' and Goldsmiths' Hall.

mark of the beast: In *Hemp for the Flaxman: or, A Friday Feast Kidnapped, Apr. 21, 1682* (Leyden, Printed for the benefit of the Sweet Singers) [H 1426], there is a concluding section entitled *Arsy Versy: or Riddle of Riddles* ("All head, all feet; all Rump, yet body all") the last line of which undoubtedly suggested the phrase here: "Say, Reader, are not these all marks o' the beast." The beast is, of course, Antichrist, or the antichristian power.

56. *all o'er Geneva:* completely, wholly Calvinistic.

64. *Death and the cobbler:* Both deal in souls (soles). Cf. Shakespeare, *Julius Caesar,* I.i.

65. *He:* Monmouth. The stanza gives an ironic view of the highly significant moves of the government in checking Monmouth's growing popularity. In Sept. 1682 the

Where ev'ry *Huzza* by new martial law
Was fight, kill, and slay and deserv'd hang and draw.
    His jockies were loons
    And traitors, Godswoons!
And he's packing the cards to play for three croons.   70
Then brave dammee boys, come caper and jump,
For the bold Tory knave of clubs turns up trump.

9.

A great City match at Guildhall was made,
Which twixt four rich burghers of London was play'd.

Duke undertook what was, in effect, a Northern Progress, with the ostensible purpose of going to the races at Wallareg Sands, "but Charles remembered that, in Oliver's days, his own loyal gentlemen had met at horse races and cock matches under color of which they furthered their designs for his restoration" (D'Oyley, *Monmouth*, p. 196). Spies were sent along by Secretary Jenkins, and a company of foot reinforced the garrison at Chester Castle. At the race on Tuesday, 12 Sept., Monmouth " 'rid for and won the 12-stone plate' of £60 value, beating young [Colonel] Whitley, [Henry] Booth, and Bellingham [his friends and supporters]. Matthew Anderson, returning to Chester that night, 'saw the city as it had been in flames,' so many were the bonfires because his Grace had won" (ibid., p. 198). The Chester crowd got out of hand, breaking into the church, ringing bells till they overturned them, yelling, shooting off guns, shouting always "A Monmouth! A Monmouth!"

This was the excuse the government needed. By Monday 18 Nov., Serjeant Ramsey had intercepted Monmouth on his return journey at Stafford and arrested him on a charge of riot. On Saturday the 23rd, Charles committed him to Ramsey's custody, and on Monday he was bailed (giving surety of £20,000) but effectually bound over until his discharge on the 27th. The Northern Progress proved to be, in effect, the last opportunity for a popular uprising; Shaftesbury was right in recognizing this, but Monmouth was equally right in recognizing that such an unorganized uprising would have been doomed.

66. *Huzza:* The shout of exultation and encouragement given by the crowds in approval of Monmouth. In the quite different context of Tory victories, North remarks that "it is not to be denied but at merry meetings, good fellowship, in way of healths, run into some extravagances and noise, as that which they call Huzzaing, an usage then at its perfection" (*Examen*, p. 617).

68. *jockies:* Used both in the ordinary sense of the rider in a horse race (and perhaps referring to Monmouth's supporters who rode in the race) and in the Scots dialectical sense of a country fellow, a rustic (Wright, *The English Dialect Dictionary*).
loon: In Scots dialect, a rascal, scoundrel, scamp; an idle stupid fellow. (ibid.)

69. *Godswoons:* In Scots dialect, the oath "God's wounds."

70. *croons:* In Scots dialect, crowns, referring, of course, both to the coin and the three kingdoms. The bet, here, is in accordance with the rule in three-card Pam-Lu, that the sums wagered be divisible by three (see headnote).

74. *four rich burghers:* i.e. the two Tory candidates, Roger North and Ralph Box (or Peter Rich) and the two Whig candidates, Thomas Papillon and John Dubois.

For white wand and gold chain they wrangl'd and bawl'd,   75
Till at last the groom porters for judgment were call'd.
      But the Whigs, as they say,
      Though after hard play,
In counting their cards had two to one of the lay,
Yet brave dammee boys, come caper and jump,   80
For the bold Tory knave of clubs turns up trump.

10.

What though two to one for Dubois and Papillion
A man would have sworn would have won for a
      million;
Yet, oh, the ill luck does their fortune withstand,
The king, queen and knave were in th' enemy's hand;   85
      And at this kind of play
      A court card, they say,
Will beat ten times over deuce, cater, and tray.

---

75. *white wand:* A white wand or rod, usually called the white staff, is carried as a
symbol of office by certain high government officials, e.g. the steward of the king's
household and the lord high treasurer; hence, the office or official who carries the
white staff.
    gold chain: The symbol of the mayoralty.
    bawl'd: To shout at the top of one's voice.
    76. *groom porters:* "At the time of the Restoration, gaming had been officially
recognized by the appointment of groom-porter, an officer of the lord steward's depart-
ment to whom the superintendence and regulation of all matters relating to cards
and dice had been committed since the reign of Henry VIII, if not from a still earlier
date" (Hartmann, introd. to *Games and Gamesters of the Restoration*, p. xvii). The
"inner sanctuary of aristocratic gaming" was the lodging of the groom porter (p. xi)
but his authority gradually extended beyond the limits of the Court to a regulation
of gaming throughout the kingdom (p. xvii).
    79. *two to one:* As 82 shows, the writer has quite carefully paralleled the card
game, in which the Whigs are said to have taken two tricks to one, and the voting
for the shrieval posts. In the latter case he has hit just about the correct ratio. Taking
Luttrell's figures for the polls taken on 5 and 15 July (*Brief Relation, 1,* 203, 206),
we find that the total number of votes in Moore's and Pilkington's books comes to
3,166 (Tory) to 5,463 (Whig) and 1,434 (Tory) to 5,023 (Whig), respectively. This
averages out as roughly a two-to-one ratio.
    85. i.e. the Tories hold a pam-flush, which is much higher than the low trump-
flush held by the Whigs.
    87. *court card:* A face card.
    88. There might be a reference here to Put, where this would be a fairly good
hand. In Put (see 21 n.), the trey (3) and deuce (2) are the highest cards, though the
cater (4) is the lowest.

Then brave dammee boys, come caper and jump,
For the bold Tory knave of clubs turns up trump.   90

11.

Old Roger was there with his fiddle, they say,
To hearten the bullies and cheer up their play,
And for the kind guineas that went to the box
To cry up the gamesters he bellow'd like ox,
     And all to the tune   95
     Of Musket and Gun
Plots, treason, rebellion, and Old Forty-One.
Then brave dammee boys, come caper and jump,
For the bold Tory knave of clubs is the trump.

91. *Roger:* Roger L'Estrange, the chief Tory journalist (*Observator*) and pamphleteer, a vigorous opponent of Shaftesbury and a corrosive critic of the Popish Plot.

his fiddle: "L'Estrange was an accomplished musician, and during the protectorate Cromwell, when paying an accidental visit at the house of John Hingston the organist, found L'Estrange and a few others playing music. . . . L'Estrange's confession of participation in this little concert is responsible for his later nickname of 'Oliver's fiddler' " (*DNB*).

box: The separate box for the holder of a pam-flush.

95–96. *to the tune of:* The usual phrase found on ballads employing well-known airs. The tune to which the lyrics were set frequently reinforced the satiric purpose of the verses.

97. *Old Forty-one:* This tune, one of the most popular from 1640 on, was known by various names, most frequently *Hey then, up go we*, but also *The clean contrary way* and *The good old cause*. For a history of the song and a version of the music, see Chappell, *Popular Music*, pp. 425–29. As well, there is probably a direct allusion to one of L'Estrange's favorite arguments. "To Andrew Marvell's 'Account of the Growth of Popery and Arbitrary Government' he replied in 'The Parallel, or an Account of the Growth of Knavery under the pretext of Arbitrary Government and Popery' (London, 1678, anon., new ed. 1681, with author's name). Here he compared the policy of the contemporary Whig leaders with that of the parliamentary leaders in 1641—a comparison that became a favorite cry with the Tories" (*DNB*).

Midsummer Moon.

[*T 1011*]

Many shades of political opinion existed between the two extremes that fought loudly for the shrieval posts. Thomas Thompson, taking the position of one of the liverymen or guild members who voted in the common halls, heaps scorn upon the Lord Mayor's "betrayal" of the City and dependence on Jenkins, Halifax, and those who directed the Court's campaign. He is not so much anti-Court as pro-City, not so much pro-Whig as anti-York. Such a position must have been not uncommon during this period when national politics intruded on municipal government, but, in the course of the larger struggle, it was a position that disappeared as its exponents were increasingly forced to align themselves with the Whigs.

The poem appeared in quarto sometime after 26 June (when Pilkington and Shute were briefly in the Tower) and probably before mid-July (when the last polling for North and Box was taken). When the poem was reprinted in *z*, most of the names (all of which Thompson had with prudence partially blanked out) were given in full.

Midsummer Moon

or the Liveryman's Complaint
1682

I cannot hold! hot struggling rage aspires
And crowds my freeborn breast with noble fires.

Title: The shrieval elections take place on Midsummer Day, i.e. 24 June; investiture is on 28 Sept., the day before the Lord Mayor's election. The *OED* suggests that the phrase "midsummer moon" might refer to "the lunar month in which Midsummer Day comes" and adds that it is "sometimes alluded to as a time when lunacy is supposed to be prevalent." The latter meaning was undoubtedly in the mind of the author, whose moderate Whig sympathies soon become evident.

Whilst prudent fools squeak treason through the nose
And whine a quivering vote in sneaking prose,
My muse soars out of reach and dares despise   5
Whate'er below attempts to tyrannize.
Though I by some base Nero should be clad
In such a gown as the old Christians had,
In clouds of satire up to Heav'n I'd roll,
For he could burn my shell, but not my soul.   10
Though Nature her auspicious aid refuse,
Revenge and anger shall inspire my muse:
Nature has giv'n me a complaining part,
And bleeding England a resenting heart.

Let creeping play'rs, whose pliant fancies can,   15
Sneak to the Devil and call him gentleman.

3. *prudent fools:* In Thompson's view, the lukewarm majority of the City faction, those who refuse to speak of the real problem (i.e. James and Catholicism) and who hope to overcome Court pressure by Guildhall politics.

squeak treason: The reference is not only to the remarks made during the day-long voting and politicking when (to quote the Tory account of Roger North) "the partisans were raging about the hall and rooms" (*Examen,* p. 608); it alludes also to the events that followed Lord Mayor Moore's adjournment of the Common Hall at 7 P.M., which produced an uproar and "a terrible rage of faces made at him. . . . When the Mayor and officers were gone, the two precious [Whig] sheriffs, Pilkington and Shute, with some liverymen of their party, thought fit not to obey the Lord Mayor's adjournment but by . . . their own authority, held . . . the common hall . . . and . . . proceeded to continue the election by setting up a poll; and afterwards they finally declared the choice had fallen upon [the Whig candidates] Papillon and Dubois" (p. 608). Since both the Mayor and the Sheriffs, though elected, were king's officers, this put the City faction at least in a state of riot and quite possibly treason.

4. The physical tumult and political pressure at Guildhall during the election are particularly noted by Tory writers (see L'Estrange's descriptions of the scene in *Observator,* No. 162 [29 June 1682] and 95–96 n.), but even the delightfully biassed biographer of Papillon remarks that "the order of adjournment was imperfectly heard through the noise and clamor" (Papillon, *Papillon,* p. 216).

7. *Nero:* An allusion to James, Duke of York. Thompson implies that as Nero was responsible for the burning of Rome, so James was involved in the burning of London in 1666. There was a report in May that the Whig sheriff, Pilkington, had said that "the Duke of York had twice burnt the City and was now come to cut the inhabitants' throats" (*CSPD* 1682, p. 194). That London's immolation was a Popish Plot manqué was given official sanction by the City in 1681; and the plaque so stating was not finally removed until 1830. Cf. Pope, *Moral Essays,* III, 339–40.

15. The players were notoriously on the side of the Court, though Thompson might have been thinking specifically either of the recent opening of "the King's and Queen's theater," for which Dryden (a favorite Whig target) had written suitable verses, or of

How long has northern air so sovereign been
To purge the plot, and sanctify a sin?
'Tis well for England if at last it find
The traitor's noxious humors left behind,   20
Which long have been fomented by the spoil
Of that old-fashion'd honest fool Argyle,
Who lost a noble fortune on pretence
Of a fond thing the Whigs call conscience.
His fall and Thynne's, if rightly understood,   25
Were only doom'd to flesh the hounds in blood.
The way's chalk'd out, though fear retard the blow;
'Tis plain that once a rogue and ever so.
Treason's the gangrene of a mounting soul,

---

the union of the acting companies on 14 May 1682 when they merged into the Duke's company under Killigrew and Davenant (Nicoll, *A History of Restoration Drama, 1660–1700*, p. 26).

17. While there may be ironic overtones of the evil spirits that traditionally came from the North, the allusion is probably intentionally ambiguous, referring both to Dudley North by a play on his name and to York, who ruled strictly in Scotland as Royal Commissioner from Oct. 1680 until March 1682.

19–23. The Test Act, adopted by the Scottish Parliament in July 1681, was used to attack Archibald Campbell, the ninth earl of Argyle, who, as Ogg succinctly puts it, was "an object of dislike to the executive because of his Whig sympathies, and the occasion of both envy and enmity on the part of his many neighbors, anxious to share in the forfeiture of his great estates" (*Charles II*, p. 637).

24. Argyle subscribed to the Test "in so far as it was consistent with itself and with the Protestant faith." This stand, as well as his view that the royal family should not be exempted from the Act, brought upon him the full fury of James. On 9 Nov. 1681, he was "committed on charges of treason, perjury, and assuming the legislative power, and convicted on evidence which, as Halifax said, would not have hanged a dog in England. Sentence of death and forfeiture was pronounced December 23; but a few days before, the prisoner had succeeded in making his escape" (Ogg, *Charles II*, p. 637).

25. For the Whig interpretation of Thynne's murder, see *A Hue and Cry after Blood and Murder* and headnote. The implication is, of course, that the removal of Argyle, the chief exponent of Protestantism in Scotland, and of Monmouth, the Protestant Duke, are to prepare the way for a Papist coup.

27. *fear:* i.e. of civil war and overthrow of the monarchy itself. The line recalls *The Popish Fables* (1682) [P 2950], a Whig pamphlet that is given a Tory analysis in *Observator*, No. 167 (8 July 1682); "Whig," quoting from *The Popish Fables,* says: "The *Observators,* at their first coming out, chalked as fair a way to a Fanatical Plot for the Irish O Hones to walk in as may be."

29. The figure of the gangrened body politic would have been popularly associated with sectarian complaint, if only on the basis of Thomas Edwards' oft-printed *Gangraena* (1646), a work which L'Estrange had turned to his own purposes just at this time (*Observator*, No. 153 [12 June 1682]). Two days later (*Observator*, No. 154

Which, if not soon cut off, infects the whole.   30
Though Heav'n in anger sometimes may relieve,
Pardons still do not follow a reprieve.
Not fell Charybdis, Godwins, and the Oar,
If Fate ordain't, shall keep a prince from shore,
Since he that would by brother's blood be crown'd   35
Shall (though in egg-shell frigate) ne'er be drown'd.

[14 June 1682]), he pointed to Settle's recent (1681) provocative use of the image: "Truly I thought that the game [i.e. civil strife] had more than begun when three mercenary prostitutes, the author, the printer, and the publisher of the *Character of a Popish Successor* had branded him [i.e. York] in print for a 'gangraen'd branch of royalty.' "

31–36. Though at first reading this passage may seem confused, it is quite witty in its own way. The writer's purpose is, first, to overcome the Tory pamphleteers' claim that York's escape from drowning on 6 May 1682 was a proof of divine approval and, secondly, to continue his strong condemnation of York. The whole of his attack turns on the unexpressed half of the popular proverb "He that is born to be hanged shall never be drowned" (Tilley, *Proverbs*, B. 139), which the imagery of 32 suggests. The same literal use of the proverb is found in Fielding's *Jonathan Wild*.

31. The author might well have had in mind the "eucharistic verse or two" offered up on this occasion in *Heraclitus Ridens*, No. 69 (23 May 1682):

They lie that say, there is no providence,
    But all things are contriv'd by giddy chance,
As some men ween, but men of little sense.
Atheists and Cargillites, what think you now?
    Will you this miracle allow?
Are ye convinc'd, ye Whigs, your prayers are tricks,
    When "GOD WITH US" you own?
Are you not fool'd in all your politics,
When you would undermine a crown?
Heav'n laughs at your attempts, and tells you loud,
The sons shall live t'avenge the father's blood.
    Whatever Hell or rebels dare,
    The royal brothers are Its tender care.

33. *Charybdis:* A dangerous whirlpool on the coast of Sicily, opposite the Italian rock Scylla. Used allusively of anything likely to cause shipwreck of life.

Godwins: i.e. the Goodwin Sands. The reference is to York's escapes in the Third Dutch War. If meant precisely, the incident took place on 16 May 1672 (see Evelyn, *Diary*, 3, 614–15 and notes; John Glover to Williamson, *CSPD* 1671–72, pp. 582–83; and *Journals and Narratives of the Third Dutch War*, ed. Anderson, p. 12). On the previous evening, at about 5 P.M., the Allied Fleet under York moved past Dover "towards the Holland coasts at the back of the Goodwin" (Richard Watts to Williamson, *CSPD* 1671–72, p. 583). An engagement here would probably have proved disastrous. Thus, Captain Francis Digby, writing to the Earl of Bristol on the following day, fervently hoped that the English would "shun fighting amongst the sands, as the only thing which can endanger this fleet" (ibid., p. 595).

If "Goodwin Sands" is being used as a name for the whole of this campaign, it

Which stock'd seraglios and rich grand viziers,
Th' industrious Tory truck for officers?
In sober sadness, sirs, how goes the price?
Are sheriffs lately grown good merchandise?   40
Sure, brethren, we may fear the cause is low
When you for cordials unto Turkey go.
When nothing else the desperate game retrieves,

---

might well refer to the famous engagement against de Ruyter at Sole Bay which took place on 28–29 May. (de Beer [Evelyn, *Diary*, *4*, 432, n. 1] uses the name Solebay and says Gunman was master of the *Prince*.) York was in the thick of the fighting throughout, engaged de Ruyter's *Zeven Provincien* and Van Nes' *Eendracht* in the center of the line, and had twice to shift his standard—on the 28th from the crippled flagship, the *Prince* (whose captain, Sir John Cox, had been killed) to the *St. Michael*, and on the same day, about 5 P.M., from the *St. Michael* to Spragge's *London*. Amid the subsequent conflicting critiques, James' role was generally appreciated, and he was rewarded with a Vice Admiralcy and command of the Red Squadron.

the Oar: For James' narrow escape when the frigate *Gloucester* broke up on the Lemon and Oar Sands, see the headnote to, *An Heroical Poem Upon His Royal Highness' Arrival*.

37–38. A difficult passage. The sudden change of subject from York to Dudley North (see following note), along with the grammatical confusion, suggest that there may be some lines missing. By expansion, the meaning here might be: With which stocked seraglio and with which Grand Vizier does the industrious Tory truck for [shrieval] officers?

The earlier career in Turkey of Sir Dudley North (1641–91), as told in his correspondence and reflections (North, *Lives*, *2*, pp. 7–170), constitutes a fascinating example of English mercantilism abroad from 1660 to 1680. Undoubtedly his nomination to the shrievalty was encouraged by his brother, Sir Francis North, who was Chief Justice of Common Pleas from 1675 to 1682, a close adviser of the King, and Lord Chancellor from 20 Dec. 1682. In the *Examen*, Roger North remarks: "While these intimidations [of Whigs against anyone's accepting the Lord Mayor's pledge] run high, the Court at a loss for a good man, the citizens busy as bees, some persuading others, but none inclined to stand, everyone wanting courage to bear the brunt, Sir George Jeffreys, the Recorder, or through him some of the citizens, insinuated that the Lord Keeper's brother, a Turkey merchant, lately arrived from Constantinople and settled in London, rich and a single person, was every way qualified to be sheriff at this time, in case he could be prevailed with to stand, as they hoped might be done by the Lord Keeper's means, if he would endeavor to persuade him. This extremely took with the King and soon set him at ease, for he found no formalizing scruples on the Lord Keeper's part; and as for the citizen, he was made to understand that there was no hazard at all" (p. 601).

38. *truck:* To have dealings in; to traffic. The author seems to imply that the Tory candidates are eunuchs; certainly his suggestion here and in the following lines is that they are slaves.

41. *brethren:* This may be directed either to the predominantly loyalist Aldermen, who were properly so addressed, or sarcastically to the Tory politicians, whose archenemies, the dissenting sectarians, referred to each other by this term.

You'll choose the city circumcised shrieves:
To whom, if you would take advice from me,   45
Good Father Elliot should a chaplain be.
Some mufties too you might have wafted o'er,

46. The story of the Rev. Adam Elliot represents one of Titus Oates' more spectacular failures. Elliot had been at Caius College, Cambridge, during Oates' brief stay there. Elliot took his B.A. in 1668 and went abroad on a kind of Grand Tour. On his return journey, in 1670, he was captured by Moorish pirates and taken to Sallee, in the kingdom of Fez, where a renegade named Hamet Lucas bought him in hopes of a ransom. Elliot managed to escape in Nov. and eventually return to England. Two years later, he was ordained by the Bishop of London and settled in Dublin.

In Sept. 1679 he was called to London as a witness in litigation over an estate and suddenly found that there was a warrant out for his arrest as a Jesuit. Miss Lane suggests that Oates met Lord North (the unsuccessful party in the litigation) in Whitehall and, having listened to his case and hoping both for reward and for revenge of youthful grudges, "immediately took North to the King, and to his Majesty imparted the information that this man Elliot was really a very dangerous Jesuit disguised in a parson's gown" (Oates, p. 216). As Elliot himself reconstructed the scene: "Oates told his Majesty . . . that he believed he [Elliot] had more malice in him than all the Jesuits who were hanged; nay more, says he, he is a circumcised Jesuit. God bless us, says his Majesty, What sort of Jesuit is that? A Jesuit who is no Christian but a Turk, replied the Salamanca Devil" (A Modest Vindication of Titus Oates, the Salamanca Doctor, from Perjury, by Adam Elliot, M.A., 1682 [E 543], cited in Lane, Oates, pp. 216–17). Oates swore out a warrant, but Lord North obviously withdrew at once, leaving Titus with no recourse but to admit that the whole affair was a mistake.

Elliot returned to Ireland, and thus the affair would have ended had not the parson given voice to his view of Oates in such strong terms that he was fined £200. Oates' memory suddenly improved on hearing of this in April 1680, and he thereupon swore new charges in the Court of Delegates; these began with every possible sin of youth and ended with the assertion that, in addition to being a circumcised Jesuit, Elliot "as he confessed, did give poison to his Master or Patron when he was a slave" (ibid., p. 27, cited in Lane, Oates, p. 236).

The case did not come up until the beginning of 1682, and the Fates were particularly unkind to Oates. "To begin with, the Emperor of Morocco's ambassador was on a visit to England, and in his train was Hamed Lucas, the identical 'murdered' master of the Rev. Adam Elliot. The legal authorities had the bad taste to choose this of all moments to hear Titus' suit against Elliot . . ." (Lane, Oates, p. 284). Elliot produced not only the "murdered man" but also a large number of college acquaintances who attested to his behavior at the time. "Finally," says Miss Lane, citing Elliot, "so anxious was Elliot to establish his own innocence that he proved, 'by a demonstration not altogether consistent, I confess, with the gravity of my profession,' that he had never been circumcised."

On 1 July, just about the time of the shrieval tumults, Elliot's action for slander was brought before Chief Justice North. Oates had no defense and, as Thompson's Loyal Protestant and True Domestick Intelligence for 1 July reported, "the jury withdrew and after an hour's debate (in tenderness to the Doctor's low condition) brought in £20 damages and costs of suit against Doctor Oates."

47. mufties: Mohammedan priests or expounders of the law; in Turkey, restricted

But that with bishops we were stock'd before:
High rampant, swearing bishops, tite and true,
Brisk bishops, who have their seraglios too;   50
Who'll bid, e'er ghostly codpiece find rebuke,
Two hundred pounds a year above a duke;
Who, if their piety were open set,
Are verier Turks than Bishop Mahomet;
Who, arm'd with sword for pen and mail for gown,   55
With cogent blows knock reeling Error down.
Had you some aids of janizaries got,
Or some bold troops from the timariot,
These better would have merited rewards
Than all your ruby-nos'd and whoring guards,   60
Who, though to fight they could not find a heart,
Most nobly would discharge the plund'ring part.
Then we shall get as loyal sheriffs, when
The lousy regiments are liverymen.

---

to the official head of the religion of the state and to deputies appointed by him in some of the larger cities.

49. *tite:* Quick, swift. Though quite rare as an adjective, its meaning and presence seem justified by "brisk" in 50.

57. *janizaries:* The word is being used quite precisely by the writer if 60 and (by association) 74 have any connection. The janizaries were a body of Turkish infantry acting as the sultan's guard and the main part of the standing army. They were composed partly of tributary children and partly of voluntary renegades. The phrase is frequently found in anti-papist writing ("janizary jesuits," "Romish janizaries." etc.).

58. *timariot:* The holder of a timar, or soldier's share, of land in a conquered country.

60. The question of papists in the King's Guard had been a particular point of attack during the early days of the Popish Plot. At the end of Oct. and beginning of Nov. 1678, the House of Lords actively recommended the matter to Monmouth, who "appointed three officers to attend the King wherever he goes, and to suffer none but his own servants to come near the King" (*HMCR, 11,* Part II, The Manuscripts of the House of Lords, 1678–88 [London, 1887], pp. 53–54). Two years later, a full examination of lists of officers in the army and navy was instituted (ibid., pp. 199–201). A year later (1681), the Whigs argued that holding a parliament at Oxford entailed real danger "from papists at Oxford and [they] had even suggested that some of this danger would come from papists in the King's own guards" (Brown, *Shaftesbury,* p. 278). One of the three Whig objectives (besides exclusion and annual parliaments) was "restoration of the traditional freedom of Englishmen from 'guards and mercenary soldiers' " (ibid.).

64. *lousy:* Probably used here in its stronger figurative sense of dirty, filthy, obscene, rather than the more general abusive sense of mean, scurvy, vile, or contemptible.

Now you by law may freely take a purse,   65
For one upon the bench will vouch it, sirs.
Claw me, and I'll claw thee; what, he's his brother!
And one good turn, ye know, requires another.
For that old fox most prudently decreed
To get a pow'rful friend in time of need,   70
That when he Newgate fate approaching sees,
He may persuade him to refund his fees;
Or, if they cannot here securely trade,
Sneak back with him, and turn a renegade.

Poor Tories! have you none but him in store   75
Who's now been thumb'd so oft he'll hold no more?
Can you provide no better partner than
An unbeliever for a Mussulman?

66–67. The references is to Francis North. See note to 37 above.

68. There might be a play on words here. A tourn or turn is the "tour, turn, or circuit made by the sheriff of a county twice in the year, in which he presided at the hundred court in each hundred of the county" (*OED*).

71–72. i.e. Dudley North, as sheriff of London, would be responsible for imprisoning the Chief Justice when the latter's crimes came to light. The Chief-Justiceship of Common Pleas, according to Roger North, was worth about £4,000 per year.

74. A renegade is an apostate from any form of religious faith, especially a Christian who becomes Mohammedan. There was a lively interest at this time, to judge from Evelyn and Luttrell, in the "renegado Englishman" who acted as interpreter for Ahmed Hadu during the latter's colorful embassy from Jan. to July 1682. The particular renegade in this case was probably Hamet Lucas, the man "murdered" by Elliot. Actually, he was not English though he had twice deserted from the English garrison at Tangiers. (See Evelyn, *Diary, 4*, 265, n. 6. For a full account of the embassy and Hamet Lucas' part in it, see the very thorough study by Routh, *Tangiers*.)

75–76. The reference is to the Tory candidate, Ralph Box, who was maneuvered into the other shrievalty by the constant adjournment and reconvening of Common Halls which denied confirmation to North and election to Box. On 24 and 27 June and 5, 7, and 15 July, the commonalty indicated either by poll or by temperament their support of Papillon and Dubois. Despite all efforts to retain some veneer of enfranchisement, Moore finally had to declare in effect that only the count in his books was valid. To the utter consternation of the Court party, Box fined off on 5 Sept., and the scene of popular pressure and official disregard ended only on the 19th, when Peter Rich was named North's colleague.

76. *thumb'd:* The word here means something soiled or worn with the thumbs in using or handling and plainly refers to Box's two previous unsuccessful attempts for the shrievalty. In 1680 Box ran with Humphrey Nicholson, merchant tailor, against Cornish and Bethel, and the Tory candidates were firmly defeated. In the following year, the same two Court candidates ran against Pilkington and Shute and were completely routed by a more than four-to-one vote. (For results, see Sharpe, *London and the Kingdom, 2*, 472–74.)

Those are but mongrel Turks (to tell you true)
Who love not Christian better than a Jew;   80
And, if they will not take a friend's advice,
Shall ne'er come into Mahomet's Paradise.

   Degenerate London! Slave to mighty pelf!
Degenerate London! Stranger to thyself!
Are these thy senators? thy fathers sage?   85
Sure, if they are, they dote with gold and age.
There was, alas! there was a time when we
Esteem'd our lives below our liberty;
When, if our dying country we could save,
We h'd sung on tombs and triumph'd on the grave,   90
Joyfully fall'n on her beloved face,
And perish'd in our mother's dear embrace.
That nobler ardor long ago is fled;
The slaves are living, and the heroes dead.
We peep into the hall, and whoop, and then,   95
Fools as we went, like fools come back again:
For shrieves, like larks in falling skies, we gape,

85–86. Too frequently, we forget that there were scarcely a half-dozen Whig alder-
men and a score of Tories. North says that "all of the alderman but five (for no
more were factious) advised [Moore] to adjourn" (*Examen*, p. 606). Even in 1683, after
the Charter had been suspended by the Quo Warranto proceedings, Charles replaced
only eight of the aldermen. Six of these—Sir John Lawrence, the Whig leader in the
Corporation, Clayton, Ward, Shorter, Gold, and Cornish—were in open opposition to
the Tories; the remaining two—Alleyn and Frederick—had more recently shown a
disposition to favor the Nonconformists and Whigs" (Beaven, *Aldermen*, 2, 109–10).
The aldermen represented, on the whole, the foremost merchants of the City.

   87–94. The evocation of the spirit of 1641 is surprisingly direct.

   95–96. The ludicrousness of the frustrating Common Halls must have been particu-
larly bitter for the Whigs, whose polls were constantly nullified by Moore's adjourn-
ments. North's account of the first assembly on 24 June is strongly pro-Tory but
quite descriptive: "This was Midsummer work indeed, extreme hot and dusty, and the
partisans strangely disordered every way with crowding, bawling, sweating, and dust;
all full of anger, zeal, and filth in their faces; they ran about up and down the stairs
so that anyone not better informed would have thought the place rather an huge
Bedlam than a meeting for civil business" (*Examen*, pp. 606–07). Six times in three
weeks this scene was to be reenacted. Indeed, upon Box's fining off, it was performed
anew on 19 Sept., when Peter Rich was declared sheriff.

   97. A combination, probably intentional, of a phrase reportedly used by Secretary
Jenkins, with at least three proverbs. In *The Matters of Fact In the Present Election
of the Sheriffs* [M 1304], we were told that Moore agreed to poll for both shrievalties
but "resumed the pretense of his having chosen one sheriff . . . after he heard the

And dance attendance on the courtier's ape;
Who (poor good-natur'd soul) can neither have
Honesty for the fool nor wit for knave.   100
He's a strange piece of linsey-woolsey ware,
Just such another thing as bishops are.

When he on lofty ten-toes did advance,
And through the streets on foot-back proudly prance,
Circled around by all the ragged rout,   105
Who loud huzzas and, "Bless your lordship," shout,
Absent from Jenkins, Halifax, and all
That in his ears forever buzz and bawl,
Then he his loyal carcass did undress
And unto ghostly mother thus confess: 110

"The work is done, I ought to swear 'em too;
But oh! I shall be chidden if I do.

Secretary affirm that they must take that course, though *rueret coelum.*" This phrase
is combined by the author with the proverb which (to cite the comment in Kelly,
Scottish Proverbs, 343) is "spoken when people make silly frivolous excuses or ob-
jections": When (If) the sky (heaven) falls we shall have (catch) larks. (Cf. Tilley,
Proverbs, S 517; *Oxford Dictionary of English Proverbs,* p. 595; *English Proverbs and
Proverbial Phrases,* p. 576.) In addition, there is the proverbial phrase for the sluggard,
and Tilley's example from Palsgrave (L 71, "Do thou but gape, and I shall make larks
fall into thy mouth") is fairly close. Finally, there is an allied and self-explanatory
phrase, "You may gape long enough ere a bird fall in your mouth" (Tilley, *Proverbs,*
B 390). The fact that all three meanings are readily applicable—i.e. that frivolous
excuses have been given to the Whigs who, if they do not take action, will never
receive satisfaction—leads me to think that this is a rather clever and suggestive
quartum quid.

98. *courtier's ape:* The Lord Mayor, Sir John Moore. See headnote to the poems
on the shrieval elections.

101–02. *linsey-woolsey:* Perhaps used in the sense of being a strange medley of
talk or action, or perhaps in the sense of being neither one thing nor the other. The
lines evidently refer to Moore's religion. "He had been a Nonconformist himself,"
says Burnet, "till he grew so rich that he had a mind to go through the dignities
of the city, but though he conformed to the Church, yet he was still looked on as
one that in his heart favored the sectaries" (*History,* 2, 335). A Whig of this period
would probably not have found it difficult to think of some bishops in the same terms.

107. See headnote to the poems on the shrieval elections.

110. *ghostly mother:* There may well be the low colloquial use of "mother" as a
female bawd. This was not uncommon with a religious (particularly a Roman Cath-
olic) word. Cf. "mother abbess" (in Partridge, *Dictionary of Slang,* p. 534; *Dictionary
of the Canting Crew,* H.4ᵛ). As well, there are suggestions of "mother church" and,
by analogy, ghostly father, to whom the subsequent *confessio* should properly be made.

Somebody terrifies me twice and once,
And frights me with 'Raw-head and bloody bones!';
But if I'm good, he calls me 'Love' and 'Joy',   115
And tells me, 'There's my dainty golden boy!'
Gives me a pipe and cart to truckle in,
And strokes my head, and chucks me under chin,
And also promis'd the next time he comes
To bring his pocket full of sugar-plums.   120
Nay, once in verity he pass'd his word
To make my honorable knaveship, lord.
Spite of my teeth, he made me truant play,
And to Whitehall kidnapp'd my lord away;
There such paw words so terribly he said,   125
As with strange proclamations fill'd my head.
I'll imitate great Lucifer and be
A tyrant far more absolute than he,
Who never could a Common Council call,
Nor domineer like me in Heaven's Guildhall,   130
Nor yet in the Crown Office put the stars,
Nor angels prosecute for rioters.

113. *twice and once:* The use is uncertain, but cf. *Macbeth,* IV.i.2: "Thrice and once the hedge-pig whined."

114. *'Raw-head and bloody bones':* In the seventeenth century, the name of a bogy used to terrify children. (See Ned Ward, *The London Spy,* ed. A. C. Hayward [1927], p. 73.) Speaking of the Popish Plot on 8 Oct. 1684 (No. 146), the *Observator* remarks that " 'tis nothing so saucer-ey'd, nothing so Raw-head-and-bloody-bones, that it was; but people go to bed nowadays and sleep quietly."

117. *to truckle in:* To move on truckles or castors, but probably here employed in the pejorative sense of trafficking or dealing with. Certainly the overtones of submitting from an unworthy motive, yielding meanly or obsequiously, and acting with servility, are all implied (cf. *OED,* truckle, v., 2b, 4, 5).

124. *my lord:* i.e. me, my lordship.

125. *paw:* Slang: improper, naughty, obscene.

126. Possibly a reference to Moore's Proclamations, or perhaps to Charles II's Order of Council, issued 13 July, directing Moore to begin the election *de novo* (see Echard, *History, 3,* 661).

131. On Monday morning 26 June, the King summoned the Lord Mayor, the Court of Aldermen, and the two sheriffs, Pilkington and Shute, to the Crown office where the proceedings of the previous Saturday were examined. With a swiftness that did not go unnoticed by Whig pamphleteers (see 257–58 below, and *Song, or Satire* beginning "Presto popular Pilkington"), the 24 privy councillors signed a warrant against the two sheriffs and ordered them committed forthwith to the Tower as "promoters and encouragers of the late enormous riot" (Echard, *History, 3,* 660 and 670).

Well, if at last I find the House too hot,
And Master Jeffrey needs must go to pot,
Worst come to th' worst, it only shall be said,   135
I wisely hang'd myself to save my head."

Thus said, on gilded couches sinking down,
Sleep seiz'd his corpse, and laid his empty crown.
Through all the tedious hours of baleful night,
Guilt gnaws his soul with many a ghastly sprite.   140
Disloyal Morpheus did at first present
The horrid specter of a parliament;
Five hundred heads adorn its mighty chest,
Millions of noble hearts inform the breast,
Millions of hands defend the sacred throne,   145
Bravely resolv'd to make its grave their own.
Poor he at their tribunal quivering stood;
Guilt lock'd his veins, and fear congeal'd his blood;
But what was done or said by him, or these,
I cannot tell you till their masters please.   150

The next that gave his memory a rub,
Were two produc'd in City sweating-tub,

133. *House:* i.e. Commons.

134. *Jeffrey:* i.e. Sir George Jeffreys, with whom the writer will soon deal at length.
The pun in this line becomes obvious when we recall that Jeffreys was a notoriously
heavy drinker. Indeed, drinking was almost the death of him in 1689 when, trying
to flee England in disguise, he got as far as Wapping where "he went into a cellar
to take a pot" (Edward Foss, *The Judges of England* [9 vols. London, 1848–64], 7,
240). While there, he was recognized and almost lynched by the mob.

136. There is the additional ironic sense that those convicted of treason, if they
were of sufficient rank, could beg for beheading rather than the more ignominious
death by hanging and quartering. Charles had granted this to the Viscount Stafford
on 7 Dec. 1681.

142–45. The image, though not an unusual conceptualization of the body politic,
recalls the frontispiece to Hobbes' *Leviathan*. For the Whigs' dependence on what
North calls the "after-game" of a parliament, see headnote to the poems on the
shrieval elections.

150. Evidently a reference to the prohibition against publishing the proceedings
of a parliament. Jeffreys, as Recorder, tried to prohibit by judicial fiat any person from
exposing "to the public knowledge anything that concerned the affairs of the public"
without authority from the King or his officers (H. W. Woolrych, *Memoirs of the
Life of Judge Jeffreys* [London, 1827], p. 56).

152. The heat and press of the Common Hall is mentioned constantly. The "two"
that come into Moore's dream might well be among those mentioned by Luttrell:

Who, that they might appear for North and Box,
Were us'd like rotten courtiers with a pox;
Within his bagnio they were forc'd to stay   155
Till, chok'd with heat, their souls did melt away;
Bequeathing him the people's weighty hate,
Sure omen of a far severer fate.

The next that discompos'd his lordship's naps
Was a whole show'r of dreadful shoulder-claps;   160
Action they still atop of action pack,
Almost enough to break a camel's back;
Hundreds of thousand pounds! St. James defend us,
Or these unconscionable Whigs will end us.

So great a noise these Counter-devils did keep   165
As fright his doughty lordship out of sleep.
For a court journey he again provides,
Saddles his cane, and then gets up and rides;

"Several persons, as Mr. King a furrier, Mr. Levens a tobacconist, a Quaker, and others, being taken sick with the great heat at Guildhall at the choice of the sheriffs, are since dead" (*Brief Relation, 1,* 209 [22 July 1682]; see also *The Matters of Fact,* p. 3). If the Mr. King in Luttrell's note is Thomas King, he was alive enough in Oct. to bring an action against Moore (*CSPD* 1682, p. 512).

In the following lines, the author plays with the literal and slang uses of several words. Thus, "city sweating-tub" here refers to the Guildhall; but also a sweating-tub was formerly used in the treatment of venereal disease (cf. "pox" in 154). Partridge (*Dictionary of Slang,* p. 914) notes a late nineteenth-century use of "tubbing" meaning imprisonment, which might also be relevant here (cf. n. 155).

155. *bagnio:* All three definitions in the *OED* have application: 1. a bath, a bathing house, esp. one with hot baths, vapor baths, and appliances for sweating, cupping, and other operations; 2. an oriental prison, a place for slaves, a penal establishment; 3. a brothel, a house of prostitution.

160–62. *shoulder-claps:* A shoulder-clapper is an officer charged with the arrest of an offender, a bailiff, sheriff's officer. One of the principal threats against both North and Box was that of crippling litigation (see North, *Examen,* pp. 611–12); indeed, following the Common Hall of 15 July, the Whigs tried to bring the full weight of "actions" on their main target, Moore (see Luttrell, *Brief Relation, 1,* 207; *Observator,* particularly No. 175 [22 July], No. 176 [24 July], No. 178 [26 July]). As "Whig" remarks in No. 175, "Only seventeen [actions] in hand, but more to follow. They talk of 300"; and later he threatens that "My Lord will have a thousand actions upon him." For an example, see the brief in *CSPD* 1682, p. 512.

163. *St. James:* Both *4°* and *z* read "St. J———s," perhaps recalling 107, which has "J———s," while at the same time invoking York. That Secretary Jenkins and the Court did indeed defend Moore in legal actions is indicated by *CSPD* 1682, p. 512.

165. *Counter:* The prisons attached to the London courts.

To the Cabal he hastily does go,
Still crying, "Westminster" and "Lambeth, ho!"   170
What there he did, fanatics must not tell,
But if you'd know, pray ask Sir Lionel.

Room for the chap-fall'n mouth, or else 'twill swear
By all the Aps from Saint Cadwallader,

169. *Cabal:* Originally the political government of Clifford, Arlington, Buckingham, Ashley Cooper, and Lauderdale. By this time, the word was used pejoratively for any political group (cf. Papillon, *Papillon,* p. 208, where Lady Moore uses it for the Whig faction). Here the reference is clearly to the Privy Council.

170. *"Westminster":* The location of government offices in general and Jenkins' in particular.

"Lambeth": The residence in London of the Archbishop of Canterbury.

172. *Sir Lionel:* i.e. Sir Leoline Jenkins.

173. *chap-fall'n:* Not only does the literal meaning of "the lower jaw hanging down as an effect of extreme exhaustion" (*OED*) apply to "the mouth," but the figurative sense of "crestfallen" would also be valid since Jeffreys had been forced by the City Whigs to resign his recordership in 1680 and had not been re-elected Chairman of the Middlesex Sessions in Feb. 1682.

mouth: Though the term has been applied to Scroggs (Foss, *Judges of England,* 7, p. 169) and Sir George Treby (*Observator,* No. 168 [10 July 1682]), it was more commonly the nickname of Jeffreys who, as Recorder of London, had referred to himself as "the mouthpiece of the City." (See also *Westminster Wedding or the Town Mouth, POAS,* Yale, 2, 351–55, and cited at length in Woolrych, *Memoirs,* pp. 37–40.) Jeffreys, who began his practice in London as a Whig sympathizer, early turned to the Court, becoming rapidly Recorder (1678), Chief Justice of Chester (1680), and King's Serjeant (1681). The Whigs' anger at his defection (if not betrayal) was aggravated both by his leading the attack on the City charter and, in the present instance, by his activity in behalf of Moore and the Court candidates. Jeffreys not only proposed Dudley North, but also allowed his house in Coleman Street near Guildhall to be used as Tory headquarters during the Common Halls. (Cf. North, *Lives, 1,* 223; Hyde, *Judge Jeffreys,* p. 126.) The final blow, however, was Jeffreys' (and Saunders') legal advice to Moore that the Lord Mayor had every right to adjourn the Common Hall. (See Sharpe, *London and the Kingdom,* p. 481, n. 2.) It was this point, argued at length in the trial for riot of Pilkington et al. (see Howell, *State Trials, 9,* esp. 219–98) that made the subsequent pollings for the sheriffs illegal and riotous.

174–79. The mock-Welsh that follows is a gibe at Jeffreys who, in 1681, was created a baronet. Hyde (*Judge Jeffreys,* p. 15, n. 3) notes that two manuscript pedigrees were compiled at this time which quite disprove "the opinion spread by his enemies that he was a person of low birth." The best comment here would be the statement of one of Jeffreys' biographers, Seymour Schofield: "The Jeffreys were a solid and respectable county family, and as Welsh families are not, as a rule, guilty of understating their antiquity, the clan modestly claimed descent from Tudor Trevor, Earl of Hereford, and so linked themselves up with the assemblage of kings, princes and demigods from whom this celebrity was doubtless derived" (*Jeffreys of "The Bloody Assizes"* [London, Thornton Butterworth], p. 14).

174. *Saint Cadwallader:* Cadweladr Vendigaid (the Blessed), seventh-century king

Prute's hur creat cranfather, if hur enquire,   175
And Adam's cranfather was Prutus' sire.
Famous ap Shenkin was hur elder prother,
Some Caledonian Sycorax hur mother,
Or some she-deel more damn'd than all the rest,
At their black feast hur lustful sire compress'd;   180
Thence this incarnate cacodemon rose,
Whose very face his parents' image shows:
His shape was all inhuman and uncouth,
But yet he's chiefly devil about the mouth.
With care they nurs'd the brat, for fear it should   185
Grow tame, and so degen'rate into good;
With City Charters him they wrapp'd about,
And Acts of Parliament for swaddling-clout.
As he grew up, he won a noble fame,
Well worthy of the brood from whence he came;   190
Cherishing Spite and hugging Discord fell,
He was the best beloved brat of Hell.
Oft with success this mighty blast did bawl
Where loudest lungs and longest swords win all,
And still his clenched arguments did end   195
With that home thrust, "He is not Caesar's friend."
Sometimes, that jaded ears he might release,
Good man! he has been fee'd to hold his peace.
Hear him, but never see him, and you'd swear
He was the crier, not the counsellor.   200

---

of the Britons, moves, half historically, half mythically, through most of the Welsh chronicles.

175. *Prute's:* Brut or Brutus, legendary great-grandson of Aeneas, was first king of the Britons, and founder of Troia Nova (i.e. London).

177. *ap Shenkin:* The comic name for the pretentious Welshman, i.e. the son of Jenkin. The same mock-genealogy is given by Henry Fielding in *The Grub Street Opera.*

178. *Caledonian:* Jeffreys' mother, Margaret, was the daughter of Sir Thomas Ireland of Lancashire (Cf. Woolrych, *Memoirs,* p. 2).

Sycorax: An unusual word, not found in the *OED* but probably related to psychagogue, a necromancer. The suggestion might well have come from Shakespeare's *Tempest,* where the witch Sycorax is the mother of the malevolent monster, Caliban.

179. *she-deel:* i.e. a succubus.

181. *cacodemon:* An evil spirit. The use of the word for a person precedes the first reference in the *OED* by 29 years.

200. As King's Serjeant, Jeffreys was the Crown's counsel.

He roars as if he only chanc'd to find
Justice was now grown deaf as well as blind.
This demi-fiend, this hurricane of man,
Must shatter London's glory (if he can);
This engineer must, with his forked crown   205
For battering ram, beat all her bulwarks down.
And him our prudent praetor wisely chose
To splutter law and the dinn'd rabble pose.
They have a thousand tongues, yet he can roar
Far louder, though they had a thousand more.   210
Unto long-winded Cook he scorns to go,
But pleads, "His Majesty will have it so."
Counsel alone, for such a client fit,
As fam'd for honesty as he for wit.

    "Well," quoth Sir George, "the Whigs may think me rude,   215
Or brand me guilty of ingratitude;
At my preferment they (poor fools) may grudge,
And think me fit for hangman more than judge;
But though they fret, and bite their nails, and bawl,

204. A reference to the Quo Warranto proceedings, Charles' maneuver of recalling
city charters in order to reissue more favorable versions.
    205. Jeffreys' second marriage, in 1679, was to Lady Anne Jones, a widow, daughter
of Sir Thomas Bludworth, ex-Lord Mayor. In Woolrych's tactful phrase, she "was a
dame of most slippery courses, if we are to credit rumor" (*Memoirs*, p. 316). See also
The Westminster Wedding, POAS, Yale, 2, 351–55.
    207. *praetor*: Either the Lord Mayor or Leoline Jenkins, the Secretary of State for
the South (see headnote to the poems on the shrieval elections).
    209. Foss (*Judges of England*, 7, 227) refers to his "voluble tongue and stentorian
voice," and Woolrych (*Memoirs*, p. 18) cites support from the trial records.
    211. Cf. *Jeffreys' Elegy*, by N. H. (1689) [H 98], quoted in Woolrych (*Memoirs*, p. 12):

    Methought I saw a lawyer at his book,
    Studying Pecunia, but never Cooke;
    He scorned Littleton, and Plowden too,
    With mouldy authors he'd have nought to do.

214. Jeffreys' often cruel witticisms were notorious. In Parliament, Henry Booth
(later Lord Delamere and Earl of Worrington) attacked Jeffreys for his conduct in the
Chester Assizes, for having "behaved himself more like a jack-pudding than with the
gravity which beseems a judge: he was mighty witty upon the prisoners at the bar;
he was very full of his jokes upon people that came to give evidence . . . but would
interrupt them because they behaved with more gravity than he" (Hyde, *Judge Jeffreys*,
p. 99). Whatever one's opinion of Jeffreys' conduct on the bench, there can be little
doubt that he must have been a brilliant trial lawyer.

I'll slight them, and go kiss dear Nelly Wall.   220
Dalila is to court return'd, and I,
Bless'd with her influence, all the world defy.
I'm made, whilst Samson wantons in her lap:
Such favorites are whores, so charming is a clap."

 But hold! what makes the gaping many run?   225
Is France defeated? or is Rome undone?
Is Portsmouth nun, or Kate a mother grown?
Will conscientious Comyn swear for none?
Have poets quite forgot to smooth, and glose,
And lead admiring cullies by the nose?   230
Have we a war with Monsieur? peace with Spain?
Or have we got a parliament again?
All in good time, when Heav'n and Charles shall please.
But 'tis a wonder greater far than these:
Were not our shrieves the greatest sots alive   235
To question my Lord Mayor's prerogative,
Who is (if all that Tories say be true)
The wisest lord that ever London knew?
And aided by some musty laws, dispute
With him that is, or would be, absolute?—   240

220. *Nelly Wall:* Companion to the Duchess of Portsmouth. Perhaps an allusion to Jeffreys' questionable conviction of Justice Doughty in 1680. See Irving, *Life of Judge Jeffreys* (New York, Longmans, Green), pp. 115–17; and *HMCR, Verney Papers,* p. 478.

221. *Dalila:* Louise de Kéroualle, Duchess of Portsmouth, mistress to Charles II. Her influence at Court was remarkable; it was she who checked Monmouth, maneuvered York, and pushed forward her favorites. Thus *On the Duchess of Portsmouth's Picture, Sept. 1682* (Case 211 (1) (c), p. 51; cited also in Woolrych, *Memoirs,* p. 33) refers to her as "Monmouth's tamer, Jeffreys' advance" (13). For her favors to Jeffreys, see Hyde, *Judge Jeffreys,* pp. 50, 55, 97.

227. *Kate:* Catherine of Braganza, the childless wife of Charles II.

228. *conscientious Comyn:* Eustace Comyns, or Comins, one of the Irish witnesses in 1680. For an amusing parody of his testimony, see *A Good Pook . . .* by Eustas Comyne, *His Majesty's True Evidence in Good Will and Conscience to serve King and Country: One that is more for Peace and Quietness than any Man in the three Nations* (1682) [C 5679].

236. The parallel of the municipal and the national struggles for power made the shrieval contention even more bitter. Charles' proroguing of parliaments found echo in Moore's adjournments and dissolutions of the Common Halls.

239. For the "musty laws" on which the sheriffs based the legality of their actions, see Howell, *State Trials, 9,* 264–83.

240. *him:* i.e. Moore.

Though that's (if due to one) to one alone,
Unless the Hustings could commence a throne.
Rave whilst they will, he'll make the City stay
Because 'tis great and lordly to delay.
"Our pleasure is that you no longer sit,   245
But go, and meet again when we think fit."
When will and pleasure could not aught prevail,
Away he trots to tell the woeful tale.
On marrow bones he sadly begs for pity:
"Pray, sir! I can't be quiet for the City.   250
They hunch, and punch, and hit me many a pat,
And throw one down, and dirt one's beaver hat.
Th' uncomplaisant fanatics neither care
For sage Sir John, nor Lord, nor Moore, nor Mayor."

Woe to the naughty boy that's such a noddy   255
T' abuse him who says nothing to nobody.
The shrieves must come, and in one live-long hour,

241. *one:* i.e. Charles II.

248. On 25 June, Moore reported the illegalities of the sheriffs to Charles (Luttrell, *Brief Relation, 1,* 197) at Whitehall, and Jenkins summoned the Privy Council for the following day (*CSPD* 1682, p. 268).

251–52. In the trial of Pilkington et al. for riot, a number of prosecution witnesses painted a picture of a mob that only failed to lynch the Lord Mayor because of the number of loyal friends that held it back (Howell, *State Trials, 9,* esp. 252–64). Much was made of the fact that Moore stumbled and that he lost his hat. The caustic remark of Pilkington's counsel, Sir Francis Winnington ("Here is a mighty riot upon the hat") seems borne out by Jenkins' note that "Going home he [Moore] met with no affront. They were his friends that accompanied him. Though in the great crowd his hat was lost, yet it was without harm or disrespect" (*CSPD* 1682, p. 268). It was not until the day after the Council meeting that the incident became a cause (*CSPD* 1682, p. 172, Newsletter).

257. On the morning of 26 June, Pilkington and Shute were summoned before the Privy Council at the complaint of the Lord Mayor. The extraordinary session, probably called by Jenkins (*CSPD* 1682, p. 268), found that the sheriffs "did promote and encourage a most enormous riot" and committed them forthwith to the Tower upon the warrant of 24 of the Councillors. Charles then gave instructions to Sawyer, the Attorney-General, to bring suit in King's Bench "according to the utmost severity of Law" (*London Gazette,* No. 1733 [26–29 June 1682], p. 272). The two men were, then and there, taken into custody by Derham, the Sergeant-at-Arms, and "in Sheriff Pilkington's coach, attended only by two musketeers and two yeomen, [they were] carried at high noon time through the City to the Tower" (*CSPD* 1682, p. 272). Carte claims that this show of authority was due to Ormonde, who, "ever averse to all counsels that proceeded from fear," advised against a strong guard and a surreptitious trip to the Tower by boat (Thomas Carte, *A History of the Life of James, Duke of*

Presto, they're conjur'd into enchanted Tower.
But four small devils did hoist 'em on their backs.
Behold the policy of Halifax   260
Who makes the Protestants' devotion thus:
From Hell, and Hull, and Him, deliver us.

That sham won't take, sir; for, whate'er you do,
We know our strength but know our duty too.
At these fine little tricks of state we laugh;   265
For such old birds are seldom caught with chaff.
Yet though whole droves of locusts you provide,
With ten and twenty regiments beside,
Though they should batter down our towers and walls
(As once before) with Tewkesbury mustard balls,   270
We've noble hearts dare leap into a flame,
With a bold traitor's blood to quench the same,
With parting breath curse all the friends to Rome,
And in some temple's ruins find a tomb.

Ormonde [3 vols. London, 1735–36], *2,* 524). On 27 June, the Court of King's Bench granted a habeas corpus which the Lieutenant of the Tower refused to honor (Luttrell, *Brief Relation, 1,* 199), but three days later, upon a second writ, Pilkington and Shute were admitted to bail (ibid., p. 200). The Court party's maneuver to put the Whig sheriffs out of operation during the critical Common Halls had proved only partially successful.

258. The swiftness of the Court's action is frequently noticed. See 131 n.

262. The proverb, "From Hell, and Hull, and Halifax," is given in Tilley, *Proverbs,* H 399, which cites, among others, a late (1662) but fairly clear explanation from "Fuller, *Worthies* [ed. J. Nichols, 1811] Yorkshire, II, 494: This is part of the beggars' and vagrants' litany . . . Hull is terrible unto them as a town of good government. . . . Halifax is formidable unto them, for . . . thieves . . . stealing . . . cloth are instantly beheaded with an engine." The great cloth center of Halifax had power, under the Gibbet Law, of executing anyone guilty of stealing any goods worth more than thirteen pence. The gibbet, which somewhat resembled a guillotine, was first used under this law in 1541, "and the right was exercised in Halifax longer than in any other town, the last execution taking place in 1650" (*EB, 12,* 844). Historically, Thompson may be alluding to the Marquis of Halifax's Yorkshire origin, or perhaps to his part in the removal of Monmouth as Hull's governor (which was accomplished at the end of 1679). The proverb appears also in *A Litany for St. Omers* [L 2532]: "From Halifax, with Hull and Hell" (9).

268. The trained bands were called out to maintain order during the Common Halls and, later, during the investiture of the Tory sheriffs.

270. *Tewkesbury mustard balls:* As Oates explained in *The Narrative of the Popish Plot* (1679): "The deponent saith that by Tewkesbury mustard-balls, we are to understand fire-balls" (p. 48). They were composed of a "notable biting sauce" and meant for the firing of Westminster (Lane, *Oates,* p. 100).

Nor you familiars shall forgotten be,   275
Although unworthy of my verse and me;
You who that honorable fool command,
And finely manage him by sleight of hand.
Billy, look to't; e'er parliament come on,
Let you and neighbor Jemmy get you gone.   280
Rouse up, ye Tories of the factious age,
Implicit clappers to the bawdy stage:
Duncomb's an ass to think these mighty men
Would take such store of pains for nine or ten;
When your dear patrons to preferments rise,   285
Moloch must have a larger sacrifice;
Hundreds of hecatombs shall grace his shrine,
Whilst you huzza in blood instead of wine;
Whilst from their holes the waspish Whigs you burn,
And every signpost to a gibbet turn.   290
Degenerate Albion! Ah! is this thy son?

279–80. Probably the Aldermen, Sir James Edwards and Sir William Pritchard. See
Matters of Fact: "Nor must Sir J. E. and Sir W. P. &c. think to escape being called to
account, not only for abetting the Mayor in all these invasions upon the privileges of
the City, but for exciting him unto, and hurrying him upon them" (p. 4).

283–84. Charles Duncombe (later alderman, sheriff, and mayor) was a zealous sup-
porter of North's right to confirmation during the polling (see *CSPD* 1682, pp. 263–64).
It was probably about the time of the 14 July polling that Duncombe made the rather
tactless remark which Henry Care (*Weekly Pacquet, 4,* No. 31 [21 July 1682], p. 248)
was quick to publish: "If we may believe what a printed paper relates and names the
person, one of the sticklers confessed lately that the business so struggled for was to get
'sheriffs to hang up half a score that were uneasy.'" To the writer of *The Matters of
Fact,* the election of Tory sheriffs meant the encouragement of Papists and masquerade
Protestants, a denial of the Popish Plot and general slaughter. "And whereas Mr.
Duncombe was contented a few days ago with the lives of 9 or 10, nothing less will
now serve them than the destroying of scores, if not hundreds" (p. 4).

285–90. The description echoes those found in Oates, but the opinion that the ad-
vent of the Papists would be followed by a general massacre of Protestants was popu-
larly held. For L'Estrange's use, at this time, of the Moloch image, see *Observator,* No.
175 (22 July 1682).

288. *huzza:* North (*Examen,* p. 617) remarks: "At all the Tory healths, as they were
called, the cry was reared of *Huzza!,* which at these great and solemn feasts made no
little noise and gave advantage to the Whigs, that liked not such music, to charge the
Tories with brutality and extravagance." Care is particularly annoyed at the custom;
see, esp., *Weekly Pacquet, 4,* No. 34 (11 Aug. 1682), p. 272.

291. *son:* The reference here would seem to be either to Moore, who had betrayed
London, or James, who had turned Catholic. Despite 294, this is not a treasonous refer-
ence to Charles II, the author being in favor of Monmouth's succession (cf. 415–18).

This thy degenerate offspring, Albion?
Canst thou without a cloud of blushes see
The follies of thy spurious progeny?
Is not the man a hero, bold and brave,   295
That damns his race and dooms his grandchild slave?
Does not our loyal lord deserve to pass
For what he is indeed, a loyal ass?
Are not our dearest friends, the plodding Whigs,
Old dogs at politics and state intrigues,   300
Who split again upon the self-same shelves,
And sweat to twist a rope to hang themselves?
One would have thought the port wherewith he goes,
And chain and all, enough to fright his foes!
'Tis true, he scorns to fear or take affront   305
But looks as big as Bully Rodomont.
For who the valor and the force can tell,
That waits upon the name of colonel?
But yet, to curb fanatics' discontent,
Guards must be drawn up ready to present;   310
Yet though he's so courageous, he's so wise,
That none but friends know where his valor lies.
Poor souless thing! alike contemn'd and curs'd,
By some Court-sneaking devil inform'd at first,
Under what sickly planet wert thou born,   315
Doom'd at thy birth thy nation's plague and scorn?
Did sullen Saturn rule the sooty sky,

294. *spurious:* As a counterpoise to Monmouth's illegitimacy, exclusionists often played on the legal or metaphorical sense of the word. Thus the reference here would be to one who is not properly qualified or constituted, one who is false, a counterfeit or a sham (cf. *OED*).

295–96. *man:* i.e. Moore. The order of the text is followed here, though greater unity would result from placing these lines after 302.

299. As a slightly left-of-center legalist, the author is forced to condemn the extremists of both parties. To a comparatively moderate Whig, Shaftesbury's Association would have been abhorrent.

plodding: There was a contemporary confusion (perhaps intentionally made here) with the verb "plot" (cf. *OED*, v.4).

304. *chain:* The mayor's badge of office.

306. *Rodomont:* A bragger or boaster; the name of the boastful Saracen leader in Ariosto's *Orlando Furioso*.

308. *colonel:* Moore was Colonel of the Yellow Regiment from 1682 to 1687 (Beaven, *Aldermen*, 2, 99).

Or frowning Mars his car run rumbling by?
No manlike power would then vouchsafe to sway;
Some woman-god usurp'd th' unlucky day;   320
Unconstant Luna's force did then prevail
In close conjunction with the Dragon's tail.
Poor souless thing! thee cross-grain'd nature gave
To make the land a scourge, the Court a slave;
Thy country's bane, the statesman's wooden tool,   325
More fool than knave, and yet more knave than fool.
Like farting Pythia, thou art nothing else
But a mere trunk to Satan's oracles:
Still mayst thou live, but live in fear and pain,
And live to see a parliament again.   330

    Ah, too, too happy London! didst thou know,
And bless the arm divine that made thee so;
Planted by Heav'n in a luxuriant soil,
The paradise of all this fruitful isle;
With air-invading turrets proudly crown'd,   335
With Thames' oozy arms begirt around,
With silver Thames, who smooths his aged face
When hasting to his darling's dear embrace;
Bearing the traffic of the home-spun west
As a love-token to adorn her breast.   340
On his proud neck, he takes the irksome chain,
And still rolls back to kiss her shores again;
Indulgent mothers so, long tales will tell,
And give their parting sons a long farewell!
The gentle Naiads for her sight prepare,   345
And in their crystal mirrors curl their hair;
Their purling streams and bubbling rills advance,
And round the sedges deck'd with osiers dance;
Their brooks and ponds of scaly subjects drain

327. *Pythia:* The priestess of Apollo at Delphi who delivered the oracles.

328. *trunk:* Probably used in the sense of a body apart from the soul or life (cf. *OED* sb.3).

341. *chain:* Perhaps a metaphorical allusion to London Bridge, but more likely a reference to the chain used to prevent enemy vessels from coming into the harbor.

345. *Naiads:* The river nymphs.

For presents to enrich their sovereign.   350
The stately Nereids, with the swelling tide,
Rich freights from all the universe provide;
Whate'er of rarities the East can shew,
With all the glittering entrails of Peru,
Cargoes of myrrh and frankincense they bring,   355
And pearls and diamonds for an offering;
And when a storm is rais'd, to make their peace,
E'en their own corals and their ambergris.
Nor yet this cabinet, though bright, had been
Admir'd, but for the nobler gems within;   360
Not all the Indies charms enough can find
To please and satisfy a virtuous mind;
For wealth without our liberties would be
But painted chains and gilded slavery.
To make her happiness complete and whole,   365
The gods inspir'd her with a generous soul;
Her freeborn offspring still was great and brave,
Too low for rebel, but too high for slave;
Who both of right and duty sense did feel,
And could bow low, but rather burst than kneel.   370

    Amongst this purer wheat some tares did breed,
Some cockle, and encroaching darnel seed;
A vip'rous brood, who smiling poison give
To those indulgent friends who made 'em live;
Cut out for France, or some ignobler place,   375
Where tyrants' chains are counted no disgrace.
Nature found stuff for men and wrought it right,

351. *Nereids:* The sea nymphs.

354. The bullion of South America dazzled the contemporary mind. On 9 Oct., shortly after the date of this poem, *The Domestic Intelligence (or News both from City and Country Impartially Related),* No. 145 (9–12 Oct. 1682) reported that "several new mines are discovered in Peru, affording gold in more abundance than what has hitherto been known; 300 Spaniards and 200 of the natives daily labor."

368. The association of the rebel with excessive height probably comes from a conceptualization of his attempt to rise above his superior or some legitimately higher power (cf. *OED,* a. and sb. 2, and the adverb *rebel-high*).

372. *darnel:* A weed that grows among corn. Like tares and cockle, it belongs to the *genus Lolium.* The image was particularly popular during the fourteenth century in anti-Lollard literature.

But Heaven denies to give a human sprite.
Some sparks of fire she like Prometheus stole,
And, wanting better, gave a chicken's soul;   380
Or what did by late transmigration pass
From some contented slave or golden ass.
These (bleeding London) all thy bliss destroy,
These stab thy hopes, and murder all thy joy:
These not content with what themselves could do,   385
To please the Devil, would damn their neighbors too.

But thou (great Charles!) whose glorious Wain does rove
Round our horizon, next to none but Jove,
With royal goodness hear their humble suit,
Who fain would love thee, if thou'dst let 'em do't.   390
I beg no favor, I expect no bays;
Bare truth gets frowns, gilt lies have coin and praise.
Could I the art of thy great laureate win,
To wash a Moor, or blanch a blacker sin,
Then might I nobly swear and whore in state,   395
And e'en bid fair for wealth in spite of fate;
But though my threadbare muse would fain be trying,
Yet all, like him, have not the gift of lying.

Oh, hear thy bleeding subjects' groans and sighs,
If not their tongues, yet hear their flowing eyes;   400
Pity their too well-grounded griefs and fears,
Mov'd by the silent rhetoric of their tears.
Oh let the charming Devil tempt on in vain;

387. *Wain:* Charles' Wain (originally churl's wain) is composed of the seven brightest stars of Ursa Major, and is known now as the Dipper. The phrase was a particular favorite of the political poets of the 1640s.

391. *bays:* Probably an indirect allusion to Dryden, who was ridiculed under the name of Bayes in Buckingham's famous play, *The Rehearsal.*

393. *laureate.* John Dryden, whose *Absalom and Achitophel* had gone through seven London editions since its publication in mid-Nov. 1681 (see Macdonald, *Dryden Bibliography,* pp. 18–26).

394. *wash a Moor:* A punning variant of "paint an Ethiop white." In point of fact, Dryden (or more likely his collaborator, Nahum Tate) concluded *The Second Part of Absalom and Achitophel* with a fulsome praise of Moore (Ziloah) and a condemnation of "the viler pair," Pilkington and Shute.

blacker sin: Most likely a reference to Dryden's treatment of Charles II's adultery in *Absalom and Achitophel,* 1–20.

Appear thyself, and break th' ignoble chain;
Shake the Court ear-wigs from thy pester'd throne,   405
Shake off thy little kings, and reign alone.
So mayst thou see thy flatterers fall, and see
Those that are friends to law are friends to thee;
So mayst thou bring poor England glad relief,
To right her wrongs and banish all her grief,   410
Till crown'd with suns and beams of peaceful day,
Attendant angels thee to bliss convey;
Thither, though late, (late let it be) remove,
And change this diadem for one more bright above.
May thy surviving image ever be   415
(If possible) as much belov'd as thee.
May after-ages his great sons admire,
For England's darlings and the world's desire;
For sworn eternal foes to France and Rome,
In a long, long succession down to th' day of doom.   420

405. *earwig:* An insect so called from the notion that it penetrates into the head through the ear; hence an ear-whisperer, flatterer, parasite. Cf. Dryden's description of Shaftesbury in *The Medal* "A vermin wriggling in the usurper's ear" (31).

pester'd: In addition to its usual meaning, to encumber or obstruct, there is probably the sense "to annoy, as with vermin, or to infect" (*OED*).

415. *surviving image:* Although the author tries to avoid any controversial stand on the succession by carefully pluralizing *great sons* in 417 and *England's darlings* in 418, the latter phrase and the subsequent call (419) for a Protestant, anti-French king inevitably point to his support of Monmouth.

Cethegus' Ghost

[S 6176]

In Sept. 1682, Ralph Box, who had been North's running mate during the stormy sessions at the Guildhall, officially "fined off" from the post, much to the consternation of the Court party. While Box, a grocer, undoubtedly disliked the prospect of interminable law suits, there was certainly economic pressure brought to bear upon him, not unlike that which Josiah Keeling, the bailiff who revealed the Rye House Plot, claimed had involved him earlier in the Pritchard-Papillon affair: "The particular argument that [Goodenough] used to persuade me to [arrest the Lord Mayor] was this, That I having a trade and dealing among that sort of people, they would think ill of me if I did not do it" (Howell, *State Trials, 10,* 327). Added to this was the anticipated danger of Whig revenge from what North aptly calls an "after-game in Parliament" (p. 611).

Though the Court party attempted to leave a legal loophole by accepting his £400 as money for the use of the City rather than as a fine (Luttrell, *1,* 217), Box did not change his mind. Once again, feelings ran high, "the Tories blaming him on one side, and the Whigs gathering heart on the other, promising themselves success; but the more moderate persons like not these proceedings, dreading the ill consequences that such heats and divisions may occasion" (ibid). On Tuesday 12 Sept., petitions were presented to the Court of Aldermen demanding that Papillon and Dubois be sworn. Moore dissolved the crowded hall, only to be faced with petitions and counterpetitions when the Court met two days later. It was thereupon decided, to the shouts of "No North! No Common Hall!" (see *Observator,* No. 209 [21 Sept. 1682]), that there would be an election on the following Tuesday, 19 Sept., for "another person to serve sheriff with Mr. North" (Luttrell, *1,* 219). Charles put off his trip to Newmarket in order to be close at hand for the crucial contest.

The scenes of the previous June and July were reenacted: the crowd, the confusion, the cross-purposes of Pilkington (taking a poll for the two Whig candidates) and Moore (who declared Rich the winner). Certainly there was no longer any doubt of Whig plans. Their refusal to compromise their legal position by voting in Moore's books showed plainly that they felt quite certain that a Parliament would ultimately grant them both posts. For the Court party, this unbending position made it reasonably simple to outmaneuver the opposition. For Charles, there was now one more excellent reason for not summoning a parliament.

Luttrell's notation on the Huntington Library copy reads: "Ag[ains]t the Whigs. 20 Sept. 1682." The author (Caleb Calle?) assumes the mask of an extreme nonconformist and sustains the irony throughout the poem. The sequel, *Cethegus' Apology for Non-Appearance upon his Conjurer's Summons,* follows immediately in the present volume.

A SUMMONS FROM A TRUE PROTESTANT CONJURER
TO CETHEGUS' GHOST,
TO APPEAR SEPTEMBER 19, 1682

Rise from the dead, Cethegus, at our call;
Lend a kind vote at our next common hall.
Thy voice of old in Rome was deem'd divine,
Surpassing our great patron's, Catiline.
"The ills we have committed safe can't be   5
Without attempting worse for liberty."
Shall we, like vassals, fetter'd be by law;

1. *Cethegus:* Reputedly the "Hotspur" of the Catilinarian conspiracy. Cf. Jonson's characterization in *Catiline.* The idea of Cethegus' ghost is found in the Epistle Dedicatory of Caleb Calle's free translation of Sallust, *Patriae Parricida* [S 409], in 1683: "And may not we as well imagine that Catiline or Cethegus is now rais'd from the dead, and like Mahomet's pigeon inspires men with the horrid principles of blood and rebellion?" [A6v]. For further discussion of the use of the Catilinarian conspiracy see *An Ironical Encomium.*

2. *common hall:* The general meeting of a corporation or guild.

5-6. Cf. Jonson, *Catiline* (Catiline's opening speech):

The ills that I have done cannot be safe
But by attempting greater.

(I.79–80)

For another example of the use of Catiline, see *Ironical Encomium,* 5–10 n., 77–78 n., 79 n.

7. Cf. *Ironical Encomium,* 15, though the idea is not uncommon.

We, who of nought that's mortal stand in awe?
Shall we (true Israel) by Sauls humbl'd be;
We, who can scarcely own theocracy?   10
Brutus was brave, and his impulse divine,
When first from Rome he chas'd the royal line;
And something like't we did, ere forty-nine.
But those blest reformation days soon pass'd,
And Charles' return our blooming hopes did blast.   15
On bishops' lands we saints did freely feed,
 Till Batt, the vile apostle, made us bleed;
Shepherds and sheep cashier'd, th' admitted goats
Who led our flocks astray; till up rose Oates—
Oates, grand retriever of our reformation,   20
Savior o' th' true protesting part o' th' nation!
He taught us by his blest discovery
To form a method for new liberty;
And to secure a stronger combination,

9. Cf. I Samuel 9–14. The Book of Samuel was traditionally the source for concepts of monarchical supremacy. Cf. James I, *The Trew Law of Free Monarchies*.

10. Cf. I Samuel 8, where the Israelites reject theocracy in favor of an earthly monarchy.

11. *Brutus:* Probably Lucius Junius Brutus, a symbol of republicanism, who expelled Tarquinius Superbus and established the early republic (509 B.C.). According to tradition, this was due to the rape of Lucretia by Sextus Tarquinius, the son of the king. Cf. Shakespeare's *Rape of Lucrece*. There may be a confusion in the author's mind: cf. *An Ironical Encomium,* 35, where the reference seems to be to Marcus Brutus.

12. *royal line:* i.e. the Tarquinii.

13. *ere forty-nine:* Charles I was beheaded on 30 Jan. 1649, i.e. 1648, o.s.

16. i.e. through sequestration during the Commonwealth period.

17. *Batt:* Uncertain. Perhaps William Bates, a moderate nonconformist and "reputed one of the best orators of the age" (Edmund Calamy, *The Nonconformist's Memorial,* ed. Samuel Palmer [3 vols. 2nd ed., London, 1802], *3,* 116). Though he was among the 2,000 who refused the Act of Uniformity in 1662, Bates had taken part in the negotiations for the restoration of Charles II, been chaplain to the King, and headed the group which took the oath in order to escape the severe deprivation of the Five Mile Act.

18. Those who refused the oath supporting the illegality of taking arms against the King or of altering the government of the Church or state were not to come within five miles of any city, or parliament borough, or of the church where they had served. It was in this manner, the poet suggests, that the extreme nonconformists lost the land that they had acquired under Cromwell.

21. Oates' title for himself was Savior of the Nation. "True Protestant" was the common term for Dissenter.

We mildly styl'd it an association.   25
But this intrigue was stifled in its birth,
And prov'd th' abortive of our teeming mirth.
This point thus lost, no favor can we hope
(For Ignoramus noos'd the joiner's rope);
And long'd-for Commonwealth is this day lost   30
Unless retriev'd by Brutus' or thy ghost.
Rise then, Cethegus, dear Cethegus, rise;
Pym, Hampden, Strode, all Brutus' dear allies,
From holy Macchiavel to more holy Hobbes
(The grand duumvirate for republic jobs);   35
Rise, Milton, who to make the worst cause good,
Didst dare bespatter a blest martyr's blood;
Rise Peters, Nol, Scroop, Scott, Hell's modern furies;
Meet Satan, fire and brimstone, and Whig juries;

25. *association:* The famous Association found among Shaftesbury's papers and one of the principal documents against him in the treason trial.

27. *th' abortive:* The fruitless, imperfect, or unsuccessful result of an endeavor.

29. Stephen College, "the Protestant joiner" (i.e. cabinet-maker), was indicted at the Old Bailey for seditious words and actions during the Oxford Parliament. The grand jury, selected by the Whig sheriffs, Bethel and Cornish, rejected the indictment with an "Ignoramus," whereupon (on the pretext that the action had taken place in Oxford) College was there indicted on 12 July 1681, before a grand jury that returned a true bill. The trial, held on 17 Aug., "was one of the most unfair in a period abounding in judicial murder" (Ogg, *Charles II*, p. 627), and College was hanged on 31 Aug., "the first martyr of the Whig cause" (p. 628).

33. *Pym, Hampden, Strode:* Parliamentary leaders of the Puritan block during the reign of Charles I. John Pym (1584–1643), most outstanding of the group, spearheaded the attack on Charles and his ministers; John Hampden (1594–1643) is most famous for his fight against Charles I's ship money; William Strode (1599?–1645) was a violently outspoken and bitterly zealous opponent of the King and his ministers. All three were among the Five Members whom Charles I sought to impeach on 3 June 1642.

34. *Macchiavel . . . Hobbes:* Though specific works could be cited, the names were virtually eponymous. The first had been so for at least a century; for "the monster of Malmesbury," see S. I. Mintz, *The Hunting of Leviathan* (Cambridge, 1962). At this particular period, the names were frequently applied to Shaftesbury.

36–37. The reference is most likely to *Eikonoklastes*, Milton's answer to the "Royalist bible" (George Sensabaugh, *That Grand Whig Milton* [Stanford, 1952], p. 47) *Eikon Basilike*, reputedly by Charles I; however the writer might also have had in mind the *Pro populo* controversy, or *Paradise Lost*, II.113–14: "and could make the worse appear/ The better reason."

38. *Peters, Nol, Scroope, Scott:* Hugh Peters (1598–1660), the militant and politically active independent divine; one of the foremost spokesmen of his day; executed as a

With zeal hell-hot, outvie Vesuvio's fires,   40
Calcining what against our cause conspires:
Without these aids (no trust in holder-forth)
We're gone, gone, gone, by C——— laws, Dudley North.

---

regicide. *Nol:* the nickname of Oliver Cromwell. *Scroope:* Sir Adrian Scrope or Scroope (1601–60), an officer of the parliamentary army and one of the regicides. *Scott:* Thomas Scott or Scot, another regicide, head of the Commonwealth's intelligence service, a rabid republican.

40. *Vesuvio's:* Mount Vesuvius, near Naples, had just been reported as erupting. See Luttrell, *Brief Relation, 1,* 221 (20 Sept. 1682).

42. *holder-forth:* A somewhat contemptuous term for a preacher or orator.

43. *C——— laws:* Possibly "Charles' laws," "court laws," or "City laws." The first might recall Charles II's determination, as expressed to the Oxford Parliament, to rule strictly by law (*LJ, 13,* 746); the second would be an uncommon phrase; the last might refer to the rights of the Lord Mayor to govern the common halls and nominate one of the sheriffs.

Though destroying the meter, "Clarendon's laws" would also be applicable. These are the statutes that followed the Act of Uniformity and can be attributed to Clarendon "only in the sense that, after 1663, [he] was the most notable exponent of the view that sedition and dissent were inseparable" (Ogg, *Charles II,* p. 206). This, of course, is the ironist's point.

Dudley North: Nominated sheriff by Moore, North was anathema to the Whig faction, and his confirmation was the center of the political strife.

Cethegus' Apology

[C 1784]

Cethegus' Apology, the sequel to the preceding poem, is in the long-established satiric genre, the informal convocation. The form, allowing condemnation of living figures through association with popular villains already damned, illustrates at once the most basic form of irony (blame by praise) as well as the contemporary desire to find historical parallels to actual situations.

A second not uncommon device is found in the false colophon, which is here blatantly ironic but which, during the stricter censorship of the Commonwealth period, was used by fugitive presses both to give an air of authority to their publications and to make trouble for the more legitimate, nonroyalist printers. The close identification of a bookseller or printer with a political or religious group increased throughout the 1680s to a point where the bias of a work can often be determined merely by seeing who printed or sold it. The rule is, of course, not infallible; but, in a period when the presses were without any check short of a legal action on the uncertain charge of scandal, the writers' vituperation had to have at least the sympathy of the equally liable printer and publisher. We find, fairly consistently, that Fifth Monarchist material is being done by the Smiths at the Elephant and Castle, that the pro-sectarian Care is associated with Langley Curtis and then Astwood, and that L'Estrange's strongly royalist *Observator* was published (save for six months) by the Bromes.

While the writer of this poem is definitely anti-Whig, his position is, on the whole, that of a moderate loyalist. Luttrell purchased his copy on 28 Sept. 1682, which must have been within a day or two of its appearance.

CETHEGUS' APOLOGY
FOR NON-APPEARANCE
UPON HIS CONJURER'S SUMMONS.

That we appear'd not at thy friendly call,
Know, 'twas not want of will nor want of gall
(This the sole talent is of souls in thrall);
But we, once slaves to arbitrary fate,
Can't sham the laws of our coercive state.   5
Then muse not if I don't at summons come
To thunder in Guildhall, as erst in Rome.
Thy friendly lines receiv'd and humbly kiss'd,
In token of applause our furies hiss'd;
And we, known friends to your association,   10
Hell's faction cited to swift consultation.

4–5. A similar view is given in *T. Thynn's Ghost*, 1681/82 (Z, pp. 150–58; W', pp. 78–80, beginning "In dead of night when the pale moon"):

> No factions there [in Hell] disturb the State
> Which is preserv'd by steady fate;
> Unalterable laws they have
> Which the Almighty Godhead gave.

5. *sham:* To cheat, trick, deceive; to impose upon, take in, hoax. "The word first appears as slang . . . about 1677, and immediately came into very frequent use." [*OED*]. For Tory excursus on the word, see *Observator*, No. 94 (28 Jan. 1681/82) and North, *Examen*, p. 231.

8. See headnote to *Cethegus' Ghost*. A newsletter for 19 Sept. (*CSPD* 1682) describes the scene as follows: "Today at a Common Hall the Whigs and Tories appeared in great numbers, one for choosing a sheriff to hold with North and the other for opposing it. About 10 the Lord Mayor came on the hustings and the Common Crier made the usual proclamation but, before he had finished, there was such a confused noise of No North, No Hall, that he could not be heard. However he went on and finished it and then the Lord Mayor retired to the Council Chamber" (p. 412).

9. *our furies:* The gloss printed in the margin reads: Yelping, "No N[orth]." Cf. *Poem to the Right Honorable Sir John Moore* ("Hail, loyal sir, whom Providence design'd") [P 2710], which Luttrell purchased on 30 Sept.: "Thou hast quite quell'd the hot spur'd Whiggish Furies."

10. *association:* When Shaftesbury was arrested on 2 July 1681, his papers were also ordered to be taken. The loose papers that Sergeant Gwyn found "in my Lord Shaftesbury's closet above stairs" were put in a velvet bag, which soon reached the hands of Leoline Jenkins, the Secretary of State for the South. Among these, according to Jenkins' testimony, was the famous paper of association, by which the signers agreed "never [to] consent that . . . James Duke of York . . . be admitted to the succession." To this end, they agreed to obey "such orders as we shall from time to

From Korah down to Knox, all came on breast,
With later imps shut out from Baxter's Rest.
Thus met, we first condol'd, that souls born free,
Like yours, should be retrench'd by monarchy,   15
Since Hell's sole privilege is anarchy.
We piti'd the rejection of your choice;
The people's (if not God's) is sure our voice.

---

time receive from this present [i.e. 1681] Parliament whilst it shall be setting, or the major part of the members of both Houses subscribing this Association when it shall be prorogued or dissolved; and obey such officers as shall by them to set over us" (Howell, *State Trials, 8,* 779–87). This seemed, indeed, to be 1641 again, and Court sympathizers throughout England signed an " 'abhorrence' of 'the association soe positively sworne to be found in the Earle of Shaftesbury's closett' " (Brown, *Shaftesbury,* p. 293).

12. *Korah:* The son of Izhar who, "with certain of the children of Israel, two hundred and fifty princes of the assembly, famous in the congregation, men of renown" (Numbers 16:2) rebelled against the divinely chosen Moses and were subsequently punished for their plot. Dryden used the name in *Absalom and Achitophel* for Titus Oates.

Knox: John Knox (1505–72) the militant leader of the Scottish Reformation. As Mackay remarks in the *DNB,* "At his best he resembled a prophet of the Old Testament, not an evangelist of the New. At his worst he was a political partisan and ecclesiastical bigot, who could see no merit in an opponent, and could overlook any faults in a follower."

on breast: abreast.

13. *Baxter's:* Richard Baxter (1615–91), one of the great and popular divines of the period, attempted to avoid (to use the title of one of his tracts) the "Schism Detected in Both Extremes." Baxter's "more moderate English Presbyterianism, which was forced by legislation into the camp of active dissent" (Ogg, *Charles II, 1,* p. 214), had long been opposed to excess. "I abhor," he said, "unlimited liberty and toleration of all; and think myself able to prove the wickedness of it" (*Plain Scripture Proof,* 1651; cited in Whiting, *Studies in English Puritanism,* p. 45).

Of Baxter's voluminous writing, one of his most popular works was *The Saints' Everlasting Rest* (1650), which went through at least thirteen editions by 1688. From such rest, Baxter excludes the anarchic sects, "the later imps," i.e. those with whom demons were supposed to be familiar.

16. *privilege:* The special right, or immunity, of Parliament had been one of the central points of contention during the Stuart era.

17. i.e. Dubois and Papillon, the Whig candidates.

18. Variations on the "vox populi vox dei" phrase had been used since the 1640s for titles of sectarian pamphlets. In his report to Secretary Jenkins (*CSPD,* 1682,), James Harris writes that "Col. Danvers, Major Massie, Capt. Thymbleton, old Oates, Capt. Spurraway and [Francis] Smith, the Baptist bookseller, who sold and printed *Vox et Lacrimae Anglorum* [by George Wither, 1668 [W 3208]], *Vox populi* [probably, *Vox Populi: or the peoples claim,* 1681, [V 729]], the *Account of the Sheriffs' Election,* and *Remarks on the Comet* this last August are grand intimadoes, frequent meeters and distributors of the like factions new to most counties in order to animate the mobile to join with them" (p. 405).

On quick debate—time must not now be spent!
(At this consult Bradshaw was president)—   20
Resolv'd: —— No devil like an human wit,
None for Guildhall debates below so fit.
     On north-side of an useless, tuberous pile,
A wight lives, chief Whig-leader of your isle;
Known to men worthy, hugg'd by worthy men,   25
Who all infernal wiles has in his ken.
To him was granted, in year forty-three,
By patent, Hell's last arch-monopoly:
All governments to vex, in all admir'd to be.
To him you have appli'd; he's all in all;   30
Our furies need not, whilst his fill your hall.
On, then! All Hell's extempore effusions
Shall help to aggravate that day's confusions;
We'll make such medley with our fiend-land prayer,
That ours with yours sent up, shall blast your air.   35
Cartwright with our Ignatius shall join tones,

20. *consult:* In the seventeenth century, "a secret meeting for purposes of sedition or intrigue, a cabal" (*OED*). The word was particularly charged at this time, since the very heart of Oates' testimony rested on the accusation that there was a "General Consult" of the Jesuits at the White Horse Tavern on 24 April to plot the death of the King.

Bradshaw: John Bradshaw (1602–59) was Lord President of the Parliamentary commission for the trial of Charles I in 1649. He presided at the trial and pronounced the death sentence. He later tried other leading royalists and was President of the Council of State from 1649–52. At the Restoration, his body, along with those of Cromwell, Ireton, and Pride, was exhumed, hanged, mutilated, and reburied at Tyburn.

23–24. In July 1676, Shaftesbury moved to Thanet House in Aldersgate Street, less than a quarter of a mile north of St. Paul's Cathedral, the "useless, tuberous pile." The move not only made him a resident of the city, but Thanet House itself soon became the meeting place for leaders of the Country party (Brown, *Shaftesbury,* p. 263).

25. The reference is to the famous list, ascribed to Shaftesbury, of members of Parliament who were for his policies ("worthy men") and against them ("men worthy" i.e. to be hung). See North, *Examen,* pp. 112–13.

27. At the start of the Civil War, Shaftesbury sided with Charles I. As the result of discontent and conflicting motivations (see Brown, *Shaftesbury,* p. 45), he joined the parliamentary forces on 14 Feb. 1644 (1643 o.s.) and soon received command of the forces in Dorsetshire.

28. *patent:* A license to manufacture, sell, or deal in an article or commodity to the exclusion of other persons.

36. *Cartwright:* Probably Thomas Cartwright (1535–1603), whom Strype describes as "the head and most learned of that sect of dissenters then called puritans" (cited

Theresa with Mall Hawkins send up groans,
Jesuits and Whigs shall all be unisons.
Rest sure of Hell's best wishes all and one,
From Cain to Mahomet and Muggleton.   40
Meanwhile, by poll and noise assert your right
By Hell, 'tis yours, although John Moore deny't.
Let then no foils heroic souls dismay;
Expect fresh aids ere Sherman's martyr's day.

---

in *DNB*). Cartwright lectured (1569) and wrote (1572) vigorously against the Anglican constitution and hierarchy and for a Presbyterian standard. He was, in a sense, if not the founder at least the authority for much of the later Puritan movement.

If the reference is to a contemporary, it might well be to Thomas Cartwright (1634–89) who at this time was Dean of Rippon, though he was to achieve the bishopric of Chester under James II in 1686. Cartwright's opportunism was notable, even for this period. Although "puritanically educated under Presbyterian parents" (Wood, *Athenae Oxoniensis, 4,* 251) he managed by 1681 to be the intimate of the Duke of York and his family. His extreme position in favor of divine right caused him to be "looked on as a man that would more effectually advance the design of popery, than if he should turn over to it" (Burnet, *History, 1,* 696).

Ignatius: St. Ignatius of Loyola (1491–1556), founder of the Society of Jesus. If the first Thomas Cartwright is being referred to, the writer would be damning the extremist sects of both sides—a not unusual position for moderates during this period. If he has the later Cartwright in mind, he would be comparing him to the contemporary view of Jesuits as masters of pretence, delusion, and intrigue. This position, which tends, when most strident, to come from pro-Whig writers, is given extensive treatment throughout the Courant section of Henry Care's *Weekly Pacquet,* but see especially pp. 183–84, and 201–02 (i.e. 191–92) for 26 Jan. and 2 Feb. 1682/83.

37. *Theresa:* The printed gloss reads: "A Whig Nun." The reference is probably to St. Theresa (1515–82), the Carmelite nun, whose trances and visions (considered by the sisters to be possession by the devil) led her to found the stricter convent of Descalzos at Avila, despite the great opposition of the established Order.

Mall Hawkins: The printed gloss reads: "The wonderful praying maid of St. Ives, burnt afterwards for a witch at New England."

40. *Muggleton:* Lodowicke Muggleton (1609–98) and his cousin John Reeve (1608–58) considered themselves "the two last prophets of the only true God" on the authority of personal communication "by voice of words from Jesus Christ." As messengers of the new dispensation (following directly in the line of Moses and Aaron, Christ and the disciples), they felt themselves able both to damn eternally and to proclaim a quasi-Manichean, anti-Trinitarian enthusiasm that denied the efficacy of prayer, oaths, morality and the new astronomy. See Whiting, *Studies in English Puritanism,* pp. 242–58.

42. *John Moore:* Lord Mayor of London. See headnote to the poems on the shrieval elections.

44. *Sherman's martyr's day:* The printed gloss reads: "St. Michael's Day." This is 29 Sept., the day after the sheriffs took office. The date was also in the minds of men of this world. The newsletter of 16 Sept. to John Squier at Newcastle (*CSPD* 1682)

Disdain the slights o'th' man you style Lord Mayor;   45
His shall be fallible, as Peter's chair.
In this assurance, braves, your heads up lift,
Dominion's yours by Satan's deed of gift.
And this firm tie endears us to your state:
Both covenants love alike, alike allegiance hate.   50

Printed for the assigns of Jack Thumb and L. C., sworn
stationers to the Luciferian order.

---

announced that "His Majesty goes not to Newmarket till after Michaelmas, by which
time the sheriffs will be chosen and sworn" (p. 401). The phrase alludes to a dispute
between Edmund Sherman, one of the church warders of All Saints, Barking, and
Jonathan Saunders. Saunders (according to Sherman) had set up a statue of St.
Michael that he bowed before and prayed to during the service. An indictment was
brought against the church warders for image worship, probably at Sherman's insti-
gation, whereupon he pulled down the statue and burnt it as "an abominable badge
of superstition and . . . Popery." Sherman's two pamphlets, *The Birth and Burning
of the Image Called St. Michael* (26 May 1681) [S 3382] and the *Second Part* (10 June
1681) [S 3383], were strong reactions to Saunders' *Fiery Apparitions seen on several
days about Tower Hill, A New Narrative of a Fiery Apparition,* and the *Sham-Indict-
ment Quasht* [S 747]. Further publicity was given the incident by Nathaniel Thompson's
defense of Saunders in *The Loyal Protestant and True Domestic Intelligence.*

46. *His:* i.e. the Lord Mayor's Chair. See 44 n.

Peter's chair: i.e. the Papacy, which claimed infallibility.

50. *covenants:* An allusion to the Solemn League and Covenant of Sept. 1643, which
united the English Parliamentarians with the Scottish Church. The military support
from the north was one of the decisive factors in the subsequent reversals and final
defeat of the royalist forces.

allegiance: This is, perhaps, a reference to the oath of allegiance and supremacy,
but it may also allude to the professions of allegiance to the King that were part of
the Addresses of Abhorrence that followed the discovery of the Paper of Association.

Jack Thumb: i.e. John Starkey, the strongly pro-Whig bookseller. Roger L'Estrange
(who may have thus baptized him) explains the nickname in *Observator,* No. 139
(17 May 1682):

   Tory. But we must have a touch at John Starkey's Advertisement before we part.
   Pray, read it whole there as it lies.
   Whig. ". . . [The *Observator* and *Heraclitus Ridens*] are pleased to give [me]
   the nickname J. Thumb because I had the misfortune to lose one with a pistol
   bullet. . . . Nor was I born in Ireland, as they maliciously insinuate, but in
   Leicestershire . . ."
   Tory. . . . But what is that story of the thumb?
   Whig. I have heard of a thumb that was lost upon an Epsom expedition against
   tyranny and popery.
   Tory. Aye, but I took that for an Irish thumb.

Whig. And yet ye see 'twas a Leicestershire thumb.

L. C: Langley Curtis, one of the more radical of the London booksellers, the publisher of an almost unending series of sectarian pamphlets and (until 18 Aug. 1682) of Henry Care's *Weekly Pacquet.* From 25 Aug. until 4 May of the following year, he had William Salman write a continuation of the *Pacquet* in direct competition with Care.

His old enemy L'Estrange was probably exaggerating when he remarked, just after Curtis had been fined £500 and sent to the pillory for *Lord Russel's Ghost,* that "he has been the publisher of more desperate libels than half the town beside" (*Observator, 2,* No. 21 [25 Feb. 1683/84]).

JOHN DRYDEN

Prologue to The Duke of Guise

[*D 2338*]

To counteract Dryden's ingenuity and wit, Whig opponents attempted on occasion to show that he had gone so far beyond the bounds of propriety that he was in fact libelling the monarch he claimed to be supporting. Christopher Nesse, the Calvinistic preacher, asserted that the poet had "notoriously traduced" the King and the kingdom by his "scurrilous reflections" in the "profane" *Absalom and Achitophel*. (See *A Whip for the Fool's Back* . . . and *A Key [With the Whip]* . . . [Macdonald, Nos. 202–03].) Such criticism Dryden dismissed with light mockery in *The Medal's* "Epistle to the Whigs."

Far different, however, were the exceptions that Whig writers took to the historical parallels in *The Duke of Guise,* to the analogies between Paris and London, between Guise and Monmouth, and (more damagingly) between Henry III and Charles II. At least four attacks appeared (Macdonald, Nos. 221–23, 224); and to two of these (*A Defence of the Charter* . . . , by the lawyer Thomas Hunt, and *Some Reflections Upon* . . . *The Duke of Guise,* by Shadwell and and unknown collaborator) Dryden felt it necessary to reply with *The Vindication* (Macdonald, No. 130), in which he stressed the fact that the play was "not a parallel of the men, but of the times." His embarrassment may well have resulted from inadvertent inconsistencies; but, even granting that historical parallelism may prove less tractable than biblical, we should recall that Dryden had first worked on this material in the 1660s, that "for some while [he] balanced precariously before he launched the powerful Tory poem of *Absalom and Achitophel*," and that Lee, his collaborator, had "an essentially Whiggish character" (R. G. Ham, *Otway and Lee* [New Haven, 1931], p. 164).

The Prologue (Macdonald, No. 101), which reflects none of the events of the last months of 1682, was probably written between 24 June (when the shrieval elections began) and 18 July (when the play was temporarily prohibited) or, at the latest, 28 Sept. (when the Tory Sheriffs were installed). Unlike the play, the prologue is certainly not "balanced precariously"; its position is unequivocally anti-Whig.

Luttrell's copy is dated 30 Nov. and 4 Dec. 1682; the former very likely indicates the day of the first performance (Macdonald, pp. 126, 143), the latter (added after the phrase "Written by Mr. Dryden: Spoken by Mr. Smith") may refer either to the date when William Smith first delivered it or to the date of publication.

PROLOGUE

to Dryden and Lee's
The Duke of Guise, a Tragedy

Our play's a parallel: the Holy League
Begot our Cov'nant; Guisards got the Whig.
Whate'er our hot-brain'd Sheriffs did advance
Was, like our fashions, first produc'd in France;
And, when worn out, well scourg'd, and banish'd there,   5
Sent over, like their godly beggars, here.
Could the same trick, twice play'd, our nation gull?
It looks as if the Devil were grown dull;
Or serv'd us up, in scorn, his broken meat,
And thought we were not worth a better cheat.   10
The fulsome Cov'nant, one would think in reason,
Had giv'n us all our bellies-full of treason;
And yet, the name but chang'd, our nasty nation
Chaws its own excrement, th' Association.

1-2. In *The Vindication,* Dryden states that "our intention therefore was to make the play a parallel betwixt the Holy League plotted by the house of Guise and its adherents, with the [Solemn League and] Covenant plotted by the rebels in the times of King Charles the First, and those of the new Association which was the spawn of the old Covenant" (S.-S., *Dryden, 7,* 155). For a fuller treatment, see John Northleigh, *The Parallel* (1682) [N 1301].

3. *Sheriffs:* Thomas Pilkington and Samuel Shute, the Whig sheriffs.

6. *their godly beggars:* An allusion to the Whig nominees, Thomas Papillon and John Dubois, men of French Huguenot background. See the reference to the "Whiggish Walloons" in *An Ironical Encomium,* title n.

9. *broken meat:* Fragments of food left after a meal.

14. *Chaws:* Cf. *The Medal,* 147.

Association: An allusion to the treasonable paper, allegedly found in Shaftesbury's study, calling for armed resistance to York's succession.

'Tis true we have not learn'd their pois'ning way,   15
For that's a mode but newly come in play;
Besides, your drug's uncertain to prevail;
But your true Protestant can never fail
With that compendious instrument, a flail.
Go on; and bite, ev'n though the hook lies bare;   20
Twice in one age expel the lawful heir;
Once more decide religion by the sword,
And purchase for us a new tyrant lord.
Pray for your King, but yet your purses spare;
Make him not two-pence richer by your prayer.   25
To show you love him much, chastise him more;
And make him very great, and very poor.
Push him to wars, but still no peace advance;
Let him lose England to recover France.
Cry freedom up with popular noisy votes;   30
And get enough to cut each other's throats.
Lop all the rights that fence your Monarch's throne;
For fear of too much pow'r, pray leave him none.
A noise was made of arbitrary sway;
But, in revenge, you Whigs have found a way   35
An arbitrary duty now to pay.
Let his own servants turn to save their stake;
Glean from his plenty, and his wants forsake.

15. *their pois'ning way:* The Prologue to *The Spanish Friar* mentions "the new-found poisoning trick of France" (46). Kinsley explains that "the Chambre Ardente had condemned the Marquise de Brinvilliers for poisoning four of her family in 1676, and Catherine Deshayes, La Voisin, had been executed in February, 1680" for poisoning.

19. *a flail:* For a description of the "Protestant flail," see North, *Examen,* pp. 572–73; illustrations of the instrument (a weighted piece tied to a short wooden handle) are given in Lane, *Oates,* opp. p. 240 and *POAS,* Yale, 2, opp. p. 12; it was commemorated in verse in this year [P 3833].

27. The classic attack of parliamentarians is concisely given in *The Commons' Petition to the King* ("In all humility we crave"), which concluded:

> And if he pleases to lay down
> His scepter, dignity, and crown,
> We'll make him for the time to come
> The greatest prince in Christendom.

(5–8)

29. i.e. by voting supplies for war at the cost of royal prerogative.

36. Probably a reference to party dues, such as those charged for the abortive Whig Feast of 21 April 1682.

But let some Judas near his person stay
To swallow the last sop, and then betray.   40
Make London independent of the Crown:
A realm apart, the Kingdom of the Town.
Let Ignoramus juries find no traitors,
And Ignoramus poets scribble satyrs.
And, that your meaning none may fail to scan,   45
Do what in coffee-houses you began:
Pull down the master, and set up the man.

41. In opposition to the King's attempt to recall its Charter by a Quo Warranto, London contended that its rights and privileges were based on ancient law and independent of the Crown.

43. *Ignoramus juries:* See the Medal poems and the poems on the shrieval election.

45. *scan.* Assess.

46. For an excellent summary of the coffee-houses as "nurseries of sedition," see Ogg, *Charles II, 1,* 101–02; also Defoe's *Review,* 12 March 1713. The principal gathering place for Whig sympathizers was Kid's coffee house, the Amsterdam.

47. The leaders of the various factions of the Whig party had their own clubs, which met at different places in the City. Within these select groups, the talk, according to the report of Samuel Oates, Junior (*CSPD,* 1682, pp. 236–38), very frequently dealt with ways to "pull down the master."

JOHN DRYDEN AND NAHUM TATE

The Second Part of
Absalom and Achitophel

[D 2350]

The first part of *Absalom and Achitophel* appeared in 1681, probably on 17 Nov., the day celebrating Queen Elizabeth's anniversary and one which the Opposition had appropriated for its famous Pope-burning procession. Almost a year later, on or about 10 Nov. (both dates are Luttrell's), *The Second Part* was published. Yet the curious fact is that—with the exception of the obviously appended last ten lines—the poem refers solely to events that occurred before the end of May; indeed, the poem seems to culminate in the panegyric to the Duke and Duchess of York upon their return to London on 7 May, three weeks after James' shipwreck on the *Gloucester*. The occasion for this unusual delay of at least five months between the poem's composition and its publication may be found in the last ten lines, for these refer to the shrieval contention in tentative terms that seem to indicate that, though there has been an apparent Tory victory, the issue is far from settled. In the *"battaille rangée"* for the sheriffs' posts, a Whig victory would have proved hard indeed on poets who had taken the Yorkist Tory position that is set forth in *The Second Part*. It is, then, perhaps more than coincidence that the period of delay is almost precisely that of the critical struggle for the shrieval offices.

E. S. de Beer, in an important article (*"Absalom and Achitophel:* Literary and Historical Notes," *Review of English Studies,* 17 [1941], 298–309), has pointed out that as early as 1677, Lee had publicly suggested to Dryden, in a poem prefixed to *The State of Innocence,* that he should

> The troubles of majestic Charles sat down:
> Not David vanquish'd more to reach a crown.
> Praise him as Cowley did that Hebrew king;
> Thy theme's as great, do thou as greatly sing.

Again, there is the well-known story printed by Tonson (*Miscellany Poems*, 4th ed. 1716 [Macdonald, No. 49]) that "In the year 1680, Mr. Dryden undertook the poem of *Absalom and Achitophel* upon the desire of King Charles the Second." Malone (*1*, i, 141–42), who says that Tate related this story and that it is therefore probably so, set the date almost as late as possible, i.e. about Feb. 1680/81. This seems unnecessary if we consider—as the evidence would seem to show—that Dryden had been working on an *Absalom* since before Nov. 1680 and that he revised his material in the second half of 1681, fitting his poem to the more delicately balanced situation and aiming it at that now all-important "honest party," the yet-uncommitted man "of the more moderate sort" (*Absalom and Achitophel*, "To the Reader"). What is being suggested here is that the first part of *Absalom and Achitophel* had been in hand longer than is ordinarily thought, and that *The Second Part* may well contain *disjecta membra* of the first (as evidenced, for example, in the fact that the description of Arod—i.e. Waller—would certainly seem to have been written prior to 15 Nov. 1680).

The question of authorship is equally knotty. In the 1716 *Miscellany*, Tonson, the publisher, supplied a more or less complete "Key" to the names in the two parts, and added, concerning *The Second Part*, that 310–509 "were entirely Mr. Dryden's compositions, besides some touches in other places." Scott, whose contempt for Tate's poetry seems boundless, defined these "touches" as whatever he thought worthwhile in the poem, and pointed to the "dreary waste" of what remained as proof that Tate's verses are "flat, common-place, and uninteresting" (Scott-Saintsbury, *Dryden*, *9*, 321). By this totally arbitrary method, he asserted that "much of the charcter of Corah [69–102] is unquestionably Dryden's; so probably is that of Arod [534–55] and the verses generally descriptive of the Green Ribbon Club [522–33] which precede it" (ibid.). Subsequent editors have followed Tonson and Scott, but such a position now seems in need of revaluation. The *whole* of *The Second Part* is impregnated with phrases found elsewhere in Dryden and, while it is true that the majority come from the first part, many come from other works and, in one or two instances, from works that Dryden was to write in later years. The subjective criterion of excellence is, then, only a partial guide at best.

Those lines in *The Second Part* which, by historical allusion, seem definitely earlier than the rest and might therefore qualify as *disjecta membra* of the first part are just those which would have been too partisan to sustain the wit and sweet reasonableness of *Absalom and Achitophel*'s appeal to those moderates who, reacting to the excesses of the Popish Plot and Whig aggressiveness, were just beginning to listen sympathetically to less frenetic voices. The thematic difference tends to bear this out. The first *Absalom* is a poem of persuasion; the second, a poem of attack. The Jews, who in the first part foolishly replaced kings through error, have lost their meekness and become willfully besotted by zeal or drink in the second. The latter opens not with the witty concession of the first part, but with the theme of property, the baseness of it, and its avaricious opposition to royal prerogative. Treachery has supplanted ambition, rebellion has replaced restlessness. It is not now misguided patriotism but innate evil that rules the Opposition: Og (Shadwell) is born unruly; the mob is "born drunk," as opposed to becoming so in the first part. Again, in *The Second Part*, David is more aggressively Godlike and noble; he (and his authority) are present throughout the poem, whereas he comes in only as the final, divine voice in the first part. Indeed, *The Second Part* has another hero, one that could not have appeared in a poem of persuasion in November 1681. James Duke of York, is the real hero of Part II, and the subsidiary heroes tend to be those of the far more extreme Yorkist faction. James is the culmination of *The Second Part* as Charles was of the first, and God's sanction is seen in his divine salvation from shipwreck.

The Second Part, then, represents a greater polarization, one that would have been incompatible with the tone and intention of the first but which was, however, quite in keeping with the partisan verse of the preceding and subsequent years. In his address "To the Reader" of the first *Absalom,* Dryden himself had warned that "They who can criticize so weakly as to imagine I have done my worst may be convinced, at their own cost, that I can write severely with more ease than I can gently." *The Second Part,* with its louder mobs, its starker contrasts, and its assertion that the Whigs' goal is the destruction of monarchy, demonstrates the "easier" and commoner writing which aims more at polemic than persuasion.

The Second Part of
Absalom and Achitophel

A Poem

Si quis tamen haec quoque, si quis
Captus amore leget.

Since men, like beasts, each other's prey were made;
Since trade began, and priesthood grew a trade;
Since realms were form'd, none sure so curst as those
That madly their own happiness oppose;
There Heaven itself and Godlike kings in vain   5
Show'r down the manna of a gentle reign;
While pamper'd crowds to mad sedition run,
And monarchs by indulgence are undone.
Thus David's clemency was fatal grown,
While wealthy faction aw'd the wanting throne.   10
For now their sov'reign's orders to contemn
Was held the charter of Jerusalem;
His rights t'invade, his tributes to refuse,

Epigraph. Virgil's Sixth Eclogue, 9–10, are appropriate for a poem seeking favorable notice because of the fame of its predecessor. The beginning of 9 ("non injussa cano") was probably omitted in order to avoid the suggestion of official inspiration; likewise, the conclusion (that the name of Virgil's subject, Varus, would be suitably praised) was not considered relevant. Dryden's rather inadequate translation of these lines, in their context, reads:

> My past'ral muse her humble tribute brings;
> And yet not wholly uninspir'd she sings.
> For all who read, and reading not disdain
> These rural poems and their lowly strain,
> The name of Varus oft inscrib'd shall see
> In every grove and every vocal tree.

6. *manna:* Exodus 16:13–36; Numbers 11:7–9, and esp. Psalm 78:23–25. See also *The Medal,* 131.

8–9. Cf. *Absalom and Achitophel,* 146–47.

10. During the Exclusion Parliaments of 1679–81, the Whigs followed the classical parliamentary tactic of withholding subsidies until concessions were granted. The City members were predominantly wealthy merchants of the anti-Court party.

12. *charter of Jerusalem:* Throughout 1682, both the Crown and the City were preparing to argue the crucial case of the London (here, Jerusalem) charter. See headnote to poems on the Quo Warranto proceedings.

13. *His rights t'invade:* The Whigs announced that a feast would be held at Haberdashers' and Goldsmiths' Hall on 21 April 1682 (to counter the pro-York Artillery Feast on the previous day), but Charles prohibited it on the grounds that the proclamation of feasts was a royal prerogative.

A privilege peculiar to the Jews;
As if from heav'nly call this license fell,   15
And Jacob's seed were chosen to rebel!

    Achitophel with triumph sees his crimes
Thus suited to the madness of the times;
And Absalom, to make his hopes succeed,
Of flattering charms no longer stands in need;   20
While fond of change, though ne'er so dearly bought,
Our tribes outstrip the youth's ambitious thought;
His swiftest hopes with swifter homage meet,
And crowd their servile necks beneath his feet.
Thus to his aid while pressing tides repair,   25
He mounts and spreads his streamers in the air.
The charms of empire might his youth mislead,
But what can our besotted Israel plead?
Sway'd by a monarch whose serene command
Seems half the blessing of our promis'd land;   30
Whose only grievance is excess of ease;
Freedom our pain, and plenty our disease!
Yet, as all folly would lay claim to sense,
And wickedness ne'er wanted a pretense,
With arguments they'd make their treason good,   35

---

his tribute to refuse: The specific allusion might be to the City's collection of market money, one of the charges made by the Crown in the Quo Warranto against the London charter.

14. *Jews:* i.e. English. English Protestants had done much to advance Hebraic and Old Testament studies (as, for example, Thomas Godwin's school text, *Moses and Aaron,* which reached its twelfth edition in 1685); English sectarians tended to identify themselves with the Jews as the chosen people, and with the prophets who had received the word of God immediately.

17. *Achitophel:* Here, as in *Absalom and Achitophel,* the Earl of Shaftesbury. For the biblical background, see *Absalom Senior,* 870 n. Shaftesbury's triumph—his release from an indictment of high treason by the famed London "Ignoramus" grand jury —marked the end of his active political career. See the Medal poems.

19. *Absalom:* Here, as in *Absalom and Achitophel,* the Duke of Monmouth. For the biblical background, see *Absalom Senior,* 272 n. For 19–20, cf. inter al., *Absalom and Achitophel,* 303–04.

21. Cf. *Absalom and Achitophel,* 216–19.

22. *tribes:* Sects.

24. Possibly an echo of *Absalom and Achitophel,* 453.

26. An allusion to Monmouth's first "Western progress" of Aug–Oct. 1680, described at length in *Absalom and Achitophel,* 727–52.

29–32. Cf. *The Medal,* 124–26.

And righteous David's self with slanders load:
That arts of foreign sway he did affect,
And guilty Jebusites from law protect,
Whose very chiefs, convict, were never freed,
Nay, we have seen their sacrificers bleed!   40
Accusers' infamy is urg'd in vain,
While in the bounds of sense they did contain;
But soon they launch'd into th' unfathom'd tide,
And in the depths they knew disdain'd to ride.
For probable discoveries to dispense,   45
Was thought below a pension'd evidence;
Mere truth was dull, nor suited with the port
Of pamper'd Corah, when advanc'd to court.
No less than wonders now they will impose,
And projects void of grace or sense disclose.   50

    Such was the charge on pious Michal brought;
Michal that ne'er was cruel e'en in thought,

37. *foreign:* i.e. French.

38. *Jebusites:* i.e. Roman Catholics.

39. *chiefs:* On the evidence of Oates and Prance, Parliament ordered the five popish lords—Arundell, Belasyse, Powis, Petre, and Stafford—sent to the Tower on 21 Oct. 1678. Stafford was impeached 30 Nov. and executed on 29 Dec. 1680, but the others remained in prison until 1684.

40. As Luttrell's gloss indicates, these are the "popish priests" who were executed for their putative part in the Popish Plot.

41. *Accusers' infamy:* Quite apart from the general disdain in which the Irish witnesses were held, the principals had highly unsavory reputations. Oates had been accused of sodomy; Prance of bribery and theft; Dangerfield of highway robbery and counterfeiting; Bedloe of impersonation.

48. From 31 Oct. 1678 until 31 Aug. 1681, Titus Oates (Corah) was lodged in an apartment at Whitehall and given an annual pension of £1,200 (Lane, *Oates*, pp. 130, 276). He was, of course, the idol of the anti-Court faction, who considered him, as he considered himself, the "savior of the nation" (Pollock, *The Popish Plot*, p. 227, and Lane, *Oates*, pp. 130, 276; cf. 75–96 n.). For the biblical background of Corah, see *Absalom Senior*, 730 n.

51. *the charge:* Both Oates and Bedloe asserted that the Queen had reluctantly consented to the Jesuits' plan to assassinate Charles. (Ogg, *Charles II*, pp. 574–75; Lane, *Oates*, pp. 135–41, 203; Janet Mackay, *Catherine of Braganza* (London, 1937), pp. 200–37.

Michal: Biblically, the wife of David, whose early devotion to him (I Samuel 19:11–17) was followed by many years of enforced separation. It was after this alienation that Michal, having chided David for dancing before the Ark, was cursed with childlessness (II Samuel 6:20–23). Historically, Catherine of Braganza, the childless wife of Charles II, whose practice of Roman Catholicism made her the object of much radical sectarian attack.

The best of queens and most obedient wife,
Impeach'd of curst designs on David's life!
His life, the theme of her eternal pray'r,   55
'Tis scarce so much his guardian angel's care.
Not summer morns such mildness can disclose,
The Hermon lily, nor the Sharon rose.
Neglecting each vain pomp of majesty,
Transported Michal feeds her thoughts on high.   60
She lives with angels, and, as angels do,
Quits heav'n sometimes to bless the world below;
Where, cherish'd by her bounties' plenteous spring,
Reviving widows smile, and orphans sing.
Oh, when rebellious Israel's crimes at height   65
Are threaten'd with her lord's approaching fate,
The piety of Michal then remain
In Heaven's remembrance, and prolong his reign!

    Less desolation did the pest pursue,
That from Dan's limits to Beersheba slew,   70
Less fatal the repeated wars of Tyre,
And less Jerusalem's avenging fire;
With gentler terror these our state o'erran,
Than since our evidencing days began!
On every cheek a pale confusion sat,   75
Continued fear beyond the worst of fate!
Trust was no more, art, science, useless made,
All occupations lost but Corah's trade.
Meanwhile, a guard on modest Corah wait,

66. *lord's . . . fate:* i.e. the ultimate demise of Charles II, who alone (like Moses) stands between his criminally rebellious people and a righteously vengeful God.
69. *the pest:* The 1665 plague.
70. *Dan to Beersheba:* Cities at the extreme north and south of Palestine.
71. *the repeated wars of Tyre:* The wars with Holland (Tyre) in 1665–67, 1672–74.
72. *Jerusalem's avenging fire:* The London (Jerusalem) fire of 1666.
77–78. The return to a state of primal nature, anarchy and fear, seems based on Hobbesian analysis. Kinsley cites *Leviathan*, I.13.
79–96. "[Oates] was now in his trine exaltation, his plot in full force, efficacy, and virtue; he walked about with his guards (assigned) for fear of the Papists murdering him. . . . Whoever he pointed at was taken up and committed, so that many people got out of his way as from a blast, and glad they could prove their two last years' conversation. The very breath of him was pestilential and, if it brought not im-

If not for safety, needful yet for state.   80
Well might he deem each peer and prince his slave,
And lord it o'er the tribes which he could save:
E'en vice in him was virtue—what sad fate
But for his honesty had seiz'd our state?
And with what tyranny had we been curst,   85
Had Corah never prov'd a villain first?
T' have told his knowledge of th' intrigue in gross
Had been, alas, to our deponent's loss.
The travel'd Levite had th' experience got
To husband well, and make the best of 's plot;   90
And therefore, like an evidence of skill,
With wise reserves secur'd his pension still;
Nor quite of future pow'r himself bereft,
But limbos large for unbelievers left.
And now his writ such reverence had got,   95
'Twas worse than plotting to suspect his plot.
Some were so well convinc'd, they made no doubt
Themselves to help the founder'd swearers out.
Some had their sense impos'd on by their fear,
But more for int'rest sake believe and swear: 100
Ev'n to that height with some the frenzy grew,
They rag'd to find their danger not prove true.

   Yet, than all these, a viler crew remain,
Who with Achitophel the cry maintain;
Not urg'd by fear nor through misguided sense   105
(Blind zeal and starving need had some pretense),
But for the *Good Old Cause* that did excite

---

prisonment or death over such on whom it fell, it surely poisoned reputation and
left good Protestants arrant Papists, and something worse than that, in danger of
being put in the Plot as Traitors" (North, *Examen*, p. 205.)

83–94. Oates, who had sworn himself in and out of the Roman Catholic religion,
exhibited an astonishing improvement in memory as one deposition after another
was accepted.

97. *Some:* Certain embarrassing gaps and contradictions in Oates' evidence came
out in the subsequent trials of 1679, but, until the Wakeman Trial, Oates was helped
along at such moments by Lord Chief Justice Scroggs (see Howell, *State Trials*, 7,
esp. 244–45, 247, 251; Lane, *Oates*, pp. 141–202).

103. *than:* i.e. more than.

107. *Good Old Cause:* Originally the popular appellation for the Parliamentarian

Th' original rebels' wiles, revenge, and spite.
These raise the Plot, to have the scandal thrown
Upon the bright successor of the crown,   110
Whose virtue with such wrongs they had pursued,
As seem'd all hope of pardon to exclude.
Thus, while on private ends their zeal is built,
The cheated crowd applaud and share their guilt.

    Such practices as these, too gross to lie   115
Long unobserv'd by each discerning eye,
The more judicious Israelites unspell'd,
Though still the charm the giddy rabble held.
E'en Absalom, amidst the dazzling beams
Of empire and ambition's flattering dreams,   120
Perceives the Plot (too foul to be excus'd)
To aid designs, no less pernicious, us'd.
And (filial sense yet striving in his breast)
Thus to Achitophel his doubts express'd:

    "Why are my thoughts upon a crown employ'd,   125
Which once obtain'd, can be but half enjoy'd?
Not so, when virtue did my arms require,
And to my father's wars I flew entire.

---

and Cromwellian governments of the Interregnum, the phrase was used by the Court
partly to associate the Whigs generally with the republican faction of extremists.
    109. *These raise the Plot:* Noyes' note suggests that these lines charge Shaftesbury
with instigation of the Plot but, while the accusation has been made in the past,
few historians have seriously considered it (see Lane, *Oates*, pp. 108–09). North's
evaluation seems correct and explicates the verb: "I find nothing of his Lordship's
midwifery in the bringing forth that discovery, for that seemed left to a lower order.
But it is more than probable he was behind the curtain and, after the chief throes
were over, he was the dry-nurse and . . . took the charge of leading the monstrous
birth till it could crawl alone" (*Examen*, p. 95). This was also Dryden's view in
Absalom and Achitophel, 208–13.
    110. *the bright successor:* The Roman Catholic James, Duke of York. Shaftesbury,
taking advantage of the furor aroused by the Popish Plot, attempted vainly to have
passed an act excluding James from the succession.
    117. *The more judicious:* i.e. the moderates, to whom the whole of the first part of
Absalom and Achitophel appeals.
    128. *my father's wars:* Monmouth had been sent to quell the uprisings in Scotland
that followed the murder of Archbishop Sharp. He successfully routed the rebels—
who evidently had some hopes of treating with him—at Bothwell Bridge on 22 June
1679. The political implications of Monmouth's command are set out in North, *Ex-
amen*, pp. 81–83.

My regal pow'r how will my foes resent,
When I myself have scarce my own consent?   130
Give me a son's unblemish'd truth again,
Or quench the sparks of duty that remain.
How slight to force a throne that legions guard,
The task to me; to prove unjust, how hard!
And if th' imagin'd guilt thus wound my thought,   135
What will it when the tragic scene is wrought?
Dire war must first be conjur'd from below;
The realm we'd rule we first must overthrow.
And, when the civil furies are on wing
That blind and undistinguish'd slaughters fling,   140
Who knows what impious chance may reach the King?
Oh, rather let me perish in the strife
Than have my crown the price of David's life!
Or if the tempest of the war he stand,
In peace some vile officious villain's hand   145
His soul's anointed temple may invade,
Or, press'd by clamorous crowds, myself be made
His murtherer; rebellious crowds, whose guilt
Shall dread his vengeance till his blood be spilt.
Which if my filial tenderness oppose,   150
Since to the empire by their arms I rose,
Those very arms on me shall be employ'd,
A new usurper crown'd, and I destroy'd.
The same pretense of public good will hold,
And new Achitophels be found as bold   155
To urge the needful change, perhaps the old."

He said. The statesman with a smile replies
(A smile that did his rising spleen disguise):
"My thoughts presum'd our labors at an end,
And are we still with conscience to contend,   160

146. Cf. Shakespeare, *Macbeth*, II.3.:

Most sacrilegious murther hath broke ope
The Lord's anointed temple, and stole thence
The life o' th' building
                    (68–70)
147–49. The reference is to a judicial murder, as in the case of Charles I.

Whose want in kings as needful is allow'd
As 'tis for them to find it in the crowd?
Far in the doubtful passage you are gone,
And only can be safe by pressing on.
The crown's true heir, a prince severe and wise,   165
Has view'd your motions long with jealous eyes,
Your person's charms, your more prevailing arts,
And mark'd your progress in the people's hearts;
Whose patience is th' effect of stinted pow'r,
But treasures vengeance for the fatal hour;   170
And if remote the peril he can bring,
Your present danger's greater from the King.
Let not a parent's name deceive your sense,
Nor trust the father in a jealous prince!
Your trivial faults, if he could so resent   175
To doom you little less than banishment,
What rage must your presumption since inspire?
Against his orders your return from Tyre?
Nor only so, but with a pomp more high,
And open court of popularity,   180
The factious tribes——"
                                    "And this reproof from thee?"

161–62. Cf. *Absalom and Achitophel*, 224–25.

165–70. Cf. *Absalom and Achitophel*, 441–46.

165. *true heir:* During the Exclusion controversy, there developed a distinction between the true heir (i.e. the next in blood to the throne) and the legal heir (i.e. the next in line who was Protestant and therefore not legally disqualified through adherence to Roman Catholicism).

175–81. When Charles fell ill in Aug. 1679, he sent for York, despite Monmouth's efforts to persuade him to the contrary. James' arrival on 15 Sept. was followed by Monmouth's being deprived of his generalship and his being ordered out of the kingdom. He left London on 24 Sept. for Utrecht and the Hague (Luttrell, *Brief Relation*, *1*, 21; *DNB*) but, not receiving royal permission to return, and having "all his places (except master of the horse) taken from him, . . . as is said, by the means of His Royal Highness," the Duke of York (Luttrell, *Brief Relation*, *1*, 27), Monmouth took it upon himself, once James had gone back to Scotland, to return to England. He reappeared in London at midnight 27 Nov., and "His Majesty, learning of [his] arrival . . . , hath signified his displeasure thereof by refusing to see him and forbidding him to come within the verge of the Court; yet the people were well pleased at his coming, testified by their ringing of bells and making bonfires at night" (p. 29). By 15 Dec., Charles had revoked Monmouth's last office, the mastership of the horse (p. 30; see also Kinsley, *Absalom and Achitophel*, 700 n.).

The prince replies. "Oh, statesman's winding skill!
They first condemn that first advis'd the ill!"

"Illustrious youth," return'd Achitophel,
"Misconstrue not the words that mean you well.   185
The course you steer I worthy blame conclude,
But 'tis because you leave it unpursu'd.
A monarch's crown with fate surrounded lies,
Who reach, lay hold on death that miss the prize.
Did you for this expose yourself to show,   190
And to the crowd bow popularly low?
For this your glorious progress next ordain,
With chariots, horsemen, and a numerous train;
With fame before you like the morning star,
And shouts of joy saluting from afar?   195
Oh, from the heights you've reach'd, but take a view;
Scarce leading Lucifer could fall like you!
And must I here my shipwrack'd arts bemoan?
Have I for this so oft made Israel groan?
Your single interest with the nation weigh'd,   200
And turn'd the scale where your desires were laid?
Ev'n when at helm a course so dang'rous mov'd
To land your hopes, as my removal prov'd?"

"I not dispute," the royal youth replies,
"The known perfection of your policies,   205
Nor in Achitophel yet grudge or blame
The privilege that statesmen ever claim;
Who private int'rest never yet pursu'd,

182. *winding:* Tortuous, crooked, wily.
189. Noyes paraphrases the line: "Those who reach for the crown, but miss that prize, receive death."
190–91. Cf. *Absalom and Achitophel,* 688–89.
192–93. Cf. *Absalom and Achitophel,* 729–30.
194–95. Cf. *Absalom and Achitophel,* 733–34.
202. The image is also used for Shaftesbury in *Absalom and Achitophel,* 159–62.
203. *my removal:* During April 1679, Shaftesbury accepted the post of Lord President of the Privy Council, but his adamant stand on exclusion, his support of Monmouth's succession, his violent objections to prorogation and dissolution, and finally his open opposition to Court policy, led to his dismissal six months later (*DNB;* Brown, *Shaftesbury,* pp. 258–64).
208–09. Kinsley notes the similarity to *Absalom and Achitophel,* 179, 206. His note

But still pretended 't was for others' good.
What politician yet e'er scap'd his fate,   210
Who saving his own neck not sav'd the State?
From hence on ev'ry hum'rous wind that veer'd,
With shifted sails, a sev'ral course you steer'd.
What form of sway did David e'er pursue,
That seem'd like absolute, but sprung from you?   215
Who at your instance quash'd each penal law
That kept dissenting factious Jews in awe:
And who suspends fix'd laws, may abrogate;
That done, form new, and so enslave the State.
E'en property, whose champion now you stand   220
And seem for this the idol of the land,
Did ne'er sustain such violence before,
As when your counsel shut the royal store;
Advice, that ruin to whole tribes procur'd,
But secret kept till your own bank 's secur'd.   225
Recount with this the triple cov'nant broke,

to the latter cites the Epistle Dedicatory to *All for Love* (1678): "He who has often changed his party, and always has made his interest the rule for it gives little evidence of his sincerity for the public good. 'Tis manifest he changes but for himself and takes the people for tools to work his fortune."

212–13. Cf. *The Medal,* 79–80.
214–15. Cf. *The Medal,* 77–78.
216, 218. *Who:* i.e. he who.

216–17. Shaftesbury, in mid-March 1672, supported the Declaration of Indulgence, granting toleration to both Catholics and Dissenters, and vainly tried to defend the government's position on 5 Feb. 1673 (Brown, *Shaftesbury,* pp. 196, 204; *DNB*). The Declaration tended, in effect, to suspend some of the force of the "fix'd laws" of the Act of Uniformity. As he moved into opposition in the closing months of 1673, Shaftesbury supported the Test Act, though it entailed a reversal of his former stand.

223–25. In order to obtain funds for the Dutch War, in early 1672, Charles, evidently on the advice of Clifford, suspended payment on £1,400,000 lent him by the London bankers, and reduced the interest from 12 per cent to 6 per cent. Shaftesbury, then Lord Ashley, as a Commissioner of the Treasury, Chancellor of the Exchequer, and a member of the Cabal ministry, received much of the blame, and was attacked for having carefully withdrawn his own funds before the stop was announced. It would seem, however, that he had no such personal investment and, indeed, had opposed the move, listing among his objections the ruin it would bring to trade, to the King's credit, and to the widows and orphans whose funds would ultimately suffer; nonetheless, he did again defend the government in Feb. 1673. (See Brown, *Shaftesbury,* pp. 194–95, 204; also Noyes and Kinsley.)

226. *triple cov'nant:* The Triple Alliance of England, Sweden, and Holland against France in 1668. Shaftesbury was active in breaking the alliance and encouraging the

And Israel fitted for a foreign yoke;
Nor here your counsel's fatal progress stay'd,
But sent our levi'd pow'rs to Pharaoh's aid.
Hence Tyre and Israel, low in ruins laid,   230
And Egypt, once their scorn, their common terror made.
E'en yet of such a season we can dream
When royal rights you made your darling theme;
For pow'r unlimited could reasons draw,
And place prerogative above the law;   235
Which, on your fall from office, grew unjust.
The law 's made king, the King a slave in trust:
Whom with statecraft (to int'rest only true)
You now accuse of ills contriv'd by you."

　　To this Hell's agent: "Royal youth, fix here;   240
Let int'rest be the star by which I steer.
Hence to repose your trust in me was wise,
Whose int'rest most in your advancement lies;
A tie so firm as always will avail,
When friendship, nature, and religion fail;   245
On ours the safety of the crowd depends;
Secure the crowd, and we obtain our ends,

Third Dutch War (1672–74), thus assisting Louis XIV's program of territorial and religious expansion. When he delivered his famous *Delenda est Carthago* speech to Parliament on 5 Feb. 1673, he probably had no hint of the secret Treaty of Dover between Charles and Louis; certainly, his move to the anti-French opposition in 1673 makes more rhetorical than real the charge of 227, a repetition of *Absalom and Achitophel*, 175–77, and an echo of *The Medal*, 65–70. (See Ogg, *Charles II*, pp. 365, 371–72; Brown, *Shaftesbury*, pp. 203–04; and Noyes and Kinsley.)

229–30. For the assistance given the French and the growing opposition in Parliament, see Ogg, *Charles II*, pp. 372–88. Holland was subjected to military attack from France from 1672 until the Treaty of Nijmwegen in 1678.

232–35. The allusion, though general, would seem to refer specifically to Shaftesbury's defense of Court policy and prerogative during the first half of 1673; on 9 Nov., he was dismissed from office (Brown, *Shaftesbury*, pp. 202–15).

237. Similar arguments are associated with Shaftesbury in *Absalom and Achitophel*, 409–18 (verbal echoes are found in 766, 775); for the relationship of these with Hobbesian doctrine, see Kinsley's note to *Absalom and Achitophel*, 759–810; also *The Medal*, 82–83.

240. *Hell's agent:* Cf. *Absalom and Achitophel*, 373.

241–45. The theme of self-interest, found in *Absalom and Achitophel*, 501–04, and broadening into a general motive in *The Medal* (88–90), here becomes an infernal bond.

Whom I will cause so far our guilt to share,
Till they are made our champions by their fear.
What opposition can your rival bring   250
While Sanhedrins are jealous of the King?
His strength as yet in David's friendship lies,
And what can David's self without supplies?
Who with exclusive bills must now dispense,
Debar the heir, or starve in his defense;   255
Conditions which our elders ne'er will quit,
And David's justice never can admit.
Or, forc'd by wants his brother to betray,
To your ambition next he clears the way.
For if succession once to naught they bring,   260
Their next advance removes the present king:
Persisting else his senates to dissolve,
In equal hazard shall his reign involve.
Our tribes, whom Pharaoh's pow'r so much alarms,
Shall rise without their prince t' oppose his arms: 265
Nor boots it on what cause at first they join,
Their troops, once up, are tools for our design.
At least such subtle covenants shall be made,
Till peace itself is war in masquerade.
Associations of mysterious sense,   270
Against, but seeming for, the King's defense,
E'en on their courts of justice fetters draw,
And from our agents muzzle up their law.
By which, a conquest if we fail to make,
'T is a drawn game at worst, and we secure our stake."   275

250–62. The three last parliaments (Sanhedrins) of Charles' reign attempted to
force him to exclude Monmouth's "rival" (the Duke of York) by refusing to grant the
supplies that the King so desperately needed. Charles' parliamentary response was to
prorogue or dissolve his parliaments; his financial recourse was, in part at least, to
the subsidies of Louis XIV.

269. Cf. *Absalom and Achitophel*, 751–52.

270. *Associations:* The reference is to the famous Paper of an Association, reputedly
found in Shaftesbury's study at his arrest on 2 July 1681.

272–73. The impaneling of Whig juries which rejected government attempts at
legal retribution was in the hands of Whig sheriffs in London from 1680 to 1682. The
first notable instance of an "Ignoramus" was the trial of Stephen College in July
1681; the most famous was, of course, the trial of Shaftesbury himself on 24 Nov. of
that year.

He said, and for the dire success depends
On various sects, by common guilt made friends,
Whose heads, though ne'er so diff'ring in their creed,
I' th' point of treason yet were well agreed.
'Mongst these, extorting Ishban first appears,   280
Pursu'd b' a meager troop of bankrupt heirs.
Blest times, when Ishban, he whose occupation
So long has been to cheat, reforms the nation!

280. *extorting Ishban:* The biblical name may be an invention, though this would
not be in keeping with either of the *Absalom* poems. Perhaps the allusion is to Eshban,
merely mentioned as one of the four sons of Dishon (Genesis 36:26; I Chronicles 1:41),
but even more applicable would be Eshbaal (i.e. Ishbosheth), the youngest son of Saul
who, after the slaughter at Gilboah, was his legitimate heir. His powerful kinsman,
Abner, took him across the Jordan to Mahanaim, slowly rebuilt the dominion of Saul's
house, and made him king, as a rival to David. With Abner's death, this last repre-
sentative of Saul's house (save for Mephibosheth), was assassinated and the kingdom
was united under David.

Historically, Ishban is Sir Robert Clayton (1629–1707), who rose from an apprentice
scrivener to become one of the most powerful London merchant-bankers. He served as
an alderman from 1670 until his death (with the exception of the 1683–89 period), was
a London M.P. from the time of the Exclusion Parliaments, and served as Sheriff
(1671–72) and Lord Mayor (1679–80) of London. The splendor and pageantry of his
procession on 29 Oct. 1679 is recounted in *London of Luster* by Thomas Jordon
[J 1035]. The regal sumptuousness found in the household of this steadfast Whig awed
even his friend John Evelyn, who took the Countess of Sunderland there on one
occasion "that she might see the pomp and ceremony of this Prince of Citizens, there
never having been any who, for the stateliness of his palace, prodigious feasting, and
magnificence, exceeded him." Three days later (21 Nov. 1679), Evelyn returned with
the Earl of Ossory to "a feast and entertainment that might have become a king."
(Evelyn, *Diary, 4,* 185–87 and notes thereto; also J. T. Page, "Lord Mayors of London
who were Natives of Northamptonshire," *Northamptonshire Notes and Queries* 2 [1886–
87], 229–38.)

"Extorting" (i.e. obtaining from a reluctant person by violence, torture, intimidation,
or abuse of legal or official authority) is employed with witty ambiguity, for its ob-
ject may be either money (see 292 n.) or statements. Clayton, along with other Whig
City officials, was charged by Fitzharris with having "extorted from him by threats his
previous declaration concerning the Popish Plot, and used the most urgent means to
compel him to impute the guilt of Godfrey's murder to Danby, and to fix an accession
to the Popish conspiracy on the Queen and Duke of York. The man was executed
adhering to this last story. Clayton, and the others accused of such infamous practices,
exculpated themselves in a pamphlet entitled 'Truth Vindicated'" (S.-S., *Dryden, 9,*
337) by the City Recorder, Sir George Treby [T 2107]. An attack analogous to the one
developed here may be found in *A New Ballad of London's Loyalty,* 25–32, POAS,
Yale, *2,* 433.

281–85. Evelyn remarks, on 18 Nov. 1679, that "some believe him guilty of hard-
dealing, especially with the Duke of Buckingham, much of whose estate he had swal-

Ishban of conscience suited to his trade,
As good a saint as usurer e'er made.   285
Yet Mammon has not so engross'd him quite,
But Belial lays as large a claim of spite;
Who, for those pardons from his prince he draws,
Returns reproaches and cries up the Cause.
That year in which the city he did sway,   290
He left rebellion in a hopeful way.
Yet his ambition once was found so bold
To offer talents of extorted gold,
Could David's wants have so been brib'd to shame
And scandalize our peerage with his name;   295
For which, his dear sedition he'd forswear,
And e'en turn loyal to be made a peer.

Next him, let railing Rabsheka have place,
So full of zeal he has no need of grace;

---

lowed" (*Diary, 4,* 186). The public nature of this charge is seen in the concluding stanza of *The Litany of the D[uke] of B[uckingham]* ([L 2536]; see *POAS,* Yale, 2, 199).

289. *the Cause:* See, 107 n.

292–95. The charge, though general, may have been based on Clayton's "swallowing" the estates of nobles such as Buckingham and Peterborough (Evelyn, *Diary, 4,* 110–11); it was incorporated in *The Last Will and Testament of the Charter of London* (1683) [L 531]; reprinted in *Somers Tracts, 8,* 392–94; and cited in S.-S., *Dryden, 9,* 338–39), where Clayton is bequeathed all remaining common stock "to purchase Paddington Manor . . . since there are no dukedoms to be purchased."

298. *railing Rabsheka:* Biblically, a servant of Sennacherib, King of Assyria, very likely the Chief Cupbearer, as the Hebrew implies (*A Dictionary of the Bible, 2,* 988). Rabshakeh, perhaps a deserter or apostate, appeared with a great Syrian host before the walls of Jerusalem in the fourteenth year of Hezekiah's reign. Falsely claiming God's sanction for Assyrian victories, and railing at the emissaries "in the Jew's tongue," Rabshakeh vainly attempted to terrify the populous into open rebellion. With Isaiah's counsel, Hezekiah successfully resisted the Assyrians. (II Kings 18:13–19:37 and Isaiah 36–37.)

Historically, Sir Thomas Player, a zealous Whig, was Chamberlain of London, (succeeding his father in 1672) and a City M.P. in the Westminster and Oxford Parliaments. He was Colonel of the Orange Regiment of the Trained Bands, and Leader of the Honorable Artillery Company from 1669 until the Duke of York took exception to him in 1677. When York returned from Brussels upon news of Charles' illness in Aug. 1679, it was Player who, with "a set speech on the horrors of Popery" and the Plot, demanded that the Lord Mayor double the City guards to prevent another burning of London and massacre of its citizens. While railing thus, he sought to increase the terror by saying "that he durst hardly go to sleep, for fear of awaking with his throat

A saint that can both flesh and spirit use,   300
Alike haunt conventicles and the stews:
Of whom the question difficult appears,
If most i' th' preachers' or the bawds' arrears.
What caution could appear too much in him
That keeps the treasure of Jerusalem!   305
Let David's brother but approach the town,
"Double our guards," he cries, "we are undone."
Protesting that he dares not sleep in 's bed,
Lest he should rise next morn without his head.

Next these, a troop of busy spirits press,   310
Of little fortunes, and of conscience less;
With them the tribe, whose luxury had drain'd
Their banks, in former sequestrations gain'd;
Who rich and great by past rebellions grew,
And long to fish the troubled streams anew.   315
Some future hopes, some present payment draws,
To sell their conscience and espouse the Cause.
Such stipends those vile hirelings best befit,
Priests without grace, and poets without wit.

---

cut." (Beaven, *Aldermen, 1,* 291; *DNB;* Scott-Saintsbury, *Dryden, 9,* 340; *Hatton Correspondence, 1,* 194–95).

In the Tory verse of the period, Player's name is constantly linked with that of Madam Cresswell, the proprietress of London's most notorious brothel in Moorfields, usually with the insinuation that he had long been deeply in her debt. *The Last Will and Testament of the Charter of London* leaves to him "all the manor of Moorfields, with all the wenches and bawdy houses thereunto belonging, with Mrs. Cresswell's for his immediate inheritance, to enjoy and occupy all from the bawd to the whore downward, at 19s. in the pound cheaper than any other person, because he may not exhaust the chamber by paying old arrears, nor embezzle the stock by running into new scores." According to *A New Ballad of London's Loyalty*, 33–36 (*POAS*, Yale, 2, 433–34), the debt was £300.

305. As Chamberlain, Player was Treasurer of the City of London. When he absented himself from the investiture on 28 Oct. 1682 of the Tory Lord Mayor, William Prichard, rumor had it that he had absconded with £400,000 of the City's funds. His strong support of the Whig sheriffs and his work in defense of the London Charter eventually led to his prosecution as one of the rioters during the shrieval elections (Howell, *State Trials, 9,* 187ff.) and forced him to relinquish his office four months later on 11 Sept. (Luttrell, *Brief Relation, 1,* 262–63, 278).

313. *former sequestrations:* i.e. the seizure of royalists' properties during the Interregnum.

Shall that false Hebronite escape our curse,   320
Judas, that keeps the rebels' pension-purse;
Judas, that pays the treason-writer's fee;
Judas, that well deserves his namesake's tree;
Who at Jerusalem's own gates erects
His college for a nursery of sects;   325
Young prophets with an early care secures,
And with the dung of his own arts manures!
What have the men of Hebron here to do?
What part in Israel's promis'd land have you?

Here Phaleg, the lay Hebronite, is come,   330
'Cause, like the rest, he could not live at home;

320. *Hebronite:* Scot. In the city of Hebron, between Jerusalem and Beersheba, David first established his government, dwelling there during the seven and a half years he reigned over Judah (II Samuel 5:5) prior to becoming King of all Israel. The analogy with Charles II's earlier reign in Scotland (from 1651) is evident.

321. *Judas:* According to biblical tradition, Judas Iscariot was the steward and almoner for the apostles (John 12:6, 13:29). Likewise, there would appear to be an intentional conflation with Judas of Galilee, the leader of a popular revolt in 6 A.D. "His fiery eloquence and the popularity of his doctrines drew vast crowds to his standard, by many of whom he was regarded as the Messiah and the country was for a time entirely given over to the lawless depredations of the fierce and licentious throngs who had joined themselves to him; but the might of Rome proved irresistible: Judas himself perished, and his followers were dispersed though not entirely destroyed" (*A Dictionary of the Bible, 1,* 1160).

Historically, Robert Ferguson, the Scots dissenting minister, nicknamed "the Plotter." Ejected from his living in 1662 by the Act of Uniformity, Ferguson became a nonconformist preacher in Moorfields and taught grammar at Islington. By 1666, he was beginning to give up religious controversy for polemics, and his connection with the Scotch Rising was the first example of his radical conspiracies that were highlighted by his central position not only in the Rye House Plot and the Monmouth Rebellion, but in almost every extremist movement during the reigns of Charles, James, and William (Kitchin, *L'Estrange,* p. 170). Ferguson's character, like his life, is veiled in mystery; indeed, it is still uncertain whether he was simply a conspirator or actually a double agent. Evaluations of him vary from the violent reaction of Scott (S.-S., *Dryden, 9,* 342-47) to the extreme sympathy of James Ferguson (*Ferguson*). Burnet's portrait seems best to fit the facts as we have them: "Ferguson was a hot and a bold man, whose spirit was naturally turned to plotting; he was always unquiet and setting on some to mischief. . . . He was cast out by the Presbyterians, and then went among the Independents, where his boldness raised him to some figure, though he was at bottom a very empty man. He had the management of a secret press, and of a purse that maintained it, and he gave out most of the pamphlets writ on that side, and with some he passed for the author of them" (*History, 2,* 358).

330. *Phaleg:* Biblically, little is known of Peleg, other than that he was a son of

Who from his own possessions could not drain
An omer even of Hebronitish grain;
Here struts it like a patriot, and talks high
Of injur'd subjects, alter'd property;   335
An emblem of that buzzing insect just,
That mounts the wheel, and thinks she raises dust.

Eber and brother of Joktan, and that he was so named because "in his days the earth was divided" (Genesis 10:25, 11:16; I Chronicles 1:19; Luke 3:35).

Historically, too, his identity remains in doubt. Using Tonson's "Key" (1716), Scott posited the traditional identification with a certain James Forbes (Scott-Saintsbury, *9*, 347–48) on the basis of an incident recounted in Carte's *Life of Ormonde*, *2*, 444–45), wherein the young Earl of Derby so abused his tutor while they were staying in Paris in 1673 that Ormonde had to replace the unfortunate man with the firmer Colonel Thomas Fairfax.

In the poem, however, Phaleg is placed between two of the most radical members of the Independent sectarians—Ferguson and Johnson—and, though 342–45 appear to parallel the incident in Carte, the injustice and inappropriateness of the attack (noted by most editors) is increased if we consider that the poem portrays a Scot whose unproductive lands at home force him to seek his living in England, who is closely and volubly connected with the Whig party, who is extremely thin in appearance with a reputation for lechery and cuckoldry, who has been "a waiting man to trav'ling nobles" though so unsuccessfully that he was "bastinado'd" and sent home to learn manners, and, finally, who, at present, "reads politics" to Monmouth.

The problem is complicated by the currency of the name. The most frequent confusion is with James Forbes, the nonconformist preacher of Gloucester who left Scotland in 1653, assisted in the publication of factious pamphlets in 1664 (*CSPD*, 1664–65, pp. 8, 19, 24), was imprisoned for six months at Gloucester under the Five Mile Act in 1680 (*CSPD*, 1681, pp. 45–6; *Observator*, No. 99 [15 Feb. 1682]), and may have been interrogated in connection with the Rye House Conspiracy (*CSPD*, July–Sept. 1683, pp. 90, 92, 100, 106). However, not only is it highly doubtful that Ormonde would have chosen as governor to his grandson-in-law a nonconformist so intransigent that he had been frequently sought and on one occasion excommunicated, but James Forbes had been licensed to preach at Stinchcombe in Gloucestershire on 3 Feb. 1673 (*CSPD*, 1672–73, p. 513), just five months before the young Earl and his governor went abroad (*CSPD*, 1673, p. 443), and he says of this period: "I had five years [1672–77] quiet exercise of my ministry, wonderfully hid; when others in most places around us were in great troubles" (Matthews, *Calamy Revised*, p. 205; misdated in Kitchin, *L'Estrange*, p. 352). Indeed, the James Forbes interrogated in 1683 might well have been, inter alios, James Forbes (a son of Viscount Granard?), "a very simple fellow," in Monmouth's opinion, but one who was most closely associated with the Duke during the difficult period at the end of Nov. 1683 (D'Oyley, *Monmouth*, pp. 245, 247).

Clearly, a totally different identification can be entertained, but, though names such as Sir Thomas Armstrong's present themselves as possibilities, it would appear that further study of the Monmouth circle is needed before there can be a definitive solution.

333. *omer:* A Hebrew measure of capacity, the tenth part of an ephah, or, roughly, five pints.

336–37. Kinsley refers to LaFontaine, *Fables*, VII, 9 in the 1678 translation.

Can dry bones live? or skeletons produce
The vital warmth of cuckoldizing juice?
Slim Phaleg could, and at the table fed,   340
Return'd the grateful product to the bed.
A waiting-man to trav'ling nobles chose,
He his own laws would saucily impose,
Till bastinado'd back again he went,
To learn those manners he to teach was sent.   345
Chastis'd, he ought to have retreated home,
But he reads politics to Absalom;
For never Hebronite, tho' kick'd and scorn'd,
To his own country willingly return'd.

But leaving famish'd Phaleg to be fed,   350
And to talk treason for his daily bread,
Let Hebron, nay, let hell produce a man
So made for mischief as Ben-Jochanan.

338–39. Ezekiel 37:1–10.

353. *Ben-Jochanan:* If there is a biblical reference here, it is probably to Jeremiah 41:11–43:6, where Johanon defies Jeremiah's command to remain in Israel and flees into Egypt with the remnant of Judah. More likely, the name was taken as a "translation" of Johnson.

Historically, the Rev. Samuel Johnson (1649–1703), a native of Warwickshire whose "humble parentage" is unknown, was educated at St. Paul's School, London (where he became librarian) and then entered Trinity College, Cambridge, though he did not graduate. On 1 March 1670, Robert Bidolph gave him the rectory of Corringham, Essex, a living worth £80, half of which Johnson paid to a curate when he went to London. (*Some Memorials* prefixed to his *Works*, 1710, p. iii). There, the study of constitutional law which he had undertaken at Bidolph's suggestion probably helped him obtain the position of domestic chaplain to Lord Russell, whom, it was said, he influenced deeply. Though Johnson claimed that he never carried his politics into the pulpit, his Palm Sunday sermon, preached on 13 April 1679 before the Whig Lord Mayor, Clayton, and the aldermen, strongly supported the Country party's anti-Yorkist exclusion policy and began Johnson's active political life. In 1682, the year when his famous *Julian the Apostate* appeared (371 n.), Johnson was referred to as "formerly a reader in Covent Garden" (*CSPD*, 1682, p. 253). The government did not move against him until 3 Aug. 1683 (*CSPD*, July–Sept. 1683, pp. 246, 248), when they attempted to prove the sequel, *Julian's Arts* (which Wing records as the 1689 edition [J 832]), a libel; but Johnson refused to divulge the location of the 3,000 copies he had had printed and was sent to the Gatehouse at the end of Sept. though soon bailed by friends (*Some Memorials*, pp. v–vi; *CSPD*, July–Sept. 1683, p. 432). The government, on the basis of the Oxford Decree (*London Gazette*, No. 1845 [23–26 July 1683]; also Gillett, *Burned Books*, pp. 516–20), next attacked the first *Julian*. Johnson was indicted on 6 Nov. 1683, found guilty two weeks later, and on 11 Feb. 1684 the book was

A Jew of humble parentage was he,
By trade a Levite, though of low degree: 355
His pride no higher than the desk aspir'd,
But for the drudgery of priests was hir'd
To read and pray in linen ephod brave
And pick up single shekels from the grave;
Marri'd at last, and finding charge come faster,   360
He could not live by God, but chang'd his master;
Inspir'd by want, was made a factious tool;
They got a villain, and we lost a fool.
Still violent, whatever cause he took,
But most against the party he forsook;   365
For renegadoes, who ne'er turn by halves,
Are bound in conscience to be double knaves.
So this prose-prophet took most monstrous pains
To let his masters see he earn'd his gains.
But as the Dev'l owes all his imps a shame,   370
He chose th' Apostate for his proper theme;

---

ordered to be burned and Johnson to pay 500 marks fine (Luttrell, *Brief Relation, 1,*
287, 288, 300), which was tantamount to perpetual prison for the impoverished
preacher. Yet, even in prison and even in James' reign, Johnson continued his attacks.
On 21 June 1686, he was tried for two seditious libels, and he was sentenced on 16
Nov. not only to 500 marks fine but to be defrocked, pilloried and thrice whipped
(Luttrell, *Brief Relation, 1,* 381–82; Howell, *State Trials, 9,* 1339–54). After the Revolu-
tion, though "the proceedings against him were declared illegal and he received a
pension of £300 yearly, with £1,000 in money and a post for his son" (Scott-Saintsbury,
9, 351), he resolutely maintained his independence, still "firmly [adhering] to his dar-
ling doctrine of the power of the people over kings" (*Hatton Correspondence, 2,* 213).
   371. In crushing response to a sermon on "the sovereign power" by the orthodox
George Hickes (preached 1681, printed 1682 [H 1845]; *DNB*), there appeared about 18
June 1682 (*Observator,* No. 157 [19 June 1682]) *Julian the Apostate: being a short
Account of his Life, the Sense of the Primitive Christians about his Succession, and
their Behaviour towards him, Together with a Comparison of Popery and Paganism*
[J 829-30], a treatise giving a theoretical justification of the Exclusion Bill based on
nullification of the Anglican doctrine of passive obedience. Johnson tried to show how
the primitive Christians opposed the efforts of the pagan emperor, Julian, to alter the
established religion. Passive obedience, he argued, applies only to countries in which
the Christians are in the minority and the laws are opposed to them; in countries in
which Christianity is the established religion, subjects are obligated to prevent its
extirpation.
   Probably Scott is correct (*Dryden, 9,* 349) in saying that Johnson "has fairly made
out his case" and that the poem's attempted reply (384-91) is weak indeed. Contem-
porary readers must have seen at once the implied parallel between Julian and James,

With little pains he made the picture true,
And from reflection took the rogue he drew:
A wondrous work, to prove the Jewish nation
In every age a murmuring generation;   375
To trace 'em from their infancy of sinning,
And show 'em factious from their first beginning;
To prove they could rebel, and rail, and mock,
Much to the credit of the chosen flock;
A strong authority, which must convince,   380
That saints own no allegiance to their prince;
As 'tis a leading card to make a whore,
To prove her mother had turn'd up before.
But, tell me, did the drunken patriarch bless
The son that show'd his father's nakedness?   385
Such thanks the present Church thy pen will give,
Which proves rebellion was so primitive.
Must ancient failings be examples made?
Then murderers from Cain may learn their trade.
As thou the heathen and the saint hast drawn,   390
Methinks th' Apostate was the better man;
And thy hot father (waiving my respect)

---

the Catholic Duke of York. At least two editions appeared, both published by Langley
Curtis and one of them printed by John Darby (who was also to print *Julian's Arts*
in early Sept. 1683). The Yale copy of [J 829] may represent a third edition, having
118 pages of text, whereas Wing's entry describes a copy of 94 pages. As well, a fourth
edition seems to have been printed by Richard Chiswell about the end of May 1683
(*CSPD*, July–Sept. 1683, p. 432).

  Johnson's tract occasioned a shower of replies: Edward Meredith ridiculed the piece
in *Some remarks upon a late popular piece of nonsense called Julian the Apostate*
(1682) [M 1784], to which there was a counterreply in kind, probably by Johnson, *The
Account of the Life of Julian the Apostate Vindicated* (1682) [A 319]; George Hickes'
Jovian; or an Answer to Julian the Apostate (1683) [H 1852–53], and John Bennet's
Constantius the Apostate (1683) [B 1884] both of which Johnson tried to answer with
Julian's Arts; Thomas Lang's *Vindication of the Primitive Christians* (1683) [L 2985];
and John Northleigh's "Remarks" in *The Triumph of our Monarchy* (1685) [N 1305],
to which Dryden contributed some commendatory verses (Kinsley; Macdonald, *Dryden
Bibliography*, pp. 41–42).

  382. *a leading card:* That which is played first; here, with the sense of a leading
case, one which sets a precedent; and also, perhaps, in an ironic sense, with reference
to the Quaker concept of a directing influence or guidance.

  384. *the drunken patriarch:* Noah. See Genesis 9:18–27.

  392. *thy hot father:* St. Gregory Nazianzenus, whose invective against Julian is
used by Johnson (Kinsley; see also Noyes' more extended note, and Macaulay, *History*,
2, 759–60).

Not of a mother church, but of a sect.
And such he needs must be of thy inditing;
This comes of drinking asses' milk and writing.   395
If Balak should be call'd to leave his place
(As profit is the loudest call of grace),
His temple dispossess'd of one, would be
Replenish'd with seven devils more by thee.

   Levi, thou art a load, I'll lay thee down,   400
And show rebellion bare, without a gown;
Poor slaves in meter, dull and addlepated,
Who rhyme below ev'n David's psalms translated.
Some in my speedy pace I must outrun,
As lame Mephibosheth, the wizard's son;   405

---

396. *Balak:* Biblically, the King of the Moabites at the time that the children of
Israel were ending their journey in the wilderness. Fearing their numbers, Balak
sought to hire Balaam to curse them, but instead the prophet blessed them thrice and
foretold their prosperity (Numbers 22–24). "According to Gesenius, the name signifies
inanis, vacuus" (*A Dictionary of the Bible, 1*, 163). According to Tonson's "Key"
(1716), Balak is "Barnet" (i.e. Gilbert Burnet, the buzzard of *The Hind and the Pan-
ther*, III, 1121), but 396–99 offer so brief and so general a portrait that even the con-
temporary Luttrell was unable to gloss them.
   400. *Levi:* i.e. one of the priestly tribe.
   403. *David's psalms translated:* The much-maligned metrical psalter of Thomas
Sternhold and John Hopkins (completed 1562) was superseded by the version of
Nahum Tate and Nicholas Brady in 1696. Shadwell's name had elsewhere been asso-
ciated with both of the earlier translators; at just about this time, Dryden linked him
with Sternhold in concluding *Religio Laici* (456), and five years earlier Settle, then
anti-Shadwell, referred to him as a "Hopkin-rhymer" (Preface to *Ibrahim*, 1677).
   405. *lame Mephibosheth, the wizard's son:* Biblically, the son of Jonathan and, at
the time of David's victories, the last of the house of Saul. Mephibosheth had been
crippled in both legs at the age of five when his nurse, hearing of the defeat on Gil-
boah, escaped with the child but dropped him in her flight (II Samuel 4:4). Seventeen
years after David had restored Mephibosheth to wealth and honor at court, the revolt
of Absalom occurred. According to Mephibosheth's servant, Ziba, who met the fleeing
David with food, wine, and asses, his master had remained in Jerusalem hoping to
regain the throne of his grandfather, Saul (II Samuel 16:1–4). According to Mephibo-
sheth, Ziba had betrayed him, taking the asses so that the lamed man was unable to
ride out and join David in his time of need (II Samuel 19:24–30; see also *A Dictionary
of the Bible, 2*, 324–27). An additional reason for the use of the name may be its
meaning as "utterance of Baal."
   Historically, Mephibosheth is the minor poet and dramatist Samuel Pordage (1633–
91?), the "limping Pordage [who was] . . . violently suspected for *The Medal Revers'd*"
(*Observator*, No. 119 [5 April 1682]), which sought to answer Dryden's *The Medal*, and

To make quick way I'll leap o'er heavy blocks,
Shun rotten Uzza as I would the pox,
And hasten Og and Doeg to rehearse;
Two fools that crutch their feeble sense on verse,
Who, by my Muse, to all succeeding times   410
Shall live, in spite of their own dogg'rel rhymes.

———

for *Azaria and Hushai,* an attempted reply to *Absalom and Achitophel* (see headnote to *The Medal Revers'd*). Pordage's father, John (1607–81), had been an early and ardent follower of the German mystic, Jakob Boehme; he was also a student of astrology, and had become rector of Bradfield, Berkshire. Though cleared of charges of heresy in 1651, he was again accused in 1654 on a panoply of charges, not the least of which were necromancy and having converse with spirits. On 8 Dec., he was ejected from his ministry and not reinstated until the Restoration; throughout his life, he promulgated Boehmenism, contributing greatly to the founding of the Philadelphians (*DNB;* Whiting, *Studies in English Puritanism,* pp. 298–300).

407. *rotten Uzza:* Though all texts have printed "Uzza" and editors have referred to the well-known episode (II Samuel 6:6–8 and I Chronicles 13:7–11) where he attempts to prevent the ark from falling as it is brought into Jerusalem and is struck down by God for touching it, the inapplicability of the reference is outstanding. More likely, in light of the adjective, the line alludes to Uzziah, the King of Judah whose early reign was exemplary but who, growing proud in his strength, sought to invade the priest's offices and burn incense on the altar. In his anger, as he opposed Azariah and the eighty priests, "the leprosy even rose up in his forehead. . . . And Uzziah the king was a leper unto the day of his death, and dwelt in a several house being a leper, for he was cut off from the house of the Lord . . . and Jotham his son reigned in his stead" (II Chronicles 26:16–23).

Tonson's "Key" (1716) identifies "Uzza" merely as "J. H.," a unique use of initials which suggests not only (as Kinsley indicates) that "J. H." was alive in 1716, but also that he was probably in a position of some power. This would confirm the identification adopted by Noyes (p. 1042, on the basis of V. de Sola Pinto's comment in *Sir Charles Sedley* [London, 1927] p. 146) that the person referred to is John Grubham Howe (1657–1722), a politician who reached his zenith during Anne's reign but who, even in 1716, must have been formidable. During his twenties, however, he was "the notorious 'Jack How,' author of many contemporary lampoons" (Brice Harris, "Robert Julian, Secretary to the Muses," *ELH, 10* [1943], 304, n. 42; also Macaulay, *History, 3,* 1334–36, and *POAS,* Yale, 2, 206, n. 9) and constantly mentioned in the pasquils of the period as a young fop who, in verse, with modish scurrility defamed female reputations or commented on the times. The *Satire on the Court Ladies* (1680; A"), 28, recommends "for smutty jests, and downright lies, Jack Howe"; and the expected counterblast (recalling "rotten Uzza" and "the pox") is found in *To Julian* ("Dear Julian, twice or thrice a year") where Howe, called Julian's patron, is said to have written "a prologue lawfully begotten" which, though it has been worked on by a number of wits,

Yet Swan says he admir'd it scap'd,
Since 'twas Jack Howe's, without being clapp'd.
(47–48)

Doeg, though without knowing how or why,
Made still a blund'ring kind of melody;
Spurr'd boldly on, and dash'd through thick and thin,
Through sense and nonsense, never out nor in;   415
Free from all meaning, whether good or bad,
And, in one word, heroically mad:
He was too warm on picking-work to dwell,
But faggoted his notions as they fell,
And if they rhym'd and rattl'd, all was well.   420

412–13. The lines would seem to elaborate on 54–55 of *The Medal of John Bayes,*
published about 15 May 1682 (Luttrell's date, given in Macdonald, *Dryden Bibliog-
raphy,* p. 232), which takes much the same attitude toward Dryden:

> In verse, thou hast a knack with words to chime,
> And had'st a kind of excellence in rhyme,

412. *Doeg:* Biblically, the reference is to the informer and opportunist who was the
"chief of Saul's herdmen ('having charge of the mules'). He was at Nob when
Ahimelech gave David the sword of Goliath, and not only gave information to Saul,
but when others declined the office, himself executed the King's order to destroy the
priests of Nob, with their families to the number of 85 persons, together with all their
property (I Samuel 21:7; 22:9, 17, 22; Psalm 52)" (*A Dictionary of the Bible, 1,* 447).
   Historically, Elkanah Settle (1648–1724) who, though previously a Court poet, had
for several years been writing for Shaftesbury and the City Whigs. In 1683, when it
was evident that the King would win the struggle, Settle again became a Tory; in
1668, when James II was tottering, he once more became a Whig. As Kinsley observes,
"the name of the Edomite . . . Doeg ('fearful, uneasy'; I Samuel 22) accords with what
is known of his character.
   Settle's early success with *The Empress of Morocco* (1673) [S 2678] provoked an at-
tack, *Notes and Observations on the Empress of Morocco* (1674) [D 2320], which he
believed had been written by Dryden, Shadwell and Crowne, and which he answered
with *Notes and Observations . . . Revised* (1674) [S 2702]. The portrait here, however,
finds its motivation in his anticourt activities, in his organization of the Pope-burning
processions of 17 Nov., in the strong suspicions that he had a hand in *The Medal
Revers'd* and possibly *Azaria and Hushai* (see R. G. Ham, "Dryden versus Settle," *MP,*
25 [1928], 409–16 and headnote to *The Medal Revers'd*), in the suggestion here that he
might have written the scurrilous *Medal of John Bayes,* and in the certainty that he
was the author of *Absalom Senior,* with its equally coarse attack on Dryden.
   414–20. As Noyes and Kinsley note, many of these charges are to be found in *Notes
and Observations:*

> What stuff may not a silly unattending audience swallow, wrapped up in rhyme;
> certainly our poet writes by chance, is resolved upon the rhyme beforehand, and
> for the rest of the verse has a lottery of words by him, and draws them that come
> next, let them make sense or nonsense when they come together he matters not
> that (p. 2).

And, again, in the Postscript:

> He would persuade us he is a kind of fanatic in poetry and has light within

Spiteful he is not, though he wrote a satyr,
For still there goes some *thinking* to ill-nature:
He needs no more than birds and beasts to think;
All his occasions are to eat and drink.
If he call rogue and rascal from a garret,   425
He means you no more mischief than a parrot:
The words for friend and foe alike were made;
To fetter 'em in verse is all his trade.
For almonds he'll cry whore to his own mother,
And call young Absalom King David's brother.   430

----

him, and writes by an inspiration which (like that of the heathen prophets) a
man must have no sense of his own to receive.

The same charge had been made in line 48 of *A Session of the Poets* (see *POAS*, Yale, *1*,
354). Settle, too, had complained about poets who "can write against all sense, nay
even their own" (*Prologue to "The Heir of Morocco,"* 9).

418. *picking-work:* The collecting of worthwhile scraps or gleanings. (Not in *OED*.)

419. Malone (I, 1, 170) felt that the idea of the line came from Flecknoe's *Enigmati-
cal Characters* (1658) [F 1213]: "For his [a schoolboy's] learning, 'tis all capping verses
and faggoting poets' loose lines, which fall from him as disorderly as faggot-sticks when
the band is broke" (p. 77).

429. In April 1682 appeared *A Character of the True Blue Protestant Poet* [C 2028],
recounting how Otway, "a man of the sword as well as the pen, finding himself most
coarsely dealt withal" in *A Session of the Poets* (also entitled *A Trial of the Poets for
the Bays,* which Settle was said to have written in 1676) challenged Settle to a duel. To
avert this, Settle "presently took pen, ink, and paper out of his pocket" and "writ these
following words, (viz.) I confess I writ the *Session of the Poets,* and am very sorry for't
and am the son of a whore for doing it. Witness my hand E. S." (See Noyes, Kinsley;
also R. G. Ham, *Otway and Lee* [New Haven, 1931], pp. 110–11 and "Dryden versus
Settle," *MP*, 25 [1928], 409–16). In the following year, the story was reiterated and rein-
forced ("He has twice given it out under his hand that his mother was a whore," p. 7)
in *Remarks Upon E. Settle's Narrative* [R 943] (see Macdonald, *Dryden Bibliography,*
p. 239). Settle denied his authorship of *A Session of the Poets* in *A Supplement to the
Narrative* (1683) [S 2720] (Macdonald, ibid.; and David Vieth, *Attribution in Restora-
tion Poetry* [New Haven, 1964], p. 318).

Kinsley notes the similarity to Shakespeare's *Troilus and Cressida,* V.ii.193–95, but
the poem, picking up the parrot image of 426, uses a proverbial phrase that had been
associated with pamphlet wars at least since the time of the Skelton (see Tilley, *Prov-
erbs,* A 220).

430. Settle had identified Absalom with the Duke of York in *Absalom Senior.* In
concluding the prefatory "Epistle to the Tories," he begged the favor "that you'll give
me the freedom of clapping but about a score of years extraordinary on the back of
my Absalom," and pointed out that Dryden had brought in Zimri, who had lived in
the time of Moses, and Stephen, who had been martyred "so many ages after." (See
also *Absalom Senior,* 239, 271 and notes; and S.-S., *Dryden, 9,* 357–58 and notes.)

Let him be gallows-free by my consent,
And nothing suffer, since he nothing meant;
Hanging supposes human soul and reason;
This animal 's below committing treason.
Shall he be hang'd who never could rebel?   435
That's a preferment for Achitophel.
The woman that committed buggery,
Was rightly sentenc'd by the law to die;
But 'twas hard fate that to the gallows led
The dog that never heard the statute read.   440
Railing in other men may be a crime,
But ought to pass for mere instinct in him:
Instinct he follows, and no farther knows,
For to write verse with him is to *trans-prose*.
'T were pity treason at his door to lay,   445
Who *makes heaven's gate a lock to its own key.*
Let him rail on; let his invective Muse
Have four and twenty letters to abuse,
Which if he jumbles to one line of sense,
Indict him of a capital offense.   450
In fireworks give him leave to vent his spite;

437–40. The allusion is to the ribald Cavalier ballad of 1647 [F 1659–60] (collected in *Rump* and reprinted in 1677) entitled, *The Four Legg'd Elder; or a Relation of a Horrible Dog and an Elder's Maid.* While fundamentally a corrosive attack on sectarianism, the Rabelaisian narrative culminates with the punishment of Jane and Swash:

Hers was but fornication found,
  For which she felt the lash,
But his was buggery presum'd,
  Therefore they hanged Swash.
                    (Stanza 10)

444. *trans-prose:* See note to the title of *Absalom Senior: or Achitophel Transpos'd.* The word recalls the satire on Dryden in *The Rehearsal* I.i. where Johnson remarks, "Methinks, Mr. Bayes, that putting verse into prose should be called transprosing."
  446. A misquotation of the opening couplet of *Absalom Senior:*

In gloomy times, when priestcraft bore the sway
And made heav'ns gate a lock to their own key.

451–52. Settle, as Whig City poet, had charge of the famous Pope-burning processions which Dryden had described in the *Prologue to the Loyal Brother* (18–40). The pro-Court periodical *Heraclitus Ridens* (No. 50 [10 Jan. 1682]) effectively ridiculed his work:

Jest. For instance, I knew a lusty fellow who would not willingly be thought valiant, who has an indifferent hand at making of crackers, serpents, rockets and

Those are the only serpents he can write.
The height of his ambition is, we know,
But to be master of a puppet show:
On that one stage his works may yet appear,   455
And a month's harvest keeps him all the year.

Now stop your noses, readers, all and some,
For here's a tun of midnight work to come;
Og, from a treason-tavern rolling home.

---

other playthings that are proper on the fifth of November; and has for such his skill received applause and victuals from the munificent gentlemen about Temple Bar.
Earnest. And he, I'll warrant, is made Master of the Ordnance?
Jest. True; and I think he's very fit for it. But he's . . . design'd Poet Laureate too.
Earnest. These two offices . . . may well enough be supplied by one man; the poet to make ballads in peace, and betake himself to other business in war.
Jest. Nay, his squibs and his poems have much what the same fortune; they crack and bounce, and the boys and girls laugh at them.

454. *to be master of a puppet show:* Kinsley points out "Settle's association with the actress Elizabeth Leigh, with whom he contracted in 1681 'to write or compose a certain interlude or stage play.' Elizabeth Leigh was the daughter of a Mrs. Mynn who kept booths at Bartholomew Fair and Southwark Fair; and later, at least, Settle was writing drolls for Mrs. Mynn (Hotson, pp. 274–6). In *The Vindication: or The Parallel* (1683) Dryden jibes at the Whigs, who 'must take up with Settle, and such as they can get: Bartholomew Fair writers . . .' (Malone, ii, 132–3)."

Further evidence that Settle was engaged in such work is found in the deposition of Joshua Bowes on 11 Nov. 1682 (*CSPD*, 1682, p. 536):

Settle likewise showed him two letters signed by Sir Thomas Player, as he told him, one directed to Sir Henry Thompson at York, commonly called Judgment Sir Harry, and the other to Sir John Hewly, to desire them to encourage Settle, who designed to carry down one Coish and others to act some plays or drolls in York. To make them more willing, Sir Thomas told them how eminently serviceable Settle had been to the public (as he termed it) and the deponent believes that his service consisted of writing [*The Character of a Popish Successor* and *Absalom Senior*].

Settle's career did, in fact, end in Bartholomew Fair, a descent that was set in verse by both Edward Young in his *First Epistle to Pope* (1730) and Alexander Pope in *Dunciad* III, 35–348, esp. 283–88. See also *The Satires of Dryden* ed. J. C. Collins (London, 1903), p. 114.

458. *a tun of midnight work:* Very likely a reference to the midnight cart, the cart for carrying away night soil (*OED;* though this would predate the earliest entry by 16 years). Cf. *Mac Flecknoe*, 103.

459. *Og:* Biblically, the King of Bashan who was destroyed with all his people by the Israelites under Moses (see especially Deuteronomy 3:1–13). He was famed, indeed

Round as a globe and liquor'd ev'ry chink,   460
Goodly and great, he sails behind his link.
With all this bulk there's nothing lost in Og,
For ev'ry inch that is not fool is rogue:
A monstrous mass of foul corrupted matter,
As all the devils had spew'd to make the batter.   465
When wine has given him courage to blaspheme,
He curses God, but God before curs'd him;
And if man could have reason, none has more,
That made his paunch so rich, and him so poor.
With wealth he was not trusted, for Heav'n knew   470
What 'twas of old to pamper up a Jew;
To what would he on quail and pheasant swell
That e'en on tripe and carrion could rebel?
But though Heav'n made him poor (with rev'rence speaking),
He never was a poet of God's making.   475
The midwife laid her hand on his thick skull,
With this prophetic blessing: *Be thou dull!*
Drink, swear, and roar, forbear no lewd delight
Fit for thy bulk, do anything but write.
Thou art of lasting make, like thoughtless men: 480
A strong nativity—but for the pen.

---

legendary (*A Dictionary of the Bible*, 2, 593–94), for his size, which is set down in Deuteronomy 3:11:

> For only Og King of Bashan remained of the remnant of giants; behold his bed-stead was a bedstead of iron; is it not in Rabboth of the children of Ammon? nine cubits was the length thereof, and four cubits the breadth of it, after the cubit of a man.

Historically, Thomas Shadwell, the Whig poet whom Dryden considered the author of the scurrilous attack, *The Medal of John Bayes* (see headnote to the poem, and Macdonald, *Dryden Bibliography*, pp. 232–33). Dryden had satirized Shadwell in *Mac Flecknoe,* which, though written approximately six years before this (see the headnote to *Mac Flecknoe, POAS,* Yale, *1,* 376–78), was printed in 1682. That poem, as Scott points out (Scott-Saintsbury, *9,* 362), struck at Shadwell mainly as a literary figure; here, he is ridiculed chiefly as a political hack, with the emphasis throughout on his size, his bulk, his rank grossness. For Dryden's subsequent prose elaboration on Og, see *The Vindication: or the Parallel* (1683) [D 2398] (Macdonald, No. 130) and Scott-Saintsbury, *7,* 180–81 (quoted in part in Kinsley).

472. Possibly a reference to Numbers 11–12, where the rain of quails is followed by the sedition of Miriam and Aaron.

477. *Be thou dull!*: "Apparently the midwife's blessing is confined to these three words, which are printed in italics in the early editions" (Noyes).

481. *nativity:* Birth considered astrologically; a horoscope.

Eat opium, mingle arsenic in thy drink,
Still thou mayst live, avoiding pen and ink.
I see, I see, 'tis counsel given in vain,
For treason botch'd in rhyme will be thy bane;   485
Rhyme is the rock on which thou art to wreck,
'T is fatal to thy fame and to thy neck.
Why should thy meter good King David blast?
A psalm of his will surely be thy last.
Dar'st thou presume in verse to meet thy foes,   490
Thou whom the penny pamphlet foil'd in prose?
Doeg, whom God for mankind's mirth has made,
O'ertops thy talent in thy very trade;
Doeg to thee, thy paintings are so coarse,
A poet is, though he's the poets' horse.   495
A double noose thou on thy neck dost pull,
For writing treason, and for writing dull.
To die for faction is a common evil,
But to be hang'd for nonsense is the devil.
Hadst thou the glories of thy king express'd,   500
Thy praises had been satire at the best;
But thou in clumsy verse, unlick'd, unpointed,
Hast shamefully defi'd the Lord's anointed.
I will not rake the dunghill of thy crimes,
For who would read thy life that reads thy rhymes?   505

482. *Eat opium:* Shadwell very likely died from an overdose of opium, to which
he had long been addicted.

mingle arsenic: "Occasionally, as among the Styrians, individuals acquire the habit
of arsenic-eating, which is said to increase their weight, strength and appetite, and
clears their complexion" (*EB*, 2, 653).

489. The allusion may be to the verses (Psalm 23?) read by the chaplain to the
criminal just prior to execution.

494. *thy paintings:* Dryden was later to write on the close alliance between the
literary and graphic arts in his preface ("A Parallel of Poetry and Painting") to his
translation of C. A. Du Fresnay's *De Arte Graphice* [C 2458] (Macdonald, No. 139 a–b;
Scott-Saintsbury, *17*, 289–355), the epigraph of which was the much reverenced Horatian
phrase "ut pictura poesis erit." The force of the concept is treated in Hagstrum,
The Sister Arts.

504–05. Cf. *The Vindication: or The Parallel:* "I do not delight to meddle with
his course of life and his immoralities, though I have a long bead-roll of them. I have
hitherto contented myself with the ridiculous part of him, which is enough, in all
conscience, to employ one man" (S.-S., *Dryden, 7,* 180).

But of King David's foes, be this the doom,
May all be like the young man Absalom;
And for my foes, may this their blessing be,
To talk like Doeg, and to write like thee.

Achitophel each rank, degree, and age,   510
For various ends, neglects not to engage:
The wise and rich for purse and counsel brought,
The fools and beggars for their number sought;
Who yet not only on the town depends,
For e'en in court the faction had its friends.   515
These thought the places they possess'd too small
And in their hearts wish'd court and king to fall;
Whose names the Muse, disdaining, holds i' th'dark,
Thrust in the villain herd without a mark,
With parasites and libel-spawning imps,   520
Intriguing fops, dull jesters, and worse pimps.
Disdain the rascal rabble to pursue,
Their set cabals are yet a viler crew.
See where involv'd in common smoke they sit,
Some for our mirth, some for our satire fit: 525

506–07. "And the king [David] said unto Cushi, Is the young man Absalom safe? And Cushi answered, The enemies of my lord the king, and all that rise against thee to do thee hurt, be as that young man is" (II Samuel 18:32).

512–21. Though general in nature, the poet may have specific persons or groups in mind; thus, 512 would seem to refer to Whig merchants and magnates of London (Clayton, Pilkington, Papillon, etc.), and 515 to men such as Buckingham and Essex; finally, in 521, the intriguing fop may be Jack Howe (see 407 n.), while the pimp may allude to Ford, Lord Grey of Wark.

524. *See where:* The center of Whig organization from at least 1676 was the Green Ribbon Club, whose name, says the Tory Roger North, came from "the signal of a green ribbon, agreed to be worn in their hats in the days of street engagements, like the coats of arms of valiant knights of old" (*Examen*, p. 572). The club was located in the King's Head Tavern, at the junction of Fleet Street and Chancery Lane,

> a center of business and company most proper for such anglers of fools. The house was double balconied in the front, as may yet be seen, for the clubsters to issue forth in fresco with hats and no perukes, pipes in their mouths, merry faces, and diluted throats, for vocal encouragement of the canaglia below, at bonfires, on usual and unusual occasions (ibid.).

The membership, as J. R. Jones has pointed out ("The Green Ribbon Club," *Durham University Journal*, 49 [N.S. *18*, 1956], 17–20),

> made up a cross-section of the first Whig party. There were peers, mainly of

These gloomy, thoughtful, and on mischief bent,
While those for mere good-fellowship frequent
Th'appointed club, can let sedition pass,
Sense, nonsense, anything t' employ the glass;
And who believe, in their dull honest hearts,   530
The rest talk treason but to shew their parts;
Who ne'er had wit or will for mischief yet,
But pleas'd to be reputed of a set.

But in the sacred annals of our Plot,
Industrious Arod never be forgot: 535
The labors of this midnight-magistrate

---

doubtful reputation like Grey, and old puritans such as Bethel . . . and Barbon.
. . . The City also contributed wealthy merchants, minor politicians, and lawyers
. . . Shadwell . . . was a member. But the largest section consisted of men with
residences in the country but some connections in London (p. 20).

526–33. North indignantly describes the temper of the club in 1680:

The conversation . . . was chiefly upon the subject of braveur in defending the
cause of liberty and property, and what every Protestant and Englishman ought
to venture and do rather than be over-run with popery and slavery . . . the
pastime . . . was very engaging to young gentlemen, and one who had once tasted
the conversation could scarce quit it. . . . The Pope himself could not make
saints so readily as they papists. . . . And a lewd atheistical fellow was as readily
washed clean and made a zealous Protestant . . . And these [members], besides
tutoring, were carriers up and down, or dispersers of seditious talk, at proper
times, as blood from the heart, to nourish sedition all over town" (Examen, pp.
572–73).

534–35. Cf. Absalom and Achitophel, 630–31.

535. Arod: Biblically, the founder of one of the families of God (Genesis 46:16;
Numbers 26:17). Paranomasia may be intended, since "a rod" is a symbol of power
or tyrannical sway, an instrument of punishment, a symbol of office, etc.
Historically, Sir William Waller (d. 1699), the son of the parliamentary general and,
from the end of 1678, a justice of the peace closely associated with Oates and, accord-
ing to North, "a great inquisitor of priests and Jesuits, and gutter (as the term was for
stripping) of popish chapels; in which he proceeded with . . . scandalous rigor . . .
In a word, he was called the Priest Catcher" (Examen, p. 277). Waller was best known
for his part in the Meal Tub Plot and in the Fitzharris affair. (See below, An Elegy
on . . . Sir William Waller, headnote and 14 n., 17 n.)

536. magistrate: As justice of the peace, Waller's first information is dated 17 Jan.
1679 (CSPD, 1679–80, p. 37); according to Luttrell (Brief Relation, 1, 39), he was
deprived of his commission by the King about the second week of April 1680. (The
event is probably the subject of Dagon's Fall, or The Knight Turned out of Com-
mission [D 111] dated 12 April 1680 ["Good God! What means this sudden alteration?"];
but see also Edmund Warcup's Journal, K. Feiling and F. R. Needham eds., EHR, 40
[1925], p. 247.) In any event, there are no further informations in the CSPD of 6
April 1680 until the arrest of Fitzharris on a warrant from Secretary Jenkins on 28

May vie with Corah's to preserve the State.
In search of arms he fail'd not to lay hold
On war's most powerful dang'rous weapon, GOLD.
And last, to take from Jebusites all odds,   540
Their altars pillag'd, stole their very gods.
Oft would he cry, when treasure he surpris'd:
" 'Tis Baalish gold in David's coin disguis'd."
Which to his house with richer relicts came,
While lumber idols only fed the flame;   545
For our wise rabble ne'er took pains t' enquire
What 'twas he burnt, so 't made a rousing fire.
With which our elder was enrich'd no more
Than false Gehazi with the Syrian's store;
So poor that, when our choosing-tribes were met,   550
Ev'n for his stinking votes he ran in debt:
For meat the wicked, and as authors think,
The saints he chous'd for his electing drink.

Feb. 1681 (*CSPD*, 1680–81, p. 189, and 3 March 1681, p. 194–95; see also Howell, *State Trials*, 8, 227, 374).

537–38. A negative survey of the Justice's zeal is given in *An Elegy on . . . Sir William Waller*, passim. In Jan. 1679 Waller, making a search of the Savoy, found in the lodgings of Thomas Pickering (who Tonge and Oates said was one of the many assassins hired to murder Charles II) a gun of "Italian make, which is said to be that designed for killing the King" (Luttrell, *Brief Relation, 1*, 7). Apparently, Oates too had been searching the Savoy, hunting for Benedictines (Lane, *Oates*, pp. 99 and 125; *An Elegy . . . on Sir William Waller*, 76–77 and notes).

538–44. "You cannot imagine what a trade they two [i.e. Waller and Gill, the constable] drove in beads, pictures, reliques, and crucifixes; and now and then, a piece of altar-plate—for they'd smell you the tang upon't of a superstitious use" (*Observator, 2*, No. 21 [25 Feb. 1684]; see *An Elegy on . . . Sir William Waller*, 62 n., and a similar suggestion of duplicity by North quoted in the headnote).

545–47. "Have we not seen a worthy knight . . . deliver up the picture of Christ in the arms of His mother, and only served for a piece of ornament or furniture in a private family, in triumph to the flames; and the multitude hoiting about it and throwing stones at it" (*Observator*, No. 189 [15 Aug. 1682]; see also *An Elegy on . . . Sir William Waller*, 68–72 and n.). With 545 compare *Absalom and Achitophel*, 97.

549. After Elisha had cured the Syrian king, Naaman, of leprosy, the prophet's servant, Gehazi, falsely using the name of his master, concocted a story whereby the grateful Naaman gave him silver and garments. Discovering this, Elisha cursed Gehazi and his descendants with the leprosy that had been Naaman's (II Kings 6:20–27).

550–53. Waller ran for all three Exclusion Parliaments. In the first election, he was defeated despite his tremendous popularity with the mob and expenditure (according to rumor) of £1,000 (*Fitzherbert Papers, HMC* 13th Report, vi, 13, dated 20 Feb. 1679). In his petition to the Parliament, Waller claimed that the bailiff had falsified

Thus ev'ry shift and subtle method pass'd,
And all to be no Zaken at the last.   555

Now, rais'd on Tyre's sad ruins, Pharaoh's pride
Soar'd high, his legions threat'ning far and wide.

---

the returns (*CJ, 9,* 571a, 20 March 1679), but before he could be heard, the King had dissolved the Parliament.

He stood again for Westminster in Sept. 1679 and again was declared defeated. "The reason was that many of the King's servants who came from Windsor were admitted to poll" (*CSPD,* 1679–80, p. 246; see also *CJ, 9,* 654a) and his arrest on 26 Feb. 1680 may indicate his increasing financial difficulties (*CSPD,* 1679–80, p. 399). Almost as soon as this much-prorogued Parliament sat, Waller again filed a petition (*CJ, 9,* 638a, 25 Oct. 1680), this time successfully, for he won his seat on 15 Nov. (ibid., p. 654a), was almost immediately presented (ibid., p. 655a), and was shortly serving on such important committees as that dealing with the impeachment of Seymour, and another delegated to get evidence against the lords in the Tower (ibid., pp. 664a–b, 26 and 27 Nov.).

On 10 Feb. 1681, Waller and Sir William Poultney stood virtually unopposed for Westminster, and L. S., writing *A Faithful Account . . . of the Election of Sir William Poultney and Sir William Waller* (1681) [S 108], significantly observes in conclusion that "in the whole management of this affair, the inhabitants did not put their designed representatives to the least expense; the people did not here sell their votes and souls for treats and wine, nor was there any here that would have purchased such votes if there had any been found to expose them to sale" (p. 4).

553. *saints.* The term applied to those sectarians that were said to consider themselves among the elect. Here, the reference would seem to be to those Whigs who financially backed Waller's first and second campaigns and who apparently were never paid back.

chous'd: Cheated, tricked; the word connotes absconding from fraudulently incurred debts (see Ben Jonson, *Works,* ed. Herford and Simpson, *10,* 61, *Alchemist,* I.ii.26 n.). According to Warcup's *Journal* for 15 May 1681 (*EHR, 40,* 254), Waller had previously fled to Holland, and so would have forced his creditors to compound. This would have occurred after his second campaign (Sept. 1679) and before he was seated (15 Nov. 1680), and there is confirmation in the report of an informer who found Waller in Utrecht in June 1680 (*CSPD,* 1680–81, p. 135).

On 9 May 1681, six weeks after the dissolution of the Oxford Parliament, he was again arrested for debt (Luttrell, *Brief Relation, 1,* 84) but received no help from his former Whig supporters who were angered by his remaining to testify at the Fitzharris trial and feared he might go over to the King (*EHR, 40,* 254).

555. *Zaken:* Biblically, an elder elected to the Sanhedrin (Godwin, *Moses and Aaron,* pp. 190–91); or, in historical terms, a member of parliament, which is how Tonson glosses the word. It cannot refer to a justice of the peace, as Noyes and Kinsley suggest, since that is an appointive and not an elective post; and certainly 550–55 deal with elections and unpaid debts. Clearly, then, the whole of the Arod portrait must have been written before Waller was ever seated as an M.P., when he had absconded to Holland to avoid the huge debts piled up in two apparently futile elections; in short, before 15 Nov. 1680. After that date, Commons not only made him a "zaken," they made him a very prominent one; and three months later, the "choosing tribes" of Westminster elected him "zaken" (along with Poultney) against almost no opposition.

556–67. The foreboding atmosphere here described would seem best to fit the period

As when a batt'ring storm engender'd high,
By winds upheld, hangs hov'ring in the sky,
Is gaz'd upon by ev'ry trembling swain,   560
This for his vineyard fears, and that his grain,
For blooming plants, and flow'rs new opening; these
For lambs ean'd lately, and far-lab'ring bees;
To guard his stock each to the gods does call,
Uncertain where the fire-charg'd clouds will fall: 565
E'en so the doubtful nations watch his arms,
With terror each expecting his alarms.
Where, Judah, where was now thy lion's roar?
Thou only couldst the captive lands restore;
But thou, with inbred broils and faction press'd,   570
From Egypt needst a guardian with the rest.
Thy prince from Sanhedrins no trust allow'd,
Too much the representers of the crowd,
Who for their own defense give no supply
But what the crown's prerogatives must buy;   575
As if their monarch's rights to violate
More needful were than to preserve the State!
From present dangers they divert their care,

---

between the Peace of Nijmwegen (1678) and the *réunion* (1681) which marked the renewal of Louis XIV's policy of expansion.

563. *ean'd:* born.

568–71. England's Spanish alliance as well as Charles' promises to William of support in case of an invasion of Flanders were put under strain when Louis violated the Treaty of Nijmwegen by taking Strasbourg and Casale in Sept. 1681. The pressure became even more intense when Luxembourg was invested in Nov. and besieged the following month.

> Charles was so harassed by the difficulty of honoring his private promises and his public commitments that he begged Barrillon [the French Ambassador] to extricate him: "You know what devils my members of parliament are," said the King; "for God's sake get me out of this fix, or I shall have to summon parliament." The appeal was not in vain; if Charles could not get money from parliament, he could get money from the threat to summon parliament (Ogg, *Charles II*, pp. 622–23).

It was largely Charles' pressure that caused Louis to raise the siege.

574–77. Possibly, these lines refer to the situation of 11–27 Nov. 1681 when Commons decided that supplies for the admittedly endangered garrison at Tangier should wait upon Charles' consent to an Exclusion Bill. (Ogg, *Charles II*, pp. 603, 605.) The reference, however, may be general, since the pattern was almost traditional. Noyes notes a similar idea in the Epilogue to *The Unhappy Favorite*, 8.

And all their fears are of the royal heir;
Whom now the reigning malice of his foes   580
Unjudg'd would sentence, and, ere crown'd, depose.
Religion the pretense, but their decree
To bar his reign, whate'er his faith shall be!
By Sanhedrins and clam'rous crowds thus press'd,
What passions rent the righteous David's breast!   585
Who knows not how t' oppose or to comply;
Unjust to grant, and dangerous to deny!
How near in this dark juncture Israel's fate,
Whose peace one sole expedient could create,
Which yet th' extremest virtue did require   590
E'en of that prince whose downfall they conspire!
His absence David does with tears advise,
T' appease their rage; undaunted he complies.
Thus he who, prodigal of blood and ease,
A royal life expos'd to winds and seas,   595
At once contending with the waves and fire
And heading danger in the wars of Tyre,
Inglorious now forsakes his native sand
And like an exile quits the promis'd land!
Our monarch scarce from pressing tears refrains,   600
And painfully his royal state maintains,
Who now embracing on th' extremest shore
Almost revokes what he enjoin'd before;
Concludes at last more trust to be allow'd

579–81. While the lines might apply to any one of the three Exclusion Parliaments (March–July 1679; Oct. 1679–Jan. 1681; 21–28 March 1681), the specific allusion would seem to be to the second Exclusion Bill which was read for the first time on 4 Nov. 1680. It "not only debarred James from the succession, but declared him guilty of high treason if he should exercise authority or return to England after 5 Nov. 1680." In opposing the Bill, Secretary Jenkins claimed that it "was contrary to natural justice because it condemned without conviction and without . . . defense; it was contrary to the principles of their religion, since it dispossessed a man of his right for no other reason than that he differed in point of faith" (Ogg, *Charles II*, p. 602).

592. *His absence:* York was "exiled" on three occasions during the exclusion crisis: first, from 4 March–2 Sept. 1679, when he lived in the Low Countries; secondly, 27 Oct. 1679–24 Feb. 1680, when he went to Scotland as High Commissioner; finally, from 21 Oct. 1680–4 March 1682, when, being forced to leave because Charles was about to summon a parliament, he returned to Scotland. According to 625–28, it is York's first "exile" that is being described.

594–97. James, as Lord High Admiral, had commanded the fleet in its victory over

To storms and seas than to the raging crowd!   605
Forbear, rash Muse, the parting scene to draw,
With silence charm'd as deep as theirs that saw!
Not only our attending nobles weep,
But hardy sailors swell with tears the deep!
The tide restrain'd her course, and, more amaz'd,   610
The twin stars on the royal brothers gaz'd:
While this sole fear——
Does trouble to our suff'ring hero bring,
Lest next the popular rage oppress the King!
Thus parting, each for th' other's danger griev'd,   615
The shore the King, and seas the Prince receiv'd.
Go, injur'd hero, while propitious gales,
Soft as thy consort's breath, inspire thy sails;
Well may she trust her beauties on a flood
Where thy triumphant fleets so oft have rode!   620
Safe on thy breast reclin'd, her rest be deep,
Rock'd like a Nereid by the waves asleep;
While happiest dreams her fancy entertain,
And to Elysian fields convert the main!
Go, injur'd hero, while the shores of Tyre   625
At thy approach so silent shall admire,
Who on thy thunder still their thoughts employ,
And greet thy landing with a trembling joy.

On heroes thus the prophet's fate is thrown,
Admir'd by ev'ry nation but their own;   630
Yet while our factious Jews his worth deny,
Their aching conscience gives their tongue the lie.
E'en in the worst of men the noblest parts
Confess him, and he triumphs in their hearts,
Whom to his king the best respects commend   635

Opdam at Lowestoft (1665) during the Second Dutch War, and over de Ruyter at
Sole Bay (1672) during the Third Dutch War. He resigned his post in 1673 as a result
of the Test Act, to which he refused to subscribe.
611. *twin stars:* Castor and Pollux.
618. *thy consort:* Mary of Modena (1658–1718) married James in 1673.
625–28. When James left England in March 1679, he went first to Antwerp, then
was briefly at The Hague before settling in Brussels.
629–30. Matthew 13:57.

Of subject, soldier, kinsman, prince, and friend;
All sacred names of most divine esteem,
And to perfection all sustain'd by him;
Wise, just, and constant, courtly without art,
Swift to discern and to reward desert;   640
No hour of his in fruitless ease destroy'd,
But on the noblest subjects still employ'd;
Whose steady soul ne'er learnt to separate
Between his monarch's int'rest and the state,
But heaps those blessings on the royal head,   645
Which he well knows must be on subjects shed.

On what pretense could then the vulgar rage
Against his worth, and native rights engage?
Religious fears their argument are made;
Religious fears his sacred rights invade!   650
Of future superstition they complain,
And Jebusitic worship in his reign.
With such alarms his foes the crowd deceive,
With dangers fright, which not themselves believe.

Since nothing can our sacred rites remove,   655
Whate'er the faith of the successor prove,
Our Jews their ark shall undisturb'd retain,
At least while their religion is their gain,
Who know by old experience Baal's commands
Not only claim'd their conscience, but their land.   660
They grutch God's tithes, how therefore shall they yield
An idol full possession of the field?
Grant such a prince enthron'd, we must confess
The people's suff'rings than that monarch's less;
Who must to hard conditions still be bound,   665

650. As Secretary Jenkins pointed out in his speech against the second Exclusion Bill on 4 Nov. 1680, "the kings of England held their right from God alone, and no power on earth could deprive them of it" (Ogg, *Charles II,* p. 602).

659. *Baal's:* Oliver Cromwell's.

661. *grutch:* A variant of "grudge," used in the sense of "begrudge," "be unwilling to give."

God's tithes: Quakers in particular suffered greatly for the witness that they early bore against tithing by the Church of England.

And for his quiet with the crowd compound.
Or should his thoughts to tyranny incline,
Where are the means to compass the design?
Our crown's revenues are too short a store,
And jealous Sanhedrins would give no more.   670

As vain our fears of Egypt's potent aid;
Not so has Pharaoh learn'd ambition's trade,
Nor ever with such measures can comply
As shock the common rules of policy.
None dread like him the growth of Israel's king,   675
And he alone sufficient aids can bring;
Who knows that prince to Egypt can give law,
That on our stubborn tribes his yoke could draw.
At such profound expense he has not stood,
Nor dy'd for this his hands so deep in blood;   680
Would ne'er through wrong and right his progress take,
Grudge his own rest and keep the world awake,
To fix a lawless prince on Judah's throne,
First to invade our rights and then his own;
His dear-gain'd conquests cheaply to despoil,   685
And reap the harvest of his crimes and toil.
We grant his wealth vast as our ocean's sand,
And curse its fatal influence on our land,
Which our brib'd Jews so num'rously partake

666. *compound:* To come to terms and pay for. The word was emotionally charged because of its use during the Interregnum, when Committees of Compound took over the holdings of royalists in lieu of the heavy fines that the government had imposed.

671. James' pro-French feelings were strengthened by his conversion to Roman Catholicism at some time prior to 1672; his marriage to Mary of Modena "finally bound [him] to the policy of Louis XIV" (*DNB*). When Thomas Pilkington, as M.P., proposed York's impeachment for high treason on 11 May 1679, the first and fourth of his seven charges dealt with the Duke's French sympathies and, though the impeachment was not carried out, the preamble to the first Exclusion Bill (15 May 1679) condemned James equally for his Catholicism and for having "advanced the power of the French king to the hazard of these kingdoms" (Ogg, *Charles II*, pp. 588–89 and n. 10).

689. *our brib'd Jews:* A number of the leaders of the anti-Court party in Commons received Louis XIV's bribes through Ruvigny early in 1678, even while Barrillon was bribing the Court. "The opposition, hitherto clamorous for war against Louis, now began to fear that the troops for which they voted might be turned against themselves, and accordingly some of them found it in their interest to act in accordance with French dictates" (Ogg, *Charles II*, p. 551).

That ev'n an host his pensioners would make.   690
From these deceivers our divisions spring,
Our weakness, and the growth of Egypt's king.
These with pretended friendship to the State
Our crowd's suspicion of their prince create;
Both pleas'd and frighten'd with the specious cry   695
To guard their sacred rights and property.
To ruin, thus, the chosen flock are sold,
While wolves are ta'en for guardians of the fold.
Seduc'd by these, we groundlessly complain,
And loathe the manna of a gentle reign.   700
Thus our forefathers' crooked paths are trod;
We trust our prince no more then they their God.
But all in vain our reasoning prophets preach
To those whom sad experience ne'er could teach;
Who can commence new broils in bleeding scars,   705
And fresh remembrance of intestine wars,
When the same household mortal foes did yield,
And brothers stain'd with brothers' blood the field;
When sons' curs'd steel the fathers' gore did stain,
And mothers mourn'd for sons by fathers slain!   710
When thick as Egypt's locusts on the sand,
Our tribes lay slaughter'd through the promis'd land,
Whose few survivors with worse fate remain
To drag the bondage of a tyrant's reign:
Which scene of woes, unknowing, we renew,   715
And madly e'en those ills we fear pursue;
While Pharaoh laughs at our domestic broils,
And safely crowds his tents with nations' spoils.
Yet our fierce Sanhedrin, in restless rage,
Against our absent hero still engage,   720
And chiefly urge (such did their frenzy prove)
The only suit their prince forbids to move,

700–02. See 6 and n.; 702 may refer to the murmuring Israelites upon whom God
rained manna (Exodus 16) or to their later idolatrous worship of the golden calf
(Exodus 32).

705. The religious and social strife of the Civil War was regularly recalled by Court
party writers of the 1680s. These lines recall particularly *I Henry IV*, I.i, 1–33.

714. *a tyrant's:* Oliver Cromwell's.

722. *The only suit:* The Exclusion Bill.

Which, till obtain'd, they cease affairs of state,
And real dangers waive for groundless hate.
Long David's patience waits relief to bring,   725
With all th' indulgence of a lawful king,
Expecting till the troubl'd waves would cease,
But found the raging billows still increase.
The crowd, whose insolence forbearance swells,
While he forgives too far, almost rebels.   730
At last his deep resentments silence broke;
Th' imperial palace shook, while thus he spoke:

"Then Justice wake, and Rigor take her time,
For lo! our mercy is become our crime.
While halting Punishment her stroke delays,   735
Our sov'reign right, Heav'n's sacred thrust, decays;
For whose support e'en subjects' interest calls—
Woe to that kingdom where the monarch falls!
That prince who yields the least of regal sway,
So far his people's freedom does betray.   740
Right lives by law, and law subsists by pow'r;
Disarm the shepherd, wolves the flock devour.
Hard lot of empire o'er a stubborn race,
Which Heav'n itself in vain has tri'd with grace!
When will our reason's long-charm'd eyes unclose,   745
And Israel judge between her friends and foes?
When shall we see expir'd deceivers' sway,
And credit what our God and monarchs say?
Dissembl'd patriots, brib'd with Egypt's gold,
Ev'n Sanhedrins in blind obedience hold;   750
Those patriots' falsehood in their actions see,
And judge by the pernicious fruit the tree.

727. *Expecting:* Waiting, deferring action.
743–44. Cf. *Absalom and Achitophel,* 45–46.
749. See 689 and n.
752. Parliament failed repeatedly in its attempts to assert its right of impeachment, most notably in the case of Danby (1675 and 1678–79). Though numerous impeachments were voted, Charles' countermoves prevented them from proceeding to trial in all instances save one, that of the aged Lord Stafford (one of the five Popish lords), who was found guilty and executed for complicity in the Popish Plot on the evidence of Oates and others in the closing weeks of 1680.

If aught for which so loudly they declaim,
Religion, laws, and freedom, were their aim,
Our senates in due methods they had led   755
T' avoid those mischiefs which they seem'd to dread;
But first ere yet they propp'd the sinking State,
T' impeach and charge, as urg'd by private hate,
Proves that they ne'er believ'd the fears they press'd,
But barb'rously destroy'd the nation's rest!   760
Oh! whither will ungovern'd senates drive,
And to what bounds licentious votes arrive?
When their injustice we are press'd to share,
The monarch urg'd t' exclude the lawful heir;
Are princes thus distinguish'd from the crowd,   765
And this the privilege of royal blood?
But grant we should confirm the wrongs they press,
His sufferings yet were than the people's less;
Condemn'd for life the murd'ring sword to wield,
And on their heirs entail a bloody field.   770
Thus madly their own freedom they betray,
And for th' oppression which they fear make way.
Succession fix'd by Heav'n, the kingdom's bar,
Which once dissolv'd, admits the flood of war;
Waste, rapine, spoil, without th' assault begin,   775
And our mad tribes supplant the fence within.
Since then their good they will not understand,
'Tis time to take the monarch's pow'r in hand;
Authority and force to join with skill,
And save the lunatics against their will.   780
The same rough means that swage the crowd, appease
Our senates raging with the crowd's disease.

762. *licentious:* Unrestricted by law, decorum, or morality.

769. The subject of "Condemn'd" would appear to be "peoples" in the preceding line.

770. Cf. 708.

773. *bar:* Though used here in the sense of a barrier controlling entrance, the word is given another meaning in 774 (a barrier of sand across a river or harbor), but returns to the first sense in 776.

775. *without:* From the outside.

776. *supplant the fence:* Uproot the defense or barrier.

780–83. Cf. *Absalom and Achitophel,* 787–89.

Henceforth unbias'd measures let 'em draw
From no false gloss, but genuine text of law;
Nor urge those crimes upon religion's score   785
Themselves so much in Jebusites abhor.
Whom laws convict (and only they) shall bleed,
Nor Pharisees by Pharisees be freed.
Impartial justice from our throne shall show'r,
All shall have right, and we our sov'reign pow'r."   790

He said; th' attendants heard with awful joy,
And glad presages their fix'd thoughts employ.
From Hebron now the suff'ring heir return'd,
A realm that long with civil discord mourn'd,
Till his approach, like some arriving god,   795
Compos'd and heal'd the place of his abode;
The deluge check'd that to Judea spread,
And stopp'd sedition at the fountain's head.
Thus, in forgiving David's paths he drives,
And chas'd from Israel, Israel's peace contrives.   800
The field confess'd his pow'r in arms before,
And seas proclaim'd his triumphs to the shore;
As nobly has his sway in Hebron shown
How fit t' inherit godlike David's throne.

785–86. While it had been long argued that the extreme left-wing sectaries were using the same tactics as the most zealous Jesuits, L'Estrange had most recently popularized the idea in his *Observator*, with the suggestion that both groups were working for similar ends.

788. *Pharisees:* Whigs. Here, the allusion is to the "Ignoramus" juries. See headnote to the Medal poems.

791–92. Cf. *Absalom and Achitophel*, 937–38 and 1026–27.

793. *Hebron:* Scotland. See 320 n. James, who had been named High Commissioner of Scotland in Sept. 1679, returned finally to England on 11 March 1682.

798. Generally, James continued the policies of Stuart consolidation that Lauderdale had pressed. In July 1681, he had presided over a meeting of the Scottish parliament which passed a test act of such complexity that Argyle subscribed to it "in so far as it was consistent with itself and the Protestant faith." This gave James the excuse for imprisoning and sentencing to death (23 Dec.) the Whig leader on charges of treason, though the Earl soon escaped to Holland (Ogg, *Charles II*, p. 631).

799. Prior to the July 1681 Parliament James "adopted the conciliatory tone sanctioned by the King" in both political and religious affairs (*DNB*).

801–02. In the field, James had achieved fame under Turenne (1652–55) and with the Spanish forces in Flanders (1657–58); on the sea, he had won the battles of Lowestoft (1665) and Sole Bay (1672) in the Dutch Wars.

Through Sion's streets his glad arrival 's spread,   805
And conscious Faction shrinks her snaky head;
His train their suff'rings think o'erpaid to see
The crowd's applause with virtue once agree.

Success charms all, but zeal for worth distress'd,
A virtue proper to the brave and best;   810
'Mongst whom was Jothran, Jothran always bent
To serve the crown, and loyal by descent;
Whose constancy so firm, and conduct just,
Deserv'd at once two royal masters' trust;
Who Tyre's proud arms had manfully withstood   815
On seas, and gather'd laurels from the flood;
Of learning yet no portion was deni'd,
Friend to the Muses, and the Muses' pride.

Nor can Benaiah's worth forgotten lie,
Of steady soul when public storms were high;   820

805. On 8 April 1682, the King and Duke arrived in London from Newmarket and
"were waited on by most of the nobility in town, and at night was ringing of bells,
bonfires, etc." (Luttrell, *Brief Relation, 1*, 177). L'Estrange (*Observator*, No. 122 [12
April 1682]) also reports the celebrations, admitting, rather reluctantly, that "To give
the devil his due, the Whigs where I was were pretty quiet, so long as the fire was
blazing."

811. *Jothran:* While there are several Jothams in the Bible (Judges 9; II Kings 15,
and II Chronicles 27; I Chronicles 2:7) and while Dryden uses the name for Halifax
in *Absalom and Achitophel* (probably alluding to Judges 9), there is no Jothran.

Historically, Jothran has generally been identified as George Legge (1648–91), the
son of the ardent royalist colonel William Legge, who had been educated at West-
minster and King's College, Cambridge, and, between the ages of 17 and 25, had
served with such distinction in the Dutch Wars that he rose from lieutenant to com-
mander of the *Royal Katherine*. In 1668, he joined York's household, and by 1683 was
known as one of the Duke's favorites (Evelyn, *Diary, 4*, 314). At the same time, he had
been serving Charles in a number of posts, culminating, on 28 Jan. 1682, in his ap-
pointment as master-general of the Ordnance. On 2 Dec. 1682, he was created Baron of
Dartmouth, and in Aug. of the following year, as admiral of a fleet and governor of
Tangier, was sent to Africa to evacuate and raze that town. (See *The Tangiers Ballad*.)

Luttrell identified Jothran as Prince Rupert in his copy of the poem, probably on
the basis of 814, which he would have taken to refer to Charles I and Charles II. This
is the natural association, but the proximity of York and Legge, both in the text and
in history, would seem to militate against it.

819. *Benaiah:* Biblically (II Samuel 23:20–23; I Chronicles 11:22–25), "the son of a
valiant man" who, having demonstrated his personal courage, was "set by David . . .
over his bodyguard, . . . occupying a middle rank between the first three of the

Whose conduct, while the Moor fierce onsets made,
Secur'd at once our honor and our trade.

Such were the chiefs who most his suff'rings mourn'd,
And view'd with silent joy the prince return'd;
While those that sought his absence to betray,   825
Press first their nauseous false respects to pay:
Him still th' officious hypocrites molest,
And with malicious duty break his rest.

While real transports thus his friends employ,
And foes are loud in their dissembl'd joy,   830
His triumphs, so resounded far and near,

Giborim or 'mighty men' and the thirty valiant men of the armies" (*A Dictionary of the Bible, 1,* 185).

Historically, Colonel Edward Sackville, "who had served at Tangier with great reputation, both for courage and judgment," was a "particular friend of the Duke of York" (S.-S., *Dryden, 9,* 380). As M.P. in the first Exclusion Parliament, he was accused in Commons by Oates and Tonge of complicity in the Popish Plot, "which raised a new flame in that place" (Echard, *History,* p. 970). Four days later (25 March 1679), Oates again appeared in the House,

> declaring he [Sackville] said, "they were sons of whores who said there was a plot and that he was a lying rogue that said it." Whereupon the Colonel was immediately sent to the Tower and ordered to be expelled the House, with a petition to the King to be made incapable of having any office. But, in a short time, upon his submission, he was discharged from his imprisonment but not restored to his seat in the House (ibid., p. 971).

By the end of 1680, Sackville, as commander-in-chief of the Tangier garrison, had arranged for a six months' truce with the Moors and for a Moorish embassy to London (Luttrell, *Brief Relation, 1,* 60–61). By Aug. 1681, he was acting as governor, in place of Sir Palmes Fairborne who had been killed there; his commission was given on 4 Sept. and two months later, he was preparing to depart for London to present himself (ibid., *1,* 110, 123, 141).

Luttrell first identified Benaiah as the Marquis of Worcester (Henry Somerset) then, realizing the inapplicability and finding that Bezaleel (94) very likely referred to Worcester, he replaced it with the equally questionable gloss: "Duke of Ormond."

823–31. A similar description is given in 14–25 of the *Prologue to His Royal Highness* (Macdonald, No. 98), which Dryden wrote for York's "first appearance at the Duke's Theater since his return from Scotland," on 21 April 1682, when Otway's *Venice Preserved* was performed.

825–26. Luttrell's gloss reads "Earl of Anglesey," and his entry for 10 April 1682 explains his identification of Arthur Annesley (1614–86), who was "of Presbyterian inclination and a friend of Monmouth's" (Kinsley, p. 1929): "The Earl of Anglesey went to wait on His Royal Highness but met with a cold reception and was denied to

Miss'd not his young ambitious rival's ear.
And as when joyful hunters' clam'rous train
Some slumb'ring lion wakes in Moab's plain,
Who oft had forc'd the bold assailants yield   835
And scatter'd his pursuers through the field,
Disdaining, furls his mane and tears the ground,
His eyes enflaming all the desert round,
With roar of seas directs his chasers' way,
Provokes from far, and dares them to the fray;   840
Such rage storm'd now in Absalom's fierce breast:
Such indignation his fir'd eyes confess'd.
Where now was the instructor of his pride?
Slept the old pilot in so rough a tide,
Whose wiles had from the happy shore betray'd,   845
And thus on shelves the cred'lous youth convey'd?
In deep revolving thoughts he weighs his state,
Secure of craft, nor doubts to baffle fate;
At least, if his storm'd bark must go adrift,
To balk his charge, and for himself to shift,   850
In which his dext'rous wit had oft been shown,
And in the wreck of kingdoms sav'd his own;
But now with more than common danger press'd,
Of various resolutions stands possess'd,
Perceives the crowd's unstable zeal decay,   855
Lest their recanting chief the cause betray,

---

kiss his hand, he having been for the bill in parliament against his succession to the crown" (*Brief Relation, 1,* 177).

831. L'Estrange's account of York's welcome to London on Saturday, 8 April 1682, is given in *Observator,* No. 121 (10 April 1682). Care's indirect but daring comments may be found in the Courant section of the *Weekly Pacquet* for 14 and 21 April 1682. Luttrell's comments (*Brief Relation, 1,* 177) show his usual objectivity and moderation.

832. *his . . . rival's:* i.e. Monmouth's.

833-40. The simile would seem to echo *Absalom and Achitophel,* 447-52, but cf. also *Annus Mirabilis,* 381-88, which derives from Virgil, *Aeneid,* IX, 397-98, translated by Dryden as IX, 1072-77. The reference to "Moab's plain" (834) may come from Numbers 22:1, the Balaam story, which twice (23:24; 24:9) uses the simile of the lion for Israel.

843. Cf. *Absalom and Achitophel,* 971.

844-46. Cf. *Absalom and Achitophel,* 159-62.

847. *he:* i.e. Shaftesbury.

855-56. This may possibly be an allusion to Monmouth's attempt to secure a reconciliation with his father in May 1682. See J. R. Jones, *The First Whigs* (Oxford, 1961), p. 197.

Who on a father's grace his hopes may ground,
And for his pardon with their heads compound.
Him therefore, ere his Fortune slip her time,
The statesman plots t'engage in some bold crime   860
Past pardon: whether to attempt his bed,
Or threat with open arms the royal head,
Or other daring method, and unjust,
That may confirm him in the people's trust.
But failing thus t' ensnare him, nor secure   865
How long his foil'd ambition may endure,
Plots next to lay him by, as past his date,
And try some new pretender's luckier fate;
Whose hopes with equal toil he would pursue,
Nor cares what claimer's crown'd, except the true.   870
Wake, Absalom, approaching ruin shun,
And see, Oh see, for whom thou art undone!
How are thy honors and thy fame betray'd,
The property of desp'rate villains made!
Lost pow'r and conscious fears their crimes create,   875
And guilt in them was little less than fate;
But why shouldst thou, from ev'ry grievance free,
Forsake thy vineyards for their stormy sea?
For thee did Canaan's milk and honey flow;
Love dress'd thy bow'rs, and laurels sought thy brow;   880
Preferment, wealth, and pow'r thy vassals were,

861. *to attempt his bed:* While there may be no specific reference here, in Nov. 1679, after Monmouth made his unauthorized return to England, he "paid assiduous court to Nell Gwyn, the staunchest supporter of Protestantism in the inner circles of Charles' court" (Ogg, *Charles II,* p. 645); see also Allen Fea, *King Monmouth* (London, 1902), p. 82.

862. Again, although this may be general, it would seem to allude to Monmouth's "western progress" of autumn 1680, which Dryden aptly described:

Thus in a pageant show a plot is made,
And peace itself is war in masquerade.
    (*Absalom and Achitophel,* 751–52)

It is interesting that there is no reference here to his far more aggressive second progress just two years later which ended with his return to London on 23 Sept. under arrest for riot and breaking the peace.

868. Quite possibly, William of Orange. See Jones, *The First Whigs,* pp. 129–30, 136–37, 194–96.

And of a monarch all things but the care.
Oh, should our crimes again that curse draw down,
And rebel arms once more attempt the crown,
Sure ruin waits unhappy Absalon,   885
Alike by conquest or defeat undone!
Who could relentless see such youth and charms
Expire with wretched fate in impious arms:
A prince so form'd, with earth's and heav'n's applause,
To triumph o'er crown'd heads in David's cause?   890
Or, grant him victor, still his hopes must fail,
Who, conquering, would not for himself prevail.
The faction, whom he trusts for future sway,
Him and the public would alike betray;
Amongst themselves divide the captive State,   895
And found their hydra-empire in his fate!
Thus having beat the clouds with painful flight,
The piti'd youth, with scepters in his sight
(So have their cruel politics decreed)
Must by that crew that made him guilty, bleed!   900
For, could their pride brook any prince's sway,
Whom but mild David would they choose t' obey?
Who once at such a gentle reign repine,
The fall of monarchy itself design;
From hate to that their reformations spring,   905
And David not their grievance, but the king.
Seiz'd now with panic fear the faction lies
Lest this clear truth strike Absalom's charm'd eyes;
Lest he perceive, from long enchantment free,
What all beside the flatter'd youth must see.   910
But whate'er doubts his troubl'd bosom swell,
Fair carriage still became Achitophel;
Who now an envious festival installs,

891–906. Noyes suggests that "these lines are evidently inspired by a passage in *The Medal* . . . 287–317."

903. *who:* Those who, i.e. the republicans of "the faction."

905. *that:* i.e. monarchy.

906. Cf. *Absalom and Achitophel,* 512.

913. *envious festival:* The Whig Feast, scheduled to take place on 21 April 1682, was meant to outshine the Tories' Artillery Company Feast of the previous day to which York was formally invited. See the headnote to "Poems on the Whig Feast."

And to survey their strength the faction calls,
Which fraud, religious worship too must gild—   915
But oh how weakly does sedition build!
For lo! the royal mandate issues forth,
Dashing at once their treason, zeal, and mirth!
So have I seen disastrous chance invade
Where careful emmets had their forage laid;   920
Whether fierce Vulcan's rage the furzy plain
Had seiz'd, engender'd by some careless swain;
Or swelling Neptune lawless inroads made,
And to their cell of store his flood convey'd;
The commonwealth broke up, distracted go,   925
And in wild haste their loaded mates o'erthrow:
Ev'n so our scatter'd guests confus'dly meet
With boil'd, bak'd, roast, all jostling in the street;
Dejected all, and ruefully dismay'd,
For *shekel* without treat or treason paid.   930

Sedition's dark eclipse now fainter shows;
More bright each hour the royal planet grows,
Of force the clouds of envy to disperse,
In kind conjunction of assisting stars.

914. *survey their strength:* The invitations were "by tickets of which any man might have one for a guinea" (Luttrell, *Brief Relation, 1,* 179). Probably between 300 and 800 tickets were sold and, while Janeway's estimate "that there would have been near 1,000" (*Impartial Protestant Mercury,* No. 104 [18–21 April 1682]) is high, the Whigs would undoubtedly have had the larger gathering.

915. According to the ticket, the feast was one of thanksgiving, "it having pleased Almighty God by His wonderful providence to deliver and protect his majesty's person, the Protestant religion, and English liberties (hitherto) from the hellish and frequent attempts of their enemies (the Papists)" (quoted in Luttrell, *Brief Relation, 1,* 179). The feast was to be preceded by a sermon at St. Michael's in Cornhill; L'Estrange suggests that "the lessons for that day were the story of Absalom and Achitophel" (*Observator,* No. 129 [27 April 1682]), but the actual text would seem to have been the provocative "Curse ye Meroz" (see *Absalom Senior,* 139 n.).

917. On 19 April, Charles' order in Council prohibited the Whig Feast as a "manifest derogation of his right" to name days of public thanksgiving, and as "tending to raise destructions and confederacies."

920. *emmets:* ants.

921. Cf. Dryden's translation of the *Aeneid* II, 960–61.

925–31. A similar view is given in the poems on the Whig Feast and *The Loyal Feast* [L 3346] (quoted in part by Scott-Saintsbury, *9,* 386); also see Otway's Prologue to Aphra Behn's *The City Heiress.*

Here, lab'ring Muse, those glorious chiefs relate   935
That turn'd the doubtful scale of David's fate;
The rest of that illustrious band rehearse,
Immortaliz'd in laurel'd Asaph's verse.
Hard task! yet will not I thy flight recall;
View heav'n, and then enjoy thy glorious fall.   940

First write Bezaleel, whose illustrious name
Forestalls our praise, and gives his poet fame.
The Kenites' rocky province his command,
A barren limb of fertile Canaan's land;
Which for its gen'rous natives yet could be   945
Held worthy such a president as he!
Bezaleel with each grace and virtue fraught;
Serene his looks, serene his life and thought;
On whom so largely Nature heap'd her store,
There scarce remain'd for arts to give him more!   950

935. Cf. *Absalom and Achitophel*, 898.

938. *laurel'd Asaph:* Biblically, chief of those "whom David set over the service of song." Asaph was considered David's equal in songs of praise and prophecy (II Chronicles 29:30; Nehemiah 12:46), a seer who could "prophesy with harps, with psalteries, and with cymbals" (I Chronicles 25:1–2). When the ark was brought in to David's tent, Asaph headed those whose office it was "to record, and to thank and praise the Lord"; it was into his hands that David delivered his psalm of thanksgiving (I Chronicles 16:4–7).

Historically, Dryden, who had been Charles' poet laureate since 1668. The stories reported by Tonson (that Dryden undertook *Absalom and Achitophel* at the behest of Charles) and by Pope ("that King Charles obliged Dryden to put his Oxford speech into verse and to insert it toward the close of his *Absalom and Achitophel*") may be fortuitous analogues to I Chronicles 16:4–7.

941. *Bezaleel:* Biblically, "the artificer to whom was confided by Jehovah the design and execution of the works of art required for the tabernacle in the wilderness (Exodus 31:1–6). His charge was chiefly in all works of metal, wood, and stone" (*A Dictionary of the Bible, I,* 208).

Historically, Henry Somerset (1629–1700), first styled Lord Herbert, then third Marquis of Worcester (from 1667), and (from Dec. 1682) first Earl of Beaufort. He was created Lord President of the Council of Wales and the Marches (i.e. "the Kenites rocky provinces," 943). Somerset's "tabernacle in the wilderness" was Badminton, an estate he had acquired in 1653 at which he entertained the King and Queen ten years later. The "patriarchal life" there (to use Kinsley's apt phrase) was incisively described by Francis North following his visit in 1680 (North, "Life of the Lord Keeper Guilford," in *Lives, I,* 271–77; reprinted in full in Scott-Saintsbury, *9,* 388–91). In 1682, Somerset built the present mansion in Palladian style on the site of the old manor house.

To aid the Crown and State his greatest zeal,
His second care that service to conceal;
Of dues observant, firm in ev'ry trust,
And to the needy always more than just;
Who truth from specious falsehood can divide,   955
Has all the gownmen's skill without their pride.
Thus crown'd with worth from heights of honor won,
Sees all his glories copi'd in his son,
Whose forward fame should every Muse engage,
Whose youth boasts skill deni'd to others' age: 960
Men, manners, language, books of noblest kind,
Already are the conquest of his mind;
Whose loyalty before its date was prime,
Nor waited the dull course of rolling time:
The monster *Faction* early he dismay'd,   965
And David's cause long since confess'd his aid.

951. Somerset's "zeal" led him to oppose the Exclusion Bill with such vehemence that in 1680 the House charged him (along with Halifax and Clarendon) of Catholic sympathies (Burnet, *History, 1,* 484). Later, he took an active part in the Quo Warranto proceedings against municipal charters and in the suppression of conventicles in the counties under his control (Ogg, *Charles II,* pp. 635, 639).

956. *gownmen's:* Lawyers, barristers, or judges.

958. *his son:* Charles Somerset (1660 or 1661–98), eldest surviving son of Henry Somerset, styled Lord Herbert (1667–82) and then Marquis of Worcester. Though it is not mentioned here, he was married in early June 1682 to Rebecca, the daughter of Sir Josiah Childs, who gave a dowry rumored to be between £25,000 (Luttrell, *Brief Relation, 1,* 192) and £30,000 (Evelyn, *Diary, 4,* 306).

962–66. Charles Somerset was fully involved in his father's attempt to control the area. In 1679, as a former knight of the shire, he tried unsuccessfully to stand for Monmouthshire in the elections for the second Exclusion Parliament. Gentry opposition, however, forced him to stand for Monmouth town, but even then, the strongly Whig Committee of Elections in Parliament displaced him. (See Jones, *The First Whigs,* pp. 101–02). Another instance of the cooperation of the two men can be found in their suppression of nonconformists in their region; it was so effective that the son could write Secretary Jenkins on 14 Jan. 1682 that "soon not a single Dissenter would be heard of in . . . Somerset" (Ogg, *Charles II,* p. 639, and *CSPD,* 1682, pp. 24–25).

967. *Abdael:* Biblically, "the son of Guni, chief of the house of their fathers" (I Chronicles 5:15). Historically, the undistinguished Christopher Monck (1653–88), second Duke of Albemarle, who succeeded to the title in 1670 upon the death of his father, the famous general whose efforts were the immediate cause for the peaceful restoration of the monarchy (969–71).

Albemarle, who had succeeded Monmouth as captain of the Life Guards at the end of Oct. 1679 (Luttrell, *Brief Relation, 1,* 27), was chosen chancellor of Cambridge ("the prophets' school") on 8 April 1682 (ibid., 177), displacing Monmouth who had held the position since 1674. With fitting pomp, the new chancellor was installed on

Brave Abdael o'er the prophets' school was plac'd;
Abdael, with all his father's virtue grac'd;
A hero who, while stars look'd wond'ring down,
Without one Hebrew's blood, restor'd the crown.   970
That praise was his; what therefore did remain
For following chiefs but boldly to maintain
That crown restor'd? and in this rank of fame,
Brave Abdael with the first a place must claim.
Proceed, illustrious, happy chief, proceed;   975
Foreseize the garlands for thy brow decreed;
While th' inspir'd tribe attend with noblest strain
To register the glories thou shalt gain:
For sure the dew shall Gilboah's hills forsake,
And Jordan mix his stream with Sodom's lake,   980
Or seas retir'd their secret stores disclose
And to the sun their scaly brood expose,
Or swell'd above the clifts their billows raise,
Before the Muses leave their patron's praise.

Eliab our next labor does invite,   985
And hard the task to do Eliab right.
Long with the royal wanderer he rov'd,
And firm in all the turns of fortune prov'd!
Such ancient service and desert so large,

---

11 May 1682 at London (ibid., 184). Lines 977–78 may refer to the future "glories"
set forth on this occasion in *A Panegyric on His Grace the Duke of Albemarle* [P 259].

979. Cf. II Samuel 1:21, David's lament for Saul and Jonathan: "Ye mountains of
Gilboa, let there be no dew."

985. *Eliab:* Among the numerous Eliabs in the Bible, the most likely seems to be
the briefly mentioned Gadite leader (1 Chronicles 12:1, 8–9) who came to David
(Charles) while he was in the wilderness (exile) because of Saul (Cromwell). There
may, however, be some conflation with David's oldest brother (I Chronicles 2:13; I
Samuel 16:6), though, aside from the implied compliment of consanguinity and the
mention of the marriage of a daughter (II Chronicles 11:18), the references (I Samuel
17:13, 28) would seem neither flattering nor applicable.

Historically, Henry Bennet (1618-85), first Earl of Arlington:

> Sir Henry Bennet was the constant attendant of Charles II during his exile:
> after the Restoration, he became a member of the Cabal administration, and
> secretary of state. He was finally lord chamberlain [from 1674, see 990], and
> through many turns of politics retained the favor of Charles II. (S.-S., *Dryden, 9,*
> 394)

For a description of Arlington in his later years, see Evelyn, *Diary,* passim, but espe-
cially *4,* 116–20.

Well claim'd the royal household for his charge.   990
His age with only one mild heiress bless'd,
In all the bloom of smiling nature dress'd,
And bless'd again to see his flow'r alli'd
To David's stock, and made young Othniel's bride!
The bright restorer of his father's youth,   995
Devoted to a son's and subject's truth:
Resolv'd to bear that prize of duty home,
So bravely sought (while sought) by Absalom.
Ah prince! th' illustrious planet of thy birth
And thy more powerful virtue guard thy worth,   1000
That no Achitophel thy ruin boast.
Israel too much in one such wreck has lost.

991–92. Isabella Bennet (c. 1667–1723) completely captivated Evelyn, who described her at five as "a sweet child if ever there were any," at ten as "that wise and charming young creature" who was "worthy for her beauty and virtue of the greatest prince in Christendom" (phrases which he embellished two years later), and at sixteen (after her first child) as "more beautiful (if it were possible) than before" (*Diary*, *3*, 622; *4*, 117, 119, 184, 451).

993–94. On 1 Aug. 1672, Isabella (then age five) was married to Henry Fitzroy (then age nine), the natural son of the King by "that infamous adultress" (Evelyn, *Diary*, *4*, 97), Barbara Villiers, Duchess of Cleveland. There was a remarriage on 6 Nov. 1679, when Isabella was twelve (ibid., pp. 184–85), but it was not until April 1681 that "the espousals were . . . completed by the Duke's bedding her, she being now fourteen years old" (Luttrell, *Brief Relation*, *1*, 77).

The match, as the Countess of Arlington told Evelyn (*Diary*, *4*, 184), was carried out because "the King would have it so and there was no going back." Neither side considered itself "bless'd." Evelyn's indignation reflects the Bennets' feeling; the Duchess of Cleveland tried to prevent the match (S.-S., *Dryden*, *9*, 395) in favor of an alliance with the heiress of the wealthy Northumberlands or with one of the natural daughters of Louis XIV (Evelyn, *Diary*, *4*, 184, n. 5).

994. *Othniel:* Biblically, the younger brother of Caleb. When Joshua honored Caleb's claim to Hebron, Caleb, in order to control the region, offered his daughter to whoever would capture the city of Dehir (Joshua 15:13–19). Othniel succeeded "and received with his wife in addition to her previous dowry the upper and nether springs in the immediate neighborhood" (*A Dictionary of the Bible*, *2*, 651).

Historically, Henry Fitzroy (1663–90), made Earl of Euston (1672) and then first Duke of Grafton (1675). He, observed Evelyn, "affects the sea, to which I find his father intends to use him; he may emerge a plain, useful, robust officer; and were he polished, a tolerable person, for he is exceedingly handsome, by far surpassing any of the King's other natural issue" (*Diary*, *4*, 185). Scott (S.-S., *Dryden*, *9*, 396) suggests that Charles "endeavored to set Grafton, though inferior in all personal accomplishments, in opposition to [Monmouth] in the hearts of the people." While Grafton undoubtedly received certain honors (see Luttrell, *Brief Relation*, *1*, 69, 149, 151, and S.-S., *Dryden*, *9*, 395), Scott's oft-repeated phrase seems a bit too strong. Charles set forth only one real counterbalance to Monmouth, the Duke of York.

E'en envy must consent to Helon's worth,
Whose soul (though Egypt glories in his birth)
Could for our captive ark its zeal retain,   1005
And Pharaoh's altars in their pomp disdain.
To slight his gods was small; with nobler pride,
He all th' allurements of his court defi'd:
Whom profit nor example could betray,
But Israel's friend, and true to David's sway.   1010
What acts of favor in his province fall,
On merit he confers, and freely all.

Our list of nobles next let Amri grace,
Whose merits claim'd the Abbethdin's high place;

1003. *Helon:* Biblically, the father of Eliab (Numbers 1:9; 2:7; 7:24, 29; 10:16). The choice is remarkably inept.

Historically, Louis de Duras (c. 1638–1709), who was born in France (Egypt, 1004) of a Huguenot family (1005). He was the "brother of the French marshals Duras and De Lorge, a nephew to the famous Marshal Turenne . . . and retained his religion, or the form of it, when both his brothers [perhaps the "example" of 1009] conformed to the Catholic church" (S.-S., *Dryden, 9,* 396). When he became naturalized in 1665, he sacrificed his position as Marquis de Blanquefort (perhaps the "profit" of 1009), but soon attached himself to York as colonel of the Duke's guards (1667). He was created Baron Duras of Holdenlig in 1673 and four years later succeeded his father-in-law as second Earl of Feversham. "The Duke of York's opportune return from Flanders [in 1679] is said by Sir John Reresby [*Memoirs,* p. 187] to have been planned by this nobleman; who is, therefore, introduced here with singular propriety" (ibid.).

1006. *Pharaoh's:* Louis XIV's. In the following two lines, *his* refers to the French monarch.

1013. *Amri:* Possibly Omri. Of the four men of this name, the best-known (I Kings 16:16–30) is certainly the least applicable. The remaining three (I Chronicles 7:8; 9:4; 27:18) are merely names in genealogies, though perhaps the last, who was chief of the tribe of Issachar in the reign of David, would have some relevance.

Historically, Heneage Finch (1621–82), first Earl of Nottingham, Solicitor General (1660), Attorney General (1670), and Shaftesbury's successor as Lord Keeper (1673) and Lord Chancellor (1675–82) (Kinsley, p. 1931). His contemporary reputation was very high and even Burnet refers to him as "a man of probity, and well versed in the laws. . . . He was an incorrupt judge and in his court he could resist the strongest applications even from the King himself, though he did it nowhere else" (*History, 2,* 42–43). In addition to sitting on almost every major case from 1660, "as a law reformer . . . he must hold the highest place, since to him we owe the most important and most useful act of the reign—the Statute of Frauds" (Foss, *Biographical Dictionary of the Judges of England* [London, 1870], p. 253). Finch's eloquence was famous; he was "the silver tongu'd lawyer," "the English Cicero" and Pepys, Evelyn, and Burnet all mention his persuasive powers (see ibid., p. 252).

1014. *Abbethdin:* E. S. de Beer ("Absalom and Achitophel: Literary and Historical Notes," *Review of English Studies,* 27 [1941], 298–309) notes that Dryden, who used

Who, with a loyalty that did excel,   1015
Brought all th' endowments of Achitophel.
Sincere was Amri, and not only knew,
But Israel's sanctions into practice drew;
Our laws, that did a boundless ocean seem,
Were coasted all, and fathom'd all by him.   1020
No rabbin speaks like him their mystic sense,
So just, and with such charms of eloquence:
To whom the double blessing does belong,
With Moses' inspiration, Aaron's tongue.

Than Sheva none more loyal zeal have shown,   1025
Wakeful as Judah's lion for the crown;
Who for that cause still combats in his age,
For which his youth with danger did engage.
In vain our factious priests the cant revive;
In vain seditious scribes with libel strive   1030
T' enflame the crowd, while he with watchful eye

---

the term in *Absalom and Achitophel,* 188, very probably acquired it from Thomas
Godwin's *Moses and Aaron,* "a general companion to the Bible first published in
1625" (p. 303, n. 1) which appeared for the thirteenth time by 1678 (STC 11951–5;
[G 976–83]), frequently bound with *Romanae Historiae Anthologia* or Francis Rous'
Archealogia Attica or both. Godwin states that "in the civil consistories, consisting of
seventy judges, . . . [the] Abbethdin [was termed] the Father of the Senate" (ibid.)
or "house of judgment. See the Jewish Encyclopedia under *bet din*" (Noyes' note to
Absalom and Achitophel, 188).

1020. *coasted:* Traversed all parts of, explored, scanned, marked out.

1025. *Sheva:* Biblically, the scribe or royal secretary to David (II Samuel 20:25).
Historically, Roger L'Estrange (1616–1704), the principal Tory pamphleteer and
journalist. During the Civil War, he fought for Charles I, was imprisoned, went into
exile, and finally (1653) returned to England. From 1659, he began writing prolifically,
in hopes of helping to restore the monarchy. His pen, therefore, rarely rested. In
1663 he became "surveyor of the inprimery," had the power to license books and the
sole right to publish a newspaper. His rigorous censorship was aimed especially at
the sectarians (1029) and Whigs (1030–31) who dissented from, or opposed, Court
policy. During the heat of the Popish Plot, he wrote against the witnesses and, during
1681, was forced to leave England. Upon his return, he began his major work, *The
Observator,* which ran from 13 April 1681 to 9 March 1687. The principal grist for
his mill were the Whig newspapers (1033), pamphlets, and poems, which he pulver-
ized with remarkable effectiveness.

1026. "Among the Hebrews, and throughout the Old Testament, the lion was the
achievement of the princely tribe of Judah" (*A Dictionary of the Bible, 1,* 1667; cf.
Genesis 49:8–10). There may also be a reference to the lion on the royal arms.

Observes, and shoots their treasons as they fly.
Their weekly frauds his keen replies detect;
He undeceives more fast than they infect.
So Moses, when the pest on legions prey'd,   1035
Advanc'd his signal, and the plague was stay'd.

Once more, my fainting Muse, thy pinions try,
And strength's exhausted store let love supply.
What tribute, Asaph, shall we render thee?
We'll crown thee with a wreath from thy own tree!   1040
Thy laurel grove no envy's flash can blast;
The song of Asaph shall for ever last!
With wonder, late posterity shall dwell
On Absalom and false Achitophel:
Thy strains shall be our slumb'ring prophets' dream;   1045
And, when our Sion virgins sing, their theme.
Our jubilees shall with thy verse be grac'd;
The song of Asaph shall for ever last!
How fierce his satire loos'd; restrain'd, how tame;
How tender of th' offending young man's fame!   1050
How well his worth, and brave adventures styl'd;
Just to his virtues, to his error mild.
No page of thine that fears the strictest view,
But teems with just reproof, or praise, as due;
Not Eden could a fairer prospect yield,   1055
All paradise without one barren field:
Whose wit the censure of his foes has pass'd;

1032. *Observes:* An allusion to L'Estrange's periodical, *The Observator.*

shoots . . . fly: Cf. Dryden, *Aureng Zebe*, III.i ("Youth should shoot . . . [joys] as they fly") and Pope, *Essay on Man*, 13 ("shoot folly as it flies").

1033. *weekly frauds:* The reference is very likely to the two Whig weeklies, Richard Janeway's *True Protestant Mercury* and Henry Care's *Weekly Pacquet of Advice from Rome.*

1035–36. For the ten plagues of Egypt, see Exodus 5–12.

1041. "The thunder was anciently supposed to spare the laurel" (Scott-Saintsbury, 9, 401).

1042. This theme (repeated at 1048, 1058, 1064) and the passage as a whole (especially 1059–64) are strongly reminiscent of the passage on Asaph in the conclusion of *Old England* (404–11), a poem herein ascribed to Tate (pp. 183–84).

1046. *Sion:* Synonymous with Jerusalem. *Sion's rock* (1063) is "one of the various names of Mount Hermon" (*A Dictionary of the Bible, 4,* 3055).

1050. See *Absalom and Achitophel,* "To the Reader," 32–46 (Kinsley).

The song of Asaph shall for ever last!
What praise for such rich strains shall we allow?
What just rewards the grateful crown bestow?   1060
While bees in flow'rs rejoice, and flow'rs in dew,
While stars and fountains to their course are true,
While Judah's throne and Sion's rock stand fast,
The song of Asaph and the fame shall last.

Still Hebron's honor'd happy soil retains   1065
Our royal hero's beauteous dear remains;
Who now sails off, with winds nor wishes slack,
To bring his suff'rings' bright companion back.
But ere such transport can our sense employ,
A bitter grief must poison half our joy;   1070
Nor can our coasts restor'd those blessings see
Without a bribe to envious destiny!
Curs'd Sodom's doom for ever fix the tide
Where by inglorious chance the valiant di'd!

1065. *Hebron's:* Biblically, the city where David established the seat of his government during his reign over Judah (II Samuel 5:5). Historically, Edinburgh, or Scotland in general. See 320 n.

1066. *remains:* i.e. the remaining member of a family; here, Mary, Duchess of York. This use of the plural noun for a singular subject is unusual.

1066–1102. On 3 May, York, ending his final "exile," set off for Scotland in order to bring back the Duchess. On the following day, he boarded the frigate "Gloucester" which, early on the morning of the 6th, struck the Lemon and Oar Sands and split. Accounts of what happened thereafter vary with the writer's political bias (for a Whig interpretation, see *Midsummer Moon,* 33–36). J. S. Clarke (*The Life of James the Second* [2 vols. London, 1816], *1,* 731) presents the pro-Yorkist version: James, having gotten aboard the accompanying yacht,

> such was the modesty and respect of those who attended him, many whereof were persons of quality . . . that no one offered to go into it but whom his Highness pleased to call himself . . . ; but other boats coming to their rescue, most of the persons of quality and his Royal Highness's servants got off also, and many more might have been saved had not the timorousness of the boatmen hindered their coming near the ship . . . ; those therefore who were thus abandoned (though ready to be swallowed up) gave a great huzza as soon as they saw his Royal Highness in safety, to the no less honor of the English seamen for their intrepidity and zeal than the Duke's for having gained so great an esteem amongst them, when such endeavors were used to render him the object of all men's hatred.

1073. Sodom, according to one tradition, was submerged after its burning (see *A Dictionary of the Bible,* 2, 1338ff.).

Give not insulting Askalon to know,   1075
Nor let Gath's daughters triumph in our woe!
No sailor with the news swell Egypt's pride,
By what inglorious fate our valiant di'd!
Weep, Arnon! Jordan, weep thy fountains dry,
While Sion's rock dissolves for a supply!   1080
Calm were the elements, night's silence deep,
The waves scarce murm'ring, and the winds asleep;
Yet fate for ruin takes so still an hour,
And treacherous sands the princely bark devour;
Then death unworthy seiz'd a gen'rous race,   1085
To virtue's scandal and the stars' disgrace!
Oh! had th'indulgent pow'rs vouchsaf'd to yield,
Instead of faithless shelves, a listed field;
A listed field of Heav'n's and David's foes,
Fierce as the troops that did his youth oppose,   1090
Each life had on his slaughter'd heap retir'd,
Not tamely and unconqu'ring thus expir'd.
But destiny is now their only foe,
And dying, e'en o'er that, they triumph too;
With loud last breaths their master's scape applaud,   1095
Of whom kind force could scarce the fates defraud,
Who for such followers lost (O matchless mind!)
At his own safety now almost repin'd!
Say, royal sir, by all your fame in arms,
Your praise in peace, and by Urania's charms,   1100

1075–76. From David's lament for Saul and Jonathan (II Samuel 1:20): "Tell it not in Gath, publish it not in the streets of Askelon; lest the daughters of the Philistines rejoice, lest the daughters of the uncircumcised triumph." Askelon and Gath, two cities of the Philistines, may not have specific application.

1079. While the Jordon very likely signifies the Thames, the Arnon, a river forming the south boundary of Causan, is difficult to locate. It may perhaps be the Tweed or the Forth.

1085. "In this shipwreck perished the Earl of Roxburghe, Mr. Hyde, a son of the great Clarendon, the Lord O'Brien, the Laird of Hopetoun, Sir Joseph Douglas, [and] Colonel Macnaughton" (Scott-Saintsbury, 9, 403).

1088. *shelves:* Sandbanks in the sea or river rendering the water shallow or dangerous.

listed: Connected into lists for tilting.

1090. i.e. the Commonwealth forces of the Civil War and Interregnum.

1100. *Urania:* The heavenly or spiritual (as opposed to the pandemic) Venus, here standing for the Duchess of York.

If all your suff'rings past so nearly press'd
Or pierc'd with half so painful grief your breast.

    Thus some diviner Muse her hero forms:
Not sooth'd with soft delights, but toss'd in storms,
Not stretch'd on roses in the myrtle grove,   1105
Nor crowns his days with mirth, his nights with love;
But far remov'd, in thund'ring camps is found,
His slumbers short, his bed the herbless ground;
In tasks of danger always seen the first,
Feeds from the hedge, and slakes with ice his thirst.   1110
Long must his patience strive with Fortune's rage,
And long opposing gods themselves engage,
Must see his country flame, his friends destroy'd,
Before the promis'd empire be enjoy'd.
Such toil of fate must build a man of fame,   1115
And such, to Israel's crown, the godlike David came.

    What sudden beams dispel the clouds so fast,
Whose drenching rains laid all our vineyards waste?
The spring, so far behind her course delay'd,
On th' instant is in all her bloom array'd;   1120
The winds breathe low, the element serene;
Yet mark what motion in the waves is seen,
Thronging and busy as Hyblaean swarms,
Or straggl'd soldiers summon'd to their arms!
See where the princely bark, in loosest pride,   1125
With all her guardian fleet, adorns the tide!
High on her deck the royal lovers stand,
Our crimes to pardon ere they touch'd our land.
Welcome to Israel and to David's breast!
Here all your toils, here all your suff'rings rest.   1130

1104–06. The contrast would seem to be with the Duke of Monmouth, whose long affair with Lady Henrietta Wentworth at Toddington was widely known.

1116. *And such:* i.e. in a manner paralleling James' suffering.

1123. *Hyblaean swarms:* "The honey from the hills about Hybla, in Sicily, is celebrated by the ancient poets: hence *Hyblaean swarms* means swarms of bees. Cf. [Absalom and Achitophel, 697]" (Noyes, *Dryden*, p. 974).

1125. James and Mary returned to London on 27 May and "the King came on purpose that day from Windsor to meet them, to the unspeakable joy of them all" (Clarke, *Life of James the Second, 1,* 732).

This year did Ziloah rule Jerusalem
And boldly all sedition's surges stem,
Howe'er incumber'd with a viler pair
Than Ziph or Shimei to assist the chair;
Yet Ziloah's loyal labors so prevail'd   1135
That faction at the next election fail'd,
When e'en the common cry did justice sound,
And merit by the multitude was crown'd.
With David then was Israel's peace restor'd;
Crowds mourn'd their error, and obey'd their lord.   1140

1131. *Ziloah:* Biblically, this may possibly be Shiloh, often taken as the Messianic Prince of Peace (Genesis 49:10): "the scepter shall not depart from Judah, nor a lawgiver from between his feet, until Shiloh come; and unto him shall the gathering of people be."

Historically, Sir John Moore, the Lord Mayor of London during the period of the shrieval elections. (See the headnote to the poems on the shrieval elections.)

While this passage (1131–38) is an obvious addition referring to the long contention for the shrieval posts that lasted from 18 May until 28 Sept. 1682, it is difficult to say at just what point it was written.

1133. *the viler pair:* The two Whig sheriffs, Samuel Shute and Thomas Pilkington.

1134. *Ziph:* Biblically, known only as a son of Jehaleleel (I Chronicles 4:16). Historically, Samuel Shute, the less active of the two sheriffs.

Shimei: Biblically, Shimei cursed David and his party as they fled from Absalom, but David would not let Abushai slay him. After David's restoration, Shimei was pardoned but ever under suspicion (II Samuel 16:5–13; 19:18–23; see also *Absalom Senior*, 696 n.). Historically, Thomas Pilkington, the Whig sheriff who led the opposition to the Court's ultimately successful attempt to control the vital posts of sheriff; see the headnote and the poems on the shrieval elections. In *Absalom and Achitophel*, Shimei had been the more factious Slingsby Bethel; see 585–629.

1139–40. Cf. the concluding lines (1130–31) of *Absalom and Achitophel*.

A Message from Tory-Land

[*S 134 A*]

As is indicated by this poem's persona, a papal nuncio of sorts, the Whig writers were beginning to understand the persuasive power of wit. The light, internally rhymed lines, set to a tune which comes from Durfey's *The Royalist* (Chappell, *Popular Music,* p. 619a) but which had been separately printed [D 2772], actually constitute quite a corrosive attack on the Court party propagandists with their strong inclinations toward Romanism.

Luttrell's copy is dated 11 July [1682], though the lack of reference to the intense political battles being fought in London suggests that R. S. might have written it earlier in the year.

The text is based on *f″,* collated with *k″.*

A Message from Tory-Land

to the Whig-Makers in Albion

1.

From Rome I am come, His Holiness sent me
To you his fast favorites, to compliment ye.
Saint Peter's successor, his friends doth impute ye,
Expecting you'll firmly abide in your duty,
And daily scribble, nibble, quibble;   5
Your mother defend, you suck'd at her nipple.
She who did breed you, lead you, feed you,
Claims your assistance now she doth need you.

2.

And with me I bring the Pope's dispensations,
To furnish you all on any occasions;   10

6. *mother:* Mother Church, the oldest or original church from which all others have sprung.

339

Then swear and forswear as occasion requires,
And cities inflame with your Catholic fires.
If you can't turn 'em, scorn 'em, burn 'em;
Else with your sanctifi'd daggers adorn 'em.
Bring to perfection distraction, and faction;   15
The Pope will account it a glorious action.

3.

I come to encourage projectors and actors,
His Holiness' implements, and the Church factors.
Your zeal for the cause is put to a trial,
When you at the gallows can die in denial: 20
Thousands of crosses, masses, passes
To mount your bless'd souls to Peter's embraces.
You his indicters, biters, and writers,
Have done him more service than armies of fighters.

4.

Poor Towser return'd when the Parliament ended;   25
His politic wit our cause still befriended,
For his flying pen so swift is in motion,
More bless'd with the craft of St. Giles' devotion.

11. A reference to the Irish witnesses who first attested to the Popish Plot and later were used as evidences against Shaftesbury in his arraignment for high treason.

12. By parliamentary decree, the Catholics were made responsible for the fire of London (1666).

14. *sanctifi'd daggers:* Either the huge knife which Oates said Father Conyers meant to employ on Charles II (Lane, *Oates,* p. 100) or, perhaps, the short French dagger which Dangerfield said Mrs. Cellier gave him to kill Shaftesbury (Care, *History of the Damnable Popish Plot,* 1680 [C 522], pp. 332–33).

18. *factors:* agents.

20. Not one of those who suffered as a result of Oates' discoveries would admit to the existence of a Popish Plot, despite offers of leniency.

21. Pickering, for example, was to have 300,000 masses as a reward for shooting Charles II, according to Oates (Lane, *Oates,* p. 94).

25. *Towser:* The Whigs' nickname for Sir Roger L'Estrange, the Tory pamphleteer, from about the time (Oct.–Nov. 1680) that public opinion forced him into a brief exile. He returned in Feb. 1681 (just after the dissolution of the second Exclusion Parliament) and two months later (just after the dissolution of Charles' final Oxford Parliament) began his most effective enterprise, *The Observator.*

28. *the craft of St. Giles' devotion:* Grub Street, the resort of hack journalists, poets, and pamphleteers, was just a little to the east of St. Giles Cripplegate. It is now Milton Street (not named for the poet) and runs north from Fore Street.

Thy *Observator*'s matter, scatter;
In Rome he's a saint that in Albion's a traitor;   30
Since these dissenters ventures, enters,
Toss the Plot back, we'll swear't at adventures.

5.

The chief of our foes are now out of favor.
This, this is the time, there ne'er was a braver!
Our politics now hath an excellent face on't;   35
Then down with these Whigs, nor bate 'em an ace on't.
Those dull romances, Prance's fancies,
To Catholic Nat much credit advances;
Let his pen rogue on, tug on, jog on,
Were Albion our own, stand clear Hogan Mogan!   40

6.

Godfrey's murder was rarely contriv'd,
To kill himself, he walk'd abroad while he liv'd.
Heraclitus, Nat, and the brave *Observator,*
Ingeniously each hath stated the matter.
For if to fright us, Titus indict us,   45
These valiant heroes stand up to right us;
Those who were string'd, swing'd, hang'd,
As innocent babes were certainly wrong'd.

29. *Observator:* Accented, as often, on the third syllable.

32. *Toss the Plot back:* An allusion to the Meal Tub Plot, which claimed that the Popish Plot was a device of the Whigs to seize power.

at adventures: At hazard, at random, recklessly.

33. *The chief of our foes:* By this time, Shaftesbury and Monmouth had been stripped of all their offices.

36. *bate . . . an ace:* To make the slightest abatement.

37. Miles Prance's confession of involvement in Godfrey's murder was printed as *A True Narrative and Discovery* [P 3177] and *The Additional Narrative* [P 3170]. Nathaniel Thompson, who was strongly suspected of Catholic leanings, replied by printing *A Letter to Mr. Miles Prance* [F 537], stating that Godfrey had committed suicide. For this, he and his collaborators, William Pain and John Farwell, were fined and pilloried (Howell, *State Trials, 8,* 1359-86).

40. *Hogan Mogan:* A contemptuous reference to the Dutch, specifically "The High Mightinesses" (Hoogmogendheiden), the States General.

43. The three principal Court party newspapers at this time were *Heraclitus Ridens,* "Nat" Thompson's *Loyal Protestant,* and L'Estrange's *Observator.*

48. Cf. *The Jesuit's Justification, proving they died as innocent as the child unborn* (1679) [J 718], repr. in *Roxburghe Ballads, 4,* 238-39.

7.

But dear Madam Cellier's intrigue did miscarry;
You see that 'tis dangerous to be unwary.   50
These heretics must by all means be destroy'd,
And all the Church rights by us be enjoy'd.
Yet if we arm us, ram us, damn us
These heretic dogs will find Ignoramus.
Still it miscarries, it tarries, it varies;   55
Yet never were days so bless'd as Queen Mary's.

8.

Cloud the Whigs' evidence with high derision,
And make it your care to foment division;
Divide if you can the prince from the people,
And that will advance the crown that is triple.   60
Now is the time boys, mine boys, thine boys;
Eclipse but the Whigs, the Tories will shine boys.
But if you'll root 'em, smoot 'em, blot 'em,
Cut the Duke's legs, and swear the Whigs cut 'em.

9.

If mortal assistance should happen to fail ye,   65
As't did to St. Coleman, St. Whitebread, St. Staley,
St. Pickering, St. Grove, or such holy martyrs,
Stand fast to the cause, ne'er value your quarters.

49. *Madame Cellier's:* The "Popish midwife" and central figure of the abortive Meal Tub Plot.

54. *Ignoramus:* An allusion to the Whig grand jury which defeated the Court's attempt to try Shaftesbury for high treason.

56. *Queen Mary's:* i.e. the reign of Philip and Mary, and the period of persecution of Protestants that followed in 1555.

60. *crown that is triple:* The three-tiered papal crown.

63. *smoot:* A variant of the verb *smut*, to blacken, smudge.

64. *Cut the Duke's legs:* On 25 Jan. 1682, the picture of the Duke of York was mutilated by vandals, who cut out the portion below the knees. See *The Whigs' Exaltation,* 45–49 n., for a fuller account.

66–67. All five men were Catholics who were hanged, mutilated, and quartered during the early months of the Popish Plot scare. Edward Coleman (tried 27 Nov. 1678), the Duchess of York's secretary, had carried on a treasonable correspondence with Père La Chaise and others; Whitebread (tried 13 June 1679) was a Catholic priest; William Staley, a goldsmith (tried 21 Nov. 1678), was convicted of treasonable words against the

You shall be when dead, painted, sainted;
With Purgatory you shall ne'er be acquainted.   70
When you are tortur'd, quarter'd, martyr'd,
Y'are canoniz'd saints; all pardon is granted.

10.

There ne'er was more hope since the Spanish invasion
To bring in subjection this heretic nation;
And now should it fail and our plot be defeated,   75
'Tis vain to expect 'twill e'er be completed.
Win it and wear it, clear it, share it,
Possession's the due reward of your merit,
You shall have guineas, and it no sin is
To build up with blood on the Protestant —— Finis.   80

King and was the first to be executed; Thomas Pickering, a Benedictine lay brother,
and John Grove, a servant to some of the London Jesuits, were both tried on 17 Dec.
1678.

73. *Spanish invasion:* In 1588.

JOHN DEAN

Iter Boreale

[*D 493*]

John Dean, a London bookseller, wrote and sold a number of poems and ballads strongly supporting the Court. This one, with its opening parody of sectarian rhetoric and its mock-mourning, reinforces the lyrics with the tune and achieves further impact by employing the title of Robert Wild's famous poem of 1660 (*POAS*, Yale, *1*, 3–19; for a discussion of the *Iter* poems, see *r″* (*V*), pp. 154–55). The version of the song to which Dean refers is that written by Matthew Taubman in his musical, poetical tribute *An Heroic Poem to . . . the Duke of York* [T 239] and there entitled "The Duke's Return from Scotland." In *k″*, there is a separate printing of Taubman's song with the statement: "To a new playhouse tune." The music is supplied in both cases, but in all probability Taubman's *Heroic Poem* (acquired by Luttrell on 4 July) appeared after the broadside version, which had been printed for P. Brooksby in West Smithfield. The song was reprinted in 1685 in *180 Loyal Songs* (*c*).

Slingsby Bethel, the leader of the extreme republican wing of the Whig party, had been sheriff of London in 1680–81 (see headnote to the Poems on the Shrieval Elections). Dryden had pilloried him in *Absalom and Achitophel* under the name of Shimei (who "loved his wicked neighbor as himself"), and Burnet's portrait is scarcely more flattering:

> but as he was a known republican in principle, so he was a sullen and willful man, and run the way of a sheriff's living [which could cost as much as £5000 per year for entertainment] into the extreme of sordidness, which was very unacceptable to the body of the citizens, and proved a great prejudice to the party (2, 254).

During his shrieval tenure, Bethel had done much to sustain the impanelling of Whig juries and had been head of the radical Queen's Arms club (*CSPD*, 1682, pp. 236–38), and during 1682 he

344

was in litigation over the report that he had announced that he himself would have executed Charles I rather than see him go unpunished. It is small wonder, then, that Bethel, foreseeing the victory of the Tory shrieval candidates and knowing from personal experience what kind of juries would result, prudently decided that it was time to leave London. According to another broadside entitled *Iter Boreale (or Esquire Sparepenny's Departure to the North)* [I 1092], he left on 3 July; on 9 Sept., Secretary Jenkins heard that he had gone from Durham for Newcastle (*CSPD*, 1682, p. 382). Eventually, he settled in Hamburg (1682–89), the city where he had received mercantile training in his younger days. For the exultant Tories, Bethel's departure was the first real evidence that the Whig control was beginning to break; and, indeed, the ensuing months saw an ever-increasing number of Opposition leaders seeking refuge on the Continent.

Dean's verses were printed for "C. Tebroc," the usual reversal of Charles Corbet, another London bookseller. Luttrell's copy is dated 11 Aug. 1682, which would be about three weeks after it became known that Bethel had fled to Hamburg (Luttrell, *1, 209*).

ITER BOREALE

or

Tyburn in Mourning for the Loss of a Saint.
A New Song to the tune of "Now the Tories that glory"

1.

Behold great Heaven's protection!
Jehovah frowns for to see
Pretended zeal claim election
In rights of monarchy.
Great Charles in spite of all treason,   5
Preserves his kingdoms in peace;

3. Thomas Papillon and John Dubois, the Whig candidates for the shrieval posts, claimed election on the basis of the votes taken in the books of the Whig Sheriffs, Pilkington and Shute, who were in charge of the polling. The Court supported the right of the Lord Mayor, Sir John Moore, to convene or dissolve a Common Hall, and claimed that North and Box, the Court party candidates, had been chosen according to the count in Moore's books. (See headnote to the Poems on the Shrieval Election.)

He rules by law and by reason,
Whilst Whig melts in his own grease.
　　Ignoramus is out of doors;
　　Fly, oh fly, ye base sons of whores!   10
　　Poland or Holland will hide such bores
　　Who rebellion have sown;
　　For nothing but royalty, loyalty,
　　Shall in our isle be known.

2.

The Bethelites are in mourning   15
To see their sire so cold.
Zounds! who thought of adjourning
A zealot so factious bold?
To prayers, ye pestilent Whigs!
The devil may hear you in time!   20
What think you by Oliver's jig?
(Gad, 't brings my song into rhyme!)
　　Hamburg once again take thy own;
　　Tyburn long for thy son doth groan,
　　Cromwell's disturb'd with her making moan,   25
　　Curses the sins brought him there.

9. *Ignoramus:* The name applied to the Whig grand jury which had refused to indict Shaftesbury. Papillon and Dubois had been members, and the former had been particularly vociferous in his opposition.

11. *Poland or Holland:* Both countries had elective monarchies; at this time their rulers were John III and William III. As well, the mention of Poland was probably meant to recall the rumor that Shaftesbury had coveted the position to which John Sobieski had been elected in 1674; while the mention of Holland, England's longtime commercial and military foe, evoked thoughts of a country composed of "Whiggish" municipalities. Both countries had been torn by civil strife.

bores. Modern *boors,* i.e. persons who are rude, ill-bred, or unmannerly.

15. *Bethelite:* See headnote.

17. *Zounds!:* A euphemistic abbreviation for the oath "by God's wounds."

21. *Oliver's jig:* For Old Nol's (i.e. Cromwell's) Jig, see Chappell, *Popular Music,* pp. 449-50. As well, a jig is a trick or a cheat.

23. *Hamburg:* For Bethel's earlier connections with, and escape to, Hamburg, see headnote. Hamburg was "a hotbed of sectarian extremism and the haven of many English exiles" (*POAS,* Yale, 2, 125, 46-47 n.; see also 46 n. below).

24-26. By a bill of the Convention Parliament, "Cromwell's body was disinterred . . . and hung on the gallows at Tyburn on 30 January 1661. . . . The head was then set on a pole on top of Westminster Hall, and the trunk buried under the gallows" (*DNB*).

Then let us be merry, drink sherry,
The zealots no longer fear.

3.

Whine louder, ye priests of the zealous,
For Heaven is deaf to your prayers.   30
Why do ye deceive us, and tell us
You travel in Heaven's affairs?
What Saint e'er came, or professor,
From grave, to teach to dethrone
Your lawful King and successor   35
Whom next to Heaven we own?
    If these be tricks of your Whiggish tribe,
    No Saint will ever the devil chide,
    Though in the bottom of Hell he hide:
    Such lovers of kings the wrong way.   40
    Then hey boys, trounce it and bounce it,
    For monarchy gets the day!

4.

Must nine-penny esquire be forgotten?
Oh, do not to memory bring
Those Hamburg sayings, were hot ones: 45
Damn'd rogue, didst thou murder the King?

33. *Saint:* The word was used derisively to refer to certain puritanical sects that considered their adherents to be among the elect.

professor: One who makes open declaration of his allegiance to some principle, or religion.

40. *the wrong way:* This and "Then hey boys" (41) are meant to recall one of the most popular songs of the century, known both as *The Clean Contrary Way,* and *Hey, then* or *Hey, boys, up go we* (see Chappell, *Popular Music,* 425–29 and the headnote to D'Urfey's *The Whigs' Exaltation*). The chorus line, with its reversal of meaning, is seen in the fifteenth-century song "Cujus Contrarium Verum Est."

43. *nine-penny esquire:* Bethel's parsimony was notorious, particularly when contrasted with the lavish feasts that sheriffs were expected to give. The phrase, elsewhere applied to Bethel (see headnote), may refer to the price of an inexpensive meal at an ordinary (cf. *The London Cuckolds* [L 2894A] and *Observator,* No. 45 [20 Aug. 1681]) or to the price that Bethel was accustomed to pay for his bottle of wine (*CSPD,* 1682, p. 238).

46. The Muddiman Newsletter for Thursday, 4 May 1682, announced that "Mr. Bethel hath revived his suit and declared against Captain Harvey for words that the said Captain affirmed to have been spoken formerly by Mr. Bethel at Hamburg im-

Must still the zealous o'errule us;
Shall Council gowns be above
Majesty, sword, mace? then tell us
Who better than Moore can love.   50
   Loyalty burneth within his breast;
   Religion is his chief interest;
   The City he would with peace invest:
   Were they not blinded with zeal.
   Then hey boys, laugh it and quaff it;   55
   Let Moore to the King appeal.

5.

Be gone, base sons of the nation,
That love not the power of kings;
Go seek Dad Bethel's new station,
'Twill hold ten thousand such things.   60
Go mourn the sin of rebellion
You would set up in the City;
Take with you your new friend Papillion,
The rest of the old Committee.
   Let love and loyalty once more reign   65
   Within your breasts for great Charlemagne,

---

porting that rather than an executioner should be wanting for the late king, he him-
self would . . . perform that office, or words to that effect" (see also Luttrell, *Brief
Relation*, *1*, 187). Fourteen days later, the Captain very wisely obtained permission to
have the case "tried by a jury from another county" (Muddiman Newsletter, 18 May
1682).

48. *Council:* The Aldermanic Council.

55. The line is taken directly from stanza 1, l. 13 of *The Duke's Return from Scot-
land* ("Now the Tories that glory") in Taubman's *An Heroic Poem to . . . the Duke
of York* [T 239].

56. The Lord Mayor had, in fact, complained to Charles the day after the first
Common Hall (25 June) about the riotous action of the Sheriffs in continuing to poll
after he had dismissed the count. As a result, Pilkington and Shute were sent to the
Tower (26 June), though they were released on bail on the 30th.

60. *ten thousand such things:* Probably a reference to the "ten thousand brisk boys"
from Wapping who, according to Shaftesbury, were willing to rise in rebellion to sup-
port his cause (Brown, *Shaftesbury*, pp. 299–300).

63. *new friend Papillion:* Cf. *Ironical Encomium*, 80. This anglicized spelling of the
Huguenot name occurs often.

64. *old Committee:* i.e. the military Committee of Safety that ruled England in 1659.
Bethel had been connected with it and appointed to the Council in Jan. 1660.

66. *Charlemagne:* Charles the Great, i.e. the King.

And for the Prince, that's come home again,
Who our peace will support.
Then hey boys, drink it, ne'er shrink it,
Here's a health to the King and Court.   70

67. *the Prince:* The Duke of York finally returned to England on 27 May 1682.

A Poem to Her Royal Highness

[P 2706]

"St. James'. August 15, 1682. This morning between the hours of 7 and 8, Her Royal Highness was delivered of a daughter, to the extraordinary joy of all the whole Court, which was further manifested by ringing of all the bells in Westminster, St. Martins, etc. About 7, a messenger was dispatched for Windsor to acquaint His Majesty, His Royal Highness, etc. of the joyful news." So Nat Thompson reported the birth of the fifth child of Mary of Modena, duchess of York, in *The Loyal Protestant,* No. 195 (17 Aug. 1682). The four previous children had all died, and the fact that "Her Highness and daughter [were] in health" did much to alleviate the disappointment that York and his followers must have felt at not having a male heir. At 3 P.M., the following day, the child was christened Charlotte Maria by the Bishop of London, with the Duke of Ormonde as godfather and the Princess Anne and Countess of Arundel as godmothers.

The speed with which this poem appeared (Luttrell's copy is dated 17 Aug.) did not detract from the savagery of its conclusion nor from the effective attack it makes on the Tory persona who is the narrator.

The text is based on *k″* and *f″*.

A POEM TO HER ROYAL HIGHNESS

Upon the Birth of her Daughter

Madam!
By all our thunder-thumping lies! by Jove!
By all the gods that rule the spheres above!
We are all lost. Kind Heaven have mercy on us,
Your lying down has quite and clean undone us.   5
Who e'er did think the angry planets would

2. *thunder-thumping lies:* The phrase is found also in *Advice to the Painter from a Satyrical Night-Muse (POAS,* Yale, 2, 496): "Their thunder-thumping lies, and oaths so sharp" (31).

Turn bonny blue-cap to a silken hood?
Alas! alas! to what an ebb we're brought!
Are all our vows and prayers come to nought?
Now he believes his father De'il can lie;
How basely false is Thompson's prophecy!   10
While all the grinning Whigs do burst with laughter
To see the monarch son should prove a daughter.
We had design'd in racy gossips' bowls
And christ'ning caudles to refresh our souls;   15
When the majestic boy should once appear,
We'd swim in wine, and would carouse in beer,
And feast our bellies with the richest cheer.
Proving a girl, alas, it proves our woe!
Our feast is spoil'd, and all our cakes are dough.   20
We did design to revel in the street,
And highest skies with fireworks to greet;
With shouts your laboring self to entertain,
As neighbor heathens do the moon in pain;

7. *blue-cap:* A Scotsman. James, with his duchess, had gone to Scotland as High Commissioner in Oct. 1679. He and his wife returned to England on 27 May 1682.

silken hood: i.e. female headdress. Yorkists, of course, wanted a male heir.

10. *Thompson:* Nathaniel Thompson, an ardent Court party propagandist and printer, was strongly suspected of being Roman Catholic. In addition to producing the periodical *The Loyal Protestant,* he printed a great number of pamphlets and broadsides, including some on the "loyal apprentices'" feast referred to in 34.

14. The writer has caught Thompson's idiom quite effectively; cf. *The Loyal Protestant's* account of the apprentices' feast or Barillon's entertainment for the birth of the Dauphin's son (Nos. 192–93 [10 and 12 Aug. 1682]). As opposed to the picture given here, Thompson describes Charing Cross as the scene of joyous celebration on the evening of 15 Aug., with "ringing of bells, bonfires, drinking of healths, . . . great quantities of wine and other strong drink given amongst the people, and squibs in so great numbers that the people were forced to shut up their shops for fear [of] fire" (No. 195 [17 Aug. 1682]).

14. *racy:* Of wines or other liquors, having a characteristically excellent taste, flavor, or quality.

gossips': Godfathers or godmothers, as well as those friends (usually female) given to idle talking. A gossip's cup or bowl is the same as a caudle (15), i.e. a warm drink of thin gruel, mixed with wine or ale, sweetened and spiced.

20. The author attempts to draw a parallel between the allegedly frustrated christening party and the prohibited Whig feast of 21 April 1682. Cf. *A Congratulatory Poem on the Whigs' Entertainment,* 5: "Thy wine is spilt, thy pies and cakes are dough."

24. Possibly a reference to the connection between the moon and childbirth, seen in mythology in Diana, goddess of the moon, who, in her second title of Lucina, was also the goddess of childbirth.

Each loyal Tory with his gloating mate   25
The lad's nativity would celebrate.
Tantivy boys to dance, their clerks to sing,
Had all design'd within a holy ring,
And witty females were to be spectators.
Towser had made a crown of *Observators*   30
For the brisk boy to wear; but now the elf
May bravely take it up and wear't himself.
Nay, t'other day, when lords and tailors met,
And loyal 'prentices in rank were set,
To Hans-in-kelder they did quaff each glass,   35
And whoe'er did refuse, was dubb'd an ass.
Grandees would find corals to rub his gums,
And 'prentices would find him sugar plums,
And this they did confirm with loyal oaths,
But Whip-stitch he did hope to make him clothes.   40
    But we're deceiv'd; for Madam in your arms
Is held a girl, that is all over charms.
A girl, though fair, yet is the bane of bliss;
'Tis gloomy woman darkens Paradise.
Women, though fair, yet ugly are their wills,   45
Born to do mischief, and triumph in ills.
Madam, how many longing hearts did groan
With tedious sighs to see your wish'd-for son?

27. *Tantivy boys:* The Whigs' derogatory nickname for High Churchmen and Tories. See *The Whigs' Exaltation,* 5 n.

30. *Towser:* The Whigs' name for Sir Roger L'Estrange, the prolific Tory writer, whose best-known work at this time was the witty periodical *The Observator.*

33. On 9 Aug., at noon, there had been "the most noble and splendid feast of the loyal young men and apprentices" at Merchant Tailors' Hall, "there being about fifty several tables few of which contained less than sixty persons. . . . The nobility that were there were most splendidly accommodated at the upper end of the great Hall" (*The Loyal Protestant,* No. 192 [10 Aug. 1682]).

35. *Hans-in-kelder:* Dutch, literally Jack-in-cellar; an unborn child.

36. After reporting the royal healths that were drunk, Thompson adds that there were no disorders "save only that an intruding, impudent Whig or two having crowded themselves amongst the loyal assembly were hissed and turned out" (*The Loyal Protestant,* No. 192 [10 Aug. 1682]).

37. *corals:* Toys made of polished coral, given to infants to assist them in cutting their teeth.

40. *Whip-stitch:* An overcast stitch; the word is here employed as a name for any tailor.

But if it be a maid, we'll cheer our hearts,
And once again rely upon our arts: 50
Nature shall never our pledg'd hopes destroy;
I'll swear if it be a maid, we'll make't a boy.
But 'twas a boy, the fault is only this,
The midwife circumcis'd the babe amiss.
And if it be cut off, we won't complain;   55
The child is young and it may grow again.
But if it be a maid, what need we care?
We make no use of the porphyry chair.

    Then rouse up all you Tories of our isle!
Fortune on us can never choose but smile;   60
We have the best of all her pleasant gifts,
Her lucky hand doth help us at dead lifts.
And if untimely death by chance destroy
The happy infant, either maid or boy,
Yet will we revel at a well-set board,   65
And drink a loyal health to Royal Charles the Third.

58. *porphyry chair:* A chair used in the installation of a pope; specifically the *sedes stercoraria,* a chair of porphyry marble, in the cloister of St. John Lateran (*OED* and citation). A female pope (Pope Joan) was supposed to have ruled as John VIII in the ninth century; afterwards, according to legend, the porphyry chair was constructed in such a way that the sex of a newly elected pope could be ascertained.

62. *at dead lifts:* In extremities; in conditions when one can do no more.

63–64. The Duchess, who had lost her four previous children, was indeed to lose this one too. On Thursday night, 5 Oct., when York returned from Newmarket, the seven-week-old princess had been taken with a "dangerous indisposition." She died about 6 P.M. the following evening from "the gripes and convulsion fits . . . to the regret of their Royal Highnesses" (*CSPD,* 1682, pp. 461–62).

A New Song on the Strange and Wonderful Groaning Board

[N 770]

L'Estrange ended his newssheet of 13 Sept. 1682 in a particularly amiable mood. Observator suggests to Whig that

> you and I should go see the Groaning Board now, when we have done our morning's chat. Why really they say't has put the virtuosi beside their Latin.
> *Whig:* I'll tell ye how 'tis. They take a hot iron, and if ye touch't at one end, it groans at t'other; and if ye touch't in the middle, it quivers and trembles as if 'twere in agony.

In *The Anatomy of Plants* (1682) [G 1945], Nehemiah Grew pointed out that these boards were of elm, a wood with ample "air vessels" which acted as little wind-pipes and made a "big or groaning noise" when heat was applied.

For Court party writers, the comic analogy of the board to their descriptions of the sectarian preachers was reinforced by the crowd's awe and wonder at this "prodigy." Here was, in fact, an opportunity to associate the uncritical acceptance of fantastic plots with the superstitious fears promulgated by radical sects such as the Fifth Monarchists.

The text is based on *f"*, which Luttrell acquired on 2 Oct. 1682.

A NEW SONG ON THE STRANGE AND WONDERFUL GROANING BOARD

1.

What fate inspired thee with groans,
    To fill fanatic brains?
What is't thou sadly thus bemoans,
    In thy prophetic strains?

354

2.

Art thou the ghost of William Prynne,   5
   Or some old politician,
Who, long tormented for his sin,
   Laments his sad condition?

3.

Or must we now believe in thee
   Th' old cheat transmigration,   10
And that thou now art come to be
   A call to reformation?

4.

The giddy vulgar to thee run,
   Amaz'd with fear and wonder;
Some dare affirm, that hear thee groan,   15
   Thy noise is petty thunder.

5.

One says and swears you do foretell
   A change in Church and State;
Another says you like not well
   Your master Stephen's fate.   20

5. William Prynne (1600–69), a prolific Puritan pamphleteer, whose outspoken attacks on government made him a martyr to the parliamentary cause in the 1630s.

10. *transmigration:* The idea of the transmigration of departed souls, especially into trees, is virtually universal. Famous literary examples occur in Vergil and in Dante; in this particular case (as L'Estrange's Observator lightly remarks) we may have "some of the old folks, perhaps in Ovid's *Metamorphoses,* that were turned into trees; and this may be one of the planks" (No. 204 [13 Sept. 1682]).

18. There is a distinct genre of "strange and wonderful" literature, prodigy pamphlets that told of apparitions, comets, monstrous offspring, visions in the sky, and the like, that were "warning pieces" to England of great changes soon to take place. Many of these instances were brought together in the *Mirabilis Annus* books that were published by the famous Anabaptist bookseller, Francis "Elephant" Smith, in support of his radical religious doctrines. (See Muddiman, *The King's Journalist,* pp. 153–61; also Brown, *Fifth Monarchy.*)

20. Stephen College, who was tried and executed for treason at Oxford in Aug. 1681, was by trade a joiner (i.e. a woodworker or cabinet maker) and in this sense he is the Groaning Board's "master." L'Estrange closes his conversation on the same note (*Observator,* No. 204 [13 Sept. 1682]):

> *Whig:* Well, these occult qualities are wonderful things. I have known strange things done by sympathy.

6.

Some say you groan much like a Whig,
    Or rather like a Ranter;
Some say as loud and full as big
    As conventicle canter.

7.

Some say you do petition,   25
    And think you represent
The woe and sad condition
    Of old Rump Parliament.

8.

The wisest say you are a cheat;
    Another politician   30
Says 'tis a mystery as great
    And true as Hatfield vision.

Observator: I'll tell ye no lie now. It was observed, when College suffered at Oxford, that all the conventicles here about the town fell a-groaning upon 't; and a long shovel-board table, where the True-Protestants used to meet in consultation, trembled and quivered from one end to t'other. And this is seven and forty miles off, now.

22. *Ranter:* In specific use, the term refers to members of a sect of Antinomians which arose about 1645.

23–24. Tory writers constantly ridiculed the preaching style of the dissenting sects. See, for example, *Observator,* No. 110 (11 March 1682).

25. *petition:* On 27 Oct. 1680, Commons resolved that it was "the right of English subjects to petition the king for the calling and sitting of parliaments, and that to represent such petitioning as sedition was to betray the liberty of the subject" (Ogg, *Charles II,* p. 602). Those who were opposed were known as Abhorrers or Addressers.

28. *Rump Parliament:* The remnant of the Long Parliament which sat from Dec. 1648 until April 1653 and again from May 1659 until Feb. 1660.

32. *Hatfield vision:* In 1680, there was published *A True and Perfect Relation of Elizabeth Freeman . . . of a Strange and Wonderful Apparition which . . . commanded her to declare a message to His Most Sacred Majesty* [W 2248] as it was taken "from the maid's own mouth by me, Richard Wilkinson, schoolmaster of Hatfield." The "maid of Hatfield" was to convey the prophesy that the royal blood would be poisoned on 15 May; the Whig-inclined apparition returned on the following day (25 Jan.) with the command to "tell King Charles from me and bid him not remove his Parliament and stand to his Council." Tory comment appears in *Heraclitus Ridens,* No. 5 (1 March 1681). Dryden makes reference to her in the Epilogue to *The Unhappy Favorite* (see Kinsley's note).

9.

Some say 'tis a new evidence
  Or witness of the plot,
And can discover many things,   35
  Which are the Lord knows what!

10.

And lest you should the plot disgrace
  For wanting of a name,
Narrative Board henceforth we'll place
  In registers of fame.   40

33. *evidence:* One who furnishes testimony or proof; a witness.

39. *Narrative Board:* "Narrative" had become the regular term for Whig pamphlets telling of plots. So, for example, Oates' *A True Narrative of the horrid plot* [O 59], Mansell's *An Exact and True Narrative of the late Popish Intrigue* [M 514], or *Mr. Thomas Dangerfield's Particular Narrative* [D 192].

[*L 3365*]

The conventional exordium of this poem transfers the narrator rapidly to a *locus amoenus* where ordered nature is uncorrupted by the unnatural rebellion of London's factious Whigs. Here (echoing somewhat the device of Juvenalian satire), the narrator encounters "a man of most inviting honesty," who dramatically reveals his idealistic Cavalier loyalty by warning against these new-model rebels and by recounting his own experiences with their predecessors in Commonwealth times. So thorough and so effective is his attack on their treachery and perversion of both natural and human law that his own rejection of the world becomes justified in his concluding question: "How are they fit for man's society?" By implication, both narrator and speaker, as *honnêtes hommes,* must flee from the general corruption where (to quote a Whig writer) "universal leprosy taints all."

The text is based on *f''*. Luttrell's copy is dated 25 Oct. 1682.

A LOYAL SATIRE AGAINST WHIGGISM

As I did travel lately from the town,
Through distant roads and deserts scarcely known,
From whose dark thickets, when I'd made my way,
A new-found world as well as new-born day
I thought appear'd, where Nature rul'd alone.   5
No art or help, no gaudy pomp was shown,
But every plant, each bush and spreading tree,
Did grow without man's care or industry.
There as I stood and cast my eyes around,
Pleas'd with the sight of that delightful ground,   10
Something from midst the walks did towards me make,
Which nearly did resemble human shape.
Soon as it nigher came, it prov'd to be
A man of most inviting honesty,

An aspect courteous, and a brow serene,   15
Of humane nature and most humble mien;
His hoary head did veneration bear,
And his face spoke his noble character.
Joyful I was in those strange parts to find
A front that did foretell so brave a mind.   20
For, asking me transactions of the town,
I told him what disorders late were done;
What wild distractions and misshapen fears,
And what a cloud of faction round appears;
What daring treasons were but now maintain'd   25
By Shrieves and City, both in faction train'd;
And how the bloody-minded Whigs do aim
To play again their old king-killing game.
Which when the good old man heard me relate,
In flowing tears he mourn'd his country's fate,   30
And gave me this advice:

                    "Beware, my son,
Lest by the wiles of traitors thou'rt undone;
For I have known th' experience of those times
When loyalty was thought the worst of crimes,
And when rebellion with a daring eye   35
Was cover'd by the veil of sanctity.
But thou art young; therefore I'll plainly show
How thou a monster Whig may'st surely know.
It somewhat favors man: so have I seen,
When on a Christmas evening we have been   40
On frolics bent, a thing of such like note,
With hairy chin, diminish'd hanging coat,

26. *Shrieves:* The text gives *Sh.* which Luttrell glosses as Shaftesbury; however, not only would this make a hypermetric line, but Shaftesbury's full portrayal in 137ff. would be weakened by such an early, casual reference. Specifically, the reference would be to Pilkington and Shute. (See headnote to the Poems on the Shrieval Elections.)

33. *those times:* i.e. the Interregnum.

40. "In 1644 the English Puritans forbad any merriment or religious services by an act of Parliament, on the ground that it was a heathen festival, and ordered it to be kept as a fast. Charles II revived the feast, but the Scots adhered to the Puritan view" (*EB*).

42. Samuel Butler's *The Character of a Fanatic* contains a great many of the phrases and characteristics found throughout this poem.

Broad hat, stiff band, and a malicious eye,
Which at a distance fully seem'd to be
The very villain that sequester'd me;   45
It rais'd my wonder, but as't tow'rds us press'd,
What should it prove but a baboon well dress'd;
For so morose are they, and more precise:
As we're in truth, they're positive in lies.
What one but says, the other straight will swear;   50
Let it be right or wrong, or foul or fair,
It is all one, since they the Godly are.
Vile hypocrites, who're only good in show,
Whose whole religion lies in seeming so!
For were their souls laid open to our view,   55
We should not find amongst 'em all one true!
Therefore beware," again the old man said,
"Lest by their flattering tongues thou art betray'd;
But if they find you loyal, wise, and brave,
They'll leer, and smile, and smiling dig your grave.   60
Such is their malice, spite, and mortal hate
'Gainst all that love their country, Prince, and State.
Now, gentle youth, let any man of wit
Weigh right their cause, and well consider it,
They'll find conceal'd a lurking Jesuit.   65

  "Morals and Whigs are inconsistent things:
The one still saves, the other still kills kings.
Morality would teach 'em to obey,
And make 'em happy under sovereign sway;
Make 'em speak well of, and do good to all,   70
Envious tow'rds none, but love in general.

45. *sequester'd me:* The phrase probably means "confiscated my estates"; but it may also have the sense of "excommunicated me" or even "kept me apart from society."

48. *precise:* Here, a term of opprobrium, connected with *precisian*, i.e. rigidly precise or punctilious in the observance of rules or forms; puritanical. By extension, there is the hypocrisy of mental reservation (*OED, precision:* "You can neither tie them by promise nor by oath; for if they promise or swear, 'tis with a mental precision.").

65. The argument that the Whigs were accomplishing the goals of the Jesuits by using, and indeed going beyond, their methods, was one of the strongest of the Tories' appeals to the moderates. Roger L'Estrange stressed this point throughout *The Observator* in his condemnation of the "popish Whigs." Both parties, at one point or another, claimed that Jesuits had infiltrated the anti-Court party and were acting as *agents provocateurs*.

"The very herds do due submission yield
To the imperial lion of the field;
No mutinies or factions do they know,
But pay allegiance where they ought to do.   75
'Tis only Whig, that worser beast than they,
That does pretend to sense, and disobey;
He that, although he hears his brother's name
Unjustly wrong'd, won't vindicate his fame,
But rather blow those ashes into fire   80
Which were before just ready to expire.
Oh! where is then his justice? does it lie
In things like these, or acts of charity?
There I have known 'em well. Ye poor, beware!
Better ye starve than ask for mercy there;   85
For 'stead of helping, they will spurn your grief,
Contemn your sorrows, and forbid relief.
Once one of these did my assistance crave
For certain sums, which I most frankly gave
Without the least distrust; his note or bond,   90
(For who would think that man could do such wrong)
Which when I call'd for in, in rage he says,
Nay vows, he never saw me in his days.
By this I only warn thee to be wise;
Ne'er trust 'em, for they're all deceit and lies: 95
Whilst still they seem to act on pious grounds,
Ye cut your throat to gain an hundred pounds.
'Tis interest alone that they adore,
Almighty interest, and a secret whore
Can touch the lechers so, that they again   100
Shall hug and fleer as if they're jurymen.
Oh, that bless'd time! Then, then the cause did rise,
And full revenge for Tory injuries!

101. *hug:* Used also in the sense of "to congratulate or felicitate oneself" (*OED*).
fleer: Gibe, sneer; laugh in coarse, impudent manner.
jurymen: i.e. members of the Whig "Ignoramus" jury, who (according to the author) could sneer at the Court and the law.
102. *time:* The period of Whig control of the grand juries.
cause: Court party propagandists regularly tried to identify the Whigs with the Good Old Cause, the phrase connected with the Commonwealth movement.
103. *Tory injuries!:* i.e. those suffered since the Restoration.

It was not right, but faction did prevail;
A well-grown Whig of verdicts ne'er could fail.   105
Oh, then, ye common hirelings, cheats, and knaves,
Heroes in stews, stabbers, and alley-braves,
Turn, turn t'embrace so good, so safe a cause.
There you may act your murders with applause:
Kill but a Tory, and you serve the laws.   110
Nay, though 'tis prov'd that 'twas your dire intent
To seize your King at Oxford Parliament,
Yet bring it up to town, and you shall be
Prais'd by a jury for your loyalty;
Though at the very moment oaths they take   115
That all they do is mere for conscience sake."

    At this he paus'd, and somewhat weary grown,
In a fine od'rous grotto we sat down;
And then he thus went on:
                        "Think not, dear youth,
That what I've said is malice more than truth;   120
For Heaven can tell from such vile thoughts I'm free,
And all is out of sense of honesty.
Which did they know, they would not dare to own
The hellish principles of forty-one,
Nor in their tubs of treason still declare   125
That kings elective by the people are;
Nor would they now (but Whig is still the same)
Foment divisions, and blow up the flame.
But jealousies, suspicion, guilt, and fear
Do on their disaffected brow appear;   130
Their business is to raise commotions higher,
Lay open breaches, people's hearts to fire
With wild chimeras of tyrannic pow'r,

107. *stews:* Brothels.

109–10. The author may have in mind the Whig peer, the Earl of Pembroke. See Carr, *The Murder of Sir Edmund Godfrey,* esp. pp. 338–43.

116. *mere:* This adverbial form is uncommon. The text (*f"*) has *meer,* which may be a misreading of *meet.*

124. *forty-one:* The rebellion of 1641.

125. *tubs:* Applied contemptuously or jocularly to pulpits, especially of nonconformist preachers.

126. *elective:* i.e. as in the case of Poland or Holland.

And of another bloody massacre:
Or now, which is so much the nation's cry,   135
The eminent increase of Popery.
' 'Tis Popery that round our city waits;
'Tis Popery that taints our magistrates;
'Tis that alone that makes our nation fear
A Popish miss, and Popish successor,'   140
Cries out old Belial's heir, the noble peer,
Whose little bulk with treason's so o'ercast
That it is vanish'd in the mist at last:
He that's reserv'd so long only to be
A fitter pattern of Hell's cruelty,   145
Where with his faction, when he groveling lies,
They may too late cast up repenting eyes,
And ask forgiveness of that Prince, whose name
They made it still their business to defame;
Whilst he shall dazzle with a crown so bright,   150
Their guilty heads shan't bear that glorious light,
But from his presence sink, and howl in dismal night.

"Another tenet Whig does surely hold
Is to rail at these times, and praise the old;
To cry out on the nation's horrid pride,   155
And cast all sins upon the Tory side;

134. *another bloody massacre:* The reference may be either to the Irish Uprising of 1649, put down so vigorously by Cromwell, or to the St. Bartholomew Massacre in France (1572).

137. Probably a reference to the various assertions of the Popish Plot that there were 50,000 Catholics secretly waiting in London to rise, an "army of Spanish pilgrims" that had landed in England, and 40,000 Irish and 8,000 Scottish Catholics who were ready to rebel.

138. While the reference may be to the Court-appointed judges generally, Whig wrath had fallen particularly on Justice Scroggs following the acquittal of Wakeman, the Queen's physician.

140. *Popish miss:* Louise de Kéroualle, Duchess of Portsmouth.
Popish successor: The Duke of York.

141. *the noble peer:* The Earl of Shaftesbury.

143. Sometime around the beginning of the month (Oct.), Shaftesbury disappeared. Whether it was from fear of arrest (Luttrell, *Brief Relation, 1,* 227) or an attempt to further the proposed uprising (Brown, *Shaftesbury,* pp. 299–300) is uncertain; he was probably hiding out both at Lord Essex's and in the City.

144–52. Cf. Milton, *Paradise Lost,* I.26–81.

As if that formal looks and dress precise
Mayn't hide a heart more proud than ever lies
In those that wear more handsome decencies.
Then whoring, drinking, swearing, to our charge   160
They all impute, and lay our crimes at large.
And crimes they are, but such with them are done:
Jenny can tell how well the tap did run.

    " 'Tis thus that faction moves; 'tis these foul ways
That make rebellions, broils, and threat'ning days;   165
These are the men from whom all trouble springs;
'Tis they that ruin states; 'tis they that ruin kings;
Though he be ne'er so gracious, just, and good,
One that wa'n't pleas'd e'en with traitors' blood;
And though whole hecatombs could ne'er atone   170
For royal blood, and an usurped throne;
Yet, like the Almighty, with a giving hand
Pours favors still on an ungrateful land.
And how do they requite him now at last?
'Tis well, 'tis well, Acts of Oblivion pass'd.   175
Sure 'twas enough to have a father slain,
Not to attempt it in the son again;
But they who are not grateful cannot be
Ever expected to have honesty.
The very beasts do gratitude profess;   180
Oblige them once, what kindness they'll express
By every sign, and in their language say,
'Rather than you shall die, we'll be the prey.'
Now to be Whig and grateful ne'er was known;
It is enough to make their Charter none.   185

157. *formal:* Chiefly in reproachful use: unduly precise or ceremonious; stiff.

163. *Jenny:* Possibly Jane Roberts (see J. H. Wilson, *A Rake and his Times* [New York, 1954], p. 133), though it is not certain that she was Shaftesbury's mistress.

169. *wa'n't:* A contracted form of *was not* (this predates the earliest quotation in *OED* by twenty years).

175. *Acts of Oblivion:* Discussed and passed by the Convention Parliament in 1660 (Ogg, *Charles II*, p. 154).

185. *Charter:* In order to regain control of the City offices, Charles proceeded against the Charter by a writ of Quo Warranto, claiming that there had been violation by various officials. The action, begun at the end of 1681, was finally settled in the King's favor in 1683 (see Howell, *State Trials, 8,* 1039–1358).

For if such bounteous graces of their Prince
Can't raise a grateful nor a loyal sense,
But they who, after all, his pow'r disown,
His favors slight, and undermine his throne,
First bring him low, to seize at last his crown;   190
Who're such to kings, oh! what will they then be
To fellow creatures of their own degree?
How are they fit for man's society?"

A New Ballad,

or

The True-Blue Protestant Dissenter

[*N 571*]

While witty and incisive in its own right, this poem echoes strongly the highly popular *Geneva Ballad* ("Of all the factions in the town") which went through three editions when it appeared in 1674 [G 515–17] and was ascribed, though without firm evidence, to Samuel Butler (see *POAS,* Yale, *1,* 313). The use of previously popular poetry, like the use of politically charged tunes (*The Geneva Ballad* is set "To the Tune of Forty-eight"), allows an additional area of attack without actually engaging in parody. (See, for example, D'Urfey's *The Whig's Exaltation,* pp. 9–10.)

A comparison of this poem with *The Geneva Ballad* shows the following line correspondences: 1–2 with 26–27; 3 with 23; 4 with 25; 23 with 28; 24–28 with 38–42; 29–35 with 50–56; 37 with 65; 44–46 with 16–18; and 96–98 with 47–49. *The True-Blue Protestant Dissenter,* however, does more than bring its original up to date, for it adds to the already established condemnation a far greater measure of dramatic quality through the monologue.

The text is from *k″* and must have been written sometime after the end of October, 1682, when Shaftesbury, defeated, went into hiding.

A New Ballad,

or

The True-Blue Protestant Dissenter:

With their sad Lamentation for their late loss
in Aldersgate Street.
To the tune of "The Downfall of Anthony"

Title. True-Blue: Specifically applied to the Scottish Presbyterian or Whig party in the seventeenth century (the Covenanters having adopted blue as their color in contradistinction to the royal red).

Aldersgate Street: The location of Thanet House, Shaftesbury's residence in the City.

1.

When Jeroboam's calves were rear'd,
And church was neither lov'd nor fear'd;
When treason had a fine new name,
And pulpits did like beacons flame;
　　When sent by teacher of the Word,　　　　　　　5
　　The rabble, arm'd with gun and sword,
　　Did fight the battles of the Lord;

2.

Dissenter (now grown a great rabby)
Was then in's swaddling-clouts a baby:
Dissenter, son of Presbyter,　　　　　　　　　　10
Who was undoubted son and heir
　　Of Puritan, who was the son
　　Of Calvin, he was christen'd John,
　　And sign'd with hot iron at Noyon.

3.

From whence, as sober men descant,　　　　　　　15
Knaves learn'd to burn Board Protestant,
That with a doleful sigh and groan,
Foretells the Good Old Cause must down;
　　And from this Calvin John, the great

1. *Jeroboam's:* Tetrasyllabic. Jeroboam, like Absalom before him, rebelled against the House of David. He succeeded in winning over ten of the twelve tribes, but Rehoboam, Solomon's son and the legitimate heir, held Jerusalem through the loyalty of the tribes of Judah and Benjamin. Fearing that the pilgrimages to Jerusalem would make the people sympathetic to Rehoboam, Jeroboam made two calves of gold and, establishing two temples served by a new, non-Levitic priesthood, seduced the people into idolatry. The war between the two kings continued "all their days" until God, angered at the idolatry, cut off the House of Jeroboam and drove the Israelites from the land of their fathers (I Kings 12–14).

4. *beacons:* Quite probably an allusion to the famous set of Beacon pamphlets of 1652 (Thomason Tracts E 675 [14] and [29]) which attempted to inflame the populace with warnings of the secret designs of Jesuits plotting to re-establish Roman Catholicism. See also *Absalom Senior,* 457 and n.

8. *rabby:* Variant form of *rabbi.*

14. *Noyon:* Calvin was born at Noyon in Picardy on 10 July 1509. Though he met with ecclesiastical opposition there in the course of his early career, he was not branded.

16–18. See headnote to *A New Song on the Strange and Wonderful Groaning Board.*

Learn'd Doctor T.O., as some relate,   20
Found a way in at boy's back gate.

4.

Dissenter, brat of Presbyter,
That gospel-comet, that dog-star,
Whose very preaching slew more men
Than Bonner with fire, stake, and chain: 25
   He with wild zeal, and lungs like Boreas
   Once fought and taught, and 'tis notorious!
   Murder'd his king to make him glorious.

5.

Dissenter in his tub begins,
And bawls out loud, "Friends, leave you sins";   30
But, rallying up his Saints in swarms,
He whispers, "Boys, stand to your arms!
   Stand to your arms, by Tory rude
   Our gods can never be subdu'd;
   Money, I mean, and Multitude."   35

6.

Next, in a rage and frantic fume,
He bellows out, "Beware of Rome,
The Pope and arbitrary power,
Like dragons fierce, will us devour.
   O hellish Popish Plot! down, down!"   40

20. *T.O.:* Titus Oates.

21. John Lane, who had been one of Oates' servants, brought an indictment against him on 19 Nov. 1679 for sodomy. The charge was made not merely for sensationalism; had Oates been found guilty his entire testimony would have been rendered legally invalid. The grand jury ignored Lane's bill and he and two others were found guilty of attempting to scandalize Oates and Bedloe. (See Pollock, *The Popish Plot,* p. 339; Lane, *Oates,* pp. 30–31, 224–26, 290; and Howell, *State Trials, 7,* 763–811.)

25. Edmund Bonner (1500?–69), Bishop of London, took a leading part in the Marian persecutions.

28. *his king:* Charles I.

29. *tub:* The contemptuous or jocular term applied to the pulpit of a nonconformist or sectarian preacher.

31. *Saints:* The term used by certain sects for its membership which was considered to be of the elect under the New Covenant.

Then whispers, "Boys (let's not be known),
We have contriv'd plot of our own."

7.

Dissenter, speaking words like these,
Doth give his handkerchief a squeeze;
With pleasing twang then tunes his prose,   45
Drawing John Calvin through his nose.
   He tells the sisters, if plot take,
   The righteous, as before, will make
   The greatest in the kingdom shake.

8.

But (Oh alas!) who can forsee   50
The wild intrigues of Destiny?
In steps a fatal messenger
Acquaints the Tubster, Noble Peer
   Absconds himself. The dire affright
   Perplex'd the audience; yet the Knight   55
   O'th' Tub bawl'd on with all his might.

9.

"Thou little mortal of three names,
Pilot of plots, and sire of shams;
Thou subterranean, secret spring,
That mov'st all engines 'gainst the King;   60
   If thou forsake us, we despair:
   The Tory sheriffs, and new mayor
   Will th' righteous all to pieces tear.

51. Probably a reference to the Calvinist doctrine of predestination.

53. *Noble Peer:* Shaftesbury, recognizing the desperate condition of the Country party and unable to incite his followers to more desperate action, went into hiding in Nov. 1682 in order to avoid the vengeance that was certain to be leveled against him.

55–56. *Knight O' th' Tub:* A sectarian preacher. The phrase is analogous to "knight of the post," one who stands in a pillory.

57. *mortal of three names:* Anthony Ashley Cooper.

59–60. For contemporary interest in engines and fanciful devices run hydraulically, see Evelyn, *Diary, sub* Water-works, Fountains, and Music (mechanical instruments).

62. *Tory sheriffs:* The central political contest of 1682 ended on 28 Sept. 1682 with the swearing-in of Dudley North and Peter Rich, the Court party candidates who had

10.

"Woe, woe be now to all our Clubs,
And Colonels of Plot-Meal-Tubs!   65
Now Salamanca woe to thee,
And thy illustrious family!
    Who unto thee, thou stubborn Whig,
    Who whilom look'd so bold and big;
    Thou wilt be taught another jig!   70

11.

Jails, dungeons, racks" (he knock'd his breast,
Inspir'd as prophet, and as priest)
"Ropes, halters, hatchets, pillories
Present themselves before our eyes:
    Oh true blue Protestant rioters!   75
    Off goes your heads, and eke our ears."
The sisters pour'd out floods of tears.

---

been maneuvered into victory over Papillon and Dubois. (See Poems on the Shrieval Election.)

new mayor: Sir William Pritchard was declared Lord Mayor on 22 Oct. following the scrutiny of the poll for that contested office (Luttrell, *Brief Relation, 1,* 225–27, 229, 231–32).

64. *Clubs:* The groups of politically sympathetic persons that met at coffeehouses and taverns in London. The most famous of these were the Whigs' Green Ribbon Clubs (North, *Examen,* pp. 562–64); for obvious reasons, they periodically changed their place of meeting (see *CSPD,* 1682, pp. 236, 237).

65. *Colonels:* Roderick Mansell, in whose chambers Thomas Dangerfield said he found papers revealing the Protestant (Meal Tub) Plot on 22 Oct. 1679. Proof that the papers had been put there by Dangerfield led to the chaos of charges and counter-charges of sham plots.

66. *Salamanca:* Titus Oates claimed a doctorate in theology from the University of Salamanca. For the University's denial, see *Observator,* No. 127 (21 Oct. 1682).

67. *illustrious family:* Samuel Oates, Titus' father, was an Anabaptist preacher with a somewhat questionable reputation (see Pollock, *The Popish Plot,* p. 4; Lane, *Oates,* passim); Samuel, Jr. and Constant, Titus' brothers, were supplying information to the Secretaries of State (see Lane, *Oates,* pp. 284–85, 287–89; *CSPD,* 1682, passim).

70. *jig!:* A lively dance or song; also a fidgety movement; in slang, a trick. Here, the implication would seem to be that the dance will be at the end of a rope.

76. *ears:* The punishment for seditious preaching included the cutting off of the guilty party's ears. The most famous case had been that of the Independent, Henry Burton, in 1636.

12.

"Associate, mount, raise the rude rabble;
Reform the kingdom to a Babel;
Cry up false jealousies and fears; 80
Turn paring-shovels into spears!
  Yet, brethren, boast your innocence,
  Religion being your pretence,
  Torture the text to any sense.

13.

"And cry aloud, 'We love the king,' 85
Though we intend not such a thing;
For our designs do drive us rather
To serve him as we serv'd his father;
  Whom we (his subjects good and true)
  Made stand at's gate to public view 90
  In white cap, and in waistcoat blue."

14.

Tubster concludes, and so will I,
Affirming that the azure sky
Will fall, and larks find a hard trial,
When dissenter turns subject loyal. 95
  Oblivion Acts change not his case:
  No clemency, no laws of race
  Make white this Ethiopian's face.

78. *Associate:* The famous Bill of Association, the principal paper against Shaftesbury in his treason trial, pledged its signers to absolute rejection of York, by force of arms if necessary.

90. Charles I was executed at Whitehall on the afternoon of 30 Jan. 1649.

94–96. Tilley, *Proverbs,* S 517: "When (If) the sky (heaven) falls we shall have (catch) larks."

96. *Oblivion Acts:* Principally, the Bill of General Pardon, Indemnity, and Oblivion of 29 Aug. 1660, which consigned all acts of hostility between king and parliament to perpetual oblivion (Ogg, *Charles II,* pp. 154–55).

JOHN DRYDEN

The Prologue to the King and Queen

[*D 2339*]

More properly subtitled in the *Miscellany Poems* (third edition, 1702 [Macdonald, No. 42c]) "upon the Union of the two Companies," these verses mark the actual amalgamation of the King's and Duke's players into the new King's Company, following the agreement which had been reached on 14 May 1682. The union of the two rival theaters had not been easily arrived at: some great names had to disappear, a great deal of the old liberty of action was sacrificed, and disputes on the stage property continued for many months.

The conventional analogy of stage and state—almost as time-honored as the topos of the world-turned-upside-down (18)—applied with particular force in mid-November when the new King's Company first acted together and when the Court party for the first time in years fully controlled the government of London.

The text is based on *f″* and collated with the 1702 *Miscellany;* Luttrell's copy is dated 16 Nov. 1682. Kinsley's notes contain minor imprecisions; the text is printed also in William B. Gardner, *The Prologues and Epilogues of John Dryden* (New York, Columbia University Press, 1951) and in *Rare Prologues and Epilogues,* ed. Autrey Nell Wiley (London, Allen & Unwin, 1940).

Prologue to the King and Queen

at the Opening of their Theater

Since faction ebbs, and rogues grow out of fashion,
Their penny-scribes take care t' inform the nation
How well men thrive in this or that plantation;

1. By mid-November, the Court party controlled the offices of lord mayor and sheriff in London, Bethel had fled, Shaftesbury had disappeared, and the principal Whig leaders were under the real threat of crushing litigation.

2–3. Advertisements on the colonies were not uncommon. For the two mentioned here (4–5), see *The Impartial Protestant Mercury.* In No. 93 (10–14 March 1682), there

How Pennsylvania's air agrees with Quakers,
And Carolina's with Associators: 5
Both e'en too good for madmen and for traitors.

Truth is, our land with Saints is so run o'er,
And every age produces such a store,
That now there's need of two New Englands more.

What's this, you'll say, to us and our vocation?   10
Only thus much, that we have left our station,
And made this theater our new plantation.

The factious natives never could agree;
But aiming, as they call'd it, to be free,
Those playhouse Whigs set up for property.   15

---

is notice of "An account of the Province of Carolina in America, together with . . .
useful particulars to such as have thoughts of transporting themselves thither"; and,
beginning in No. 105 (21–25 April 1682), "the Pennsylvania Free Society of Traders"
announced that "their book and attendance of some of them" would be thrice weekly
at Bridges' Coffeehouse to receive subscriptions.

4. "The grant to Penn of Pennsylvania received the royal signature March 14, 1681.
Penn sailed from Deal in the *Welcome* with 100 comrades on Sept. 1, 1682, and landed
at New Castle on 27 October" (Thorn-Drury's note, given in Gardner, *Prologues*, p.
287).

5. Shaftesbury, whom the Crown had tried unsuccessfully to indict on the basis of
the Association paper found in his study (see the Medal Poems), was one of the original
eight lord proprietors of the Carolinas and, with Locke, strongly influenced the plan-
tation's 1669 constitution (Gardner, ibid.; Ogg, *Charles II*, pp. 673–74). In 1681, prior
to his treason trial, Shaftesbury wrote to Arlington from the Tower, offering to go and
live in Carolina if he were released with a pardon (Brown, *Shaftesbury*, pp. 288–89;
Howell, *State Trials, 8,* 765 n.).

6. The "madmen" are the enthusiast Quakers with their doctrine of the inner light;
the "traitors" are those who were sympathetic to the Association.

7. *Saints:* The term used by certain puritanical sects to refer to their adherents,
whom they considered to be among the elect.

13. *the factious natives:* For some of the difficulties involved in the union, see Nicoll,
Restoration Drama, p. 296, n. 2–3, and pp. 327–28.

14–15. The rhyme words play on the Whigs' platform of "liberty and property."

15. *Those playhouse Whigs:* In addition to theater politics, Dryden may be alluding
directly to Whig dramatists such as Settle and Shadwell.

set up for: To have as one's object or goal; or, to claim (though this predates the
quotations given in *OED*).

property: For the fate of the all-important theater property, see Nicoll, *Restoration
Drama,* p. 296, n. 3, p. 298, n. 1, and Mohun's petition (p. 328).

Some say they no obedience paid of late,
But would new fears and jealousies create,
Till topsy-turvy they had turn'd the state.

Plain sense, without the talent of foretelling,
Might guess 'twould end in downright knocks and quelling;   20
For seldom comes there better of rebelling.

When men will, needlessly, their freedom barter
For lawless pow'r, sometimes they catch a Tartar.
(There's a damn'd word that rhymes to this call'd Charter.)

But since the victory with us remains,   25
You shall be call'd to twelve in all our gains
(If you'll not think us saucy for our pains).

Old men shall have good old plays to delight 'em
And you, fair ladies and gallants that slight 'em,
We'll treat with good new plays, if our new wits can write 'em.   30

We'll take no blund'ring verse, no fustian tumor,
No dribbling love, from this or that presumer,
No dull fat fool shamm'd on the stage for humor.

For faith, some of 'em such vile stuff have made
As none but fools or fairies ever play'd;   35
But 'twas, as shopmen say, to force a trade.

23. *catch a Tartar:* Kinsley cites Tilley (*Proverbs,* T 73), and *Dictionary of the Cant-ing Crew* "instead of catching, to be catched in a trap." Dryden is drawing the parallel to the Whigs' unsuccessful play for power in 1680–82.

24. *Charter:* The word does more than rhyme. At the end of 1681, Charles moved against the London Charter by a writ of Quo Warranto on the grounds of lawless actions and violations of the original charter (see Howell, *State Trials, 8,* 1039–1358).

26. *call'd to twelve:* Kinsley states that the phrase means "invited to participate."

29. *gallants:* Accented on the second syllable.

30. "Only during the period when the theaters were united between 1682 and 1695 was there such a 'reviving of the old stock of plays' that 'the poets lay dormant' and 'a new play could hardly get admittance'" (Nicoll, *Restoration Drama,* p. 27, quoting Powell's preface to *The Treacherous Brothers,* 1689).

33. *dull fat fool:* Probably Shadwell. Cf. *Mac Flecknoe,* 187–96. For Shadwell's in-terest in the Jonsonian comedy of humors, see his dedication of *The Virtuoso* (26 June 1676), the relevant portions of which are quoted by Gardner (*Prologues,* p. 290).

We've giv'n you tragedies, all sense defying,
And singing men in woeful meter dying;
This 'tis when heavy lubbers will be flying.

All these disasters we well hope to weather; 40
We bring you none of our old lumber hether:
Whig poets and Whig Sheriffs may hang together.

38. Operatic versions of tragedies, burlesques upon them, and often incongruous use of music were stock parts of the Restoration theater. See, for example, Nicoll, *Restoration Drama*, p. 37 and n. 9, pp. 59–63.

41. *lumber:* Useless or cumbrous material.

hether: i.e. *hither,* the reading in 1702 *Miscellany.*

42. *Whig Sheriffs:* Dryden alludes to Thomas Pilkington and Samuel Shute, who vainly tried to control the election of their successors (see the headnote and Poems on the Shrieval Elections). Though not serious candidates for Tyburn (to take one sense of Dryden's "hang together"), both men were soon to be tried for riot (Howell, *State Trials, 9,* 187–298); the former, Pilkington, was shortly (24 Nov.) to be found guilty of *scandalum magnatum* for words spoken against York and ordered to pay the astonishing sum of £100,000 (Luttrell, *Brief Relation, 1,* 236, 240).

Reversing the conventional topos of the world-turned-upside-down, this poem employs the persona of a converted and "loyal" Shaftesbury. While it is true that the title uses the stock Tory gibe that Shaftesbury coveted the Polish throne to which Sobieski had been elected in 1674, the body of the poem shows the penitent Earl dissociating himself from the extremists and demagogues of his party. So farfetched is this that the fantasy of a world-turned-rightside-up seems at times to dissolve into an outright apologia, or into irony that has overreached itself. Indeed, at line 39 (or even at line 37), it would be possible to consider that the remainder of the poem is spoken by the author, and that the preceding lines alone are Shaftesbury's "recital." The text, however, gives no warrant, either by punctuation or paragraphing, for such a change, and one must therefore consider that the concluding lines are meant to stress the vast distance that separates the historical Shaftesbury from the converted and avidly "loyal" persona of the poem.

By 19 Nov., the date when Luttrell acquired this poem, Shaftesbury had been in hiding for almost a month, his defeat made certain by the election of a Tory Lord Mayor, Sir William Pritchard, on 24 Oct.

The text is based on *f"* and collated with *b;* it is found also in *k"* and *l"*.

THE CASE IS ALTER'D NOW

OR

the Conversion of Anthony, King of Poland
Published for the Satisfaction of the Sanctified Brethren

E'en as a lion, with his paws uprear'd,
As he would tear in pieces all the herd,
So, of late days, you Whigs as rampant were;
An honest Tory scarce to speak did dare.

Nay, it was almost an offensive thing;   5
The bellman scarce dar'd cry, *God save the King!*
Thou, my dear Titus, and the Popish Plot,
Did'st fire my zeal and make my head so hot
That then I whispered loud unto the nation,
"Now, now's the nick of time for Reformation!"   10
You huff'd and hector'd at a lofty rate,
When parliaments of your own mettle sate;
As if you had o'ergrown the King and laws,
And were beginning a new Good Old Cause.
But remedy in season did appear,   15
And stopp'd the fury of your hot career.
Thus for a while I danc'd to my own pipe,
Till I was grown Association-ripe.
But then addresses from each county came,
And loyalty did soon put out the flame.   20
Then was the time that Tyburn claim'd his due,
But had it not, for want of such as you;
Yet it had some small satisfaction giv'n,
By the deserved death of traitor Stephen.

6. *bellman:* The town crier.

11. Months later, Oates was being taunted in the same way. L'Estrange reports a coffeehouse argument in which Oates took part:

> There passed some words, it seems, about Vienna and Salamanca, and some such stories. And the Doctor opened his mouth and out came, "Impudent fellow!" and "Impudent rascal!" The gentleman told him to this effect, that he must never use those paw names but when he had a parliament at his elbow to back him. And upon this saying, the Doctor's wrath rose against him. (*Observator*, No. 399 [6 Sept. 1683]).

15. From the acquittal of Wakeman (18 July 1679) to the time of the poem, a series of increasingly positive moves by Charles checked Oates and his more ardent supporters.

17. *danc'd to my own pipe:* Followed my own lead; acted after my own desire or instigation.

18. *Association:* The treasonous paper, said to have been found in Shaftesbury's study, was the basis of the Court's indictment of the Earl (see the Medal Poems).

19. *addresses:* Following the disclosure of the Association paper, the Court party encouraged a new wave of "loyal addresses" which voiced abhorrence of the principles of the document and, by strong implication, of Shaftesbury and the City faction. (Two views of the dispute can be found in *Observator*, Nos. 112–13 [16 and 18 March 1682] and Oldmixon, *A Complete History of Addresses*.

24. *Stephen:* Stephen College, the "Protestant joiner," had been found guilty of treason and hanged at Oxford in Aug. 1681.

Cabals and factious clubs so rife were grown,   25
And old rebellious seed so thick were sown,
I hop'd ere this, the day would be my own.
In coffee-houses you did domineer,
And prattled treason without wit or fear.
Reason and loyalty you overruled,   30
And settled nations whilst your coffee cool'd.
The point you argu'd with a surly face,
And he that did not yield and give you place
Was term'd by you a Tory, void of grace.
One house, one town, one kingdom scarce could hold   35
Tory and Whig, Sir Whig was grown so bold.
For this recital, sirs, pray do not blame us;
We ne'er balk'd justice by our Ignoramus.
No, no, you meant no harm, I oft was told;
No more did your rebelling sires of old.   40
Thus, for a while, with factious rage you burn'd;
But, Heav'n be thank'd, the scales at last are turn'd;
The wheel, at length, is mov'd a little round,
And its worst pieces lowest to the ground.
The State has found a way to cool our fevers,   45
Quench our new lights, and curb our strong endeavors;
And we are taught compliance with more ease,
To *What*, and *When*, and *How* the King shall please.
We to your private meetings now can come,
And seize your holder-forth, and send you home;   50
Meet you at Guildhall, or elsewhere; and then,

25–26. For a Tory evaluation of the intriguings of the old republican factions, see
Observator, passim; also *CSPD, 1682,* pp. 236–38.

28. See, for example, *Observator,* No. 125 (20 April 1682) or No. 399 (6 Sept. 1683) for
Oates' coffeehouse rhetoric.

38. The writer has Shaftesbury dissociate himself even from the Whig grand jury
that returned the treason indictment Ignoramus, and that, according to these lines,
used Shaftesbury only to forward their own rebellious ends.

39. The apparent shift in tone that occurs here is discussed in the headnote.

46. *new lights:* Novel doctrines (especially theological or ecclesiastical) the partisans
of which lay claim to superior enlightenment. The phrase tended to be connected with
the Quakers and their doctrine of the inner light.

49. *private meetings:* i.e. the illegal conventicles.

50. *holder-forth:* A contemptuous reference to the sectarian preachers or speakers.

51. *Guildhall:* The place in which elections took place. The atmosphere at the
election of Pritchard as Lord Mayor (Luttrell, *Brief Relation, 1,* 226, 231) contrasted

Help you make choice of loyal honest men.
The memory and name of Moore be bless'd,
That loyal precedent for all the rest.
Let faction cease, and loyalty get ground,   55
Till not one Whig be in the nation found;
Then we'll rejoice, as in the days of yore,
And Salamanca's shall be known no more.

---

sharply with the tumult of the previous months (see headnote and Poems on the Shrieval Elections).

53. *Moore:* It was through the agency of Sir John Moore, the Lord Mayor during the preceding tumultuous months, that the Court was able to impose its authority in the shrieval elections.

54. *precedent:* All texts have *president,* a possible reading; however, such "forms arose in English through practical identity of pronunciation, and consequent confusion, with *president*" (*OED*).

58. *Salamanca's:* Oates assumed a divinity degree from the University of Salamanca, despite that institution's statements to the contrary (see *Observator,* Nos. 225, 227, 237 [17 and 21 Oct., 8 Nov. 1682]).

To The Loyal Londoners

It is difficult to give a precise date to this bitterly ironic Whig poem with its persona of the jeering, threatening and triumphant Tory. The *terminus a quo* would seem to be 9 August 1682 (stanza 2), but the *terminus ad quem* might be June 1683 (24) or even as late as the actual loss of the Charter in early October. While dates given in printed collections of political verse must be treated with extreme caution, *l*'s 1682 is not unlikely, provided we remember that the year could run to 25 March.

To The Loyal Londoners

1.

Prepare, oh you cits, your Charter to lose:
  You're catch'd in a noose
   That is laid;
  You're betray'd, you're betray'd,
   By those lords you ador'd;   5
Your sons shall be sold, your daughters be whor'd,
Your wives turn'd to bawds. For who is't will pity
Such hungry baboons that have eat up the City?

2.

  Now open your eyes,
  See your 'prentices rise,   10

1. *cits:* Citizens.
 2. *catch'd:* There may be a play on the name of the public executioner, Jack Catch or Ketch. *O″* reads *ketcht*.
 4–5. If written after mid-June 1683, the reference would be to those noblemen—Monmouth, Essex, Grey and Russell—who were involved in the Rye House Plot.
 10. On 9 Aug. 1682, the "loyal apprentices" held their annual feast at Merchant Tailors' Hall. As he had done previously, Charles sent a brace of bucks and a large number of nobles. (See *The Loyal Protestant*, Nos. 191–92 [8 and 10 Aug. 1682]; also Luttrell, *Brief Relation, 1,* 212.)

Your wives and your daughters obey;
   For the bucks which they eat
   Were provocative meat;
For a brace more their god they'd betray.

3.

A Catholic prince   15
   With an oath can dispense,
When his sword's sharp point shall advance;
   Then throw off your shoes
   And put on sabots,
For England is model'd by France.   20

4.

Your ruling by law
   Is as weak as a straw
When e'er he his measures shall alter;
   Your shrieves and lord mayor

15. *A Catholic prince:* The violently Tory persona would be an admirer of France and absolute monarchy. Ostensibly, therefore, this refers to Louis XIV; by implication, the Whig writer is alluding to the Duke of York and probably to Charles.

16. *an oath:* The coronation oath supporting the Church of England.

19. *sabots:* The wooden shoe worn by French peasants. Pronunciation is indicated by O'''s *sabbues.* The Tory L'Estrange, attacking the Whigs' fears that led them to exchange "a visionary bondage for a real," attacks the English fear of the French at the time of Charles I in the same terms: "They were afraid of French shoes and slavery. . . . And what came on't? They only shifted councils by introducing the King's murderers into the place of his friends" (*Observator*, No. 249 [29 Nov. 1682]). For John Ayloffe's daring use of the symbol, see *POAS, 1,* 284; a later reference may be found in *A New Litany in the Year 1684,* 11.

21. *ruling by law:* The phrase is probably used in the dual sense of governing by parliament and acting through grand juries in the law courts. Through French subsidies, and through his recently gained control of the municipal offices, Charles was able to check both of these areas of Whig pressure.

24. As soon as he had the City firmly in hand, Charles proceeded with legal actions against the Whig leaders. On 24 Nov. 1682, the former sheriff, Pilkington, was found guilty of *scandalum magnatum* (Luttrell, *Brief Relation, 1,* 240); on 8 May 1683, the former sheriffs Pilkington, Shute, Cornish, and Bethel, along with other City Whigs, were found guilty of riot during the shrieval elections at the Guildhall on 24 June 1682 (see Howell, *State Trials, 9,* 187–298 and headnote to Poems on the Shrieval Elections); and on 19 May 1683, the former Lord Mayor, Sir Patience Ward, was found guilty of perjury (ibid., 299–350 and *The Great Despair of the London Whigs,* 4 n.).

Shall each have a share   25
Of a sanctifi'd popish halter.

5.

Hark! hark! the time's come!
Sound trumpet, beat drum!
Do ye wonder, ye curs, do ye wonder?
'Tis the guards who do wait   30
At your base City gate
And want but the word for to plunder.

30. Charles' guards were strongly suspected of being Catholic.
31. *base City gate:* Perhaps Ludgate, the lowest gate on the Fleet, which led to
Westminster.

Satire, or Song

The closing days of 1682 saw the virtual rout of the Whig party in London. Its most radical spokesman, Slingsby Bethel, had fled several months before; by October, Shaftesbury had dropped out of sight and, at the end of the following month, sailed secretly to Holland. The more conservative leaders stayed on, only to be crushed by courts that they had briefly checked through carefully impanelled grand juries. The astonishing efforts of the Whig sheriff Pilkington (as well as Shute) and of the Whig nominee Papillon (and his running mate Dubois) had ended only in the final bitter election of the Court candidates, North and Rich.

The possibility of an avenging parliament—or indeed of any parliament—faded daily with the realization of all that the "secret" French subsidies implied. The last hope lay in recapturing the London mayoralty; but, here again, the apparent victoy of Alderman Cornish became another bitter defeat when the number of disallowed votes gave the office to William Pritchard. The comparatively few men— Clayton, Player, Ward, and so on—who had been able, by chance and by devising, to keep the London administration in Whig control, were, during 1683, dismissed from their offices and facing trial on a variety of charges.

For non-Whigs, the close of 1682 may well have seemed moderation's moment of triumph. Revenge had not yet made their victory bleak, nor had the desperation of the Rye House Plot yet darkened their outlook.

The text of the poem is based on the unique example in *Z'*.

SATIRE, OR SONG

1.

Presto popular Pilkington,
Shit upon Sheriff Shute;

1. *Presto:* Convey or transfer by magic. During the shrieval elections, York had sought to intimidate Pilkington with a charge of *scandalum magnatum*. On 24 Nov.,

The fools will give no more milk in town,
All the poor Whigs are mute.
Shaftesbury, that old cat of state   5
That lately leapt from the nation,
With Slingsby, that huge maggot pate,
Gave in an association.
Tony has tapp'd his old kilderkin,
And begun forty-one again,   10
Drinks a health to Old Nick again.
    Oh beware brave York!
Oh little Anthony, Anthony!
Where wilt thou put in thy cork?

2.

Cuckoldy Clayton no less ill,   15
And Patience is quite worn out;
Sir Thomas is gone to Cresswell,

---

with the municipal offices safely in Court hands, Pilkington was tried and found
guilty. Unable to pay the enormous damages of £100,000, he was sent off to prison.
Cf. also *Midsummer Moon*, 257 and n.

3. *give . . . milk:* Probably used in the sense of "give down milk," i.e. to give
assistance or profit. "The truth was, the way in which the sheriffs lived made it a
charge of about £5,000" (Burnet, *History*, 2, 253).

6. "Shaftesbury left England on November twenty-eighth and it was surmised in
London four days later that he was definitely out of the country, though his exact
whereabouts was unknown" (Brown, *Shaftesbury*, p. 301).

7. *Slingsby:* For Bethel's flight, see headnote to *Iter Boreale*.

8. *gave in:* Handed in, delivered.

association: An allusion to the treasonable paper calling for armed resistance to
York's succession. This paper, said to have been found in Shaftesbury's study, con-
stituted the strongest piece of evidence in the Court's case against the Earl.

9. *kilderkin:* A cask for liquids, fish, etc. This almost inevitable allusion to the
tap in Shaftesbury's side shows a certain witty variation in the use of the Dutch term.

10. *forty-one:* Throughout 1682, Court writers regularly pointed out the relationship
of that year to 1641, when the Parliament took up arms against Charles I.

15–17. Sir Robert Clayton, Sir Patience Ward, and Sir Thomas Player were all
ardent members of the opposition party. Clayton had been Lord Mayor in 1679 and
was succeeded by Ward; Player was Chamberlain of the City 1672–83. There is some-
thing of all three, but particularly the first, in Crowne's depiction of the Podesta
in *City Politics*.

17. *Cresswell:* "On Tuesday last [29 Nov. 1681] the famous Madam Cresswell was,
on a trial by Nisi Prius at Westminster, convicted after above thirty years' practice
of bawdry, some of her does most unkindly testifying against her" (*Impartial Protestant
Mercury*, No. 64 [29 Nov.–2 Dec. 1681]). L'Estrange strongly suggests that she had

> And somebody has the gout.
> Cornish is balk'd in ambition,
> And Gold has met with allay;   20
> Poor Middlesex lost the petition,
> And Pritchard has won the day.
> Duboys with his shuttle is shrunk away;
> Papillion pimp'd with a punk away;
> All the Tories are drunk today;   25
>   Hey boys then up go we!
> Ah little mobilly mobile,
> Where's your mutiny?

3.

> The *Raree Show* will be sung no more,
> College is dead of the cramp;   30
> And Oates resolves he will hang no more,
> Howard has struck 'em damp.

---

political scruples, obtained her money from "True-Protestant concupiscence" and was particularly attached to a certain notable Whig (*Observator*, No. 78 [7 Dec. 1681]).

18. *gout:* The disease from which Shaftesbury suffered; also, slang for venereal disease.

19–20. The Whig candidates in the mayoral election of 29 Sept. 1682 were Aldermen Henry Cornish and Sir Thomas Gold. Though both appeared to have won over Pritchard and Sir Henry Tulse (*CSPD*, 1682, p. 453), after an inspection of the votes (ibid., p. 487; also Luttrell, *Brief Relation, 1*, 231) and a second common hall, Pritchard was declared the victor.

21. *petition:* Possibly a reference to the London and Middlesex petitions against the installation of North and Rich as sheriffs; these were presented Sept.–Nov. 1682 (see *CSPD*, 1682, pp. 443, 556, etc.). It may also refer to the official petition, published during Ward's mayoralty, calling for a parliament. This was one of the Court's legal bases for rescinding the City's charter (Howell, *State Trials, 8*, 1085–86, 1097–98, 1131–37).

23. *with his shuttle:* John Dubois was a weaver by trade. For further information on him and on Papillon, see headnote and notes to Poems on the Shrieval Elections.

26. "Hey boys, up go we" was the contemporary title of a highly popular Royalist ballad ("The Clean Contrary Way"). See Chappell, *Popular Music*, pp. 425–29. For two examples, see *The Whigs' Exaltation* and *The Tories' Confession*.

27. *mobilly mobile:* The two words are homophonous. In keeping with the text, I have given the first as an adjectival nonce-word.

29. *Raree Show:* The title of the highly popular, highly libellous ballad of Stephen College, the "Protestant joiner," who was hanged for high treason on 31 Aug. 1681 at Oxford. See *POAS*, Yale, *2*, pp. 426–31.

32. Probably Charles Howard, who appeared for the defense in the Popish Plot trial of Richard Langhorne, a Catholic barrister. Howard denied having seen Oates

Escrick is gone away in the dark,
Rebels will riot no more;
And Armstrong, that bully ruffian spark,   35
Will call Monmouth the son of a whore.
Down goes old Ignoramus;
A North wind is risen to shame us;
A Rich will now quite defame us.
  Grave House of Commons meet!   40
Oh little property, property,
Liberty always sweet.

---

at his lodgings in Arundel House during the crucial period of the alleged "Grand Consult" of the Jesuits (Lane, *Oates,* pp. 53–54, 196, 261–62).

33. *Escrick:* Lord William Howard of Escrick had been sent to the Tower in mid-1681. He was released with Shaftesbury on 14 Feb. 1682 and remained out of the public eye until the Rye House Plot (Luttrell, *Brief Relation, 1,* 100, 164, etc.).

35. *Armstrong:* Sir Thomas Armstrong (1624?–84), a daring Royalist during the Commonwealth period, had by this time become an intimate of Monmouth and, according to Sprat, "a debauch'd atheistical bravo" (*DNB*).

36. *son of a whore:* Though a stock ruffian oath, this reflects the opinion of Lucy Walter held by many who were not of Monmouth's faction.

37. *Ignoramus:* The term used by the London grand juries to indicate that they do not consider an indictment to be a true bill. Since the Sheriffs impanelled the grand jury, the defeat of the Whig candidates entails the downfall of juries refusing to allow the Court's cases to be tried.

38–39. *North . . . Rich:* Dudley North and Peter Rich, the newly elected Tory Sheriffs.

40. The final hope of the Whigs lay in a parliament; Charles never allowed them to realize that hope.

Medals of 1682 by George Bowers commemorating: (1) James, Duke of York and (2) his escape from the wreck of the *Gloucester;* (3) the arrival of the Moroccan ambassador, Hamet Ben Hadu, for discussions on (4) the port of Tangier; (5) the arrival of the Bantam ambassador, Keay Naia-Wi-Drai.

An Heroic Poem upon His Royal Highness' Arrival

[H 1590]

At the beginning of May 1682, James, once more permitted to be at Court, prepared to sail for Scotland to bring back his wife Mary. On the 4th, his yacht, the *Mary* put into Margate Road and James boarded the frigate *Gloucester*. Early in the morning of the 6th, the *Gloucester* struck the Lemon and Oar Sands and split. Luttrell says she lost

> a plank of the ship so that they had eight foot water in a moment. The ship being absolutely lost, the boat thereof was let down, into which the Duke entered, and as many persons of quality as it would well hold, and were carried safe to the other ships which, on the news hereof, sent out their boats immediately. But they came too late, for the ship was quickly under water and many perished in her. (*1*, 184–85)

The losses were said to run to about 140 men, and property of the Duke to the amount of £30,000.

Following the royal couple's return to London on 27 May, the presses poured forth panegyrics eulogizing the Duke and Duchess and (a telling argument against the sectarians) seeing the direct interposition of God in York's salvation. Dryden, Otway, and Lee, to name but a few of the known writers, contributed to this flood of encomia. Caleb Calle pictured a descending angel that bowed twice to "Heaven's peculiar care" before delivering himself of his sacred message of salvation (*On His Royal Highness' Miraculous Delivery and Happy Return,* 2 June 1682 [C 299]) ; and the author of *A Pindaric Ode on their Royal Highnesses Happy Return from Scotland after his Escape at Sea,* 27 May [P 2254B] recounted how York's comrades eagerly gave up their lives and were borne to Heaven in an ecstacy of joy at the Duke's deliverance. Matthew Taubman collected his admirable Yorkist and anti-Whig songs, added a few new ones, and, with a preface of adulation, issued his pamphlet *An Heroic Poem to His Royal Highness the Duke of York on his Return from*

Scotland. With some choice songs and medleys on the times [T 239] on 4 July. There were a few anti-Yorkist voices that suggested that, second only to his desire to save himself, the Duke's principal concern had been in salvaging as much of his property as he could; but such comments were drowned in the Tory paeans of joy, thanksgiving, and welcome.

With wit and insight, the writer of the following mock encomium begins by employing the same image and tone that one finds in the encomia; then, incorporating from almost every preceding panegyric ideas and phrases that were probably as sincere as they were vapid, he extends the inanities to their logical absurdity. The resultant comic irony sustains even the last fifteen lines of direct attack on Tory mendacity, which, for the poet, is but an extension of their praise.

The text is based on *f''*; Luttrell's copy was acquired 20 Dec. 1682.

An Heroic Poem upon His Royal Highness' Arrival

Hail to great Neptune, monarch of the sea!
Whose dread command the stubborn winds obey;
And hollow storms that the clouds' bowels tear,
At his grave nod do dwindle into air.
Hail to the powerful beings of the skies!   5
To the winds' god! and wat'ry deities!
"Peace to your briny region," mortals say,
And on your rocky altars incense lay,
Since you grew kind, when equal was your pow'r
To save the perishing or to devour.   10

1. The author's salutation is in sharp contrast to the most fulsome of the eulogists. In Calle and the *Pindaric Ode,* Neptune is accused of stirring up a storm through jealousy of James' glory at sea.

8. Yorkist writers used the image of the altar, but with almost sacrilegious adulation. Taubman concludes the opening stanza of a song "On the Duke's Return after Shipwreck" (p. 15) with

> We sigh'd in the shade for the sun we adore,
> And now with fresh incense our altars run o'er.
> (5–6)

Calle goes even further:

> Let all your incense on his [James'] altars shine,
> Adore his name as you would things divine.
> (55–56)

But oh! the horror of the darken'd main!
But worse the treachery it did contain.
Well might the frigate sink, the sailors cri'd
When all the water was be-whiggifi'd;
When sails conspir'd poor seamen to undo;   15
Nay, every rope was a fanatic too;
The compass presbyterian, which by fits
Makes the winds veer as do a Tory's wits:
Poor loyal Tories, the curst whiggish helm
Into the boundless ocean did o'erwhelm.   20
One curses fate and ships; another raves,
And 'stead of Whigs does fisticuff the waves;
Another damning sinks, and swears he'll go
To firk their coxcombs in the lake below.
Perfidious waves yet threat to trace the sky,   25
Contemn the gods, and spit on majesty,
Daring the nymphs their actions to control,
Wildly upon their wat'ry axles roll.
But kinder Heaven does say it is its will
The storm should cease, and bids the sea be still;   30
Sends out its halcyon from the ark above,

14. The author probably got the idea for the following lines from the poem *To His Royal Highness at his Happy Return from Scotland,* written about 30 May "by a person of quality":

> Heaven, who declares in wonder so divine
> Care of succession, in the rightful line,
> That it protects you with a guardian hand
> From Whiggish Lemans both of sea and land.
>   (62–65)

The verses are as serious as the pun in the last line is unintentional. Almost all the Tory writers stress the parallel of the storm at sea and the political storm on land.

24. *to firk their coxcombs:* To beat their heads; or, to drub, or drive away their fools.

the lake below: Probably Avernus, though Styx and Acheron are occasionally referred to as lakes.

31. The halcyon is a bird of which the ancients fabled that it bred about the time of the winter solstice in a nest floating on the sea, and that it charmed the wind and the waves so that the sea was specially calm during this period. Calle had used the image both in the opening ("And birds of calm sat brooding on the wave") and in the conclusion:

> No more let civil wars torment our isle,
> Let all things with halcyon quiet smile.
>   (98–99)

Which does return with wreaths of grateful love.
Heroic art! to save a monarch's brother:
But still one deity is kind to t' other.
    Welcome, great sir, to our too happy land;   35
Welcome from th' dire fate of treach'rous sand!
At whose approach the town does gently bow,
And fawning courtiers charm'd they know not how;
It makes the duller Tories' heart alive,
And dying prosecutions to revive.   40
Now, rampant Tories, drink! let full bowls pass
With healths and oaths to sweeten every glass,
And once again prepare a sumptuous feast
To entertain the happy welcome guest:
Prepare the dainties of the wat'ry main   45
As Neptune's present to his glorious train;

32. Though the halcyon is usually indentified with the kingfisher, the author prob-
ably connected it with the dove that Noah sent from the Ark on the basis of the
second stanza of Taubman's popular song, "York and Albany" (p. 13):

> The wand'ring dove that was sent forth
>   To find some landing near,
> When England's Ark was toss'd on the flood
>   Of jealousy and fear,
> Returns with olive branch of joy
>   To set the nation free
> From Whiggish rage that would destroy
>   Great York and Albany.
>   (9–16)

34. The line attacks the sacrilegious tone found, for example, in Calle, or the
Pindaric Ode (see 8 n.), or Taubman, who, in his introductory verses (p. iii) suggests
that

> . . . we due reverence to our kings may learn,
>   Restor'd divinely as divinely born.
>   (75–76)

40. *dying prosecutions:* The reference may well be to James' earlier charge of
scandalum magnatum against the former Whig Sheriff, Thomas Pilkington. On 4
Nov., Luttrell heard that the case was to be brought to trial, and on the 24th, the
jury found for York and ordered Pilkington to pay £100,000 damages (Luttrell, *Brief
Relation, 1,* 236, 240; see also headnote and Poems on the Shrieval Elections).

41. A number of Taubman's ballads are drinking songs with "healths and oaths"
in behalf of York and Charles.

43. *a sumptuous feast:* The Duke of York had been guest of honor at the Artillery
Company's feast at the Merchant Tailors' Hall on 20 April. (For divergent accounts
of the Tory feast, see *Impartial Protestant Mercury,* Nos. 105–07 [28 April–2 May
1682] and *Observator,* No. 133 [6 May 1682]; also the Poems on the Whig Feast.)

And every kind of beasts that you are able,
Except of asses—those may wait at table.
(Damn'd prodigality, when you're so poor,
To feast your duke, are forc'd to starve your whore;   50
And most of you, one may be bold to swear,
For one day's feast are doom'd to fast a year.)
Yet swear the Whigs are factious and debate
In private halls the overtures of state;
As true as you are loyal (that's a lie!),   55
They are a people drown'd in treachery;
Swear with an Irish brow and charming grace
Their looks do speak rebellion in their face.
You have at villainies a gracious wink;
Tories may act what others dare not think.   60
Let fly your oaths, and ranting curses too,
The worst, we know, such tools as you can do.

54. *overtures:* Overturnings, overthrows. An erroneous, obsolete use, apparently due to association with *over*. This use postdates the *OED*'s latest quotation by about 50 years.

55. Contemporary pronunciation would have made the first syllable of *loyal* homonymous with the last word in the line.

57. *swear with an Irish brow:* An allusion to the Irish witnesses who swore against Shaftesbury at the time of his treason indictment (see the Medal poems, and Howell, *State Trials, 8,* 759–828).

59. *gracious:* Besides employing the word in its usual sense of "acceptable," "pleasing," or "indulgent," the author very probably wishes us to recall its use as a stock epithet in referring to royalty, their actions, etc.
wink: Signal; intimation (*Dictionary of the Canting Crew*).

60. As Lord Chief Justice Pemberton explained to the grand jury at the proceedings against Shaftesbury, by 35 Edward III it was treason to "compass, imagine, or intend" the death or overthrow of the king, though the law could not be applied until there had been an overt act. By 13 Car II, this overt act did not have to be committed; that is, if suspects were caught before they acted, or if they spoke treason, they would be subject to the law. Two witnesses were still needed, it is true; but by the logic of this later law, one could be executed merely for thinking certain thoughts.

62. *tools:* Implements fit for any turn; the creatures of any cause or faction; a mere property, or cat's foot (*Dictionary of the Canting Crew*).

An Essay upon the Earl of Shaftesbury's Death

Shaftesbury's death meant many things to many people. "Ormonde's comment was 'Whether his death be better for the King's affairs or no is not agreed upon. I am of those that believe it cannot be worse.' James Stuart, who thought what he wanted to think, said, 'I do not hear he is at all regretted by his own party' " (Brown, pp. 303–04). The latter comment, while undoubtedly exaggerated, is quite perceptive; Shaftesbury and the party had probably grown sufficiently apart that "the most eminent politician of his time" now represented only a faction within the opposition party that he had done so much to create. Biographies and elegies appeared, but no national mourning, no civil disturbance, was forthcoming from the Whigs. Practically speaking, the party had lost its leader months before his death.

With sympathy and skill, the writer uses this very situation as the central theme of his ode: "Silence denotes the greatest woe." By this means, he not only separates himself and his subject from any connection with the period of Cromwellian tyranny, but also achieves a tone of restraint that permits analogies to classical and biblical leaders.

AN ESSAY UPON THE EARL OF SHAFTESBURY'S DEATH

Whenever tyrants fall, the air
And other elements prepare
To combat in a civil war:
Large oaks up by the roots are torn;
The savage train,   5
Upon the forest or the plain,
To a procession through the sky are borne;
Sulphureous fire displays
Its baneful rays.

4. See Edmund Waller's *Upon the Late Storm, and Death of . . . Cromwell* [W 532–33], the relevant lines of which are given in *Shaftesbury's Farewell*, 33 n.
8. *sulphureous:* Modern usage would very likely be "sulphurous," which, poetically employed, would apply to thunder and lightning.

Then from the hollow womb   10
Of some rent cloud does come
The blazing meteor or destructive stone.
Distant below, the grumbling wind,
Pent up in earth, a vent would find,
But failing, roars   15
Like broken waves upon the rocky shores.
The earth with motion rolls;
Those buildings which did brave the sky,
Now in an humble posture lie,
While here and there   20
A subtle priest and soothsayer
The fatal dirges howl.
Thus when the first twelve Caesars fell,
A jubilee was kept in Hell;
But when that Heaven designs the brave   25
Shall quit a life to fill a grave,
The sun turns pale and courts a cloud,
From mortals' sight his grief to shroud,
Shakes from his face a shower of rain,
And faintly views the world again.   30
The tombs of ancient heroes weep,
Hard marble tears let fall;
The genii, who possess the deep,
And seem the island's fate to keep,
Lament the funeral.   35
Silence denotes the greatest woe,
So calms precede a storm;
Deep waters smoothest are we know,
And bear the evenest form.
So 'tis when patriots cease to be,   40
And haste to immortality:
Their noble souls blest angels bear
To the ethereal palace there,

21. *subtle:* Skilful, clever; cunning, sly.
23. *twelve Caesars:* The Roman emperors down to Domitian, who are thus grouped in Suetonius' *Lives.* They are here referred to as types of absolute monarchs.
27. *The sun turns pale:* There is a possible echo of Luke 23:45.
33. *genii:* The tutelary gods or attendant spirits.

Mounting upon the ambient air,
While wounded atoms press the ear   45
    Of mortals who far distant are.
Hence sudden grief does seize the mind,
    For good and brave agree;
Each being moves unto his kind
    By native sympathy.   50
So 'twas when mighty Cooper died,
    The Fabius of the Isle:
A sullen look the great o'erspread,
The common people looked as dead,
    And nature droop'd the while.   55
    Living, religion, liberty,
A mighty fence he stood;
    Peers' rights and subjects' property
None stronglier did maintain than he,
For which Rome sought his blood.   60
Deep politician, English peer,
That quash'd the power of Rome,
The change of State they brought so near,
In bringing Romish worship here,
Was by thy skill o'erthrown.   65
    'Less Heaven a miracle design'd,
    Sure it could never be,

---

45. For contemporary theories on the transmission of sound, see A. Wolfe, *A History of Science, Technology, and Philosophy in the 16th and 17th Centuries* (New York, 1935), pp. 287–89. The atomic theory, held by Gassendi and in part by Derham, was just being disproved by Guericke, whose recently invented (1650) air pump was the basis for the later experiments of Boyle, Papin, and Hauksbee.

52. *Fabius:* Quintus Fabius Maximus, after having been named dictator by the people of Rome, carried out his famous defensive action of harassment against Hannibal, which won him the title of *Cunctator* ("the delayer"). His caution and prudence set him in opposition to more aggressive policies and, particularly in later life, to young men such as Scipio. The author might well be attempting to establish Shaftesbury as a model of restraint in his campaign against Charles, in contrast to Russell, Grey, Essex, and so on.

56. *Living:* i.e. *when living.*

57. *fence:* A bulwark, defense (*OED*, though this postdates the latest quotation by 130 years).

60. Probably the specific reference is to Thomas Dangerfield's alleged plan to assassinate Shaftesbury as part of the Meal Tub Plot (cf. Brown, *Shaftesbury,* p. 265).

One so gigantic in his mind,
That soar'd a pitch 'bove human kind,
So small a corpse should be.   70
Time was, the Court admir'd thy shrine,
And did thee homage pay;
But wisely thou didst countermine,
And, having found the black design,
Scorn'd the ignoble way.   75
Having thus strongly stemm'd the tide
And set thy country free,
Thou, Cato-like, an exile prid'st,
'Mongst enemies belov'd resid'st,
Whilst good men envy thee.   80
And as the sacred Hebrew seer,
Canaan to view desir'd;
So Heav'n did show this noble peer
The end of popish malice here,
Which done, his soul expir'd.   85

68–71. Dryden's famous portrait in *Absalom and Achitophel* contrasts the great wit (163) with the "pygmy body" (158).

71–74. Shaftesbury, who had helped in the negotiation of Charles' restoration, was Chancellor of the Exchequer from 1661–72. After going into full opposition, he accepted the office of President of the Privy Council (April 1679), but Charles probably wished thus to circumvent him. He was dismissed in Oct. of the same year.

78. *Cato:* Marcus Porcius Cato (95–46 B.C.), the type of virtuous public servant and the model of Stoic republicanism. When Caesar triumphed and Cato found himself unable to establish his national ideal of a free state, he died with his principles, though (unlike Shaftesbury who was a Christian) by his own hand.

prid'st: Art proud to be, takest pride in being.

79. Though the English had fought three wars with the Dutch in as many decades, the two countries were allied by their Protestantism.

81. *Hebrew seer:* Moses, see Deuteronomy 32:48–52.

The Last Will and Testament of
Anthony, King of Poland

[L 514]

After acquiring his copy of this poem on 16 Oct. 1682, Luttrell wrote on it, "A libel against the Lord Shaftesbury and several of that party. A virulent, prophane thing." The form of the "last will and testament," long popular in political verse (cf. the relevant entries in Wing [L 514–33]), allowed the writer to itemize his victim's alleged errors, portray him as unrepentant to the end, and show who his heirs of evil were. Generally, such a poem was an *omnium gatherum* of stock charges, spiced with a "virulent, prophane" tone that produced strong invective, if not *saeva indignatio*. It is not far from the mock "last words," and indeed, it was only eight days later that Luttrell bought his copy of *The King of Poland's Last Speech to his Countrymen* [K 570].

In this attack, all the stock comments are brought together: the Tory gibe that Shaftesbury coveted the Polish throne to which Sobieski was elected in 1674; the reference to the silver tap which drained the liver cyst that had been operated on in 1668; the consequent nickname of "Potapski" which (according to the later *T"*) combines "*Po,* from Poland or Polish king, *tap* [because of the] . . . silver tap . . . , and *ski* . . . a form in Poland proper to the king and all the nobility thereof"; the treasonous paper of an Association which was said to have been found in his study; the charge that the Earl developed the Popish Plot; the assertion that he planned, through demagogues, fanatics, and republicans, to bring in a new commonwealth through civil strife. All these are bound together not only by the form of a mock testament, but, even more, by the items being disposed of: with a certain shock, one realizes the author is parceling out the mutilated remains of someone who has suffered a traitor's death. In this particular case, only the entrails may be allowed burial; and for this, the author fittingly changes to the epitaph tetrameter, which contrasts sharply with the brutality of the sense of the lines.

As the number of texts testify, the poem was quite popular, and there was the inevitable reply. The deposition of a certain Joshua Bowes (*CSPD*, 11 Nov. 1682) furnishes a rare insight into the production and distribution of such manuscript verse:

> Elkanah Settle gave him the enclosed libel, the title of which is *Mac's Triumph, in imitation of the King of Poland's Last Will and Testament*, beginning "My game is won, then, Patrick, tell me why," and ending, "Then let my praise be tuned to Roger's fiddle." He [Bowes] was desired by Settle not to give it to any but such as he knew to be Whigs. The deponent then mentioned the Earls of Essex, Anglesey, Macclesfield and Stamford, Lords Grey, Herbert and Gerard and some others, which Settle liked very well and conditioned with the deponent for half the profit.
>
> Settle to the deponent's knowledge composed the enclosed libel, for he showed to the deponent piecemeal, now about 6 lines and afterwards 8 or 10 more, and in the deponent's presence corrected several words in the old copy and in his sight put commas to the enclosed and said that, if that took, he would make others. . . .
>
> The deponent asked Settle who Mac was. Settle answered the Duke of York and that by Carnegie was meant a countess who formerly had clapped the said Duke.

The Last Will and Testament of
Anthony, King of Poland

My tap is run; then Baxter, tell me why
Should not the good, the great Potapski die?
Grim Death, who lays us all upon our backs,

1. *tap:* See headnote. The gloss of *T"* remarks that "The common saying is, 'My glass is run,'" but cf. Chaucer's Prologue to the *Reeve's Tale*, 38–41.

Baxter: Richard Baxter (1615–91), probably the most famous of the Presbyterian divines, left the Anglican Church a few days before the Act of Uniformity was passed (1662). An active force in the Civil War (see Leo Solts, *Saints in Arms* [Stanford, 1959]), a prolific writer (the best known of his tracts being *The Saints' Everlasting Rest*), and the most popular nonconformist preacher, Baxter embodied the highest principles of moderate dissent.

2. *Potapski.* See headnote. For a full treatment of the theme, see *A Modest Vindication of the Earl of Shaftesbury* [M 2375], reprinted in *Somers Tracts*, 8, 313–18.

Instead of scythe doth now advance his axe;
And I, who all my life in broils have spent,   5
Intend at last to make a settlement.
    Imprimis: For my soul (though I had thought,
To 've left that thing I never minded, out)
Some do advise, for fear of doing wrong,
To give it him to whom it doth belong.   10
But I, who all mankind have cheated, now
Intend likewise to cheat the devil too:
Therefore I leave my soul unto my son,
For he, as wise men think, as yet has none.
    Then for my Polish crown, that pretty thing,   15
Let Monmouth take't, who longs to be a king;
His empty head soft nature did design
For such a light and airy crown as mine.
    With my estate, I'll tell you how it stands:
Jack Ketch must have my clothes, the King my lands.   20
    Item: I leave the damn'd Association
To all the wise disturbers of the nation;
Not that I think they'll gain their ends thereby,
But that they may be hang'd as well as I.
    Armstrong (in murders, and in whorings skill'd,   25

4. *axe:* i.e. for execution (cf. 20).

14. Cf. Dryden's famous description in *Absalom and Achitophel:*

> And all to leave what with his toil he won
> To that unfeather'd, two legg'd thing, a son;
> Got while his soul did huddl'd notions try,
> And born a shapeless lump, like anarchy.
>
>   (169–73)

16. James, Duke of Monmouth, was the Whigs' choice of successor to the throne in place of the Catholic Duke of York.

20. By law, those convicted of treason forfeited their entire estate to the crown. By custom, the executioner (at this time, the famous Jack Ketch) received the clothes which the condemned man wore at the time of his death.

21. *Association:* See headnote and the Medal Poems.

22. Luttrell's gloss reads: "to the Parliament."

24. This is not in conflict with 4, since the punishment for treason included hanging, drawing, emasculation, disemboweling, beheading, and quartering. Most of these are referred to in the course of the poem.

25. *Armstrong:* Sir Thomas Armstrong (1624–84) had been knighted at the Restoration for his work and suffering in behalf of the Royalist cause. He became an intimate of Monmouth and, according to prejudiced writers, "led a very vicious life" as a "debauched, atheistical bravo" (Burnet and Sprat, quoted in *DNB*). In 1679, he and

Who twenty bastards gets for one man kill'd),
To thee I do bequeath my brace of whores,
Long kept to draw the humors from my sores;
For you they'll serve as well as silver tap,
For women give, and sometimes cure, a clap.   30
    Howard, my partner in captivity,
False to thy God and King, but true to me,
To thee some heinous legacy I'd give,
But that I think thou hast not long to live;
Besides, thou'st wickedness enough in store   35
To serve thyself, and twenty thousand more.
    To thee, young Grey, I'll some small toy present,
For you with any thing can be content;
Then take the knife with which I cut my corns;
'Twill serve to pare and sharp your Lordship's horns,   40
That you may rampant Monmouth push and gore
'Till he shall leave your house, and change his whore.

Monmouth joined an English regiment in Flanders, Armstrong having earlier been granted a royal pardon for having killed the brother of Sir Carr Scroope at the Duke's playhouse (*A True Relation of the Behavior and Execution of Sir Thomas Armstrong* [T 2934]). As M.P. for Stafford in 1679 and 1681, he aligned himself with the Shaftesbury faction and was evidently in the Earl's confidence at this time. He was eventually executed (20 June 1684) for complicity in the Rye House Plot.

   29. *silver tap:* See headnote.

   31. *Howard:* William Howard, Baron of Escrick, "had learned his preaching from the Anabaptists and his plotting from Cromwell's Guards" (Ogg, *Charles II*, p. 642). In 1681, he was sent to the Tower "on the false charge preferred by Edward Fitzharris of writing the *True Englishman*" (*DNB*). There he was joined by Shaftesbury, who had been committed on a charge of treason, and the two tried unsuccessfully to petition for trial or bail under the Habeas Corpus Act. Through the influence of Algernon Sidney, Howard was released in Feb. 1682 and joined the anti-Court forces. The writer's words (35–36) were to prove all too true; Howard, when arrested for complicity in the Rye House Plot (1683), turned state's evidence and was largely responsible for the conviction of at least Sidney.

   37. *Grey:* Forde, Lord Grey of Werk, was in the inner circle of Whig politics. He was, as well, constantly involved in the most sensational gossip of the time. First, there was the persistent rumor of an affair between Monmouth and his wife, Lady Mary Grey (the daughter of the Earl of Berkeley); then there was his secret, romantic, and pathetic liaison with his sister-in-law, the eighteen-year-old Lady Henrietta Berkeley, which culminated in her running away from home (Aug. 1682) and the charge against him of debauchery. The ensuing trial (23 Nov. 1682) proved to be one of the most dramatic courtroom scenes of the period (see Howell, *State Trials, 9,* 127–86). See also *The Western Rebel*, 46; *POAS*, Yale, *4*.

On top of Monument let my head stand,
Itself a monument, where first began
The flame that has endanger'd all the land.   45
But first to Titus let my ears be thrown,
For he, 'tis thought, will shortly lose his own.
I leave old Baxter my envenom'd teeth
To bite and poison all the bishops with.
Item: I leave my tongue to wise Lord North,   50
To help him bring his *What-de-call-ums* forth;
'Twill make his Lordship utter treason clear,
And he in time may speak like Noble Peer.
My squinting eyes let Ignoramus wear,
That they may this way look, and that way swear.   55
Let the cits take my nose, because 'tis said,

43. *Monument:* The London Monument, which commemorated the fire of 1666, was erected near the spot where the conflagration began (Bell, *The Great Fire,* p. 208).

my head: The heads of traitors were impaled on spikes, usually on London Bridge but occasionally at Westminster.

45. *The flame:* In this case, the anti-Catholic fervor with which Shaftesbury fired the country. The most convinced soon came to believe that the conflagration of 1666 had been caused by Jesuits and an inscription to that effect was engraved on the Monument in June 1681, by order of the Common Council, during the mayoralty of the Whig Sir Patience Ward. For Alexander Pope, the column still stood "like a tall bully [that] lifts the head, and lies." (cf. Bell, *The Great Fire,* pp. 208–09.)

46. *Titus:* i.e. Titus Oates, the discoverer of the Popish Plot.

my ears: The punishment for libel included cutting off one or both of the offender's ears. The most notable sufferer had been William Prynne, who, in the 1630s and 1640s, was considered a martyr to the Parliamentary cause.

50. *North:* Francis North (1637–85), Chief Justice of Common Pleas (1675–82) and Lord Chancellor (1682). In the following year he was created Baron Guilford. His inclusion here is surprising, since he was a firm adherent of the Court and had advanced his brother Dudley as that party's candidate to the hotly contested shrieval post.

51. Roger North stresses Francis' extreme shyness as a youth (*Lives, 1,* 45–47), and his extraordinary caution when older: "For, although all the company understood him perfectly well, yet his sense was so couched that, if it had been delivered in the center of his enemies, no crimination, with any force, could have been framed out of it; and this way he used with his intimate friends as with strangers" (p. 307). *T",* which is perhaps more exegetical than informed, says, "A blundering fellow who was a plotter and lord chancellor. He was wont to cry to anything he could not readily tell 'What-de-call-um, What-de-call-um.' "

53. *Noble peer:* A stock sobriquet for Shaftesbury.

54. *Ignoramus:* The name applied to the Whig Grand Jury that returned the treason indictment against Shaftesbury "Ignoramus" and thus blocked the Court's action.

56. *cits:* Citizens.

That by the nose I them have always led;
But for their wives I nothing now can spare,
For all my lifetime they have had their share.
 Let not my quarters stand on City gate,   60
Lest they new sects and factions do create;
For certainly the Presbyterian wenches,
In dirt will fall to idolize my haunches.
But that I may to my old friend be civil,
Let some witch make them mummy for the devil.   65
 To good King Charles I leave (though, faith, 'tis pity)
A poison'd nation and deluded City,
Seditions, clamors, murmurs, jealousies,
False oaths, sham stories, and religious lies.
There's one thing still which I had quite forgot,   70
To him I leave the carcass of my plot;
In a consumption the poor thing doth lie,
And when I'm gone 'twill pine away, and die.
 Let Jenkyns in a tub my worth declare,
And let my life be writ by Harry Care.   75
And if my bowels in the earth find room,
Then let these lines be writ upon their tomb.

Epitaph upon his Bowels.

Ye mortal Whigs, for death prepare,
For mighty Tapski's guts lie here.

58. Since all the other steps of a traitor's execution are referred to, this may be an oblique reference to the cutting off of the privy members.

60. *my quarters:* See 24 n.

71. *my plot:* The direction, if not the initial idea, of the Popish Plot was frequently ascribed to Shaftesbury.

74. *Jenkyns:* William Jenkyn (1613–85), the ejected minister, was a rigorous Presbyterian who continued to preach privately even after his meetinghouse in Jewin Street was disturbed. His funeral sermon on Lazarus Seaman (1675) provoked a pamphlet exchange that continued through 1681.

tub: A term of obloquy for the pulpit of a nonconforming preacher.

75. *Harry Care:* Care was one of the principal writers for the Whigs. His most regular production at this time was *The Weekly Pacquet of Advice from Rome* which, with its appended *Courant,* was the party's answer to L'Estrange's *Observator.* Actually, the earliest life was probably that of S. N., *Rawleigh Redivivus* [N 72], which was printed in 1683.

76. *bowels:* Ordinarily, the bowels of a traitor were to be taken out and burnt before the victim's eyes.

Will his great name keep sweet d' y' think?   80
For certainly his entrails stink.
Alas! 'tis but a foolish pride
To outsin all mankind beside,
When such illustrious garbage must
Be mingled with the common dust.   85
False Nature! that could thus delude
The cheater of the multitude,
That put his thoughts upon the wing,
And egg'd him on to be a king;
See now to what an use she puts   90
His noble great and little guts.
Tapski, who was a man of wit,
Had guts for other uses fit;
Though fiddle-strings they might not be
(Because he hated harmony),   95
Yet for black puddings they were good;
Their master did delight in blood:
Of this they should have drank their fill,
(King Cyrus did not fare so ill).
Poor guts, could this have been your hap,   100
Sheriff Bethel might have got a snap;
But now at York his guts must rumble
Since you into a hole did tumble.

96. *black puddings:* Sausages made of blood (cf. 97) and suet. The mixture is stuffed in animals' entrails.

101. *Sheriff:* The word might quite possibly have been pronounced monosyllabically, as in its alternate form, *shrieve.*

Bethel: Slingsby Bethel, the leader of the extreme republican wing of the Whig party, had been sheriff in 1680–81. He fled north in early July 1682, probably recognizing by then that, without the shrieval posts, Charles' control of the municipal government was inevitable.

snap: A slight or hasty meal, a snack; also, a scrap, fragment or morsel.

102. *York:* By 9 Sept., Leoline Jenkins had heard that Bethel, a Yorkshire man, had been at Durham and later Newcastle (*CSPD,* 1682, p. 382). Eventually, Bethel managed to arrive in the free city of Hamburg, where he had been earlier in his life (1637–49).

guts must rumble: Bethel's parsimony was a constant target for Tory gibes (see *Iter Boreale*).

1683

A Supplement to the Last Will and Testament
of Anthony, Earl of Shaftesbury

[S 6187]

This poem, with its themes of mock-mourning, confession, and testament, is a codicil to (and, very likely, by the writer of) *The Last Will and Testament of Anthony, King of Poland*. If it lacks some of the virulence of the earlier poem, it supplies a fuller survey of the Whig party and a more careful analysis of Shaftesbury's political position in the final months of his life.

A SUPPLEMENT TO
THE LAST WILL AND TESTAMENT
OF ANTHONY, EARL OF SHAFTESBURY

with his last words, as they were taken in Holland,
where he died January the 20th, 1683

Mourn! England, mourn! let not thy grief be feign'd:
The tap so long upon the lees is drain'd.
The cringing pillar of the State and Church
Is fall'n, and left his proselytes i'th' lurch.
Alas! what will become o'th' reformation,   5
The Popish Plot, and black Association,
Our rights and liberties, and Good Old Cause,
Patch'd juries, and the Ignoramus laws?
What will become o'th' Saints in tribulation,

Title. The date is a bit in error; Shaftesbury died on the morning of 21 Jan.
6. *Association:* The paper of an Association, said to have been found in Shaftesbury's study, called for resistance to the accession of the Catholic Duke of York. (See the Medal Poems; and, for the text of the Association, Howell, *State Trials, 8,* 781–87.)
7. *Good Old Cause:* The motto of the Commonwealth's-men.
8. Shaftesbury's indictment for high treason was presented to a Middlesex grand jury that had been carefully chosen by the Whig sheriffs. Their "Ignoramus" prevented any further action. Luttrell has emended *Patch'd* to *Pack'd.*
9. *Saints:* Certain sectarians who considered themselves among the elect.

If Tory-loyalty comes into fashion?   10
The Salamanca doctor must take post,
If Thompson and L'Estrange must rule the roast;
And Monkey Care, Gotham, and Snivelling Dick
Must from the Hague e'en follow to Old Nick.
    "In vain we strive to shun th' appointed fate,   15
That on the knave, as well as fool, does wait.
Though I," said he, "have drawn infectious breath,
And liv'd this eighty years in spite of death,
Had I been hang'd but fifty years agone,
Less treason had ensu'd, less mischief done.   20
But as there is an evil genius waits
On private men, so there's in public states—
The universal tempter of mankind
That always in the ditch will lead the blind,
Of sin and faction the allotted bane,   25
And for that very cause has leave to reign:
Else Belzebub, long since, I'd been thy due,
But that he fear'd I should supplant him too.
Thus, like the Devil, I was born a curse

11. *Salamanca doctor:* Titus Oates encouraged the idea that he had taken a D.D. from the University of Salamanca. For that institution's vigorous denial, see *Observator*, No. 227 (21 Oct. 1682).

12. *Thompson and L'Estrange:* Nathaniel Thompson and Roger L'Estrange, the most prolific and most violent Tory propagandists of the period, were perhaps best known through their journalistic writing. Thompson produced the aggressive *Loyal Protestant*, while L'Estrange wrote the devastatingly witty *Observator*. Both also engaged fully in the pamphlet wars that were raging.

13. *Care, Gotham, and . . . Dick:* Henry Care, Langley Curtis, and Richard Janeway were writers and publishers of anti-Court material as strident, if not so witty, as that of their Tory opposites. Care was principally involved in *The Weekly Packet of Advice from Rome,* with its appended *Courant,* but he probably also had a hand in *Impartial Protestant Mercury.* Curtis and Janeway were the publishers but may well have done some of the writing.

14. Both sides had been punished for libel (see e.g. Howell, *State Trials,* 7, 959, 1111–30; *8,* 1359–98), but, though I have not found that any of the three Whigs had been forced to seek refuge in Holland, Court control of municipal offices threatened direct persecution, or at least a cessation of the kind of favoritism that had freed Janeway in May 1682 (Luttrell, *Brief Relation, 1,* 186).

18–19. In point of fact, Shaftesbury was just sixty-one and a half years old at his death; as well, his first "treason" (if the author has in mind Cooper's change from the royalist to the parliamentary side circa Feb. 1644) would have been about thirty-nine "years agone."

To all mankind. My lord and master, worse 30
Betray'd, like Judas, while I kept the purse.
  "Yet still, in every state, I walk'd secure,
Grave with the king, and jocund with the whore;
And never did one lucky mischief brew,
But grateful laurels still adorn'd my brow; 35
In every state have so successful been,
As fame alone were the rewards of sin.
  "And all this while, not the severest law
Could find me faulty, though they found a flaw.
Still by my arts, or Ignoramus friends, 40
I guiltless seem'd, and still pursu'd my ends.
For what was all this specious pretence
Of subjects' rights, and safety of the prince,
Religion, liberty, association,
But to betray all, and enslave the nation? 45
Which by so many plots I did enthrall,
Whilst the blind rabble worshipp'd me as Baal.
  "But now the mist is vanish'd from their eyes;
They see my crimes through all its thick disguise
(Though, for the Saints and brethren, I dare say, 50
I could have kept in ignorance to this day).
Once sons of light, but now the Saints are blind,
While Tories, Janus-like, have eyes behind.
  "Thus, all my shams discover'd, I, poor I,
Was forc'd, although my wings were clipp'd, to fly. 55
Nay, though no legs I had, my gait was fleet,

31. Judas kept the purse for Jesus (John 12:6, 13:29). Shaftesbury had been Chancellor of the Exchequer from 1661–72, Lord Chancellor 1672–73.

36. Shaftesbury sat, for example, on the Council of State in both 1653–54 and 1659 and just two decades later, in 1679, was the President of Charles II's Privy Council.

43–44. All these phrases were slogans of Shaftesbury's party; so too 71–72, 74–75.

47. *Baal:* A false god, or idol. See *Absalom Senior,* 79 n.

52. *sons of light:* Perhaps a reference to the Quaker doctrine of guidance through the "inner light."

53. *behind:* i.e. that look back to 1641.

56–61. Shaftesbury, who was crippled with gout, ague, and a suppurating liver cyst, must have had great difficulty in moving about. To some contemporaries, he was the "little limping peer," and Ormonde, on 2 Dec. 1682, wondered how "a man of his age, infirmity, and wealth could be frighted out of his country, unless he knows more of himself than appears to me" (Brown, *Shaftesbury,* pp. 268, 301).

56. *gait was fleet:* Modernization may be hiding a possible play on words here. The

Oblig'd to travel, though I had no feet;
From justice (all my crimes laid at my door)
Found power to run, who could not crawl before.
   "Old and decrepit, gouty toes, scarr'd shins,   60
Turn pilgrim in my dotage for my sins.
My strength and action gone, I mount the stage
With all the frailties that attend on age,
And nothing left me but the constant will
And natural inclination to do ill.   65
Glad to sham off with all my vanquish'd hope,
To save that neck that would disgrace a rope.
   "My hopes are fled; let death wind up the charm;
Life's but a plague when I can do no harm.
Your canting words no longer will prevail;   70
Your liberty and property is stale;
The rights and privileges of the nation
Are but cast suits when loyalty's in fashion.
Your plots and perjuries will do no more;
Your slavery and arbitrary pow'r   75
Are, like my banish'd self, thrown out of door.
   "What now remains but that the tap should burst?
Who can do any more, that has done his worst?
That the proud foe rejoice not in my fall,
Now heart, break heart, and baffle Ketch and all.   80
But ere I fall a victim, though too late,
In a vile nation, to a viler fate,
I thus bequeath the remnant of my estate.
   "My former will, as Fate's decretals, stands,
But something's due unto the Netherlands   85
For their civilities, since here I fled:

---

broadside reads: "my Gate was Fleet" and it is conceivable that there is an allusion
to the Fleet prison for debtors near Ludgate.

60. *scarr'd shins:* Perhaps as the result of past attacks of venereal disease.

80. *Ketch:* Jack Ketch, the public executioner from about 1663 until his death in
1686.

84. *My former will:* See headnote.

86. *civilities:* Despite his desire in 1673 for the "utter destruction" of Holland in
the Third Dutch War, Shaftesbury was generally welcomed and, by 12 Dec. 1682,
had been made a burgher of Amsterdam. (See *The Dispatches of Thomas Plott and*

Foul linen, stinking fish, and mouldy bread.
To th' States, because they are a free-born nation,
I do bequeath my new Association,
That perfect model of true anarchy   90
And charm against all monarch tyranny;
Though to live here (had it so pleas'd the Fates),
I had been king, or th' Devil had had the States.

"My heart, with faction flam'd, that source of evil,
I leave to my old club that haunts the Devil;   95
As fickle and as false as is your own
Sworn enemy, to all that sways the throne.

"My lungs, my Ignoramus friends, are yours;
But for my sleights, I leave 'em to the boors,
To blow the bellows of each new sedition,   100
On any change of faction or religion.

"My tap and spigot were dispos'd before,
Or that had serv'd some Belgic common-shore;
A sovereign cure for an hydroptic nation
To stop, or else let out, the inundation;   105
To drown the monsieur for his late abuses,

Thomas Chudleigh, ed. F. A. Middlebush [Ph.D. dissertation, University of Michigan]
1926, p. 196 and n. 1, p. 197.)

88. *States:* The States General, the legislative assembly of the Netherlands; the
Netherlands.

89. *new Association:* See also *Shaftesbury's Farewell, or The New Association.*

95. *club:* Probably the famed Green Ribbon Club, which had formal headquarters
at the King's Head Tavern. (See J. R. Jones, "The Green Ribbon Club," *Durham Uni-
versity Journal, 49* [N.S. *18*], Dec. 1956, pp. 17–20; also North, *Examen*, p. 572.) How-
ever, in the Preface to *The Duke of Guise*, Dryden refers to "the Associating Club of
the Devil Tavern" (S.-S., *Dryden, 7,* 163–64), and there may have been an Old Devil
(ibid., p. 181) as opposed to the Young Devil Tavern (between the two Temple gates)
where the Rye House conspirators met on occasion.

99. *sleights:* Deceitful, subtle, or wily dealing or policy; artifice, strategy, trickery.
boors: Peasants (particularly Dutch or German); any rude, ill-bred, coarse fellow.

102. *tap:* See *The Last Will and Testament,* 29 and headnote.

103. *common-shore:* Originally, the "no man's land" by the waterside where filth
was allowed to be deposited for the tide to wash away; then, used interchangeably with
"common sewer," a drain through which all or a large part of the sewage of a town
passes. For the intermediate form of the word, see the textual note.

104. *hydroptic:* Charged with water.

106. The Dutch War with England and France began in 1672; two years later the
English withdrew, but the French continued until the Treaty of Nijmwegen (1678).
The French had been able to overrun large portions of the country and had defeated

And vent out all their venom through the sluices.

"I leave my brains to that incestuous crew,
The lordly tribe who lofty treasons brew:
Those hot-brain'd fiery Catilines of State   110
Who their own and the nation's ills create,
And will, I fear, like me, repent too late.

"To Bethel and his brethren I resign
The axe which baffled Fate predestin'd mine,
To do that execution they would bring   115
On monarchy and an indulgent King.

"To th' Salamanca beagle of the Plot,
I leave a halter as his proper lot,
For his ill management, while Tory striv'd,
Of an ill plot that was so well contriv'd.   120

"And lastly, to those friends who were at strife,

---

the Dutch fleet in the Mediterranean (1676), but William of Orange's defense and eventual counter-offensives kept Holland entire.

107. *sluices:* In 1672, William III was able to save the province of Holland and the city of Amsterdam by opening the sluices.

108. *incestuous crew:* The reference is primarily to Ford, Lord Grey of Werk, whose sensational affair with his sister-in-law, Lady Henrietta Berkeley, culminated in a trial for debauchery on 23 Nov. 1682 (Howell, *State Trials, 9,* 127–86). There was also the persistent rumor that Grey was being cuckolded by Monmouth (cf. *The Last Will and Testament,* 37–42); such "incest," though somewhat less of kin, was more of the party kind.

110. *Catilines:* Lucius Sergius Catiline, who revolted in 63 B.C. against Rome, was the type of the profligate conspirator and reckless incendiary (see, e.g., *The Loyal Scot,* 25).

113. *Bethel:* Slingsby Bethel, one of the sheriffs in 1681, headed the republican faction of Shaftesbury's party; he had fled from London in July 1682 when it became evident that the Court would control the City (see *Iter Boreale*).

116. Bethel was reputed to have said that "rather than the old King [Charles I] should have wanted an executioner, he would have done it himself" (Luttrell, *Brief Relation, 1,* 187); and reports from informers suggest that the old Oliverians still thought of the short, sharp way to a commonwealth (*CSPD,* 1682, pp. 236–38).

117–18. The metaphor is frequently connected with the Popish Plot. In 1679, the anti-Court pamphlet *An Appeal from the Country to the City* (ascribed to Charles Blount [B 3300]) states that "had we not had some such good huntsmen as the . . . Earl of Shaftesbury and our late Secret Committees to manage the chase for us, our hounds must needs have been baffled and the game lost." Shaftesbury is said to have remarked, enigmatically, "I will not say who started the game, but I am sure I had the full hunting of it" (Ferguson, *Ferguson,* p. 42).

121. *those friends:* The allusion (see 124) would seem to be to those who had been foremost on the "Ignoramus" jury: Sir Samuel Barnardiston (the foreman), Thomas Papillon, and John Dubois. The last two had been the Whig shrieval candidates in

Losing themselves to save a wretched life,
I do bequeath my sledge as the just fee
Of their accumulated perjury.
  "These, with my gouts and pains, I leave to those   125
Who did my long deserved fate oppose:
Their too-officious kindness prov'd a curse;
To hang is bad, to die unpiti'd's worse;
Since I had rather fall'n a martyr there
Than rot, and moulder in effigy, here.   130
  "You the trustees of this my dying will,
If you in villainy would prosper still,
Be sure you justly every point fulfill."

1682. At the time of this poem, the full force of Charles II's legal revenge was being felt by the Whig leaders.

123. *sledge:* The conveyance used for carrying a traitor to his place of execution.

128–30. For the relationship of Shaftesbury to the party at this time, see the head-note to *An Essay Upon the Earl of Shaftesbury's Death.*

130. *effigy:* Accented on the second syllable. There seems to be a conflation of the practice of executing escaped traitors in effigy and the famed "laying in state" of Shaftesbury's body in Amsterdam, where the coffin had "a glass over the face in order that the common people might not touch it, as they were inclined to do, 'by reason it lay with a very smiling countenance'" (Brown, *Shaftesbury,* p. 304).

Shaftesbury's Farewell

[S 2909]

Amid the clamor of partisan verse that surrounded Shaftesbury's life and death, examples of sympathetic yet critical poems are surprisingly few. One thinks at once of Dryden; the Dryden not of *The Medal,* but of *Absalom and Achitophel,* with its changes from witty invective to the subtle though biased analysis of character that is so justly famous:

> For close designs and crooked counsels fit,
> Sagacious, bold, and turbulent of wit,
> Restless, unfix'd in principles and place,
> In power, unpleas'd, impatient of disgrace.
> A fiery soul, which, working out its way,
> Fretted the pygmy body to decay
> And o'erinform'd the tenement of clay.
>
> (152–58)

Shaftesbury's Farewell seems at times to echo the earlier Dryden poem and may, as well, contain an allusion to *The Medal;* yet basically its characterization is independent. As well, the poem is unusual not only because it appeared at this date and on this occasion, but also because of the tone of pity, loss, and harm that informs the writer's indignation.

The text is based on *l″* (copies in *f″* and *k″*) and collated with *b.* Luttrell's copy is dated 3 Feb. 1683.

Title. Association: The Association was to be a league of those opposed to the Catholic Duke of York's accession, who would, if necessary, take up arms against him and obey the commands of the parliamentary exclusionists. The consequence of such an action could only have been a repetition of the Civil War. The "new" association is explained in the final line of the poem.

SHAFTESBURY'S FAREWELL

or

The New Association

Greatest of men, yet man's least friend, farewell:
Wit's mightiest, but most useless, miracle;
Where Nature all her richest treasures stor'd,
To make one vast unprofitable hoard.
So high as thine no orb of fire could roll,   5
The brightest, yet the most eccentric, soul;
Whom, 'midst wealth, honors, fame, yet want of ease,
No pow'r could e'er oblige, no State could please.
Be in thy grave with peaceful slumbers bless'd,
And find thy whole life's only stranger: rest.   10
Oh, Shaftesbury! had thy prodigious mind
Been to thyself, and thy great master kind,
Glory had wanted lungs thy trump to blow,
And pyramids had been a tomb too low.
Oh, that the world, great statesman, e'er should see   15
Nebuchadnezzar's dream fulfill'd in thee!
Whilst such low paths led thy great soul astray,
Thy head of gold mov'd but on feet of clay.
Yes, from rebellion's late inhuman rage,
The crimes and chaos of that monstrous age,   20
As the old patriarch from Sodom flew,
So to great Charles his sacred bosom, thou;

2–10. Cf. Dryden, *Absalom and Achitophel:*

> Great wits are sure to madness near alli'd,
> And thin partitions do their bounds divide;
> Else, why should he, with wealth and honor bless'd,
> Refuse his age the needful hours of rest?

(163–66)

16. Nebuchadnezzar's dream was of an image whose "head was of fine gold, his breast and his arms of silver, his belly and his thighs of brass, his legs of iron, his feet part of iron and part of clay." The dream and its interpretation are found in Daniel 2:31–45. The writer of the ironic *Panegyric on the Author of Absalom and Achitophel* (*POAS*, Yale, 2, 503–04) likens Dryden's panegyrics first on Cromwell and later on Charles II to "Daniel's dream," being "A head of gold to his old feet of clay" (69).

21–22. *the old patriarch:* For Lot's flight to the safety of Zoar at the time of Sodom's destruction, see Genesis 19:22. For Shaftesbury's part in the restoration of Charles II, see Brown, *Shaftesbury,* pp. 69–99.

But, oh! with more than Lot's wife's fatal fault,
For which she stood in monumental salt.
Though the black scene thy hasting footstep flies,   25
Thy soul turns back, and looks with longing eyes.
Ah, noble peer, that the records of fame
Should give Herostratus and thee one name;
Great was his bold achievement, greater thine:
Greater, as kings than shrines are more divine;   30
Greater, as vaster toils it did require
T' inflame three kingdoms, than one temple fire.
     But where are all those blust'ring storms retir'd,
That roar'd so loud when Oliver expir'd?
Storms that rent oaks, and rocks asunder broke,   35
And at his exequies in thunder spoke?
Was there less cause when thy last doom was giv'n
To waken all the revellers of heaven?
Or did there want in Belgia's humble soil
A cedar fit to fall thy funeral pile?   40
No; die, and heav'n th' expense of thunder save,
Hush'd as thy own designs, down to thy grave.
So hush'd, may all the portents of the sky
With thee, our last great comet's influence, die;

23–24. See Genesis 19:26.
27. *records:* Accented on the second syllable.
28. Herostratus is said to have burned the temple to Artemis in Oct. 356 B.C., in order to acquire eternal fame, even if that fame was based upon a great crime. The image is found frequently (e.g. *An Ironical Encomium,* 4).
33. A reference to Edmund Waller's *Upon the Late Storm, and Death of . . . Cromwell* [W 532–33], which begins:

> We must resign. Heaven his great soul does claim
> In storms as loud as his immortal fame;
> His dying groans, his last breath, shakes our isle,
> And trees uncut fall for his funeral pile. . . .
>   On Oetas' top thus Hercules lay dead,
>   With ruin'd oaks and pines about him spread

In 1682, the Whigs had reprinted *Three Poems Upon the Death of . . . Cromwell* (originally published in 1659), in order to embarrass Waller, Sprat, and Dryden (see Macdonald, *Dryden Bibliography,* Nos. 3a and 3d i-ii).
39. *Belgia:* Used loosely as an appellation for the Netherlands.
44. The Yorkist author of *A Panegyric on their Royal Highnesses* [P 264] compared the Duke and the Earl, in 1682, as follows:

> . . . in his [York's] face you will see the rising sun,
>   T'other's a comet blazing o'er the town,

May this one stroke our low'ring tempests clear,   45
And all the fiery trigon finish here.
With thee expire the democratic gall;
Thy sepulchre and Lethe swallow all;
Here end the poison of that vip'rous brood,
And make thy urn like Moses' wondrous rod.   50
So may our breaches close in thy one grave,
Till Shaftesbury's last breath three nations save;
And dying thus, t' avert his country's doom,
Go with more fame than Curtius to his tomb.

    But is he dead! How! Cruel Belgia, say!   55
Lodg'd in thy arms, yet make so short a stay!
Ungrateful country! Barbarous Holland shore!
Could the Batavian climate do no more?
Her Shaftesbury's dear life no longer save?
What! a republic air, and yet so quick a grave!   60
Oh! all ye scatter'd sons of Titan weep;
This dismal day with solemn mournings keep;
Like Israel's molten calf your Medals burn,

Portending mischiefs seeming to explain
The former tragic scene design'd again.

(57–60)

45. *low'ring:* There is a confusion between *lour, lower* ("to look dark and threaten-ing"), and *lower* ("to bring or come down"). If the writer recognized the distinction, probably the first was intended. *b* gives *lowring*.

46. *trigon:* In astrology, a set of three signs of the zodiac, distant 120° from each other, as if at the angles of an equilateral triangle; triplicity. The first trigon is com-posed of the Aries, Leo, and Sagittarius and is therefore called the fiery triplicity. Harvey, in *Pierce's Supererogation,* gives, perhaps, a pertinent use of the phrase: "His zeal to God and the Church was an aery triplicity; and his devotion to his Prince and the State, a fiery trigon." (See *OED,* esp. quotations for 1819 and 1599.)

50. *Moses' wondrous rod:* See Exodus 4:2–4.

54. *Curtius:* "Marcus Curtius, a legendary hero of ancient Rome. It is said that in 362 B.C. a deep gulf opened in the Forum, which the seers declared would never close until Rome's most valuable possession was thrown into it. Then Curtius, a youth of noble family, recognizing that nothing was more precious than a brave citizen, leaped, fully armed and on horseback, into the chasm, which immediately closed again" (*EB*).

56. *short a stay:* Shaftesbury arrived at Amsterdam in early Dec.; he died on the 21st of the following month.

58. *Batavian:* Pertaining to Holland or to the Dutch.

61. *sons of Titan:* The Titans and their sons had rebelled against Uranus and en-throned Cronus. He, in turn, was overthrown by Zeus, but one faction of the Titans refused to submit and were finally conquered and hurled down to Tartarus.

63. *Israel's molten calf:* "And all the people broke off [their] golden earrings . . . and brought them unto Aaron . . . [and he made] a molten calf" (Exodus 32:1–6).

And into tears your great *Laetamur* turn;
Oh! wail in dust, to think how Fate's dire frown   65
Has thrown your dear Herculean column down.
    Oh, Charon! waft thy load of honor o'er,
And land him safely on the Stygian shore.
At his approach, Fame's loudest trumpet call
Cromwell, Cook, Ireton, Bradshaw, Hewson, all,   70
From all the Courts below, each well-pleas'd ghost;
All the republic legions' numerous host,
Swarm thick, to see your mighty hero land,
Crowd up the shore, and blacken all the strand;
And, whate'er chance on earth, or pow'rs accurs'd,   75
Broke all your bonds, your Holy Leagues all burst,
This union of the Saints no storm shall sever:
This last Association holds for ever.

Medals: An allusion to the famed memento of Shaftesbury's release from the Tower on 1 Dec. 1681, following the grand jury's refusal to accept the Court's bill of indictment for treason (see *The Medal*).

64.   On the reverse, a tow'r the town surveys;
       O'er which our mounting sun his beams displays.
       The word, pronounc'd aloud by shrieval voice,
       Laetamur, which in Polish, is rejoice.
                                (The Medal, 12–15)

70. All were regicides and leaders during the Commonwealth period.

76. *Holy Leagues:* With the signing of the Solemn League and Covenant on 25 Sept. 1643, the Scots entered the Civil War against Charles I; following the King's capture, however, they were repelled by English religious and political trends, and in 1648 began what is at times referred to as the Second Civil War.

77. *Saints.* Certain sectarians who considered themselves among the elect.

The King of Poland's Ghost

[K 569]

The dialogue, the ghost, and the infernal scene, long connected with political verse, here receive an interesting treatment in that the subject of the poem, Shaftesbury, never comes near the center of the stage and never talks—though he is thoroughly discussed. By this indirection, an attempt is made at an additional dramatic level.

The text is based on *l''*, collated with *b*. Copies of the broadside are found also in *f''* and *k''*. The poem is dated 7 Feb. 1683 by Luttrell.

THE KING OF POLAND'S GHOST

or

A Dialogue betwixt Pluto and Charon upon his Reception

Pluto.   Hold, Stygian sculler! What hast brought me here?

Charon.   The soul, sir, of your long-wish'd noble peer.

Pluto.   What? not the King of Poland's?

Charon.   Yes, 'tis it.

Pluto.   You old tarpaulin, will you ne'er learn wit?

          Who bid you touch at Danzig, and be hang'd;   5

          D'ye think my Furies long to be harangu'd?

Charon.   Stop the mistake, and let your passion cease.

          He ne'er came there, for Poland's still in peace;

Title. King of Poland: It was a stock Tory gibe that Shaftesbury coveted the elective throne of Poland to which John Sobieski had succeeded in 1674. For a fuller treatment of the theme, see *A Modest Vindication of the Earl of Shaftesbury* [M 2375], reprinted in *Somers Tracts, 8,* 313–18.

2. *noble peer:* A Tory sobriquet for the Earl of Shaftesbury.

4. *tarpaulin:* A seaman, tar (*Dictionary of the Canting Crew*).

5. *Danzig:* While virtually a free city at this time, Danzig was nominally subject to Poland; it was represented in the diets and at the election of kings.

8. *Poland's still in peace:* By his military victories, John III (Sobieski) had concluded the favorable Treaty of Oliva with the Turks in Oct. 1676. However, less than eight weeks after this poem appeared, Sobieski allied himself with Austria in a united front that stopped the Turks at the famous Second Siege of Vienna.

But I suppos'd you waited for your prey,
And therefore Amsterdam'd him in his way.   10

Pluto.   Pox on your zeal, you did it for your fare.
Could'st think I want incendiaries here?

Charon. No, no, sir; I have passengers enough
That spoke their places and gave earnest too;
And though y' had boutefeus enough before,   15
Yet such as this ne'er touch'd th' infernal shore:
Sulla, Sejanus, Catiline, and Noll,
Must give our politician the wall.
They, cruel wretches, sought imperial sway
By fire and slaughter, ours a milder way.   20
They fought e'en like your Furies for a crown;
He by petitions softly bowls it down.
Kings may be fell'd and never hurt a limb,
And Pluto's self fall gently under him.
But sir, you're safe, for ere he came at Styx,   25
He drew and rack'd off all his politics.

Pluto.   I can't tell that. Coopers are cunning blades;
We devils scarce can dive into their trades:
The lees of one rich pipe may ferment more,
And I am plaguy loth to lose my power.   30

Charon. Fie Pluto! y'are too jealous of your peer,

10. *Amsterdam'd him:* Shaftesbury died at Amsterdam on 21 Jan. 1683.

12. *incendiaries:* Those who inflame men politically, who kindle strife or sedition.

14. *earnest:* Money given as an installment for securing a contract.

15. *boutefeus:* Incendiaries.

17. *Sulla, Sejanus, Catiline:* Romans who fought against the established government of their time (see headnote to *An Ironical Encomium*).

Noll: Oliver Cromwell.

18. *give . . . the wall:* Give way to; acknowledge the superiority of.

22. *petitions:* During 1680, Shaftesbury attempted to bring concerted effort on the Court by flooding it with petitions calling for a parliament (Ogg, *Charles II*, p. 602; also Oldmixon, *A Complete History of Addresses*).

23–24. Opposite 24, but probably applying to 23, is the printed gloss: "See the noble peer's speech." I have been unable to locate the phrase.

26. *rack'd off:* Drew off (wine, cider, etc.) from the lees.

27. *Coopers:* Generally, those who make or repair casks; also (and with reference to the preceding line) those who rack off, bottle, and retail wine; wine-coopers. Shaftesbury's family name was Cooper.

29. *pipe:* A large cask used for wine. There is probably an allusion, as well, to the silver tap which Shaftesbury was forced to have in order to drain a liver cyst (Brown, *Shaftesbury*, p. 185).

He that hath been your drudge this fifty year.
If you begin to slight old servants thus,
'Twill be a great discouragement to us.

Pluto. Why did'st not take Elysium in thy way?   35
Charon. Why sir, the keeper feign'd he'd lost his key,
And would not slip the lock for all my pray'rs.
I touch'd besides at Purgatory stairs
(The Trimmer's Office, as some term it well,
Because it squints both toward Heav'n and Hell),   40
But 'twould not do.

Pluto.   No? What could they object?
He seems the very founder of the sect.

Charon. 'Tis true, but they urg'd 'twas like an inn
Where folks a while were baited for their sin,
Then like cur'd lunatics turn'd out again.   45
And they alleg'd my charge was past all cure,
And nothing in the world was e'er said truer;
For 'tis not all the Saints in Heav'n and earth,
Were he once in, could ever pray him forth.

Pluto. Well, Charon, I forgive thee, for I see   50
Thou speak'st both for thy client and thy fee.
But how stand causes on the British shore
Since they have lost the bauble they adore?

Charon. Why, they resent it in a various way,
And some there are who do not stick to say   55
That the elm-board foregroan'd this fatal day;

32. *fifty year:* Even from a Tory viewpoint, this is a slight exaggeration. It was not until the end of 1643 or the beginning of 1644 that Shaftesbury resigned his royalist commission and took charge of the parliamentarian forces in Dorset.

39. A trimmer was one who inclined to each of two opposite sides as interest dictated. Fittingly, the word has two applications: Halifax (to whom it was often applied) considered it a complimentary term for a moderate (cf. "The Character of a Trimmer," *Works*, p. 48); for most, however, it was a "hateful distinction" synonymous with "Whig" (Evelyn, *Diary*, *4*, 439). Dryden, in the Epilogue to *The Duke of Guise* (1682), recognized them as "Damn'd neuters, in your middle way of steering" and employed a somewhat similar image alluding to Erasmus (see Gardner, *Prologues*, p. 297):

> We Trimmers are for holding all things even:
> Yes—just like him that hung 'twixt Hell and Heaven.

56. *elm-board:* For the popular "prodigy," see *A New Song on the Strange and Wonderful Groaning Board;* also, *The Last Words and Sayings of the True-Protestant Elm-Board* [L 534].

That th' Albion rocks relent and change their hue;
And e'en Tyburn puts on mourning too.
Your dear friend Titus clothes himself in crape,
(Masculine Titus) your outdoing ape,   60
Who's got above the dispensation of a feeble rape.
Others there are who are not troubled much,
But rather seem beholding to the Dutch;
For this one kindness they to Britain do
Commutes for Chatham and Amboyna too.   65

58. *Tyburn:* The place of public execution for London and Middlesex. The line echoes the subtitle of John Dean's *Iter Boreale,* "Tyburn in mourning for the loss of a Saint."

59. *Titus:* The relationship of Oates and Shaftesbury, even with regard to the Popish Plot, has never been made clear. The Earl is reputed to have said, cryptically and cynically: "I will not say who started the game, but I am sure I had the full hunting of it" (Ferguson, *Ferguson,* p. 42).

60. *Masculine Titus:* Probably an ironic reference to Oates' reputed homosexuality. The charge of sodomy unsuccessfully brought by John Lane in 1679 was advanced by others in Jan. 1683, but apparently with little foundation. (See Lane, *Oates,* pp. 30–31, 66, 224, 290, and Luttrell, *Brief Relation, 1,* 248.)

61. The allusion may be to the incident on 26 Sept. 1682, when "Thompson's newssheet regaled its readers with a comical and highly improper story of [Oates'] being accosted in Moor Fields by 'a popishly affected gentlewoman'" (Lane, *Oates,* pp. 288–89).

65. *Chatham:* The chief naval station of England, which had undergone a direct attack in June 1667, during the Second Dutch War.

Amboyna: One of the Molucca Islands where, in Feb. 1623, the Dutch tortured to death several of the English merchants. In 1654, following the First Dutch War, Holland agreed to pay £300,000 to the descendants of the victims, as compensation for the massacre. Dryden treated the original incident dramatically in *Amboyna* (1673).

The Quo Warranto Poems

Charles II's attempts to rescind the franchises and liberties of London by a writ of Quo Warranto against the City's Charter began quietly at the end of 1681. The action was undoubtedly undertaken because "the London [Ignoramus] juries were at this time notorious to the whole nation for partiality" (James Wright, *A Compendious View*, 1685 [W 3692], p. 146); but "the great contest about the Sheriffs" in 1682 must have convinced the Court not only that the City itself would have to be politically subdued but also that London's Quo Warranto constituted a test case for corporations throughout England (see William Gough, *Londinum Triumphans*, 1682 [G 1411], pp. 371–72).

On 18 Jan. 1682, the London Common Council, formally served with the writ, "showed no signs of dismay; they scarcely realized, perhaps, at the outset the true significance . . . or the consequence it was likely to entail" (Sharpe, *London and the Kingdom*, 2, 477). Many thought it referred only to specific persons or customs (Luttrell, *1*, 153), but nonetheless a committee was established to consult with counsel and prepare a defense. The political tumults of 1682 underscored, for both sides, the tremendous importance of the impending legal contest. As the proceedings amply demonstrate (Howell, *State Trials, 8*, 1039–1358), both Court and City lawyers made full use of the twelve months that intervened before the first hearing on 7 Feb. 1683; but the delay may well reflect Charles' fine sense of timing. By the beginning of 1683, he had won the political battles for the municipal offices and could move into the legal arena when he wished, with the firm backing of the Sheriffs and Mayor, with the added confidence of picked judges, and with the fortuitous confusion of the opposition that resulted from Shaftesbury's death.

When the case was first argued by the King's Solicitor, Heneage Finch, and the City Recorder, George Treby, it soon became obvious that the very nature of corporation and the body politic was the fundamental point at issue. In effect, the two philosophies that contended in the reality of the law court exemplify the basic political separation of the period: on the one hand, those who saw the municipal government both as an extension of the central monarchy and as an incorporation representing and involving all its members by its actions; and, on the other, those who conceived of the corporation (though not its real holdings) as immortal, and of the office (though not the officeholder) as unpunishable. If Treby won the day, it was because of his brilliant attack on the very logic of the government's action.

The second, and final, hearing began on 27 April. For six hours the Attorney General, Sir Robert Sawyer, spoke, replying to Treby's objections and reinforcing the Crown's legal position. On the following day, the City's chief counsel, Henry Pollexfen, spent a similar length of time in advancing opposing opinion and precedent. Judgment was pronounced (but not entered) on 12 June, and two days later the London Common Council decided (by 18 votes) to present a submission to the King. When it was presented on 18 June, the Lord Keeper, Francis North gave Charles' terms (Howell, *State Trials, 8,* 1273–83), the most important being that those elected to the key offices must be approved by the King, who would appoint someone if forced to disapprove the City's choice more than twice. The terms were accepted by a vote of 104–86 on 20 June; but by 27 Sept., the Lord Mayor (Pritchard) was putting to the Council the question of surrendering the City's Charter. Legal advice was sought and, when the same lawyers again presented their viewpoints on 2 Oct., Treby (arguing that the Council would be legally responsible for all losses if they went against their oaths by surrendering) carried the vote 103 to 85. On the following day, judgment was entered, and by the 4th, Charles had replaced Treby and eight "factious" aldermen (Bevan, *Aldermen, 2,* 109–10). Before the month was out, Sir Henry Tulse, commissioned by the King to act as Lord Mayor, was sworn in. The Charter remained suspended until 3 Oct. 1688.

The Charter

[*C 3722*]

The Charter was probably written in the second half of 1682, possibly in late Oct., though the author's grasp of the overall implications of the famous case makes it difficult to date the poem by comparing it to the printed versions of the City's plea (entered 13 June [C 4358]), the Crown's replication (3 July [R 1047]), the City's rejoinder (19 Oct. [C 4362]), or Attorney General Sawyer's surrejoinder (c. 8-17 Nov. [S 6195]). Indeed, the author anticipates arguments (152–57) not used by Treby and Pollexfen until the case was heard in 1683. A date late in Oct. would allow for the possible reference to Halley's comet (172), the presentation of the City's rejoinder to the Crown's specific charges, the treatment of Shaftesbury as a mere symbol of Whig duplicity rather than as an active power to be feared, and the sudden public awareness (after the hurly-burly of the shrieval elections) of the magnitude of the case which had been quietly building up during the past year. Not until 28 Oct. (*Observator*, No. 232) did L'Estrange take up the matter fully, and then Observator's arguments and tone were not unlike those in *The Charter*:

> Y'are come to give laws already: creating and empowering of officers; setting up invisible prerogatives; cutting out work for parliaments; giving directions when to convene or prorogue them; passing your judgments upon alliances; calling for justice upon delinquent abhorrers and addressers (which is a good step toward the power of life and death). You have begun with a Medal, as an earnest of your coining of money, too; and I will not despair of seeing a stamp with twelve Ignoramus heads upon it, over a court of justice, gaping and crying *Laetamur*, or rather *Jubilate*.

Probably what makes *The Charter* most difficult to date is the author's strongest point, his ability to see the pattern of past events reflected in the legal contention over the Charter; and this insight might well be what allows him to arrive at his comic, and optimistic, conclusion.

THE CHARTER

A Comical Satire

[*Author*]   As Sampson's strength up in his hair was ti'd,
Rebellion's strength was in the Charter hid;
Late in a trumpet treason every punk   15
Could speak; now't must be whisper'd through a
      trunk.

[*Whig*]   "By Charter, brother traitor we could free;
Now there's no privilege for perjury.
Next time, my Lord, beware the Medal-house.
Though we'd be damn'd for't, we can't save your
      souse: 20
We've done as much for you as men could do;
Ventur'd our souls, and lost our Charter too."

[*Shaftesbury*]   "And is that all? Come, ben't crestfall'n, make shift,
And bear up, I'll help you at a dead lift.
Something may yet be done, though we daren't
      touch   25
On Meal-Tub Plots lest caught i'th' bolting-hutch."

[*Whig*]   "How says your Lordship (for your Honor's free,

15. *punk:* "A little whore" (*Dictionary of the Canting Crew*).

16. *trunk:* A pipe used as a speaking-tube or ear-trumpet.

17. *brother traitor:* i.e. the Earl of Shaftesbury whose indictment for high treason had been rejected by a Whig grand jury in Nov. 1681.

19. *Medal–house:* Probably the Mint. The famed medal commemorating Shaftesbury's release was engraved by George Bower, "Engraver to the Mint and Embosser in Ordinary." (See *The Medal*, especially "Epistle to the Whigs," note e.)

20. *souse:* Various parts of a pig, or other animal, especially the feet and ears, prepared or preserved for food by means of pickling. There is a macabre parallel to the fate of traitors whose dismembered remains were frequently dipped in pitch.

24. *dead lift:* A crisis or emergency (though this post-dates the last example in the *OED* by 50 years).

26. *bolting-hutch:* The place at which the sifting (here, of evidence from the Meal Tub) would occur. The Court party claimed that this was a counterplot, i.e. that the Whigs had fabricated an apparently anti-Whig plot which, when acted on by the Court, was then to be exposed as a Court connivance.

Capital member of our Company;
And you know well 'tis out of fashion,
For tradesmen to sink in desperation)?   30
Methinks, though we broke at State (for sins),
We may drive our old trade of cony-skins,
And kidnapping. Sell brock- and dog-skin muff,
And country captains cheat with horse-skin buff.''

[*Shaftesbury*]   ''We must employ our talents, still, devise   35
A hundred prodigies, and prodigious lies;
The hook of Popery won't take small
Fish now (fie on't!). The French have quite marr'd
    all;
The Whore of Babylon, and Antichrist,
He hath ground to powder and spoil'd our grist.   40
Who would have thought that Unchristian King
Would stop our mouths with such a Christian
    thing?
    But yet we'll sigh, and groan, and shake the
    head;
In time rebellion may be brought to bed,
With good midwifery, and the good wives' aid,   45
To whom such tales as these must still be said:
How a child spoke as soon as born we'll tell

28. *Company:* Shaftesbury was a member (made free) of the Skinners' Company. Lines 32–34 exploit this connection.

32. *cony-skins:* Rabbit skins; a cony is also slang for a dupe or gull.

33. *kidnapping:* During 1682, there was a great stir about the number of young boys who had been spirited away to the plantations, principally Jamaica, though there were hints that Carolina (the colony with which Shaftesbury was connected) was also involved. The principal offender was John Wilmore, who had been head of College's "Ignoramus" jury and was deeply involved in City politics. (See Luttrell, *Brief Relation, 1,* 187–88, 233; also *Observator,* sub Wilmore, and advertisement in No. 128 [26 April 1682].) Wilmore was freed by an "Ignoramus" jury (see J[ames] W[right], *A Compendious View,* p. 146).

brock: Badger.

34. *buff:* Leather made of buffalo or ox hide; used especially for the heavy coats worn by soldiers.

39–42. Possibly a reference to Louis XIV's moves against Spain and the Hapsburg Empire.

47. A number of the more radical sects, particularly the Fifth Monarchists, dwelt heavily on "prodigies" and "wonders" (not unlike those given here) as signs that "the Saints' government was now at prime." The principal publisher of the *Mirabilis Annus* books and similar pamphlets was Francis Smith. (See Muddiman, *The King's Journal-*

(Perhaps before, to ears that could hear well);
Tell Northern men how six suns did appear
At once i'th' South; to Southern, eight moons
    there.   50
    Then for a touch of prophecies we'll say
The Isle o' Brazeel but the other day
Appear'd to a good master of a ship,
Where an old woman that gave Death the slip
E'er since the deluge, told him that the time   55
Of the Saints' government was now at prime.
Down goes Baalam, Ashteroth, and Dagon;
Down goes Bel, and then up goes the dragon."

[Author]   But now let's jibe the sail, and catch the wind,
And make a tack to fetch you up behind.   60
There was a time (they say) since the world stood,
You had a Charter never to be good.
    Have you forgot your routs and riots, when
You forc'd the best of kings and best of men
To fly from's royal palace and betake   65
Himself to forest shelter and the brake?

---

ist, p. 152 and illustrations; Whiting, *Studies in English Puritanism,* esp. pp. 238–41; and Brown, *Fifth Monarchy.*)

52. *Isle o' Brazeel:* The legendary island of Brazil or Brasil was supposed to be located in the Atlantic Ocean.

57. *Baalam, Ashteroth, and Dagon:* Various false gods and objects of idol worship in the Old Testament. The first two are the principal male and female divinities of the Phoenicians; the last, the national god of the Philistines.

58. *Bel . . . dragon:* Bel, the name of a chief deity in Babylonian religion, is the counterpart of the Phoenician Baal. The dragon was representative of primeval chaos. Daniel, according to the apocryphal story, convinced King Astyages that Bel was a mere image of brass and proved it was not divine by causing it to burst asunder.

60. The City's response to the three major charges brought against the Charter was basically the same in each case: "that the City of London is, and time out of mind hath been, an ancient city; and that the citizens of that city are, and by all that time have been, a body corporate and politic . . . (Howell, *State Trials, 8,* 1042; also 1047, 1049).

63ff. Throughout 1641, the militant members of the Long Parliament made use of the London mobs to intimidate their opponents. The specific allusion here is probably to the series of events subsequent to Dec. 1641, when a mob appeared at Westminster to terrorize the peers. Charles I thereupon attempted to arrest the five leading members of the opposition; "the City took up their cause and Charles, finding that force was against him, left Whitehall on 10 Jan., never to return till he came back to die" (*DNB*).

When the divine magicians of your town
Chang'd you to wolves and dogs to hunt him down?
 Have you forgot how you the Queen did force,
And high-born issue, to a sad divorce   70
From their royal father? Have you forgot
How you made th' Crown and Miter go to pot?
First clamor, then petition, last you bring
Rebellion, a complete sin-offering.
Say, Obadiah, tell me if you please,   75
Had you a charter for such tricks as these?
 Once more, beloved: Have you forgot when
    drums
Beat up for bankrupt and religious thrums?
When hungry Levites and starv'd 'prentices
Salli'd from their dark cells and penthouses,   80
And like the plagues of Egypt spread all o'er,
Some for to stench us, all for to devour?
Have you forgot how you did stab the King
And Church with bodkin, thimble, spoon, and ring,
And, like the Indians, prostitute yourselves   85
For th' devilish idol of your Cause and elves?
Say, Ananias, tell me if you please,
Had you a charter for such tricks as these?
Surely the Act of Amnesty is split

67. *divine magicians:* Puritan preachers, particularly in London, were largely responsible for the direction and fervor of politics.

69–70. Henrietta Maria had left England early in 1642, Charles II was in Paris from July 1646, and James escaped to Holland two years later.

72. *Crown and Miter:* King and bishops.

75. *Obadiah:* Like Ananias (87), an Old Testament name, indicating a staunchly Puritan or sectarian background.

77. *beloved:* The writer sarcastically employs sectarian pulpit rhetoric.

78. *thrums:* Applied contemptuously to persons meanly or raggedly dressed.

79. *Levites:* A term used frequently for the Puritan and sectarian preachers because of their tendency to base their teaching on Old Testament texts and Hebraic studies.

81. *plagues of Egypt:* For the ten plagues, see Exodus 7–11.

84. In order to finance the Parliamentary forces in the 1640s, the women of London were urged to donate whatever personal articles they owned that were of silver or gold. See, for example, *Upon Bringing in the Plate* ("All you that would no longer") in *Rump, 1,* 87–89; also, *The Essex Ballad, POAS,* Yale, 2, 323, 74 n.

86. *elves:* malignant beings, imps, demons.

89. *Act of Amnesty:* i.e. the Act of Free and General Pardon, Indemnity and Oblivion (1660), reprinted in part in *English Historical Documents, 1660–1714, 3,* 164–65.

On those claim pardon, won't renounce the
    guilt.   90
A realm divided 'gainst itself can't stand,
Nor city, if by such as you 'twere mann'd;
In vain are oaths and witnesses if th' shrieve
Can pack a jury that will not believe.
The Pope and Conclave sure have chang'd their
    nests   95
And took their quarters up within your breasts;
Their high prerogatives, to you resign'd,
Can damn the innocent, and saint the fiend;
Or else your conscience and religion
Are inspir'd with Mahomet's pigeon;   100
A race of checker-work that's intertex'd
With the worst Christian and worst Jew mix'd,
A kind of circum-uncircumcised kind,
Can swear the body, and not swear the mind.
(As senators, for to get in, must swear,   105
Then keep their first vow, to depose the heir).
And all this's done by virtue of the Bull
Of Magna Charta, and a tub-pulpit full.
    Sons of Oedipus, we know you enough;
The mark of Cain is graven on your brow!   110
Not for the churches nor for the Crown land,
But for the twelve apostles 'tis you stand.

---

spilt: Spoiled, rendered useless, misused, wasted.

90. i.e. on those who claim pardon and won't . . . etc.

91. Matthew 12:25; Mark 3:24–25; Luke 11:17.

94. For the packing of anti-Court, "Ignoramus" juries, see Poems on the Shrieval Elections and Medal Poems.

100. *Mahomet's pigeon:* Legend had it that the writings of Mohammed were inspired by the Divine Spirit that came to him in the form of a pigeon or dove, resting on his shoulder and speaking the words into his ear. Disbelievers maintained that the prophet put grains of corn in his ear for his trained bird.

101. *intertex'd:* Woven together, intertwined.

105–06. *senators:* i.e. those members of parliament who swore allegiance to the King but were intent on excluding the Duke of York from the succession.

108. *tub:* Applied contemptuously to the pulpit of a nonconformist preacher.

109. *Sons of Oedipus:* Eteocles and Polynices, who deposed and imprisoned (or, according to another account, drove into exile) their father, the ruler of Thebes.

111. L'Estrange also touches upon this point (*Observator,* No. 232 [28 Oct. 1682]).

112. *twelve apostles:* Perhaps a reference to the Whig jury. *Apostles* may be gen-

St. Paul for London, St. Peter for Rome,
Judas for th' suburbs till the day of doom.
'Tis not the first time you have show'd your liege   115
How you hate idols but love sacrilege;
'Tis hard to say, to whom we're most in debt,
To the Jesu-, or to the Judas-it.
Lions and unicorns support our arms,
But these are th' beasts that do support our
        harms.   120

[Whig]   "Now to the Quo Warranto we must plead.
          Help, P., W., T.; lend 's all your aid,
          For if that be lost, we're all bewray'd!
          O divine Charter, it would burst our heart
          If th' ark from Israel should thus depart!"   125

[Judge]   "But don't bring pleas as vast as th' Book of Martyr
          To obstruct justice and prolong your Charter.
          Speak to th' point, good brother. What canst say
          To keep this Charter ever and for ay?"

[Whig   "Please you, my Lord, our Charter's sacred made   130
lawyer]   By grants so many none can it invade;
          Of twenty kings and senates hath the seal."

[Author] The Pope had more before he did rebel
          Against the law of God and of the king;

---

erally used for anyone who comes to plant a faith; Judas (114) might be termed an apostolic, a member of a heretical sect.

114. *th' suburbs:* The main area of Whig strength and London low life.

119. *arms:* i.e. the heraldic arms of Great Britain.

122. *P., W., T.:* The leading counsels for the City were Henry Pollexfen, Richard Wallop, and Sir George Treby, the recorder of London.

126. *pleas:* The pleas proved to be vast indeed, though on both sides. See Howell, *State Trials, 8,* 1039–1288.

Book of Martyr: The popular title of John Foxe's *Acts and Monuments* (1559; in English 1563), a huge work concentrating on the Marian martyrs to Protestantism, though its attack on Catholic persecution begins with the earliest period of the Christian church. Luttrell notes (*Brief Relation, 1,* 193, 230) that the City's plea ran to 200 pages and its rejoinder to 100 pages.

131–32. The number is not too greatly exaggerated. See Howell, *State Trials, 9,* esp. 1041–50.

133–35. The reference might well be to the contention between Henry VIII and

He was confiscate for the self-same thing.   135
The law's the rule of peace, it doth not jar
In'tself, 't hath no repugnance, nor war.
If kings themselves can't give their crowns away,
Then kings by law can't themselves betray.

[*Judge*]   "Look you, brother; here you have misus'd   140
Your Charter, and the known laws abus'd.
Riots and routs, you that should them suppress,
You have promoted to a great excess;
You have pick'd juries, pack'd them for your Cause,
And this destroys the fundamental laws;   145
You that should schism and faction quell, support
Unlawful meetings, and to them resort.
What shall I say of oaths? You allegiance swear
Today, tomorrow would expel the heir.
Whose crimes beyond all precedents go,   150
Forfeit their chattels, and their Charter too."

[*Whig*   "To this we answer: Let the sinner die;
lawyer]   A tooth for a tooth, and eye for eye.

Clement VII, which led ultimately to the Act of Supremacy (1534) and confiscation of papal lands and benefices.

140. The speaker would seem to be a judge. Such remarks were the gist of the Crown's argument and, while not voiced by any of the justices in the report of the trial, are confirmed by their final decision. The tone is not dissimilar to the King's reply (delivered by Lord Keeper North) to the City's petition for mercy, presented on 18 June 1683 (Howell, *State Trials*, *8*, 1273–83).

141. *the known laws abus'd:* Apparently an allusion to the specific charge that the City had illegally levied money (Howell, *State Trials*, *8*, 1051–61).

142. *Riots and routs:* A general reference to the disturbances connected with the shrieval elections, which led to a trial for riot against the Whig leaders on 8 May 1683 (Howell, *State Trials*, *9*, 187–291). The original Quo Warranto challenged the City's right to choose its sheriffs, and contemporary comment makes it quite clear that the Crown's frustration in the law courts was one of the principal reasons for the attack on the Charter (North, *Examen*, pp. 628–29; J[ames] W[right], *A Compendious View*, p. 146, etc.). Later this was dropped in favor of the specific charge that the City had voted and caused to be printed (on 13 Jan. 1681) a petition against Charles' recent prorogation of Parliament, which gave official support to public dissension.

147. *Unlawful meetings:* Politically, the Common Halls, which became illegal assemblies when they refused to dissolve on the Lord Mayor's order; religiously, the conventicles to which sectarian Whigs belonged.

152–57. This, quite succinctly, summarizes the views of Treby and Pollexfen (Howell, *State Trials*, *8*, 1139 and 1235), their point being that a charge of treason might be

Let the transgressors of the law be lash'd,
But do not let the law itself be dash'd;   155
Things that have sanction of long time, and great
Authority, should not be lightly set."

[*Author*] In days of old, when subjects' innocence,
Virtue, and goodness did oblige their prince,
The greatness of the monarch's mind was such,   160
They thought good subjects could not have too
    much;
But yet they ne'er intended public wrong
By private act: that's but an ill-tun'd song;
They us'd their charter merely to support
The government, you to betray the fort;   165
And 'twas not Sodom's sins, but 'twas the men
Cast town and charter in the sulph'rous fen.
Your oracle hath spoke, and 't must be so:
Carthago delenda est, down 't must go.
    Where now do all our learn'd Chaldeans keep?   170
Be all our soothsayers and 'strologers asleep?
I'th' blazing star's predictions was a flaw,
Or you said *antichrist* for *anti-law.*
Oft men of art by figure take that scope
To mean the Charter when they nam'd the Pope.   175
Well, there's no help for't now; she must be
    stripp'd,
That's caught a-whoring, and severely whipp'd.

---

brought against the individual alderman as a private citizen, but it could not be brought against him in his corporate capacity, as a representative of the London citizenry. The individuals who were aldermen could be indicted, but the corporate body, the aldermanic council, could not be.

168–69. Shaftesbury made his famed pronouncement supporting complete destruction of the Dutch when he was chancellor in 1673. Afterwards, the phrase was frequently recalled by his opponents in order to embarrass him (Brown, *Shaftesbury,* pp. 203, 215, 258).

170. *Chaldeans:* Astrologers, soothsayers, seers.

172. *blazing star's:* The reference is probably to Halley's comet, which appeared from 15 Aug. to 19 Sept. 1682, though an equally sensational comet had been seen from 12 Dec. 1680 until at least 12 Jan. 1681. For the reactions of the superstitious and the almost superstitious, see Howell, *State Trials, 9,* 150 and Evelyn, *Diary, 4,* 235.

173. *you said:* The precise publication is uncertain, but political interpretation of "prodigies," especially by sectarians, was common practice (see 47 n.).

The doubt of tyranny late turn'd your maw;
How do you like this governing by law?
When lunatics are in their frantic fits,   180
'Tis the best expedient to reduce their wits.
     Son of a slave! is't not enough to cheat
Fools of their money, but you must defeat
Them of their souls, duties to their God and
     Prince?
Was this the trade you're bound to ten years
     since?   185
Sell your poldavis, pack up your false ware,
And be content to cheat your chapmen there.
You ne'er were 'prentice to a statesman sure!
Say some great knave, to draw thee to this lure,
Should stroke thee on the addle head, and cry: 190
[*Shaftesbury*]   "Come, honest Tom, thou know'st better than I,
We're like to have sad times you see.
Religion groans, and bleeding liberty.
The honest subject he must be disgrac'd,
And every sober officer displac'd.   195
We can't keep feast nor fast for th' nation's good,
But all's misconstru'd and misunderstood.
The Plot is vanish'd, and the Duke appears.
Tom, ha'n't we cause for jealousies and fears?"

178. *doubt:* Fear.
maw: Stomach, belly.
182. *Son of a slave!:* Perhaps the writer has in mind Thomas Papillon, the principal
Whig candidate in the shrieval contest of 1682. His French background would make
him "son of a slave" (though for his father's history, see *DNB*); his connection with the
Mercers Company and the Navy may account for the "poldavis" remark (186); his
election as an M.P. for Dover in 1672 (though see Beaven, *Aldermen,* 2, 117) may ac-
count for the "ten years" (185). As well, there is the appellation "Tom" (191), and the
zeal (202) and tone of his reply (204ff.), which can be found in his life and writings
(Papillon, *Papillon*).
182–83. See 141 n.
186. *poldavis:* Or poldavy, a coarse canvas or sacking originally woven in Brittany
and formerly much used for sailcloth.
187. *chapmen:* Purchasers, customers.
189. *some great knave:* Presumably Lord Shaftesbury.
196. For Charles' action in Council on 19 April 1682, see the headnote to Poems on
the Whig Feast.
198. *the Duke:* York had arrived in London on 27 May 1682, and his influence rose
steadily from then on.

Perhaps thou sigh'st then till thy buttons crack,   200
And (as thy soul was tort'ring on the rack)
From the Vesuvius of thy smoking zeal,
Thou bellow'st forth this lamentable peal:
[*Papillon*]   "Ah! My dear Lard! Happy the womb that bore
An heart so noble; Israel can deplore   205
In such sad times as these, when woes us shroud,
That Moses will conduct us in a cloud!
We are all grieved with extremities,
And Pharaoh's deaf to all our plaints and cries!
Our wills with bridle, and our mouths with bit,   210
Are held by force: our Sanhedrins shan't sit:
We can't stoop down to Baal; Saints that have right
To judge the earth are ravish'd of their might;
Our hands are fetter'd, and our hearts complain
That free-born spirits should be thrall'd in
    chain.   215
These, and ten thousand grievances, we have;
But you must save poor dying souls from grave.

204. The extent of sectarian sacrilege that is here suggested can be seen by comparing this line with its probable source, Luke 11:27–28.

205. *Israel:* i.e. England. Here, and at 207 and 211, the writer makes use of Dryden's *Absalom and Achitophel* to turn biblical analogues against the text-ridden sectarians.
deplore: Give up as hopeless, despair of having.

207. *Moses:* Monmouth. Dryden uses the same allusion when Achitophel first appeals to Absalom:

> Thy longing country's darling and desire,
> Their cloudy pillar and their guardian fire,
> Their second Moses
>
> (232–34)

These attempts to hedge Monmouth with divinity are not uncommon among the supporters of the Protestant Duke. For the cloud as the symbol of God, see Exodus 13:21; 16:10; 19:9; 24:15–16, 18; etc.

209. *Pharaoh:* Charles II. If we can assume that Papillon has made the change from Dryden's Pharaoh (Louis XIV) intentionally, then he is strongly attacking the pro-French policy of the Court. For French subsidies and bribes to both parties, see Grose, "Louis XIV's Financial Relations with Charles II and the English Parliament," pp. 177–204; also Dalrymple, *Memoirs,* Appendix, pp. 314–19.

211. *Sanhedrins:* Parliaments.

212. *Baal:* Used generically for any idol.

Saints: The term used by certain sectarians that considered themselves among the elect.

Sweet Lord, but Orpheus, who should take the pain
To bring Eurydice from Hell again?"

[*Shaftesbury*] "How, drooping?" quoth my Lord. "Hold up, good
                         Tom;   220
Of my spirit of sulphur take a dram.
Though at a slight or two, we're almost gone,
He's a poor juggler that ha'n't more tricks than one.
I'll call my familiar:—Presto appear!
He comes—and whispers in my ear."   225

[*Presto*] "Courage, Monsieur, and do not be dismay'd;
From Pluto's Council Board, I'll still bring aid.
Stand but your ground and doubt no overthrow,
Whilst there's a Fury in the deep below.
A thousand ways, a thousand wiles we'll try: 230
In town must set the Stygian company,
Whose country factors must retail their wares
From house to house, as do the Scotchmen theirs;
Complain of taxes in time of wars,
In peace, of trade and evil councillors.   235
Invet'rate lechers, when their lust departs,
To keep the sports up, they must use new arts."

[*Shaftesbury*] "We must the Crown's prerogative impair,
The negative voice in th' Commons declare;

218. *but:* If not; other than.
Orpheus: Probably Monmouth.
221. *spirit of sulphur:* Sulphuric oxide, or oil of sulphur (*OED*, though this ante-dates the earliest entry by 22 years).
222. *slight:* A display of contemptuous indifference or disregard (*OED*, though this an-tedates the earliest entry by 19 years); there is probably a homonymous pun on sleight, a piece of subtle dealing or policy intended to deceive or mislead, a feat of jugglery.
224. *familiar:* A demon or evil spirit supposed to attend at a call.
Presto: An interjection used by conjurers and jugglers in various phrases of com-mand; also, the name given to a familiar spirit.
228. *doubt:* Fear.
232. *factors:* Used in a dual sense of partisans or adherents; and those who buy and sell for other persons, mercantile agents, or commission merchants.
233. *Scotchmen:* Most of the peddlers of the period would seem to have been Scots-men. During the Whig conspiracy, many sympathizers were able to move about un-noticed as peddlers.
236–37. For the reputed sexual aberrations of Shaftesbury, see Otway, *Venice Preserved* (1682), III.i.

Slight all the King's alliances, disgrace 240
Foreign ambassadors in every place;
Say that Ben Hadu Ottor's scarce half-mann'd
(Though wiser far) than all our knaves i'th' land.
We are all brethren, and we now must plow
With all our heifers; might and main must bow. 245
Every new moon, a new Parliament can't
Remind the folk that they're the government;
We shall have one at last I'm sure, and then
We'll make such senators shall make us men.
The tide may turn, states have their ebb and
    flow, 250
And we may catch them when the water's low;
Children must be provided for, and wars
May hap (Crowns themselves are not free from
    cares);
Then money must be had; our silver coin

240. Tory writers frequently charged Shaftesbury with the full responsibility for the breaking of the Triple Alliance (see also 168–69).

240–41. *disgrace Foreign ambassadors:* The representatives, particularly of France and Spain, were frequently subject to affronts from the unsympathetic Londoners. The incident might be of a minor, spontaneous nature like that which occurred at Barillon's celebration of the Dauphin's birth (*Loyal Protestant,* No. 193 [12 Aug. 1682]), or it might involve a major embarrassment, as when Don Pedro Francisco, the nephew of the Spanish ambassador and a member of his entourage, was arrested and jailed for debt (*CSPD,* Jan.–June 1683, passim).

242. *Ben Hadu Ottor:* The Moorish ambassador, Mohammed Ohadu, was in England from 29 Dec. 1681 until 23 July 1682. He was lionized by the Court and seems (according to accounts in the newspapers and poems) to have led a fairly gay life. (See Routh, *Tangiers,* pp. 223–28; *Tangier's Lamentation,* 38 n., etc.) Considering the size of his entourage, the courage which he displayed at horsemanship, and the hints that he was enjoying the English "ladies' kindness," *half-mann'd,* in these senses, could only be ironic. On the other hand, the word, as used in falconry (tamed, made tractable), had come into colloquial speech, and this may be the meaning that the writer has in mind.

244–45. These lines may come from Judges 14:18; "And [Sampson] said unto them, 'If ye had not plowed with my heifer, ye had not found out my riddle.'"

252–54. *Children:* i.e. Charles' illegitimate offspring.

wars: The hope of the anti-Court party was that some extraordinary expense would force the King (as it had forced his father) to convene a parliament. So, too, Achitophel in Dryden's poem:

    And every shekel which he can receive
    Shall cost a limb of his prerogative.
    To ply him with new plots shall be my care,

Shall buy good part of Pharaoh's golden mine.   255
We are all tradesmen now, and what we give
'T shall be but bart'ring for prerogative.
Fetch the Addressers up, and scour the coast
Of all the Tories and abhorring host;
Hang up the judges, and grand juries clap   260
Close in jails, that stood i'th' royal gap!"

[*Papillon*]   "Dawn but that day," quoth Tom, "and we will
                 sing,
                 A headless Council, and a headless King."

[*Shaftesbury*] "Hold!" quoth my Lord, "too fast, now you
                 ramble."

[*Papillon*]   Quoth Tom. "To keep pace wi' y', I must am-
                 ble."   265

[*Author*]   Bless me, my stars! Can such as these men be
                 The bulwarks of our Church and liberty?
                 Send them to the Morocco in exchange
                 For's ostriches and lions; they're beasts more
                 strange.
                 The French, 'tis said, fees anyone that's rare;   270
                 Pray cross the waters and to him repair:
                 If there be any spirits that excel
                 You in sedition, they must come from Hell.
                 We know the idol of your Charter's dear

Or plunge him deep in some expensive war,
Which, when his treasure can no more supply,
He must, with the remains of kingship buy.
                 (391–96)

258. *Addressers:* Those opposed to the Petitioners' request for calling a new (i.e. ex-
clusionist) parliament.

259. *abhorring host:* Those who signed addresses stating an abhorrence of the prin-
ciples set forth in the Association Paper that was said to have been found in Shaftes-
bury's study.

263. *headless Council:* i.e. the Privy Council. Shaftesbury had been removed as presi-
dent in 1679; his objections in 264 suggest that he still coveted the office.

269. Ben Hadu's presents for Charles included two lions and twenty ostriches (Routh,
Tangier, p. 221).

To you as Laban's gods to Rachel were   275
In her pollutions, which she slily hid
Because all search there modesty forbid;
But your pollutions in your Charter reign,
And hope it shall your wickedness maintain.
No time, no, nor authority, can give   280
Such sanction as to make corruption live.
    But Master Ignoramus, make right view,
And sure 'tis not your Charter squints, but you;
There's no such thing as *the King's friends shall
      bleed,*
And's mortal enemy's for treason freed.   285
You're fine fellows to judge th' twelve tribes; I fear
By Magna Charta you will scarce sit there:
Cabbage twice-boil'd's stark naught, and th' dis-
      course,
You know, in pulpit still the same, is worse.
    Consider, rabby (you are wise and sage),   290
Rebels and jubilees thrive but once an age:
Alas, you know it was but th' other day
With drum and trumpet, fool and knave, this play

275–77. Genesis 31:19; 30–35. When Rachel, Laban's daughter, fled with Jacob, she stole the images of her father's gods. When Laban caught up with Jacob, he searched throughout the encampment. "Now Rachel had taken the images and put them in the camels' furniture, and sat upon them. . . . And she said to her father 'Let it not displease my lord that I cannot rise up before thee; for the custom of women is upon me.' And he searched, but found not the images."

284. *King's friends:* The allusion might be to Viscount Stafford and others who had been put to death during the Popish Plot furor, or to such men as the Earl of Danby and the Popish lords who were still in the Tower.

285. *mortal enemy's:* This probably refers to Shaftesbury; though men such as Stephen College and Shaftesbury had both been freed by an "Ignoramus" from London grand juries. The Crown succeeded in getting a conviction against the former by moving the trial to Oxford.

286. *twelve tribes:* i.e. of Israel.

288–89. i.e. these same political arguments are even more unbearable when expounded from the pulpit.

290. *rabby:* A contemporary spelling of rabbi; or perhaps a familiar shortening of the personified rabble. The dissenting sects were considered partial to Old Testament and Hebraic studies.

291. *jubilees:* "This week was published here a bull for an universal jubilee granted by the Pope" (*London Gazette,* No. 1702 [9–13 March 1682]).

292. *th' other day:* i.e. the Civil War against Charles I.

Was acted to our cost of lives and ore.
Pack up your nawls, we'll be deceiv'd no more.   295
    Grant some great lord or two did chance to jar
(With cedars well as shrubs such chances are),
But yet methinks the twigs should grateful be
To th' root that gave them all their bravery.
Malice ne'er wants for mischief; and revenge   300
Is dearer much to mortals than the fringe
Of Heaven, the soul of body and 'state;
And ev'ry nerve's employ'd to serve its hate.
The cunning and the crafty must be bought;
The young and sportive, they are easy caught;   305
The discontented must be left alive
With hopes of his ambitious retrieve;
Sticks of all sorts and sizes it must get
To make the flame and to increase the heat;
And still Religion makes the oven red,   310
Or else quite spoil'd's the batch of gingerbread.
    Then crawl the insects forth, their kingdom's
       come:
Still where the carrion is those creatures roam,
And buzzing up and down the town they cry,
"For liberty, and for the truth, we'll die."   315
    What snake-hair'd jury with infernal brand,
Broke loose from Hell thus to inflame the land?
Take a survey of all the world beside,
Subjects are slaves, each English seems a dride.
If Heaven should bid a subject to implore   320
What bliss we want, he could not ask for more.

---

295. *Pack up your nawls:* "To pack up one's awls: cf. *all* B.I.b. (It is possible that the phrase originated with this word, or in a pun on *all* and *awl*.)" (*OED* [sub *awl* 2. c.], which then cites one example from 1674: "I then call to pay, And packing my nawls, whipt to horse, and away.").

308. *it:* i.e. rebellion.

315. After 315, *b* inserts 60 lines expounding the Whigs' rebelliousness during the last few years, and attacking the turbulent rabble that does not realize that "All others' birthright, bondage is; but we/Surfeit with cates and glut with liberty."

316–17. These lines are found in *b* as 350–51.

319. *dride:* Meaning uncertain. If the text is correct, the verses would seem to call for a word meaning "lord" or "ruler," and one might be tempted to connect it with *dright,* but no instance of that word appears after the mid-fifteenth century.

Oh, the unhappy state of happiness!
They enjoy more that do enjoy much less.
Rome in its pomp and pride could never show
Men of that bulk of wealth in England flow;   325
And every cottager lives frank and free
As Jove. Here's a perpetual jubilee.
Hear one great truth an English poet sings:
We have one emperor, and a million kings.

[*Author to*   But you that are now of th' new livery
the   And old leaven, look for no thanks from me.
Livery-men]   Keep to your gods; on damned Bradshaw call,   410
Implore the shades of Ireton and Noll
To come improv'd from Hell and be so good
To set crack'd men with plunder up, and blood.
The rabble shall no longer rule this town;
Rebellion's Charter now must go down, down.   415

325. After *wealth* supply *that*.

328–29. I have been unable to locate the specific allusion, but cf. *The Parliament Dissolved at Oxford, March 28, 1681* [P 501], beginning "Under five hundred kings three kingdoms groan;" *POAS*, Yale, 2, 411–13. This view of parliament is not unusual.

330–407. There follows a series of stock tributes: 32 lines in praise of a Christ-like Charles; 18 lines in defense of York (twenty lines in *b*); six lines to those lords who have remained untainted; 10 lines to the loyal gentry; and 12 lines to those members of the London Common Council and Court of Aldermen who have faithfully maintained their allegiance to the King.

409. *old leaven:* I Corinthians 5:6–8, which concludes: "Therefore, let us keep the feast not with old leaven, neither with the leaven of malice and wickedness; but with the unleavened bread of sincerity and truth." The phrase, denoting traces of an unregenerate condition, was often applied to prejudices of education inconsistently retained by those who had changed their political or religious opinions.

410. *Bradshaw:* John Bradshaw (1602–59) presided at the trial of Charles I and pronounced his death sentence.

411. *Ireton:* Henry Ireton (1611–51), Cromwell's son-in-law and his staunch supporter in the Army, regularly attended Charles I's trial and signed the warrant for his execution.

Noll: Oliver Cromwell (1599–1658), the Lord Protector of the Commonwealth, was active in the prosecution of Charles I. Following the Restoration, Bradshaw, Ireton, and Cromwell (as well as Thomas Pride) were attainted, and their bodies exhumed, hanged, and buried at Tyburn.

413. *crack'd:* Bankrupt; of flawed moral character or reputation.

plunder: Specifically, the wealth gained through sequestration of estates or royalists' compounding.

But yet we'll beg the King that he would please
To give another on good terms as these.
    Countries o'ergrown with beasts of rapine be
Ti'd to destroy the common enemy,
And bound by charter yearly to afford   420
So many fox or wolf skins to the lord.
London, once bounded in walls, is now boundless
Grown from a city to a wilderness;
More and worse vermin lurk in 'ts holes and dens
Than wolves in Tory-land or frogs in fens.   425
If they renew their Charter, may they pay
A rebel's head for quit-rent every day,
And a whore's liver, till the town be found
Honest and (like the loyal country) sound.
    Now we have done, we have not done. What's
      there?   430
See how the mutinous women appear!
Nip insurrections in the bud. Drums beat
A parl, and let us with the females treat.
What would the good wives have? Forbear
    slaughter!

[*Women*]   "Then," quoth the Amazons, "we'll keep our Char-
      ter."   435

    And thus pleads first a mousetrap maker's wife:
[*1 Wife*] "Before we'll lose our honor, we'll lose life;
Honor, than food or raiment priz'd more high;
For it we'll live and for it we will die.
Farewell Charter, farewell gentility."   440

419. *Ti'd:* Bound or obliged (to do something).

425. *Tory-land:* Ireland.

427. *quit-rent:* A rent, usually of a small amount, paid by a freeholder or copy-holder, in lieu of services which might be required of him.

428. *liver:* The organ was considered the seat of love and of violent passions generally.

430. The line strongly echoes the refrain of John Donne's *A Hymn to God the Father* and *To Christ:* "When thou hast done, thou hast not done,/For, I have more."

Next comes a bouncing butcher's wife i'th' van,
With a cow-killing pole-ax in her hand,
[*2 Wife*]   "D'y' think we'll lose our Charter and be styl'd *Fro,*
As fisherwomen be in Bore-land, and well so?
Master Punch kills an ox and twenty sheep   445
Each week i'th' year, and I the stall do keep;
Shall all this blood (besides a freeman's wife)
Now lose its honor? By my butcher's life,
For our noble Charter we will stand and fall,
For if we lose our arms, we then lose all."   450

Then spoke a chandler's wife with ale-stuff'd
    lungs,
As big as tun, foaming at all her bungs:
[*3 Wife*]   "D'ye think I'll sit at bar all day for th' fees
I get by porter's penny bread and cheese,
And see the slaves, like clowns in Sussex, come,   455
And cry 'Dame, where is your husband? at home?'
Shall double drink so give place to feeling?
Shall't be Madame Creswell, and not Miss Keel-
    ing?"

[*4 Wife*]   Quoth Mistress Fough: " 'T would be a stinking
             life

442. *pole-ax:* Originally, a battle-ax, a halbert; also, an ax with a hammer at the
back, used to fell or stun animals (though this predates the earliest example in the
OED by about 37 years).

443. *Fro:* i.e. Frow, a Dutchwoman.

444. *Bore-land:* A bore (or boor, or bauer) is, specifically, a Dutch or German
peasant.

451. *chandler:* A petty shopkeeper, usually dealing in groceries and provisions.

452. *bung:* The hole (or the stopper) in the bulge, or "mouth," of a cask.

458. *Madam Creswell:* On 22 Nov. 1681, "the famous Madam Creswell was . . .
convicted after above 30 years practice of bawdry, some of her does most unkindly
testifying against her" (*Impartial Protestant Mercury,* No. 64 [29 Nov. to 2 Dec.
1681]). Whether sentence was pronounced is uncertain. There was a persistent rumor
that Sir Thomas Player, the London chamberlain, was in her debt (*Observator,* No. 78
[7 Dec. 1681]; *Last Will and Testament of the Charter of London* [L 531], reprinted
in *Somers Tracts, 8,* 393).
Miss Keeling: Identity uncertain.

459. *Fough:* Or Faugh, is an exclamation of abhorrence or disgust.

If I were not Master Gold-finder's wife.   460
If farewell Charter, then farewell to all
The nobility of Pin-makers Hall.
Stand to your arms, both life and limb shall go

To save our honor, and our Charter too."

A reverend matron in whose loyal face   465
Was every touch of modesty and grace,
Hearing their grievances, ventur'd the crowd,
And thus she spake, and thus their ears they bow'd:

[Matron]   "Dear Sisters of the Livery, appease
The boisterous bellows of your passions; cease.   470
You know that oftentimes untimely fears
Unform the men, and them transform to hares;
And jealousy's our sex's cursed spell,
Transforms us angels to the hags of Hell.

"The last old Charter which you so deplore   475
Was granted to us in the days of yore,
And many an odd thing was in't; 'twas done
When th' land with Popery was overrun,
And now by law 'tis so repugnant found,
That th' law itself is in that Charter drown'd.   480
But there's another in the mint for you,
According to your heart's desire, *New, New;*
Not after the old superstitious fashion,
But new, according to the Reformation.
For we, that were but mistresses before,   485
Shall now be masters, lords, and something more.
Moreover, 'tis provided, all the geese
In London shall have two ganders apiece;
Double mann'd; and if that be not *satis,*
You shall have your boys on Sundays, *gratis.*"   490

460. *Gold-finder:* "Emptier of jakes or houses of office" [i.e. privies] (*Dictionary of the Canting Crew*).

462. *Pin-makers Hall:* The allusion is difficult. The Pinners Company had used the refectory of Austin Friars for their hall in the time of Henry VIII, but, during Elizabeth's reign, had merged with the Wire Drawers under the name of the Girdlers of London. Girdlers Hall had been in disrepair since 1643 and was totally destroyed by the London Fire (Bell, *The Great Fire*, pp. 6, 108, 338).

490. *boys:* Helpers, apprentices, servants.

> This said, they shout, and make the welkin ring;
> [*Women*]   Cri'd, "Damn th' old Charter, and God save the
>   King!"

492. *welkin:* The sky, the firmament. From the sixteenth century on, the word had only literary (chiefly poetic) use in standard English.

The Great Despair of the London Whigs

Probably written shortly after the court gave its judgment against the City on 12 June 1683, this poem has been found only in *b*.

THE GREAT DESPAIR OF THE LONDON WHIGS

for the Loss of the Charter

Then is our Charter (Pollexfen) quite lost?
Is there no aid from the new-sainted post?
Are our sham plots and perjuries all in vain?
If not, we'll summon Patience back again.
Saints' prayers to Heaven we've found will not prevail,   5
But more propitious Hell will never fail.
   Then let almighty Titus—for you know
He needs must be a magic doctor too;
For how do you think at Salamanca he

1. *Pollexfen:* Henry Pollexfen (1632?–91) was best known for his work as a defense lawyer, having been counsel to College, Fitzharris and, in the following year, to Sacheverell and Sandys.

2. *post:* Perhaps the whipping post or pillory. The term "knight of the post," which is probably being alluded to here, refers to a notorious perjurer, one who gets his living by giving false evidence. The "new sainted post" would therefore be Sir Patience Ward (see 4 n.).

4. *Patience:* Sir Patience Ward, one of the Whig leaders in the City and Lord Mayor prior to Moore, had testified at the *scandalum magnatum* trial of Pilkington on 24 Nov. 1682 that he had not heard the former sheriff say, on the particular occasion in question, that the Duke of York was responsible for the burning of London and would cut the citizens' throats. On 19 May 1683, Ward was brought to trial for perjury and, after five hours of conflicting testimony skillfully maneuvered by Jeffreys (Howell, *State Trials*, 9, 299–350), the jury gave a private verdict of guilty, "which they affirmed the 21st in open court" (Luttrell, *Brief Relation*, *1*, 259). "But before the day for sentence, he thought it best to go out of the way, having had intelligence they intended to set him in the pillory" (Howell, *State Trials*, 9, 350). Ward may have hidden in London (*Observator*, No. 365 [28 June 1683]) before fleeing to Holland; he did not regain his former rank until the accession of William III.

5. *Saints':* The appellation used by certain sectarians that considered themselves among the elect.

9. *Salamanca:* Titus Oates, the discoverer of the Popish Plot, encouraged the notion that he had received a degree of Doctor of Divinity from the University of Salamanca

Could take such an invisible degree,   10
Unknown to all the University—
Let him raise up the once great Tapski's ghost,
With his retinue, all that num'rous host
Of brave heroic spirits, who could die
For treason, and rebellion justify: 15
Amongst those, Stephen, condemn'd by wicked laws,
The proto-martyr for the last Good Cause.
Advance you brave arch-traitors from the grave,
Who made slaves princes, and your Prince a slave:
Bradshaw and Cromwell, those two glorious names   20
That raise dull treason up to active flames.
Let these infernal worthies then be back'd
By Zimri and the jury that he pack'd
With all the fiery zealots of the town,
But chiefly our great patriot of renown,   25

---

while in Spain in 1677. In Oct. 1682, Roger L'Estrange had published the absolute
denial of that ancient institution in *Observator*, Nos. 225 and 227 (17 and 21 Oct.
1682), with the attestations in No. 237 (8 Nov. 1682). See also Lane, *Oates*, pp. 56–58.

10. Cf. Dryden, *Absalom and Achitophel:*

> And gave him his rabbinical degree,
> Unknown to foreign university.
> (658–59)

12. *Tapski:* A common Tory nickname for Shaftesbury, who had died 21 Jan. 1683.
For the derivation of the sobriquet, see the headnote to *The Last Will and Testament
of Anthony, King of Poland;* see also *The King of Poland's Ghost.*

16. *Stephen:* Stephen College, "the Protestant joiner," had been a zealous believer
of the validity of the Popish Plot. In 1681, his ballads and pamphlets led to a charge
of high treason which, though thrown out by a London jury, was found against him
at Oxford where he was executed.

17. *Good Cause:* i.e. the "Good Old Cause," the Commonwealth.

20. *Bradshaw:* John Bradshaw (1602–59) had been Lord President of the parlia-
mentary commission that condemned Charles I and other leading royalists.

Cromwell: Oliver Cromwell, Lord Protector (1653) of the Commonwealth, had
been active in the prosecution of Charles I. Bradshaw and Cromwell (along with
Ireton and Pride) were attainted in 1660, whereupon their bodies were exhumed,
hanged, and buried beneath Tyburn.

23. *Zimri:* George Villiers (1628–87), second Duke of Buckingham; see *Absalom and
Achitophel*, 544. Though Buckingham was one of the Whig leaders in the City,
there is evidently a confusion here between Zimri and Shimei, who, in Dryden's
poem (585), represents Slingsby Bethel, the Whig sheriff responsible in 1680 for
packing the "Ignoramus" juries.

25. *patriot:* Monmouth.

To whom we'll give some pretty Polish crown
(Not that we promis'd him, for all our zeal
Is only how to raise a commonweal).
With this cabal we'll fool all equity,
And gain what law has lost by polity.   30
Here godlike Tapski once shall speak again,
And what he speaks Fates shall oppose in vain;
For if alive he treason taught so well,
What a vast traitor now he's school'd in Hell!
Could Cromwell once by force assume the crown,   35
And sha'n't this angry ghost relieve one town?
Sha'n't Ignoramus, who with no ado
Could save great Tapski, save our Charter too?
    But what are only councils now? The course
That we would take in this distress is force;   40
But the militia now, alas, is gone;
'Tis odds to what we had in forty-one.
The Saints are all sequester'd of their right,
The City govern'd by a Jebusite;
What then should we distressed rebels do?   45
Is it too late? can't we for pardon sue?
Why, good King Charles' clemency may spare
Though we in two rebellions had our share,
Nor need we hang ourselves like Judas for despair!

26. Cf. *The Last Will and Testament*, 16–17: "Then for my Polish crown, that pretty thing,/Let Monmouth take't."

37–38. The most famous check which the Whig grand juries of London gave to the King was their refusal to consider as a true bill the treason indictment which the Crown had brought against Shaftesbury on 24 Nov. 1681 (see the Medal Poems).

41. *militia*: Following the Restoration, Charles II made certain that these auxiliary forces (to be distinguished from the far more effective professional army) remained firmly under his control in order to prevent any repetition of the parliamentary dominance that had occurred in the Civil War of 1641. (For the Militia Acts of 1661 and 1662, and Dryden's comments on "the rude militia" [*Cymon and Iphigenia*, 399–408], see *English Historical Documents, 1660–1714*, pp. 793–96.)

44. *Jebusite*: In *Absalom and Achitophel*, 86, Dryden's term for Roman Catholics. Whig propaganda held that those sympathetic to the Court were Catholic. The "Jebusite" in this instance is Sir William Prichard, the Lord Mayor.

46. For the London Common Council's petition of submission on 14 June, see headnote to the Quo Warranto poems. Earlier, on 22 May (three weeks prior to the judgment on the Charter), the Council had discussed the possibility of such a petition, but nothing had been done (Luttrell, *Brief Relation, 1*, 260).

But let's, like Origen, since other hopes are past,   50
Hope the poor Devil may be sav'd at last.

50–51. "I have not so much as an uncharitable wish against Achitophel, but am content to be accused of a good-natured error, and to hope with Origen that the Devil himself may at last be saved" (*Absalom and Achitophel*, "To the Reader," ed. Kinsley, p. 216, 51–53). Origen (ca. 185–ca. 254) was one of the most distinguished, influential, and controversial theologians of the ancient church. His doctrine of the ultimate restoration of all things was part of a system that led to his degradation in his own time and the anathematizing of his teaching in 553.

The Character of a Trimmer

[C 1995A]

Among many clear indications of the extent of the Court's victory, not the least is the significant change of personae that carried on the dialogue in L'Estrange's newssheet. Observator remained; but Whig, whose blind fanaticism had evoked an equally strident conservatism, gave way to Trimmer, a more subtle antagonist whose apparent moderation masked a character composed of compromise, pusillanimity, and specious logic. For ten successive numbers (240–49 [13–29 Nov. 1682]), L'Estrange attempted to anatomize his opponent, but in so doing he had to develop a new vocabulary and new images. Yet, since his target was closer to his own position, he had to elevate the cannon of his rhetoric and aim his salvoes with far greater care. On the one hand, therefore, he seeks to establish all of the stock images of the political Laodicean (the boat-balancer, the weathercock, the bat, and so on); while, on the other hand, he tries to distinguish between virtue, moderation, and trimming:

> Moderation . . . is that by which we govern ourselves in the use of things that a body may have too much of . . . but it is ridiculous to talk of moderation in a case that admits of no excess. Did you ever hear of any man that was too wise, too temperate, too brave, too loyal, too pious, too continent, too charitable? (No. 247 [25 Nov. 1682])

While Observator has some difficulty maintaining this position, he has none in separating himself from the trimmer. "You are upon the point of what the government ought not to do; and I'm upon the question, on the other side, of what the subject is bound to do." At best, the trimmer sins by omission:

> He that is a member of the community and withdraws his service from the public is, in my opinion, little less criminal than he that by downright treachery and corruption betrays it.

And 'tis much a case whether a town is lost by confederacy or
by desertion. (No. 245 [22 Nov. 1682])

But, more frequently, the trimmer's moderation "is only the cover
of a vice"; a desire for gain, or (as Dryden also suggested at this
time in *The Vindication of "The Duke of Guise,"* S.-S., 7, 182) a
disguise for "secret Whigs." Halifax's famous defense, which has
the same title as this poem, did not appear in print until 1688. *The
Character of a Trimmer, neither Whig nor Tory* [C 1995B], which
was printed "For T. S., 1682," is a prose defense of the moderate's
position.

The text is based on *l″* (dated 1683) and checked with another
copy in *k″*.

THE CHARACTER OF A TRIMMER

Hang out your cloth, and let the trumpet sound;
Here's such a beast as Afric never own'd:
A twisted brute, the satyr in the story,
That blows up the Whig heat and cools the Tory;
A State hermaphrodite, whose doubtful lust   5
Salutes all parties with an equal gust;
Like Iceland shoughs, he seems two natures join'd,

1. *cloth:* The painted cloth set before a fair tent depicting the "monster" on
exhibition within.

2. For the great interest in exotic animals, see Evelyn, passim; particular interest
in those from Africa may have been stimulated by the Moroccan Ambassador's gift
of lions and ostriches (*Diary, 4,* 266).

4. As an equal and opposite reaction to the Trimmer's suggestion, Observator wants
to continue "loyal" writing, since "it does blow the coal on the one side and puts it
out on the other" (No. 240 [13 Nov. 1682]).

5. "the hermaphrodite Trimmer is the only thing we have to fear" (*Observator,*
No. 243 [18 Nov. 1682]).

6. *gust:* a keen relish, appreciation, or enjoyment. The connotation of sensual out-
burst would seem to have been extended into the sexual; cf. *Absalom and Achitophel,*
19–20.

7. *Iceland shoughs:* An Iceland is a shaggy sharp-eared white dog, formerly in
favor as a lap-dog in England; a shough (sometimes "shock") refers to the same
species, though it was more generally applied to shaggy dogs and, more specifically,
to poodles. A contemporary (1688) description explains that "an Iceland dog [is]
. . . curled and rough all over. . . . These curs are much set by with ladies who
. . . trim off all the hair of their hinder parts. . . . Some call them shoughs" (*OED*).

Savage before and all betrimm'd behind,
And the well-tutor'd curs like him will strain,
Come over for the King, and back again.   10
'Tis such a sphinx, the Devil can't unriddle:
A human schism upward from the middle,
And splits again below, which gives us light
To the sole point that can all sects unite.
Thus did the fam'd Dutch double-monster trim,   15
And that cleft soul's pythagoriz'd in him.
    Noah (whom for the sake of wine we love)
Sav'd Nature's breed by mandate from above,
But all the learned sages do agree
He kept his ark from mules and leopards free: 20
All such mix'd animals he scorn'd to float,
And would not save one trimmer in his boat.
    Beasts feed on beasts, and fishes fish devour,
And o'er weak birds the winged tyrants tower;
But this same land-fish with his feather'd fins   25
Commits both air, and earth, and water, sins;
Complies with those that fly, and walk, and dive,

11. *sphinx:* In Greek mythology, the hybrid monster, usually described as having the head of a woman and the (winged) body of a lion, which infested Thebes until the riddle it propounded was solved by Oedipus.

15. *Dutch double-monster:* Perhaps an allusion to the union of the two principal political groups of the Dutch Republic under the Prince of Orange in 1672.

16. *pythagoriz'd:* Passed, or changed, by transmigration.

17. Genesis 9:20–21.

20. The leopard was erroneously thought to be a hybrid resulting from the cross-breeding of a lion and a pard, or panther.

23–24. Cf. Rochester, *A Satire against Mankind:*

> Birds feed on birds, beasts on each other prey,
> But savage man alone does man betray.
>
> (129–30)

25. Dryden, in the epilogue to *The Duke of Guise* (Gardner, *Prologues,* p. 136 and Scott-Saintsbury, *Dryden,* 7, 133) describes trimmers as:

> Damn'd neuters, in their middle way of steering,
> Are neither fish, nor flesh, nor good red herring;
> Not Whigs nor Tories they; nor this, nor that;
> Not birds, nor beasts; but just a kind of bat,
> A twilight bird, true to neither cause,
> With Tory wings but Whiggish teeth and claws.
>
> (39–44)

26–28. "These amphibious participators of both interests . . . join at last with them that have the better on't" (*Observator,* No. 240 [13 Nov. 1682]).

But fastens only upon those that thrive.
  In short, his only art is to inveigle,
Flatter the popular power as well as regal,   30
Like a State Janus or a Church spread-eagle.

30. In *Observator,* No. 246 (23 Nov. 1682), Trimmer concludes: "I am utterly against all reflections upon the King; but for the rest, it may do well enough to tell the people who are their friends and who are their enemies." Thus, he feels it his function to "do good offices betwixt the King and his people by making the best of what one does and the best of what the other" (*Observator,* No. 248 [27 Nov. 1682]).

31. *Church spread-eagle:* The image is based on the symbol of the Holy Roman Empire, the double-headed spread-eagle which, like Janus, looks both left and right.

The omnibus title of the Rye House Plot covers, in point of fact, two rather separate actions, each of which had its subdivisions. The first of these occurred at the end of 1682, from the time that Shaftesbury went into hiding in the last weeks of September until he fled to Holland in early December. Totally defeated, driven to ever more desperate schemes, the aging, harried Shaftesbury must have viewed with helpless torment the inevitable course of affairs: national political contol had been obliterated through Charles' financial independence from parliaments; the very center of Whig power had been wrested from the party by the Court's victories in the municipal elections; and, even more bitter, the party had slipped out of the control of the man who, as the spokesman for Commonwealth principles that were now fading into history, had translated religious dissent into political action. Time had worked against Shaftesbury, had dazzled him with great expectations of a political inheritance on which for a while he traded brilliantly but which, when he most needed to convert it into the current coin of real power, proved but an inheritance of wind. The general prosperity, the abhorrence of renewed civil strife, the gradual disappearance of sectarian zeal and Oliverian republicanism, the subtle separation of religion and politics, these and countless other factors must have driven Shaftesbury to extremes. "We believed," said Howard, who had turned Crown's evidence, "his frenzy now grown to that height that he would rise immediately and put his design in execution, so we endeavored to prevent it." Howard claimed to have told Monmouth at the time that "this man is mad and his madness will prove fatal to us all. He hath been in a fright from being in the Tower and carries those fears about him that cloud his understanding." Certainly, if Howard's account is to be trusted, Shaftesbury's desperation had led him to the absurd claims that "above ten thousand brisk boys are ready to follow me whenever I hold up my finger," and that in 24 hours there would be five times that number that could "possess themselves of Whitehall by beating the Guards."

Shaftesbury, however, was now dependent on a distinctly different group. The older group, which he personified, had fled, had died, or were bracing themselves for the Stuart revenge; the new party leaders—Monmouth, Essex, Russell, Sidney, Howard—"methoded" every move, theorized on the nature of republicanism, or thought in terms of political advantage. To refer, therefore, to the Plot even under the more general term of the "Whig Conspiracy" hides the fact that by mid-1683 there was a different kind of Whig, and that Charles now aimed at this second group while his lawyers did all they could to connect it with its outmoded and discredited predecessor.

If in October 1682 Shaftesbury had seemed mad, it was the madness of Cassandra. He must have recognized that each day, as well as increasing the danger of discovery of a *coup d'état*, represented a strengthening of the Court's position that incalculably outweighed the petty securities that might be gained. When the discovery came in June 1683, he was proved correct: the reaction very strongly suggests that, within that vast majority of uncommitted moderates, sympathy had swung heavily away fom the anti-Court party.

The political complexities and personal conflicts of the Whig Conspiracy can perhaps best be understood by reading the full accounts, with the peripheral material, given in Howell's *State Trials* (9). Here, perhaps, one need only reemphasize the fact that there were two fairly distinct actions: one, the attempted assassination of the King and Duke of York that was to have taken place at the Rye House, near Hoddesdon in Hertfordshire; the other, with which Shaftesbury had been briefly but desperately engaged, the attempted insurrection that was to begin principally in London and receive support from dissident Scots under Argyle. It seems fairly clear that the Whig leaders—Monmouth, Essex, Russell, Sidney, Howard, Grey, and probably Hampden—all engaged, more or less actively, in the projected insurrection. Likewise, their ignorance, or at least their disapproval, of the plans for an assassination seems reasonably certain, despite the Crown's attempts to link the two plots through Robert Ferguson, one of the two men—the other being the more surreptitious John Ayloffe—who might have been intimate with both groups. (See Ferguson, *Robert Ferguson, the Plotter* esp. p. 156.) The assassination was to be the work of virtually unknown zealots, men such as Richard Goodenough (who had been under-sheriff to Pilkington), Richard Nelthorp, Nathaniel Wade, Richard Rumbold, Robert West, Col. Rumsey, John Rouse, Captain Walcot, and the pathetic joiner, William Hone. Some informed; some suffered; others fled, eventually engaging in Monmouth's ill-fated rebellion and, in turn, suffering or informing.

For those in the assassination plot, one can feel a certain awe at their zeal and determination, no matter how wild were the schemes that they are alleged to have considered (see Sprat, *True Account*, pp. 50–51, 110–12); but for the three principal sufferers of the insurrection conspiracy, there is a sense of pathos and tragedy that evokes a sympathetic response. The drama of Essex's death, the nobility of Russell's character, the abuse of Sidney's defense, all these make an appeal which grows stronger when we forget or suppress the historical situation. To those contemporaries that considered them guilty, however, such appeals must have been quite secondary to the fundamental fact that they had attempted to commit that most heinous of crimes, high treason against the king.

The Eight Lay Witnesses Slain (post 1688?): Godfrey (Popish Plot); Essex, Russell, Sidney, Cornish, Armstrong (Rye House Plot); Monmouth, Argyle (1685 uprising).

An Elegy on the Earl of Essex

[E 415]

The services of Arthur Capel, Earl of Essex (1631–83), to the English crown, at least until 1680, seem models of devoted and outstanding conduct. His youthful engagement in the royalist cause, his brilliant embassy to Denmark in 1670, his exemplary work as Lord-Lieutenant of Ireland (1672–77) and as head of the Treasury Commission (1679), stand in sharp contrast to the general practices of others. In England, Essex's association with the anti-Court party probably originated in his opposition to the Danby ministry, and his ever deeper involvment very likely stemmed from his feeling that a Catholic prince represented England's greatest danger. Though he differed often with Shaftesbury, he remained at the center of opposition and, after the old Earl's death, was counted among the Whig leaders.

A series of indeterminables lead up to the dramatic moment of Essex's death on 13 July. One cannot, for example, be certain whether he contemplated active insurrection, or how far he was influenced by Sidney's political ideas, or to what degree his imprisonment in the Tower affected his mind. His death, which many first heard dramatically revealed by Howard during the Russell trial, immediately became a point of political faith. For the Tory, guilt had driven Essex to suicide; for the Whig, dark hints of murder and bloody razors being thrown from a Tower window evoked memories of Godfrey and the Popish Plot. This may explain in part the violent reaction to the event. The mock elegy given here forgets Essex's service, unjustly connects him with Robert Devereux, and heartily approves his course of action if not the act itself. On the other side, the Whigs' attempt to establish a charge of murder ended in failure on 7 Feb. 1684 with the conviction of Laurence Braddon and Hugh Speke for subornation of witness.

The text is based on *h''*, a copy of which is also in *k''*. Luttrell's copy is dated 14 July 1683. I have not seen the Edinburgh edition [E 416], printed the same year.

AN ELEGY ON THE EARL OF ESSEX

Who cut his own throat in the Tower
July 13, 1683.

How many strange uncertain fates attend
The wand'ring pilgrim to his journey's end.
Earth turns to earth; water, air, and fire,
Against the breath inform'd them, do conspire;
As every man were his own fatal Catch,   5
'Tis in his hands to forward the dispatch;
Some in the field of Venus, some of Mars,
Some meanly hang themselves, some hang an arse.
But mighty Essex, his victorious arm,
With griefs oppress'd, receives the swift alarm;   10
A meaner foe than steel he scorns to own,
Or fall by any hand but by his own.
Achitophel may hang himself, and Oates
With Judas swing, and some may cut their throats,
Whom black despair may urge; but Essex, he   15
The first that cut his throat for 's loyalty.
Oh, that despair should 'tend such fiery zeal!
This mighty Sampson of the commonweal,
Rais'd to defend, and set his Israel free
From Popish rage, Philistian tyranny,   20
To shake the pillars of the Church and State;
He crowns it with his own untimely fate.
     Essex the famous general (that name,

5. *Catch:* That by which anything is caught or held; there is, also a pun on the name of Jack Catch or Ketch, the public executioner.

8. *hang an arse:* Hold back, be reluctant, be tardy.

11. *meaner foe:* i.e. the hangman's rope.

13. *Achitophel:* Shaftesbury. The name generally derives from Dryden's *Absalom and Achitophel* (150 *ad fin.*), but in this specific case the writer might have had in mind Dryden's remarks at 53–55 in "To the Reader" (Kinsley, p. 216). Both men are referring to II Samuel 17:23, a passage which the later writer might well have used for its appropriateness of tone if not of facts.

Oates: Titus Oates, the principal discoverer of the Popish Plot.

14. *With Judas swing:* See Matthew 27:5.

21–22. See Judges 16:29–30.

23. *Essex the famous general:* Robert Devereux, the third Earl of Essex (1591–1646) was, nominally at least, commander-in-chief of the parliamentary forces in the

So dear recorded in the books of fame,
With royal blood, and fatal conquests cloy'd)   25
Ten thousand of the King's best friends destroy'd ;
But thou'rt the first, and shall recorded be,
That rid him of one secret enemy.
What fitter victim could great Essex bring,
T' atone his crime against an injur'd king?   30
   But here thy rage too desperate appears,
To die a martyr to thy doubts and fears.
Oh, dire revenge! Oh, too officious steel!
To make that wound which time can never heal.
Had'st thou but few days courage to withstand,   35
Jack Catch had done the business to thy hand.
   But, oh, despair more desperate than thy guilt,
That durst not trust thyself to stand the tilt
Lest thy false tongue should through thy throat impart
The bloody treasons that oppress'd thy heart.   40
This must convince the world, and thy wrong'd prince;
Thou with thy guilt had rather hurry hence
Than stay to justify thy innocence.

---

opening years of the Civil War. His generalship, reputedly not of the best, ended in 1644 with the defeat of his army in Cornwall. In point of fact, no relationship existed between Devereux and Capel, the former being the last earl of the sixth creation, the latter the first of the seventh. Capel's father, Lord Capel of Hadham, had been a staunch royalist leader whose sacrifices culminated with his beheading on 9 March 1649. "By one of those strange instances of retributive justice which are not rare in history, the son of the murdered man succeeded to the honors of him [i.e. Devereux] who had benefited most by the spoliation of his father's lands" (*DNB*).

  36. *to thy hand:* Without exertion on your part.

  38. *tilt:* Combat, contest; encounter; also, a public dispute or discussion.

ALGERNON SIDNEY'S FAREWELL

[A 923]

Though the matter of Russell's political intentions and the legality of his trial have occasioned a great deal of partisan debate (see, for example, Harold Armitage's *Russell and Rye House* [Letchworth, 1948]), such questions are rarely evoked in the case of Algernon Sidney (1622–83). Sidney's life demonstrates his unequivocal republican principles as clearly as his execution testifies to a blatant distortion of the law. It is not unlikely, of course, that Jeffreys, now Lord Chief Justice, felt that there was such a clear and present danger in Sidney's political theories and in his involvement in the conspiracy, that these overruled the exigencies of the treason laws. This, however, scarcely excuses his allowing, as evidence of an overt act (even under the law of 25 Edward III, where "the compassing or imagining the death of the king" was high treason), the private notes that Sidney had penned in answer to Filmer's *Patriarcha,* on the basis that "scribere est agere." (For the transcript, opinions and consequences of the trial, see Howell, *9,* 817–1022; also *DNB, sub* Sidney.)

These verses reflect the somewhat ambivalent feeling of the Court party toward Sidney: a grudging admiration for the integrity of the old republican and a wholehearted detestation of the principles in which he believed.

Sidney had been indicted on 7 Nov. 1683, tried on the 21st, sentenced on the 26th, and executed on 7 Dec., the day on which Monmouth was forbidden the Court. Of the so-called Council of Six, three were dead by the end of the year; Monmouth, shortly to go into exile, would die on the block; Howard had turned informer; only Hampden managed to survive politically. The times called for moderation, compromise, and trimming.

Luttrell obtained his copy of this poem on 8 Dec., the day after Sidney's execution.

ALGERNON SIDNEY'S FAREWELL

Welcome, kind Death: my long tir'd spirit bear
From hated monarchy's detested air;
And waft me safe to th' happier Stygian land
Where my dear friends with flaming chaplets stand;
And seat me high at Shaftesbury's right hand.   5
There worshipping, my prostrate soul shall fall.
Oh! for a temple, statues, altars, all!
Volumes, and leaves of brass; whole books of fame!
For all are due to that immortal name.
For my reception then, great shades, make room,   10
For Sidney does with loads of honor come.
No braver champion, nor a bolder son
Of thunder, ever grac'd your burning throne.
Survey me, mighty Prince of Darkness, round:
View my hack'd limbs, each honorable wound,   15
The pride and glory of my numerous scars
In Hell's best cause, the old republic wars.
Behold the rich, grey hairs your Sidney brings,
Made silver all in the pursuit of kings.
Think of the royal martyr, and behold   20
This bold right hand, this Cyclops arm of old,
That labor'd long, stood blood and war's rough shock,
To forge the ax and hew the fatal block.
    Nor stopp'd we here. Our dear revenge still kept
A spark that in the father's ashes slept,   25
To break as fiercely in a second flame
Against the son, the heir, the race, the name.

5. This line is the center of a rather daring and, on the whole, successful inversion of the Creed's "He ascended into heaven and sitteth at the right hand of the Father." (Cf., also, Mark 16:19; Colossians 3:1.)

20. *the royal martyr:* On 4 Jan. 1649, Sidney was appointed one of the commissioners for the trial of Charles I. Though he attended three preliminary meetings of the court, he refused to serve because, he said, of "these two points: first, the king could be tried by no court; secondly, that no man could be tried by that court" (*DNB*).

27. *the son, the heir, the race, the name:* i.e. Charles II, James Duke of York, the Scots in general, and the Stuarts in particular.

Revenge is God-like, of that deathless mold,
From generation does to generation hold.
Let dull religion and sophistic rules   30
Of Christian ignorants, conscientious fools,
With false alarms of Heaven's forbidding laws,
Blast the renown of our illustrious cause:
A cause (whate'er dull preaching dotards prate)
Whose only fault was being unfortunate.   35
Oh, the blest structure! Oh, the charming toil!
Had not Heav'n's envy crush'd the rising pile,
To what prodigious heights had we built on!
So Babel's tower had Solomon's church outshone.
    True! my unhappy blood's untimely spilt;   40
And some soft fools may tremble at the guilt.
    As if the poor vicegerent of a God
Were that big name that our ambition aw'd!
A poor crown'd head, and Heav'n's anointed! No!
We stop at naught that souls resolv'd dare do,   45
And only curse the weak and failing blow,
Whilst like the Roman Scaevola we stand,
And burn the missing, not the acting, hand.
Nay, the great work of ruin to fulfill,
All arts, all means, all hands are sacred still.   50
No play too foul to win the glorious game:

28. *Revenge is God-like:* Cf. Deuteronomy 32:35; Psalm 94:1; Romans 12:19.

34. *whate'er dull preaching dotards prate:* Probably a reference to the sermons preached on 9 Sept., the official day of thanksgiving for the King's "deliverance from the late conspiracy." See also *A Merry New Ballad: In Answer to "Old Rowley the King,"* 20 n.

42. *the poor vicegerent of a God:* i.e. the King.

47. *Scaevola:* Gaius Mucius Scaevola, a legendary hero of Rome, when threatened with torture after an unsuccessful attempt to assassinate the besieging king, Lars Porsena, thrust his right hand into an altar fire and kept it there until it was consumed in order to demonstrate the determination of his comrades to carry out the assassination. Porsena was so impressed that he withdrew his forces, and Gaius Mucius was rewarded and received the name Scaevola ("left-handed").

48. *missing:* Possibly used in the sense of "that which fails to hit or strike its target" (*OED*). There is also the possible implication that the burnt right hand is missing as the result of a punishment for robbery. There would seem to be the suggestion that "the acting hand" is engaged in left-handed (i.e. underhanded, sinister) dealings.

Witness the great, immortal Teckley's fame.
In holy wars 'tis all *True Protestant*
Kings to dethrone, and empires to supplant;
Nay, and the Antichristian throne to shake.   55
Curst monarchy! 'tis famous even to make
The Alcoran the Bible's cause assume,
And Mahomet the prop of Christendom.
Such aid, such helps, sublime rebellion wants:
Rebellion, the great shibboleth of Saints,   60
Which current stamp to Reformation brings;
For all is *God With Us* that strikes at kings.
Now Charon, land me on th' Elysian coast,
With all the rites of a descending ghost.
A stouter, hardier murmurer ne'er fell   65
Since the old days of stiff-neck'd Israel;

---

52. *Teckley:* In reaction to the rigorous religious and political persecutions of the Hapsburgs, the Hungarian Protestants under Count Imre Tököli (regularly anglicized to Teckley) revolted against Leopold I and thrice fought against him between 1678 and 1682. In that year, they allied themselves with the Turks (or, rather, against the Holy League of Innocent XI) in a war that culminated in the famous siege of Vienna of 14 July to 12 Sept. 1683. The Dissenters in England looked with sympathy on Teckley and his "malcontents," and considered that his alliance with the Mohammedan infidels was more than offset by his Protestantism and anti-Catholicism. Tory propagandists made much of these strange bedfellows: see, for example, *Observator*, No. 204 (13 Sept. 1682), 228 (23 Oct. 1682), 399 (6 Sept. 1683), and 420 (13 Oct. 1683); also *The Rebels' Association in Hungary* [R 598], which is based on the Whig Conspiracy; and Dryden's Epilogue to Lee's *Constantine the Great* (ca. 12-14 Nov. 1683).

    53. *Observator:* . . . Is not the Hungarian True-Protestant rebellion the very same with the English True-Protestant rebellion? And their calling in the Mahometan Turks to their brotherly assistance every jot as warrantable as our calling in the Christian Turks, the Scottish Covenanters, to our brotherly aid and assistance? Is not the Alcoran as sacred as the old Solemn League or the modern Association? And is not the faith and honor of those Turks more to be confided in than we have found the faith and honor of these? (No. 228 [23 Oct. 1683]).

    55. *Antichristian:* Roman Catholic; papal.

    56. *famous:* This would seem to be used as an expression of approval, though it predates the earliest example in the *OED* by about 115 years.

    57-58. For L'Estrange's suggestion that such ideas could be found in Marvell's *Growth of Popery* and Samuel Johnson's *Julian the Apostate*, see *Observator*, No. 204 (13 Sept. 1682).

    60. *Saints:* The term applied by certain sects to their members to indicate their being among the elect under the New Covenant.

    62. God With Us: The motto of the Commonwealth.

Since the cleft earth in her expanded womb
Op'd a broad gulf for mighty Corah's tomb.
Methinks I saw him, saw the yawning deep.
Oh! 'twas a bold descent, a wondrous leap!   70
More swift the pointed lightning never fell.
One plunge at once t' his death, his grave, his Hell.

68. *mighty Corah's tomb:* To punish Corah and his followers for rebelling against Moses, God caused the earth to "open her mouth and swallow them, with all that appertain unto them, and they [went] down quick into the pit" (Numbers 16:30). Corah, along with Cain and Balaam, typified those who "despise dominion and speak evil of dignities" (*A Dictionary of the Bible, 2, 50*; also Jude, 11). For Dryden, Corah was Titus Oates (*Absalom and Achitophel*).

70. Sidney's courage and resolution were with him to the end:

When he came on the scaffold, instead of a speech he told them only that he had made his peace with God, that he came not thither to talk but to die; put a paper into the Sheriff's hand and another into a friend's, said one prayer as short as a grace, laid down his neck and bid the executioner do his office. (Evelyn, *Diary, 4,* 353).

A History of the New PLOT: Or, A Prospect of Conspirators, their Designs Damnable, Ends Miserable, Deaths Exemplary;

E. Shaftsbury Dictating his measures

Max: Worthy
Worth: Next:

Arthur Late Earle of Essex Cut his own Throat.

E. Shaftsbury at Consult Hastens the Damnable Plot to be put in Execution.

L.d Will: Rusels Execution in Lincolns Inn Fields.

Septemb. 9th. meet to be observed as a day of Thanksgiving us being thrown out all England, &c.

Tho: Walcot. Will: Hone. John Rouse.

The Kings of a Traitor.

Executed at Tiburn.

The Frog and Mouse at Variance which Shall be King both.

The Morall.
So Factious Men Conspiring doe Contend
But Hasten their own Ruin in the End.

17. Aug. 1683.

A brief Account of the late Treasonable Conspiracy,

AGainst His Majesties Sacred Person and Government,

By promoting Seditious Libels, and other wicked Arts, to incite to a dislike and hatred of his Sacred Person, the Heads of which Party having no other Design but the Destruction of Himself and Government.

Law, viz. Thomas Walcot, William Hone, John Rouse, and the Lord William Russell. Arthur late Earl of Essex, being Committed to the Tower, for High Treason, Killed himself.

Shaftsbury's curfed Defign, how laid, is Explained by his Book of Worthy Men, and Men Worthy, thus,

'Tis an Alphabetical Digeftion of all the Counties of England, juft in Order of a Parliament-Tax, in the Statute-Book; with a Lift of the tho' a Member of a Society. 14. An Oath Superadds no Obligation to Paſt; and a Paſt Obliges no further then it is-Credited. 15. If a People Sinfully Difpoſeſs One Prince; and contrary to a Former Oath, Covenant with Another, the Later Covenant ftands. 16. All Oaths are Unlawful. 17. The Taker Swears in his own Senſe. 18. Dominion Founded in Grace. 19. Civil Powers Uſurp upon the Prerogative of Chriſt. 20. Kings Subject to the

Reſifteth the Power, reſiſteth Gods Ordinance; the Conſideration of which will prove the ancient Maxime true, That Chriſtianitys Confiſtency is always attended with Loyalty; which is the great Defign of this Exemplar.

Abſolom Conſpires againſt his Father, 2 Sam. 15. Chap. 18. Abſolom in the wood of Ephraim, is hanged by the hair, in a great Oak, and ſlain by Joab.

The Amalekite that ſtood upon Saul and ſlew

Subjects, who foreſaw what this method would produce; ſhewing with great Courage, Duty and Affection, readily to defend His Majeſties Royal Perſon and Government.

By which means, theſe Factions loſt ground: Hence being deſperately reſolved to betake themſelves to Arms, by force to overturn the Government.

Different Intereſts and Opinions joyn in this villanous Enterprize.

Contriving a general Inſurrection in this Kingdom, and alſo in Scotland, &c.

Conſpiring to Aſſaſſinate His Sacred Majeſty, and Royal Brother.

Alſo to Maſſacre the Magiſtrates of the City of London, &c.

But the Divine Providence hath wonderfully ſhewed it ſelf, in a gracious Preſervation, from this damnable and horrid Conſpiracy, &c.

About the Beginning of October laſt, the Principal Conſpirators met to agree, how to Maſter the Guards, and to Sieze His Majeſties Sacred Perſon, &c.

Some other Villains were likewiſe carrying on that horrid and Execrable Plot of Aſſaſſinating His Sacred Majeſty, and his Deareſt Brother, at their return from Newmarket; That being deferred, it was after agreed, at His Majeſtys next going to Newmarket. The Place appointed was the Houſe of one Richard Rumbold, a Malſter, called the Rye, near Hodſdon, in the County of Hertford.

Fourty Perſons were in this Aſſaſſination to be Actors, &c.

This Blow was to be followed with a Maſſacre, of the Officers of State, the preſent Lord Mayor and Sherriffs, and the Magiſtrates moſt eminent for their Loyalty, &c.

The late Earl of Shaftsbury, who had preſt firſt to a ſudden Riſing, ſent to know the Conſpirators reſolution, and finding they intended farther preparation, conveyed himſelf ſecretly into Holland, to avoid the danger of his being diſcovered.

Divers of the Conſpirators are fled from Juſtice.

Others have been Committed, Tryed, Convicted, Attainted, and Executed according to be Hang'd, &c. Into this Book were Enter'd the Names of the moſt conſiderable Men in the Kingdom, and Ranged in their proper Counties under the One, or the Other Head, accordingly as they ſtood Enclin'd: Inſomuch that it was, Effectually, a Compendium, and a Ready Eſtimate of the Strength and the Intereſt of Both Parties.

Some affect to be Maſters of new Hereſies, by fair ſhews, though for baſe Ends, that are the Churches Troublers: Such the Apoſtles With reaches, Would to God they were even Cut Off, Gal. 5, 12.
And to mark them that cauſe Diviſions, Rom. 16. 17.
Thoſe little Foxes that ſpoil the Vines, Cant. 2. 15.

I would have old Babylon broken down, and all new Babels kept down; that we may not be burthened with New Jeſuitical Plots, of Factions and Schiſm; leaſt pleaders for Liberty turn Libertines, to begin and foment Conſuſions.

For not to dwell in Rome, but to have Rome dwell in us is as great a ſin, and the High-way to Deſtruction in this Caſe Engliſh or Italian Babylonians are all one.

The Twenty Seven Propoſitions Condemned and Executed by the Conſent of the Univerſity of Oxford, which are as follows.

THE Firſt Propoſition is, That the People are the Fountain of Power. 2ly, There's a mutual Compact, and the Power Forfeitable upon Breach of Truſt. 3dly, Power Forfeitable for Miſgovernment. 4ly, The King one of the Three Eſtates. 5. Birthright gives no Title. 6. Subjects may Covenant for Defence, without, and Againſt the Supreme Magiſtrate. 7. Self Preſervation is the Sovereign Law. 8. Reſiſtance Lawful for Religion. 9. Againſt Paſſive Obedience. 10. Poſſeſſion is a good Title. 11. The State of Nature is a ſtate of War, in which every man hath a Right to all things. 12. The Foundation of Civil Authority is this Natural Right. 13. Every man retains a Right of Defending himſelf againſt Force, King, and Tyrants to Death; and if they fail, the Power devolves to the People. 24. God's People are to expect New Revelations for a Rule of their Actions, and upon an Inward Motion from God may deſtroy Tyrants. 25. The Preſident of Phinehas is to us inſtead of a Command. 26. The Murderers of Charles the Firſt, were the Inſtruments of Gods Glory. 27. Charles the Firſt making War upon his Parliament; was Lawfully Reſiſted, and no longer King.

DAvid's Subjects Loyal, did eſtimate him better worth than Ten Thouſand of his Subjects, 2 Sam. 18. 3.

By the only Wiſe God, the great King of Kings, Monarchy was firſt eſtabliſhed. Moſes was a Monarch and King in Jeſhurum, Deut. 33. 5.

Joſhua and the reſt of the Judges or Dukes, were Virtually tho' not Formally Kings.

The Habit of Saintſhip, or if Intereſt and a long Sword, and ſtrong Arm will not do: For Powers are Ordain'd of God, and not of men, (and this in the New-Teſtament dayes) Rom. 13. 4. 6.

Note, God foretold Iſrael of their having a King, Deut. 17. 14, 15. And this King was not choſen by the People, but by Lot, 1 Sam. 10
And when Samuel ſhewed the People him whom the Lord had choſen, &c. The People ſhoute, and ſaid, God Save the King: or as the Hebrew Margent, Let the King Live.

Conſult Scripture and you will find, that Judgments have Dogg'd at the heels of all ſuch Subjects as have either ſecretly or openly Riſen up in Conſpiracy or Rebellion againſt their Lawful Kings. Had Zimri peace who Slewhis Maſter? 2 Kings 9. 31.

Hence let the Original of Kingly Power teach us, in Conſcience towards God, to ſtand in Defence of our King.

To Strengthen this, let us reflect back upon the Judgments that overtook the Inſtruments of our late Kings Murther.

Gods Providence takes a ſpecial Care of the Safety of Princes, and that he is immediately concerned to avenge their Blood; that ſeeing the Powers that be, are ordained of God, it follows, That not only he that Rebels, but even he that ſtead, 1 Kings 15. 28, 29.
Ela the Son of Baaſha, that ſlew Nadab, Zimri his Servant, Conſpired againſt him, and ſlew him after he had Reigned two years, 1 Kings 16. 8, 9, 10.

Zimri Reigned but ſeven days, who ſlew Ela, and when the People Encamped, heard ſay, Zimri hath Conſpired, and alſo ſlain the King, the Souldiers made Omri, the Captain of the Hoſt, King, Zimri deſperately Burnt himſelf, at Tirza in the Palace of the Kings Houſe, 1 Kings 16. 5, &c.

Ahab the Son of Omri is ſlain at Ramoth Gilead, the Dogs lick up his Blood, 1 Kings 22. 34, 38.

Jehoaſh is ſlain by his ſervants, that made a Conſpiracy, 2 Kings 12. 20.

Amaziah ſlew his ſervants that had ſlain the King his Father, 2 Kings 14. 5.
2 Chron. 33, 24, 25. King Amon's Servants Conſpire and ſlay him in his own houſe, but the People of the Land ſlew all them that had Conſpired.

The New Teſtament is not ſlack in foretelling the laſt Ages, Perilous Times, and mark'd them out, Rom. 16.

As ſervers of their own Bellies, deceiving the Hearts of the People. Satans Miniſters are Transformed, Gal. 5. 19, &c.

Windy Doctrines of men, cunning Craftineſs, and lying in wait to deceive, Eph. 4. 14.

But Timothy Exhorts eſpecially, Supplications, Prayrts, and Interceſſions eſpecially for Kings, 1 Tim. 2. 1.

And 2 Tim. 3. is expreſs concerning theſe perilous Times, Traytors, Heady, High-minded, Reprobates, Seducers, Itching Ears, turned into Fables, Chap. 4 3, 4.

Titus 1. 10. &c. Vain Talkers and deceivers, ſubvert whole houſes: Their mind and Conſcience being defiled, abominable and diſobedient to every Good work.
2 Pet. 2. 1. 10. Falſe Teachers, deſpiſers of Government, Preſumptuous, Self-willed, that ſpeak Evil of Dignities, Scoffers, walkers after their own luſts.
Jude v. 8. 19. Renders ſuch, Filthy Dreamers, Deſpiſers of Dominion, Evil ſpeakers of Dignities, Senſual, Separatiſts, not having the Spirit.

LONDON, Printed for Randolph Taylor, 1683.

A History of the New Plot, 17 August 1683, containing the official account of the Whig Conspiracy, the twenty-seven propositions of Oxford, and Biblical citations in support.

An Elegy on Sir William Waller

[*E 430*]

Though one finds mock elegies and astrologers' predictions occurring regularly in the political writing of the period, the device of the ante-mortem elegy, which buries the victim alive, is rather unusual. The most effective example did not appear until 1708: Swift's famous annihilation of the Whig astrologer John Partridge, who had, just 25 years before, attempted to prophesy the Duke of York out of existence.

In point of fact, Sir William Waller did not die until 1699. Politically, however, his life began and ended with the Popish Plot. His alliance with Oates undoubtedly had much to do with his becoming Justice of the Peace for Middlesex, and, to Tories at least, he was

> a great inquisitor of priests and Jesuits, and gutter (as the term was for stripping) of popish chapels; in which he proceeded with that scandalous rigor as to bring forth the pictures and other furniture of great value and burn them publicly; which gave occasion to suspect, and some said positively, that under this pretense he kept good things for himself. In a word, he was called the Priest Catcher." (North, *Examen*, p. 277)

The high points of Waller's political life were undoubtedly his taking of Edward Fitzharris and his part in the Meal Tub Plot, but the zeal and persistence with which he carried out his less spectacular arrests struck terror into the heart of many a fugitive priest. (See, for example, Henry Foley, *Records of the English Province of the Society of Jesus* [London, 1879], 5, 625.) In April 1680, Charles found an excuse to relieve him of his position as Justice of the Peace (Luttrell, *1*, 39; and *Dagon's Fall* [D 111]), but he was nonetheless returned for Westminster a second time in 1681. Waller's estimation of the extremes to which the Popish Plot might have gone is perhaps best illustrated by the report that in Jan. 1681 he was in Holland purchasing arms (*CSPD*, 1680–81, p. 135). Though his foresight in this instance came to naught, it served him well in the middle of the following year, when he decided to retire to Holland. He was there when Shaftesbury arrived at the end of 1682, and sometime after the Earl's death, he moved on to Bremen where, according to Lord Preston (*HMC 7th Report,* pp. 347, 386) and the *Observator* (2, No. 21 [25 Feb. 1684]), he became the governor and a "second Cromwell" to the Whig exiles who gathered around him. Wisely, he took no active part in Monmouth's rebellion, though it undoubtedly had his moral and even perhaps his financial backing; rather, he waited until 1688, when he joined the Prince of Orange's invasion, though William never saw fit to give him any employment. If Waller's political foresight kept him far from the dangers of battle, it also kept him far from the victor's reward. Only for a brief period, as a lieutenant of Titus Oates, did this man of radical thought but conservative action have political life. By Aug. 1683, when it was clear that he was not actively involved in the Whig Conspiracy, he could indeed be buried alive with very little fear that there would be a spiritual or political reanimation.

The text is based on *h″*, printed by Nathaniel Thompson and purchased by Luttrell (who noted that it was "a scandalous, abusive thing") on 21 Aug. 1683.

AN ELEGY ON THE MUCH LAMENTED

SIR WILLIAM WALLER,

Who Valiantly Hang'd Himself at Rotterdam

"Rise, grim Alecto, rise ('tis fit to choose
For hellish matter an infernal muse);
Thou who at Fox Hall didst inspire those sots,

1. *Alecto:* One of the three goddesses of vengeance charged with punishing "every transgression of natural order, and especially . . . offences which touch the foundation of human society." (Seyffert, *Dictionary of Classical Antiquities,* p. 224). The writer must have felt that Alecto ("She who rests not") was particularly suitable to his material.

3. *Fox Hall:* i.e., Vauxhall, the district on the south bank of the Thames where Christopher Kirby (or Kirkby, one of the first believers of the Popish Plot) had his lodgings (Lane, *Oates,* p. 83). Titus Oates moved there at the beginning of Sept. 1678, and it was here in "the Plot house" that he and the fanatic preacher, Dr. Israel Tonge, wrote out the famous *Narrative.*

Tonge, Oates, and Kirby, to contrive their plots;
Who didst through wondrous labyrinths of ill   5
Conduct Sir Godfrey safe to Primrose Hill;
And by mysterious ways and oaths most quaint,
Of an old faggot make us a young saint.
Plots thou canst make and mar: thou Stygian whore,
Assist me once! I'll ne'er invoke thee more."   10
    The hell-born dame assents: her head she shakes,
Pregnant of plots and periwigg'd with snakes;
At her right ear an Oates and Bedloe hung,
And at her left Prance, Everard, and Tonge.
Thus gravely she recounts what the curs'd elf,   15
Sir Waller, confess'd ere he hang'd himself.
    " 'Good Father Ferguson,' quoth he, 'now I

6. *Sir Godfrey:* Sir Edmund Berry Godfrey (1621–78), Justice of the Peace for West-minster, took Oates' first depositions of the Plot. A month later, his body was found on the south side of Primrose Hill. His death, which lent substance and sensationalism to Oates' discoveries, has never been fully explained. (See Carr, *The Murder of Sir Edmund Godfrey.*)

7. *oaths:* Principally of Miles Prance and William Bedloe, whose evidence put the blame directly on the Catholics.

quaint: Clever, ingenious; cunning, crafty.

8. *an old faggot:* Godfrey's gaunt features are quite striking. His portrait is repro-duced as a frontispiece to Carr's book.

a young saint: The anti-Court party virtually canonized Godfrey as the Protestant proto-martyr of the Plot. His particular day was 17 Nov., when the Pope-burning pro-cessions took place. (See Luttrell, *Brief Relation, 1,* 144; North, *Examen,* pp. 570–79.)

14. *Everard:* Edward Fitzharris, "a notorious papist," was said to have plotted an insurrection and disturbance. To assist him in writing an inflammatory libel (*The True Englishman Speaking Plain English*), "he proferred Mr. [Edmund] Everard a great sum of money." Toward the end of Feb., however, Everard, "ingeniously dis-covering it, a way was contrived for Sir Willam Waller and Mr. Smith to overhear [Fitzharris]," who was immediately sent to Newgate on a charge of high treason (Lut-trell, *Brief Relation, 1,* 68–69). He was tried on 9 June and, despite attempts to im-plicate Lord Howard of Escrick, was found guilty, and executed on 1 July. (For the legal contention between Commons and the law courts, as well as the trial and its implications, see Howell, *State Trials, 8,* 223–446.)

15. *elf:* Often used for a malignant being, an imp, or demon.

17. *Ferguson:* Robert Ferguson, the Scottish dissenting minister who was at the very center of both aspects of the Whig Conspiracy, would have been the logical per-son to have taken Waller's "confession." The two were together in Holland at the end of 1682 (when Ferguson arrived with Shaftesbury), and again, after the Conspiracy was discovered and Ferguson once more fled to the Continent. In the following months, the exiles congregated at Bremen, where Waller, now the leader, became for them "a second Cromwell." (See *HMCR, 7th Report,* e.g. pp. 347, 386.)

Do mean to make confession verily.
  " 'When willing senators wisely were afraid
Of horrid scarecrows they themselves had made;   20
When chapel of St. Stephen and place of peers
Were overflow'd with sudden floods of fears;
When easy mortals stopp'd their ears and eyes
With uncouth tales and incoherent lies;
When knaves and thieves and cheats grew rich by plots,   25
I wisely worshipp'd Bedloe and great Oates,
Because I scarely then was worth ten groats.
These, my right worthy patrons, with great ease,
Soon made my worship Justice of the Peace.
  " 'Arm'd with this power (as if I had a charter   30
To rob and spoil), I gave no mortal quarter:
Even aged matrons, in my nightly trade,
I grop'd; such might be priests in masquerade.
My skill herein was great; I got the start
Of Brother Chamberlain in his own art.   35
And with my co-adjutors at my tail—
Gill, Merry, Jones, Snow, Chetwyn, Prance, Mansell—

21. *chapel of St. Stephen:* The meeting chamber of the Commons in Westminster Palace.

place of peers: House of Lords.

24. Even as late as 1681, Waller was able to act on what was evidently anonymous information. L'Estrange remarks (*Observator,* No. 2 [16 April 1681]: "Commend me to the unknown hand that gave Sir William Waller the intelligence of an insurrection intended by the prentices on the 20 of May. Honest Ovington and King were clapped up about it." (For earlier "conspiracies" which Waller checked, see *CSPD,* 1679–80, pp. 424, 432.)

25. *knaves and thieves and cheats:* Though the categories are quite broad, the writer might have had in mind Oates, Dangerfield, and Prance.

27. *groats:* The groat (equal to about four pence) ceased to be issued after 1662; the word was used figuratively for any small, almost worthless, amount.

29. *Justice of the Peace:* According to the *CSPD,* Waller probably became a J.P. in the last weeks of 1678.

35. *Brother Chamberlain:* Sir Thomas Player, a Whig, had succeeded his father as Chamberlain of London in 1672. To the Chamberlain's court belong "the receipts of the rents and revenues of the City . . . and the business of apprentices over whom he hath a great authority" (*Angliae Notitia* [14th ed.], Second Part, p. 203).

37. Some of Waller's "myrmidons" (as North calls them in *Examen,* p. 262) can be identified. Of the first, L'Estrange remarks that "Waller and Gill the constable were a pair of active rabbit-suckers and demolishers of popery as well in coin as in crucifixes" (*Observator,* No. 451 [6 Dec. 1683]; see also 2, No. 21 [25 Feb. 1684]). Thomas Merry was willing to sell out to both sides at once, though the Court (according to Mrs.

In obscure holes and lanes I briskly blunder'd,
And every Papist that I found I plunder'd.
Even Protestants themselves 'scap'd not my gins: 40
Though they were Guelphs, their goods were Ghibellins.
John Gadbury's maps and globes were not protected;
Such as I lik'd were popishly affected.
    " 'Now see me on a steed, more big by far
Than that my rebel sire bestrid in war;   45
Towards Tothill Fields the way I do traverse,
With a rude rout of miscreants at my arse.
To th' fields we come. Lo, Parson Farrington,

Wall) considered "he was not worth the looking after, for he was thought an incon-
siderable rascal" (Howell, *State Trials, 8,* 367). Jones and Snow must remain in ob-
livion. The doings of Walter Chetwynd (or Chetwyn) can be found throughout *CSPD,*
1679–80, where he is constantly in the company of men such as Dugdale and Speke;
he is quite likely the same Chetwyn who was J.P. and deputy lieutenant in Stafford-
shire, who helped Warcup search Lord Stafford's residence, Tart Hall, for priests, and
whose name came up in the trial of the five popish lords (Pollock, *The Popish Plot,*
p. 271; *CSPD,* 1679–80, p. 377). The ex-Catholic Miles Prance, following his discoveries
of the Godfrey murder, became one of Waller's "priest-catchers." Colonel Mansell
achieved prominence when Dangerfield "discovered" papers of a plot in his room, and
his counteraccusations led to Waller's finding the famed Meal Tub papers at Mrs.
Cellier's.

40. *gins:* Schemes; stratagems; tricks.

41. *Guelphs . . . Ghibellins:* The two principal parties in medieval Italian politics,
the former supporting the popes, the latter the emperors. Dryden uses the words
similarly: "Thy doublet and breeches are Guelph and Ghibellines to one another"
(*Wild Gallant,* I.i).

42. *John Gadbury:* The astrologer (1627–1704), whose Tory and Catholic inclinations
involved him in the Meal Tub Plot (see *DNB;* Pollock, *The Popish Plot,* pp. 205, 240;
also, above).

45. *my rebel sire:* Sir William Waller (1597?–1668) was a parliamentary general until
1645, when his zealous Presbyterianism led him into ever-greater opposition to the
Commonwealth government until, in 1659, he was actively engaged in bringing about
the Restoration.

46. Waller's "progress" takes him to Tothill Fields, then to Lady Dormer's, from
there to the New Palace Yard at Westminster and so north to the Savoy. Thus it is a
relatively short, but profitable, trip.

48. *Parson Farrington:* Probably William Farrington, "a silk weaver, a fellow of
notorious loud conversation who preached on Sundays and Thursdays 'to near 1,000
auditors.' " Charles complained of his folly in "preaching in the playhouse" (the Old
Theater in Vere Street?); on his death "Calamy speaks of him as 'too well known
about London for the scandal he brought upon religion by his immoralities' " (A. G.
Matthews, *Calamy Revised* [Oxford, 1934], p. 191).

Like a brave Knipperdolling, marches on,
With hat erect on cane ('twas to seem taller),   50
He cries: "I' th' name of Gad, a Waller, a Waller!"
As when to warn men to Bear-Garden plays,
Exalted Pug from 's Rosinante surveys
Attendant crowds of dogs, thieves, bums, and boys,
Expressing in his pleasant face his joys: 55
Like Pug look'd I when Billing and his blades
Denuded their dull, sullen, loggerheads,
Throwing their everlasting caps to th' sky,
Bawling "A Waller!" with a full-mouth'd cry.
   " 'Environ'd with my rogues, I bent my course   60
To Lady Dormer's, where, without remorse,

49. *Knipperdolling:* An adherent of Bernhard Knipperdolling, a leader of the Mün-
ster Anabaptists (1533–35); an Anabaptist; hence, a religious fanatic.

52ff. The apparently long-standing practice of the Bear Garden is referred to by
Rochester, *Tunbridge Wells* (1674):

> So the Bear Garden ape, on his steed mounted,
> No longer is a jackanapes accounted,
> But is, by virtue of his trumpery, then
> Call'd by the name of "the young gentleman."
>   (162–65)

53. *Pug:* A cant term, probably here used merely in the figurative sense of an ape
or a monkey, though L'Estrange applies it specifically to the Whig printer Benjamin
Harris.

Rosinante: The name of Don Quixote's horse; hence a hack, a jade.

54. *bums:* Bumbailiffs, a contemptuous synonym of "bailiff." Ned Ward, in *The
London Spy,* refers to "the vermin of the law, the bum."

56. *Billing:* Though there is a Quaker named Billing involved in the disturbances
on Guy Fawkes Day (*CSPD,* 1682, p. 528), this is, more likely, a man named Billington.
The Observator inquired about him:

> Was he not one of Will. Waller's ferrets, at the fetching up of Bedingfield
> the Jesuit that died here at the Gate-House and rose again at Newark a
> matter of forty years younger than he lay down?
>
> *Whig.* He was no such friend of Sir William Waller's as you would have him,
> for I have heard this Mr. Billington several times threaten to arrest Sir
> William for the charge of that expedition. (No. 217 [4 Oct. 1682])

59. On 7 Feb. 1685 (*Observator,* 2, No. 215), L'Estrange recalled the time when
"nothing was as it should be that had not Oates' blessing along with it. A Smith! A
Waller! A Bethel! was still the cry wherever Titus had to do." For a more sympathetic
view of the parliamentary election and "triumph," see *A Faithful Account of . . . the
Election of Sir William Poulteney and Sir William Waller* (London, Printed for
T. Davies, 1681).

61. *Lady Dormer:* The Dormer family contained many notable Catholics (see Henry
Foley, *Records of the English Province of the Society of Jesus* [London, 1879], 5). In

Spoons, tankards, pictures, plates I took away
(Alas! such popish trinkets were just prey!);
And after narrow search, like cunning fox,
I seiz'd a priest hid in a pepper-box: 65
The priest to Newgate had his mittimus;
The box, being silver, did belong to us.
Then in New Palace Yard of Westminster,
I most courageously did make a fire,
And, true-dissenter-like, in zealous scorn,   70
At noonday did my saviour's picture burn:
A worthy prank of reformation work,
That outdoes Father Jew and Brother Turk,
And tells the Christian world I durst act what
My grandsire Pilate would have blushed at.   75
  " 'With gun, I and my knaves to th' Savoy came;
Like skillful thieves in Pickering's house we roam;

------

this instance, the reference may be to Mary (1655–1709), the second wife of Lord
Charles Dormer, second Earl of Carnarvon (1632–1709). I have been unable to locate
the London residence of the Dormers, though Lord Dormer was baptized at St. Benet's,
Paul's Wharf.

62. Waller was regularly charged with "rifling [Catholics'] houses of goods under
the notion of searching after papers and chapel-stuff, called by him popish trinkets"
(Dalrymple, *Memoirs*, quoted in Wood, *3*, 818; also *Observator*, No. 189 [15 Aug. 1682]).
On 25 Feb. 1684 (*Observator*, *2*, No. 21), L'Estrange lamented sarcastically that "the
chief merchant that negotiated his [i.e. Waller's] matters is long since dead and gone.
(I speak of Gill the constable.) And you cannot imagine what a trade they two drove
in beads, pictures, reliques, and crucifixes; and now and then, perhaps, a piece of
altar-plate—for they'd smell you the tang upon't of a superstitious use."

66. *mittimus:* A warrant for arrest; a dismissal from office or station.

68–72.

    Whig. . . . Have we not seen a worthy knight . . . deliver up the picture of
        Christ in the arms of His mother, that only served for a piece of ornament
        or furniture in a private family, in triumph to the flames; and the multi-
        tude hoiting about it and throwing stones at it. . . .
    Tory. Oh! Tis an excellent way of fleshing a whelp of the True-Protestant-Dis-
        senting-Reformation, to enter him upon a picture, and let him worry his
        prince and his religion in effigy (*Observator*, No. 189 [15 Aug. 1682]).

76. In Jan. 1679, Luttrell (*Brief Relation*, *1*, 7) noted that "Sir William Waller,
searching at the Savoy, hath found several popish books and priests' vestments, and in
Pickering's lodgings found a gun, Italian make, which is said to be that designed for
killing the King." Oates had earlier brought the area under suspicion and search when
he stated that the Benedictine convent (next to Somerset House) was a center of the
Popish Plot (Lane, *Oates*, pp. 99, 125).

77. *Pickering's:* Thomas Pickering, according to Tonge and Oates, was one of the
many assassins hired to kill Charles II. His assignment was to shoot the King. After

Closets and trunks we break; one did unfold
Full fourscore pieces of Egyptian gold.
"Good quids," quoth I. "My brethren, not a word.   80
All this is ours; we're people of the Lord.
This gun we bought i' th' Minories, 't must be laid,
And we must find't out in Pickering's bed.
Then early in the morning let's repair
To tell our patriots at Westminster   85
(Not of the fourscore pounds we stole in gold)
That Pickering's gun is found, and in safe hold;
This gun, clos'd up in featherbed so dark,
That dext'rous gunner us'd in James's Park.
And if their honors vote to have't laid by,   90
'Twill serve a surer marksman with one eye."
    " 'My Sanch-Panch Prance and I, in Lent,
A journey took to Newark upon Trent,
To seize old Bedingfield, who, like a fop,
Forsook 's quiet grave to keep a ribbon shop.   95
He was grown young again; say what ye will,

---

having "dogged" Charles for eight years, Pickering and his partner, Grove, reputedly attempted the assassination several times in St. James' Park, where Charles very frequently walked. However, loose flints, mis-firings, Pickering's forgetting to load the pistol, and Grove's cold, all prevented the fulfillment of the dire plan that Oates had outlined (Lane, *Oates*, pp. 77, 79, 94–95). Pickering was executed for high treason on 9 May 1679.

80. *quids:* Money, cash (though this antedates the citation in *OED* by 17 years).

82. *Minories:* The Minories, a street between Aldgate and Tower Hill, received its name from the house of the nuns, or minoresses ("sorores minores"), of the Franciscan order, the Poor Clares. The street was famous for its gunsmiths (see N. G. Brett-James, *Growth of Stuart London*, pp. 33–35, 95; Louis Zettersten, *City Street Names* [3rd ed. London, 1926?], pp. 110–11).

91. *a surer marksman:* The printed gloss reads "Rumbold," i.e. Colonel Richard Rumbold, the owner of the Rye House and, according to the Court's witnesses, "the principal promoter of the assassination plot. . . . Rumbold was commonly called Hannibal by the conspirators 'by reason of his having but one eye' " (*DNB*). He escaped to Holland in June 1683 but was captured with Argyle's forces in 1685 and executed.

94. *Bedingfield:* Father Bedingfield, the Duke of York's confessor, died in prison before he could be tried on Oates' accusations. In Jan. 1680, there was "the startling rumor that 'notwithstanding the jury who sat upon Mr. Bedingfield, the Jesuit, in the Gate House, and found him to be dead and was buried accordingly, yet we have an account that Sir William Waller found him alive at Newark, and has committed him to the Gate House by that name, but it is discoursed that this Bedingfield will prove himself but a cobbler' " (*The Protestant Domestic Intelligence* [10 Feb. 1680], quoted in Lane, *Oates*, p. 334).

These cunning Jesuits will be Jesuits still.
The mayor and we robb'd him of all his things:
Two spoons, one old plate, horse, ribbons, gloves, rings.
" 'But why should I my mighty deeds declare?   100
I'll hang myself now in this wild despair.
Why do I live? Brave Anthony is gone,
And Essex with his razor cries, "Ah Hone!"
Bold Walcot's hang'd, and close behind his breech
Stands noble Russell, making a true speech.   105
All-killing Armstrong and bold Grey are fled;
Prince Monmouth sneaks, and dares not show his head.
All's lost. Go Ferguson, get a rope. Go, go!
Here's a convenient beam will serve us two:'
Then at one swing himself Sir Waller hurl'd   110
To 's fellow traitors in the other world."

102. *Brave Anthony:* Anthony Ashley Cooper, the Earl of Shaftesbury, leader of the anti-Court party, died in Amsterdam on 21 Jan. 1683. Waller was not present at his death though he had been close to the Earl during his self-imposed exile.

103. *Essex:* Arthur Capel, Earl of Essex, was found dead in the closet of his Tower cell with his throat cut on 13 July 1683. The inquest's decision that he committed suicide [A 175] has found general acceptance, though many Whigs at the time claimed he had been murdered. (See headnote to *An Elegy on the Earl of Essex*.)

Ah Hone: A triple pun: *1.* a whetstone used for giving a fine edge to cutting tools, especially razors; *2.* the Scottish and Irish exclamation of lament, Ohone, i.e. oh! alas! *3.* William Hone, the joiner, who confessed to his part in the assassination plot, was executed with Walcot and Rouse on 20 July 1683.

104. *Walcot's:* Captain Walcot asserted to the end that he only meant to engage the King's guard at the Rye House, and had no intention of killing the King himself. See Howell, *State Trials, 9,* 668–74.

105. *Russell:* William, Lord Russell, executed on the following day (21 July), delivered to the Sheriff a paper stating his position (Howell, *State Trials, 9,* 685–93); it was printed that evening. Many persons felt that Burnet had composed it (Luttrell, *Brief Relation, 1,* 271, 277), and action was taken against John Darby, the printer, who later stated that he had run off 20,000 copies of the speech (*CSPD,* 29 Sept. 1683).

106. *Armstrong:* Sir Thomas Armstrong had the reputation of being a "bravo." He had killed the brother of Sir Carr Scroope in a playhouse encounter several years before, and was deeply embroiled in the assassination plot. He escaped in mid-1683 but was captured at Leyden in May and executed in England, as an outlaw and traitor, on 20 June 1684. (See the headnote and poems on Armstrong's execution.)

Grey: Forde Lord Grey of Werk also fled to Holland in 1683. Though he commanded Monmouth's horse at Sedgmoor in 1685, his evidence against his associates saved his life.

107. *Monmouth:* At this time, Monmouth was in hiding, possibly at Toddington. For his return to the Court on 25 Nov., and the subsequent disfavor (see *A Merry New Ballad in answer to "Old Rowley the King"*).

Tangier's Lamentation

[*T 135A*]

For Charles II and England, Tangier was the dowry of a marriage
that had promised so much and proven so fruitless. The dreams of an
African empire and the plans for control of the Mediterranean
hinged on the successful development and expansion of the former
Portuguese installation. Into this effort, England poured men and
money, combatting the Moorish troops of the tyrant Mulaï Ismâïl,
rebuilding the town, establishing its outlying forts, and undertaking
the necessarily ambitious improvement of the harbor. Tangier's his-
tory has been thoroughly and ably told by E. M. G. Routh (*Tangier,
England's Last Atlantic Outpost, 1661–1684*), who supplements vast
documentary evidence with the striking contemporary illustrations of
Thomas Phillips and Wenceslaus Hollar. In Routh's book we can
trace the fading of Charles' hopes that led to his decision in July 1683,
to demolish totally the work of more than two decades; indeed,
Dartmouth's mission of destruction seems an almost inevitable prod-
uct of the party struggle that divided England and prevented the
King from summoning a parliament after March 1681. Many of the
Whigs, though they believed that Tangier was a profitable venture,
also recognized that Catholicism was rife in both its government and
its battle-hardened army; even more important, they felt (albeit in-
correctly) that Tangier was a lever by which they would pry from
Charles concessions on exclusion before voting him the money and
supplies that could save the outpost. Charles came pathetically close
to realizing his dream, but the combined pressures of domestic strife
and foreign wars forced upon him the realistic conclusion that "the
brightest jewel of his crown" had to be not only abandoned but
utterly pulverized.

The true purpose of Lord Dartmouth's mission was kept so secret
that the Admiralty itself was not informed until after the 21 ships
had set out; and Pepys, who, with Colonel Kirke and the engineer
Henry Shere, accompanied the young admiral as a special consultant
and supplied sufficiently pessimistic evaluations to justify the destruc-

A Prospect of Tangier and the Mole before it was demolished, 1683. Drawing by Thomas Phillips.

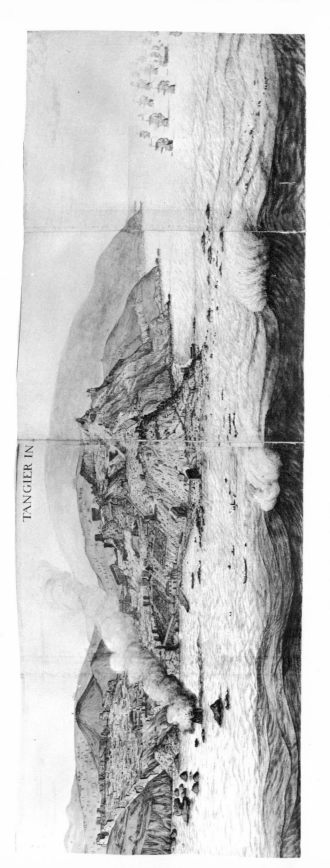

TANGIER IN

Tangier in Ruins, February 1684. Drawing by Thomas Phillips.

tion, was not told of the King's decision until he had been on board for five days (Routh, pp. 247–48). On 4 Oct., Dartmouth formally announced his plans to the inhabitants of Tangier, but official publication only appeared in England with the simultaneous arrival of refugees aboard the *Swallow* and the hospital ship *Unity* (ibid., pp. 254, 261–62, and *London Gazette*, No. 1877 [12–15 Nov. 1683]). Four days later (Thursday, 16 Nov.), the Mayor of Tangier and others arrived at Spithead on the *St. David* (*London Gazette*, No. 1879 [19–22 Nov. 1683]). The evacuation of civilians was carried out so smoothly that by 5 Nov. practically all the townspeople had left Tangier (Routh, p. 262). Here, perhaps, is where the writer of this poem got the date that appears in the title; in point of fact, however, the construction of the harbor had been so solid that it was not until three months later that the final demolition took place (ibid., pp. 264, 363).

Whoever wrote these verses was sufficiently familiar with Tangier so that he could imagine, with reasonable accuracy, the destruction of the town many months before it occurred. As well, he was sufficiently attached to the place that he set his "half-melancholy, half-ironical verses" (ibid., p. 265) to the tune of the *Tangier March*. (The music is given in *c*, with two earlier sets of lyrics; see also *r″* (V), pp. 473 and 476 n. 1. The tune is also used for *The Whigs in Mourning for the Loss of Their Charter* [W 1658A].)

The text is based on *g″*, and collated with *c* and *r″* (V). Luttrell obtained his copy on 24 Nov. 1683.

TANGIER'S LAMENTATION

on the Demolishing and Blowing-up of the
Town, Castle, and Citadel
November the 5th, 1683

1.

Let the Moors repine,
Their hopes resign,
Now the pagan troops are cheated;

1–3. "Ali Benabdala [the Moorish commander besieging Tangier], realizing that he could not hope to prevent the destruction of the fortifications, nor to take the city

Let foot and horse
Disband their force,   5
Since Tangier is defeated.
Alas, Tangier! what sudden doom
Hath wrought this alteration,
That thus thy march should now become
Thy fatal lamentation?   10

2.

Now, alas, Tangier!
That cost so dear
In money, lives, and fortunes,
See how the States,

---

before it and the harbor were ruined, was perforce contented to let events take their
course" (Routh, *Tangier*, p. 264).

4–5. The Whigs wished to abandon Tangier so that Charles could not build up a
standing army of seasoned fighters; they therefore refused to grant money on the ex-
pectation that the King would be forced to recall and disband his troops (see Routh,
Tangier, pp. 239–42). The Duke of York wished to abandon the port in order to have
"three thousand loyal troops within call . . . in upholding his right to the throne
against the claims of Monmouth" (ibid., p. 243). When the troops finally did return in
1684, they were not disbanded. For their later use, see ibid., pp. 339–42.

7–8. Charles might have been able to overcome the ever greater need for men and
money, as well as the pressure from both the Shaftesbury and York factions, but the
rejection by Mulaï Ismâïl, the Emperor of Morocco, of the Whitehall treaties forced
him to give up all hope of maintaining the port.

9. *thy march*. See headnote and Routh, *Tangier*, p. 265.

13. In 1683, the Tangier Commissioners estimated all expenses for the next twelve
years at £4.8 million. While this sum was undoubtedly exaggerated in order to furnish
another argument for withdrawal, the cost of the mole (see 45 n.) had already come
to £340,000. In so far as lives are concerned, no figures are available save for casualties
in certain military operations; but these, combined with disease, etc., must have gone
well into the "thousands" mentioned in 59. Finally, while the repatriation of Tangier's
Englishmen certainly involved some loss, no really great "fortunes" (in the material
sense of the word) lay buried in the town's ruins. (See Routh, *Tangier*, pp. 148–49, 258–
59.)

14–16. i.e. it would have been a kinder fate to have been overcome by an enemy in
battle than to be deliberately destroyed by one's own forces. *States* probably refers to
the States General, the Netherlands, England's chief maritime rival during the seven-
teenth century. At just the moment when Charles was attempting to make a treaty
with Mulaï Ismâïl, "in 1682, the Dutch bought from him [Ismâïl] a treaty of peace
and commerce at the price of six hundred quintals of the best powder, and a large
and richly furnished State coach" (Routh, *Tangier*, p. 233). Used less specifically, *States*
could apply to France (rumored to be joining the Moors for an attack on Tangier) or
Spain (which feared the proximity of the English) (see Routh, *Tangier*, pp. 233, 270).

The kinder fates,   15
For thy own fate importunes.
Had this been plotted by the Moors,
    Alas! it were no matter;
But blown up thus by thy own store,
    Thou'dst better swum in water.   20

3.

The old port, Tangier,
    Where for good cheer
We never paid extortion;
    Which, whilst it stood,
    Was once thought good   25
To be a monarch's portion;
Whilst English hearts thy walls possess'd,
    They scorn'd e'er to surrender,
Now to the foe is left a nest
    For serpents to engender.   30

4.

Alas! what now
    Must seamen do
When they come ashore to lord it,
    For a little fresh store,
    And a little fresh whore,   35
Which Tangier still afforded?
No ambuscade of treacherous Moor,
    Nor shall Ben Ottor's highness,
Court any more the British shore,
    To try the ladies' kindness.   40

19. *store:* In this case, military supplies, material; specifically mines, powder, etc.

23. Tangier, by proclamation, was a "Free Port" (Routh, *Tangier,* p. 148).

26. *a monarch's portion:* Tangier was part of the dowry of Catherine of Braganza.

35. For this aspect of life, see Routh's description, *Tangier,* pp. 213–14, 276.

37. Both in major engagements (see Routh, *Tangier,* pp. 61–68) and in daily harassment (see ibid., pp. 280–81), the Moors' most effective tactic was ambush.

38. *Ben Ottor's:* Hamet ben Haddu Ottor, or, more correctly, Mohammed Ohadu (or Ben Hadu), the Moorish ambassador, arrived in England on 29 Dec. 1681 and did not leave until 23 July 1682. During his entire stay, he was lionized and Moors "became the fashion of the season." Routh gives a good account of his stay (*Tangier,* pp. 223–28), but this can be filled out by the newspaper accounts and the hints (as here) that the Ambassador was enjoying the English "ladies' kindness."

5.

It would grieve your heart
Should I impart
The gold and precious matter
That lies oppress'd
In every chest   45
Drown'd underneath the water;
But now the mole that forc'd the main,
The mole so gay and bonny,
Is with the chests blown up again,
But ne'er a cross of money.   50

6.

Of how many souls,
And large punch bowls,
Has this been the undoing?
How many ton
Of precious coin   55
Lie buri'd in the ruin?
Had this been done some years ago,
Of horsemen and postillions,
'T had sav'd some thousand lives the blow,
And sav'd besides some millions.   60

7.

When the pile took fire
Above the spire,

45. *chest:* The mole—the massive piers that were to create an artificial harbor at
Tangier—was first undertaken by Sir Hugh Cholmley in 1663. In 1676, he was suc-
ceeded by Henry Shere who had for six years advocated the use of great wooden chests
(some of them to be as large as 83′ x 30′ x 20′ and weighing 1,000 tons) filled with stones
and cement and sunk in place, a procedure successfully employed by Genoese engineers
and quite contrary to Cholmley's more conventional idea of a solid breakwater built
of debris. The plan and views of the mole, as well as a detailed drawing of one of
Shere's chests, are given in Routh's chapter (*Tangier,* pp. 343–64) on this "greatest
engineering work till then attempted by Englishmen." The mole proved far more diffi-
cult to destroy than had been anticipated, and when it had finally been demolished, the
rubble completely filled the harbor.

50. *cross:* A coin; money. There may be an allusion to the game of pitch and toss,
in which one throws or casts up a coin which then comes down cross or pile (cf. 61),
i.e. heads or tails.

62. *spire:* Probably that of Peterborough Tower, the highest point in Tangier.

I wish (for th' good o' th' nation)
  The walls well cramm'd,
  With rebels ramm'd   65
Of the Association:
All Bethels of a Commonwealth,
  Each sullen Whig and Trimmer,
That boggle at a loyal health,
  Yet will not balk a brimmer.   70

8.

Now Heav'n preserve
(While rebels starve)
The King and 's royal brother,
  While traitors fly,
  And others die,   75
Impeaching one another:
That gracious prince, that values more
  His subjects' lives and pleasure
Than all the wealth of Afric's shore,
  And Tangier's buried treasure.   80

66. *Association:* In order to block the Duke of York's attainment of royal powers, Essex had proposed in Parliament that the possibility of an association be investigated. Later, the famed Paper of an Association, which urged a resistance to York's succession (by force if need be), was the basis of the Court's unsuccessful attempt to obtain an indictment of treason against the Whig leader, the Earl of Shaftesbury.

67. *Bethels:* Slingsby Bethel, the leader of the most radical faction of the Whig party, had been Sheriff of London in 1680–81. Prudently, he fled to Hamburg in July 1682, when it became fairly evident that the Court party would soon dominate municipal politics. See Poems on the Shrieval Elections and *Iter Boreale.*

69. *loyal health:* A toast to the king as opposed to a full drink (*brimmer,* 70) for its own sake.

73–75. These verses appeared while the Whig Conspiracy still gripped the attention of England. Grey, Armstrong, Ferguson, and many others had fled to the Continent; Russell, Walcot, Rouse, and Hone had already been executed, and Sidney's sentence was shortly to be carried out; Howard, West, Keeling, Bourne, and Shepard had turned Crown's evidence. On 26 Nov. (two days after Luttrell obtained this poem), Monmouth officially came out of hiding and surrendered himself to Secretary Jenkins.

79. Dartmouth wrote to Jenkins on 11 Aug. 1683: "I cannot but think it best for His Majesty to save the lives and estates of his subjects before any necessity or dishonorable misfortune happen to the place. . . . By the help of God, I will so order it [the abandoning of Tangier] that it shall be no reproach to His Majesty nor any future annoyance to Christendom, at least in our age" (cited in Routh, *Tangier,* p. 246).

80. *Tangier's buried treasure:* As in 43, the reference is to the vast sums that had literally been sunk in the harbor.

Song. Old Rowley the King

Using a highly popular tune that was " 'ancient' in 1575" (Chappell, *Popular Music*, p. 792), a tune that had been given, since the late Commonwealth, a series of relatively genial anti-Puritan lyrics (ibid., p. 265), the writer of this particular version reviews the political situation in the last two months of 1683 with a delightful "plague on both your houses" attitude that he voices through the King himself. So far as is known, the ballad was never printed, though it circulated in manuscript. Indeed, it is not at all unlikely, as Professor Brice Harris has suggested in his article on "Robert Julian, Secretary to the Muses" (*ELH, 10* [1943], 294–309), that the distribution of manuscript copies of these verses led to the "captain's" indictment (31 May 1684; Luttrell, *1,* 309), and later conviction (12 Nov.; Luttrell, *1,* 319–20), with the sentence "to pay 100 mark fine; to stand in the pillory at Westminster, at Charing Cross, and at Bow Street; and be bound for his good behavior for life." Obviously, the Court was not amused; and Julian, who had already lost an ear for peddling libels (Harris, p. 295), heard all the more clearly the strong voice of authority. Literally, if not gracefully, this Wits' plaything bowed out of his public life and into the mists and myths of poetic allusions.

The authorship remains unknown, since a copyist's ascription of it to Charles Sackville, Earl of Dorset (see *Z,* p. 765, and Harris, p. 304, n. 40, and p. 305, n. 45) seems as weak as the Court's ascription of it to Julian (Luttrell, *1,* 309).

Song. Old Rowley the King

To the Tune of "Old Simon the King"

1.

"This making of bastards great,
And duchessing every whore,

1–2. Charles ennobled the following: James Scott (also known as Crofts, and Fitzroy), Duke of Monmouth and Buccleugh (by Lucy Walter); Charles Fitzcharles, Earl of

     The surplus and Treasury cheat,
       Have made me damnable poor,"
         Quoth old Rowley the King,   5
         Quoth old Rowley the King,
           At Council Board,
           Where every lord
       Is led like a dog in a string.

2.

     "And as my wants grow more,   10
       The factions likewise do;
   The cudden son of a whore
     You see outreaches me too,"
         Quoth old Rowley the King,
         Quoth old Rowley the King.   15
          "Not Ketch's ax

Plymouth (by Catherine Pegge); Charlotte, Countess of Yarmouth (by Lady Shannon); Charles Fitzroy, Duke of Southampton and Cleveland, Henry Fitzroy, Duke of Grafton, George Fitzroy, Duke of Northumberland, Anne, Countess of Sussex, Charlotte, Countess of Lichfield (by Barbara Villiers, Countess of Castlemaine and Duchess of Cleveland); Mary Tudor, Countess of Derwentwater (by Margaret or Mary Davis); Charles Beauclerk, Duke of St. Albans (by Nell Gwynne); and Charles Lennox, Duke of Richmond (by Louise de Kéroualle, Duchess of Portsmouth).

3. In Jan. 1683, Halifax, probably angered by Sunderland's advancement and alliance with Rochester, made public a fraud of £40,000 in the management of the Treasury, of which Rochester was principal Commissioner. The subsequent dispute divided the Court, and Rochester, strongly supported by the Duke of York and the Duchess of Portsmouth, was the apparent victor. In Nov. of the following year, however, Rochester was "kicked upstairs," to use Halifax's phrase (Foxcroft, *A Character of the Trimmer*, p. 201), into the Lord Presidency of the Council. Two versions of Halifax's charges are available, that of Burnet, *History*, 2, 339–41, and that of Reresby, *Memoirs*, pp. 288–95; the affair is well summarized in Ralph, *History*, 1, 704–06.

5. *Rowley:* A somewhat disrespectful, though usually affectionate, nickname for Charles. Rowley was the name of the King's stud horse.

7. *Council Board:* i.e. the Privy Council, the members of which are listed in *Angliae Notitia* (15th ed.), 1, 187–88.

12. *cudden:* A born fool, a dolt.

son of a whore: Monmouth, "the Protestant Duke," had been quite deeply involved in the Rye House conspiracy's plans for insurrection, though he might have been unaware that the plot included attempts on the lives of Charles II and York.

16–18. Following the discovery of the plot, Monmouth went into hiding, perhaps at Toddington (D'Oyley, *Monmouth*, p. 233). During July, the month in which a number of the conspirators suffered traitors' death under the ax of Jack Ketch, the public executioner, Monmouth "received a message that if he would come in his offence would be condoned" (ibid.). Halifax might have been the messenger then, as he was in Oct.,

Nor Halifax
You see can bring him in."

3.

Then Keeper Guilford cri'd,
"Good Sir, why fret you so?   20
Leave all to York and Hyde,
And see what they can do."
Thinks old Rowley the King,
Thinks old Rowley the King,
"Gud's fish these fools   25
Have been the tools
From whence all mischiefs spring."

4.

The double Duke then bows
And cries, "Give ear to me:

---

when the negotiations led to Monmouth's private letter of submission on 24 Nov. (ibid., pp. 237–44). When the letter was made public (*London Gazette,* No. 1880 [22–26 Nov. 1683]), Monmouth disowned it and then, probably under Halifax's direction, submitted anew his statement on the plot. But on the following morning, he regretted his action, and Charles, in a fury, returned the paper. Monmouth gave no further support to the Court and left England at the beginning of the year.

17. This line may refer either literally to the earlier attempts to bring Monmouth into Court or figuratively to the later attempts to have him support the Court's view of the Rye House conspiracy.

19. *Keeper Guilford:* Francis North (1637–85) became Keeper of the Great Seal on 20 Dec. 1682 and was raised to the peerage as Baron Guilford on 27 Sept. 1683.

21. Monmouth "saw now, he said, that the Duke of York, his implacable enemy, had a mind to ruin him, and that he had been brought back to Court 'only to do a job'" (D'Oyley, *Monmouth,* p. 247; see also York's letter of 4 Dec. 1682 to William of Orange, quoted on p. 248, and Monmouth's note, on p. 244). The pressure on Monmouth must have been particularly strong; by 7 Dec., he was forbidden to enter the Court (Roberts, *Life, 1,* 173).

Hyde: Laurence Hyde (1641–1711), created Earl of Rochester on 29 Nov. 1681, worked with York against Halifax and his policy of reconciliation (Roberts, *Life, 1,* 152).

25. *Gud's fish:* God's fish, a mild oath which Charles frequently employed.

25–27. To what extent Charles was constrained by his brother's faction is difficult to determine. The Monmouth pocket-book, or diary, notes that the King stated that he had been inclined to save Lord Russell, but was forced to allow the execution, "otherwise he [Charles] must have broke with [the Duke of York]" (James Wellwood, *Memmoirs* [London, 1700], pp. 375–76; also Roberts, *Life, 1,* 151 n., and D'Oyley, *Monmouth,* p. 244).

28. *double Duke:* James, Duke of York and Albany.

Suppress the Whigs, and use laws   30
   That knock down popery."
      Quoth old Rowley the King,
      Quoth old Rowley the King,
         "My Lord, we know
         How all things go;   35
   You've got our art for to trim."

<h3 style="text-align:center">5.</h3>

Then Rochester declar'd
Expedients might be found;
His brother and colleagues star'd,
   At which a loud hum went round.   40
      Then thinks old Rowley the King,
      Then thinks old Rowley the King,
         "Expedients and shifts
         Were his father's gifts
   And are all the sense he left him."   45

<h3 style="text-align:center">6.</h3>

Then Holy Orders spoke,
   Like oracles out of Hell,
"Let conventicles be broke
   And all things will go well."
      Then thought old Rowley the King,   50
      Then thought old Rowley the King,
         "These lawn-sleev'd lords,
         With lukewarm words,
   Wise Heav'n may trust, not him."

36. *for to trim:* To move cautiously between two alternative interests.

39. *His brother:* Henry Hyde (1638–1709), second Earl of Clarendon.

44. *his father's:* The religious and foreign policies of Edward Hyde (1609–74), first Earl of Clarendon, led to his impeachment and banishment in 1667.

46. *Holy Orders:* Probably Henry Compton (1632–1713), Lord Bishop of London and a member of the Privy Council.

48. The writer stresses the similarity of views between the Anglican Church's desire to suppress forcibly the illegal meetings of dissenters and nonconformists and the Catholic Duke of York's recognition that the religious laws can be used for political ends.

53. *lukewarm:* The implied charge against the Anglican Church is that of Laodiceanism (if not of a downright latitudinarianism) in accepting the Catholic position.

7.

The Council then did rise,   55
    The usefuller dogs did bark;
The devil a lord more wise,
    For everything's in the dark.
        Says old Rowley the King,
        Says old Rowley the King,   60
            "To sit only and prate
            Of tricks of State
        Is a very insipid thing."

Enter Old Rowley at Portsmouth's Lodging.

8.

"Sir, Monmouth is fit for a roy,   65
    And Richmond for another.
Will you both your babes destroy
    For one poor cully brother?"
        "Soft and fair," quoth Rowley the King,
        "Soft and fair," quoth Rowley the King,   70
            "The fool I must please
            Or not be at ease,
        But I'll have a trick for him.

9.

"Though having two queens be dear,
    And rarely more than one do appear,   75

56. *The usefuller dogs:* Charles "took delight to have a number of little spaniels follow him" wherever he went (Evelyn, *Diary, 4,* 410).

64. *Portsmouth's:* Louise Renée de Kéroualle (1649–1734), Charles' principal mistress, was Duchess of Portsmouth.

65. *roy:* King. The use of French here not only suggests the Duchess' background but also creates a pun on one of the names by which Monmouth was known, Fitzroy.

66. *Richmond:* Charles Lennox, Duke of Richmond, the son of Charles and Portsmouth.

68. *cully:* A dupe, gull, or simpleton.

74–75. Portsmouth "became the queen while the Queen herself, happy to be relieved of affairs of state that she had never understood, stayed in her apartments, or was rowed down the river, or listened to the counsels of her peculiar confessors" (John Lindsey [J. St. Clair Muriel], *Charles II and Madame Carwell* [London, 1937], p. 195).

I'll make two: and then 'tis clear
One has got a son and heir
For brave old Rowley the King,
For brave old Rowley the King;
And when I've done,   80
My bother and son
May end their tricks in a string."

In Answer to Old Rowley the King

If *Old Rowley the King* is written from a moderate Whig position, the *Answer* develops that of a moderate Tory, for, though it concentrates its attack on Monmouth and Halifax, it also stresses the weaknesses of both the King and his Privy Council. The events set forth in the *Answer* all have to do with Monmouth's situation between 25 Nov. 1683, when he officially returned to Court, and 7 Dec., when he was again in disfavor. It is not improbable that these lines were written within, or very soon after, that period; certainly they would seem to have been composed prior to Monmouth's flight to the Continent at the beginning of the year.

A Merry new Ballad
In Answer to Old Rowley the King

1.

"Our rebel party of late
　　Upon all their ruins reckon'd;
But rebels again are in date
　　Under Shaftesbury the Second,"

2. *reckon'd (upon)*: Counted up, evaluated; counted on (almost in the sense of "resigned themselves to"). In *V* and *r"*, there is the reading *recond*, to be connected perhaps with the verb "to recon," to remember or call to mind. *F*'s *reclin'd* should probably be rejected through its failure to rhyme.

3. *in date*: In fashion (cf. "out of date").

4. *Shaftesbury the Second:* Following Shaftesbury's death, it was, most ironically, George Savile, Marquis of Halifax, who became, willynilly, the spokesman for a large number of the now leaderless Whigs, principally because of his open opposition to the Rochester-York faction at the time of the Treasury fraud in early 1683 (see *Old Rowley the King*, 3 n.). Ralph points out that "all the malcontents, who expected from the broils of the Cabinet to derive some advantage to themselves, now showed a disposition to forgive Lord Halifax his apostasy and all the mischiefs it had occasioned, and extolled him as the censor of the age; insomuch that he himself, though not insensible of their praises, grew fearful of the consequences, as that it might create a jealously elsewhere which might injure him more essentially than this transient gale of popularity could serve him" (*History, 1,* 706).

484

> Says Perkin that would be king,   5
> Says Perkin that would be king.
> " 'Twas you, my lord,
>   And your good word,
> Did us this happiness bring.

2.

> "No more will I skulk for fear   10
>   Of scarecrow proclamation;
> Nor do I come to swear
>   For this my preservation,"
>   Says Perkin that would be king,
>   Says Perkin that would be king.   15
>   "The world shall know
>   I scorn to bow,
> Or recantations sing.

3.

> "My pardon so neatly obtain'd,
>   Has fool'd their declaration;   20

5. *Perkin:* Monmouth's nickname proved somewhat prophetic. Perkin Warbeck (1474–99) claimed to be Richard, Duke of York, the son of Edward IV. He was recognized as Richard IV of England by several rulers, among whom was James IV of Scotland. Warbeck's attempted invasion in 1497 led to his capture, his confession of the imposture and, finally, his execution in Nov. 1499.

7–9. For Halifax's role in "bringing in" Monmouth, see *Old Rowley the King,* 16–18 n. The Duke officially returned to Court on 25 Nov., though, through Halifax's efforts, he had met with the King a month before (*DNB*).

11. On 29 June, a royal proclamation was issued, offering £500 reward for the capture of Monmouth, Grey, Armstrong, and Ferguson (Luttrell, *Brief Relation, 1,* 263). Monmouth had gone into hiding, and it was not until 13 Oct. that Halifax located him. In the intervening period, "the Attorney General had orders to prosecute him to outlawry" (Roberts, *Life, 1,* 151).

12. *to swear:* i.e., as a witness against those conspirators still to be tried. (See Roberts, *Life, 1,* 161; also Sprat, *Copies* [S 5029], p. 136, often found with Sprat, *True Account* [S 5066].)

13. As Roberts remarks, however, "Monmouth had now betrayed his associates and had become an informer in order to purchase his safety and immunity from punishment" (*Life, 1,* 163).

18. *recantation:* See *Old Rowley the King,* 16–18 n. For Monmouth's three letters, see Sprat, *Copies,* pp. 137–41; also D'Oyley, *Monmouth,* pp. 237–39, 241–42, 246.

20. *declaration:* It was not until 9 Sept., after a number of the conspirators had already been put to death, that, "by His Majesty's declaration," a day of thanksgiving was officially celebrated. Luttrell (*Brief Relation, 1,* 279) goes on to remark

Which point so handsomely gain'd,
 We're in our former station,"
  Says Perkin that would be king,
  Says Perkin that would be king.
   "You've got much credit,   25
   My lord, who did it:
   The rogues gather under your wing.

4.

"It joys my heart to spy
 Each Whig perk up his head,
And in every Tory's eye,   30
 His sad defeat to read,"
  Says Perkin that would be king,
  Says Perkin that would be king.
   "The town's our own;
   The plot's run down   35
   And made a ridiculous thing.

5.

"Hereafter we'll be wiser,
 And carry our bodies swimming.
Be still my trusty adviser;
 We'll show 'em a trick for their trimming,"   40

---

that "at one or two churches here in town was given up a note to the reader to this effect following:

> You hypocrites, forbear your pranks
> To murder men, and then give thanks;
> Forbear your tricks, pursue no further,
> For God accepts no thanks for murder."

The verses, with a reply, were printed shortly after [C 6237] and are reprinted in *r"* (V), 299. See also *Observator*, No. 403 (14 Sept. 1683).

 22. *our former station:* For the reception of the prodigal son, see Roberts, *Life, 1,* 161, and D'Oyley, *Monmouth,* pp. 243–44. In the brief period between his submission and his banishment from Court, Monmouth, as Luttrell noted, "hath been mightily caressed at Court, to that degree that some persons have thence imagined there was no plot" (*Brief Relation, 1,* 293).

 25–27. See 4 n.

 35. *plot's:* The reference is to the Rye House Plot.

 38. *swimming:* i.e. swimmingly, with easy, smooth progress, with uninterrupted success.

 40. *trimming:* Modifying, or compromising, according to expediency. Halifax person-

Says Perkin that would be king,
Says Perkin that would be king.
"When the Parliament sits,
Let 'em look to their hits;
We'll make all England ring.   45

6.

"Pull you down Rochester!
Let me alone with York!
Ere he shall rule our godly land,
  We'll first bring in the Turk,"
    Says Perkin that would be king,   50
    Says Perkin that would be king.
    " 'Tis not succession
    Shall give him possession;
His sinking shall make us swim.

7.

"The lawn-sleev'd Church shall fall,   55
  And Holy Kirk shall rise.
Hang bishops in ropes, they're all Vice-Popes,
And o'er souls tyrannize,"

---

ified—and defended—the position of the trimmer (see *The Character of a Trimmer*).

43. From the time of the Oxford Parliament (March 1681) on, the anti-Court groups counted ever more heavily and ever more hopelessly on "the after-game" of Parliamentary revenge; however, by avoiding extraordinary expenses (e.g. war) and by receiving French subsidies, Charles was never forced to summon the legislative body.

44. *look to their hits:* Look to their chances (though this predates the earliest entry in *OED* by approximately sixteen years).

46–47. The political struggle against the Catholic faction was fought, in the matter of administration, between Halifax and Rochester, and, in the matter of succession, between Monmouth and York.

49. For the alleged sympathy of the Dissenters for the Turks, and their preference for the infidels rather than Christians, see L'Estrange's attack on Holwell's *Appendix to . . . Catastrophe Mundi* [H 2515] and his mocking account of Oates' ignominious defeat at Sam's coffee house, *Observator*, No. 399 (6 Sept. 1683). From 17 July–12 Sept. 1683, the famous siege of Vienna engaged the attention of all of Europe. The successful relief of the city by forces under Charles of Lorraine and John Sobieski led to successes of the Christian forces in Hungary during the closing months of 1683.

55. *lawn-sleev'd Church:* The Anglican Church, with reference to its bishops and episcopacy.

56. *Holy Kirk:* The Church of Scotland, distinguished by its Presbyterian structure.

Says Perkin that would be king,
Says Perkin that would be king.   60
"Atheism free
And debauchery
We'll into fashion bring.

8.

"Though Walcot and silly Hone,
Like fools, confess'd and were hang'd,   65
Russell and Sidney, like Saints, li'd on,
And all the conspiracy sham'd,"
Says Perkin that would be king.
Says Perkin that would be king,
" 'Tis no matter for laws,   70
We'll keep up the Cause,
That more religious thing.

61. *Atheism free:* "There was another company of Lord Shaftesbury's creatures that met in the Temple in the chambers of one West, a witty and active man, and believed to be a determined atheist" (Burnet, *History,* 2, 357).

62. *debauchery:* One of the leaders of the group, Forde, Lord Grey of Werk, had been tried and found guilty on 23 Nov. 1682 (Howell, *State Trials, 9,* 127–86) of debauching his sister-in-law, Lady Henrietta Berkeley. As a result of extracurial compromise, judgment was never asked for.

64. On 12 July 1683, Captain Thomas Walcot was found guilty of treason, as was William Hone, on the following day. Walcot did not deny being involved in the plans for an insurrection, and Hone pleaded guilty to the conspiracy. They were executed, along with John Rouse, on 20 July at Tyburn. (The trials are given in Howell, *State Trials, 9,* 519–70, 571–78.)

66. Russell was tried on the morning of 13 July and, despite an able defense, was found guilty. He was executed on 21 July, maintaining the illegality of his condemnation and not owning the conspiracy. (For his trial, and comments thereon, see Howell, *State Trials, 9,* 577–818.) Sidney's trial and conviction on 7 Nov. 1683 has proved even more debatable, for here the requisite second witness was papers found in his study which were, he claimed, private notes replying to Sir Robert Filmer's *Patriarcha; or, the Natural Power of Kings,* 1680 [F 922]. He was sentenced on 26 Nov. and executed on 7 Dec., just the period of Monmouth's submission and return to Court.

Saints: A term used by certain Protestant sects to show that their members were considered among God's elect under the New Covenant.

67. *sham'd:* This is the reading of the majority of texts though the word was thought to be closely related to *shamm'd,* the reading of *F.* A contemporary discussion of the relationship and connotations of *sham* are given by North (*Examen,* pp. 231–32).

71. *the Cause:* The Commonwealth was frequently referred to as the "Good Old Cause." Here, as in the time of Charles I, the appeal would seem to be to a "higher law."

9.

"And though we should rebel,
  The danger's ne'er the more;
We know before full well
  Old Rowley will quit the score,"
    Says Perkin that would be king,
    Says Perkin that would be king.
      "Though Caesar resents,
      He straight relents,
    And the law has then no sting.

10.

"The King too we'll abuse,
  And call the Council fools;
As how indeed can we choose,
  When they're made such pitiful tools?"
    Says Perkin that would be king,
    Says Perkin that would be king,
      And this same ballad
      Will stick in each palate,
    And Whigs shall merrily sing.

76. *Old Rowley:* Charles II. See *Old Rowley the King,* 5 n.
quit the score: Pay the bill, requite the obligation.
83. *Council:* The Privy Council. See *Old Rowley the King,* 7–9, 25–26, 55–58, for a similar view.

The Last Horse Race at Dorset Ferry, 24 August 1684. Drawn by Francis Barlow, 1687.

TOM DURFEY

The Newmarket Song, 1684

[N 932]

Under Charles' aegis, Newmarket and horse racing reached their glory and became almost synonymous words. The town, set within the downs, had been a favorite hunting resort of James I; under Charles, its famous course—the Rowley Mile and the Ditch—became the center of Court and country recreation, of booths and gambling and holiday mood (see the frontispiece to Vol. *1* of J. P. Hore's thorough study, *The History of Newmarket and the Annals of the Turf . . . to the end of the seventeenth century* [3 vols. London, 1886]; also the illustrations facing pp. 16 and 38 in Frank Siltzer, *Newmarket: Its Sport and Personalities* [London, 1923]). Here at Newmarket, the King

> let himself down from majesty to the very degree of a country
> gentleman. He mixed himself amongst the crowd, allowed every
> man to speak to him that pleased; went a-hawking in the morn-
> ings, to cock matches in the afternoon (if there were no horse
> races) and to plays in the evenings, acted in a barn and by
> very ordinary Bartholomew-Fair comedians (Reresby, *Memoirs*,
> p. 259).

Charles visited Newmarket each Spring and Fall, and the opening verses would seem to indicate that the ballad was written for the gathering in March. Ebsworth (*r''* (V), p. 143) states that the song was sung before the King in 1682, but, though that was a brilliant season (Hore, *3*, 18–34), Durfey's treatment of the Plot and the poem's tone of general calm strongly suggest that the lines were composed very close to the date of printing, probably for the coming visit in March 1684. In support of this is the fact that neither of the 1684 broadside printings adds the "selling point" that the song was "sung to the King there"; this appeared only when the ballad was reprinted in Durfey's *Wit and Mirth* (ed. 1719, 2, 51–55).

For Durfey, the golden glow of a settled State permeates this period. The royal visit in that Spring of 1684 was to last from 1 to 22 March (Hore, *3*, 88), and, though the weather proved "unseasonable and dirty," James hunted, the races were run, and Charles conferred the George and Garter on one illegitimate son, George Fitzroy (the recently created Duke of Northumberland), and the governorship of Wight on another, Henry Fitzroy, Duke of Grafton. Surrounded by "seven dukes at once," by the newly married Prince of Denmark, by the Court and Court ladies and by "an abundance of company," Charles stayed out "the full time he intended" and did not return to Whitehall for three weeks. "The weather," wrote Sunderland to Jenkins, "is cruel cold and yet [the King and Duke of York] are not weary of this place" (*CSPD*, 1684–85, pp. 305, 317, 321; Hore, *3*, 48; *HMC Ormonde*, NS 7, 212).

Durfey set his verses to a long-popular tune, one that had been recently revived for *Old Rowley the King* (see headnote) and the *Answer;* but in Durfey's lyrics, party feeling fades. Whigs are damned more from habit than passion, and Tories are admired but not apostrophized. Fanatic sham has ended; the tone of moderation and monarchy is broken only by the healthy, masculine invective of the country squire saddling up to ride off for Newmarket's "sporting and game" (his dramatic forebears can be found in Shadwell's Prig [*A True Widow*, 1673] and Howard's Swiftspur [*The Man of Newmarket*, 1678]).

The music is given in *g″* (Luttrell's copy [N 933], which is dated 16 Jan. 1684) and in Durfey's *Wit and Mirth*.

THE NEWMARKET SONG

To the Tune of "Old Simon the King," 1684

1.

The Golden Age is come;
   The winter storms are gone;
The flowers do spread and bloom,
   And smile to see the sun,
Who daily gilds each grove   5
   And calms the angry seas.

Dame Nature seems in love,
  And all the world's at ease.

"You rogue, go saddle Ball,
  I'll to Newmarket scour.   10
You never mind when I call;
  I should have been there this hour!

"For there is all sporting and game,
  Without any plotting of state.
From Whigs, and another such sham,   15
  Deliver us, deliver us, O Fate!

"Let's be to each other a prey;
  To be cheated be ev'ryone's lot,
Or chous'd any sort of a way
  But by another damn'd Plot.   20
Let cullies that lose at the race
  Go venture at hazard and win;
And he that is bubbl'd at dice,
  Recover't at cocking again:

"Let jades that are founder'd be bought;   25
  Let jockeys play crimp to make sport;

15–16. The lines are based on the frequent political litanies with their three
verses of complaint and the final "Libera nos, Domine."

19. *chous'd:* Duped, cheated, tricked.

21. *cullies:* Dupes, gulls; simpletons.

22. *hazard:* "The most bewitching game that is played on the dice," says Charles
Cotton in his *Compleat Gamester* (1674); and he remarks that it is properly named,
"for it speedily makes a man or undoes him; in the twinkling of an eye either a man
or a mouse" (*Games and Gamesters of the Restoration*, pp. 82–84).

24. *cocking:* Cockfighting had "gained so great an estimation among the gentry"
that Cotton, who proposed it "before all other games," gave a full discussion on
breeding, matching and caring for fighting cocks (*Compleat Gamester*, pp. 100–14).
He also reprints *An excellent . . . Copy of Verses upon Two Cocks' Fighting*, by
Dr. R. Wild.

25. *jades that are founder'd:* Worn-out horses that have an inflammation of the foot,
resulting usually from overwork.

26. *jockeys:* Anyone who manages or has to do with horses; a horse dealer; a crafty
or fraudulent bargainer, a cheat.

play crimp: "To lay or bet on one side and (by foul play) to let 'tother win, having
a share of it"; *to run a crimp* is "to run a race or horse match foully or knavishly"
(*Dictionary of the Canting Crew*).

For, 'faith, it was strange, methought,
　　To see vintner beat the Court.

2.

"Each corner of the town
　　Rings with perpetual noise: 30
The *Oyster*-bawling clown
　　Joins with *Hot Pudding-pies;*
And both in consort keep
　　To vend their stinking ware;
The drowsy god of sleep   35
　　Hath no dominion there.

" 'Hey boys!' the jockeys roar,
　　'If the mare and the gelding run,
I'll hold you five guineas to four
　　He beats her, and gives half a stone.'   40

" 'God d———me,' quoth Bully, ' 'tis done,
　　Or else I'm a son of a whore;
And fain would I meet with the man
　　Would offer it, would offer it once more.'

"See, see the damn'd fate of the town!   45
　　A fop that was starving of late,
And scarcely could borrow a crown,
　　Puts in to run for the plate.
Another makes chousing a trade,
　　And dreams of his projects to come,   50
And many a crimp match has made
　　By bribing another man's groom.

"The townsmen are Whiggish, God rot 'em,
　　Their hearts are but loyal by fits;
For, should you search to the bottom,   55
　　They're as nasty as their streets.

40. *gives half a stone:* i.e. gives a handicap of seven pounds.

48. *the plate:* In horse racing, a prize consisting of a silver or gold cup or the like given to the winner of a race.

51. *crimp:* Fraudulent, "fixed" (not in *OED*, but see 26 n.).

56. On 8 Oct., during Charles' final visit to Newmarket, the Duke of York wrote to his niece, the Countess of Lichfield, describing the races and adding that "I never saw this place so dirty as it is now" (*Memoirs*, p. 300, cited in Hore, *3*, 91).

3.

"But now all hearts beware.
   See, see on yonder downs!
Beauty now triumphs there,
   And at this distance wounds.   60
In the Amazonian wars
   Thus all the virgins shone,
And, like the glittering stars,
   Paid homage to the moon.

"Love proves a tyrant now,   65
   And there doth proudly dwell;
For each stubborn heart must bow,
   He has found a new way to kill.

"For ne'er was invented before
   Such charms of additional grace,   70
Nor has divine Beauty such pow'r
   In ev'ry, in ev'ry fair face.

" 'Od's bud,' cries my countryman John,
   'Was ever the like before seen?
By hats and by feathers they've on,   75
   Ise took 'em e'en all for men.
Embroider'd and fine as the sun,
   Their horses and trappings of gold;
Such a sight I shall ne'er see again,
   If I live to a hundred years old.'   80

"This, this is the country's discourse,
   All wond'ring at this rare sight:
Then Roger, go saddle my horse,
   For I will be there tonight."

57. Durfey seems to have in mind some specific "divertissement," but I have been unable to locate it in the accounts of the visit.

73. *'Od's bud:* An attenuated form of the oath "God's body."

On 10 or 12 Oct. 1683 (cf. *Observator*, No. 418 [10 Oct. 1683] and W. H. Hart, *Index Expurgatorious Anglicanus*, 1872–78, p. 283), the most active of the Whig booksellers, Langley Curtis, "[did] print and publish and cause to be printed and published, a . . . scandalous libel concerning the pretended ghost [of Lord William Russell] . . . entitled *The Night Walker of Bloomsbury*" [N 1154]. Printed on both sides of this single folio sheet was a conversation between a vintner, a tallow chandler, a brace of fishmongers, and a printer, as reported "in dialogue between Ralph and Will." The sedition lay principally in the writer's assertion that the Tory vintner, with his companions' assistance, had pretended to be Russell's ghost and, standing near the deceased lord's house in Bloomsbury Square, had groaned out the complaint (found in most Tory propaganda at this time) that Burnet had written the paper delivered by Russell to the Sheriffs at the time of his execution (Luttrell, *1*, 271; see also *Elegy on . . . Waller*, 105 n). All had ended, claimed the writer, when the watch administered "a palt o' the pate and the thigh" which exposed the Tory sham.

Though *The Night Walker* was scarcely more than a screed (it is reprinted in Hart, pp. 283–89), it gave the Court the opportunity simultaneously to reinforce its position on Russell's "paper," to expose a Whig counter-sham, and to silence Curtis—for a while at least. In *Observator*, No. 419 (11 Oct. 1683), L'Estrange carefully printed the depositions of those involved so that the public could see how Whig malice could distort a bit of innocent horseplay—the bet that Rutland, master of the Fountain Tavern, would walk around Bloomsbury Square and home with a cloth over his head and another around his middle—in order to discredit the government.

"Curtis was found guilty on February 14, 1684, and was sentenced on April 21 to stand on the pillory in Bloomsbury Market from eleven to one o'clock, with a placard above his head stating his offense in large letters. He was fined £500 and sent to Marshalsea prison until the fine was paid and security given for his future good behavior. At

the same time, the 'libel' was to be burned by the common hangman"
(Gillett, *Burned Books*, p. 521). The government had once more
moved successfully to embarrass and silence the opposition.

Assuming the mask of his victim, the writer exposes the Whig
politics behind the plots of the last five years, stressing the convicted
or alleged perjurers of that period and suggesting a pattern of shams
of which *The Night Walker* is merely an inept example. The ballad
appeared on or before 16 Jan. 1684 (Luttrell's date) and was probably
meant to swing public opinion against the yet untried Whig book-
seller.

The broadside, printed by John Dean with the music, has been
found only in *g''*. Luttrell marks it "a scandalous thing."

LANGLEY CURTIS HIS LAMENTATION IN NEWGATE

Who lies there in danger of his ears for printing and
publishing sedition and treason, for this five years past

A Song

1.

Come Whigs out of fashion,
Of me take compassion;
My ears are in danger, my case may be yours:
Long, long have I reigned, disturbing the nation;
Now, now am made captive to the higher pow'rs: 5
With Pacquet and pamphlets,
Abus'd Church and chaplets,
With Care's damn'd Courants did abuse the king so,
That none can defend us

3. *ears:* A person convicted of libel could by law have his ears cropped, though this
punishment had fallen into disuse by this time.

6. *Pacquet:* Curtis published Henry Care's *Weekly Pacquet of Advice from Rome*
until 18 Aug. 1682—"for 195 weeks (baiting but one)." Following this rupture, a
rival publication of the same name was issued for 38 numbers by William Salmon.

7. *chaplet:* A string of beads, especially one used for counting prayers, one
third of the length of a rosary.

8. *Care's damn'd Courants:* From 23 Dec. 1681 until the periodical finally expired
on 13 July 1683, Care appended to his *Weekly Pacquet* a two-page *Courant*, which
was meant to offset the popularity of the informal and effective *Observator*.

Till Tyburn befriend us,   10
And send us a-hunting for Tapski below.

2.

The loss of our Charter,
And College the martyr,
His flails are all seiz'd and our arms made a prey,
We have lost Ignoramus, both Jew, Turk, and Tartar;   15
No plots nor cabals to recover the day.
Since Tony left squinting,
Our cause has been sinking,
And our party for Tyburn advancing, you know;
There's none can defend us   20
Till Tyburn befriend us,
And send us a-hunting for Essex below.

3.

The law for a livery
Will put me i' th' pillory,

10. *Tyburn:* The usual place for public executions in London.

11. *Tapski:* The common Tory nickname for the Earl of Shaftesbury, who had died in Amsterdam on 21 Jan. 1683. For an explanation of the sobriquet, see the headnote to *The Last Will and Testament of Anthony, King of Poland.*

12. *Charter:* After almost two years of legal and political contention, the London Charter was finally lost on 3 Oct. 1683 (see headnote to the Quo Warranto poems.)

13. *College:* Stephen College (1635?–81), "in the excitement of the Popish Plot, sold 'Protestant flails,' short pocket bludgeons to repel anticipated Romanist assassins" (*DNB;* see headnote and illustration to College's *Truth Brought to Light, POAS,* Yale, 2, 12). His zeal in pamphleteering (23) and in coming armed to the Oxford Parliament led to his arrest in London. When the indictment against him was thrown out by a Whig grand jury (July 1681), the case was moved to Oxford, where, a conviction for treason having been obtained, the "proto-martyr of the Plot" was executed on 31 Aug.

14. Following the discovery of the Conspiracy, the houses of the leading Whigs were searched for arms with some success.

15. *Ignoramus:* The term applied to the London grand juries which, during 1681–82 when they were impanelled by Whig sheriffs, blocked the Court's legal actions by rejecting its bills of indictment.

17. *Tony:* Anthony Ashley Cooper, Earl of Shaftesbury.

22. *Essex:* The circumstances surrounding the death of Arthur Capel, Earl of Essex, are discussed in the notes to *An Elegy on the Earl of Essex;* see also *A New Ballad to the tune of the Irish Jig,* 37–48.

23. *livery:* A suit of clothes, formerly sometimes a badge or cognizance (e.g. a collar or hood) . . . by which [retainers] may be recognized. In law, there is the additional meaning of legal delivery. For the Whig inclinations of the London livery companies, see *The Charter,* 408–29.

A damn'd hard, wooden ruff for a Saint of the Cause.   25
Had a Tory my place, I would flear and look merrily;
With hardened brickbats I'd pelt him with blows.
          When my head peepeth thorough,
          The Tories will hollow;
At poor Langley Curtis cry *O Raree Show.*   30
          Now none will defend us
          Till Tyburn befriend us,
And send us a-hunting for Russell below.

4.

          Poor Colly was whipp'd, too,
          For stretching an oath or so;   35
And damn'd Tory Rutland, too hard for us all:
These daily misfortunes will all our designs undo;
Would his Fountain Tavern would sink, burn, or fall.
          But, alas, I am jailed,
          And must not be bailed;   40
As we serv'd the Papists, must we be serv'd so?
          There's none will defend us
          Till Ketch does befriend us,
And send us a-hunting for Walcot below.

5.

          Would I were with Patience,   45
          I'd keep in his stations,

25. *a Saint of the Cause:* A sectarian who favors the Commonwealth ("The Good Old Cause").

26. *Tory:* Nathaniel Thompson, Curtis' Tory counterpart, had already been sentenced to stand in the pillory on 5 July 1682 for asserting in print that Sir Edmund Berry Godfrey had committed suicide. (See Howell, *State Trials, 8,* 1359–89.)

28. *thorough:* i.e. through.

30. Raree Show: i.e. a peep show. This was also the title of the most notorious of Stephen College's libellous verses (see *POAS,* Yale, *2,* pp. 425–31), for which the printer-publisher, Francis Smith, was sentenced to the pillory on 18 June 1684 (Luttrell, *Brief Relation, 1,* 311).

33. *Russell:* William, Lord Russell, was convicted of complicity in the Whig Conspiracy and executed at Lincoln's Inn Fields on 21 July 1683.

36. *Rutland:* The vinter, master of the Fountain Tavern in Holborn, whose prank caused all the commotion. See headnote.

43. *Ketch:* Jack Ketch, the public executioner.

44. *Walcot:* Captain Thomas Walcot's involvement in the Rye House Plot led to his execution for treason on 20 July 1683 at Tyburn.

45. *Patience:* Sir Patience Ward, the Whig Lord Mayor in 1680–81, had been found

And save both my ears, for the Doctor may want:
I fear they'll be cropp'd if I live till next sessions;
Then Prance for his swearing may sweat and look blank.
     But after a collar,   50
     Oft cometh a halter;
My neck like my ears are in danger, you know.
     There's none can defend us
     Till Ketch doth befriend us,
And send us a-hunting for Sidney below.   55

6.

     Poor Arnold is pounded,
     For lying confounded,
By Worcester, which he did most basely defame.
Poor Giles he was pillor'd, 'cause Arnold was wounded,
Though by his own hands, Sir, in Jack-an-Apes Lane.   60
     Now Giles he is bailed,

---

guilty of perjury on 19 May 1683, but fled (eventually to Holland) before his sentence could be imposed (see *The Great Despair of the London Whigs for the Loss of the Charter,* 4 n., and *A New Ballad,* 50 n.).

47. *the Doctor:* Probably Titus Oates, the principal discoverer of the Popish Plot, who claimed a doctorate in divinity from the University of Salamanca.

49. *Prance:* The evidence of Miles Prance, along with that of William Bedloe, led to the conviction of Green, Berry, and Hill for Godfrey's murder (5 Feb. 1679). He subsequently supported the testimony of Dugdale and Bedloe against the Jesuits Harcourt and Fenwick, and later attached himself to the "priest-catcher," Sir William Waller. On 15 June 1686, he pleaded guilty to perjury.

55. *Sidney:* Algernon Sidney, the Whig leader, had been executed on 7 Dec. 1683 for treason. The headnote to *Algernon Sidney's Farewell* reviews the questionable legality of his trial and conviction.

56–58. On 22 Nov. 1683, John Arnold, a Monmouthshire justice of the peace and a rabid anti-Catholic (Pollock, *The Popish Plot,* pp. 273–74), was sentenced to pay £10,000 damages to the Marquis of Worcester (who had been created Duke of Beaufort on 2 Dec. 1682) for defamatory remarks made in July and Aug. of 1682. (A full Tory review is given by L'Estrange in *Observator,* Nos. 446–47 [29–30 Nov. 1683].) Arnold, according to the not-unbiassed Ailesbury (*Memoirs, 1,* 130), "would have had [the sum] remitted on the spot on a submission, but he chose rather imprisonment." The Welsh J.P.—who was counted among the most zealous of the "priest-catchers" (*CSPD,* 1680–81, p. 381)—evidently was willing to attempt subornation in order to obtain the downfall of Worcester, who had been Lord Lieutenant and then Lord President of Wales (*CSPD,* 1680–81, pp. 461–62, 559).

59–60. Sometime between 10 P.M. and 2 A.M. on the night of 15 April 1680, Arnold's cries were heard in Jackanapes Lane and Bell Yard. According to Arnold, he had left the Devil Tavern, had walked up Bell Yard, and had been assaulted by three men,

And Arnold is jailed;
There may lie and rot too, for ought that we know.
There's none will defend us
Till Ketch doth befriend us,   65
And send us all head-long to th' old Rump below.

7.

Mowbery and Balderen
Swore more like friends than men;
They both have been perjur'd ten thousand times o'er:
They had but one wife, and she still lay between them,   70
They being our Saints, though she could be no whore.
Dangerfield swore, too,

---

who had thrown a cloak over his head, dragged him into the narrow lane, and there tried first to stab him to death and (when his whalebone bodices protected him) then attempted to cut his throat. By happy circumstance, the wounds were not grave, and Arnold said he chanced to see one of his assailants, whom he later identified as John Giles, a Monmouthshire man who heartily detested the Justice. There is a good deal of evidence that the whole affair was a sham and that Arnold's wounds were either self-inflicted or carefully given him by those who wished to see the Popish Plot furor stirred up again by a repetition of the Godfrey incident (see Pollock, *The Popish Plot*, pp. 394–99, and *CSPD*, 1679–80, p. 480). Though none of this came out at the trial on 14 July 1680, Giles' witnesses contradicted Arnold's on every point; nonetheless, the jury (which was constantly reminded of the Godfrey parallel by the prosecution) found Giles guilty, and he was sentenced on 17 July to stand in the pillory at Lincoln's Inn Fields, near Jackanapes Lane, then at Grey's Inn, and finally in the Strand "on three several days." In addition he was fined £500 and had "to find sureties for your good behavior during life" (Howell, *State Trials*, 7, 1160). When first pilloried on 26 July, the crowd pelted him so severely with bricks and stones that he was protected on his two subsequent exposures "by a great guard of constables and watchmen" (Luttrell, *Brief Relation, I*, 53, 55; see also Giles' petition, *CSPD*, 1679–80, p. 591).

59. *pillor'd:* Pilloried.

66. *Rump:* The remnant of the Long Parliament that sat Dec. 1648–April 1653 and again May 1659–Feb. 1660.

67. *Mowbery and Balderen:* Lawrence Mowbray (or Mowbrey) and Robert Bolron (or Boldron) were the principal evidences of the Yorkshire, or northern, plot that involved Sir Thomas Gascoigne and his family. They were remarkably unsuccessful not only in Yorkshire, where their questionable past might have worked against them (see Pollock, *The Popish Plot*, p. 199; Luttrell, *Brief Relation, I*, 111, 173–74), but also in London, where the octogenarian Gascoigne was also acquitted (see Howell, *State Trials*, 7, 959–1044).

72. *Dangerfield:* Thomas Dangerfield was the chief informer in the Meal Tub Plot; however, in the trials of Elizabeth Cellier and the Earl of Castlemaine, his criminal record of 16 convictions (for which he had been branded, pilloried, and outlawed) led

All sorts of oaths, black and blue,
Though he had been carted and pillor'd before.
Yet still they escaped,   75
Though worse no Hell raked;
Then why may not I, that can rebel no more?

8.

Yet that fortunate hour,
They got out of the Tower
(Both Wildman and Trenchard, old Charlton and all).   80
I may find friends, too, though Jeffreys look'd sour,
And pardon, perhaps, when I come to Whitehall;
Guineas five thousand, too,
(For printing of treason) due,
Like some for plotting (a kind of recompence).   85
While others for loyalty
In the jail daily die,
I'll into the the country and live like a prince.

Chief Justice Scroggs to denounce his evidence as unworthy of credit (see Howell, *State Trials*, 7, 1049–54, 1102–03).

75. The informers escaped punishment by obtaining a royal pardon before testifying.

80. *Wildman . . . Trenchard . . . Charlton:* Major John Wildman, John Trenchard, and Francis Charlton, all of whom were deeply involved in one way or another with Whig party politics, were taken into custody in the weeks following the discovery of the Conspiracy (Luttrell, *Brief Relation, 1,* 263, 274). Since no evidence was found against them, they were bailed on 28 Nov. 1683 (ibid., p. 292) and discharged on 12 Feb. 1684 (ibid., p. 301).

81. *Jeffreys:* Charles had elevated Sir George Jeffreys to the post of Lord Chief Justice on 29 Sept. 1683.

83. *Guineas five thousand:* The allusion might be to the printer's bill found on Charlton (Ferguson's cousin and evidently the financier of the Conspiracy, according to James Ferguson in *Ferguson,* pp. 80, 132–33, 162), which showed £23 still due on a bill of £56 for such treasonable pamphlets as *The Black Box* and *The Indictment of the Duke of York.* There were also promises of a yearly fee of £100 and costs for "an engine made on purpose for the service" (ibid., p. 55, and Sprat, *Copies* [appended to *The True Account*], p. 85).

85. *some:* This may allude to the Scots who had been promised £10,000 to obtain men and arms for the uprising; on the other hand, it may simply be a variant of *sum* and refer to Curtis' alleged activities in the Whig Conspiracy.

A New Ballad

In a period when Tory writers exulted over the Rye House revelations and the post-Shaftesbury disillusion of their opponents, the Whig press remained all but silent. One of these rare expressions of opposition can be found in this remarkable little ballad which, with finely controlled irony, begins in the manner of so many Tory songs and then, with a *Realpolitik* and with increasing sharpness, converts past Whig defeats into motives for action.

Ebsworth asserts that the author was "the Honorable William Wharton, son of Philip fourth Baron Wharton. . . . He was killed in a duel, Dec. 1689, after having won a small reputation for ballad-making like his more notorious brother, 'Tom Wharton' " (*r″* (V), 448). While the suggestion is an interesting one, Ebsworth gives no evidence for it and I have not found any in the manuscript or later printed versions of the song.

As the copy text, I have used *B″*, collating it with *U′, d, j, m*. In *B″*, there is an interesting note that may suggest one of the possible channels of distribution for political verse that, or one reason or another, was not published in print:

> Mementum. I had this ballad of a bookseller at the Miter in Fleet Street next the Devil Tavern (whose name I know not) on Friday afternoon 6th June 1684, and returned it him again next morning by my coachman, sealed up under a covert, wherein was written: 7th June 1684. I here enclosed return you the paper I had yesterday from you, which I do not think on second reading to be so witty as I thought it at first; and in some places I can't make sense of it.

While we might question the writer's sense of economy or integrity, his note would seem to suggest that the bookseller-stationers served as outlets—and very likely as copyists—for manuscript verses.

Though the poem might possibly have been composed as early as Dec. 1683, a more likely date would be about the beginning of Feb. 1684, when Braddon and Speke were tried for subornation (41). Nor would this conflict with the date given in the later printed versions, since the "1683" given there in the title could well be calculated in Old Style.

A New Ballad

To the tune of The Irish Jig

1.

'Twere folly if ever
The Whigs should endeavor
Disowning their plots, when all the world knows 'em;
Did they not fix
On a Council of Six   5
Appointed to govern, though no body chose 'em?
Those that bore sway
Knew not one would obey.
Did Trincalo make more ridiculous pother?
Monmouth's their head   10
To strike monarchy dead.
They chose themselves viceroys all o'er one another.

2.

Was't not a damn'd thing
For Russell and Hampden

5. *Council of Six:* In order to prevent either stagnation or precipitousness among the Whigs, according to Lord Howard's confession, "it was thought necessary that some few persons should be united into a cabal or council, which should be as a concealed spring both to give and to guide the motion of the machine" (reprinted in Howell, *State Trials, 9,* 434). The members, he said, were Monmouth, Essex, Russell, Sidney, Hampden, and himself.

6. During Russell's trial (Howell, *State Trials, 9,* 612), the following exchange occurred:

    Lord Russell. Pray, my lord [Howard], not to interrupt you, by what party (I know no party) were they chosen?

    Lord Howard. It is very true, we were not chosen by community but did erect ourselves by mutual agreement, one with another, into this society.

    Lord Russell. We were people that did meet very often . . . He says it was a formed design, when we met about no such thing.

9. Possibly an allusion to Shakespeare's *Tempest,* where the jester, Trinculo, takes part in the comic homage offered by Caliban to Stephano. James, Duke of Monmouth, was referred to by this name in *A Canto on the New Miracle wrought by the D. of M. curing a young Wench of the King's Evil . . . 1681* [C 463]. On the other hand, the reference may be more general. In *Trincalo Sainted or the Exaltation of . . . Nathaniel*

To serve all the projects of hot-headed Tony? 15
    But more untoward
    To appoint my Lord Howard
By his own purse and credit to get men and money;
    That at Knightsbridge did hide
    Those brisk boys unspi'd 20
That at Shaftesbury's whistle were ready to follow;
    When aid he should bring,
    Like a true Brentford King,
Was here with a whoop, and gone with a hollow.

3.

    Algernon Sidney, 25
    Of Commonwealth kidney,
Composed a sad libel (aye, marry, was it!),
    Writ to occasion
    Ill blood in a nation,
And therefore dispers'd all o'er his own closet. 30
    'Tis not the writing
    Was prov'd, nor inditing,

Thompson [T 2282], Trincalo would seem to be a current name for a yelping dog and is connected with Towzer (the name given Roger L'Estrange).

15. *hot-headed Tony:* For the rashness of Shaftesbury in the final months of 1682, see headnote to Poems on the Whig Conspiracy and Howell, *State Trials, 9,* 432, 604–06.

19. In Act V of *The Rehearsal,* the heralds announce to the two kings of Brentford (see 23–24) that "the Army's at the door, and in disguise . . . having, from Knightsbridge, hither march'd by stealth."

20–21. According to Howard, Shaftesbury asserted that "there is above ten thousand brisk boys are ready to follow me whenever I hold up my finger" (Howell, *State Trials, 9,* 604).

23–24. In Act V of *The Rehearsal,* the first king of Brentford sings out:

So firmly resolv'd is a true Brentford king
To save the distressed, and help to them bring,
That, ere a full pot of good ale you can swallow,
He's here with a whoop, and gone with a hollow.

Buckingham was burlesquing lines in Dryden's *Tyrannic Love,* IV.i.

27. *a sad libel:* Since Howard was the only witness against Sidney, the Crown introduced, as the necessary second evidence, private notes answering Filmer's *Patriarchia.* See headnote to *Algernon Sidney's Farewell.*

30. *closet:* A study, a small room for retirement or privacy.

31–32. Though these notes were almost certainly Sidney's, he never admitted that he had composed them and the Crown proved no more than "a similitude of hands" (see Howell, *State Trials, 9,* 853–67, 901).

And though he urg'd statutes, what was it but fooling,
>> Since a new trust is
>> Plac'd in the Chief Justice   35
To damn law and reason by overruling?

4.

>> What if a traitor,
>> In spite of the State, Sir,
Will cut his own throat, from one ear to t'other?
>> Why should a new freak   40
>> Make Braddon and Speke
To be more concern'd than his wife or his brother?
>> A razor all bloody,
>> Thrown out of his study,
Is evidence strong of his desperate guilt, Sir!   45
>> So Godfrey, when dead,
>> Full of horror and dread,
Ran his sword through his body up to the hilt, Sir.

---

33. Sidney, throughout his trial, argued brilliantly on the basis of past law both as to the basis of the charge against him and the admissibility of the notes (e.g. Howell, *State Trials*, 9, 860–66; 876–79).

35. *Chief Justice:* Jeffreys had been appointed Lord Chief Justice on 29 Sept. 1683. For his summation, see Howell, *State Trials*, 9, 888–95.

37. *a traitor:* For the circumstances surrounding Essex's death, see headnote to *An Elegy on the Earl of Essex*.

39. One of the many points that aroused Whig suspicions of foul play was the extent of the wound. At the inquest, Robert Andrews, a surgeon, testified that Essex's throat was "cut from one jugular to the other, and through the windpipe and gullet, unto the vertebrae of the neck, both jugular veins being also quite divided" (*An Account How the Earl of Essex Killed Himself* . . . [A 175]).

40. *freak:* A capricious humor, notion, whim, or vagary.

41. *Braddon and Speke:* The attempts of Laurence Braddon and Hugh Speke to establish the Whig view of Essex's death led to their conviction for subornation of witnesses on 7 Feb. 1684. The entire story is revealed in the course of their trial (Howell, *State Trials*, 9, 1127–1215).

42. Evidently, Lady Essex believed the Earl had killed himself and "therefore desired the business might fall. . . . Brother Capel [Henry] excused himself, pretending to be indisposed, which looked very odd" (*Diary of Henry, Earl of Clarendon* [Oxford, 1763]; quoted in Howell, *State Trials*, 9, 1233–34).

43–44. The story of the bloody razor being thrown from a Tower window, then quickly picked up by a maid who ran out, with the subsequent alarm, was principally the evidence of the thirteen-year-old William Edwards. The boy's later testimony in court led to the conviction of Braddon and Speke for subornation. The informations and later evaluations of the case are given in Howell, *State Trials*, 9, 1225–1332.

46. *Godfrey:* Sir Edmund Berry Godfrey, the Justice of the Peace who took Oates' first depositions, was found dead on 17 Oct. 1678 at the south side of Primrose Hill,

5.

Can the case be thought hard
Of Sir Patience Ward,   50
Who lov'd his own rights more than those of His Highness?
O disloyal ears,
As on record appears,
Not to hear, when 'twould do the Papists a kindness!
An old doting cit,   55
With his Elizabeth wit,
Against the French mode, for freedom to hope on;
Those ears that told lies
Were less dull than his eyes,
And both of them shut when all others' were open.   60

6.

All Europe together
Can't show such a father,
So tenderly nice of a son's reputation,
As our good King is
Who labor'd to bring his,   65

---

strangled and with a sword plunged through his body. Since his death gave substance
to the Popish Plot, some Tory writers (principally Thompson, but indirectly L'Estrange)
suggested that a general despondence had led him to commit suicide. (For the trial of
Thompson, Farwell, and Pain, and a review of the evidence, see Howell, *State Trials,
8*, 1359–98.)

50. *Sir Patience Ward:* In the course of the vengeance by law which the Court
followed, Ward, a former Whig lord mayor (1680) and sheriff (1670), was charged with
having deliberately perjured himself at Pilkington's trial for *scandalum magnatum*
on 24 Nov. 1682. Ward had stated that he had not heard the Sheriff say that the Duke
of York "hath burnt the City and is come to cut our throats"; indeed, Ward claimed
that all talk about James had ended before Pilkington had entered the room. Other
witnesses had sworn to the contrary; the jury had found for the Duke to the full sum
of £100,000; and now, on 19 May 1683, the Court moved against Ward. The defense
tried to show that Ward's version of the event had no greater discrepancies than those
shown by the Crown's own witness, but, the jury finding to the contrary, Ward fled to
Holland before sentence was imposed. (The trial is given by Howell, *State Trials, 9*,
299–352.)

55. *cit:* Citizen. Ward was fifty-four at the time.

56. *Elizabeth:* The meaning is probably loyal, honest, patriotic. Whigs generally
looked on the Elizabethan period as a golden age.

57. *French mode:* i.e. the government's pro-French policies as well as the Court's
dependence on French fashions and manners.

62. For a full description of the preparations, the terms, and the termination of
Monmouth's brief reconciliation with Charles during 25 Nov. to 7 Dec. 1683, see *A
Merry New Ballad: In Answer to Old Rowley the King.*

By tricks, to subscribe to a sham declaration.
    'Twas with good reason
    He pardon'd his treason,
To obey (not his own, but) his brother's command, sir;
    To merit whose grace   70
    He must in the first place
Confess he's a villain under his hand, Sir.

7.

    While fate the Court blesses
    With daily successes,
And giving up charters goes round like a frolic;   75
    While our Duke Nero,
    The Church's blind hero,
By murders is planting his faith apostolic;
    Some modern sages,
    More wise than past ages',   80
Would ours establish by Popish successors.
    Queen Bess ne'er thought it,
    And Cecil forgot it—
'Twas lately found out by the prudent Addressors.

75. During the early months of 1682, a great number of towns willingly yielded their charters to the King, but when London contested the Court's Quo Warranto, the resignations ceased (see Gough, *Londinum Triumphans* [G 1411]). Once the case was lost, "all towns and corporations . . . strove to . . . outrun each other to the throne of majesty" in order to surrender.

76. *Duke Nero:* The implication of this not uncommon Whig comparison is that James was responsible for the burning of London as Nero had been for the burning of Rome.

78. *murders:* In the Whig view, these would probably include the judicial murders of at least Russell and Sidney (if not all those connected with the Whig Conspiracy) and the outright murder of the Earl of Essex.

83. *Cecil:* The reference would seem to be either to the famed William Cecil, Lord Burghley (1520–98), who served as a diplomat under Philip and Mary (1554–58) but who, as Elizabeth's chief minister, followed a rigorously anti-Catholic line after Elizabeth's excommunication in 1570, or to Burghley's son Robert, Earl of Salisbury (1563?–1612), whose career as a statesman reached a critical point in 1601 when " 'Essex accused [him] of having said that the infanta of Spain was the right heir to the crown of England.' " Following the discrediting of the charge and the punishment of Essex, "Cecil allowed himself to enter into communication with James I, precisely as his father had done with Elizabeth" (*DNB*).

84. *the prudent Addressors:* Those who sent in addresses of loyalty to the Crown and abhorrence of the conspiracy following the discovery of the Whig plot in mid-1683. (For a later Whig account, see Oldmixon, *A Complete History of Addresses*, pp. 60–88.)

THOMAS SHADWELL

The Protestant Satire

While *The Protestant Satire* attacks L'Estrange and Dryden and goes on to ridicule the power struggle between Halifax and Rochester, it aims principally at describing the legal enormities committed by the Tory-controlled courts. The cannon of the law, with which the Whigs had been able to hold the King's forces in check, had been recaptured by Charles by the close of 1682, wheeled into position at the opening of 1683, and used with merciless effect on the anti-Court party in the months that followed. The desperate plans of the Whig Conspiracy had supplied new targets and justified attacks on all who had been connected with the Opposition.

L'Estrange and Dryden, as the chief Tory propagandists in prose and verse, are thoroughly, though rather conventionally, pilloried. But the single theme remains: L'Estrange "undermines," and Dryden has only "reproach" for, the country's laws; and (even worse) the two are merely by-products of the Court's corruption of the courts, apologists for a government that, in the Whig Conspiracy trials, had made a travesty of justice. The second half of the poem shows to what levels the Whigs, denied press, parliament, and position, had come by the summer of 1684. By this time, the only choice left them was between the two long-time rivals for power, Halifax—the "trimmer," the apostate from the Whig cause—and Rochester—the Yorkist, the leader of the High Church faction. The bleakness of the Whig position was such that the poet is forced to back Halifax, not so much out of approbation as desperation; of the two evils, Halifax is the lesser. He at least is anti-French; he at least is seeking some balance of political forces; he at least is for a strict accounting of revenues. Halifax did, in fact, attain dominance during that summer, but for the poet he was chief minister to a government that practiced judicial murder, preached Erastianism, and plotted to bring in the Catholic Church. The leaderless and powerless Whig party, shattered in the courts by convictions for treason, riot, and *scandalum magnatum,* realized at last the full implications of the Stuart determination to rule by law. The prospect during that hot, dry summer must have been arid indeed, and the poet etched much of it with the bitter acid of corrosive irony.

The Protestant Satire was very probably written in July 1684. Numerous references to Armstrong's execution place the poem after 20 June; while the careful investigation of the Halifax-Rochester struggle fails to mention its resolution in August, when the Earl was "kicked upstairs" as lord president of the Council.

The question of authorship is more difficult to determine, but certain scraps of internal evidence suggest Thomas Shadwell: (1) the use against the Tories (84) of Dryden's line against Shadwell found in the *Second Part of Absalom and Achitophel* (479), (2) the attack on Dryden (161–263), which closely resembles the data and tone found in the attack on Dryden in *The Medal of John Bayes* (almost certainly by Shadwell), (3) the concurrence of technical words (179–80) in an image quite similar to that found in Shadwell's play *The Virtuoso*, (4) the reference to Sir Formal Trifle (184), a character from *The Virtuoso* whom Shadwell considered one of his most Jonsonian (i.e. excellent) creations, (5) the detailed allusion to *The Alchemist*, the much-admired play by Shadwell's literary god, Ben Jonson (see Shadwell, *Works*, ed. Montague Summers, *I*, lxix–lxii). Admittedly, these scraps are in no way conclusive, but they may be considered indicative.

Against this ascription to so professional a writer, there is the fact that no contemporary texts of *The Protestant Satire* are known. It was not printed until 1747 (Case 455) and appears in only one manuscript, G′ (probably in an eighteenth-century hand). However, one must not forget that, by trials for libel and *scandalum magnatum*, the government (principally under the direction of L'Estrange, who had been made a justice of the peace on 8 July 1683) had successfully prosecuted 32 writers and virtually silenced the Whig Press (Kitchin, *L'Estrange*, p. 334).

THE PROTESTANT SATIRE

or

Some Reason, Not all Rhyme
In return to several late Popish libels
Written in the year 1684

How wise and happy are we grown of late,
Since plays and ballads have reform'd the State!
Since Tories with a spleen and guilt accurst
Have had the forehead to cry *Traitor* first!
By hackney wits rising on England's ruin,   5
Have libell'd Whigs for what themselves are doing!
And while new polities their chief devise,
Cast dirt about to blind the people's eyes.

Since Roger, under loyalty's pretense,
Has outstar'd truth and bawl'd down common sense;   10
Since against powers that us'd even kings to awe
(Champions of right and guarantees of law!),
Powers that, like Heaven, will not the guilty quit,
The bully rages without fear or wit;
On whom, though he can fix no other stains,   15
By mention only his foul mouth profanes.
Since to clear Popery he seems inspir'd,
Himself still fresh and all his readers tir'd;

4. *forehead:* Assurance, impudence, audacity.
6. The subject of *have libell'd* is Tories (3).
7. *polities:* Modes of administering or managing public affairs; statecraft.
9. On 17 April 1683, Robert Stephens, a messenger of the press, cited both L'Estrange's Tory *Observator*, No. 319 (14 April), and Henry Care's Whig *Weekly Pacquet of Advice from Rome* (Luttrell, *Brief Relation, 1,* 254-55) as libels. In the course of his counterblasts (*Observator*, Nos. 323-30 [20-30 April]), L'Estrange printed the following screed, purportedly from "R.S.," though Stephens probably did not write it:

> The devil, your [i.e. L'Estrange's] master, could never have written more against the government than such a rogue as thou art—and all under the pretense of loyalty, but the truth of it is, the end of such loyalty is hanging.

For an example of L'Estrange's protestations of his "unchangeable and unwearied loyalty" at the time of the Stephens affair, see *Observator*, No. 326 (25 April 1683).

Since by long lying for that cassock cause,
And undermining all his country's laws,   20
He got the clergy's money and applause;
Since, like a vicar-general, he rules
Those ductile minds on whom the Church and schools
Have stamp'd th' indelible character of fools
(Whom, to know nothing but with words to fence,   25
Their function in all ages did dispense,
Exempt forever from the power of sense);

Since guides who must mislead have best esteem,
And those who should corrupted crowds redeem
From the lov'd yoke of their own passions' sway   30
To the far worse of other men's betray;
With reason they a pastor's name reject.
More just is that of *Priest* they so affect;
It speaks their mission right, whose myst'ry lies
In making their whole flock a sacrifice.   35
With sordid hopes and base ambition blind,
They chain the body, who should free the mind;
And of Court frowns, more than of Heaven's, in awe,
Have for Christ's gospel preach'd our statesmen's law.

Since Tory, in all courts, Chief Judge did sit,   40
Here he's the test of right, and there of wit.
Since Britain, like a fond, unwary maid,
Has been by pleasing promises betray'd;
Since she her help to cheat herself affords,
And, drunk with passion, barters things for words;   45
Since frequent parliaments, the crown's best screen,
By fines of thanks were paid for—but ne'er seen;
Since their reforming votes Addressors cloy'd,

34. *mystery:* In addition to the nontheological meaning, there is the sense of the mystical, revealed, or ritualistic.

41. The writer plays on the two meanings of *court: here* refers to the courts of law; *there* refers to the Court of Charles II.

42. *fond:* Infatuated, foolish, silly.

47. *fines:* In law, settlements, compositions paid; also, conclusions, terminations, ends. The writer is alluding to Charles II's tactic of proroguing or dissolving parliaments (with a message of thanks) after having obtained the subsidies he had requested. It should be recalled that there had not been a parliament since March 1681.

48. *their:* i.e. the frequent parliaments'.

And government by law we have enjoy'd:
Law, that makes Littleton's out of credit grow,   50
Such as nor statutes nor reports can show,
And clients equal with their counsel know.
Such Empson once, and Dudley (by ill chance
For their own necks) did loyally advance;
Such now makes Frenchmen run away from France.   55
Such sense of right has rais'd their tyrant's throne;
Under such law the conquer'd Flemings groan.
Such juries learn, ere the Chief Justice speaks;
Such sets up witnesses, and merchants breaks.
Such starves that bank that, with her daily bread,   60
Suppli'd the widow and the orphan fed.
Such, with their rights, time-serving rogues relieves;
Such perjures Ward, and wicked Will believes;
In whom th' ungrateful mercenary knave
From deserv'd halters does the coward save.   65
Such, vexing Protestants, does Papists spare,
Makes trials traps, Justice itself a snare,

Addressors: The Addressors were those of pro-Court feeling who opposed the Whig Petitioners (i.e. for recalling parliament) and who voiced their abhorrence of the Association paper found in Shaftesbury's study and later of the Whig Conspiracy (see Oldmixon, *A Complete History of Addresses,* chaps. II–IV).

50. *Littleton's:* Sir Thomas Littleton (1422–81) was a judge and legal author whose *Tenures,* with Coke's comments (1628–44), formed the basis of English law on real property.

53. *Empson . . . and Dudley:* Sir Richard Empson (d. 1510) and Edmund Dudley (1462?–1510) were statesmen and lawyers under Henry VII who, as *fiscales judices,* rigorously exacted taxes and used their positions to extort and rob. So great was their unpopularity that, upon the accession of Henry VIII, they were almost immediately indicted (on a charge of constructive treason), and the new King was forced by public feeling to allow their execution on 18 Aug. 1510.

57. *the conquer'd Flemings:* By a series of agreements culminating in the treaty of Nijmwegen (1679), the French received a large portion of southern Flanders. In 1683, they again invaded the Spanish Netherlands and met with relatively little opposition. The annexation was carried out through the Courts of Reunion (1680–83), reinforced by French troops.

60–61. The reference would seem to be to the stop on the Exchequer which was blamed chiefly on Rochester (Burnet, *History,* 2, 435).

63. *Ward:* Sir Patience Ward, the Whig Lord Mayor in 1680, had been found guilty of perjury on 19 May 1683 for the evidence he had given in the Pilkington trial (see *A New Ballad,* 49–60 and notes; also Howell, *State Trials, 9,* 299–352.)

Will: If the writer is still speaking of Ward's case, the reference might be to Sir William Hooker, who gave the most positive evidence against the Whig leader (Howell, *State Trials, 9,* 311–12).

And London's Tower a castle in the air.
Law that, from contracts sworn when they are crown'd
Can release kings and keep their subjects bound;   70
Law that, with power like Rome's blasphemous See,
From all ties that are troublesome can free,
And ev'ry virtue into vice decree;
Law that on civiliz'd people is a satyr;
Law that can justify *The Observator*,   75
And patriots, whom he calls a trait'rous gang,
Seize without proof, and without trial, hang.
In vain would Wisdom Caution's shield afford
To blunt the edge of her destroying sword.
Though fast our tongues Self-Preservation tie,   80
She into thought, like Heav'n's dread pow'r, can pry,
And punish Whigs whose ears will not comply.
All day unhurt with common sense can fight,
And, scorning fame, do anything—but right.

Care's useful wit she never could endure,   85
For whipping Babylon's old painted whore.

69–70. The Whig theorists considered that the king, in taking his coronation oath
to uphold the laws and religion, established a contract with his people. This strongly
anti-Hobbesian view was not new, but it had been recently verbalized in the papers
that had been produced as evidence of treason in the Sidney trial (Howell, *State Trials*,
9, 855–56). For Achitophel's use of the argument, see *Absalom and Achitophel*, 765–76,
and Kinsley's note.

72. For the implied similarity of royal and papal prerogative, see 148 n. on *non-obstante*.

77. *without trial:* Probably an allusion to Jeffreys' refusal to allow Armstrong a
trial. See 83 n.

81. *She:* i.e. Tory law.

82. *ears:* A possible allusion to the punishment for libel, the cutting off or cropping
of the offender's ear.

84. The line is based on the advice to Shadwell in *The Second Part of Absalom and
Achitophel:*

> Drink swear and roar, forbear no lewd delight
> Fit for thy bulk; do anything but write.
>
> (478–79)

85. *Care:* Henry Care, the writer of *The Weekly Pacquet of Advice from Rome*, had
devoted a major portion of the appended *Courants* to attacks on Catholic doctrine and
politics. Thus from 24 Nov. 1682 until 23 Feb. 1683, he subtitled this section "The
Jesuits' [later, Judaists'] Memoirs," and his last numbers rejected transubstantiation and
leveled a dozen charges against Rome (Nos. 46–47 [6–13 July 1683]).

she: Court justice; the law.

86. *Babylon's . . . whore:* The Roman Catholic Church.

Twice of his strokes the wounded hag complain'd,
And twice his hands her guilty rules restrain'd;
Hopeless, by arts of mercenary men,
To heal the gashes of his cutting pen.   90
But Hodge, who long has been her private lover
And hectors those who her intrigues discover,
All people's credit, as he please, may handle,
And rave and rail his belly-full of scandal.
Since satire's silenc'd, and good sense put down,   95
He's Libeller-in-Ordinary to the Crown;
By the same law allow'd that has preferr'd
Oates to the jail and Bomeny to the Guard;
And, op'ning our new State's tyrannic scene,
Made Jeffreys a judge, and Hickes a dean,   100
Jenner a sergeant, Pemberton a turd,
Churchill a minister, and Legge a lord.

87. *Twice . . . complain'd:* Once was undoubtedly the trial on 2 July 1680 for *The Weekly Pacquet* (2, 4) of 1 Aug. 1679 (see Howell, *State Trials, 7,* 1111–30); the other time may have been that referred to by Luttrell (see headnote) on 14 April 1683.

91. *Hodge:* Roger L'Estrange.

98. *Oates to the jail:* In 1682, Titus Oates, the discoverer of the Popish Plot, was jailed and bailed first on a counter-accusation by the Reverend Adam Elliot and then twice for debt (29 April and 14 June); he was finally found guilty of slandering Elliot on 1 July. More serious suits were yet to come: on 10 May 1684, at the time of this poem, he was sent to the Counter, where he stayed until York's charge of *scandalum magnatum* was tried on 18 June 1684, awarding the Duke £100,000 damages (Howell, *State Trials, 10,* 125–48) and sending Oates again to prison; finally there was the perjury trial of 8 May 1685, which led to his incarceration, pillorying, and whipping. (See Lane, *Oates,* pp. 285–89, 299–319.) The allusion here would probably not refer to any action later than mid-1684.

Bomeny: Paul Bomeney was the Earl of Essex's French valet who discovered his master's body in the Tower on 13 July 1683.

100. *Jeffreys:* Sir George Jeffreys, a rigorous adherent of the Court, became Lord Chief Justice on 29 Sept. 1683.

Hickes: George Hickes (1642–1715), a supporter of the Court view, received the deanery of Worcester in Aug. 1683.

101. *Jenner:* Following the rescinding of the Charter, the "very loyal, zealous" Thomas Jenner (1637–1707) was appointed Recorder of London. He was knighted shortly afterwards, and in Jan. 1684 was made King's Serjeant.

Pemberton: On 22 Jan. 1683, Sir Francis Pemberton (1625–97) was transferred from the chief justiceship of King's Bench to that of Common Pleas because of his lack of enthusiasm in the Russell trial. He was removed from the bench completely on 7 Sept. 1683, and from the Privy Council on 24 Oct.

102. *Churchill:* The reference is not clear. The Churchills qualify in their political and religious inclinations, but at this period none held a ministerial post in the strict

Law that, by bill deciding without trial,
Made Booth a rebel, Lee and Davis loyal,
Grosvenor an honest man, in spite of nature,   105
And Maxfield mangl'd for the Crown, a traitor.

---

sense of the term. Sir Winston (1620?–88) was "one of the clerks controller of the green cloth, an office of some importance at Court" (*DNB*). His son, John Churchill (1650–1722), later first Duke of Marlborough, had been very close to York and carried out a number of missions for him; he was rewarded with a Scottish baronetcy on 21 Dec. 1682 and command of the newly formed First Dragoons on 19 Nov. 1683. A distant relative, Sir John Churchill, was chosen Recorder of Bristol in Dec. 1682, with the strong backing of the King (*CSPD*, 1682, p. 582). It is possible that the writer had one of the female Churchills in mind: either Sir Winston's daughter Arabella, who was York's mistress; or John's wife, Sarah, the very close friend of Princess Anne (who appointed her one of the ladies of her bedchamber after the marriage to Prince George of Denmark in July 1683).

Legge: George Legge (1648–91), who was also in York's favor, had been created first Baron Dartmouth on 2 Dec. 1682.

103. *bill:* i.e. the bill of indictment presented to the grand jury. By this time (c. 1683), these juries would have been as solidly for the Court as they had been against it in 1681–82.

104. *Booth:* Henry Booth (1652–94), an ardent parliamentarian, was "clapped up in the Tower on account of this plot" on 13 July 1683; he was not bailed until 28 Nov. and was finally discharged on 12 Feb. 1684 (Luttrell, *Brief Relation, 1,* 269, 292, 301). Booth succeeded to the title of Lord Delamere upon his father's death on 8 Aug. 1684. He was tried by a special commission in Nov. 1685 for treason in attempting to aid the Monmouth rebellion, but was acquitted. I believe the line refers to the earlier imprisonment.

Lee: Possibly Thomas Lee, a dyer of Oldstreet, who was one of the first to turn Crown's evidence in the Whig Conspiracy (Howell, *State Trials, 9,* 387–89). His confession evidently sufficed to prove his loyalty and to stop prosecution.

Davis: Unidentified.

105. *Grosvenor:* Possibly Sir Thomas Grosvenor (1656–1700), an alderman of Chester and deputy lieutenant of Cheshire, whose sympathies were with the Court. He was a principal member of the Cheshire grand jury that set forth Macclesfield (see 106 n.) and other Whig leaders as "the principal promoters of the said seditious address and riotous reception of the Duke of Monmouth" (Howell, *State Trials, 10,* 1413).

106. *Maxfield:* Charles Gerard, created first Earl of Macclesfield in 1679, had been one of Charles I's most vigorous commanders during the Civil War, having been wounded at least four times, the last time (at Rowton Heath on 23 Sept. 1645) very seriously. He went into exile in Dec. 1646, forfeiting his estates to the Commonwealth. After the Restoration, he received a number of Court posts, but during the 1670s he became (to quote North [*Lives, 1,* 269]) "stiff of the anti-Court party," supporting Monmouth in every possible way. Following the Rye House Plot, the grand jury of Cheshire presented him as one of the disaffected party (17 Sept. 1683), in effect labeling him a traitor. Macclesfield answered by bringing a charge of *scandalum magnatum* against John Starkey, Sir Thomas Grosvenor, and seven other members of the jury on 16 April 1684 (Luttrell, *Brief Relation, 1,* 305). The case was tried on 25 Nov. 1684, and Macclesfield was awarded £10,000 damages. (See Howell, *State Trials, 10,* 1329–1418.)

Such law in Scotland, link'd with Rome's designs,
Made James' finger outweigh Charles' loins,
When, with resentments Catholic and tender,
The bishops own'd him for their Faith's Defender.   110
By such Scotch law, had Heav'n not help'd him thence,
Argyle had di'd (Oh dangerous offence!)
For daring in the Council to speak sense.
Such would change panels when they're wise or just,
And sheriffs fine if they discharge their trust.   115
Such owns all false, and turns true plots to sham,
Calls conscience cheat, and common right a flam.
This is the law that must the Gospel damn.
Vicious behind and tyrannous before,
She loves no private meetings—but to whore.   120
To worship God without her leave 's a riot;
Nor does she find, but makes men's minds unquiet.
Like a town flirt, taking a thousand forms,
Now the jilt smiles and softens, now she storms:

107. The Catholic Duke of York had been appointed Lord High Commissioner of
Scotland in Aug. 1679; he returned to England permanently on 27 May 1682.

108. In July 1681, the Scottish Parliament, presided over by James, "passed an act
securing the legitimate succession, any difference of religion notwithstanding" (*DNB*).
The issue of "Charles's loins" was, of course, York's popular rival, the Duke of Mon-
mouth.

112. *Argyle:* Archibald Campbell, ninth Earl of Argyle, subscribed to the complex
Scottish Test Act of 1681 "in so far as it was consistent with itself and with the Protes-
tant faith." This was sufficient excuse to bring a charge of treason. Argyle was sen-
tenced to death and forfeiture on 23 Dec. 1681, but he escaped to London and then
Holland, "where he corresponded with the Rye House conspirators, and fell a victim
at last after the failure of Monmouth's rebellion" (Ogg, *Charles II,* pp. 631–32).

114. *panels:* i.e. grand jury panels. Those that are "wise or just" would be the ones
impanelled by the Whig sheriffs during 1680–82.

115. The Whig sheriffs, Pilkington and Shute, claimed that the running of the
shrieval election was entrusted to their office, and it was on this ground that they con-
tinued polling after the Lord Mayor dissolved the common halls. The Court claimed
that this constituted a riotous assembly and succeeded in obtaining a judgment against
the two men and their adherents on 8 May 1683; Pilkington was fined £500 and Shute
1,000 marks (Howell, *State Trials, 9,* 187–293).

116. *true plots:* Principally the Popish Plot, which, from the time of Wakeman's
acquittal, was viewed with ever-increasing skepticism by the courts.

117. *flam:* A sham, trick, or deception.

120–21. The Conventicle Act of 1670 provided that a private, sectarian meeting for
religious purposes of more than five persons was illegal and to be dispersed, by force
if necessary. Such an assembly could be considered riotous and its members subject to

Now like the block, unmov'd and void of pow'r,   125
Now like the stork, to suitors fierce and sour,
The wrong'd whom she is bound to right, she studies to de-
    vour.
If Rye inform, like thunder lifts her voice,
But could not hear Papillion or Dubois.
With plot-wright Graham to commit murder joins,   130
But Braddon, who discovers one, she fines.
To help brave Armstrong, custom, statutes fail;

---

far greater fines than those specified in the Act. (See *English Historical Documents,
1660–1714, 7*, pp. 384–86.)

125–27. The writer has apparently attempted to derive a new moral from the oft-used Aesopic tale of the frogs who desired a king and, not content with the block of wood which Jupiter sent, complained until he sent them, to their greater grief, a stork.

128. *Rye:* i.e. the Rye House Plot, which was first discovered by Josiah Keeling on 12 June 1683.

129. *Papillion or Dubois:* The two Whig shrieval candidates fought with every legal weapon available to obtain the vital offices. On 28 Sept. 1682, they presented themselves at the investiture and were commanded to depart; as soon as the term opened (23 Oct.), they sought a mandamus against the Lord Mayor, but the courts succeeded in not giving it a hearing until 15 Nov., after the Tory municipal officers were all established in their posts (though "in an ordinary case, a mandamus would have been granted on the first motion"). Eight days later, an alias mandamus was issued (Luttrell, *Brief Relation, 1*, 224, 230, 235, 237, 239). As a last, desperate measure, on 23 April 1683, the two took out a writ against the new Lord Mayor (Prichard), several aldermen, and Sheriff North for giving a false return to the mandamus, and had the officials briefly arrested (ibid., p. 256). Once more they were blocked, and the sole result was Pritchard's counter-suit for false arrest in Nov. of 1684, which awarded the former mayor £10,000 and drove Papillon into exile in the Low Countries (ibid., p. 319).

130. *Graham:* As King's Solicitor, Richard Graham, Principal of Clifford's Inn, took part in almost every legal move that the Court made against the Whigs. He was largely responsible for creating the case against Shaftesbury and College (see *CSPD*, 1680–81, passim; Howell, *State Trials, 8*, 762–63 n.; and "The Journals of Edmund Warcup," *EHR, 40* [1925], p. 258); he was engaged in the Quo Warranto proceedings from their inception and in the trials of the Whig conspirators (see *CSPD*, 1680–83, passim).

131. *Braddon:* Laurence Braddon, the Whig lawyer, and Hugh Speke were fined £2,000 and £1,000, respectively, on 7 Feb. 1684, for suborning witnesses to prove that the Earl of Essex had been murdered by his keepers in the Tower (Howell, *State Trials, 9*, 1127–1224).

132. *Armstrong:* Sir Thomas Armstrong, who fled to Leyden following the discoveries of the Whig Conspiracy, was declared outlaw and a reward was offered for his capture. In early June 1684, he was taken in Holland and extradited; by the 14th, the courts ruled for his execution, not allowing a trial since he was considered outside the law. He suffered a traitor's death on 20 June, despite his daughter's petition and

Against Levallin neither can prevail;
Fitzharris she has right to try, but Danby could not bail
Till Rome's unerring chair clear'd ev'ry doubt,   135
And knaves whom he in prison kept, did drive their jailer
    out.
Through the dark night of records old and blind,
By the Court compass, she her way can find,
Turn with all tides, and sail with ev'ry wind.
Such law Judge Jovian alone has read: 140
Imperial law! which clears what Solon said
And will let none be happy till they're dead;
Law, that bids sovereigns safely whom they will
Rob for their pride, and for their pleasure kill;
Law, that can void Nature's great *defendendo,*   145
Indict by spleen, and prove by innuendo;
Law, that of fools and cowards can make martyrs,
And has a *non-obstante* to all charters—

---

his own plea that he had been outside the kingdom at the time of the outlawry and
by statute had a year in which to return. (Howell, *State Trials, 10,* 105–24; Luttrell,
Brief Relation, 1, 309–11.)

133. *Levallin:* Captain Levallin was one of the "four Irish ruffians" who had been
hired, according to the informer Robert Jennison, to murder Charles at Windsor
in 1679 (Luttrell, *Brief Relation, 1,* 19–20). Though information on him was ad-
mittedly scarce (*CSPD,* 1682, p. 224), the government had made no great effort to
bring him to trial.

134. *Fitzharris:* Edward Fitzharris, a Catholic, was executed on 1 July 1681 for his
libel, *The True Englishman.* The question of whether the peers or the commons had
the right to try him was settled in favor of the latter by the court trial.

Danby: Thomas Osborne, Earl of Danby, like Fitzharris, had taken part in intrigues
that involved the King and that, according to the Whig view, encouraged Popery.
Though never brought to trial, he was in the Tower from 1679 to 1684. In marked
contrast to the Fitzharris case, his continued attempt to be freed on bail was rejected
by the courts on the grounds that they were "incompetent to meddle in the matter of
an impeachment by parliament, which was a court superior to their own" (*DNB*).

135. *chair:* Seat of authority.

140. *Jovian:* In 1683, George Hickes (see 51) replied anonymously to Samuel John-
son's anonymous and highly seditious *Julian the Apostate* with *Jovian* [H 1852]. A
summary of the two works is given in Gillett, *Burned Books,* pp. 500–02.

141–42. *Solon:* Tradition assigns to the great Athenian statesman (c. 638-c. 558 B.C.)
the famous remark made to Croesus, "Call no man happy till he is dead."

145. *defendendo:* i.e. *se defendendo,* the right of self defense.

147. The allusion would seem to be to the victims of the Popish Plot; see 470.

148. *non-obstante:* In law, the first two words of a clause formerly used in statutes
and letters patent, which conveyed a licence from the sovereign to do a thing notwith-

Divine, no doubt, (though from lay eyes conceal'd)
Not made by fellow subjects, but reveal'd,   150
When monarchs ready crown'd to gaping crowds
Dropp'd like the Kings of Brentford from the clouds,
And, in a symphony of soft'ning airs,
Unheeded stole into imperial chairs;
Without or conquest made or suffrage given,   155
Seiz'd kingdoms by immediate grant from Heaven.
Hence 'tis the height of loyalty to measure
All right and wrong by great men's will and pleasure;
Hence the worst men in ev'ry house and town
Grow the best subjects of the Church and Crown.   160

Thus needy Bayes, his Rose Street aches past,
By fate enlighten'd, Tory turns at last;
Though bred a Saint, he was not call'd to fast.

---

standing any statute to the contrary; hence a dispensation from or exception to a rule. It is frequently found with reference to papal use. (See Poems on the London Charter.)

149–56. The attack on divine right takes as its main object the restoration of that Stuart doctrine with Charles and James, the two "brother kings" of Brentford.

151–54. In Act V of Buckingham's *Rehearsal*, the two usurpers, the usher and the physician, are seated in state when suddenly there is "soft music":

    K. Ush. But stay; what sound is this invades our ears?
    K. Phys. Sure 'tis the music of the moving spheres.
    [*Prince*] *Pret[ty-man]*. Behold with wonder, yonder comes from far,
        A god-like cloud and a triumphant car
        In which our two right kings sit one by one
        With virgins' vests and laurel garlands on.
    (The two usurpers steal out of the throne and go away.)
    Bayes. Look you now; did I not tell you that this would be as easy a change as the other.

159–60. When the Whig supporters of Monmouth were attacked for using as an argument the proverb that "the worst title makes the best king," they replied with the corollary given here, that "the worst men make the best (or loyalest) subjects."

161. *Bayes:* The name given Dryden in Buckingham's *Rehearsal*. (See 151–54 n.) *Rose Street aches:* On the night of 18 Dec. 1679 occurred the famous Rose Alley ambuscade in which Dryden was beaten by some ruffians. The attack was possibly carried out at the instigation of John Wilmot, Earl of Rochester, for Dryden's alleged part in Mulgrave's *Essay on Satire*. (See Shadwell's *Medal of John Bayes*, especially 95–96 and n., and Lord's summary of evidence in *POAS*, Yale, *1*, pp. 396–401.) The word *aches* was disyllabic, rhyming with *patches*.

163. The Drydens and their close relatives, the Pickerings, supported the parliamentary side during the Civil War and Interregnum. The "government of saints" (i.e. the sectarians who considered themselves among the elect) frequently celebrated their

No, he must eat, though of the Devil's carving;
He's an undaunted enemy to starving.   165
From getting money, nothing can deter him;
Any great man may damn him to prefer him.
This makes him fierce against himself dispute;
One year another's principles confute.
To varnish villainy and color nonsense,   170
In spite of all the punches of his conscience,
He honest kept as long as e'er he could—
But Privy Purse guineas cannot be withstood,
And Bayes was of Committeeman's flesh and blood.
Statesmen's false sense he parrot-like rehearses,   175
And when 'tis damn'd in prose, to rhyme transverses.

---

victories by decreeing days of national prayer and fasting. (See Shadwell's *Medal of John Bayes*, 117–18 and notes.)

168. The most literal interpretation would indicate Dryden's *Heroic Stanzas* on Cromwell (1659), which were followed in 1660 by *Astrea Redux*, "a poem on the happy restoration and return of His Sacred Majesty." Less strictly, *The Duke of Guise* would have been included by Whigs as an example of literary opportunism. (See *The Prologue to Dryden and Lee's "The Duke of Guise."*)

170. *To varnish villainy:* Probably an allusion to the lines from the *Heroic Stanzas* which Dryden's enemies constantly quoted against him:

> He [Cromwell] fought to end our fighting, and essay'd
> To staunch the blood by breathing of the vein.
>
> (47–48)

173. *Privy Purse guineas:* In 1670, Dryden received the appointments of poet laureate and historiographer, with a salary of £200 and a butt of canary wine per year. In addition, he is said by Spence to have been given "100 broad pieces" for having written *The Medal* (see headnote thereto): and probably in response to a letter to Lawrence Hyde, Earl of Rochester (written about 1683), complaining of poverty, he was appointed a collector of customs for the port of London (17 Dec. 1683) at £5 a year, plus fees.

174. Dryden's father "was a justice of the peace for Northamptonshire and is said to have been a 'committeeman' [i.e. for sequestration] under the Commonwealth" (*DNB*). For the more active career of his cousin, Sir Gilbert Pickering, see *Medal of John Bayes*, 117–18 and notes; and 226 n., below.

175–76. In Act I of Buckingham's *Rehearsal*, Bayes explains his "rule of transversion, or regula duplex":

> *Bayes* . . . I take a book in my hand . . . if there be any wit in't . . . I transverse it; that is, if it be in prose, put it into verse (but that takes up some time), if it be verse, put it into prose.
>
> *Johnson.* Methinks, Mr. Bayes, that putting verse into prose should be called transprosing.

Thus in 1682 *Achitophel* was transprosed, and five years later *The Hind and the Panther* was transversed.

Each day, with a short crust baiting his hope,
The hungry cur comes over for the Pope;
When Rome's old woodmen single out a traitor,
He's to emboss and run him down with satyr.   180
Martyrs for Magna Charta and the Bible,
He first bedevils in a coat of libel.
Such unlike pieces all mankind disdain,
'Tis copying from Sir Formal Trifle's vein;
While each invective on his foes he spends   185
Will, with a little turning, fit his friends.
'Tis sauce that serves both, for the goose and gander;
His style's the true catholicon of slander.
For all the rules in prefaces he scatters,
He rails with the same coarseness that he flatters;   190
Ne'er minding who or what 'tis he disgraces,
Bayes only turns to his drama commonplaces.
For his best flow'rs to Billingsgate beholding,
He lives upon the brokery of scolding.
Rebel and Rogue, his lines string on by rows;   195
And titles, long laid by in porters' prose,
On whom he will, this King of Verse bestows.
But against him (whose person's free from blame!)
Wit has no point and ev'ry satyr 's lame;

179. *woodmen:* Hunters. Cf. Shadwell, *The Virtuoso*, III (cited in *OED*): "I have taken more pains to single you out than ever woodman did for a deer."

180. *emboss:* To drive (a hunted animal) to extremity.

run down: To pursue (game) until caught or killed; to hunt down.

181. *Martyrs for Magna Charta:* The writer may have in mind those who defended London and the Charter (on the basis of ancient privilege going back to Magna Charta) and who were, after Oct. 1683, prosecuted on various legal grounds.

184. *Sir Formal Trifle:* "He is indeed a very choice spirit; the greatest master of tropes and figures; the most Ciceronian coxcomb; the noblest orator breathing; he never speaks without flowers of rhetoric; in short, he is very much abounding in words and very much defective in sense" (*The Virtuoso*, I).

188. *catholicon:* An electuary supposed to be capable of evacuating all humors; also a universal formula; a comprehensive treatise.

189. *For:* Despite.

192. *drama commonplaces:* In *The Rehearsal*, I.1. Bayes explains "This is my book of *Drama Commonplaces;* the mother of many other plays."

193. *flow'rs:* Embellishments or ornaments of speech.

Billingsgate: The London fish market, noted for vituperative language.

194. *brokery:* Anything second-hand or stale.

He has the sole prerogative to defame.   200
All sense of freedom and our country's laws,
All dang'rous daring to assert her cause,
All love to truth in a degenerate time,
All suff'ring virtue 's a reproach to him.
And where it makes the most attractive show,   205
"To arms!" he cries. "The colors of the foe!"
Then musters his stale topics of despite,
As once the Father of all Lies, for fight,
Rang'd Hell's black troops against the Sons of Light.
Though of the Crown's old friends he's most a hater,   210
No kind of merit's safe from his ill nature
When he's well purg'd and dieted for satyr.
On all in 's way his dunghill dirt's thrown out,
As Andrew deals Sir Reverence to the rout.
Muse, prick him till the jaded hackney feels,   215
And lash him lagging at l'Estrange's heels;
Scatt'ring at second hand, t'amuse the age,
The froth and foamings of that madman's rage,
And stumming, with his lees of sense, an empty huffing
      page.
Outfacing fact when plainest it appears,   220
He rhymes his plots and echoes all his fears.
But, though he spares no waste of words or conscience,
He wants the Tory-turn of thorough nonsense;

---

210. Dryden's detractors sought to embarrass the author of *Absalom and Achitophel* in 1681–82 by thrice republishing his *Heroic Stanzas* on Cromwell (see 168 n., and Macdonald, *Dryden Bibliography*, pp. 5–6). Charles Ward (*The Life of John Dryden* [Chapel Hill, 1961], pp. 324–26) has rejected any formal connection between the poet and Cromwell's government.

214. *Andrew:* I.e. Merry-Andrew, a clown or buffoon. In *The Epilogue . . . at Oxford* (19 March 1680), Dryden says that

Th' Italian Merry-Andrews took their place
And quite debauch'd the stage with lewd grimace.
                (11–12)

Sir Reverence: Human excrement. In the *Vindication of "The Duke of Guise"* (1683), Dryden had employed the phrase against his attackers (among whom was Shadwell): 'If I cry a Sir-reverence, and you take it for honey, make the best of your bargain.'

219. *stumming:* Renewing vapid wine by use of must.
lees: The sediment deposited in a vessel containing wine and some other liquid.

That thoughtless air that makes light Hodge so jolly,
(Void of all weight, he wantons in his folly).   225
No so forc'd Bayes, whom sharp remorse attends;
While his heart loathes the cause, his tongue defends:
Hourly he acts, hourly repents the sin,
And is all over Grandfather within.
By day, that ill-laid spirit checks; o' nights,   230
Old Pickering's ghost, a dreadful specter, frights.
Returns of spleen his slacken'd speed remit,
And cramp his loose careers with intervals of wit;
While without stop at sense, or ebb of spite,
Breaking all bars, bounding o'er wrong and right,   235
Contented Roger gallops out of sight.

    'Tis a vile trade in both, to make the brain
The belly's slave, and truck their truth for gain;
Selling man's noblest part, the baser to maintain.
But they're more mean who buy their fawning wit,   240
And in such spaniels' mouthes will stoop to spit:
State fops, who mischief to mankind are brewing,
And, with great cunning, plot their own undoing;
Project for others arbitrary sway,
To make themselves, as well as us, a prey;   245
Short-sighted owls who, caught with Fortune's lure,
For dirt and names, such power to kings assure
As makes the bribes they give 'em unsecure.
Or though (rare seen!) they for their lives could hold
Those royal smiles for which their country's sold,   250
And wear their guilty greatness to their graves,
Their sons at least must be our fellow slaves.

224. *Hodge:* Roger L'Estrange.

225. *he:* i.e. Hodge.

227. *the cause:* i.e. Court policy, though the phrase usually referred to the Commonwealth, "The Good Old Cause."

229. *Grandfather:* Dryden's maternal grandfather was Henry Pickering, Rector of Aldwinckle All Saints. The writer may have confused him in 232 with Dryden's cousin german, Sir Gilbert Pickering, who had been Cromwell's Lord Chamberlain. Dryden was said to have been in Sir Gilbert's employ during the Interregnum. (See 163 n., 174 n.; also Ward, *The Life of John Dryden*, pp. 17, 64.)

238. *truck:* Barter away (what should be sacred or precious) for something unworthy.

Like Bessus and his swordsmen, let 'em prize
Each other, and among themselves be wise,
Nay, honest too—if they can all agree   255
In Court cabals who the great k———— shall be:
If Hyde's loud birthright and divine entail,
Or Halifax's fitness shall prevail.

But what dire chance such worthies could divide,
Whom in fast friendship equal guilt had ti'd?   260
Can surplus farms effect a change so great,
And passive spirits boil with factious heat?

253. *Bessus:* In Beaumont and Fletcher's *A King and no King*, Bessus is the cowardly braggart who provides comic relief. Historically, he was a satrap of Bactria under Darius III. After Alexander defeated Darius (331 B.C.), Bessus and his fellow conspirators deposed and then killed their ruler (330). Bessus, taking the name of Artaxerxes, proclaimed himself king and attempted to organize national resistance against Alexander. In 329, however, he was betrayed to Alexander and soon condemned to mutilation and death (*EB*).

256. *k————:* Possibly *knave* or *king*, inter alia.

257. *Hyde:* Laurence Hyde, Earl of Rochester (1641–1711), was son of the famous Edward Hyde, first Earl of Clarendon (1609–74), Charles' principal minister until his downfall in 1667. From 29 March 1679, Laurence Hyde had been on the treasury commission and, failing of his hope of becoming Lord Treasurer in Aug. 1684, he left the treasury and was (to use the phrase of his enemy, Halifax) "kicked upstairs" into the lord presidency of the Council. His sister, Anne Hyde (1637–71), had married the Duke of York in Sept. 1660, an act which raised a storm of indignation against Clarendon, her father, who was accused of seeking to merge the family with the Crown (by "divine entail").

258. *Halifax's fitness:* George Savile, Marquis of Halifax (1633–95) was the sole anti-French minister at Court. The writer, as will be seen, favors Halifax only in comparison with Hyde.

259–61. Halifax and Rochester had worked together to defeat the Exclusion Bill, but they quarreled when Rochester succeeded in getting Halifax's hated brother-in-law, Sunderland, restored to his office. "Lord Halifax and Lord Hyde fell to be in open war, and were both much hated. Lord Halifax charged Hyde, who was at this time [Nov. 1681] made Earl of Rochester, of bribery for having farmed a branch of the revenues much lower than had been proffered for it" (Burnet, *History*, 2, 340–41). Halifax apparently made no direct accusation but suggested that Rochester had "been imposed upon" (North, *Lives*, 2, 202). He laid the complaint before the King in Council, offering to give Charles £40,000 more for the revenue than he was to have from the farmers.

262. The phrase "passive spirits" alludes to the Church of England's doctrine of passive obedience (see 383). Concerning Rochester, North (*Lives*, 2, 302) says that "his party was that of the Church of England, of whom he had the honor for many years to be accounted the head." The phrase is contradicted by "factious [with connotations of sectarianism] heat"; here again, North notes that "Lord Rochester was fired at"

Say, tell-troth satyr, whence these discords spring.
Coloring their own with int'rest of the King,
Two statesmen struggling for a stick I sing: 265
A stick, though in the Court's oft-changing scene
Scrap'd thin by beggars' hands, and peel'd so clean,
Fashion'd to bear a traitor's heavy weight,
And help him climb ambition's utmost height:
Those heights that turn'd their predecessor's brain,   270
While fast as he could wish he might obtain,
And over all, but Forehead-cloth, did reign:
That pow'rful wand, by whose ensnaring spell
The abler and less guilty ————— fell.

Halifax's imputation of corruption. "And no resentments could be carried higher than, upon this occasion, his were. He would neither see, hear, nor endure any thing or person that was not clear on his side" (*Lives*, *2*, 202).

265. *a stick:* The white staff, a symbol of office, in this case of the lord treasurer. Since 1679, the treasury had been under five commissioners (as opposed to a single lord treasurer). During spring, 1684, two positions on the commission fell vacant, and Rochester (the First Lord of the Commission) hoped to be appointed Lord Treasurer; indeed, as early as 13 March, Luttrell heard that Rochester was to receive the white staff (*Brief Relation*, *1*, 303). However, the Earl "had lost much ground with the King, and the whole Court hated him by reason of the stop of all payments which was chiefly imputed to him" (Burnet, *History*, *2*, 435). Halifax and Lord Keeper North tried to bring in Henry Thynne and Dudley North as commissioners without Rochester's knowledge, and the Earl in his turn attempted to block the appointments through the influence of York and Portsmouth, "but the King was not to be shaken, so he [Rochester] resolved to quit the treasury" (ibid.). It was in Aug. 1684, that Rochester was "kicked upstairs," becoming Lord President of the Council.

268. *a traitor's:* Thomas Osborne, Earl of Danby (1631–1712), Lord Treasurer from 1673 until his impeachment in 1678, received a pardon from Charles II under the great seal, but his impeachment was revived by the next parliament and, though his trial did not take place, he was kept in the Tower. His applications for bail were denied until 12 Feb. 1684, when Jeffreys became Lord Chief Justice.

270. *predecessor's:* Danby's.

272. *Forehead–cloth:* Lady Danby, formerly Lady Bridget Bertie, second daughter of the Earl of Lindsey, was famed for wearing a forehead cloth (see, e.g., *The Opening of the Session of the House of Commons*, 15–16, and *The Female Nine*, 4, both 1690, in *POAS*, Yale, *5*). "Of a penurious disposition, she was credited with exerting a sinister influence over her husband and children, and subjecting them to much petty tyranny" (*DNB*).

274. ——: The allusion may be to Arthur Capel, Earl of Essex (1631–83), who had been First Lord of the Treasury Commission from March until Nov. 1679. He died, probably by suicide, in the Tower, where he had been imprisoned for his part in the Whig Conspiracy. (See *An Elegy on the Earl of Essex*.)

Muse, raise thy voice, and in a loftier verse 275
The Court Achilles and his rage rehearse.
Conscious of greater strength to o'erturn the State,
Our ruling Agamemnon let him hate.
To toils accustom'd, with affronts untir'd,
In hopes of titles and Blue Garter fir'd, 280
Let his pride think (for desp'rate projects fit)
Nothing too hard for his mercurial wit.
Nor while each helps to sink a tott'ring throne,
Suffer his foe to take the spoil alone;
And the white staff (his services forgot), 285
That fair Briseis, be another's lot.
Though the whole Court his vain attempts deride,
Let him stand strong against the beating tide,
With the weak help of Reason on his side.
Let Reason only his assistant be 290
(Reason, as much at Court disgrac'd as he);

275–76. The lines are based on the opening of the *Iliad*. Pope's translation reads:

Achilles' wrath, to Greece the direful spring
Of woes unnumber'd, heav'nly Goddess, sing!

Court Achilles: Rochester.

278. *our ruling Agamemnon:* "There seemed a possibility [in the summer of 1684] that the moderate and humane counsels of Halifax would at last prevail" (Ogg, *Charles II,* p. 655).

280. See *Absalom Senior,* 905–1012, where the fiend that tempts Halifax (Achitophel) to the Court's side sees that this can be done because "he has pride, a vast insatiate pride." In a dream, the politic imp concludes his temptation of Achitophel with:

"Be with accumulated honors bless'd,
And grasp a Star t' adorn thy shining crest."
(999–1000)

This promise of the Order of the Garter achieves its end:

. . . the Star but nam'd
Flash'd in his eyes, and his rous'd soul inflam'd.
(1007–08)

The installation of three nobles (not including Halifax) had taken place on 8 April 1684.

286. *Briseis:* The daughter of Brises was captured by Achilles but taken from him by Agamemnon. This act occasioned the wrath of Achilles and his withdrawal from the fighting at Troy. This closely resembles the actual situation (see 262 n.) and may (if this poem was written prior to Aug.) be somewhat prophetic if Achilles' withdrawal from battle is likened to Rochester's lord presidency.

another's lot: By 12 May, Luttrell had heard that Rochester was to receive the white staff "speedily" (*Brief Relation, 1,* 308).

But call it not his choice, nor footstep find
Of former virtue in th' apostate's mind.
No love to England in his spleen be shown;
Let him not fight her quarrels, but his own.   295
Not thither bound, but, by curst Fortune's spite,
Driven and wreck'd upon the coast of right.

About his rival, let Court flatterers throng,
And (for his cause is naught) his Party there be strong.
Draw him escap'd through volleys of wind-guns,   300
Like an Alsatian bully, from his duns:
Ever in haste, and of his greatness full,
False, pettish, fearful, arrogant, and dull;
Then close and thrifty of his wit's small treasure,
A wasp in business, and a drone in pleasure.   305
But when fear checks his over-weening pride
And gentle Laury puts off angry Hyde,
When some more gen'rous wine's dear running stream
Has purg'd his choler of the fret and mellow'd all his
            phlegm,

293. *th' apostate:* An allusion to Halifax's having abandoned the Whig party at
the time of the Exclusion controversy; see *Absalom Senior* for a fuller attack on him
for this renunciation.

298. *his rival:* i.e. Rochester. Full attention is now given to Hyde, though the
transition is almost nonexistent.

300. *wind guns:* Air guns.

301. *Alsatian bully:* "Alsatia" was the cant name for the liberty of White Friars,
the refuge of debtors and criminals. It is vibrantly depicted in one of Shadwell's best
plays, *The Squire of Alsatia* (1688).

303. Burnet's characterization of Rochester seems pertinent:

> He has a very good pen but speaks not gracefully; and during all the dispute
> concerning his father [Lord Clarendon, in 1667], he made his court so dex-
> terously that no resentment appeared on that head. When he came into business
> and rose to high posts, he grew both violent and insolent, but was thought by
> many an incorrupt man. He has high notions of government and thinks it must
> be maintained with great sincerity. He delivers up his own notions to his party
> that he may lead them, and on all occasions is wilful and imperious (*History*,
> *1*, 463–64).

305. *a wasp in business:* "[He was] a person adroit in all matters of . . . business,
being observed to be always plodding at scrutiny of accounts and estimates before the
lords came [to meetings]" (North, *Lives*, *1*, 302).

307. In his earlier years as one of the Chits, Rochester had been known as
Laury and famed for his courtliness (see 303 n.).

Nothing in Nature, whether said or sung, 310
(But his slight head), be softer than his tongue.
Then let him fleering from his promise fly,
Justice evade, and helpless want deny,
With mean and impudent civility.
For the King's current cask, grown Duncombe's spoil, 315
Let him deal round to slaves, who starve the while,
The decri'd copper of his faithless smile;
Practice the flatt'ries of a courtier's face,
And play the knave with a paternal grace.
Of a belle-air in falseness let him boast, 320
And when he looks the sweetest, lie the most.
To hide from men of worth be his delight,
Where, with stripp'd whores to glut his bawdy sight,
The knave may sot secure from doing right.
To deceive friend and foe let him take pains, 325
And be throughout a statesman—but in brains.

 Confusion now, and civil war at hand,
 Seal against seal, black gown against white wand,

308–09. "He passes for a sincere man and seems to have too much heat to be false.
This natural heat is inflamed by frequent excesses in drinking" (Burnet, *History, 1,*
464). North also notes that "his infirmities were passion in which he could swear
like a cutter, and indulging himself in wine" (*Lives, 1,* 302).

313. *helpless want deny:* The stop of all payments from the treasury had been
imputed to Rochester (Burnet, *History,* 2, 435; see also 60–61).

315. *cask:* One is tempted to emend this to *cash,* but there may be the sense of a
casket (used for jewels or gold) or of a barrel (used for wine and representative of
the revenues to be had from that chief import). In this last instance, however, it was
Sir Samuel Dashwood who was involved in the questionable farming of the revenue
(North, *Lives,* 2, 202).

Duncombe: Very likely Charles (not Sir John) Duncombe, the Exchequer banker,
receiver of customs under Charles II, and intimate of Rochester's ally, Sunderland.
By his death in 1711, Duncombe was the richest commoner in England, but he had
long had an unsavory business reputation (as early as 1672, while Shaftesbury's banker,
he made £30,000 on foreknowledge of the Exchequer's closing) and was brutally un-
feeling in his politics. (He remarked to Papillon "that he could not see why people
make such a fuss [over the legal persecution of Whigs], for the Court only wanted
to hang some nine or ten persons who were obnoxious to them" [Papillon, *Papillon,*
p. 235].)

319. Rochester's father, the Earl of Clarendon, had been impeached in 1667.

328. *Seal against seal:* From 1682 to 1685, Sir Francis North, afterwards Lord Guil-
ford, was Keeper of the Great Seal; during the same period, Halifax was Lord Privy
Seal. According to Roger North (*Lives,* passim), the Lord Keeper certainly had his
differences with Halifax, but he preferred him to Rochester.

And little purses threat'ning greater stand.
What fury's this? Is it so new a thing   330
For treasurers to abuse and rob the King?
If by accounts, to bankers only known,
They help t' increase his debts, and pay their own?
If from all farms a tribute they exact,
Will not old precedents justify the fact?   335
What Danby boasted, shall we blame in Hyde?
Is not the Crown with equal reason ti'd
The portions of his daughters to provide?

Cease, heroes, cease: such mortal combats shun,
Nor, by pretending to examine, run   340
Into the dang'rous tracks of Forty-one:
Tracks that from rapine and oppressive pride
To pow'r's true end, the people's safety, guide;
From murder with a stamp of law impress'd,
And rav'ning wolves in peaceful lamb-skin dress'd: 345
Tracks that to right and reformation tend
And, if Hell fails her timely help to send,

---

black gown: If this refers to a member of the judiciary (cf. "gownsman"), then the allusion would be to North, who had been Attorney General and Chief Justice of Common Pleas prior to this. Roger North suggests that, with the retirement in 1684 of Leoline Jenkins, the Secretary of State for the South, the three remaining political heads, Halifax, Rochester, and North, fell into contention (*Lives, 1,* 237).

white staff: The allusion here is to Rochester, the anticipated Lord Treasurer.

329. *little purses:* i.e. privy purse.

334. "The Lord Rochester fired at [Halifax's investigation of the revenue farm]; for, however the matter was worded, he took it as an imputation against him; the same as saying he had been bribed to give the farmers a pennyworth" (North, *Lives, 2,* 203).

336. *Danby:* This is a blank in the original.

338. *his daughters:* As well as a son (Henry), Rochester had four daughters: Anne (married to the second Duke of Ormonde), Henrietta (married to the Earl of Dalkeith), Mary (married to the first Lord Conway), and Catherine (unmarried).

339. The whole of this section is in the strict irony of blame by praise.

341. *Forty-one:* The year in which the Civil War began; also a favorite phrase of Tory jingoists.

343. Cf. "Salus populi suprema lex."

344. Although the poet may be alluding to the executions of all those taken in the Whig Conspiracy (see Duncombe's remark, 312 n.), he seems to have had Sidney (see *Algernon Sidney's Farewell*) and especially Armstrong in mind (see 132 n., and head note to Poems on Armstrong's Execution).

In the confusion of all knaves must end.
Oh practice fruitful in fanatic treason!
Shall we force fav'rites to be judg'd by reason?—   350
A yoke, though tri'd with politic effort,
Nor you nor your forefathers could support:
Reason, to which, though your hir'd pens pretend,
When you most need it, never is your friend.
More false than France, which now your cause relies on,   355
Th' extracted venom of republic poison.
The bane of corrupt Courts in ev'ry time,
Our senate's ne'er-to-be-forgiven crime.
Will you revive their old abhor'd complaints,
And help to justify your own attaints?   360
Mingle with counsels that fly all defense,
The still-to-be-suspected aid of sense?
Is not a courtier's true elective call
The trying nothing, and approving all?
Is not your Peter still at odds with Paul?   365
Will you the fruits of your late conquests lose,
And all the traitors you have hang'd, excuse?
Will you with truths their touch has made profane,
That sacred thing, the Government, arraign?
With fatal flails that to the foe belong,   370
Break the firm order of establish'd wrong,
And by disputes, unfitting James' slaves,
Disturb the Cath'lic unity of knaves?
Shall Rome's cause languish under vain contests,

352. *forefathers:* The courtiers of Charles I.
353. *your hir'd pens:* i.e. those of Dryden and L'Estrange.
356. Here and at 358, supply *is* at the beginning of the line.
365. *Peter . . . Paul:* In the light of the reputed Romanism of the Court, the line points to the conflict between the Court party's covert Catholicism (centered at St. Peter's in Rome) and the legal religion that the King was obliged to uphold (centered at St. Paul's in London).
366. *fruits:* i.e. the legal victories (and consequent executions) that followed the Whig Conspiracy.
370. *fatal flails:* The ironic reference is to the "Protestant flail," an object which Tory propagandists referred to frequently in order to terrify their readers. According to Roger North (*Examen*, p. 572), the weapon, meant "for street and crowd work," consisted of a weight attached by a thong to a wooden handle. See also *POAS*, Yale, 2, 12.
374. *contests:* i.e. between Halifax and Rochester.

And Whig-inquiries poison loyal breasts?   375
Shall the King's service (that once useful tool)
Stop the fair progress of illegal rule?
And by Court quarrels, plots and riots cool,
While Popish spoils the Presbyterians boast
And discontented wanders Stafford's ghost?   380
Charles and his pow'r let James' creatures seize,
And with gross lies, since him it seems to please,
Blind for his safety, cozen for his ease.

But you, the leaders of the passive band,
Whose shoulders bow'd to bear oppression stand,   385
Who ev'ry change with early fawning meet,
And your necks offer to the victor's feet:
You heads of servile Issachar! take heed

375. *Whig-inquiries:* If *Whig* is being used ironically for anything that is not blindly Tory, the reference would appear to be to the renewed demands for an investigation of the farming of the revenues (see 256–58 n.). "The King determined to dissolve the farm and turn it into a management; and process was to go on in the Exchequer for it. But, before any great advance was made (for great things and great persons move slow), the King died, which ended all that affair" (North, *Lives*, 2, 204). In fact, in Jan. 1685, Halifax finally arranged to have Charles inspect the books on the first Monday of Feb., the day the King came down with his final illness (Burnet, *History*, 2, 455).

378. *plots and riots:* The corrosive irony calls into question both the plots of the Whig Conspiracy, and the charges of riotous gatherings which the Crown used to harass Pilkington and those connected with the shrieval elections (8 May 1683) as well as Sacheverell and the 20 others who objected to delivering up their city's charter (2 May 1684).

379. *Popish spoils:* The reference may be to the confiscation of Catholic religious articles, such as that carried out by Sir William Waller (see *An Elegy on . . . Sir William Waller*).

380. *Stafford's:* William Howard, Viscount Stafford (1614–80), was accused by Oates of being paymaster for an alleged Catholic army that was about to wreak havoc in England. Other witnesses swore that he had tried to persuade them to murder Charles II. He was found guilty and beheaded for treason in 1680. The text has only *S———d,* so the allusion could be to Thomas Wentworth, first Earl of Strafford (1593–1641), Charles I's vigorous administrator who was impeached by Commons in March 1641 and beheaded on 11 May. Both men seem to have been sacrificed in order to gain time in the face of what a royalist would have called mob rule. The poet ironically approves vengeance upon Stafford's murderers so that his ghost will find rest.

383. *Blind:* This is probably used in the sense of *deceive,* though there seem to be allusions to Lear here. After *Blind* and *cozen,* supply *him* (i.e. Charles II).

384. *leaders of the passive band:* Following the Whig Conspiracy, the Anglican Church issued a declaration formally inculcating the principle of passive obedience.

388. *Issachar:* Genesis 49:14–15 subtly depicts the rural, submissive character of the tribe of Issachar (the ninth son of Jacob): "Issachar is a strong ass couching down

How you the length of chosen chains exceed,
Or, for by-ends, seeking some private path,   390
Fall from the grace of your implicit faith,
Sap your own props, and with a hasty blow
In one ill hour the work of years o'erthrow.
How oft, in spite of int'rest, sense, and laws,
Has wilful blindness reinforc'd your cause?   395
And will ye now, against that faithful friend,
The foe unfollow'd, all your thunder spend?
Has not e'en doubt been *disaffection* nam'd,
By the church model of lay Popery fram'd?
Was not distrust the block still of offense,   400
And finding fault the heresy of sense?
Did not this very vice (if Hodge not lie)
Dissolve the Church and damn the monarchy?
Leave then your popular ill-boding fray,
And turn your heat a more obedient way.   405

Ah! let Hyde first (the Court's more genuine spawn,
Born to dissemble and bred up to fawn),
Out of pure love to the endanger'd Crown,
Repress his rage and lay his vengeance down.

---

between burdens: And he saw that the rest was good, and the land that it was pleasant; and bowed his shoulder to bear, and became a servant unto tribute."

392. *Sap your own props:* The precise reference is uncertain. It may well allude to the vigorous action taken by Sancroft, Archbishop of Canterbury (1617–93), when, in April 1684, he initiated the suspension of the Bishop of Lichfield, Thomas Wood. The general charge was gross neglect of duties, but one suspects that Wood's independence (he had obtained the bishopric in 1671 through the Duchess of Cleveland), as well as his sympathy to Puritanism, would have directly contradicted Sancroft's rigorous sense of ecclesiastical duty. On 19 July 1684, the instrument of suspension was read. At just about the same time, Sancroft flatly "declined to sanction a pardon, about which the King wrote to him, to the Archdeacon of Lincoln who had been convicted of simony" (H. W. Hutton, *The English Church . . . 1625–1714* [London, repr. 1934], pp. 213–14). The poet ironically condemns those actions which do not support the subordination of the Church to the political state, since he assumes that such Erastianism ("the work of years") is necessary in order to achieve the ultimate goal, Romanism.

396. *that faithful friend:* Either Charles or York, probably the former.

397. *the foe unfollow'd:* In point of fact, the "foe" (the sectarians) were being brutally harassed, jailed, and persecuted during 1684.

402. *Hodge:* Roger L'Estrange had given these arguments their widest circulation in his pamphlets against the Popish Plot and in his newssheet, *The Observator.*

And Halifax—by no engagements ti'd,   410
True only to his fear and to his pride,
Leaving by fits, and left of ev'ry side;
Who late maintain'd (while that his end did suit)
Subjects no more than servants should dispute;
How grievous e'er the government became,   415
In them 'twas saucy to pretend to blame,
And, press'd by plots and brutal force, to rout
All the remains of sense that stood it out—
Let him now practice what he preach'd before,
And in the filth, with which himself all o'er   420
Bedaub'd the Court, return to stink once more.
Charm'd with the tune he taught L'Estrange to sing,
Cease against will, reason's Whig arms to bring,
Nor through his ministers assault the King.
Like Face and Subtle, let both end debate,   425

412. This constitutes a negative definition of Halifax's famous "trimmer" position
(see *The Character of a Trimmer*). The line echoes somewhat Settle's cut at Dryden
in *Absalom Senior*: "He left not whoring, but of that was left" (1343).

415–16. Contrasting the Crown's desire for power with the people's desire for
liberty, Halifax was to write that "Power is so apt to be insolent, and liberty to be
saucy, that they are very seldom upon good terms" ("Political Thoughts and Reflec-
tions," in *Works*, p. 223).

421. *return:* Halifax had regained dominance at Court about April 1684.

422. *the tune:* Either the political doctrine of submission of the people or the
personal policy of accommodation. Since Nov. 1682, L'Estrange had been attacking the
Whig who trimmed, feeling this was "a more insidious form of Whiggery, a form no
longer clumsy and anarchic, but politic to the last degree" (Kitchin, *L'Estrange*, p. 353;
see pp. 351–57 for L'Estrange's views on the Church trimmer).

423. *will:* Royal will.

424. *his ministers:* In order to avoid lese majesty, those who attacked Court policy
aimed not at the king but at "the king's evil counselors." The phrasing of this line
is nicely ambiguous. If *his* refers to *King*, then it would be political and refer to
Rochester and his allies; if *his* refers to *reason* (423), then it would be an ethical
condemnation of the King.

425–29. *Face and Subtle:* In Jonson's *Alchemist* (1610), Face (the servant) and Subtle
(the alchemist) combine forces to cheat a series of gullible persons with promises of
obtaining the philosophers' stone. In I.1. the violent argument of the two is resolved
by their female colleague, Doll Common:

Leave off your barking and grow one again. . . .
Ha' you together cozen'd all this while,
And all the world, and shall it now be said
Yo' have made most courteous shift to cozen yourselves? . . .

And lovingly together cheat the State.
Let Portsmouth come, like Doll, with mediation,
And charge 'em, for their mutual preservation,
To join still in the ruin of the nation.

To compass this, and keep themselves in pow'r,   430
Of Irish rebels, let 'em cull the flow'r;
And round the City in half-pay maintain,
Till things are ripe for massacres again.
Nay, let 'em leave, by their success grown bold,
No law unbroke, no loyal lie untold,   435
No rogue unbought, no treach'rous trick untri'd,
No principle of honor undefi'd.
Let rooks that cheat, and women of ill fame,
In blood alliance with the Tories claim.
Bawds, pimps, and gamesters, give 'em hand and heart,   440
And not one bulker fail to play his part.
Let 'em call outlaws to support the throne,
And make the bullies of the town their own.
Let their vile cause proclaim, like infant Rome,

Fall to your couples again, and cozen kindly,
And heartily, and lovingly, as you should.

She finally gets the two

       To leave [their] faction . . .
And labor kindly in the common work.

427. *Portsmouth:* Louise Renée de Kéroualle, Duchess of Portsmouth (1649–1734), was the King's most powerful and notorious mistress. She gave strong support to the Duke of York and favored Rochester.

431–32. *Irish rebels . . . in half-pay:* The allusion is probably to the troops—largely Irish—that had been brought back from Tangiers and were kept at half-pay. By Oct. 1684, Charles and James had recalled them and held a review on Putney Heath. The Whigs now directly confronted one of their bêtes noires, a standing army under royal command.

438. *rooks:* Swindlers, cheats, sharpers.

441. *bulker:* A low-lived person; a petty thief, a shoplifter; a prostitute.

442. *outlaws:* The most recent example would have been that of James Holloway of Bristol, who fled following the discovery of the Whig Conspiracy. Holloway, attainted for outlawry, was captured on 9 April 1684, making a confession to the King that supported the government's case and involved Colonel Rumsey (Howell, *State Trials, 9,* 438–48). In marked contrast to Armstrong's treatment two months later, Holloway's attainder of outlawry was waived by the King and he was allowed to proceed to trial on 21 April. He was found guilty and executed nine days later.

Refuge to all the rakehells that will come,   445
And as fop-oglers, treated with disdain,
Asperse that virtue they despair to gain.

So while a few, despising Popish arts,
Like ancient Britons, with unconquer'd hearts
(Though left as thin as Gideon's little band)   450
On utmost bounds of their lost freedom stand;
Let some pass for fanatics, others atheists,
And none be friends to monarchy but Papists.

Let 'em black patriots with a traitor's stains,
And give him halters who refuses chains.   455
Hiding his head whose breach now bare appears,
Let small plots thicken as their great one clears.
Warn'd by three foils, and taught by public scorn,
Let 'em at last grow cunning to suborn.
Let tame, train'd rogues draw wild ones within shot,   460
And furbish up (the sheriffs being got)
A fourth edition of their Meal Tub Plot.

447. Supply *Let them* before *Asperse.*

450. *Gideon's little band:* By divine command, Gideon twice reduced the size of his army; first from 22,000 to 10,000 (Judges 7:3) and then to 300 (Judges 7:5–6).

453. *none:* The original reads *now,* and this emendation does not completely clarify a troublesome line.

454. *'em:* i.e. the Tories.
black: Blacken.
patriots: The writer would seem to have men such as Sidney, Russell, and Essex in mind.

457. *their great one:* The reference may be specifically to the Whig Conspiracy (which the writer is calling in doubt) or, more generally, to the great plot to turn England into a Catholic and absolutist monarchy.

458. *three foils:* The text does not supply enough evidence to determine definitely the three instances of aborted Court maneuvering. Since 459 suggests legal actions, the Meal Tub Plot (1679), the Shaftesbury indictment (1681), and the Whig Conspiracy (1683) from which Monmouth escaped (and which the writer is denigrating) might be proposed.

459. *grow . . . suborn:* The writer would certainly include Dangerfield, the Irish witnesses, and the turncoat evidences of the Whig Conspiracy (such as Josiah Keeling, Robert West, and Howard of Escrick) as examples of "uncunning" subornation.

461. *sheriffs being got:* i.e. to impanel a sympathetic grand jury. (For the importance of the shrieval posts in this respect, see Introduction and headnote to Poems on the Shrieval Elections.)

All Wapping for new Venners let 'em rake,
Then find the deep conspiracies they make:
Court their own traitors, promise, threat, deceive,   465
And, with still fresh assurance of reprieve,
Make 'em at Tyburn in forg'd tales persevere,
Till sudden halters stop their mouths forever.
With Popish pity, French faith, let 'em chouse
Out of their lives fool Hone and coward Rouse;   470

463. *Wapping:* The squalid dock section of London's East End was a hotbed of extreme sectarianism.

Venner: "In January 1661 a fanatic cooper named Venner, accompanied by fifty men, proceeded to set up in the streets of London the Fifth Monarchy or reign of Jesus Christ on earth. This was instantly suppressed; Venner and others were hanged, but, unfortunately, from the truth that the Fifth Monarchy men were extremists was deduced the unwarrantable opinion that all Dissenters were politically dangerous" (Ogg, *Charles II*, p. 208).

465-69. The literary analogue for this situation is found in Thomas Kyd's *Spanish Tragedy* (c. 1588), III. Pedringano is condemned to hang for murder and mounts the gallows without implicating the Duke's son Lorenzo, who, Pedringano believes, has sent a boy with his pardon. The boy, discovering he carries an empty box, remarks, "I cannot choose but smile to think how the villain will flout the gallows, scorn the audience, and descant, and all presuming of his pardon from hence." The historical analogue, for the poet, would have been the executions of the Catholic Popish Plot victims, none of whom admitted anything concerning a plot. By extension, the poet implies that these victims were duped into not revealing that York (or Charles) headed the Plot.

469. *chouse:* Cheat, trick, defraud of or out of.

470. *fool Hone:* William Hone, a laborer, first pleaded, on 12 July 1683, a muddled "not guilty" to high treason in the Whig Conspiracy, and then, on the next day, an equally muddled "guilty" (see Howell, *State Trials, 9,* 572-73). Josiah Keeling, the original discoverer of the assassination plot, and Thomas Leigh, who appears to have turned Crown's evidence to save his own life, had drawn in Hone, "who, it seems, had some heat but scarce any sense to him." As Burnet sums up, "He seemed fitter for a Bedlam than a trial." Even Robert West, the barrister turned Crown evidence, could not forebear ending his testimony with, "My lord, he hath been deluded basely, and I am sorry for the poor fellow" (Howell, *State Trials, 9,* 575).

coward Rouse: John Rouse, also tried on 12 and 13 July 1683, pleaded "not guilty" to the attempted assassination and the plot to take the Tower. The night before his execution, he told of insurrection plots at the time of the Oxford Parliament (1681) and implicated Shaftesbury and Oates (see Howell, *State Trials, 9,* 490-91). On the gallows the next day (20 July) with Walcot and Hone, he claimed he had become involved only to be able to reveal all to the King; then, rejecting all who opposed the government, he called on everyone to "pay their duty and homage to the King and those that God has set over them, and not neglect that great command to pray for the King and all that are in authority" (ibid., 682).

> In vain, each trembling for his pardon tarries,
> Hang'd to keep great men's counsel—like Fitzharris.

472. *Fitzharris:* Edward Fitzharris, the last person executed in connection with the Popish Plot (1 July 1681), became enmeshed in a tangle of double-dealing and parliamentary intrigue (see Howell, *State Trials*, 7, 223–446). Evidently, a certain Everard convinced Fitzharris to help him write a violent anti-Court libel and discussed it with him while Court party witnesses listened in on the treasonable talk. "The idea was that now, in order to save his life, he should become one of the King's Evidence, and 'confess' that he had been hired to send copies of it to the Opposition leaders, so that, these copies being found in their possession, they could be charged with high treason" (Lane, *Oates,* p. 258). There are strong grounds for the Whig suspicion (shared by the poet) that Fitzharris believed that the Court would have to protect him in order to protect itself. For an ingenious and at times subtle Tory investigation of the entire affair, see North, *Examen,* pp. 273–301, especially p. 300, where it is suggested that Fitzharris believed that his protection would come from the Whig-controlled Commons or grand juries.

The strongly Puritan background of the wealthy East India merchant Sir Samuel Barnardiston undoubtedly led to his close identification with the Whig party in parliament. He had first gained prominence on 8 May 1668, when he refused to pay a £300 fine imposed by the House of Lords for the East India Company's confiscation of the ships of an independent merchant. His commitment lasted until 10 Aug. 1668, and he emerged as a new champion of Commons' rights and privileges. Again, as the result of a contested election in 1672, he began a legal contest of major constitutional importance which finally established the exclusive right of Commons "to determine the legality of the returns to their chamber, and of the conduct of the returning officers" (*DNB;* for later contention on the decision, see *Journal of the House of Lords,* 1685–91, pp. 253–54, and Luttrell, *1,* 551–52).

Charles' legal persecution of Barnardiston probably stemmed not so much from this parliamentarianism as from a later defiance of the Court. In 1681, Barnardiston acted as foreman of that blue-ribbon panel of grand jurymen (which included also the future Whig shrieval candidates Papillon and Dubois) that returned *Ignoramus* the indictment for high treason against Shaftesbury. On 14 Feb. 1684 (two weeks after having entered a plea of not guilty), Barnardiston was brought to trial before Jeffreys on a high misdemeanor "for writing and publishing, in four several letters, to persons in the country, scandalous and seditious reflections concerning the late fanatic [i.e. Whig] conspiracy" (Luttrell, *1,* 302). That many of the statements in these letters were punishable would have seemed obvious to men of the time; quite beyond the strong anti-Court sentiment, there were expressions of sympathy and support for men who had been found guilty of high treason, and, even worse, an assertion that the Earl of Essex had been murdered. Interestingly enough, Williams, Barnardiston's lawyer, only briefly raised the question of publication (Howell, *State Trials, 9,* 1348), for these were four ostensibly personal letters of news (two to his nephew by marriage, Sir Philip Skippon, and two to intimate friends, Edward Gael and William Cavell) sent through the post to Barnardiston's native Ipswich. Jeffreys (who had ruled in Sidney's trial that *scribere est agere*) considered that Sir Samuel had made public his sentiments, and virtually ordered the jury to bring in a verdict of guilty. On 19 April, Barnardiston was sentenced "to pay the fine of £10,000, to be bound to his good behavior for life, and be committed till all this be done" (Luttrell, *1*, 305). Once again he refused to pay his fine and was imprisoned, but this time it was not until June 1688, after his business affairs had suffered greatly by his absence (Howell, *State Trials, 9,* 1371–72), that he felt forced to pay £6,000 and give bond for the residue in order to obtain his liberty (Luttrell, *1*, 441–42). The judgment against him was reversed by the Lords on 14 May 1689 (*Journal of the House of Lords, 1685–91,* p. 210).

This Tory ballad, which must have appeared shortly after Barnardiston's imprisonment, was set to Durfey's song "Hark! the thund'ring cannons roar" [D 2706] celebrating the defeat of the Turks at Vienna—an event which certain groups with Whig sympathies saw principally as a victory for Popery and arbitrary power.

The text is based on *l″* (which gives the music) and compared with *k″* and *c*. It has been reprinted in *r″* (V).

THE WHIG INTELLIGENCER

or

Sir Samuel in the Pound.

For Publishing Scandalous and Seditious Letters,
For which he was Fined £10,000 on Saturday, April 19

1.

Hark! the fatal day is come,
    Fatal as the day of doom;
For Sir Samuel there make room,
    So fam'd for *Ignoramus:*
He whose conscience could allow   5

Title. *Intelligencer:* A bringer of news, an informant, a newsmonger.
Pound: A place of confinement, a pen, a prison for debtors or offenders.
2. *doom:* Judgment.

> Such large favors you know how;
> If we do him justice now,
> > The brethren will not blame us.

2.

> Stand to the bar, and now advance
> > Morden, Kendrick, Oates and Prance;   10
> But let the foreman lead the dance;
> > The rest in course will follow.
> Tilden, Kendrick next shall come,
> > And with him receive their doom:
> Ten thousand pound, at which round sum   15
> > The Hall set up a hallow.

3.

> Brave Sir Barnardiston now,
> > Who no main would e'er allow
> To lose ten thousand at a throw,
> > Was pleas'd to all men's thinking.   20
> Ten thousand pounds! a dismal note,
> > Who before had giv'n his vote

10. John Morden and Andrew Kendrick served on the Whig grand jury which freed Shaftesbury. Morden, like many others on the panel, was a highly successful merchant, and associated with Barnardiston in the East India Company.

Oates: Titus Oates, the principal discoverer of the Popish Plot.

Prance: Miles Prance supplied the chief evidence concerning the murder of Sir Edmund Berry Godfrey.

11. *foreman:* Sir Samuel Barnardiston (see headnote).

13. *Tilden:* Unidentified.

16. *Hall:* Probably the Guildhall where Barnardiston had been tried.

18. *main:* In the game of hazard, explains Charles Cotton in *The Compleat Gamester* (1674), "there are two things chiefly to be observed, that is *Main* and *Chance;* the Chance is the caster's, and the Main theirs who are concerned in play with him. There can be no main thrown above nine and under five." The game follows the rules of modern craps fairly closely, save that the caster may have a main other than seven. If he achieves the main on his first cast, he wins; if the main comes up before he makes his chance, he loses. For other finer points of hazard, see Chapter XXXIV in *The Compleat Gamester* (reprinted in *Games and Gamesters of the Restoration*).

The figurative use (and relation to "main chance") may be seen in the *OED*'s citation (1612): "Deal merchant-like, put it upon one main and throw at all." The writer may have in mind Sir Samuel's earlier defense of the East India Company, his main or main chance, which had been fined not £10,000 but £5,000 (see headnote and *DNB* sub Barnardiston).

Not to give the King a groat
To save the Throne from sinking.

4.

"But yet there's a remedy: 25
   Before the King shall get by me,
I'll quit my darling liberty,
   Nor will I give in bail for't;
For ere the Crown shall get a groat
   In opposition to my vote,   30
I'll give 'em leave to cut my throat,
   Although I lie in jail for't.

5.

"Were't for Monmouth, I'd not grieve,
   Or brave Russell to retrieve,
Or that Sidney yet might live,   35
   Twice told, I'd not complain, sir.
Nay, what's more, my whole estate,
   With my bodkins, spoons, and plate,

23. Sir Samuel had been returned M.P. for Suffolk, during Charles' reign, in 1672, 1678, 1679, 1680. Very probably his own convictions as well as his strong Whig sympathies would have led him to withhold subsidies from the King until certain parliamentary privileges were granted.

33. *Were't:* The "it" refers to the £10,000 fine. In his two letters to Sir Philip Skippon (29 Nov. and 1 Dec. 1683), Barnardiston told joyfully of Monmouth's return to Court, of the misrepresentation of the *Gazette*'s version of the Duke's recantation (No. 1880 [22–26 Nov. 1683]), and of the consternation of "the Papists and high Tories." The letters are given in Howell, *State Trials, 9,* 1344–46.

34. In his first letter, Sir Samuel had remarked that "the brave Lord Russell is afresh lamented."

35. The second letter noted hopefully: "It is said Mr. Sidney is reprieved for forty days, which bodes well." When this proved false and the warrant for Sidney's execution was signed, he gave vent to his despair in the letter of 4 Dec. to William Cavell: "Great endeavors have been used to obtain his pardon, but the contrary party have carried it, which dasheth our hopes, but God still governs" (Howell, *State Trials, 9,* 1347).

36. *Twice told:* i.e. were his £10,000 fine counted, or reckoned, out twice.

38. Particularly at the start of the Civil War, the Parliamentary forces were extremely hard pressed for money. The mention of "bodkins" is probably meant to recall the famous incident illustrated in *A Pack of Cavalier Playing Cards (temp. Charles II, forming a Complete Political Satire of the Commonwealth,* ed. Edmund Goldsmid [Edinburgh, 1886, for the Aungervyle Society]). There, the knave of hearts shows Hugh

So I might reduce the State
    To a Commonwealth again, sir.   40

6.

"Or that Monmouth were in grace,
    Or Sir Sam. in Jeffreys' place,
To spit his justice in the face,
    For acting law and reason,
Or that the Tories went to pot,   45
    Or we could prove it a sham plot,
Or Essex did not cut his throat,
    Or plotting were not treason.

7.

"Thus I'd freely quit my coin;
    But with Tories to combine,   50
Or keep the heir in the right line
    That Popery be in fashion;
To see the Holy Cause run down
    While mighty York is next the Crown,
And Perkin's forc'd to fly the town—   55
    Oh, vile abomination!

Peters in the pulpit holding up a string of thimbles and bodkins, and saying, "Here the wives of Wappin." The text below the card states, "Hugh Peters shews the bodkins and thimbles given by the wives of Wappin for the Good Old Cause."

39–40. Barnardiston took a prominent part in the disturbances in London in 1640; indeed, "according to Rapin . . . his prominence in the crowd on this occasion gave rise to the political use of the word roundhead" (*DNB*), which the Queen applied to him.

46. In the first letter to Skippon, Barnardiston remarked prematurely that "the plot [i.e. the Whig Conspiracy] is lost here, except you in the country can find it out amongst the Addressors and Abhorrers."

47. In the same letter, Barnardiston reported that "it is generally said the Earl of Essex was murdered" and that "Mr. Braddon, who prosecuted the murder of the Earl of Essex, the information put in against him in the King's Bench, by Mr. Attorney (for a pretended subornation) etc., was not prosecuted, and the bail was discharged." These were probably the most dangerous remarks in the letters, since the assertion that Essex's death in the Tower was murder implied a belief that the order for his death had come from either the Duke of York or the King himself.

53. *the Holy Cause:* i.e. the Good Old Cause, the Puritan belief in the Commonwealth and "government of Saints."

55. *Perkin:* i.e. Monmouth (see *A Merry New Ballad, In Answer to Old Rowley the King,* 5 and n.)

8.

"Sooner than obedience owe
    To their arbitrary law,
Or my bail in danger draw
    For breach of good behavior,   60
I with Bethel, and the rest
    O'th' birds, in cage will make my nest,
And keep my fine to plot and feast
    Till Monmouth be in favor."

Printed for the Information and Terror
of all Libellers, 1684.

60. See headnote.

61. *Bethel:* Slingsby Bethel, who led the most radical wing of the anti-Court party, had been sheriff during 1680–81. He was the first important opposition leader to flee to the Continent when it became clear, in the summer of 1682, that the Court party would soon control the municipal offices. (See *Iter Boreale.*)

63. See the poems on the Whig Feast, above.

A Character of London Village

[*C 2019*]

Despite the great interest in particular persons and specific events, the poetry of the early 1680s supplies little detailed description. Here, however, we move from the playhouse to the coffee house, then ramble past the gutted cathedral of St. Paul, and across to the Bankside for a brief glimpse of Westminster. The tour is all too brief.

Luttrell purchased his copy of the poem on 3 May 1684.

A CHARACTER OF LONDON VILLAGE

By a Country Poet

A village! Monstrous! 'Tis a mighty beast,
Behemoth, or Leviathan at least;
Or like some wilderness, or vast meander,
Where to find friends one long enough may wander.
The tow'ring chimneys like a forest show,   5
At whose low branches do balconies grow.
When I came there at first, I gazed round,
And thought myself upon enchanted ground;
Or else that I (in rapture being hurl'd)
Was lately dead, and this was th' other world,   10
But was surpris'd with doubts and could not tell
Which of the two 't was, whether Heav'n or Hell?
The noise and shows my eyes and ears invade,
By coaches, cries, and glitt'ring gallants made.
My reason was convinced in a trice   15
That it was neither, but Fools' Paradise.
Ladies I saw, not handsome one in ten;
Great store of knights, and some few gentlemen;

3. *meander:* A labyrinth, maze.
6. *balconies:* Until c. 1825, this word was accented on the second syllable.

547

Fine fellows flaunting up and down the streets,
Where Fop and Flutter each the other greets: 20
Each mimic posture does an ape present,
While "Humble Servant" ends the complement.
    For garb and color there's no certain rule;
Here is your red, your blue, your yellow fool.
Most of these gallants seem to view refin'd;   25
The outside wondrous gay, but poorly lin'd.
I saw some of them in the playhouse pit,
Where they three hours in conversation sit,
Laugh and talk loud, but scarce a grain of wit.
The ladies, to ensnare, will something say,   30
Tending to show the brisk gallants their way,
But scorn as much to prattle sense as they.
Here comes a hero cover'd close from air,
By porters borne in a silk-curtain'd chair,
Whose sire in honest russet trail'd a plow,   35
And with stout flail conquer'd the haughty mow.
Next after him is, by six horses drawn,
A piece of logwood in a coach alone,
Looking like Scanderbeg on ev'ry one;
Who soon a whispering bawd softly invites   40

19. *flaunting:* Walking or moving about so as to display one's finery; displaying one-self in unbecomingly splendid or gaudy attire.

20. *Fop and Flutter:* Used generically for coxcombs or dandies. Cf. Sir Fopling Flutter in Etherege's *Man of Mode* (1676).

22. *complement:* A ceremonious or formal tribute of (mere) courtesy paid to anyone. The word has been left in its older form (cf. the doublet, *compliment*) in order not to obscure the sense of completion or ending (*OED.* I. 5: "something which when added . . . makes up a whole; each of two parts which mutually complete each other, or supply each other's deficiencies").

31. *gallants:* Accented here on the second syllable, though accented on the first elsewhere. For the suggestion that the former pronunciation implies "one who pays court to ladies, a ladies' man; a lover" (as opposed to the latter with its sense of "a man of fashion and pleasure"), cf. *OED.* B. 1 and 3.

34. *chair:* Sedan chair.

35. *russet:* A garment of coarse, homespun, woolen cloth used by peasants and country folk.

36. *mow:* A heap of grain or hay.

39. *like Scanderbeg:* For George Castriota, alias Iskander Beg (c. 1404–67), see *The Medal,* "Epistle to the Whigs," note k. It is difficult to tell whether the comparison is meant to evoke the imperiousness of the arriviste (see *OED* and 37), or the decayed state of Scanderbeg's body when exhumed by the Turks (see 38).

To a new suburb Miss, and there he lights.
But at some little distance from the place,
Handsome she seems, all cover'd o'er with lace,
That nearer shows an old and ugly face.
There goes a brisk young lass in a gay dress,   45
Here an old crone in youthful gaudiness.
Strange miracles of Nature here are plac'd!
Ill-favor'd wenches, cracks; some fair, are chaste.
The temp'rate, sick; great drinkers live in health.
Here usurers have wit, and poets wealth.   50
    The coffeehouse, the rendezvous of wits,
Is a compound of gentlemen and cits;
And not all wise, or else their wits they smother,
They sit as if afraid of one another.
So pickpocket (when deeper lifter's by)   55
Budging aloof, disowns the mystery.
In comes a cock'd-up bully, looking big,
With deep-fring'd elbow gloves and ruffl'd wig;
He turns his back to th' chimney, with a grace,
Singing and staring in each stranger's face;   60
Talks mighty things, his late intrigues, and then
Sups off his dish, and out he struts again.
And as I rambled through this quondam city,

41. *a new suburb Miss:* A young girl, oftimes from the country, who has been trapped into prostitution (see Hogarth's *Harlot's Progress*).

lights: Either (1) descends from his coach, brings his journey to an end, or (2) proceeds, has a particular place of arrival.

48. *cracks:* Prostitutes, wenches; women of broken reputation.

49. *in health:* There would seem to be a play on "health" as a toast drunk in a person's honor.

55. A deeper lifter may be a more accomplished, or more serious, thief.

56. *Budging aloof:* The meaning of this difficult phrase may simply be that the pickpocket moves away at some distance, letting the "deeper lifter" operate, and in this sense disowns (i.e. gives up) his mystery, or trade. On the other hand, a budge is "one that slips into an house in the dark and taketh cloaks, coats, or what comes next to hand, marching off with them" (*Dictionary of the Canting Crew;* see also *OED*), while the "standing budge" is the thief's "scout or perdu" (ibid.). If a verbal sense had been developed, the meaning here would be that the pickpocket or petty thief, acting as lookout, stands at a distance feigning innocence while a house is robbed.

57. *cock'd-up:* Swaggering, strutting, assertive.

62. *dish:* i.e. of coffee.

63. *quondam city:* Because of the destruction caused by the fire of 1666, London is referred to as something that formerly was or existed.

I look'd on founding Paul's with tears of pity;
But wiping off, with an auspicious smile,   65
Being like to rise the glory of this isle.
 Village, for now to you I tell my tale,
You have produc'd a mountain from a dale;
The country thought the fire had quite undone ye,
But now I find you have both zeal and money.   70
 I cross'd the Thames, much broader than the brook
Where I have bath'd and little fishes took.
From Bear Garden I Westminster might view,
And though their outside look'd of different hue,
Yet there in each is so much noise and pother,   75
I scarce knew how to difference one from th' other.
 But at the Court indeed I saw great things,
The noblest subjects and the best of kings.
 These things I did observe, and many more,
But tir'd with the relation, I'll give o'er.   80

64. *founding:* i.e. in the process of establishing a substructure or base. St. Paul's Cathedral had been almost totally destroyed by the Great Fire, and when, against Christopher Wren's strong objections, repairs were attempted, they proved futile (see Bell, *The Great Fire*, plate facing p. 182, and pp. 302–03). A patent for rebuilding was finally given in 1672, but Wren, who laid the first foundation stone without public ceremonial on 21 June 1675, had great difficulties finding a solid base on which to build (see Claude Golding, *London, The City* [London, 1951], p. 13). It was not until 1697, 22 years later, that the first service was held in the choir, and the last stone did not go into position until 1710.

67. *Village:* i.e. London.

70. *zeal and money:* London undoubtedly put great effort into rebuilding, but the contemporary statements on the Monument and in Oldmixon that the work was completed in three or four years are undoubtedly exaggerations. For some of the costs, see T. F. Reddaway, *The Rebuilding of London After the Great Fire* (London, repr. 1951).

73. *Bear Garden:* On the Bankside, opposite Queenhithe.

74. *of different hue:* The fire went only as far west as Whitefriars, leaving Westminster untouched. The buildings of the area would contrast radically with the unweathered appearance of new construction or the charred ruins of London.

76. *difference:* Differentiate, distinguish.

Tyburn's Courteous Invitation to Titus Oates

[*T 3557*]

Titus Oates' "monumental brass" remained unaffected by the change of political climate. On 28 Feb. 1684, he sent to the King and Privy Council (through Secretary Jenkins) a *Humble Petition and Complaint* [O 45] not only recalling his past services but requesting that L'Estrange should be silenced because he "hath defamed and arraigned the justice of the nation in ridiculing the said Popish Plot and the discovery and discoverers thereof, in certain scandalous and seditious pamphlets of his called *The Observator,* and in several other pamphlets." In his covering letter [O 65A], he voiced righteous indignation that "any private person could have been so bold with the government as to . . . call in question the veracity of the testimony of that evidence"; and concluded that "I hope God will put it into your hearts to do me right." Failing to obtain the action he wished, Oates brazenly had both the letter and petition printed for public consumption, probably in the last week of April 1684. (See *Observator, 2,* No. 52 [28 April 1684]. Both texts are reprinted in *Somers Tracts, 8,* 378–81.)

L'Estrange responded immediately with as thorough a flaying and anatomization of Oates as any he had ever done (*Observator, 2,* Nos. 52–62 [28 April–15 May 1684]), culminating in three numbers that set forth the contradictions in the evidence of "the quail pipe of the Cause." The old insinuations of "sodomy, buggery, perjury, blasphemy, [and] treason" were still made, but L'Estrange's principal tone was now one of controlled irony that righteously based itself on Oates' concluding prayer. "I'm for having right done him," said L'Estrange, "whatever he deserves" (2, No. 52) ; and this, he added later, "was probably the only prayer on which he and Oates ever had agreed" (Lane, *Oates,* p. 299).

Greater misfortunes were in store for Oates. On 10 May, at his regular haunt, the Amsterdam Coffeehouse, he was "arrested at the suit of his Royal Highness in an action of *scandalum magnatum* and carried to the Compter" (*CSPD,* May 1684–Feb. 1685, p. 11); two days later, "he was transferred to the King's Bench Prison, where he was

551

affronted by persons unknown; 'blows ensued, for which they were bound over.' He was ordered to plead within three or four days, but he chose to let judgment go by default" (Lane, p. 300, citing *CSPD*, May 1684–Feb. 1685, pp. 30–31). On 18 June, he was found guilty and fined £100,000 and 20s. cost.

The present poem, dated 14 May 1684 by Luttrell, echoes the *Observator*'s attack and voices the Tory hope for the ultimate elevation of the Salamanca doctor.

Tyburn's Courteous Invitation to Titus Oates

Oh, name it once again! Will Titus come?
My dearest, hopeful, that long-wish'd-for one,
For whom my triple arms extended were
To hug with close embraces, many a year.
Haste! haste! my choicest darling, whom I love,   5
And thy long-promis'd kindness let me prove.
That right thou plead'st for, which indeed's thy due,
Though others I've deni'd, I'll grant it you;
The world shall find I willingly will bear,
And dance thy carcass 'twixt the earth and air.   10
In hemp'n-string I'll lull thee fast asleep,
And prevent all the dangers of the deep.
Oh, how I love thee! 'cause I've heard thou'st been
So well acquainted with all kinds of sin,
And, with a false and strange religious guise,   15
Destroy'd the innocent, abus'd the wise.
What crafty lessons didst thou teach to men!
How to rebel, and told the time best when;
Urg'd to exclude a right and lawful heir,

Title. *Tyburn*. The place of public execution for Middlesex. In the present poem, it is the gallows (often called Tyburn tree, or the triple tree) that is speaking.

7. *that right:* See headnote.

11–12. The lines are based on the popular proverb "He that is born to be hanged shall never be drowned" (Tilley, *Proverbs*, B. 139; cf. *Midsummer Moon*, 31–36 n. and, for a later use, Fielding's *Jonathan Wild*).

19. "Oates his way of exclusion" had been commented upon in a recent *Observator* (2, No. 50 [24 April 1684]):

Trimmer: . . . I never was for murdering, or (as you call it) blunderbussing the Duke, I can assure ye.

Unthrone a king, and swore away a peer.   20
Thy zeal through two-inch-boards was plainly seen,
When Satan prompt thee t' swear against the Queen;
Besides those many guiltless souls that di'd
A sacrifice to thy Luciferian pride.
Yet, yet, beloved Titus, my dear son   25
(Reputed Savior, for thy mercies shown),
There's something still does add to make thee great:
Thy blasphemy, thy perjury; and yet
With buggery methinks I am well pleas'd,
Though done by force, for then thy pocket's eas'd.   30
By many other favors thou hast shown,
And well may'st claim my palace as thine own.
Thou'lt find me kinder far than courtiers; I
Will never turn thee out until thou die:

Observator: No, no. No more was Oates. He was only for axing of him, or taking him off by a course of law, in a High Court of Justice, or so.

20. *a peer:* William Howard, Viscount Stafford, was impeached for high treason and tried by the House of Lords 30 Nov.–6 Dec. 1680. (The account of his, trial and execution are given in Howell *State Trials*, 7, 1294–1568; Oates' testimony can be found in 1320–25, 1347–50, 1439–47.)

21–22. *two-inch-boards:* Tory poets found the proverb "He will swear (look) through an inchboard" (Tilley, *Proverbs*, I. 61) particularly appropriate to Oates' somewhat confused account of having heard and then seen the Queen in treasonous consultation at Somerset House, from behind the doors in an anteroom (see Lane, *Oates*, pp. 135–41).

22. *prompt:* An alternate form of the verb *to prompt* was *to promp*; here, *prompt* may be the derived past tense.

23. *guiltless souls:* Not one victim of the Popish Plot ever confessed to such a conspiracy, despite offers of clemency.

26. *Savior:* Oates received, from his more enthusiastic supporters, the title of "Savior of the Nation."

29. For the history of Oates' alleged perversion, and the unsuccessful legal charges of sodomy brought against him by his servants, see Lane, *Oates*, pp. 30–31, 66, 224–26, 289–90.

30. *thy pocket's eas'd:* One possible meaning is that Oates, since he forced his victims, did not have to pay them. This meaning of pocket apparently antedates the earliest entries in *OED* by about 33 years. L'Estrange constantly ridiculed Oates' claim that he was "out of pocket" £678 12s. 6d. because of expenses incurred while masquerading as a Catholic. (See, at this time, *Observator*, 2, Nos. 53, 60 [30 April, 12 May 1684].)

33–35. "On August 31st [1681], the day after College suffered at Oxford, the Lord Chamberlain's warrant was conveyed to Titus by Sir Edward Carteret, Black Rod, commanding him to remove himself and his goods from Whitehall" (Lane, *Oates*, p. 276).

And, since Whitehall has left thee, I'll provide   35
That lodging for thee, where old Noll was ti'd.

36. *old Noll:* By an order of Parliament of 4 Dec. 1660 Oliver Cromwell's body was disinterred on 26 Jan. 1661 and hanged on the gallows at Tyburn on 30 Jan., the twelfth anniversary of Charles I's execution. "The head was then set up on a pole on the top of Westminster Hall, and the trunk buried under the gallows" (*DNB*, sub Cromwell).

Brittania Mourning the Execution of Charles I. Engraving by Robert White, 1682.

The Third Part of Advice to the Painter

[*M 891*]

The convention of the political "Advice to a Painter" poems not only allowed the writer to hold "a mirror up to actuality" (Hagstrum, *The Sister Arts,* p. 121) or to express his "opinions, prejudices, and emotions" (Osborne, *Advice-to-a-Painter Poems, 1663–1856,* p. 10), but also permitted him, by selection and juxtaposition, to draw a surrealistic picture of a contemporary situation. By choosing those details which he thought significant, by ordering his scenes to give the total effect he wanted, by coloring his subjects often to the point of caricature, the writer created a tableau which, for him, was more real than actuality. Certainly the convention goes back to Horace's "ut pictura poesis" and Simonides' "poetry [is] a speaking picture," but the *pictura* was not meant to be what we would now call photographic; indeed, much of the painting of the period was highly allegorical, and the artist—whether graphic or literary—was expected to create a higher truth through his interpretation and vision.

With telling strokes, the present poem depicts first the sympathy between the Whigs and the Turkish-Hungarian forces that threatened Europe in 1683; secondly, it portrays the situation in the Netherlands, where Whig domestic turbulence had allowed Louis to carry out his aggressive policy. In the first instance, many Whigs did, in fact, support the Protestant Count Teckley's rebellion in Hungary against the oppressive measures of the Emperor Leopold; they approved of the Ottoman toleration of Hungarian Protestantism; and they condemned, out of hand, any Papal policy and saw in Innocent XI's crusade against the Turks a mere excuse to crush Teckley and reestablish the dominance of the Holy Roman Empire. But such views put them in the highly questionable position of favoring infidels above Christians—and at a time when the Ottoman Empire seemed about to pour into Europe through the gateway of Vienna. In the second instance, Louis XIV's opportunistic invasion of the Spanish Netherlands, the writer gives voice to the anti-French feeling of the period but, with equal injustice, seeks to exculpate Charles and blame

555

the Whigs for English inaction. The temper of the times has been well summarized by G. N. Clark in *The Later Stuarts:*

> England had stood aside, but these events [in Vienna and the Spanish Netherlands] were events in English history. To stand aside was to give help to Louis, and that was to alienate William of Orange, to divide the Stuart interest, and to cause one Englishman after another to turn his eyes towards the possibility of linking the cause of 'civil and religious liberty' with that of Christendom against the Turk, the Low Countries against the French, trade against armed competition. (pp. 108–09)

Like other political Advices, then, this poem can be said to hold "the mirror up to actuality" only if we recognize that the mirror itself distorts, in this case to give a Tory reflection on affairs domestic and foreign.

The text is based on *g″*, where Luttrell dates this copy 28 May 1684. M. T. Osborne notes that a copy of the poem has been recorded "with Edmund Waller's name given as the author. There appears no further evidence on which to ascribe the poem to this writer" (*Advice-to-a-Painter Poems,* No. 33, p. 50), and this is surely as mistaken as Wing's listing of the poem under Andrew Marvell.

The Third Part of Advice to the Painter

Concerning the great Turk, Count Teckley, and the
Forces against them; the French, the Spaniards,
the Dutch, and the English

Painter, once more thy pencil reassume,
And in a landskip draw me Christendom.
But first draw out the Turkish Empire; then
Paint out in colors their division.
Paint me that mighty powerful state a-shaking,   5
And their great prophet, Teckely, a-quaking,

1. The same first line is found in Marvell's *Further Advice to a Painter* (M. T. Osborne, *Advice-to-a-Painter Poems,* No. 16) and the anonymous *New Advice to a Painter* [M 875A] (Osborne, No. 27).
pencil: An artist's paintbrush.
6. *Teckely:* For the alliance of the Hungarian Protestants under Count Imre Tököli with the invading Turks, see *Algernon Sidney's Farewell,* 52 n. The connection with the

Who for religion made such bustling work
That to reform it he brought in the Turk.
Next paint our English mufties of the tub,
Those great promoters of the Tecklites Club: 10
Draw me them praying for the Turkish cause,
And for the overthrow of Christian laws.

Whigs is made even more evident in *A New Song to the tune of The Grenadiers'*
March [N 775] (beginning, "Hail to the mighty monarch, valiant Pole"), the second
part of which parallels closely the feeling of this *Advice*:

> Teckley, that Perkin Prince of War,
>   That has kept so great a stir,
>   Deluded by a renegado Fate,
> Now with his injur'd Monarch will capitulate.
>   Policy and treason ne'er agree,
>   There's no hope of remedy,
>   Since injur'd clemency is so much abus'd
>   All show of sham repentance ought to be refus'd.
>   For the Pole with rebels scorns to treat,
>   Nor can Mohammed the Great
>   Hinder Teckley's defeat,
>   Nor all the pride that the faction draws
>   Can oppose our royal cause
>   Whilst the bold resulters [? revolters] strive in vain,
>   Sobieski and Lorraine
>   Will all Hungary stain.
>   Should the[y] new conquest still pursue,
>   Then, Monsieur, gardez-vous!

The song may also be found in *c* and *r″*(V).

9. *English mufties of the tub:* Certain dissenting sects gave their support not only to
Teckley but also to the Turks, who were engaging the forces of Catholicism in Europe.
Earlier expressions of this sympathy can be found in Marvell's *Growth of Popery* and
Samuel Johnson's *Julian the Apostate* (see *Observator*, No. 204 [13 Sept. 1682]), but
with the siege of Vienna (14 July to 12 Sept. 1683), the formerly theoretical position
came under heavy attack. L'Estrange speaks of the "alliance . . . betwixt [the Whigs
at] Kid's Coffee-house and the Porte" (No. 399 [6 Sept. 1683]) and goes on to excoriate
both Oates for his prayers for a Turkish victory and "Elephant" Smith (as "father of
the Teckelites") for his obviously subversive publication in 1682 of Prince Michael
Apati's *Declaration of the Hungarian War against the Emperor's Sacred Majesty* [A
3526] (Nos. 407–08 [20 and 22 Sept. 1683]). A month before the present poem, he re-
marked that "there's the True-Protestant candlestick [Oates] just tripping away for
Hungary, and I will not despair of seeing the most Christian Dissenters under the
banner of Mahomet the next campaign" (2, No. 53 [30 April 1684]).

11–12. Oates' zeal for the Turks involved him in ludicrous encounters (*Observator*,
No. 399 [6 Sept. 1683]; *CSPD*, July–Sept. 1683, pp. 351–52) and he soon became notori-
ous as "an advocate for infidels and rebels, under the True-Protestant cloak of an
asserter of the doctrine of Jesus Christ" (*Observator*, 2, No. 58 [8 May 1684]). L'Estrange

Next paint the Turk's seraglio; then
Paint our English mufties ent'ring in:
That and rebellion is their darling sin.   15
Next draw the many guiltless souls that di'd
A sacrifice to their Lucif'rian pride;
And paint to th' life their diabolic faces,
And angry looks, for their late desp'rate cases.
But lastly, draw a fair and spacious plain,   2c
And in it gallowses to hang them on.
Now draw, in opposition to this crew,
The Germans, Poles, and Cossack forces too:
Show by thy art what they have bravely done,
Beat down the Turks and their great standard won.   25

---

recalled the incident when the Doctor "prayed so heartily at the Amsterdam Coffee House for the Turks taking Vienna and beating the Christian army. 'The Papists Christians? Ay,' says he, 'the Turks are as good Christians as they. I don't believe there's any Papist in the world's a Christian.'" The result of such highly unpopular remarks was that Titus' "face was washed with a dish of hot coffee, which, being a Turkish liquor, I suppose might be a Turkish ceremony for the introducing a Teckelite-Christian into the Turkish communion" (ibid.).

Graphically, the point is well made in the satiric portrait that surmounts the 1685 broadside, *Bob Ferguson or the Raree-Show of Mamamouchi Mufti* (beginning, "Titus, Teck. Titus, view the figure well" and ending, "Mussulman Jesuit and for him not her"). This shows Oates dressed on his right side in Jesuitical habit, and on his left side in the florid costume of the Turk (reproduced in Lane, *Oates,* facing p. 240).

16. *guiltless souls:* i.e. the victims of the Popish Plot.

18. *their:* As in the preceding line, the pronoun refers to the "English mufties."

23. At Vienna, the Christian forces were in three major groups: the Austrians and Bavarians under Charles Leopold, Duke of Lorraine; the Poles under Sobieski (John III); and the besieged under Count Starhemberg. (see *r"* (V), pp. 348–84). The "Poles and Imperialists" followed up their action with a second victory over the Turks at Barcan in Oct., and Lorraine went on to take Gran, much to the chagrin of Louis XIV, who was using the opportunity to expand his position in the Low Countries (Luttrell, *Brief Relation, 1,* 284, 286; *London Gazette,* Nos. 1869–71 [15–25 Oct. 1683]). News that the "Cossack forces" had engaged the Ottoman armies reached England on 14 March 1684:

Letters from Cracow speak of two great victories obtained by the Cossacks against the Turks and Tartars; in the battle, the Turks etc. lost near 20,000 men, and in the latter near 30,000; and that several places were revolted from the Turks and had put themselves under the protection of the King of Poland. (Luttrell, *Brief Relation, 1,* 302.)

25. In the Turkish defeat at Vienna, "even the ensign of the Vizier's authority was left behind, together with a standard [erroneously] supposed to be the sacred banner of Mohammed" (Edwin Hadder, cited in *r"* (V), p. 357).

And for the rebels' emblem draw me Hell,
Whose Luciferian fates have taught them well
What 'tis to fight their king and to rebel:
And as our God did Satan overthrow
And for rebellion him to Hell did throw,   30
So these our earthly rebels shall
Be fated here and in Hell after fall,
When kings, like terrene gods, do justly reign,
Are by good subjects held their sovereign.
Next draw the monsieurs huffing o'er proud Spain;   35
But draw them, too, upon their turn again.
Paint out their courage more by words than blows;
Blood but the monsieurs and they'll fly their foes.
And when you draw them to the life, pray draw,
Instead of El's, the cunning fox's paw.   40
Draw me the Spaniard rousing, as they would
Revenge their quarrel in the Frenchman's blood.
Draw me great Orange, whose victorious soul
Will cool their heat and monsieurs' rage control.
Next draw me Holland, pox'd with jealous fears: 45
Paint them together falling by the ears.
Distrusting one another, draw them now,
And fearful what to do, or how.

35. To no one's great surprise, Louis XIV took advantage of the involvement of the Empire with the Turkish armies to launch an invasion of the Spanish Netherlands (see Reresby, *Memoirs*, p. 296). Spain was forced to declare war in Dec., but neither Charles nor the Dutch moved, and, though Spanish resistance was more than had been expected, a 20-years truce was signed at Ratisbon in the summer of 1684 which recognized the claims of the Chambers of Reunion and granted Louis Strasbourg and the recently captured Luxembourg (see ibid., pp. 334, 338; Clark, *The Later Stuarts*, p. 108).

38. *blood:* Cause blood to flow from; wet or smear with blood.

40. *El's:* This probably represents the letter "L" (i.e. Louis XIV), given in this way in order to prevent an expansion that would have broken the meter of the line.

43–44. Following Louis XIV's invasion of Dutch territory in 1672, William of Orange was elected Stadtholder. Rejecting all thought of surrender, he blocked the French advance by flooding vast tracts. In the following year, he gained support by treaties with Austria and Spain, and the French withdrew from most Dutch territory early in 1674. William's English marriage (1677), the Treaty of Nijmwegen (1678), and a new defensive coalition with Sweden, Spain, the Empire, and several German principalities (1681) did much to check Louis' expansionism.

45. *Holland:* More correctly, the United Provinces, of which Holland was the most important.

Paint them as hector'd men by monsieur's word;
Paint them as men afraid of monsieur's sword.   50
Next draw old England rising from the dead,
And loyalty that now can show its head.
Paint me great Charles, that all the world doth awe,
Who hath declar'd he govern will by law.
Now, lastly, draw me London, that great city   55
That twice rebell'd in one age, more's the pity;
But draw them loyal now, with their new Charter,
And taking the oaths for to be true hereafter.
Draws all the loyal subjects, joyful hearts;
Draw out their loyalty in all its parts: 60
Whilst other murmuring rebels down are hurl'd,
Confounded here, and damn'd in t'other world.

49–50. The Dutch refused to come to the aid of Spain in 1683 on the grounds that
"the war, though in fact forced by Louis, had been technically declared by Spain"
(Clark, *The Later Stuarts,* p. 108).

51–52. The Spaniards had mistakenly believed that "they had two allies, but Charles
of England had long since departed from his policy of 1680, and without English help
the Dutch were not willing to fight" (ibid.). The writer attempts to put the entire
blame for English inaction on the domestic situation created by the anti-Court party.

56. *twice rebell'd:* i.e. in 1641 and 1682.

57. *new Charter:* In point of fact, no "new Charter" was forthcoming; from 3 Oct.
1683 until 3 Oct. 1688, the Charter was suspended and all appointments were made
by royal commission (see Poems on the Charter; Sharpe, *London and the Kingdom,* 2,
472–504; Beaven, *Aldermen,* 2, 109–15).

61. *rebels:* If there is a specific reference, the writer probably has in mind those who
were found guilty in the Whig Conspiracy of 1683.

Poems on Armstrong's Execution

Thomas Armstrong, who had been knighted for his daring loyalty to the Royalist cause, early attached himself to Monmouth's faction, transferring to the Duke that brash loyalty that made him at once the "bully of [the Whig] cause" and that deeply involved him in the private and public life of the youthful idol. The precise extent to which he influenced the Protestant Duke's actions is difficult to determine, since Monmouth's Whig followers tended to blame Armstrong for their hero's questionable private life, while the Court writers sanctimoniously pointed to him as a rakehell who far outdid all that Tories were reputed to have done. For differing reasons, both parties wished to avoid direct attack on Monmouth; Armstrong, therefore, was the obvious choice for his whipping boy.

Following the discoveries of the Whig Conspiracy, he fled to the Continent, and the Court promptly declared him outlaw and offered a reward for his capture. In early June 1684, he was captured at Leyden and extradited to England on the 11th; by the 14th, the courts ruled for his execution, not allowing a trial since he was considered outside the law. He suffered a traitor's death on 20 June, despite his daughter's petition, his wife's appeal, and his own plea that he had been outside the kingdom at the time of the outlawry and, by statute, had a year in which to return (Howell, *State Trials, 10,* 105–24; Luttrell, *1,* 309–11).

Of the numerous poems on Armstrong at this time, only *Sir Thomas Armstrong's Ghost* (beginning, "Thy groans, dear Armstrong which the world employ"; reprinted in *o,* p. 135 and *r″* (V), p. 488) came out in his defense. These lines may well have been written by John Ayloffe (see George de F. Lord, "Satire and Sedition: The Life and Works of John Ayloffe," *Huntington Library Quarterly, 29* (1966), 255–73, esp. p. 269), but contemporaries tended to ascribe them to another of Armstrong's friends, Robert Ferguson, who was considered the archplotter of the Whig Conspiracy; they were anatomized by L'Estrange (see especially *Observator, 2,* No. 112 [9 Aug. 1684]) and answered in *A Letter to Ferguson* [L 1703] (see also Ferguson,

Ferguson the Plotter, p. 182) and *On the Death of Sir Tho. Armstrong* [O 306] (dated by Luttrell 5 Aug. 1684).

Of the two poems given here, the first (found in *k″*) parodies the "last words" or gallows statements that were so popular at the time (Armstrong's are given in Howell, *10, 122–24*), while the second (found in *h″* and probably published on the day of execution) simply inverts the elegy and its tetrameter epitaph.

Other poems connected with Armstrong's capture and execution are:

> *The Bully Whig; or the Poor Whore's Lamentation for the Apprehending of Sir Thomas Armstrong* [B 5438] (14 June 1684)
> *Sir Thomas Armstrong's Farewell* [S 3891]
> *An Elegy on Sir Thomas Armstrong, who was executed June the 20th 1684* [E 359]

SIR THOMAS ARMSTRONG'S LAST FAREWELL TO THE WORLD: 1684.

He being condemned for high treason, and conspiring the
death of the king and the duke, and subverting the
government of these three kingdoms.

A Song. To the tune "State and Ambition."

[*S 3891A*]

1.

Adieu to the pleasure of murder and whoring,
   Of plotting, conspiring the death of a king:
Confound the temptation of bastard-adoring,
   For which I confess I deserve for to swing.
Poor Monmouth may curse me, 'twas I overrul'd   5
   In all his intrigues by Tony's black spell;
His timorous contrivance I constantly school'd,
   And told him how safe it was then to rebel.

2.

I show'd him the glimpse of a crown and a scepter,
   The strength of the crowd, and applause of the town,   10

3. *bastard:* i.e. Monmouth.

6. *Tony's black spell:* Following the Whigs' loss of the shrieval posts, Shaftesbury's
sense of urgency seems to have become almost overwhelming. He believed, accord-
ing to Lord Howard, that "ten thousand brisk boys" and "1,000 or 1,500 horse" stood
ready to follow him (Howell, *State Trials, 9*, 604, 606); and in early Oct. the conspira-
tors "believed his frenzy was now grown to that height that he would rise immediately
and put his design in execution; so we endeavored to prevent it" (ibid., 607). While
Monmouth seems to have been against the assassination plot but for insurrection,
Armstrong appears to have supported both. (See the testimony and information given
in Howell; also Ferguson, *Ferguson,* passim.)

10. Monmouth's second "Western progress" in Sept. 1682 was a bold move designed
(according to some) to culminate in a popular insurrection (*DNB*). On 16 Sept., Secre-
tary Jenkins issued a warrant for the Duke's arrest (on the grounds of riotous and
unlawful assembly), which was served on 20 Sept. at Stafford. Armstrong rode ahead
to arrange a habeas corpus (Ferguson, *Ferguson,* p. 71) and Monmouth, who arrived
in London on the 23rd, was bailed two days later. The comparatively mild response

Till glory did dazzle his soul in a rapture,
    That all things inferior appear'd but a crown.
Then I was in hopes to be second assistant;
    Therefore to un-king him our party would bring:
But now as the Devil would have it I miss'd on't,   15
    For which I before the damn'd doctor must swing.

3.

The doctor confus'd three parts of the nation:
    He murder'd thirty, I murder'd but two.
With long sword and codpiece, I made it the fashion
    Rogues, whores to advance, and the kingdom subdue.   20
Brave Monmouth I show'd him all ways of debauching,
    And ne'er let him want procurer nor whore.

---

of the city's Whigs (see *The Duke of Monmouth's Case* [D 2509], reprinted in *Somers Tracts, 8,* 403–05), in marked contrast to Shaftesbury's arrest the previous year, reflects the shift in temper during those months.

12. *but:* i.e. except.

14. That Monmouth was being used by politically ambitious men as a wedge to bring in their new commonwealth was a not uncommon opinion of the period (see, e.g., *Absalom and Achitophel,* 220–29, or Howard's testimony in Howell, *State Trials, 9,* 605).

16. *damn'd doctor:* Titus Oates, the chief discoverer of the Popish Plot, unjustly claimed a theological doctorate from the University of Salamanca.

17. *three parts:* Probably used in the sense of "three out of four equal parts"; hence, adverbially, "to the extent of three quarters, well-nigh, almost" (*OED,* though this predates the earliest entry by 27 years).

18. *He murder'd thirty:* i.e. those who were found guilty of the Popish Plot and executed for treason.

I murder'd but two: A True Relation of the Behavior and Execution of Sr. Thomas Armstrong [T 2934] states that:

> He was for several years an officer in His Majesty's troop of Horse Guards, during which time, as a soldier, he was often engaged in quarrels, either upon a mistaken point of honor or the violence of passion which puts a man's life upon the point of his own or [his] enemy's sword, either to prevent a presumptive injury or vindicate the truth of some trifling argument. Upon this account, he was forced often to fly from the severity of the law to the great mercy and clemency of an indulgent prince, whose repeated acts of favor would have obliged any but so ungrateful a wretch. The last of which mercies, more publicly known, was for killing Mr. Scroop [i.e. the brother of Sir Carr Scroope] a very worthy gentleman, in the pit at the Duke's Play-house.

Both *An Elegy on the Never-to-be-Forgotten Sir Thomas Armstrong, Knight* [E 431] and *The Bully Whig* [B 5438] refer to "murders," while *An Elegy on Sir Thomas Armstrong* [E 359] says that he had been "pardon'd thrice to keep him from the laws" (16).

Some aldermen's wives they were proud to approach him;
    I often as Grey have stood pimp at the door.

4.

Nay, many were sure that their souls would be sainted   25
    Had they but one hour his sweet Grace to enjoy;
How oft in my arms they have sighed and panted,
    Until I conveyed 'em to their princely boy.
But now all those pleasures are faded with glory,
    His Grace in disgrace and Tom is condemn'd;   30
Jack Ketch now looks sharp for to shorten my story,
    And leaves me no time to murder or mend.

5.

Yet I must confess, I was oft Monmouth's taster,
    For fear lest some fire-ship might blow up her prince,
Which caused our party to flock in much faster,   35
    All officers from the plot office advance.
Old Tony took care, too, that nothing was wanting,
    In Wapping, the Square, and Aldersgate Street;
I brought in Bess Mackrel, to help out the tapping,
    And Tony swore damn him, there's nothing so sweet.   40

24. *Grey:* Forde, Lord Grey of Werk, was another of Monmouth's intimates; his wife, Mary, was counted among the Duke's mistresses.

34. *fire-ship:* A vessel freighted with combustibles and explosives, and sent adrift among ships, etc. to destroy them; also, one suffering from venereal disease, a prostitute.

38. *Wapping:* The center of Whig strength in London.

the Square: Uncertain, though the reference is probably to Soho Square, laid out in 1681, on the south side of which Monmouth had a mansion.

Aldersgate Street: The location of Thanet House, Shaftesbury's London residence.

39. *Bess Mackrel:* Betty Mackarel began as an orange girl at the Theater Royal, by 1674 was acting minor parts, and at this time was well known for her connection with Armstrong (see J. H. Wilson, *All the King's Ladies: Actresses of the Restoration*, Chicago, University of Chicago Press, 1958, pp. 167–68). In *To Mr. Julian* ("Julian, how comes it that of late we see," X, p. 4), the writer, vilifying some of the town beaux, says:

> And all that can be said of 'em's no more
> Than calling Betty Mackrell a whore.

(32–33)

The marginal gloss reads: "Sir Thomas Armstrong's mistress." Her name alone would have made her synonymous with "whore," since "mackerel" is cant for a bawd or procuress (cf. French *maquerelle*).

tapping: The usual allusion to the silver tap that served to drain Shaftesbury's liver

6.

Sweet Betty, farewell: 'twas for thee I abjured
 My lady and children this fourteen long years;
They always were kind, but I still was obdured,
 Seeking the destruction of king, church, and peers.
Had I Grey and Mellvin now here to condole with,   45
 And their recommendations to th' cabal below,
I might have commissions in Hell to control with,
 But sure I shall find some friends where I go.

---

cyst, found in a similar context in *The Last Will and Testament of Anthony, King of Poland*, 25–30.
 45. *Mellvin:* Unidentified.

An Elegy on the Never-to-be-Forgotten Sir Thomas Armstrong, Knight

Executed for conspiring the Death of His Most Sacred Majesty,
and Royal Brother, June 20, 1684. With some Satirical
Reflections on the whole Faction

[*E 431*]

Stand forth, ye damn'd deluding priests of Baal,
And sound from out each trumpet mouth a call;
Let it be loud and shrill, that ev'ry man
May hear the noise, from Beersheba to Dan;
To summon all the faction, that they may   5
In doleful *hums* and *haws* bewail this day,
And to their just confusion howl and roar,
For the great bully of their cause is now no more.

But now methinks I hear the faction cry,
"*Ohone!* Where's all thy pomp and gallantry?   10
Thy great commands, thy int'rest and thy state?
The many crowds which did upon thee wait
When thou, like Atlas, on thy shoulders bore
That mighty world which we so much adore?"
(That pageant hero, offspring of a whore).   15

Behold, ye stubborn crew, the certain fate
That waits upon the harden'd reprobate.

1. *Baal:* The chief male deity of the Phoenician and Canaanitish nation; hence, a false god. Usually, the term was applied to Roman Catholicism (see *Absalom Senior*, 79 n.).

4. *from Beersheba to Dan:* A common biblical expression. Beersheba was in the extreme south and Dan in the extreme north of Canaan.

6. L'Estrange tells of "three or four Dissenting Academies here about the town where people are taught . . . the very tuning of their *Hums* and *Haws* by rule and method" (*Observator*, No. 110 [11 March 1682]).

10. Ohone!: A Scottish and Irish exclamation of lamentation. The writer probably had the former nation primarily in mind here.

15. Monmouth, the "pageant hero," was the son of Lucy Walter (1630?–58), the mistress to (among others) Charles II.

See the effects of treason's terrible;
In this life infamy, and i'th' next a hell.
While Heav'n attends on kings with special care,   20
The traitor to himself becomes a snare:
Drove out like Cain, to wander through the world,
By his own thoughts into distraction hurl'd,
Despis'd by all, perplex'd with hourly fear,
And by his friends push'd like the hunted deer,   25
Like a mad dog, still hooted as he ran—
A just reward for th' base rebellious man.

How often has kind Heav'n preserv'd the crown,
And tumbl'd the audacious rebel down?
How many warnings have they had of late,   30
How often read their own impending fate,
That still they dare their wicked acts pursue,
And know what Heaven has ordain'd their due?
That man who could not reas'nably desire
To raise his fortunes and his glories higher,   35
Who did enjoy, unto a wish, such store
That all his ancestors scarce heard of more,
Should by his own procuring fall so low
As if he'd studi'd his own overthrow,
Looks like a story yet without a name,   40
And may be styl'd the first *novel* in fame.
So the fam'd angels, turbulent as great,
Who always waited 'bout the mercy-seat,
Desiring to be something yet unknown,
Blunder'd at all, and would have grasp'd the crown,   45
Till Heav'n's great monarch saw they would rebel,
Then dash'd their hopes and damn'd them down to Hell.

And now methinks I see to th' fatal place
A troop of Whigs with faction in each face

22. Armstrong went into self-exile on the Continent following the discoveries of the Whig Conspiracy.

25. *push'd:* Probably used in the sense of "driven in the chase" (*OED,* though this predates the earliest example by 50 years).

30. *they:* i.e. the rebellious spirits.

41. *novel:* The word was stressed on the second syllable at this time.

48. *th' fatal place:* Tyburn, where Armstrong was executed.

And red swoll'n eyes, moving with mournful pace,   50
Pitying the mighty Samson of their cause,
Cursing their fates, and railing at the laws.
The sisters too appear, with sniv'ling cries,
To celebrate their stallion's obsequies.
From th' playhouse and from Change, how they resort,   55
From country, City, nay, there's some from Court;
From the old Countess, wither'd and decay'd,
To a Whig brewer's youthful lovely maid,
Gods! What a troop is here! Sure Hercules
Had found enough so many whores to please.   60

   Repent, ye factious rout; repent and be
Forewarn'd by this bold traitor's destiny.
Go home, ye factious dogs, and mend your lives;
Be loyal, and make honest all your wives.
You keep from conventicles first, and then   65
Keep all your wives from conventicling men.
Leave off your railing 'gainst the King and State,
Your foolish prating, and more foolish hate.
Obey the laws, and bravely act your parts,
And to the church unite in tongues and hearts;   70
Be sudden, too, before it proves too late,
Lest you partake of this bold traitor's fate.

   And if the faction thinks it worth the cost
(To keep this bully's name from being lost)

51. *Samson:* The "faction" would have seen Samson as their divinely ordained champion in the hands of the Philistines; the writer more likely is thinking of the "bully" whose exploits are given in Judges 14–16:3 and who is closely connected (as here at 60) with Hercules, who, in turn, is often identified with Baal (1) (see *A Dictionary of the Bible, 3,* 1120–21 and n.).

52. *railing at the laws:* Lord Chief Justice Jeffreys refused to allow Armstrong a trial on the grounds that he had not rendered himself but been forcibly brought to justice. Armstrong claimed that he still had several months before the year (the time allotted to those who were outlawed while abroad to come in) ran out. (For the arguments in the case, see Howell, *State Trials, 10,* 105–23.)

53. *sisters:* Female members of a sect; frequently used in a derisive or pejorative sense.

55. *th' play-house and . . . Change:* The theaters and the Royal Exchange were frequented by prostitutes.

57. The text gives *C———ss,* which would seem to be Countess, but I have been unable to identify her or the "youthful lovely maid."

60. *Had found enough:* i.e. would have found the task more than enough.

To raise a pillar, to perpetuate   75
His wondrous actions and ignoble fate,
Let 'em about it straight, and when 'tis done,
I'll crown the work with this inscription:

                    Epitaph
"Bold Fame thou li'st! Read here all you
That would this mighty mortal know.   80
First, he was one of low degree,
But rose to an hyperbole;
Famous t' excess in ev'rything
But duty to his God and King;
In oaths as great as any he   85
That ever grac'd the triple tree;
So absolute, when drench'd in wine,
He might have been the god o'th' vine.
His brutal lust was still so strong,
He never spar'd or old or young;   90
In cards and dice he was well known
T' out-cheat the cheaters of the town.

"These were his virtues: if you'd know
His vices too, pray read below.

"Not wholly Whig, nor atheist neither,   95
But something form'd of both together;
Famous in horrid blasphemies,
Practic'd in base adulteries,
In murders vers'd as black and foul
As his degenerated soul;   100
In's maxims too, as great a beast
As those his honest father dress'd;
The faction's bully, sisters' stallion,
Now hang'd and damn'd for his rebellion."

79. In *h"*, this mock epitaph (in traditional tetrameter) is separated from the rest
of the text by a rule.

86. *triple tree:* The gallows.

102. The printed gloss states that "his father was a groom"; the *DNB,* however, says
that Armstrong "was son of an English soldier serving in one of James's Low Country
expeditions, and was born at Nijmwegen, where his father was quartered, about 1624."

A New Litany in the Year 1684

One of the most durable forms for poetry of social complaint was the litany. Each line could hammer out a grievance, and the triple rhythm, echoing the General Supplication in The Book of Common Prayer, was capped by the "Libera nos Domine." Frequently it was followed by a series of positive triplets (concluding "Quaesimus te Domine"), and on occasion it would even be sung to an old ballad such as "Cavallily Man" (Chappell, *Popular Music,* p. 440).

The *New Litany,* which gives voice to Whig helplessness in the face of Charles' judicial vengeance, was probably written about July 1684. It is found only in *k.*

A New Litany in the Year 1684

From Braddon's penniless subornation,
From immoderate fines and defamation,
And from a bar of assassination,
                Libera nos Domine.

From a lawyer that scolds like an oyster wench,   5
From an English body and a mind that is French,

1. Once the municipal offices were firmly in hand, the Court effectively silenced the opposition and revenged itself upon Whig leaders through charges of *scandalum magnatum.* York had successfully prosecuted the former Sheriff Thomas Pilkington on 24 Nov. 1682 and Titus Oates on 18 June 1684; in each case the jury awarded "immoderate fines" to the amount of £100,000.

2. Laurence Braddon (along with Hugh Speke) had been found guilty of suborning witnesses to prove that the Earl of Essex had been murdered in the Tower by his keepers. The government, however, was unable to establish that any money or reward had ever been promised or given to the children whose testimony was the basis for Braddon's action. (See Howell, *State Trials, 9,* 1127–1224 for the trial [7 Feb. 1684] and judgment [21 April 1684].)

3. *bar:* i.e. a court of law. The allusion, at this time, would probably be to Jeffreys' "judicial murder" of Sir Thomas Armstrong, who had been executed for high treason on 20 June 1684. (For further details, see Poems on Armstrong's Execution.)

5. *lawyer:* Very likely Sir Robert Sawyer, the Attorney General, though the description could refer to any one of the Court's impressive battery of lawyers.

6. Probably Charles II.

And from the new Bonner upon the Bench,
　　　　　　　Libera nos Domine.

From the partial preaching that is now in fashion,
From divinity to undo a nation,   10
From wooden shoes and transubstantiation,
　　　　　　　Libera nos Domine.

From the nonsensical cant of a Loyal Addressor,
From the impudent shams of Popish professor,
And from Protestant zeal in a Popish successor,   15
　　　　　　　Libera nos Domine.

From all those Esau's within their nonage,
That would both our laws and liberties forage,
And sell their birthright for a mess of Court pottage,
　　　　　　　Libera nos Domine.   20

7. *new Bonner:* i.e. Sir George Jeffreys, at this time Lord Chief Justice of King's Bench and a zealous supporter of Court policy. Edmund Bonner (1500?–1569), Bishop of London, in his judicial capacity pushed forward with great severity the Marian persecutions.

9. *partial:* Unduly favoring one party or side in a suit or controversy, or one set or class of persons rather than another. The writer would appear to have in mind the strong Court sympathies of the regular Anglican clergy, their support of divine right and passive obedience (see e.g., G. R. Cragg, *From Puritanism to the Age of Reason* [Cambridge University Press, 1950], esp. pp. 164–65), and the contemporary prohibition of nonconformity through the rigorous suppression of conventicles.

11. *wooden shoes:* The *sabots* of the French peasantry symbolized for the English Whigs the tyranny of a Catholic monarchy. The most notable use of the symbol occurred on 28 Oct. 1673, when John Ayloffe placed a wooden shoe on the chair of Speaker Williams in the House of Commons (see *POAS*, Yale, *1*, 284; also *To the Loyal Londoners*, 19 n).

13. *Addressor:* One who supported the Court, as opposed to the Petitioners, who called for a new parliament. Addresses of abhorrence were particularly numerous and fulsome following the discovery of the Association Paper in 1681 and the disclosure of the Whig Conspiracy in 1683. (See *The Protestant Satire*, 154 n.)

15. *successor:* James, Duke of York.

17–19. Genesis 25:29:34. The writer might very well be alluding to Charles II and York in this reference to the famous incident between Esau and Jacob (i.e. James). "Jacob takes advantage of his brother's distress to rob him of that which was dear as life itself to an Eastern patriarch. The birthright not only gave him the leadership of the tribe, both spiritual and temporal, and the possession of the great bulk of the family property, but it carried with it the covenant blessing" (*A Dictionary of the Bible, 1*, 574). By this device, the writer could lay the blame for Charles' acceptance of French subsidies and for his support of the Catholic Duke as successor on the trickery of James.

> From juries that murder do justice call,
> And undoing of men a matter but small,
> And from the Star Chamber in Westminster Hall,
>   Libera nos Domine.

21. Again, the reference is most probably to the proceedings against Armstrong. The essence of these can be found in the pathetic cry of his daughter, Mrs. Matthews, who, when Jeffreys resolutely refused to allow a trial, burst out: "My lord, I hope you will not murder my father. This is murdering a man" (Howell, *State Trials, 10,* 113).

23. *Star Chamber:* "A court, chiefly of criminal jurisdiction, developed in the 15th century from the judicial settings of the King's Council in the Star Chamber at Westminster. . . . The abuse of it under James I and Charles I have made it a proverbial type of an arbitrary and oppressive tribunal. It was abolished by an act of the Long Parliament in 1641" (*OED*). The trial of Armstrong, among others, was held at Westminster Hall.

The days celebrating the discovery of the Gunpowder Plot (5 Nov. 1604) and Elizabeth's accession to the throne (17 Nov. 1558) became occasions for expression of pro-parliament and anti-Catholic sentiments. Not surprisingly, the Whigs virtually appropriated them; and it is perhaps a mark of the changing political temper that the great flurry of pamphlets and broadsides that accompanied the noisy Pope-burning processions of but a few years before had given way, by 1684, to scarcely more than this litany which no printer is known to have published. Here the tone is not so much pro-Whig as anti-Court, pointing out the deceptions and injustices of Charles' reign.

The text has been found only in *l*.

A LITANY FOR THE FIFTH OF NOVEMBER 1684

From all popish treasons, and the Gunpowder Plot,
From a perjur'd French tyrant outdone by a Scot,
And from a progeny whose coats are distinguish'd by blot,
                  Libera nos Domine.

From a popish head o'er a Protestant people,   5
From breaking of leagues either double or triple,

2. *perjur'd French tyrant:* Probably Louis XIV, whose opportunistic attacks on the Low Countries at the time when many European powers were attempting to stop Turkish aggression aroused indignation in England.

Scot: The text has merely S———, but the rhyme clearly demands that the reading be *Scot*. At this time, Whig indignation would have been based on Scottish parliaments' support of Court policy.

3. *a progeny:* Charles II's numerous illegitimate offspring.

5. *a popish head:* i.e. James, Duke of York.

6. *double:* Very likely, the allusion is to the treaty of union and defense with Spain (10 June 1680) which gave hopes of forming the nucleus of an extensive anti-French alliance (see Ogg, *Charles II,* pp. 594, 599). Much to the dismay of many Englishmen, Charles avoided war with France when Louis attacked the Spanish Netherlands by standing on the technicality that it was Spain which, in Dec., had made the formal declaration of war (see Clark, *The Later Stuarts,* pp. 108–09; and headnote to *The Third Part of Advice to the Painter*).

triple: The Triple Alliance of England, Holland, and Sweden (13 Jan. 1668) checked the expansionist policy of Louis XIV and forced him to return the conquests he had

From destroying the Church and adoring the steeple,
Libera nos Domine.

From new corporations with expedient charters,
From gates dress'd up with old Royalists' quarters,   10
From Omer's Plot expiate by Abchurch Lane martyrs,
Libera nos Domine.

From a Justice that statute law overrules,
From juries compounded of knaves and fools,
And from mercenary evidence tools,   15
Libera nos Domine.

From broken Scotch Covenants and sham Declarations,
From Loyola's fatal insinuations,
And from such as again would blow up three nations,
Libera nos Domine.   20

---

made in the Spanish Netherlands (Treaty of Aix-la-Chapelle, 2 May 1668). Louis, however, managed to bribe England and Sweden, and the principal provision of the camouflage Treaty of Dover (Dec. 1670) was that Charles would support Louis in his wars against Holland and Spain. (See Ogg, *Charles II*, pp. 333–35 and 343–50; also Clark, *The Later Stuarts*, pp. 70–73.)

7. The writer would seem to have in mind, on the one hand, the increasing intolerance of religious sects and conventicles and, on the other, the growing Catholic inclination in the Anglican stress on ritual.

9. For Charles' attack on municipal characters, see headnote to the Quo Warranto poems.

10. The former royalist, Sir Thomas Armstrong, suffered a traitor's death on 20 June 1684 for his part in the Whig Conspiracy. After execution, "his quarters were brought back in the sledge to Newgate," and, at the King's orders, "a forequarter is set on Temple Bar, his head on Westminster, another quarter is sent down to the town of Stafford for which he was a parliament man.—Quaere, how many quarters of the popish traitors were set up? and quaere, which of these fanatic plotters were not set up?" (Luttrell, *Brief Relation, 1,* 311–12).

11. *Omer's Plot:* The Popish Plot.

Abchurch Lane: The location of Thomas Shepherd's wine shop, where the Whig conspirators met.

13. *a Justice:* Sir George Jeffreys, as Lord Chief Justice of King's Bench, had been particularly harsh in the rejection of statutes on which Sidney and Armstrong based their defenses.

17. *Scotch Covenants:* On 24 June 1650, Charles II landed in Scotland and subscribed to the Covenant. Though crowned in Scone, he was forced to flee to France after the battle of Worcester (3 Sept. 1651).

sham Declarations: While this reference is vague, the writer may have been thinking of the camouflage Treaty of Dover (Dec. 1670) which omitted Charles' agreement, in the secret treaty (May 1670), to make England a Catholic nation. By 1684, this provision was largely on open secret.

18. *Loyola:* St. Ignatius Loyola, the founder of the Society of Jesus.

True and Joyful News

[*T 2507*]

When the outlawed Sir Thomas Armstrong was taken at Leyden in June 1684, there were found among his papers, letters reputedly written by the London merchant Joseph Hayes concerning a bill of exchange to the amount of 150 guineas (£161 5s. at this time) to be paid Armstrong under his alias of Henry Laurence by Hayes' brother Israel in Amsterdam. Though the Crown's lawyers produced a witness who swore he had seen the bill of exchange, and though they attempted to prove that the letters were in the merchant's handwriting, Hayes swore he had never known Armstrong, or ever lent him money, and, suggesting that the letters were forgeries, he made "remarks on the evidence which were very pertinent, as also he called several persons who testified as to his loyalty, credit, and behavior" (Howell, *State Trials, 10,* 307–20; Luttrell, *1, 321*). The jury, despite Jeffreys' summary from the bench, found the defendant not guilty. Like the Wakeman trial during the Popish Plot, this was the first clear acquittal and indicated that the strong feelings which the Whig Conspiracy had engendered were beginning to decline.

Hayes, who had pleaded not guilty at his arraignment on 3 Nov. 1684, was tried and acquitted on 21 November. Luttrell purchased his copy of the poem 26 Nov. 1684.

TRUE AND JOYFUL NEWS

or

A Word of Comfort to the
Godly Party

A Poem upon Mr. Hayes's Late Deliverance.

What! Hayes acquitted! Armstrong's magazine!
Tory turn'd Ignoramus, without spleen!
The Old Cause's grand Goliah's Pym is come,
Has slipp'd the noose, bilk'd Ketch, escap'd his doom;
The City's hope, the Charter's chief upholder,   5
Dissenters' joy, the Scriptures' best unfolder,
Is safe arriv'd. Proclaim a solemn day;
Let's halleluiahs to his praises pay,
For he's the hero of our State-Plot-Play.
The confin'd Savior of the Nation's gone,   10

Title. *Godly Party:* Derisively, the Whigs, among whom were many sectarians.
  1. *magazine:* A place where goods are laid up; a storehouse, depot. The indictment
charged that Hayes, for Armstrong's "relief and maintenance, did pay the sum of
150 [guineas]" and thus traitorously supplied and comforted an outlaw.
  2. *Tory turn'd Ignoramus:* While the phrase ironically recalls the Whig grand juries
of 1679–81 which had successfully crushed certain indictments, in point of fact Hayes
was acquitted by a regular trial jury.
  spleen: The word appears to be used in the general sense of passion, anger, spite,
or irritability.
  3. The line would seem to mean that Hayes is like Pym, the agent of the grand
Goliath (i.e. Parliament) of the (Good) Old Cause (i.e. the Commonwealth). John Pym
(1584–1643) spearheaded the Commons' attack on Charles I's government, which led
to the Civil War.
  4. *bilk'd:* Cheated.
  Ketch: Jack Ketch, or Catch, the public executioner.
  5. *Charter:* On the contest for the London Charter, see the headnote and notes
to the Quo Warranto poems. I have not come across Hayes' name in this connection,
but there was an Alderman (John?) Hayes, not mentioned in Beaven (*Aldermen*), who
came out strongly against the Court's shrieval and mayoral candidates in 1682 (cf.
Observator, Nos. 181 and 236 [29 July and 6 Nov. 1682]) and may have been related
to James and Joseph Hayes, merchants, who lived in Gracechurch Street in 1677.
(See *A Collection of the Names of the Merchants . . . of London,* 1677 [C 5204]; also,
on James Hayes, see *Observator*, No. 224 [16 Oct. 1682].)
  7. *solemn day:* The allusion is to the solemn days of prayer and thanksgiving
proclaimed by the parliament for their victories over Charles I during the Civil War.
  10. *Savior of the Nation:* Titus Oates had received this title from his supporters
for his discovery of the Popish Plot. For Oates' confinement at this time, see *Tyburn's
Courteous Invitation to Titus Oates;* also, Lane, *Oates,* pp. 296–302.

His crystal plot and mighty train's undone;
Succeeding Hayes shall be his adopted son.
Can Salamanca's brood e'er want a boy
Whilst Hayes 's the acteoniz'd fanatics' joy?
Who brings an order'd Babel on his tongue,   15
Turning sedition to the good old song
Of *All Health to Old Noll,* in each cabal,
Whose empty words the vulgar Gospel call.
The dove (precise dissenters say) 's return'd
(For whom, through fear, the City faction mourn'd)   20
With olive branches, since the floods decrease,
And fatal tidings of the raven's case;
Who boldly wing'd o'er th' surface of the deep,
Till boist'rous billows did imprison'd keep
The wand'ring messenger of the active side,   25

11. *train:* An act or scheme designed to deceive or entrap; a trick, stratagem, artifice, wile.

13. *Salamanca's brood:* Oates was regularly referred to as the doctor, or the Salamanca doctor, though that ancient university had publicly denied ever having conferred any degree upon him. His opponents used the term opprobriously and encouraged the ugly rumors of sodomy and homosexuality that had long been associated with Oates. (See Lane, *Oates,* pp. 30–31, 66, 224–26, 290.)

14. *acteoniz'd:* A nonce-word, not in *OED,* the meaning of which would seem to be "turned into a stag," i.e. as Actaeon had been metamorphosed for offending Diana. The relationship of the word to the charge of sodomy can be seen more closely in *The Sodomite; or the Venison Doctor, with his brace of Aldermen-Stags* [S 4417B], which Luttrell purchased on 13 Sept. 1684 (g").

15. For the confusion of tongues at Babel, see Genesis 11:1–9.

17. All Health to Old Noll: Old Noll was the nickname of Oliver Cromwell. I have been unable to locate the song.

19–28. These lines are based on the story of Noah, especially Genesis 8:1–14.

19. *dove:* The printed gloss identifies this as Hayes.

precise: Overexact, overnice, fastidious; strict or scrupulous in religious observance; in the 16th and 17th centuries, puritanical.

22. *the raven's case:* The printed gloss, filled out by Luttrell, reads: *D*[*r.*] *O*[*ates*]. Prior to releasing the dove, Noah had sent forth a raven, which never returned (Genesis 8:7; see also D. C. Allen, *The Legend of Noah; Renaissance rationalism in art, science, and letters* [Urbana, University of Illinois Press, 1949]). Oates had been arraigned at King's Bench on 13 Nov. for perjury; he was allowed a delay until the following term and "any counsel in England. He then asked liberty to go to them but was told that, being prisoner in execution, that could not be granted" (Muddiman, *The Bloody Assizes,* p. 155, cited in Lane, *Oates,* p. 302). Oates' black canonical habit would have encouraged the parallel to the raven.

25. *wand'ring messenger:* Probably a reference to Oates and the travels he said he had undertaken as the Jesuits' messenger for the Popish Plot (see also 46).

Whose vast fanatic ark does doubtful glide,
Longing for th' 'batement of a blest State tide.
Big with ill hopes, ill-meaning zealot's crew,
Whom no religion pleases but a new,
Can bless, speak fair, with the same breath undo.   30
Geneva's Trojan Horse, ador'd by some,
Fill'd with arm'd men, traitors suppos'd from Rome,
Whose out-swell'd Salamanca sides contain
The numerous offspring of Augusta's train.
Whitehall made room for this outlandish beast;   35
Each did admire, and for his favor press'd,
Till sable clouds of unexpected grief
O'erveil'd the state, not thinking of relief.
The mighty monster's bowels yearn'd again,
And then brought forth a wondrous plot, not men;   40
Which (Hydra-like) when spoil'd, another rose,
Debauch'd the land and its parent's heads expose;
Whose Jove-like brain a fruitful womb suppli'd,
Gave birth to Hayes and great Tom's princely pride.

31. *Geneva's Trojan Horse:* The printed gloss gives "D: T.", presumably D[octor] T[itus Oates] again.

34. *Augusta's:* The printed gloss gives "London."

35. Through the entreaties of the Privy Council, Oates had assigned to him "a pension of £600 per annum, a suite of apartments in Whitehall, and a guard for his precious person." He received this at the end of Sept. 1678; on 31 Aug. 1681 he was asked to quit Whitehall (Lane, *Oates,* pp. 107, 276).

36. *admire:* Wonder, marvel, be surprised.

39. *yearn'd:* Were deeply moved; were moved with compassion. The writer is, of course, parodying the language of sectarian preachers.

40. *plot:* Very likely, the Meal Tub Plot, which Tories said had been engineered by the Whigs.

41. *another:* The Whig Conspiracy.

42. *its parents' heads:* The allusion is to those who were seized for complicity in the Conspiracy. Their heads were, quite literally, exposed to the public following their execution for treason. While punctuation has been added here, the grammar still seems questionable.

43. *Whose:* The antecedent would appear to be the Hydra-like plot.

Jove-like brain: The allusion is to the story of the birth of Minerva, who is said to have sprung forth full grown and fully armored from the brain of Jove when Vulcan split open the god's head with an axe.

suppli'd: Took the place of; served as or furnished a substitute for; made up for the want of; replaced.

44. *Tom:* The printed gloss reads "Armstrong." For other Tory views on him, see the poems on his execution.

When Hayes, their bully-cock, the party's head,   45
And Oates, the Devil's mercury, are dead,
They, self-thought Saints, a dissolution dread.

45. *the party's head:* At this time, the Whigs were virtually leaderless; certainly, there is no indication that Hayes could be considered their head—save by default.

46. *mercury:* A messenger, peddler of news, guide, go-between, dexterous thief; (generically) a news pamphlet.

47. *Saints:* The term applied by certain sects to their members to indicate their election under the New Covenant.

1685

JOHN DRYDEN

Threnodia Augustalis

[D 2383]

With the death of Charles II, the first phase of what has been called the Augustan age came to an end. There can be little doubt that the nation as a whole regretted the monarch's passing: the Court sympathizers because they had lost a brilliant political leader; the anti-Court group because they had now to face the ruler they had so strongly sought to exclude, the ardently Catholic James II.

Naturally, what one saw during these fateful days between February 2 and February 6 when Charles lay dying depended greatly on one's political point of view. For Roger North:

> We walked about like ghosts, generally to and from Whitehall. We met few persons without passion in their eyes, as we also had. We thought of no concerns public or private, but were contented to live and breathe as if we had naught else to do but expect the issue of this grand crisis. (*Autobiography*, p. 178)

For Burnet, there were dark suggestions of poisoning, carried out by James to keep hidden his part in the alleged murder of Essex in the Tower. The most balanced evaluation, and one of the loveliest prose passages of the period, is still that of John Evelyn:

> I am never to forget the unexpressible luxury and profaneness, gaming and all dissolution, and, as it were, total forgetfulness of God (it being Sunday evening), which this day sennight I was witness of: the King, sitting and toying with his concubines, Portsmouth, Cleveland, and Mazarine; a French boy singing love songs in that glorious gallery; whilst about twenty of the great courtiers and other dissolute persons were at basset round a large table, a bank of at least 2000 in gold between them: upon which, two gentlemen that were with me made reflections with astonishment, it being a scene of utmost vanity; and surely as

they thought would never have an end: six days after was all in the dust.

Of the 78 pieces that came out on this occasion (see John Alden, *The Muses Mourn, A Checklist of Verse occasioned by the Death of Charles II*, Charlottesville, Va., [Bibliographical Society, 1958]), Dryden's, though it may have somewhat more depth and polish than the others, nonetheless demonstrates the weakness inherent in this kind of verse. We might find Dr. Johnson unsympathetic when he objects to the poem's "irregularity" of meter, and to the fact that Dryden "in the conclusion seems too much pleased with the prospect of the new reign to have lamented his old master with much sincerity"; we might even find "quaint" Johnson's strictures on the mingling of heathen and Christian gods, or of suspected humor amid the grief, but we cannot avoid his scalpel-like analysis of the principal weakness of the *Threnodia:*

> . . . it has neither tenderness nor dignity; it is neither magnificent nor pathetic. He seems to look around for images which he cannot find, and what he has he distorts by endeavoring to enlarge them. . . . There is, throughout the composition, a desire of splendor without wealth. (*Lives of the English Poets*, ed. G. B. Hill, [3 vols. London, 1905], *1, 438*)

Johnson's criticism is, in the main, quite justifiable, but the *Threnodia* must also be read as a political poem, an elegy on the old regime and a statement on the new. For his framework, Dryden follows the chronology of the fatal illness from the first attack on Monday until the King's death on Friday, interweaving the principal motifs of Charles' reign with which James was connected, until, in the final stanzas, the emphasis subtly shifts to James, suggesting at once a continuity with the past and a new order for the future.

Threnodia Augustalis appeared on or before 9 March, the date on a B.M. copy [1077.h.69(3)] mentioned by Macdonald (p. 39). The poem was first advertised in *The Observator* on 14 March, while "the Second Edition" was advertised 11 days later. Kinsley's edition has supplied the base text, though I have consulted also what Macdonald calls the first and second London editions, and the Dublin edition (Macdonald, Nos. 20a, b, c; but see Kinsley's note, p. 1961). In layout, these early editions show the varied indention of the ode forms only in stanzas 1–3, and 18, and the following text makes use of them; for the intervening stanzas, the indention is based somewhat on that suggested by Scott-Saintsbury and by Noyes.

THRENODIA AUGUSTALIS

A Funeral Pindaric Poem
Sacred to the Happy Memory
of
King Charles II

Fortunata ambo, si quid mea carmina possunt,
Nulla dies unquam memori vos eximet aevo!

I

Thus long my grief has kept me dumb:
  Sure there's a lethargy in mighty woe;
  Tears stand congeal'd and cannot flow,
And the sad soul retires into her inmost room.
Tears, for a stroke foreseen, afford relief;   5
  But, unprovided for a sudden blow,
  Like Niobe we marble grow,
    And petrify with grief.
Our British heav'n was all serene:
  No threat'ning cloud was nigh,   10
  Not the least wrinkle to deform the sky;
  We liv'd as unconcern'd and happily

Title. Samuel Johnson began his incisive critique of the poem by noting that the adjective *Augustalis* is "a term I am afraid neither authorized nor analogical," (*Lives of the English Poets, 1,* 438); however, the S.-S. Introduction (*Dryden, 10,* 61–62) contains a strong defense of the word.

Epigraph. Virgil, *Aeneid,* IX.446–47. Dryden's translation of these lines reads:

O happy friends! for, if my verse can give
Immortal life, your fame shall ever live.
(597–98)

7. *Niobe:* Niobe dared to compare herself, because of her numerous progeny of six sons and six daughters, to Leto, the wife of Zeus, who had only two offspring. To avenge this arrogance, Leto's children, Apollo and Artemis, slew all Niobe's children with their arrows. In her grief Niobe was changed to stone by Zeus in the hills of Sipylus, and the stream which washes the face of the formation makes it appear to be weeping. (See Seyffert, *Dictionary of Classical Antiquities,* p. 418).

As the first age in nature's golden scene;
   Supine amidst our flowing store,
We slept securely, and we dreamt of more: 15
   When suddenly the thunderclap was heard;
   It took us unprepar'd and out of guard,
   Already lost before we fear'd.
Th' amazing news of Charles at once were spread;
   At once the general voice declar'd,   20
    Our gracious prince was dead.
No sickness known before, no slow disease,
To soften grief by just degrees;
But like an hurricane on Indian seas
   The tempest rose;   25
   An unexpected burst of woes,
With scarce a breathing space betwixt,
This now becalm'd, and perishing the next.
As if great Atlas from his height
Should sink beneath his heavenly weight,   30
And with a mighty flaw, the flaming wall
    (As once it shall)

13. The long tradition of the golden age has its primary source in Ovid. Dryden's translation of the classical description was included in his translation of the first book of the *Metamorphoses,* printed in *Examen Poeticum* (1693).

20–21. "As soon as the news of the King's precarious state spread to the town, genuine sorrow was manifest on every face, and, fear inspiring belief, rumors of his death were rife" (Crawfurd, *The Last Days of Charles II,* p. 30, citing Chesterfield's letter to Arran and the dispatches of the Dutch ambassador, Van Citters).

22. *No sickness known before:* i.e. immediately before this fatal illness. In Aug. 1679, however, Charles had been "unexpectedly seized by a succession of ague fits" which were serious enough to have Halifax, Essex, and others recall York from his "exile" in the Low Countries. In mid-1682, there was evidently a mild recurrence (see Ailesbury, *Memoirs, 1,* 70).

28. *now:* A present point or moment of time. Dryden used the word in the same substantive way in *Eleonora* (published in March 1692):

   She vanish'd; all can scarcely say she di'd,
   For but a now did Heaven and earth divide;
   She pass'd serenely with a single breath,
   This moment perfect health, the next was death.
                       (305–08)

29. Atlas, who supported the heavens, gave his burden to Hercules (35) in order to obtain for the hero the apples from the garden of the Hesperides. Kinsley cites Ovid, *Heroides,* "Deinira Herculi," 18: "Herculo supposito sidera fulcit Atlas."

31. *flaw:* Fissure. Kinsley cites *Aeneid,* IX.970 ("Astonish'd at the flaw that shakes the land") and *All for Love,* V:

Should gape immense and, rushing down, o'erwhelm this
        nether ball;
So swift and so surprising was our fear:
Our Atlas fell indeed, but Hercules was near.   35

II

His pious brother, sure the best
  Who ever bore that name,
Was newly risen from his rest
  And, with a fervent flame,
His usual morning vows had just address'd   40
  For his dear sovereign's health;
    And hop'd to have 'em heard,
    In long increase of years,
  In honor, fame, and wealth.
  Guiltless of greatness thus he always pray'd,   45
  Nor knew nor wish'd those vows he made
  On his own head should be repaid.
Soon as th' ill-omen'd rumor reach'd his ear
  (Ill news is wing'd with fate, and flies apace),
  Who can describe th' amazement in his face!   50
Horror in all his pomp was there,
Mute and magnificent without a tear:
And then the hero first was seen to fear.
Half unarray'd he ran to his relief,
So hasty and so artless was his grief;   55
Approaching greatness met him with her charms
  Of pow'r and future state,
  But look'd so ghastly in a brother's fate,

Was it for me to prop
The ruins of a falling majesty?
To place myself beneath the mighty flaw,
Thus to be crush'd and pounded into atoms
By its o'erwhelming weight?

flaming wall: Cf. Lucretius, I.73: "flammantia moenia mundi."

38. Charles' first seizures came when he arose, before eight, on Monday morning. As soon as the King had been bled, Ailesbury, his Gentleman of the Bedchamber, went immediately to St. James' Palace to fetch the Duke of York (Ailesbury, *Memoirs, 1,* 89).

54. *half-unarray'd:* The Duke, says Ailesbury, "came so on the instant that he had one shoe and one slipper" (*Memoirs, 1,* 89).

He shook her from his arms.
Arriv'd within the mournful room, he saw   60
   A wild distraction, void of awe,
And arbitrary grief unbounded by a law.
    God's image, God's anointed, lay
      Without motion, pulse, or breath,
    A senseless lump of sacred clay,   65
      An image, now, of death,
Amidst his sad attendants' groans and cries,
   The lines of that ador'd, forgiving face
   Distorted from their native grace;
An iron slumber sat on his majestic eyes.   70
The pious Duke—Forbear, audacious muse!
No terms thy feeble art can use
Are able to adorn so vast a woe:
The grief of all the rest like subject-grief did show,
   His like a sovereign did transcend;   75
No wife, no brother, such a grief could know,
    Nor any name, but friend.

III

Oh wondrous changes of a fatal scene,
   Still varying to the last!
   Heav'n, though its hard decree was past,   80
Seem'd pointing to a gracious turn again,
   And death's uplifted arm arrested in its haste.

60–62. The scene in the bedchamber is carefully reconstructed from contemporary accounts by Crawfurd, *The Last Days of Charles II*, pp. 26–29.

62. *arbitrary . . . unbounded by law:* Dryden uses ironically these favorite terms of the anti-Court groups that objected to the Stuart doctrine of divine right and the king as "God's anointed" (63).

65. From the violence of the attacks, the copious bleedings, and the nature of the illness (which Crawfurd diagnoses as chronic granular kidney—a form of Bright's disease—with uraemic convulsions [*The Last Days of Charles II*, p. 13]), Charles lay exhausted and often speechless during his last days.

70. Commentators compare the line with *Aeneid*, X:

olli dura quies oculos et ferreus urget
somnus, in aeternam clauduntier lumina noctem.
(745–46)

81. "In the course of [Monday] afternoon, it became known that the illness had taken a favorable turn . . . the Duke was able to announce to the foreign ministers that the King was now out of danger" (Crawfurd, *The Last Days of Charles II*, p. 30).

Heav'n half repented of the doom,
And almost griev'd it had foreseen
  What by foresight it will'd eternally to come.   85
Mercy above did hourly plead
  For her resemblance here below,
And mild Forgiveness intercede
  To stop the coming blow.
New miracles approach'd th' ethereal throne,   90
Such as his wondrous life had oft and lately known,
And urg'd that still they might be shown.
  On earth his pious brother pray'd and vow'd,
    Renouncing greatness at so dear a rate,
  Himself defending what he could,   95
    From all the glories of his future fate.
With him th' innumerable crowd
  Of armed prayers
Knock'd at the gates of heav'n, and knock'd aloud;
  The first well-meaning, rude petitioners.   100
All for his life assail'd the throne,
All would have brib'd the skies by off'ring up their own.
So great a throng not heav'n itself could bar;
'Twas almost borne by force, as in the giants' war.
The prayers, at least, for his reprieve were heard;   105
His death, like Hezekiah's, was deferr'd:

86–87. Kinsley points out Dryden's previous delineations of Charles as the epitome
of mercy in *Astraea Redux* (266–69) and *Absalom and Achitophel* (326).
  95. *defending:* Prohibiting, forbidding.
  100. The source of the metaphor constitutes, as Scott noted, "a very ill timed
sarcasm on those [i.e. Whigs] who petitioned Charles to call his parliament" and in
this sense the line must mean, as Christie remarks, "that these were the first *rude
petitioners* who were *well-meaning*" (S.-S., *Dryden, 10,* 66). Within the context of the
poem, however, there would seem to be the additional interpretation that the first
prayers, offered during the initial shock and horror at the King's illness, were well
intentioned but possibly too crudely mandatory.
  104. *the giants' war:* The gigantomachia, when the Titans unsuccessfully assaulted
Heaven. The account of the struggle given by Ovid in the *Metamorphoses* was trans-
lated by Dryden and appeared in *Examen Poeticum* (1693). Citing 97–106, Dr. Johnson
(in his essay on Dryden in *The Lives of the English Poets*) felt that 100 showed
Dryden "a little inclined to merriment," while 104 indicated that he was not "serious
enough to keep heathen fables out of his religion."
  106–09. Kinsley's note reads: "The 'five degrees' are the five days of the King's
sickness. Hezekiah, 'sick unto death,' reminded God 'how I have walked before thee in

Against the sun the shadow went;
Five days, those five degrees, were lent
To form our patience and prepare th' event.
The second causes took the swift command: 110
The med'cinal head, the ready hand,
All eager to perform their part;
All but eternal doom was conquer'd by their art.
Once more the fleeting soul came back
    T' inspire the mortal frame;   115
And in the body took a doubtful stand,
    Doubtful and hov'ring like expiring flame
That mounts and falls by turns, and trembles o'er the brand.

IV

The joyful short-liv'd news soon spread around,
Took the same train, the same impetuous bound: 120
    The drooping town in smiles again was dress'd,
    Gladness in every face express'd,
    Their eyes before their tongues confess'd.
Men met each other with erected look,
The steps were higher that they took,   125
    Friends to congratulate their friends made haste,

---

truth and with perfect heart' and asked for a respite; and as a sign, God 'brought the shadow ten degrees backward, by which it had gone down in the dial of Ahaz' (II Kings 20:1–11)."

111. Dryden may have had in mind Dr. Edmund King specifically. The physician happened to be in attendance on the fateful Monday morning, and it was he who insisted that if Charles were not bled immediately, he would die. King, who had been a surgeon and happened to have his lancet with him, would not proceed without permission, since it was a capital offense to bleed a monarch without the approval of his ministers. Ailesbury evidently took the responsibility for the decision, and the physician thereupon drew 16 ounces of blood. Dr. King's action was approved by the body of physicians who were soon in attendance (indeed, by noon of the next day, an additional 18 ounces had been drawn), and the Privy Council subsequently "voted a sum of £1,000 to King, which was never paid, James finding a knighthood a more convenient method of discharging the debt" (Crawfurd, *The Last Days of Charles II*, pp. 27–28; King's portrait faces p. 26).

112. *All:* Of the 15 physicians who were consulted, at least six were in constant attendance—"all men of eminence; the presence of the least of whom, Le Sage would have said, was fully adequate to account for the subsequent catastrophe" (S.-S., *Dryden, 10,* 67).

119–27. On Monday night, "the King was seemingly recovered by that bleeding. . . . He continued so well on Tuesday . . . that the messengers were sent into every

And long-inveterate foes saluted as they pass'd.
Above the rest heroic James appear'd
Exalted more, because he more had fear'd;
His manly heart, whose noble pride   130
    Was still above
  Dissembled hate or varnish'd love,
Its more than common transport could not hide;
But like an eagre rode in triumph o'er the tide.
  Thus, in alternate course,   135
    The tyrant passions, hope and fear,
    Did in extremes appear,
  And flash'd upon the soul with equal force.
Thus, at half ebb, a rolling sea
  Returns, and wins upon the shore;   140
  The wat'ry herd, affrighted at the roar,
Rest on their fins a while, and stay,
Then backward take their wond'ring way.
The prophet wonders more than they
  At prodigies but rarely seen before,   145
And cries, *A king must fall, or kingdoms change their sway.*
  Such were our counter-tides at land, and so
  Presaging of the fatal blow,
  In their prodigious ebb and flow.
The royal soul that, like the laboring moon,   150
  By charms of art was hurried down,

---

county to carry the happy news" (Ailesbury, *Memoirs, 1,* 89). The optimism con-
tinued through Wednesday afternoon, when the physicians formally met with the
Privy Council at 5:00 P.M. "The *London Gazette* of Thursday morning, which had
gone to press after the formal meeting . . . and before the illness assumed its gravest
aspect" announced that "the physicians . . . conceive His Majesty to be in a condi-
tion of safety and that he will in a few days be freed from his distemper" (Crawfurd,
The Last Days of Charles II, pp. 33–34).

134. *eagre:* Dryden's note reads: "An eagre is a tide swelling above another tide,
which I have myself observed on the river Trent." Scott cites descriptions from
William of Malmesbury (*De Gestis Pontificum,* IV) and Drayton (*Poly-Olbion,* Song
VII), while Kinsley quotes from Browne (*Pseudodoxia Epidemica,* VII.13).

150–51. Kinsley's note reads: " 'The vain heathen had an opinion that the moon,
when she eclipsed, did labor as if in an agony, and suffer a kind of death by the
incantations of witches. . . . Besides it was generally believed that by such means
the moon might be brought down from heaven, and so, at such times, they feared
the loss of that heavenly light' (Holyday, *Juvenalis . . . Translated,* 1673, illustrating
Sat. VI, 443)."

Forc'd with regret to leave her native sphere,
Came but a while on liking here
   (Soon weary of the painful strife)
   And made but faint essays of life: 155
      An evening light
      Soon shut in night;
A strong distemper, and a weak relief;
Short intervals of joy, and long returns of grief.

V

The sons of art all med'cines tri'd,   160
And every noble remedy appli'd;
   With emulation each essay'd
   His utmost skill; nay, more, they pray'd:
   Never was losing game with better conduct play'd.
Death never won a stake with greater toil,   165
Nor e'er was fate so near a foil;
   But, like a fortress on a rock,
   Th' impregnable disease their vain attempts did mock.
They min'd it near, they batter'd from afar
With all the cannon of the med'cinal war;   170
No gentle means could be essay'd;
'Twas beyond parley when the siege was laid.
   Th' extremest ways they first ordain,
   Prescribing such intolerable pain
   As none but Caesar could sustain.   175
   Undaunted Caesar underwent

153. *on liking:* Scott's note reads, "To engage upon liking (an image rather too familiar for the occasion) is to take a temporary trial of a service, or business, with licence to quit it at pleasure."

160–61. Sir Charles Scarburgh, the King's physician, kept a detailed medical account of Charles' last illness, which has been printed and translated in Crawfurd (*The Last Days of Charles II*, pp. 56–80). The treatment included blistering agents applied to Charles' shaved head, and blistering drugs given internally; vast arrays of spices, barks, and salts, as well as "spirit of [i.e. powdered] human skull 40 drops," and "oriental bezoar stone, 2 scruples"; and it concluded with what Scarburgh ominously describes as "that most active cordial," composed of one drachm of "Raleigh's Antidote" (an extract of "an incredible number of herbs, parts of animals, and animal products, such as pearls, coral, and bezoars") in five tablespoons of pearl julip, mixed with 20 drops of succinate spirit of sal ammoniac.

Scarburgh's portrait, and a brief sketch of his very full life, may be found in Crawfurd, *The Last Days of Charles II*, pp. 52–56.

The malice of their art, nor bent
Beneath whate'er their pious rigor could invent.
In five such days he suffer'd more
Than any suffer'd in his reign before;   180
  More, infinitely more, than he
  Against the worst of rebels could decree,
  A traitor, or twice-pardon'd enemy.
Now art was tir'd without success;
No racks could make the stubborn malady confess.   185
  The vain insurancers of life,
And he who most perform'd and promis'd less,
  Even Short himself, forsook th' unequal strife.
Death and despair was in their looks;
No longer they consult their memories or books;   190
Like helpless friends who view from shore
The laboring ship and hear the tempest roar,
  So stood they with their arms across;
Not to assist, but to deplore
  Th' inevitable loss.

182–83. *rebels . . . traitor . . . enemy:* Dryden may have been indicating, respectively, those who had supported the Commonwealth, a leader of the Whig conspiracy (perhaps Russell or Sidney), and, finally, Sir Thomas Armstrong (see *Sir Thomas Armstrong's Last Farewell*, 18 n.).

188. *Short:* Dr. Thomas Short (1635–85), a Roman Catholic and strongly Tory physician, replaced Dr. Richard Lower as one of the King's physicians when Lower supported the Whigs at the time of the Popish Plot. Short was extremely successful (cf. Wood, *Athenae Oxoniensis*, 2, 858) and much admired (as literary compliments from Mulgrave, Otway, and Duke would indicate). Burnet (*History*, 2, 461–66) made much of a remark ascribed to Short to the effect that "the King had not fair play for his life." This gave strength and embellishment to the rumor that Charles had been poisoned (see also Buckingham, *Works*, "Character of Charles II," 2, 65) and Short's death this same year added further dark hints of poisoning and foul play. (See also the notes in S.-S., *Dryden, 10,* 70–73, and Kinsley, *Dryden,* p. 1962.)

Kinsley's note reads: "In the 1701 folio edition of Dryden's poems, Tonson substituted 'Short and Hobbs' for 'Short himself,' and 'he' in l. 187 is corrected to 'they' in the errata. Hobbs was Dryden's physician at least in the 1690s (see Postscript to the *Aeneis*, 111); but he does not appear in the accounts of Charles II's death, and the alteration is probably Tonson's compliment." Thomas Hobbs (b. 1663) appears as Guiacum (VI. 163) in Garth's *Dispensary* (1699).

189. On Thursday, at about 4:00 P.M., "there was a fresh access of fever with a recurrence of convulsions, more violent than before: so much so that the doctors were plunged into despair" (Crawfurd, *The Last Days of Charles II*, p. 34, citing the dispatches of the Dutch ambassador, Van Citters).

VI

Death was denounc'd; that frightful sound
  Which even the best can hardly bear.
  He took the summons void of fear,
And, unconcern'dly, cast his eye around,
    As if to find and dare the grisly challenger.   200
    What death could do, he lately tri'd,
    When in four days he more than di'd.
  The same assurance all his words did grace;
  The same majestic mildness held its place;
  Nor lost the monarch in his dying face.   205
Intrepid, pious, merciful, and brave,
He look'd as when he conquer'd and forgave.

VII

As if some angel had been sent
To lengthen out his government,
And to foretell as many years again   210
As he had number'd in his happy reign;
  So cheerfully he took the doom
Of his departing breath,
Nor shrunk nor stepp'd aside for death;
    But, with unalter'd pace, kept on,   215
  Providing for events to come
  When he resign'd the throne.
Still he maintain'd his kingly state,
And grew familiar with his fate.
Kind, good, and gracious to the last,   220
On all he lov'd before, his dying beams he cast.
Oh, truly good, and truly great,
For glorious as he rose, benignly so he set!
  All that on earth he held most dear,
  He recommended to his care   225

---

196. *denounc'd:* "Denounce" in the sense of give formal, authoritative, or official information of; announce or declare an event about to take place, usually of a calamitous nature, as war or death.

225. *his:* i.e. James'. Crawfurd states: "Charles twice recommended the Duchess of Portsmouth to James, and entreated him not to let poor Nell Gwynne starve. Then he commended his natural children to James. The Dukes of Grafton, Southampton, North-

To whom both heav'n
    The right had giv'n,
And his own love bequeath'd supreme command.
He took and press'd that ever-loyal hand
    Which could in peace secure his reign,   230
    Which could in wars his pow'r maintain;
    That hand on which no plighted vows were ever vain.
Well for so great a trust, he chose
    A prince who never disobey'd:
    Not when the most severe commands were laid;   235
    Nor want, nor exile, with his duty weigh'd;
A prince on whom, if heav'n its eyes could close,
    The welfare of the world it safely might repose.

VIII

That king who liv'd to God's own heart
    Yet less serenely died than he.   240
Charles left behind no harsh decree
For schoolmen with laborious art
    To salve from cruelty.
Those for whom love could no excuses frame,
He graciously forgot to name.   245
    Thus far my muse, though rudely, has design'd
    Some faint resemblance of his godlike mind;
    But neither pen nor pencil can express

umberland, St. Albans, and Richmond were all there. . . . Charles blessed his chil-
dren one by one, drawing them down to him on the bed" (*The Last Days of Charles II*,
p. 45, citing Barillon, Van Citters, and Chesterfield; another version of the scene is
given by Burnet, *History*, 2, 460–61).

228. *his:* i.e. Charles'

236. *exile:* Following the Restoration, James underwent two major "exiles" because
of the domestic political situation: the first, to the Low Countries in 1679; and the
second, to Scotland as Lord High Commissioner from 1679 to March 1682. For Dryden's
other lines in praise of York's devotion, see Kinsley's note to *Absalom and Achitophel*,
353, and the references therein.

239–40. "That king" who died "less serenely" than Charles was David, who asked
Solomon to take vengeance on Joab and Shimei (I Kings 2:5–6, 8–9). Cf. the Davidic
portrayal of Charles in *Absalom and Achitophel* (7) where he is "Israel's monarch,
after Heaven's own heart."

244–45. The reference is to James, Duke of Monmouth, who at this time was in
exile in Holland.

248. *pencil:* An artist's paintbrush, especially a small and fine one.

The parting brothers' tenderness—
Though that's a term too mean and low   250
(The blest above a kinder word may know).
    But what they did, and what they said,
        The monarch who triumphant went,
    The militant who stay'd,
        Like painters, when their height'ning arts are spent,   255
    I cast into a shade.
        That all-forgiving King,
            The type of him above,
        That inexhausted spring
            Of clemency and love,   260
Himself to his next self accus'd,
And ask'd that pardon which he ne'er refus'd:
For faults not his, for guilt and crimes
Of godless men and of rebellious times,
For an hard exile, kindly meant,   265
When his ungrateful country sent
Their best Camillus into banishment,
And forc'd their sov'reign's act—they could not his consent.
Oh, how much rather had that injur'd chief
    Repeated all his sufferings past   270
    Than hear a pardon begg'd at last,
Which giv'n could give the dying no relief!
He bent, he sunk beneath his grief;
His dauntless heart would fain have held
From weeping, but his eyes rebell'd.   275
    Perhaps the godlike hero, in his breast,

252–56. Dryden tactfully avoids discussing the events of the three-quarters of an hour during which James arranged to have Father Huddleston receive the King into the Roman Catholic Church and perform the last rites (see Crawfurd, *The Last Days of Charles II*, pp. 37–43).

267. *their best Camillus:* Kinsley's note reads: "M. Furius Camillus, a Roman general and 'a most devout person in point of religion,' went into exile rather than submit to an unjust fine. The parallel with the Duke of York is a close one. Camillus was 'the greatest man both in war and peace before he was banished; more famous in his banishment; . . . being restored to his country, he restored the country to itself at the same time. For which reason he was afterward . . . looked upon as worthy to be styled the second founder of the city, after Romulus' (Livy, *The Roman History . . . done into English* [1686], pp. 142, 149, 175)."

269. *that injur'd chief:* i.e. James.

Disdain'd, or was asham'd, to show
So weak, so womanish a woe
Which yet the brother and the friend so plenteously con-
    fess'd.

IX

Amidst that silent show'r, the royal mind   280
    An easy passage found,
And left its sacred earth behind;
    Nor murm'ring groan express'd, nor laboring sound,
Nor any least tumultuous breath:
Calm was his life, and quiet was his death.   285
    Soft as those gentle whispers were
    In which th' Almighty did appear,
    By the still voice, the prophet knew him there.
That peace which made thy prosperous reign to shine,
That peace thou leav'st to thy imperial line,   290
That peace, Oh, happy shade, be ever thine!

X

For all those joys thy restoration brought,
For all the miracles it wrought,
    For all the healing balm thy mercy pour'd
Into the nation's bleeding wound,   295
And care that after kept it sound;
    For numerous blessings yearly show'r'd,
And property with plenty crown'd;
For freedom, still maintain'd alive,
Freedom, which in no other land will thrive,   300
Freedom, an English subject's sole prerogative,

288. "And after the earthquake, a fire; but the Lord was not in the fire: and after
the fire, a still small voice. And it was so when Elijah heard it, that he wrapped his
face in his mantle . . ." (I Kings 19:12–13).

294–95. Scott's note reads: "King Charles's first parliament, from passing the Act of
Indemnity and taking other measures to drown all angry recollection of the Civil
Wars, was called the Healing Parliament."

298–303. It is interesting to note that Dryden has here taken up three of the four
issues summarized in the Whigs' slogans "Liberty and Property" and "No Popery, No
Slavery." Not surprisingly, he avoids the matter of "popery," substituting an appeal for
grateful loyalty.

Without whose charms ev'n peace would be
    But a dull quiet slavery:
  For these, and more, accept our pious praise;
    'Tis all the subsidy   305
  The present age can raise;
The rest is charg'd on late posterity.
    Posterity is charg'd the more,
    Because the large abounding store
To them and to their heirs is still entail'd by thee.   310
    Succession of a long descent,
Which chastely in the channels ran
And from our demi-gods began,
    Equal almost to time in its extent,
Through hazards numberless and great   315
    Thou hast deriv'd this mighty blessing down
    And fix'd the fairest gem that decks th' imperial crown.
Not faction, when it shook thy regal seat,
Not senates, insolently loud
(Those echoes of a thoughtless crowd),
Not foreign or domestic treachery,
Could warp thy soul to their unjust decree.
So much thy foes thy manly mind mistook,
Who judg'd it by the mildness of thy look;
Like a well-temper'd sword, it bent at will,   325
But kept the native toughness of the steel.

XI

Be true, O Clio, to thy hero's name!
  But draw him strictly so

305. *subsidy:* The word—considering Charles' contentions with his later parliaments for financial aid—seems somewhat infelicitous in the present poem.

307. *late:* Distant. This use of the adjective is not found in *OED*, but see the adverbial use in Dryden's translation of Virgil's *Georgics* (1697) III, 708.

311–17. For Dryden's political argument, see *Absalom and Achitophel*, 759–810, and Kinsley's note.

316. *deriv'd:* Conveyed from one to another, as by transmission, dissent, etc.; handed on.

317. *fix'd the fairest gem:* i.e. established the succession of James.

322. *their unjust decree:* The Whigs' Exclusion Bills.

325–26. These lines epitomize Charles' policy not only in the specific instances of the Popish Plot and the Exclusion Bills (318–322) but also in his reign as a whole (see, e.g., *EB*, 5, 915, sub Charles II).

327. *Clio:* The Muse of epic poetry and history.

That all who view, the piece may know;
He needs no trappings of fictitious fame.   330
  The load's too weighty: thou may'st choose
  Some parts of praise, and some refuse:
Write, that his annals may be thought more lavish than the
        Muse.
  In scanty truth thou hast confin'd
  The virtues of a royal mind,   335
Forgiving, bounteous, humble, just, and kind.
His conversation, wit, and parts,
His knowledge in the noblest, useful arts,
  Were such, dead authors could not give,
  But habitudes of those who live,   340
Who, lighting him, did greater lights receive.
He drain'd from all, and all they knew;
His apprehension quick, his judgment true;
That the most learn'd, with shame, confess
His knowledge more, his reading only less.   345

XII

Amidst the peaceful triumphs of his reign,
  What wonder if the kindly beams he shed
Reviv'd the drooping arts again,
    If Science rais'd her head,
  And soft Humanity, that from rebellion fled!   350
Our isle, indeed, too fruitful was before,
    But all uncultivated lay
  Out of the solar walk and heav'n's high way;
With rank Geneva weeds run o'er,
And cockle, at the best, amidst the corn it bore.   355

340. *But habitudes of:* The phrase would seem to mean "rather mental or intellec-
tual characteristics derived from." Dryden is pointing to the King's interest in contem-
porary experimental science, architecture, and the like.

353. Cf. *Annus Mirabilis* 639 ("Beyond the year and out of heaven's high way"),
and *Britannia Rediviva,* 306 ("Beyond the circling years, and circling year"); these de-
rive (as Scott points out) from Virgil's, "Extra anni, solisque vias."

354–55. *Geneva weeds . . . and cockle:* The same image is found in *Absalom and
Achitophel,* 194–95 ("or had the rankness of the soil been freed/ From cockle that
oppress'd the royal seed"). Kinsley cites, in this connection, Shakespeare, *Coriolanus,*
III.i.67–70; but the image was often used in connection with the Lollard movement
of the fourteenth century (see Chaucer's *Epilogue to the Man of Law's Tale* [B. 1176–
83] and Robinson's note).

The royal husbandman appear'd,
   And plough'd, and sow'd, and till'd;
The thorns he rooted out, the rubbish clear'd,
   And bless'd th' obedient field.
When straight a double harvest rose,   360
Such as the swarthy Indian mows,
Or happier climates near the line,
Or Paradise manur'd and dress'd by hands divine.

XIII

As when the new-born Phoenix takes his way,
His rich paternal regions to survey,   365
Of airy choristers, a numerous train
Attend his wondrous progress o'er the plain;
   So, rising from his father's urn,
   So glorious did our Charles return.
Th' officious muses came along,   370
A gay, harmonious choir, like angels ever young:
The muse that mourns him now, his happy triumph sung.
Even *they* could thrive in his auspicious reign;
   And such a plenteous crop they bore
Of purest and well-winnow'd grain,   375
   As Britain never knew before.
Though little was their hire, and light their gain,
   Yet somewhat to their share he threw;
   Fed from his hand, they sung and flew,
Like birds of paradise that liv'd on morning dew.   380
Oh, never let their lays his name forget!
The pension of a prince's praise is great.
   Live then, thou great encourager of arts:
   Live ever in our thankful hearts;
   Live bless'd above, almost invok'd below;   385
   Live and receive this pious vow,
Our patron once, our guardian angel now.

356–60. Dryden would appear to be referring to the post-Restoration religious laws which were meant to enforce uniformity.

364–71. Cf. *Annus Mirabilis,* "Verses to Her Highness the Duchess," 52–57.

373. Dryden is alluding to his own *Astraea Redux. A Poem on the Happy Restoration and Return of His Sacred Majesty Charles the Second.*

Thou Fabius of a sinking State,
Who didst by wise delays divert our fate,
When faction like a tempest rose 390
  In death's most hideous form,
Then art to rage thou didst oppose,
  To weather out the storm.
Not quitting thy supreme command,
Thou held'st the rudder with a steady hand, 395
Till safely on the shore the bark did land:
  The bark that all our blessings brought,
Charg'd with thyself and James, a doubly royal fraught.

XIV

Oh, frail estate of human things,
  And slippery hopes below! 400
Now to our cost your emptiness we know,
(For 'tis a lesson dearly bought)
Assurance here is never to be sought.
  The best, and best belov'd of kings,
  And best deserving to be so, 405
When scarce he had escap'd the fatal blow
  Of faction and conspiracy,
Death did his promis'd hopes destroy:
He toil'd, he gain'd, but liv'd not to enjoy.
  What mists of Providence are these 410
  Through which we cannot see!
  So saints, by supernatural pow'r set free,
  Are left at last in martyrdom to die;
  Such is the end of oft-repeated miracles.

388–90. Kinsley aptly cites Livy, *The Roman History . . . done into English* (1686), p. 559, where it is pointed out that Fabius Maximus "outdid his father's, and equalized, his grandfather's, actions. . . . Yet this same Fabius was reckoned cautious rather than eager; and as you may doubt whether he were in his nature more given to make delays, or that such delays were, in the war then in hand, very convenient to be made, so nothing is more certain than this, that 'one man by his delays restored our commonwealth,' as Ennius has it."

Even P. C. Yorke (*EB* 5, 915) admits with somewhat grudging approval that Charles' policy, in the face of the Popish Plot frenzy, "was to take advantage of the violence of the faction, to 'give them line enough,' to use his own words, to encourage it rather than repress it, with the expectation of procuring finally a strong royalist reaction."

407. *faction and conspiracy:* The Popish Plot and the Whig Conspiracy.

Forgive me, Heav'n, that impious thought;   415
'Twas grief for Charles, to madness wrought,
    That question'd thy supreme decree!
Thou didst his gracious reign prolong,
Even in thy saints' and angels' wrong,
    His fellow citizens of immortality.   420
For twelve long years of exile borne,
Twice twelve we number'd since his blest return;
    So strictly wert thou just to pay,
    Even to the driblet of a day.
Yet still we murmur, and complain,   425
The quails and manna should no longer rain;
    These miracles 'twas needless to renew;
The chosen flock has now the promis'd land in view.

XV

A warlike prince ascends the regal state,
A prince long exercis'd by fate: 430
Long may he keep, though he obtains it late.
Heroes in heaven's peculiar mold are cast;
They and their poets are not form'd in haste;
Man was the first in God's design, and Man was made the last.
    False heroes, made by flattery so,   435
Heav'n can strike out, like sparkles, at a blow;
But ere a prince is to perfection brought,
He costs Omnipotence a second thought.
        With toil and sweat,
        With hard'ning cold and forming heat,   440
    The Cyclops did their strokes repeat
Before th' impenetrable shield was wrought.
It looks as if the Maker would not own

421–23. Dryden's "twelve" and "twice twelve" are approximately correct, but, unless he had some special system of reckoning, 423 would seem to be more a matter of poetic license than mathematical exactitude.

425. Cf. Exodus 16:12–15.

430. Cf. Virgil, *Aeneid*, III.182: "nate, Ilacis exercite fatis."

435–38. A similar metaphor distnguishes brute from human creation in *The Hind and the Panther*, I.251–62.

441–42. The Cyclops acted as assistants to the Greek God Hephaestos and helped forge the miraculous shield and arms which Achilles used for his combat against Hector (*Iliad*, XVIII. 468ff.).

The noble work for his
Before 'twas tri'd and found a masterpiece. 445

XVI

View then a monarch ripen'd for a throne.
    Alcides thus his race began;
    O'er infancy he swiftly ran;
The future god at first was more than man:
    Dangers and toils and Juno's hate 450
    Even o'er his cradle lay in wait;
    And there he grappl'd first with fate:
In his young hands the hissing snakes he press'd;
So early was the deity confess'd.
    Thus, by degrees, he rose to Jove's imperial seat; 455
    Thus difficulties prove a soul *legitimately* great.
Like his, our hero's infancy was tri'd:
Betimes the Furies did their snakes provide,
And to his infant arms oppose
His father's rebels and his brother's foes: 460
The more oppress'd, the higher still he rose.
    Those were the preludes of his fate
That form'd his manhood, to subdue
The hydra of the many-headed hissing crew.

XVII

As after Numa's peaceful reign, 465
    The martial Ancus did the scepter wield,
Furbish'd the rusty sword again,
    Resum'd the long-forgotten shield
    And led the Latins to the dusty field;
So James the drowsy *genius* wakes 470

447. *Alcides:* The name of Hercules prior to his service under Eurystheus. During his infancy his enemy Juno had sent two serpents to destroy him, but the future hero strangled them with his bare hands.

464. The second of Hercules' twelve labors was the slaying of the Lernean hydra.

465. As Saintsbury commented, "Dryden's Roman history must have got a bit rusty." Ancus Martius, as Kinsley has noted, "was the fourth king of Rome and Numa's *grandson*, and led the Romans *against* the Latins. Like James II, he 'thought that the leisure and ease which Numa had, himself should hardly enjoy without some inconvenience: that his patience was tried, and being tried contemned' (Livy, *The Roman History*, 1686, p. 20)."

Of Britain long entranc'd in charms,
    Restive and slumb'ring on its arms:
'Tis rous'd and, with a new-strung nerve, the spear already
        shakes.
No neighing of the warrior steeds,
No drum, or louder trumpet, needs   475
T' inspire the coward, warm the cold;
His voice, his sole appearance, makes 'em bold.
    Gaul and Batavia dread th' impending blow;
    Too well the vigor of that arm they know;
They lick the dust, and crouch beneath their fatal foe.   480
Long may they fear this awful prince,
    And not provoke his ling'ring sword;
Peace is their only sure defense,
    Their best security his word.
In all the changes of his doubtful state,   485
His truth, like Heav'n's, was kept inviolate;
For him to promise is to make it fate.
    His valor can triumph o'er land and main;
    With broken oaths his fame he will not stain;
    With conquest basely bought, and with inglorious gain.   490

XVIII

For once, O Heav'n, unfold thy adamantine book,
And let his wond'ring senate see,
If not thy firm, immutable decree,
At least the second page of strong contingency,
Such as consists with wills originally free.   495
    Let them with glad amazement look
On what their happiness may be;
    Let them not still be obstinately blind,
    Still to divert the good thou hast design'd,
Or with malignant penury,   500
    To starve the royal virtues of his mind.
    Faith is a Christian's and a subject's test:

478. *Gaul and Batavia:* France and Holland.
482. *ling'ring:* Slow in coming into action.
502. Dryden would seem to be alluding to the conflicts that arose around York and
the Test Act.

Oh, give them to believe, and they are surely blest!
    They do; and, with a distant view, I see
    Th' amended vows of English loyalty.   505
  And, all beyond that object, there appears
The long retinue of a prosperous reign,
  A series of successful years,
In orderly array, a martial, manly train.
  Behold ev'n the remoter shores,   510
A conquering navy proudly spread;
  The British cannon formidably roars,
While, starting from his oozy bed,
Th' asserted Ocean rears his reverend head
To view and recognize his ancient lord again;   515
  And, with a willing hand, restores
    The *fasces* of the main.

Textual Notes

SIGLA

and

A Supplement to the Muses Farewel to Popery & Slavery, . . . 1690.

Case 191 (2) (c). 1690.

e. *A Collection of Poems on Affairs of State;* . . . 1689.

Case 188 (1) (a). 1689.

j. *A Second Collection of . . . Poems, Satyrs, Songs, &c. Against Popery and Tyranny*, . . . 1689.

Case 189 (2). 1689.

k. *A Third Collection of . . . Poems, Satyrs, Songs, &c. Against Popery and Tyranny*, . . . 1689.

Case 189 (3). 1689.

l. *The Fourth (and Last) Collection of Poems, Satyrs, Songs, &c.* . . . 1689.

Case 189 (4). 1689.

m. *Poems on Affairs of State:* . . . 1697.

Case 211 (1) (a). 1697.

o. *Poems on Affairs of State:* . . . 1697. [This is *m* with a continuation of almost equal length.]

Case 211 (1) (c). 1697.

s. *Poems on Affairs of State,* . . . The Sixth Edition Corrected. . . . 1710.

Case 211 (1) (g). 1710.

u. *Poems on Affairs of State,* . . . Vol. II. . . . 1703.

Case 211 (2) (a). 1703.

x. *Poems on Affairs of State,* . . . Vol. III. . . . 1704.

Case 211 (3) (a). 1704.

y. *Poems on Affairs of State,* . . . Vol. III., The Second Edition, . . . Printed for Thomas Tebb and Theoph. Sanders . . . , Edw. Symon . . . , and Francis Clay . . . M. DCC. XVI.

Case 211 (3) (b). 1716.

z. *Poems on Affairs of State,* . . . Vol. IV. . . . 1707.

Case 211 (4) (a). 1707.

c'. *A New Collection of Poems Relating to State Affairs,* . . . 1705.

Case 237. 1705.

f''. Luttrell Collection, Bindley Pamphlets, Huntington Library, Vol. 1.

g''. Luttrell Collection, Bindley Pamphlets, Huntington Library, Vol. 2.

h''. B.M. Luttrell Collection, Vol. 1.

i''. B.M. Luttrell Collection, Vol. 2.

k''. Harvard Broadsides Collection 97951.

l''. Yale Broadsides Collection.

r''. (followed by vol. no.) *The Roxburghe Ballads: Illustrating the last Years of the Stuarts,* vols. IV–VIII, The Ballad Society, 1883–1895.

The Whigs' Exaltation

Copy text: l″ [W 1657].

Collation: 4° (The Royalist, 1682 [D 2770])

1. *shall stoop*] must droop *4°*.   7. *shall*] must *4°*.   8. And hey then up go we *4°*. *This is the 4° reading throughout, save at 32, which follows l″*.   9–16. *Omitted 4°*.   17–24. *Stanza 2 in 4°*.   21. *Thus having*] When we have *4°*. 25–32. *Stanza 4 in 4°*.   26. *Cannot*] Do not *4°*.   27. *good cause*] most cause *4°*.   30. *both*] once *4°*.   33–40. *Stanza 3 in 4°*.   35. *For*] Because *4°*. 37. *in every grove*] within the groves *4°*.   38. *preach*] teach *4°*.   41–56. *Omitted 4°*.   57–64. *Stanza 5 in 4°*.   57. *windows*] window *4°*.   59. And when the bishops are run down *4°*.   60. *elders*] deacons *4°*.   61. *town*] throne *l″*.   62. *'tis too free*] to set free *l″*.   63. *its own*] her own *4°*.

Prologue to "The Heir of Morocco"

Copy text: 4° [S 2689].

Collation: f″.

15. *hero*] hew *f″*.   16. *lance*] launce *4°, f″*.   24. *asunder.*] asunder, *4°, f″*. 28. *sharps*] L'Sharps *f″*.

A Satire in Answer to a Friend

Copy text: I.

Collation: X, B′, O″, l, m, o, s, c′.

Title: A Satire *X*. A Satire in Answer to a Friend *I, O″, l*. A Satire in Answer to a Friend, 1680 *B′*.

4. *heard*] hard *l, m, o, s*.   13. *frigg*] love *X, B′, l, m, o, s, c′. my*] me *B′*.   18. *that no man's thought*] no man is thought *all except O″*.   23. *alike my lines*] my lines alike *all others*.   25. *Halifax*] *All MSS. All printed texts have* H———. *Shaftesbury*] Seymour *X. All printed texts have* S———.   27. *blust'ring*] hustling *all others. man*] men *all except O″, l*.   30. *smiling*] sniv'ling *I*.   37. *London's*] London *I*.   42. *fair*] fine *B′. hair*] mien *B′*.   47. *She's*] Sh' *I*. *Sault*] Leau *all others*.   48. *modern*] *Omitted all others*.   57. *commend*] command *X*.   58. *condemn'd*] contemn'd *X and all printed texts*.   63. *Halifax*] Peterborough *X;* P——— *l;* H———r *m, o;* H———x *s, c′. Spencer*] Spen———r *l;* S———r *m, o, s, c′*.   65. *deprav'd*] depriv'd *c′*.   66. *by*] but *o, s, c′*.   70. *fears*] fear *I, B′*.   71. *Parliament*] Parliaments *all others*. 72. *Murder*] Murders *all others. virtue*] virtues *all others*.   74. *expel'd*] expels *all others*.   75. *impious*] imperious *X and printed texts*.   76. *vein*] vane *X, l, m, o, s*.   82. *Lord*] lo *X and printed texts*.   84. *minister*] ministers *X, B′, and printed texts*.   85. *filthy*] bawdy *all others*.   86. *crown*]

frown *X*.   89. *Avoids*] Delights *X and printed texts*.   90. *parasites*] sneak-
ings *B'*, *O"*. *make*] making *I*.   101. *peer*] paire *O"*.   105. How to be very
honest is counted dull *all others*.

The Medal

Note: The text is based on Kinsley's edition (1958); some suggestions on punctua-
tion have been taken from Noyes' edition (1908).

1. *antic*] antick *all*. *Modernization has obscured the possible paronomasia.*   88.
The reason's obvious; *Int'rest never lyes*; *all*.   107. *I have followed Noyes'*
punctuation. All edd. read: And true, but for the time, 'tis hard to know   151.
their] *See 151 n.*   174. *Engender'd on*] *Noyes records a copy of 1682 with*
Enliven'd by, *a transposition of couplet 179–80 with 181–82, and the for a in 181.*
See Macdonald, Dryden Bibliography, No. 13 a i.   200. *His*] his *all*.

The Medal of John Bayes

Copy text: 4° [S 2860].

10. *Galls*] Gall's *4°*.   86. *e'er*] ere *4°*.   108. *time;*] time, *4°*.   120. *genteel*
gaity and mien] Gentile Gayety and Meen *4°*.   127. *dead*] dead, *4°*.   246.
Buckingham] B———— *4°*.   247. *against York*] against ———— *4°*.   251.
land,] Land. *4°*.   259. *Thou*] the *4°*.   264. *deceiv'd,*] deceiv'd *4°*.   289.
ours,] ours. *4°*.   324. *wit;*] Wit, *4°*.   371. Who would or Kings, or Peoples
Rights betray, *4°*.

The Tories' Confession

Copy text: f" [T 1910].

Collation: a, NN, ms (Cambridge Add MS. 7112).

Note: There were at least three broadside editions of this poem in 1682 prior to
its appearance the following year in *a*. The copy text was "Printed for
T. H." [T 1910], and another edition was "Printed for H. B." [T 1911].
Ebsworth, in *r"*(IV) pp. 268–69, reprints from "Ashmolean Collection G.16,
Article LVII" which was "Printed for John How, at the Seven Stars . . . in
Cornhill." On p. 262, Ebsworth mentions what is apparently another
edition with the same title and the same tune but bearing the simple
colophon "London: J. H., 1682." Of these printed versions, I have seen
only *f"*, a copy of which is also in *k"*. The manuscripts would seem to
derive from the printed texts.

Title: A Song against the Tories *ms;* A Song *a; omitted NN*.

3. *the game*] their Cause *ms*.   13. *abbey*] Abbed *NN*. *be*] Omitted *NN*.   19.
longer] no longer *NN*.   20. Let us truth gently tell *ms*.   23. *s————*] sware
NN.   28. *nation's pence*] nation speence *NN*. *we'd*] we'll *a*.   29. *These*]
The *ms*. *shall down*] Omitted *NN;* shall go *ms*.   30. *glorious*] goodly *a*.   35.
And] Omitted *ms*.   42. *heir?*] heir, *f", a;* heir *NN, ms*.   44. *And pox*] A pox

NN; And shake ms. off] of all. 46. *Come*] We'll *NN. souls*] hearts *NN.* 51. *we balk'd*] we'll balk *NN.* 52. *had*] have *NN.* 53. *whom*] who *all.* 55. *him*] them *NN.* 57. *these*] their *ms.* 65. *choose*] chuse *f″, a, NN;* chouse *ms.* 68. *those*] them *NN. saw*] say *NN.*

The Loyal Scot

Copy text: *l″* [L 3366].

Collation: *c.*

1. *Bread*] Bred *c.* 5. *forty*] fosty *c.* 6. *to'l*] to *l″.* 10. *au*] all *l″.* 11. *seeming*] omitted *l″.* 18. *I'se*] I *l″.* 20. *fausest*] falsest *l″.* 23. *beath*] both *l″.* 26. *au*] all *l″.* 39. *to*] unto *c.* 43. *whom*] that *c.* 46. *would*] will *c.* 47. *doon*] down *l″.* 48. *aud*] old *l″.* 62. *au*] all *l″.* 63. *to'l*] to *l″.*

Absalom Senior

Copy text: *4°* [S 2653; "revised with additions"]

Collation: *f°* [S 2652].

Substantive errors noted in the *f°* errata are indicated parenthetically.

Title: Transpros'd] Transpos'd *4°.*

4. *All*] And *f°.* 8. *Held (err.)*] Hold *f°.* 20. *murder's*] murders *4°, f°.* 21. *Cozbi*] Cozbies *f°.* 23 *et passim. human*] humane *4°, f°.* 48. *waist*] wast *4°, f°.* 49. *Internal punctuation added.* 50. *reigns*] rains *4°;* raigns *f°.* 61. *incense-fragrant*] incense fragrant *4°, f°.* 83. *soul's*] souls *4°, f°.* 84. *scorpions'*] scorpions *4°, f°.* 109. *glory's*] glories *4°, f°.* 112. *avenger's*] avengers *4°, f°.* 126. *lead,*] lead. *4°, f°.* 132. *ships (err.)*] ship *f°.* 135. *Heav'n*] Heav'n's *4°.* 136. *Rank'd (err.)*] Kindl'd *f°.* 147. *thus conquer'd (err.)*] they conquer'd *f°.* 184. *rode*] rod *4°, f°.* 196. *flames in*] flames. In *4°, f°.* 208. *Not . . . beauties' . . . nor virgins'*] Nor . . . beauties . . . nor virgins *4°;* Not . . . beauties . . . not virgins *f°.* 209. *infants'*] infants *4°, f°.* 247. *weak (err.)*] poor *f°.* 311. *a (err.)*] his *f°.* 312. *a (err.)*] his *f°.* 314. *ye (err.)*] the *f°.* 319 *were David's harp . . . choir,*] was David's Harp . . . Quire; *4°, f°.* 320. *did*] all *f°.* 324. *bind:*] bind. *4°, f°.* 325. *Joshua's*] Josheu's *4°.* 326. *side;*] side. *4°, f°.* 328. *walls,*] wall; *4°;* walls; *(err.);* walls *f°. pour*] pou'r *4°;* pour *(err.);* pow'r *f°.* 355. *glory's*] glories *4°, f°.* 398. *rods.*] rods? *4°;* rods; *f°.* 406. *renegade—*] renegade, *4°, f°.* 407. *once*] one *f°.* 408. *dress'd—*] dress'd. *4°, f°.* 417. *mischief's*] mischiefs *4°, f°.* 439. *lov'd (err.)*] Lord *f°.* 444. *masters'*] masters *4°, f°.* 461. *their*] the *4°. vengeance's*] vengeances *4°, f°.* 462. *full.*] full, *f°.* 463. *soul,*] soul. *f°.* 490. *thy*] the *4°.* 492. *cause's*] causes *4°, f°. champions*] champion *4°.* 493. *to*] do *4°.* 586. *of*] for *f°.* 623. *hidden*] bidden *f°.* 626. *an*] and *4°.* 629. *is*]in *4°.* 631. *rode*] rod *4°, f°.* 647. *Jonah*] Jonas *f°.* 680. *The metal is not*] Nor is the metal *f°.* 683. *hunter's*] hunters *4°, f°.* 694. *his*] the *f°.* 733. *rate (err.)*] loo *f°.* 772. *religion's*] religions *4°, f°.*

786. *began*] begun *4°*, *f°*.   787. *span*] spun *4°*, *f°*.   829. *multitude.*] multitude *4°*, *f°*.   837. *excluding (err.)*] encluding *4°*, *f°*. *Sanedrin's*] Sanedrims *4°*, *f°*.   857. *Sanedrin's*] Sandrims *4°*, *f°*.   872. *foe?*] foe; *4°*, *f°*.   874. *pow'r*] pow'r. *4°*, *f°*.   875. *he*] he; *4°*, *f°*.   876. *liberty;*] liberty, *4°*, *f°*.   877. *bold,*] bold: *4°*; bold; *f°*.   943. *try,*] try. *4°*, *f°*.   998. *desires*] desire *4°*.   1017. *ere*] e'er *4°*.   1019. *he draws*] draws *4°*.   1030. *Absalom pow'r, wishes, crown,*] Absolon, pow'r wishes, crown. *4°*; Absolon, power, wishes, crown. *f°*.   1091. *reveal?*] reveal! *4°*, *f°*.   1092. *kneel!*] kneel. *4°*, *f°*.   1111. *men*] them *4°*.   1118. *race*] raze *f°*.   1264. *But*] By *4°*.   1358. *must less*] much lest *4°*.   1374. *See footnote.*   1424. *sanedrins'*] Sanedrims *4°*, *f°*.

A Congratulatory Poem

Copy text: f″ [C *5830*].

Collation: ms (B.M. Add. MS. 6399).

Note: Copies of *f″* are found also in *k″* and *l″*.

Title: Whig's *f″*; Whigs *ms.*

1. *Quotation marks have been added.*   12. *rend*] tear *ms.*

An Ironical Encomium

Copy text: x.

Collation: y.

5. *pall*] paul *x.*   13. *What! Shall*] What shall *x, y.*   77. *Sulla's*] Segla's *x, y.*

A Game at Cards

Copy text: J′.

65. *ran*] run *J′.*

Midsummer Moon

Copy text: 4° [T *1011*].

Collation: z.

Note: All names in *4°* are partially blanked out; for the most part, these have been given in full in *z*. The unexpanded forms have been noted only where there might conceivably be some question or significance concerning them.

1-14. *In the original text, the whole of this passage is set in italics.*   15. *can,*] can *4°*, *z.*   16. *gentleman.*] gentleman, *4°*, *z.*   38. *officers?*] officers. *4°*, *z.*   68. *requires*] deserves *z.*   107. *Jenkins, Halifax*] J———s, H———x, *4°*, *z.*   114-15. *Quotation marks added.*   140. *sprite*] sp'right *4°*.   163. *James*] J———s *4°*, *z.*   165. *Paragraph added.*   170. *Quotation marks added.*   196. *Quotation marks added.*   204. *can*] can? *4°*, *z.*   212. *Quotation marks added.*   215-24. *Quotation marks added.*   215. *George*] G. *4°*, *z.*   240. *absolute?—*] absolute. *4°*, *z.*   245-46. *Quotation marks added.*   250-54. *Quota-*

tion marks added.   254. For sage Sir J————n, nor L. nor M————r, nor
M—a—r *4°, z.*   255. *Paragraph added.*   263. *Paragraph added.*   290.
turn] burn *z.*   292. *Albion?*] Albion! *4°, z.*   298. *loyal ass*] loyal———— *4°.*
346. *mirrors*] mirror *z.*   371. *Paragraph added.*   382. *ass*] A———— *4°.*   387.
Paragraph added.

Prologue to "The Duke of Guise"

Copy text: f" [D 2338].

Collation: ms (Chicago MS PRf1195. C72).

Note: Kinsley's text has been consulted.

2. *Whig*] Whigs *ms.*   14. *Chaws*] Chews *ms.*   20. *hook*] bait *ms.*   22. *by*]
with *ms.*   31. *throats.*] throats, *f".*   35. *a*] the *ms.*   38. *forsake.*] forsake
ms.   47. *Do what*] Doe, what *f".*

Iter Boreale

Copy text: l" [D 493].

Note: Copies are found in *f"* and *k";* the poem has been reprinted in *r"*(V).

15. *Bethelites*] Be————ellites *l".*   43. *forgotten?*] forgotten; *l".*   45. *were*]
where *l".*   46. *King*] K———— *l".*   50. *Moore*] Moor— *l".*   53. *Were*] Was
l".   56. *Moore*] Moor— *l".*   59. *Bethel's*] Be————el's *l".*   63. *Papillion,*]
Pa———— *l"*

The Case is Alter'd Now

Copy text: f" [C 870].

Collation: b.

Note: Copies of *f"* are found also in *k"* and *l".*

11. *lofty*] mighty *b.*   54. *precedent*] president *f", b.*

To The Loyal Londoners

Copy text: W'.

Collation: O", l, r"(V).

Note: r" is said to be based on a 1682 broadside, reprinted in 1689, but I have not
     seen either of these.

Title: Ballad *O".* The City-Ballad *l, r".*

1. *oh*] now *l, r".* *lose*] loose *O".*   2. *catch'd*] ketcht *O";* catcht *l;* caught *r".*
noose] nose *W'.*   7. *for who is't*] who is that *l.*   14. *they'd*] they'll *O", l.*
15–16. *In l, 15–16 are interchanged with 21–22.*   17. *his sword's*] the sword its
l.   18. *throw off your shoes*] off with your coats *l.*   19. *sabots*] sabbo's *W';*
sabbues *O";* your boots *l.*   21. *Your*] Hang *l.*   22. *Is as weak*] Tis as weak *l;*
Tis weak *r".*   23. *ere he*] ever *l.*   27. *time's*] times *W';* time *O".*
28. *beat*] and *l.*   29. *Do you wonder? O", l.*   31. *your*] the *l.*

An Heroic Poem

Copy text: f″ [H 1590].

2. *obey;*] obey. *f″.*   3. *clouds'*] clouds *f″.*   6. *winds'*] winds *f″.*   20. *o'er-whelm*] overwhelm *f″.*   36. *treach'rous*] treacherous *f″.*   41. *Now, rampant Tories, drink!*] Now rampant Tories drink, *f″.*   50. *your duke*] your ——— *f″.*

An Essay Upon the Earl of Shaftesbury's Death

Copy text: o.

Collation: l, m, s.

34. *seem*] seems *o, s.*   72. *thee*] the *m, o, s.*

The Last Will and Testament

Copy text: f″ [L 514].

Collation: k″, bds. (see note), b, u, K′, R′, T″.

Note: There are three contemporary printings: *f″* contains 4 pages, with the colophon "Printed for S. Ward, 1682"; *k″* has two pages (1 sheet printed on both sides), with the same colophon; *bds* is a broadside in Yale British Tracts (1682 + L33). Two of the manuscripts are defective: *K′* containing 1–77 (deliberately stopping at the lines of the epigraph, "which," says the scribe, "were so dull I would not write them"); and *R′,* containing 15–89. *T″* has a greatly extended title and numerous glosses, parts of which appear in the notes when relevant. For the most part, *f″, k″, b,* and *u* have proper names partially blanked out; the other witnesses supply them in the text or in marginal glosses.

Title: Anthony, King of Poland] Anthony Earl of Shaftesbury Elect King of Poland *bds.;* Anthony Ashley Cooper late of Shaftesbury who . . . thought . . . to become king of Poland . . . *T″.*

6. *last*] length *T″.*   10. *him*] Him *bds.*   20. *must have*] ought t'have *b.*   25. *whoring*] whorings *u.*   30. *give, and sometimes*] sometimes give and *T″.*   40. *horns*] h——ns *f″, k″, bds., K′.*   47. *'tis*] it's *bds. lose*] have *b,* loose *R′.*   56. *'tis*] it's *bds., R′.*   59. *lifetime*] live's time *f″, k″, b;* life's time *bds., R′.*   67. *and*] a *bds.*   80. *think?*] think! *f″, k″, b, K′, R′, T″.*   86. *Nature!*] Nature *R′, T″.*   103. *did*] do *bds.*

A Supplement to the Last Will and Testament

Copy text: f″ [S 6187].

Note: Copies are in *i″* and at Yale.

Title: 1683] 1682 *f″.*

12. *roast*] rost *f″.*   56. *gait was fleet*] Gate was Fleet *f″.*   81. *ere*] e'er *f″.*   98. *are*] is *f″.*   99. *sleights*] Leights *f″. boors*] bores *f″.*   102. *were*] was *f″.*   103. *common shore*] Commons-shew'r *f″.*

The Charter

Copy text: 4°.

Collation: b.

Note: The poem is known in two forms, that of the 1682 quarto of 492 lines [C 3722], and an expansion (to 562 lines) in b. However, since b ordinarily reprints directly and without substantive change, there may well have been a separate printing of the expanded text which I have not seen. In b, the following lines are added: 95–96, 126, 233–36, 247–50, 327–49, 352–86, 443–44. The quarto has two lines (318–19) which do not occur in b. In the text given here, prefatory and panegyric verses (1–12, 330–407) have been omitted, while speech ascriptions have been added.

1–12. *My omission.*   29. *well 'tis*] well that 'tis b.   36. *prodigies*] prod'gies 4°. 77. *drums*] Omitted in b.   94. b inserts 2 lines (95–96).   106. *their first vow*] the Covenant b.   108. *Of Magna Charta*] Charta pro Causa b. 121. *plead*] tack b.

122–23. Join my lord's kennel to the City pack
Speak, Joller, Jolly, Jewel, Whig-dog; quest
Bouncer, Bowler, Blue-lips, and the rest. (b, 124–26).

124. *our*] my b.   127. *To obstruct*] T'obstruct b.   171. *all*] Omitted in b. 173. *Or*] Omitted in b.   229. b inserts 4 lines (233–36).   239. b inserts 4 lines (247–50).   265. *wi'*] we' 4°.   277. *there*] their b.   280. No date of time, no power on earth can give b.   285. *enemy's*] enemies 4°, b.   305. *must*] they must b.   312. *crawl*] crawls 4°. *kingdom's*] Kingdoms 4°.   315. b inserts 23 lines (327–49).   316. *jury*] Fury b.   317. b inserts 35 lines (352–86).   318–19. Omitted in b.   328. *poet*] subject b.   330–407. *My omission.*   375. b inserts 2 lines (443–44).   415. *down*] Omitted in b. 437. *lose honor*] loose honor 4°, b. *lose life*] loose life 4°.   443. *lose*] loose 4°.   448. *lose*] loose 4°, b.   450. *lose*] loose 4°, b.   457. *so give place to feeling*] place to feeling so give 4°, b.   461. *then*] Omitted in 4°.   467. *their*] the b.

The Great Despair of the London Whigs

Copy text: b.

5. *we've*] w'have b.   18. *arch-traitors*] Arch-Trait. b.   23. *pack'd*] pactt; b.   48. *rebellions*] Reb. b.

Algernon Sidney's Farewell

Copy text: l″ [A 923].

Note: Copies are also found in g″ and k″.

Title: *Algernon*] Algernoon l″.

2. *monarchy's*] Monarchies l″.   22. *war's*] Wars l″.

Song: Old Rowley the King

Copy text: Z.

Collation: J, K, U', Z'.

1. *of*] my *J, Z'*.   2. *The*] With the *K*. *surplus*] Surplice *Z'*.   4. *damnable*] wonderfull *J*.   5–6. *Quoth*] Says *J*.   9. *Following this, J concludes its version with:*

> See saw sack a day
> Monmouth is a pretty boy
> Richmond is another
> Grafton is my only joy
> And why should I these three destroy
> To please a pious brother?

13. *outreaches*] Ore reacht *Z'*.   23. *Thinks*] Quoth *K*.   25. *Gud's fish*] Gud's flesh *U*.   28. *The*] Then *Z*.   30. *use laws*] use the Laws *Z'*; use/ Laws *K*. 34. *we*] you *K*.   36. You have Learnt Our to him *Z'*.   39. *and*] *Omitted in U*.   44. *gifts*] gift *Z*.   58. *everything's*] everything is *K, Z, U*.   62. *tricks*] matters *Z'*.   66. *for another*] is such another *Z'*.   67. *babes*] brats *Z'*. 69. *and*] *Omitted in U*.   74. *having*] to have *K, U*; have *Z'*.   75. *rarely*] ralely *Z*. Though no more than one appear *Z'*.   76. At last I'll make it clear *Z'*.

A Merry New Ballad

Copy text: K.

Collation: F, O, P, V, U', r'' (V).

Title: Merry] *Omitted in F*. A Merry Ballad on Pr[ince] Perkin *O, P, V, r''*. 2. *reckon'd*] reclin'd *F*; recond *V, r''* [*emended to* reckon'd].   6. *happiness bring*] happy thing *r''*.   11. *proclamation*] proclamations *all except F*.   12. *to*] into *F*.   13. *this my preservation*] that my reservation *r''*.   14–15. *king*] a king *F*.   18. *recantations*] recantation *F*.   19. *neatly*] *Omitted in P, V, r''*. 21. *handsomely*] neatly *P, V, r''*.   27. *gather*] shelter *F*.   28. *perk up*] perks up *O*; perks out *U'*.   32–33. *king*] a king *F*.   35. *The plot's*] And plots *U'*; the Clock [*emended to* Cloak] *r''*.   36. *made*] make *U'*.   39. Be you still my adviser *P, V, r''*.   40. *their*] *Omitted in P, V, r''*.   48. *godly*] goodly *r''*.   53. *Shall give*] Gives *P, V, r''*; That gives *O*.   58. *souls*] our souls *P, V, r''*.   64. *though*] *Omitted in P, V, r''*.   65. *were*] *Omitted in P, V, r''*.   66. *li'd*] di'd *F*. 67. *sham'd*] shamm'd *F*.   71. *We'll*] Let's *F, U'*.   72. *religious*] rebellious *O, P, V, U', r''*.   74. *danger's ne'er*] danger is never *F*.   75. *full*] hand *F*. 89. Will tickle each palate *F*; Shall stick in their palate *P, V, r''*.   90. *Whigs*] the Whigs *P, V, r''*. *shall*] shall it *F*.

The Newmarket Song

Copy text: k″ [N 932].

Collation: g″ [N 933], c, W&M (*Wit and Mirth*), r″ (V).

Title: Newmarket: A Song, sung to the King there W&M; The Newmarket Song. Sung to the King there. To the Tune of Old Sir Simon the King r″.

3. *the*] Omitted in W&M.   5. *each*] the W&M.   6. *angry*] air and c, W&M. 7. *Dame*] Omitted in W&M.   8. *And*] When W&M.   12. *I*] You W&M. 13. For there are sports and games W&M.   15. *sham*] shame W&M.   17– 20. *Omitted in* g″.   19. *a*] Omitted in W&M.   20. *damn'd*] Omitted in W&M.   28. *vintner*] a tinker g″; tinker W&M.   43. And would I could meet with a man W&M.   45. *see*] Omitted in g″. *fate of the*] vice of this W&M.   49. *chousing*] racing W&M.   52. *bribing*] bubbing W&M.   55. *should you*] if we should W&M.   59. How beauty try'mphs where g″.   66. *there doth*] here does W&M.   68. *found*] found out W&M.   73. *'Ods bud*] Ods but g″; Udshows W&M.   76. *e'en*] Omitted in g″. I took 'em all for men W&M.   78. *Their horses and*] On horse in W&M.   79. *sight*] show W&M.

A New Ballad

Copy text: B″.

Collation: U′, d, j, m.

Note: The text appears in all subsequent editions of m, as well as the piracy c′. It is reprinted in r″ (V).

Title: A New Song of the Times, 1683 d, j, m.

1. *if*] for d, j, m.   2. *should*] to d, j, m.   3. *Disowning*] To disown B″. *'em*] them B″; 'um d, j, m.   6. *'em*] them B″; 'um d, j, m.   7. *Those that*] Those who U′; They that d, j, m.   9. *more*] such a d, j, m.   10. *Monmouth's their*] Monmouth their U′, B″; Monmouth's the d, j, m.   12. *all*] Omitted in B″. 15. *hot-headed Tony*] the hot-headed Tory B″.   16. *more*] much more d, j, m. 17. *my*] in [?] U′.   18. *By*] With d; Of m.   19. *That*] Who U′.   21. *That*] Who d, j, m. *at*] omitted U′.   22. *When*] And when d, j, m. *he*] they B″, U′. 24. *Was here*] They were there B″; They were here U′. *hollow*] hallow B″; holoa U′.   27. *sad*] damn'd d, j, m.   29. *a*] the d, j, m.   30. *o'er his own*] over his d, j, m.   31. *'Tis not*] Tho nor U′; It was not d, j, m.   32. *nor inditing*] nor enditing B″; or indicting d, j, m.   33. *And*] Omitted in d, j, m.   36. *reason by*] reason with U′; reason too by d, j, m.   38. *State*] fate U′.   39. *Will*] Would d; Should j, m.   40. *Why should*] Shall then d, j, m.   41. *Make*] Take U′. *Speke*] Hugh Speke B″, U′.   44. *his*] a d, j, m.   48. *Ran*] Run U′, d, j, m. *up*] quite up U′.   49. Who can think the case hard d, j, m.   51. *Who lov'd his own*] Who loves his own U′; That lov'd his just d, j, m.   54. *'twould do*] to do d, j, m.   55. *cit*] chit U′.   58. *Those*] His d, j, m.   59. *Were*]

Are *U'*.   60. *And both of them*] And both of 'em *U'*; For both them were *d*, *j*, *m*. *were open*] are open *U'*.   63. *a*] his *d*, *j*, *m*.   65. *Who labor'd*] To labor *d*, *j*, *m*.   66. *to*] *Omitted in B''*, *U'*.   67. *'Twas with*] 'Twas very *d*, *j*, *m*. 70. *whose*] whole *B''*.   72. *a villain*] dishonest *j*, *m*.   73. *While*] Since *d*, *j*, *m*.   75. *up*] *Omitted in U'*. *goes*] go *d*, *j*, *m*.   76. *While*] Whilst *d*, *j*, *m*. 78. *murders*] murder *j*, *m*.   79. *Some*] Our *d*, *j*, *m*.   81. *Would ours*] Think ours to *d*, *j*, *m*.   82. *ne'er*] never *d*, *j*, *m*.   84. *'Twas*] and *U'*; But 'tis *d*, *j*, *m*.

The Protestant Satire

Copy text: G' to line 188; then *CP* (*A Collection of Poems on Several Occasions, Written in the Last Century . . . Now first Publish'd by R. Cross . . . Printed . . . [by R.] Cross 1747 [Case 455]*) *ad fin.*

Note: G', an aggregation of items dealing principally with 16th- and 17th-century theater, contains the unique MS copy of *The Protestant Satire*. Here, the poem is incorrectly bound (pp. 1–2, 5–8, 3–4), it ends at our 188, and it lacks certain lines found in *CP* (though it supplies others). There are two hands, both probably eighteenth century; one is a neat factory hand, the other (found at 99–106, 161–88, and in minor corrections) seems less professional. Evidently, the second scribe inserted the material attacking Tories other than L'Estrange. Yet, for all its complications, G' appears to be less edited than *CP*, which avoids indecorous words and tends to reduce the Alexandrine (often found at the end of one of the numerous triplets) to a more regular pentameter. *CP* probably derives from a copy that did not give names in full; in the printed version, all actual names (except at 132, 236) are partially or completely blanked out. I have noted below only those instances where names were completely deleted.

Title: In return to Mr. Bayes's Popish libels written before/the death of the late King./ ——Hic stylus haud petet ultro/Quemquam —— Hor. Sat. Lib. II. *CP*.

2. *State!*] State? *G'*.   4. *Traitor*] Villain *CP*. *first!*] first; *G'*.   6. *doing!*] doing; *G'*; doing *CP*.   12. *of right*] for right *CP*.   19. *that*] the *CP*.   28. *CP has no paragraph here.*   30. *passions'*] passions *G'*, *CP*.   31. *that*] the *CP. Parentheses added.*   35. *their*] the *G'*.   39. *Christ's gospel*] religion's *CP*. 46–47. *Omitted in CP*.   48. *their reforming votes*] num'rous counsellors *CP*. 60–65. *Omitted in CP*.   68. *Tower*] Tower—*G'*, *CP*.   70. *Can release*] Has loosen'd *CP*. *keep*] kept *CP*.   81. *thought*] thoughts *CP*. *like Heav'ns dread power*] (like Heav'n itself) *CP*.   85. *Care's*] Car's *G'*; C——'s *CP*. *useful*] pleasant *CP*.   96. *Crown*] C——n *CP*.   98. *The first scribe ends the line with etc., after which there are two columns of four lines each (99–106) written by the second scribe in the space normally left by the first scribe to indicate a new paragraph.*   101–02. *Omitted in CP*.   103. *In G' an asterisk begins this line and 107.*   114. *or*] and *CP*.   115. *fine*] fines *G'*.   122. *makes*] make *G'*, *CP*.   123. *flirt*] wench *CP*.   127. *wrong'd whom she is*] wrong'd, she's *CP*.

129. *and*] or *CP*.   130. *Graham*] Gr——— *G'*; G———s *CP*.   132. *Armstrong*] *Also given in full in CP*.   134. *has right to*] can *CP*.   135–36. *Omitted in CP*.   139. *Between 139–40, a short horizontal line, apparently put in by the second scribe, would seem to indicate that he was aware of an omission. CP inserts here:*

> True sense she hates [too prone 'tis to enquire]
> But hugs the fools, who blindfold will admire.
> Such stupid sots, who scar'd with empty sound,
> Are drove like sheep unto the statesman's pound.
> Who think, because her talk is loud, 'tis good,
> And praise her lips distain'd with martyr's blood.
> She brings forth mules by being kind to asses,
> And, like Heav'ns peace, all understanding passes.

141. *law!*] law, *CP*.   144. *pride,*] lust; *CP*.   147. *of fools and cowards can make*] turn fools and cowards into *CP*.   155. *conquest*] conquests *CP*.   158. *Following 158, CP inserts:*

> Those only understand how to obey
> Who quit their reason and their faith betray,
> Through fear and fawning give their rights away.

161. *In G', this page begins with two lines (not found in CP) from another poem, in the hand of the first scribe:*

> All beggars loyal, rakehells right prelatic,
> But wealth's a Whig, virtue a damn'd fanatic

The rest of the page is occupied by 161–88, in the hand of the second scribe. *aches*] arches *CP*.   169. *year*] year's *CP*. *confute.*] confute, *CP*.   171. *conscience,*] conscience. *G', CP*.   173. *Privy Purse*] glitt'ring *CP*.   177–78. *Omitted in CP*.   187. *both,*] both *CP*.   188. *style's the true*] style is the *G'*. 198. *him (whose*] him, whose *CP*. *blame!)*] blame, *CP*.   206. *Quotation marks added*.   216. *heels;*] heels. *CP*.   221. *echoes*] echo's *CP*.   233. *wit;*] wit. *CP*.   235. *bars,*] bars *CP*.   236. *Roger is given in full*.   241. *spit:*] spit. *CP*.   263. *spring.*] spring; *CP*.   265. *height:*] height *CP*.   272. *reign:*] reign. *CP*.   290. *be*] be, *CP*.   291. *he);*] he). *CP*.   298. *Paragraph added*. 301. *duns;*] duns. *CP*.   303. *dull;*] dull. *CP*.   307. *Hyde*] *Blanked out in CP*. 311. *Parentheses added*.   317. *smile;*] smile. *CP*.   331. *treasurers*] T———rs *CP*.   333. *own?*] own; *CP*.   336. *Danby . . . Hyde*] *Both names blanked out in CP*.   339. *Paragraph added*.   341. *Forty-one:*] Forty-one. *CP*.   358. *Hyphens added*.   369. *thing, the Government, arraign?*] Thing the Government arraign. *CP*.   373. *knaves?*] knaves. *CP*.   378. *cool,*] cool? *CP*.   380. *ghost?*] ghost. *CP*.   384. *Paragraph added*.   389. *exceed,*] exceed: *CP*. 391. *faith,*] faith; *CP*.   398. *Italics added*.   406. *Hyde*] *Blanked out in CP*. 427. *Portsmouth*] *Blanked out in CP*.   430. *Paragraph added*.   448. *Paragraph added*.   451. *stand,*] stand. *CP*.   453. *none*] now *CP*. *Papists.*] Papists:

CP.   454. *Paragraph added.*   469. *faith,*] faith *CP.* *chouse*] chouse, *CP.*
470. Out their lives, fool H———, and coward R———, *CP.*   472. *counsel—*]
counsel *CP.*

A Character of London Village

Copy text: g″ [C 2019].

Collation: b.

43. *she*] he *b.*   46. *crone*] drone *b.*

Tyburn's Courteous Invitation

Copy text: g″ [T 3557].

Collation: b.

Note: Both printings are by N[athaniel] T[hompson], the Tory printer, whom
   Whigs referred to as "Catholic Nat."

Title: b adds the Salamanca Doctor.

27–31. *Omitted in b.*

Sir Thomas Armstrong's Last Farewell

Copy text: k″ [S 3891 A].

1. *Adieu*] A due *k″.*   20. *Rogues*] Ragues *k″.*   39. *tapping*] taping *k″.*

True and Joyful News

Copy text: g″ [T 2507].

Note: Another copy is in *k″.*

3. The Old Causes grand Goliah's Pim—is come, *g″.*   5. *City's hope*] Cities
hopes *g″. Charter's*] Charters *g″.*   6. *Dissenters'*] Dissenters *g″. Scriptures'*]
Scriptures *g″.*   28. *zealot's*] zealots *g″.*   42. *parent's*] par'nts *g″.*

INDEX OF FIRST LINES

GENERAL INDEX

Italicized page numbers indicate entries in poem texts only.

Abbeville Ford, France, 185

Abhorrers, Addresses of abhorrence and allegiance, 42, 79, 93, 139, 177, 189, 272, 423, 545; reaction to Shaftesbury release, 39; against Petitioners for a parliament, 42, 92, 93, 156, 356, 436; against alleged Shaftesbury Association, 42, 92, 93, 161, 178, 269, 272, 377, 436, 515, 572; against Whig Conspiracy, 510, 515, 572; defined, 515

Account of the Life of Julian the Apostate Vindicated, The, 300

Account of the Sheriffs' Election, 269

Actors, political position, 238–39

Address from Salamanca to her Unknown Off-Spring Dr. T. O., 4

Advice to the Painter, quoted, 350

Aesop, fables of, 52, 58, 197, 520

Agincourt, France, 185

Ailesbury, Earl of. *See* Thomas, Earl of Ailesbury

Aix-la-Chapelle, Treaty of, 575

Albany, 390

Albemarle, first Duke of. *See* Monck, George

Alençon, Charles, Duke of, 186

Alexander the Great, 527

Algernon Sidney's Farewell: headnote, 458; text, 459–62

All Health to Old Noll (song), 578

Alleyn, Sir Thomas: replaced as alderman, xxxiv; as alderman, 245

Almanacs, political effects of, 221

Amboyna (island), 420

America, English colonies in, 372–73. *See also* Carolina; New England

Amnesty, Act of, 427

Amsterdam, 408–09, 410, 411, 415, 418, 500

Amsterdam Coffeehouse, 277, 551, 558

Anabaptists, 169, 370, 399; Münster, 468

Ancus Martius, 603

Anderson, Matthew, quoted, 234

Anderton, Father, alleged plot against Charles II, 126

Andrews, Robert (surgeon), quoted, 508

Anglesey, first Earl of. *See* Annesley, Arthur

Angliae Notitia, quoted, 466

Anne, Countess of Sussex, 479

Anne, Princess, 350, 518

Annesley, Arthur, first Earl of Anglesey, 397; support of Monmouth, 323–24

Annus mirabilis (*1666*), 54; books, 355, 425

Anti-Court party. *See* Whigs

Antinomians (Ranters), 356

Antwerp, 129, 315

Apati, Prince Michael, *Declaration of the Hungarian War,* 557

Apprehending of Sir Thomas Armstrong, 562

Apprentices, London, 190, 466; annual feast (*1682*), 351, 352, 380–81

Argyle, ninth Earl of. *See* Campbell, Archibald

Ariosto, *Orlando Furioso,* 257

Arlington, first Earl of. *See* Bennet, Henry

Arlington, Countess of, 331

Armstrong, Sir Thomas, 29, 297, 579, 593; biographical notes, 386, 398–99, 471, 561; flees to Continent, 477, 568; made outlaw, 485; execution without trial, 512, 516, 520–21, 532, 537, 561, 569, 571, 573, poems on, 561–70; relations with Monmouth, 561, 563; wife, 561; role in Whig Conspiracy, 563; duels, 564; mistress, 565–66; daughter, 573 (*see* Matthews, Mrs.); quartered, 575; arrest, 576; Hayes' alleged aid to, 576, 577

Arnold, John, 502–03

Arsy Versy: or Riddle of Riddles. See Hemp for the Flaxman

Artillery Company Feast, 174, 176, 178, 179, 210, 281, 326; Duke of York attends, 174, 180, 210, 390

Arundel, Earl of. *See* Howard, Henry

Arundel, Countess of, 350

Arundel House, 386

Arundell, Henry, Baron and third Lord Arundell of Wardour (*1606?–94*): biographical note, 33; imprisoned in Tower, 283

Litany for the Fifth of November 1684, A:
headnote, 574; text, 574–75
Litany for St. Omers, A, quoted, 255
Litany of the D[uke of Buckingham], The,
294
Littleton, Sir Thomas: identified, 515;
Tenures, 515
Locke, John, 202, 373
Lockhart, Sir George, 131
Lollards, 143, 599
London, xxvi, 16, 20, 91, 119, 120, 130,
141, 219, 225, 237, 251, 274, 294, 295,
322, 330, 420, 444, 467, 503, 519, 523;
comes under Court control, xxix–xxx,
194, 338, 372, 379, 381, 383, 384, 406,
410, 448, 452, 477, 511–12, 538, 546,
563, 571; shrieval elections (*1682*), xxix–
xxx, xxxiv–xxxv, 39, 170, 194–95, 215–
16, 225, 228, 278, 338, 339, 345, 359,
369–70, 376, 378–79, 383, 385, 386, 400,
402, 410–11, 421, 423, 432, 519, 563, note
to poems on, 207–16, trials for riot
during, 208, 295, 534 (*see also* Common
Halls; Moore, Sir John; Pilkington,
Thomas; Shute, Samuel); control of
juries by Whig sheriffs, xxix, 292, 405,
428, 500; Lord Mayor, selection of,
xxxiv, 207–08, prerogatives, 209, 253,
266 (*see also* Clayton, Robert; Edwards,
Sir James; Moore, Sir John; Ward, Sir
Patience); merchants, xxiv, 180, 181, 245,
281, 293, 309; Court control of judiciary,
xxxv, 207; satirized, 28–32 (*A Satire in
Answer to a Friend*), 423–43 (*The
Charter*), 547–50 (*A Character of Lon-
don Village*); Great Fire (*1666*), 32
(*see also* Great Fire); Whig party in,
32 (*see also* London Whigs); Whigs
lose control of juries, 39, 99, 511–12,
518; Bridge, 41, 258, 400; Whigs control
of, 53–54; Court efforts to control, 67–
69; Common Council, 68, 400, 421, 422,
439, petition of submission to Charles
II, 422, 446; alleged crimes of officials
of, 91, 293; Whig government praised,
91–93; municipal officers (*1681*), 92;
Whig ("Ignoramus") Grand Juries, 99,
170, 207, 219, 231, 265, 277, 292, 321,
344, 346, 361, 362, 381, 383, 405, 421,
425, 428, *430*, *437*, 445, 446, 500, 519,
540, 577, explained, 386 (*see also* Col-
lege, Stephen; Cooper, Anthony Ashley);
Aldermanic Council, 103, 175, 207–08,
209, 241, 348, 431, 439, composition of,
xxxiv, 245, members replaced, xxxiv,
422, support petition for a parliament,

190, Court of, 247, 262; Whig Feast in,
174 (*see also* Whig Feast); shrieval
elections (*1680, 1681*), 190, 208–09, 244;
Charter, rights granted to, 190, 196,
277, 295, recalled, 99–100 (*see also* Quo
Warranto proceedings); petitions, 190,
385, against prorogation of parliament,
430; relation to Commons, 207; election
procedures, 207–08, 237; power of sher-
iffs, 207–08, 253; Bishop of, 217, 242,
350 (*see also* Compton, Henry); support
of Cromwell in, 232; court prisons, 249;
described, *258;* collection of market
money by, 282; bankers' loan to Exche-
quer, 290; brothels, 295; Jesuits in, 343;
alleged Catholic army in, 363; Tory
judges, 363; Monument to Great Fire,
400, 550; in Civil War, 426–27; affronts
to ambassadors, 435; livery companies'
Whiggishness, *439–40*, 500; insurrection
plot (*1683*), 453–54; Chamberlain of,
466; rebuilding of, 550; rebellions, 560
London (ship), 241
London Gazette, The, 45; quoted, 200–01,
437, 591
London Whigs, 250, 303, 305, 377, 400–01,
578; leaders, xxviii, 445, flee England,
345; Stuart legal revenge on, 381, 383,
430, 444; defeat in shrieval elections
(*1682*), xxix–xxx (*see also* London,
shrieval elections); aldermen, xxxiv, 245;
power, xxxiv–xxxv; struggle against
Court, 32, 358, 359; pressure on Par-
liament, 32; sheriffs (*1682*), 47 (*see also*
Pilkington, Thomas; Shute, Samuel);
Shaftesbury as leader of, 160; candidates
(*1682*), 163 (*see also* Dubois, John;
Papillon, Thomas); *Feast,* 174 (*see also*
Whig Feast); strategy of Charles II
against, 174–75, 233; defeated by Court,
194, 225, 376, 378–79, 383, 386, 452,
511–12 (*see also* London, comes under
Court control), Jeffrey's role in, 139;
Pilkington's leadership of, 210 (*see also*
Pilkington, Thomas); refusal to ratify
Tory shrieval candidates (*1682*), 212,
268; actions during shrieval elections
(*1682*), 237, 249; in Parliament, 281;
merchants, 309; in Green Ribbon Club,
310; satirized, 383–86 (*Satire, or Song*),
423–43 (*The Charter*), 444–47 (*The
Great Despair of the London Whigs*);
reaction to arrest of Monmouth, 563–64.
See also London; Whigs
Longleat, Wiltshire, 15
Looking Glass for a Tory, A, 96

Wilmore, John: stewardship of Whig Feast, 34, 37, 174, 177; identified, 174; "Ignoramus" jury of, 191; trial for kidnapping, 425

Wilmot, John, second Earl of Rochester, 164; role in Dryden ambuscade, 25, 84, 522; *An Allusion to Horace*, quoted, 82, 83; *A Satire against Mankind*, quoted, 450; *Tunbridge Wells*, quoted, 468

Windsor Castle, 82, 141, 214, 312, 350, 521; improved by Charles II, 164–65; park, 215

Wing, Donald, cited, 556

Winnington, Sir Francis, 254

Wither, George, *Vox et Lacrimae Anglorum*, 269

Wonder Tavern, 182

Wood, Anthony À, *Athenae Oxoniensis*, quoted, 41, 271

Wood, Thomas, Bishop of Lichfield, suspended, 535

Woolrych, Humphrey, *Memoirs*, quoted, 252

Worcester, Charles II defeated at, 120, 137, 575

Worcester, third Marquis of. *See* Somerset, Henry

Worcester, fourth Marquis of. *See* Somerset, Charles

Worrington, Earl of. *See* Booth, Henry

Wren, Sir Christopher, 165, 550

Wynne, William, *The Life of Sir Leoline Jenkins*, 212; cited, 213

York, 306

York, Duchess of. *See* Hyde, Anne; Mary Beatrice of Modena

York, Duke of. *See* James Stuart

Yorke, P. C., *Encyclopaedia Britannica* article quoted, 601

Yorkshire, Popish Plot in, 503

Young Devil Tavern, 409

Young, Edward, *First Epistle to Pope*, 306

Young Jemmy (ballad), 233

Young Jemmy, or the Princely Shepherd (ballad), 233

Youth, youth, thou hadst better been starved at nurse, etc. (tune), 229

Zeven Provincien (ship), 241